TO SHINING SEA

TO SHINING SEA

A HISTORY OF THE
UNITED STATES NAVY

1775–1991

★

Stephen Howarth

RANDOM HOUSE

NEW YORK

Library of Congress Cataloging-in-Publication Data

Howarth, Stephen.
To shining sea: a history of the United States Navy,
1775–1991/by Stephen Howarth.
p. cm.
Includes bibliographical references and index.
ISBN 0-394-57662-4
1. United States. Navy—History.   2. United States—History,
Naval.   I. Title.
VA55.H69 1991
359'.00973—dc20   90-52889

Manufactured in the United States of America

2 4 6 8 9 7 5 3

First Edition

"A chant, for the sailors of all nations"
—WALT WHITMAN

CONTENTS

★

SAILING ORDERS:
PAST AND PROLOGUE

★

*I*t may be useful to indicate at the outset what kind of a book this is—its scope, its limitations, and its overall intent—and what kind of book it is not. It is not a disconnected series of naval adventure stories; but inevitably, frequently, and I hope entertainingly, adventures are included. It is not a sequential analysis of naval strategic development; but naval strategy and its component parts—their development, neglect, alteration, and continuity—form a recurrent theme. Nor is it an inquiry into the American naval psyche; but the reasons Americans go to sea, and their assessments of the Navy's role in peace and war, come into the narrative as well. Likewise, this is not a specialized study in naval technology over a period of two hundred years; but that too is part of the story.

In short, this is by no means a complete and utter history of the U.S. Navy, for the simple reason that the topic is so broad that even a library would be hard put to include every detail of two centuries of U.S. naval development. But this is the story of the rise, and fall, and rise again of the U.S. Navy—a naval history of a nation progressing, sometimes unwillingly, from colonial to superpower status and displaying in its growth all the contradictions and paradoxes of a colony which became an empire; which bred isolationism, yet dreamed of leading humanity to a future free of war; which once foreswore "entangling alliances," yet now heads the alliance of the Western world.

In Washington, D.C., between Constitution and Pennsylvania avenues, stands one of the elegant buildings which characterize the heart of the capital of the United States. Unlike many of the others, this building's elegance is almost all on the outside; the interior is functional and cramped, for the National Archives are the main repository of the nation's constantly growing documentary history. Most of its visitors come to see the Declaration of Independence, displayed inside the Constitution Avenue entrance, but researchers enter from Pennsylvania Avenue, passing between two allegorical statues. The inscriptions on the plinths of the statues are well chosen—a reminder on the left, an admonition on the right: "What is Past is Prologue"—"Study the Past."

There is much wisdom in those phrases; and at least some good sense, I hope, in this book. It sprang from my own study of the Imperial Japanese Navy. In writing that book I began to realize how comparatively little I knew about the U.S. Navy—how easily I accepted it as a fact of life without wondering much about its origins or development, let alone its future. I did not guess how fascinating and absorbing a story lay behind it. A project which started as a small matter of personal curiosity developed into a study of the U.S. Navy in the twentieth century; grew to include the fleet's dramatic transformation, a hundred years ago, from the Old Navy to the New; and grew further to encompass its nineteenth-century history, so different from that of Britain's Royal Navy. Having gone so far, going back to the very beginning was irresistible; and perhaps one of the most outstanding features of U.S. naval history is the intimate relationship between the fleet and the society it has served for two hundred years and more. At every stage the Navy has been the mirror of society, and so *To Shining Sea* may be read not only as a history of the U.S. Navy, but also as a naval history of the United States, tracing some of the nation's major economic, political, and social changes from the opening of the War of Independence to the Cold War's seeming end. When quoting very early sources (for example, letters and logs of the eighteenth century), I have usually modernized spelling and sometimes clarified punctuation. I think this makes them easier to read for most people nowadays, and anyone who needs to check the originals can find them without too much difficulty. Any errors of fact are, unfortunately, mine; but perhaps they may be forgiven, for some are inevitable, no doubt.

In 1906 the philosopher George Santayana remarked that progress, "far from consisting in change, depends on retentiveness." Immediately after writing that, he composed one of his most famous (but generally misquoted) sentences: "Those who cannot remember the past are condemned to fulfil it." In the unfamiliar and exciting climate of the 1990s, looking forward to the twenty-first century, it is possibly more than ever important for us all to remember the past of the fleet which is now one of the world's most potent instruments for war or peace.

At all events, what I have tried to do, within the covers of one volume, is to present a panorama (usually sympathetic) of the U.S. Navy, with most of its famous highlights and some of its infamous lowlights, both for those who have spent their life on the sea and those who have never smelled a salt breeze: for veteran and novice, professional and amateur. Of necessity I have been selective; and of necessity much of what I have selected will be familiar in isolation if not in context, from the invention of the submarine to the recommissioning of the battleship *Iowa* and beyond. Another writer's choice might well have been different in detail or generality, and a reader may feel that some things left out should have been included, or vice versa. But I trust this selection will please most people, and that even the familiar may have the odd refreshing tang.

S.W.R.H.

ACKNOWLEDGMENTS
AND DEDICATION

★

*F*ull source details of all materials cited in this book are given in the notes at the end; my debt to the various authors, archives, owners of manuscripts, libraries, and other repositories of information will be apparent, and I extend my thanks to them all. I do not think anyone has been unfairly omitted, but if so, *mea culpa*.

I am also deeply grateful to the many personnel, active and retired, of the U.S. Navy who gave freely and generously of their time to provide me with interviews and correspondence. Members of the British Royal Navy and ex-members of the Imperial Japanese Navy were likewise kind, courteous, and informative, and if I do not list them here, it is not through ingratitude; their names are in the notes, and to blazon them up front might seem unduly boastful.

Before getting under way, however, there are two names which must be carved boldly on the bow: Philip Wells and Marianne Howarth. Under the businesslike exterior of a bank manager, Philip has the heart of a modern-day patron of the arts; while to my pride and perpetual astonishment, Marianne somehow contrives to combine being a teacher, translator, and author, with being mother to our sons and my darling wife. This book has been a long project made possible only through their tolerance, confidence, and patient support; and so to Marianne and to Philip, I dedicate *To Shining Sea*.

BOOK ONE

WOOD AND CANVAS

1775–1881

PART ONE

RESTRICTION

1775 – 1793

★

With the nation,
the navy is born.
Though small, scattered,
and scarcely organized,
it contributes to the country's
independence.

1

*

WHAT THINK YOU
OF AN AMERICAN FLEET?

*O*n December 17, 1781, after nearly eight years of war, American rebels against the British crown defeated royal forces at the Battle of Yorktown and effectively secured independence for the United States. A little later, pondering all the trials that he and his countrymen had been through to achieve their liberty, one American wrote to a French friend and said, in final assessment of the victory: "It follows then, as certain as night succeeds the day, that without a decisive naval force we can do nothing definitive—and with it, everything honorable and glorious."[1]

This was a remarkable judgment for any American to have made then. During the War of Independence, most of the battles that became famous were land battles—Bunker Hill, Saratoga and all the rest. And it is an even more remarkable judgment when one considers that its author was George Washington—not a sea captain, nor even a sailor, but a general in the Continental Army. Yet he was right, and he himself had taken the first steps in creating the U.S. Navy.

The United States of America is one of the very few countries in the world which can claim with at least some justice to have had a navy of at least some sort since its very earliest days. In midsummer 1775, the thirteen colonies were still legally attached to Great Britain; but with a sense of growing crisis and a fear that the mother country might use force to try to keep them attached, Congress passed a resolution urging each colony to fit out armed vessels for its individual defense. That in itself was a historic proposal, yet the inhabitants of at least one colony felt it was inadequate. On Saturday, August 26, 1775, the members of the Rhode Island General Assembly recorded a frank and momentous decision in their journal:

This colony will most heartily exert the whole power of government, in conjunction with the other colonies, for carrying out this just and necessary war, and bringing the same to a happy issue. And amongst other measures for obtaining this most desirable purpose, this Assembly is persuaded, that the building and equipping [of] an American fleet, as soon as possible, would greatly and essentially conduce to the preservation of the lives, liberties and property of the good people of these Colonies and therefore instruct their delegates to use their whole influence at the ensuing congress for building at the Continental expense a fleet of sufficient force, for the protection of these colonies.[2]

With that resolution, so firmly worded, the Rhode Islanders stepped smartly into American naval history: Theirs was the first public, official proposal for an American fleet—a united navy for the colonies' joint protection, responsible to Congress. The resolution was more than some congressional delegates could take; Samuel Chase of Maryland has been remembered ever since for his opinion that it was "the maddest idea in the world." But George Washington agreed with it wholeheartedly—and had already begun to do something about it.[3]

Two days earlier, at Marblehead, Massachusetts (less than 60 miles north of Rhode Island), "the first armed vessel, fitted out in the Service of the United States" was hired for Continental employment.[4] The little warship was a 78-ton schooner, converted from a merchantman by the addition of four 4-pound cannon and a number of swivel guns (miniature cannon or blunderbusses mounted in pivots on the ship's rail), and she was paid for not by Congress but by Washington, out of his own pocket, to be part of the national defense.

The schooner was named *Hannah* after the wife of her owner, Colonel George Glover. It was he who wrote the note recording that proud first; and it was he who appointed her officers. The captain, Nicholson Broughton, was another resident of Marblehead, and a friend of Glover's; Glover's favorite son, John, was made first lieutenant; Hannah Glover's brother was made sailing master; and the captain's brother-in-law was made second subaltern. If nothing else, it seemed to a canny shipowner that an American navy could be a handy extension of the family business. In fact, *Hannah* was not very successful, but other hired vessels (also paid for by George Washington) quickly followed her, and by the time the first official Continental fleet sailed from the Delaware on February 17, 1776,

Washington's busy little "navy" (though never more than a handful of vessels) had already captured twenty-nine prizes.

John Adams was another of those who, like Washington, could see the possibilities offered by a national navy. On October 19, 1775, he wrote to James Warren, asking: "What think you of an American Fleet?" To forestall a rebuff, he continued:

> I don't mean 100 ships of the line, by a fleet, but I suppose this term may be applied to any naval force consisting of several vessels, though the number, the weight of metal [of the shot], or the quantity of tonnage may be small. The expense would be very great—true. But the expense might be borne, and perhaps the profits and benefits to be obtained by it would be a compensation. It would destroy single cutters and cruisers—it might destroy small concerts or fleets . . .[5]

In fact, Congress had delayed very little on the Rhode Island resolution. On October 13 it decided to make a start by commissioning two ships. At the end of the month the number was doubled, and in November, the Continental Navy's first ship was bought and named *Alfred.*

Thoughtful persuasion (and the march of events) brought doubters around. By the beginning of 1776, even Samuel Chase's imagination had been fired, and he had changed his mind completely. "I would exert every nerve," he wrote to Adams on January 12, "to fit out a number of vessels from 10 to 30 guns. I would cruise for the West India and Jamaica men. I would make prizes of every British vessel wherever found . . ." And he concluded his letter with a snort of anti-British contempt, perhaps indicating the cause of his conversion: "I have this moment seen the King's speech. I am not disappointed. Just as I expected."[6]

Impetuous Chase made it all sound very simple—build the ships, find the crews, send them out, capture the prizes. But it was all a great deal easier said than done. Others, faced with the practical task of working it into reality, quickly found difficulties.

One of the worst problems was learning, by trial and error, how to cast cannon. The skills of iron founding were well known and widely practiced, but British law had forbidden the casting of cannon in the colonies—presumably in fear of just such a rebellion as was now under way. The Continental Navy therefore went to war with only a very rough idea of how to make its main armament. The same was true of anchors—but at least they did not share the cannons' terrifying tendency to explode during manufacture. Mistakes were many and accidents common. A certain Capt. Daniel Joy, supervising the process, described a typical mishap in casting: A core, placed in the mold to make the cannon hollow, was improperly positioned, and "before the iron was all chilled the core flew up and the metal settled in the room"—a cool understatement for

what, in a confined space, would have been a dangerous explosion.[7]
Congress's first policy of centralized cannon manufacture was a failure,
so instead contracts were given to many foundries. One of the most
successful of these was the Hope Furnace in Rhode Island—another
feather in the island's cap. The Hope produced at least a dozen 18-pound-
ers, the heaviest naval guns ever cast in the colonies; but the total number
of cannon successfully made in America during the revolution would
probably not have filled more than twenty or twenty-five first-rate British
ships, and although casting continued throughout the war, the majority
of guns in American vessels were either captured or brought over from
France. Letters from 1776 show the frustration this created for would-be
naval men:

"It grieved me that the frigates cannot be got to sea. . . . They might
before this, had proper attention been paid to cannon . . ."[8]

"We have two fine frigates . . . but after so long a time, not yet ready
to put to sea . . ."[9]

"I can't sufficiently lament the seeming inattention to so important a
matter. A very fine ship lies at Portsmouth waiting only for guns. . . . This
delay disgusts the officers and occasions them to repent entering the
service . . ."[10]

"I suppose a want of anchors will be the greatest obstruction . . ."[11]

And simplest, most plaintive of all: "Where is our rigging for them,
where our guns?"[12]

The hazards of casting cannons and anchors could hold up an operation when everything else was ready, but they were only a beginning.
Probably no greater a proportion of people then than now understood the
intricacies of shipbuilding, or the differences between various types of
vessels, and no doubt Chase and others like him had to have some of it
explained.

Today, too, it is worth explaining some of these things; for when we
know a few of the technicalities concerning the kind of vessels the Americans most wanted and feared (their size, rigging, weaponry, and rating)
and the kind of vessels they were able to build, it is easier to imagine the
true nature of the maritime challenge facing the colonies.

First, the size of seagoing vessels. The Continental Navy's first purchase, *Alfred,* was a converted merchantman "of the burthen of two
hundred tons or thereabouts."[13] Nowadays, since the advent of iron ships
and steam propulsion, the standard measurement of naval craft has been
the amount of water displaced by the vessel, worked out at the rate of 35
cubic feet per ton, with all stores on board and all fuel tanks full. In 1773
(the year before *Alfred* was built), the British began using a rather complicated formula for the purpose, now known as Builders' Old Measurement. Where L was the length of the keel and B the maximum beam, the

formula was $(L - \frac{3}{5}B) \times B \times \frac{1}{2}B$ divided by 94. However, *Alfred*'s 200-ton "burthen" referred to an even older system of measurement, based on a ship's carrying capacity in terms of tuns of wine. Since one of those giant barrels would hold 252 imperial gallons, this provides the engaging thought that *Alfred* could carry about fifty thousand gallons of wine—an idea many crews would relish. In more humdrum terms, her burthen meant she would have been about 120 feet long—a middle-sized ship for the time.

The only other particular clues to her appearance are references to the armament of twenty 9-pound guns, and the fact that she was a *ship*. Then, today, and in this book, the word was and is loosely used in the way everyone understands; but strictly speaking, compared to (for example) a brigantine, a ship was a very different kind of vessel. The distinctions were simple enough, and did not necessarily relate to size. Instead, they were based on the individual vessel's style of rigging. There were six broad types. Top of the list came the ship, with three masts square-rigged, the sails aligned from one side of the craft to the other. Then came the barque, with two square-rigged masts and one rigged fore-and-aft, followed by the two-masted schooner. Both her masts would carry fore-and-aft sails, with an additional square topsail on the foremast. Next was the brig, two masts square-rigged; next, the brigantine, its foremast square-rigged and its aftermast fore-and-aft; and lastly the sloop, still the most common sailing boat, with a single mast and one or two fore-and-aft sails. There were others (the brig sloop, the ship sloop, and more), but these were the major ones.

Then the guns, one of the few elements that distinguished a warship from a merchantman—and not always then, for many merchantmen were armed. The main armament consisted of iron cannon on wooden wheeled carriages, instantly recognizable even to a modern eye. Varying in size, they were defined by the weight of the solid shot they fired, standard weights being 2, 3, 4, 6, 8, 9, 12, and 18 pounds. In the Continental Navy, 4- and 8-pounders were the most common, although they had faded out of use some twenty years earlier in the Royal Navy. *Alfred*'s 9-pounders would have been among the best in America.

Given its weight, an individual shot was remarkably small; even a 12-pounder was only 4.4 inches in diameter (easily held in two cupped hands), while the diameter of a 3-pounder was only 2.77 inches. As ever with nautical terms, the names for the parts of a cannon sound to the inexperienced ear like a foreign language, and strangely poetic—cascabel, trunnions, astragal. These, respectively, were the large round knob at the gunner's end of the cannon; the cylindrical projections in the middle of the sides, supporting and hinging the cannon on its carriage; and the strengthened ring around the cannon's mouth. One of the few words associated with cannon which is still familiar today is caliber, the diameter of the bore at the muzzle. In Europe, it had been found from experience that the ideal length for a cannon was fifteen caliber; thus, a 12-pounder would be five feet six inches from end to end. There were complicated formulae not only for the construction of the cannon, but for the carriage as well; and to begin with, the colonial Americans, with little direct experience or guidance, had to try to work all these out for themselves.

As guns were rated by the weight of their shot, so ships were rated by the number of their "great guns," the main armament. A ship's secondary armament could include swivel guns and coehorns—short mortars throwing explosive grenades, named (in a more English-sounding way) after their inventor in the late seventeenth century, the Dutch Baron van Coehoorn. Small arms were very varied, often reflecting the kind of weapons a man might keep to defend his home—pistols, muskets, cutlasses, tomahawks, pikes, grenades. But only the main armament counted toward a ship's rating, and at the time of the American Revolution British naval ship ratings fell into six groups. Sixth-rates carried anything up to 32 main guns; fifth-rates had from 32 to 50; fourth-rates, 50 to 70; third-rates, 70 to 84; second-rates, between 84 and 100; and first-rate liners carried a hundred or more main guns.

With commercial steamships today, liners are those which ply their trade on a regular route, or line. Wooden naval liners were those warships that sailed into the line of battle: With the advent of steam, their full title, line-of-battle ships, changed to the more punchy word "battleships." Normally, only ships of the first, second, and third rates were stationed in the line of battle. Very occasionally, fourth-rates joined them (in 1798, at the Battle of the Nile, H.M.S. *Leander,* a fourth-rate of 50 guns, simultaneously engaged two French third-rates carrying 154 guns between them), but generally a fourth-rate would be detached from a fleet to cruise independently, fighting enemy ships it met if possible, and if not, sending news of their whereabouts back to the main fleet. Hence, of course, the English name cruiser, a term that was also applied to a fifth- or sixth-rate if it was sent on the same kind of duty. But being comparatively small and lightly armed, these last vessels were not usually asked to face such challenges, and they never fought in the line of battle. Instead, since their main virtue was speed, they acted before a battle as scouts and lookouts, while in a battle they relayed the admiral's signals (possibly obscured by smoke) to his other liners. In Nelson's phrase, they were the eyes of the fleet. Every navy had such ships, and (allowing for different spellings in different languages) most navies called them by the same name: frigates.

Thus, thinking of those first vessels sent out to defend America, the picture becomes a little clearer. Compared to *Hannah* (78 tons, sloop-rigged with a single mast, bearing four 4-pounder guns that fired balls no more than 3 inches in diameter), *Alfred* was majestic: 120 feet long, ship-rigged with three masts, and armed with no less than twenty 9-pounders. But these were very small craft to be called men-of-war. The Royal Navy would have instantly classed *Alfred* as a sixth-rate, a small frigate; and considering that she was the best warship then available in America and that one solitary British first-rate would have five times more *and larger* guns, it is not surprising that some Americans thought the whole idea was mad.

Casting cannons and anchors, vital as it was, was unexplored territory. Building ships was not, and vessels built for the Continental Navy were often very good. When Robert Morris (soon to be superintendent of finance for the united colonies) remarked that "our frigates are really fine ships,"[14] it was not merely his own opinion.

In 1777 the thirty-two-gun *Hancock,* built in 1776 at Newburyport, Massachusetts, was captured by an overwhelming force of three Royal Navy ships mounting a total of ninety-eight guns between them. The Royal Navy liked her so much she became a British ship, renamed *Iris* and described by her captors as "the finest and fastest frigate in the world."[15] But the pressures of war frequently forced colonial shipwrights to use green, unseasoned timber—no doubt against their better judgment, for they must have known it would quickly decay and waste their labor. The worst example of this was *America,* the one and only seventy-four-gun ship built for the Continental Navy. Ordered in November 1776, she was laid down at Portsmouth, New Hampshire, in May 1777. It took five and a half years to build her, and she was never in the war. At her launch on November 5, 1782, she must have been an impressive sight: 182 feet 6 inches long on the upper deck, with a maximum beam of 50 feet 6 inches and a hold 23 feet deep. Yet she was already rotting to pieces. The process was quick and complete. In 1786 she was broken up, and it cannot have been difficult; there was not a single sound timber left in her.

It was manifestly impossible for the colonies to build a fleet of the same size or kind as the Royal Navy; resources were too few, and time was too short. Instead, the policy was to build or buy as many smaller ships as possible. Those first naval Americans desperately wished for time: time to experiment, to do trials at a reasonable pace, to create a navy slowly and steadily with the gathered experience of years to guide them. But everything had to be done at once: working out a strategy, ordering vessels and arms, establishing some kind of administration, recruiting and training officers and men. There was simply no time to spare, as Benjamin Hichborn emphasized to John Adams in the winter of 1775: "We may expect our coast to swarm with [British] transports and men of war next spring," he wrote. "Two or three frigates of two and thirty guns would be of incredible service."[16]

Under such pressure, mistakes were to be expected. One serious deficiency was ignorance of naval administration; during the eight years of the War of Independence, no less than four separate bodies were set up, one after another, to control the Continental fleet. First the three-man Naval Committee was established in mid-October 1775. After being increased to seven men two weeks later, it was renamed the Marine Committee in December and again increased to include one man from each colony. This was so cumbersome and inefficient that in 1779 the committee was dissolved and replaced by a three-man Board of Admiralty; but none of the three knew much about the sea, and their funds were very small. So in 1781, when Robert Morris became superintendent of finance for the colonies, the board looked to him for help. Reputed to be the wealthiest man in America, Morris's business flair made him a natural financial controller, but his ability did not end there; he understood more of naval needs than the whole Board of Admiralty put together. The "Admiralty" speedily acknowledged this (probably with some relief) and in September 1781 their board was dissolved. Morris became agent of marine, with sole responsibility for and authority over the fleet's organization.

Morris's abilities have always been praised, and if Congress made mistakes before choosing him, at least it was willing to keep on trying until it found the right man; but by then it was really too late. In the war overall, no more than sixty vessels of all sorts were in Continental service; and even in the year of its maximum size (1777) it contained only thirty-four craft. The fleet was always pocket-sized, and by 1781 it had almost ceased to exist. Of the thirteen frigates ordered in the hasty winter of 1775, only one survived—the twenty-eight-gun *Trumbull,* built in Chatham, Connecticut. The other dozen had all been wrecked, burnt, blown up, or captured. Apart from *Trumbull* there remained only three frigates of a later order (*Alliance, Confederacy,* and *Deane*) and a single sloop-of-war, *Saratoga,* in active service.

Confederacy surrendered in April 1781; in the same month *Saratoga* vanished, presumed lost in a gale; and in August *Trumbull* surrendered—ironically, to H.M.S. *Iris,* once the Continental *Hancock,* "the finest and fastest frigate in the world." So when Morris took over, the so-called Continental fleet consisted of only two active vessels.

However, there were far more than just those two to defend America's interests at sea. There was the navy of France, allied to America since February 6, 1778; and since the outset of the war, there had been the state navies and the privateers.

Early in 1776 John Adams expressed the hope that as well as Continental ships, those of individual colonies (the "state" navies) and private people would be "a security . . . against the depredations of cutters and tenders at least."[17] The state navies were not much good for anything else; numerically far larger than the Continental fleet at its best, their individual units were far weaker and generally included only two very basic types of vessel.

"The one is row galleys and the other is fireships," Adams wrote in that revolutionary summer. Along with floating gun batteries, he believed that these vessels would strike terror into men-of-war. The threat from fireships could indeed be great, and he hoped that since the row galleys would be low and small, it would be almost impossible for a warship to bring its guns to bear on them. Best of all, in his judgment, would be "a kind of dodging Indian fight . . . among the islands in our harbor, between such galleys and the men-of-war." He was right in part, but as he found out later, such guerrilla war was effective only to a very limited extent; and from America's viewpoint, the two main results of creating the state navies were negative.[18] During the war they took away weapons, materials, men, and time that would all have been much better used for the Continental fleet. More important, they engendered a belief in a strategy of pure coastal defense that could make an oceangoing navy unnecessary. That belief lasted longer and caused more trouble to America than any benefit the state navies brought.

In another category altogether were the privateers. In wartime most maritime countries used such vessels as an informal adjunct to official naval forces. Their virtue was their availability: By issuing private merchantmen with letters of marque (the legal authorization distinguishing a privateer from a pirate), the governor of a British colony, for example, could quickly provide himself with a useful sea arm, additional to or in place of regular warships. Allowing civilian shipowners to capture enemy craft and sell them and their contents on the open market for personal profit did, at any rate, engage all possible vessels at a time when Congress did not have the power or authority to requisition them. For the same reason, it was naturally very popular with the shipowners and their crews: "We have nothing going forward here, but fixing out privateers, and condemnation and sale of prizes sent in by them, so many that I am quite lost in my estimate of them."[19] Privateering was much more popular than naval service: It was more profitable, less risky, less disciplined, just as exciting, and everyone involved had the necessary sea skills already.

This was the system's major drawback. Since the privateers were allowed to sell their captures for their own profit, they tempted men away from the regular service and drained its limited personnel resources. Complaints on these lines began early: "Our people are entering on board privateers so fast," one American lamented, "that we shall have few hands left for the Continent."[20]

"Our own navigation is almost wholly turned into privateering," another agreed;[21] and even John Adams took up the cry. "The success of your privateers is encouraging," he wrote to James Warren in August 1776, but then he added: "We suffer inexpressibly from want of men of business—men acquainted with war by sea and land, men who have no pleasure but in that business. You have them; send them along."[22]

From the official point of view, privateers were a mixed blessing, since they were not and could not be a fully organized part of the war effort. They remained volunteers at all times, prompted mainly by the chance of personal gain, and despite their authorizing letters of marque, they could not be ordered to fight, or even to go to a particular place, unless they chose to. From their victims' point of view they had one advantage over pirates: Pirates often murdered captured crews, but privateers usually (though not always) treated them as prisoners of war and brought them back alive for ransom. Nevertheless, some privateering captains gave a very liberal interpretation to their letters of marque, seeing them as licenses to make prize of anyone's property, even if the victim was a fellow American. One complaint of such habits almost has a ring of prophecy about it, foreshadowing the Civil War by eighty years:

"Unless some measures are immediately taken to prevent the infamous practices of the privateers, America will soon be in a state of general confusion—one part warring with another, and the defenceless Southern colonies becoming a devoted prey to their more formidable Eastern neighbours."[23]

If controlling and organizing the Navy was hard, it was almost impossible with the privateers. Every letter of marque was a tossed coin that could come down, unpredictably, for or against the American cause. The privateers were far more numerous than the ships of the official navy: In their peak year of 1781 alone, almost 450 independent privateers were operating, and during the course of the war 1,697 letters of marque were issued. But for all their numbers, privateers took only three times as many prizes as the official navy. They were, in other words, comparatively inefficient, as well as risky and unreliable; yet privateering would not have been allowed if it had not been perceived as an advantage to the nation— or at least as the best that could be done under the circumstances.

In the first decades of this century, historians usually regarded the privateers as little but a damaging dissipation of America's efforts to promote the Revolution at sea. However, after the depredations of the submarine raiders of both world wars, that judgment was partly revised. The privateers were a disorganized but authentic mosquito fleet, able to dart and thrust and sting annoyingly; able to capture and bring home supplies of munitions, food, and clothing; and able, above all, to harass British shipping (especially transports) so that transatlantic supply lines became even slower and more risky than normal.

Some of the privateers' diaries and letters still survive, and there is one in particular that gives a splendidly vivid description of the appeal of privateering. Its author was an army surgeon who joined the privateer *Hope* for a single cruise at the beginning of October 1780.[24] He had the extraordinary and ominous name of Dr. Solomon Drowne; but his voyage was as successful as anyone could wish.

In twelve disappointing days of sailing, *Hope* had sighted half a dozen vessels. Some had proved to be friendly, others too fast to catch, others too strong to fight; so far, *Hope* had not caught a single prize. But Sunday, October 15, was, in Dr. Drowne's words, "a pleasant day." They saw a sail to windward, coming towards them, and decided to wait and see what happened. "More agreeable waiting for them," said Drowne, "than rowing after them." He passed the time fishing, caught a hake and a few dogfish, and then (because it was a Sunday) put on a clean shirt "in order to be something like folks ashore." Becoming impatient, *Hope*'s crew started to chase the stranger and could soon identify it as a snow—the largest contemporary type of two-masted vessel.

"Got everything in readiness to board her," Drowne continued. "There seems something awful in the preparation for an attack, and the immediate prospect of an action. She hauls up her courses and hoists English colours." He took his station in the cabin, where he would operate if necessary; but before long he heard a loud cheer outside. In spite of her "four excellent four-pounders" and a crew of ten, the snow had surrendered without a fight. From her captain's papers they learned she had sailed from Jamaica forty days before and was bound for New York. They also discovered she was carrying a privateers' dream cargo. Drowne must have taken a deep breath before he listed it all:

"149 puncheons, 23 hogsheads, 3 quarter casks and 9 barrels of rum, and 20 hogshead Muscovado sugar. Send two prize Masters and ten men on board, get the prisoners on board our vessel, and taking the prize in tow, stand towards Egg Harbour. We hardly know what to do with the prize . . ."

No wonder! All the containers mentioned except the hogsheads were of variable sizes, but the sum is worth doing, as best one may—because a hogshead held 52½ imperial gallons, while a puncheon held anything from 72 to 120 imperial gallons. So on the most conservative estimate, that entirely painless capture netted a staggering minimum of 11,935½ imperial gallons of Jamaica rum. In U.S. gallons the figure sounds even more impressive, working out as 14,325; and there were still the barrels and quarter casks, not to mention the possibility that the puncheons may have held not 72 but 120 imperial gallons each. No one outside a distillery had ever seen so much rum in one place in his life, and now it all belonged to *Hope*'s small crew, to be drunk (as no doubt a good deal of it was) or sold on the open market, with the proceeds divided among them.

Sailing homeward, Dr. Drowne's reaction was very understandable—

"Now we are terribly apprehensive of seeing a sail"—so it is pleasant to report that they all came home safe, if not sound. Their livers may have been ruined, but they had contributed a little bit to the war, and their fortunes were probably made. And that was what privateering was all about.

Coming close to turning war into sport, the privateers were glamorous, numerous, and fairly dangerous. However, though they were a nuisance to the British, in the long run their greatest value to America was in training men who, in later years, would become famous sailors in the regular service. In the short run, they did slow down British supplies; yet in spite of their numbers and Adams's ever optimistic view that they were an "infallible method of humbling the British," they never came close to breaking the supply lines permanently. In 1776, 763 transports and victualers crossed the ocean safely. Thereafter the annual total never dropped below two hundred, and even in 1782, 318 ships totaling over a hundred thousand tons made the passage successfully. Freight rates jumped from 9 shillings a ton a month before hostilities to 13 shillings in ready money during the summer of 1783; insurance shot up from 3 percent of the combined value of cargo and vessel in 1776 to 30 percent in 1778. But the ships never stopped sailing.

Of course, the privateers did not want to stop the flow altogether. Their trophies, valuable vessels and cargoes, were sold at the highest possible profit and they did not have to protect other American vessels; they were, in a word, selfish rather than patriotic. "If Virtue is the doing good to others," Dr. Drowne admitted, "privateering cannot be justified upon the principles of Virtue." But no one expected privateers to be virtuous; and if their effects on the war were limited, that simply reflected America's ability at sea when it first went to war with Great Britain.

2

★

THE REBEL FLEET WAS ATTACKED AND DESTROYED

*A*t the beginning of the War of Independence, America's varied efforts at sea may have been small, but they certainly worried the British. On arrival in New York from England, Adm. Molyneux Shuldham wrote to the Admiralty in London, expressing his concern at "the number of small armed vessels fitted out by the rebels, and which had taken many unarmed ones of ours bringing stores and supplies to this place." His voyage across the Atlantic had been terrible—sixty-one days of "almost a constant succession of storms and contrary winds, attended with the most severe weather I ever felt"—and that letter, dated January 15, 1776, was his first message back. But it was not received in London until July 14—an indication of the eighteenth-century Admiralty's problem in trying to fight a war three thousand miles away.[1]

As for the Continental Navy, the problems it faced (apart from shortage of material and pressure of time) were recruiting, retention, and leadership. The recruiting net was laid as wide as possible; men enlisted needed to be "able bodied and perfect in all their limbs and sight, of sound health without ruptures or other visible infirmities, above five feet four inches, and above sixteen and under fifty years of age: and if above forty they must be of robust constitution."[2] (The point about rupture was wise: without heavy lifting gear, rupture was a seaman's most likely injury.) But beyond the physical efforts that went with the job, those who joined the regular service often found it brutal, as this letter of complaint shows:

We cannot bear with it. We like all our officers but two, Captain Hazard and Mr. Spooner; they carry sticks with bullets in and ropes' ends to beat us with. We are kept from morning till night upon deck and have scarce time to eat. We hope that you will take it into consideration we mean to be true subjects to the country; we mean to do all that lies in our power for the country; but we are used like dogs on board the *Providence.* We hope you will find a new Captain or a new vessel.[3]

Certainly discipline was harsh, but no more so than in any other navy. As it happened, the crew of *Providence* did get a new commanding officer: The aptly named Captain Hazard was court-martialed and stripped of his rank. But, accused of embezzlement (which he called "a mere trifle indeed") and of disobeying orders ("my conscience don't accuse me of doing it knowingly"), significantly, the question of brutality did not occur at all.[4]

Hazard's letter of defense was written to the commander in chief of the Navy, Esek Hopkins, who in himself epitomized another of the flaws of the service. On November 6, 1775, he was told that the Naval Committee "have pitched upon you to take the command of a small fleet, which they and I hope will be but the beginning of one much larger." Hopkins's pay, the writer went on confidently, would be enough to give him "no reason to complain," which was fair enough—except that the writer (a member of the Naval Committee) was Esek's brother Stephen.[5] A family business could easily become nepotism, in Washington's fleet or the Continental Navy.

On the other hand, if the appointees were genuinely the best candidates, nepotism was irrelevant, and Esek Hopkins's first actions made him seem a good choice. In February 1776 he led the Continental Navy's first voyage, sailing to the Bahamas. In Nassau he captured a substantial quantity of cannon, mortars, and military stores. During the return voyage he also caught several British ships and successfully fought off a large British attack. But that was all he ever did for the Navy. Thereafter he sat in his ship and did nothing, and if seamen and captains could be disciplined, so could commanders in chief. The "old hero," as loyal John Adams called him, was not heroic enough ("the reasons given for not complying literally with his instructions were by no means satisfactory") and he was sacked.[6]

Nepotism bred incompetence, and was no way to start a navy under the urgent demands of war. Yet both remained perennial problems, and the new captain of *Providence* knew it: "I could heartily wish," he wrote, "that every commissioned officer were to be previously examined—for, to my certain knowledge, there are persons who have already been accepted into commission without abilities or fit qualification."[7]

Perhaps it is not surprising that the writer, one of the greatest leaders of the first U.S. Navy, was the self-confident and outspoken John Paul Jones. And he had more to say on the matter:

When *gain* is the ruling principle of officers in an infant Navy, it is no wonder that they do not cultivate by their precepts nor enforce by their example the principles of *dutiful subordination, cheerful unrepining* obedience in those who are under their command, nor is it strange that this principle should weaken the sacred bonds of order and discipline, and introduce the mistaken and baneful idea of licentiousness and free agency under the specious name of "Liberty."[8]

This eloquent Scot was a stickler for discipline on board because he knew its value, especially against the Royal Navy. He did not hesitate to contrast the Continental Navy with the British, in a very prophetic manner:

I propose not our enemies as an example for our general imitation—yet as their Navy is the best regulated of any in the world, we must in some degree imitate them, and aim at such further improvement as may one day make ours vie with and exceed theirs.[9]

To check Jones's remark, it is worth taking a look at the enemies. Many Royal Navy officers would have accepted that their service was the best regulated in the world, and most Americans who knew anything about it would have agreed—which was partly why they feared it. One American who disagreed was Christopher Gadsden, member of the Continental Congress for South Carolina. He explained "several times" to John Adams that "this fleet is not so formidable to America as we fear," telling Adams that in his younger days he had been an officer in the Royal Navy, "well acquainted with the Fleet."[10] In fact, Gadsden's British naval experience was limited to two years as a purser; yet his assessment of the enemy was fair. The Royal Navy had once been the "best regulated of any in the world," and it would be again; but at the time of the American Revolution, it was not—or if it was, all others must have been very badly regulated indeed.

In 1759, when John Paul Jones was twelve, the Royal Navy had excelled itself at Quiberon Bay and (with the British army) at Quebec. David Garrick extolled "this wonderful year" in his patriotic song "Heart of Oak," and Scottish-born Jones grew up half hating and half admiring the song's arrogant pride. At Trafalgar, a quarter century after the War of Independence, the Royal Navy swept the seas clear of opposition again, and then was undoubtedly the world's best-regulated fleet. But when America declared independence and Britain had to fight a far-distant war, the British Admiralty was going through a period of inefficiency, complacency, and alleged corruption. The fleet had been drastically cut after the

Seven Years' War; the administration was in a shambles. Delays in transatlantic correspondence were inevitably long, but delays in London itself
were sometimes as long. Even Sir Charles Middleton, comptroller of the
navy, raged against "the sluggish manner in which business goes through
the Admiralty" and "the notorious remissness of official correspondence"; yet even he could do little about it.[11] In transporting supplies,
different departments bid against each other for the services of too few
ships, thus artificially and absurdly inflating prices. At a moment when
twenty ships of the line were supposed to be in Portsmouth ready to sail,
their admiral found "not more than six . . . in any condition to go upon
service"; and in the West Indies, another admiral "met with every neglect
from home, and had a fleet to equip without stores, to victual without
provisions, and to man without men."[12]

Added to the disadvantage of distance and inefficiency bordering on
incompetence, the British had two further handicaps in their prosecution
of the war. First of these was that many Britons did not regard Americans
as enemies at all, but instead saw the colonists' cause as a fair one and
the colonists themselves as cousins. As one Englishman wrote to a "rebel"
overseas: 'Every friend of Liberty and the English Constitution rejoices
to hear of the firmness and unanimity of our brethren in America. By
your own virtue, valour and perseverance you are to expect a deliverance
from the yoke."[13] And when another writer felt obliged to say of Admiral
Shuldham that he "goes well convinced that he is to act in every respect
as against an enemy," it showed the enmity did not come naturally.[14]
Indeed, after one particular battle, the victorious Gov. Sir Guy Carleton
(leader of the British forces in Canada) was explicit:

> This success cannot be deemed less than a complete victory. But
> considering it was obtained over the King's subjects, that, which in
> other circumstances ought to be a proper cause of public rejoicing,
> is, in these, matter only of great concern; and therefore though it may
> be right to communicate it to the troops, yet I dare say they think
> with me, that we should suppress all signs of triumph on the occa-
> sion.[15]

Alongside this feeling of unease, another English admiral, Richard
Kempenfelt, noted the second weakness in the British attitude. He defined
it as "a vulgar notion, even with our gentry, that our seamen are braver.
. . . Ridiculous to suppose courage dependent on climate. The men who
are best disciplined, of whatever country they are, will always fight the
best."[16]

Physically distant, mentally complacent, and not entirely convinced
they should be at war at all—overall, Gadsden was right in saying the
Royal Navy was "not so formidable to America as we fear." When Jones

said, "We must in some degree imitate them," he was thinking of the Quiberon Bay–Quebec model—the Royal Navy of a generation earlier, when discipline and daring led to victory. In time, the U.S. Navy would imitate that model, and (as Jones hoped) would create "such further improvement as may one day make ours vie with and exceed theirs." But like every navy after victory, in time it would also imitate the complacency, confusion, and inefficiency.

In those highly charged days of the Revolution, however, there was one area of naval warfare in which America followed no established model at all: war under water. Eager to use all available weapons, willing to invent where none existed, the rebel colonists launched two imaginative enterprises—the brainchildren of one man—that came close enough to success to give the Royal Navy a couple of bad frights. If they had succeeded, they would have brought naval war forward, for better or worse, by a hundred years; for it was America's Continental Navy that introduced mines and a submarine into warfare.

The first the British knew of these was from a letter sent on November 16, 1776, to Admiral Shuldham: "The great news of the day with us is to destroy the Royal Navy. A certain Mr. Bushnell has completed his machine . . ."[17]

Just one week earlier, in a letter to Silas Deane, Dr. Benjamin Gale had written: "In your last you requested I would give you an account of the progress of our machine, and whether anything may be expected of it. I now sit down to give you a succinct but imperfect account of its structure, which is so complicated that it is impossible to give a perfect idea of it."[18]

Gale then proceeded to give a description that was actually so long and detailed that many years later, marine engineers were able to reproduce the object in question accurately. "The body," Gale began, "when standing upright in the position in which it is navigated, has a nearest resemblance to the two upper shells of a tortoise joined together . . ."

David Bushnell's invention was appropriately named *Turtle.* Men had been pondering the possibilities of an underwater boat since the early sixteenth century: Leonardo da Vinci sketched one in his farsighted technical notebooks. In 1578 the Briton William Bourne described the theory behind a submarine:

It is possible to make a ship or boat that may go under the water unto the bottom, and so come up again at your pleasure. . . . Anything that sinketh is heavier than the proportion of so much water, and if it be lighter than the magnitude of so much water, then it swimmeth or appeareth above the water.[19]

No one knows whether the vessel Bourne described was ever built, but his simple expression of the law of submersibility was faultless; every submarine, even the colossal nuclear *Typhoon* class of today's Soviet navy, rises and sinks on the same principle.

Between Bourne's time and Bushnell's, at least three other experimental submarines had been built, one in Holland and two in England. None had worked. In the first, the operators nearly suffocated; the second did not move; the third sank. *Turtle* did not sink. She moved laboriously but adequately; and her solo operator, Ezra Lee, did not suffocate, though he was exhausted by the effort of working her.

Turtle was egg-shaped, the pointed end going downward and ballasted by 900 pounds of lead, 200 pounds of which could be dropped off. She had two ballast tanks that could be filled with air or water; two hand-driven propellers, one for forward and one for vertical propulsion; a rudder; a snorkel breathing tube, which the German navy would reinvent in the twentieth century; a depth gauge; and a tiny conning tower with thickly glassed portholes. Apart from hydroplanes to maintain a constant depth, the odd little vessel had all the basic essentials; but ultimately it did not work.

On its top there was a detachable drill or large screw that her operator, Lee, was meant to drive into the bottom of a ship. Attached to this was a charge of 150 pounds of gunpowder—Bushnell had already established it could explode under water—with a clockwork-timed firing mechanism. When Lee set off to attack Admiral Lord Howe's flagship *Eagle,* lying off New York, he was able to see, to breathe, and to navigate. He managed to get his cumbersome craft underneath *Eagle,* and bumping around in the underwater darkness, he could hear and feel the hull. But to his extreme frustration, he could not get the drill and its attached charge to fix into the ship's bottom.

At last he gave up the attempt. It was not tried again, and since then it has usually been assumed that the cause of Lee's failure was the newly adopted British practice of putting copper sheets on ships' bottoms. These protected the hull from wood-boring teredo worms and from marine growth, thus making the ship go faster; Lee's drill likewise would have been unable to pierce the metal. In fact, *Eagle* had not been copper-bottomed at that date. All that prevented the American Revolution from being a revolution in naval warfare too was that Bushnell had not allowed for Newton's third law of dynamics—that a given force has an equal and opposite reaction. With nothing to support *Turtle* underneath, the harder Lee turned the drill, the harder he pushed himself away from *Eagle*'s hull.

Undeterred, the inventive and patriotic Bushnell proceeded with the concept of mine warfare. He set a quantity of fused barrels of gunpowder floating down the Delaware, intending them to drift onto and blow up against the moored British ships. Again the experiment failed; but it did give the British a tremendous scare, because neither they nor anyone else had ever seen such a thing before. For a while they watched the bobbing barrels, not knowing what to make of them as they approached; then one exploded prematurely, and "the danger of these machines being discovered, the British manned the wharfs and shipping, and discharged their small arms and cannon at every thing they saw floating in the river."[20]

So wrote Frances Hopkinson, a member of the Marine Committee. To him it was a comic, panic-stricken sight, and being something of a poet, a little later on he put the story into cheerful doggerel:

> *Gallants attend and hear a friend*
> *Trill forth harmonious ditty;*
> *Strange things I'll tell which late befell*
> *In Philadelphia city.*
>
> *'Twas early day, as poets say,*
> *Just when the sun was rising,*
> *A soldier stood on a log of wood,*
> *And saw a thing surprising.*
>
> *As in amaze he stood to gaze,*
> *The truth can't be denied, sir,*
> *He spied a score of kegs or more*
> *Come floating down the tide, sir.*
>
> *. . . The kegs, 'tis said, tho' strongly made,*
> *Of rebel staves and hoops, sir,*
> *Could not oppose their powerful foes,*
> *The conqu'ring British troops, sir.*
>
> *From morn to night these men of might*
> *Display'd amazing courage;*
> *And when the sun was fairly down,*
> *Retir'd to sup their porrage . . .*
>
> *Such feats did they perform that day,*
> *Against these wicked kegs, sir,*
> *That years to come, if they get home,*
> *They'll make their boasts and brags, sir.*

His complete verse went on a good deal longer in similar vein, all a lot of fun; and no doubt he was right. Back home in England, by their firesides or in pubs, the British troops probably did boast and brag about the "Battle of the Kegs," as it came to be known. But somehow, despite its importance in the experimental development of naval warfare, it is not often mentioned in modern British accounts of the war with America— maybe because, if it failed as an attack, it left Bushnell and Hopkinson and all their countrymen with the satisfaction of making the "conquering British troops" look very foolish.

Leaving such diversions aside, however, the Continental Navy had three serious functions, all of which it carried out to the best of its ability, and it is probably fair to say that without them, America would not have won its independence in the eighteenth century.

The first was well expressed in the Rhode Island resolution of 1775: Ships were to be used "in such a manner and places as will most effectually annoy our enemies." This was a modest and realistic ambition; few people dreamed of fleet actions. There were many single-ship actions, and some with a few ships simultaneously; but none had any long-term effects on the war for either side.

Beyond annoyance, the Navy's second function was in combined operations with the Continental Army. Wherever possible, ships were used to transport soldiers quickly from one theater of operations to another, or to support soldiers fighting on land. On one outstanding occasion, soldiers and sailors joined forces completely to fight side by side on land and water in one of the war's key battles—the Battle of Lake Champlain. This is how it came about.

Old England and New England share more than a name and similarities of climate; a look at a map shows that New England is halfway to being an island as well. Just over the border in Canada, the great St. Lawrence River cuts sharply in from the sea to Quebec and Montreal. South of Montreal, lakes Champlain and George, together with the Hudson River, form an almost continuous waterway to the Atlantic at New York. To the east of the lakes and river are the Green Mountains; to the west, the Adirondacks and the Catskills. The valley is the sole natural line of communication between those parts of Canada and the United States; even today it is the route of Interstate 87 from New York to the border. In 1775 and '76, it was the route by which the American colonies tried to wrest Canada from the British, and by which the British tried to isolate New England from the other colonies.

In 1775 two small American armies invaded Canada, advancing on Montreal and Quebec. Montreal was quickly taken, as the British evacuated it; the two American armies then combined under one leader, Benedict Arnold; and over the winter he besieged Quebec. On May 6, 1776, the siege was broken when the frozen St. Lawrence began to thaw and a British naval vessel came through. Through May a counteroffensive was mounted. Arnold's force slowly retreated to Crown Point, close to Lake Champlain's southern end, and there he prepared to fight for control of the lake—because whoever controlled the lake controlled the north-and-south flow of armies.

On July 5, a French spy in London wrote to the Comte de Vergennes (his country's foreign minister) in Paris about "the plans of the Royal Army in Canada." The informant revealed that British plans were "to penetrate the English colonies by way of the Lakes Champlain and George. It has been admitted that much time will be needed to build the boats required for this passage. Then, these boats will have to be carried from one lake to the other, and the Americans will have to be overcome at Ticonderoga [south of Crown Point]." The spy also pointed out the most obvious initial problem the British would have to face: "We might say that first of all the Lakes must be reached . . ."[21]

Not only men, but guns, food, and tools had to be moved—as well as one whole prefabricated ship, built and then dismantled in Canada, transported cross country, and reconstructed at the north end of Lake Champlain. Lt. John Starke, R.N., proudly called this effort a "very extraordinary and singular piece of service" taking "great exertions of ingenuity and labour." This was true; but the operation also took three months.[22] During those months Benedict Arnold was equally busy at the lake's southern end, and over the summer of 1776, with less than 50 miles of lake separating them, the opposing sides built fleets for themselves in a miniature arms race, hacking the timber from the virgin forest.

Construction was rapid and without refinement: "We build a thing called a gondola . . . in a week," wrote one of Arnold's colleagues. But both sides, especially the Americans, were badly hampered by lack of supplies. "Where is our rigging for them, where our guns?" the same colleague lamented.[23] By the beginning of October Arnold was desperate and angry. Calling his supply requisition for the first of the month a "Memorandum of Articles which have been repeatedly wrote for, and which we are in the extremest want of," he listed musket balls, buckshot, and 1,740 cannonballs; swivels, anchors, needles, and twine; nails, ropes, and yarn; "all the useless old iron that will do for langridge," for ripping an enemy's sails and rigging; "all the old junk that can be spared—1,000 tacks for sponges [to cool the cannon], 1 barrel pitch, 1 ditto tar. . . . Rum, as much as you please. . . . Clothing, for at least half the men in the fleet are naked"; and more men. But they had to be good men: "One hundred seamen," he said firmly. "No land lubbers."[24]

Certainly any landlubbers would do well to keep clear of Arnold. He might have been expected to ask for marines; today they would be regarded as essential for such an operation. However, Arnold would have nothing to do with them—some had accompanied him in the march to Quebec, and from that he had decided they were "the refuse of every regiment."[25]

If he could afford to be choosy about marines, though, he could not about his fleet. To call a gondola a "thing" was apt. They had no connection with the romantic but un-naval Venetian gondola; the ones in the battle of Lake Champlain were small flat-bottomed craft of about 53 feet in length, armed with a 12-pound gun at the bow, a few 9-pounders, and a swivel or two. Powered by oars and with a single fore-and-aft sail, they were chosen because (as Arnold's colleague Col. John Trumbull pointed out) they could be built quickly and easily. And one of those impromptu vessels still exists, for in 1935 Capt. L. F. Hagglund recovered the gondola *Philadelphia* from the mud at the bottom of Lake Champlain. Today, in a remarkable state of preservation (and with a British cannonball still lodged in her hull), she is displayed in the Smithsonian Institution in Washington, D.C.—a humble little "thing," but a relic of the very beginning of her country's navy and a direct link with America's birth by water.

By the beginning of October, Arnold's fleet consisted of fifteen units with ninety-four guns and about 700 men. In his command were four row galleys, eight gondolas, three schooners, and a single sloop; and at the north end of the lake, in addition to a fleet very like Arnold's, the British had their one prefabricated full ship, *Inflexible,* carrying eighteen 12-pounders. For every 600 pounds of shot Arnold could fire, the British could fire a thousand; and with longer range, they could give battle when they chose and be almost certain of victory.

The lilliputian arms race to win a lake sounds so like a child's game on a boating pond that its full seriousness can easily be forgotten. But each side knew the stakes, and over a century later, Adm. Alfred Mahan described it with a good phrase—it was "a strife of pigmies for the prize of a continent."[26]

Both sides accepted that if the British broke through and isolated New England, the union of rebel colonies was likely to collapse, and there would be no independence for America. Gen. Sir William Howe (Admiral Lord Howe's brother) controlled New York. Arnold was fully aware that his boats were all that stood between the city and the British fleet on Lake Champlain, "and," he said, "if they hear in time, they will doubtless attempt a junction. If they think it practicable, their fleet, I make no doubt, in the course of this month will be very formidable."[27]

The moment was closer than he realized. On October 10—the very day he wrote that report—the British felt they were ready. One of them, a man named Joshua Pell, wrote about it in his diary. With a fair north wind blowing the royal vessels swiftly to their goal, "our little squadron sailed from Pointe au Fer toward the upper or great lake." Arnold saw them coming before they saw him, which gave him the chance to assemble his fleet in the lee of Valcour Island, between the island and the lake's west shore. "About 12 o'clock on the 11th," Pell noted, "one of our armed boats espied their fleet at anchor in the Bay of Valcour. Our armed boats immediately rushed in amongst them and engaged them without waiting for orders." But, fast and confident, the ship *Inflexible*—the only ship on the lake—had sailed past the island. As she turned and beat slowly back against the wind, the major British advantage was temporarily removed.

However, one of the British sloops, *Carlton,* joined in with the armed boats "and kept on continual firing till dark, during which time we destroyed a schooner called the *Royal Savage,* and greatly damaged another."[28] At the same time the Americans were giving almost as good as they got. There were some German mercenaries in the British force, and one of them (an artillery captain named George Pausch) was sufficiently impressed to mention in his journal that "the cannon of the rebels were well served; for, as I saw afterwards, our ships were pretty well mended and patched up with boards and stoppers."[29]

Approaching one in the afternoon, the naval battle began to get "very serious," Pausch continued. "Lieutenant Dufais came very near perishing with all his men; for a cannon ball from the enemy's guns going through his powder magazine, it blew up." Dufais and his company swam to Pausch's craft. All told, there were soon forty-eight people on board, and the weight "came near upsetting my little boat, which was so overloaded that it could hardly move. In what a predicament was I? Every moment I was in danger of drowning with all on board, and in the company, too, of those I had just rescued and who had been already half lost!"

The battle on the lake was clearly quite sufficiently like the real thing for this doughty German; but happily he and his unwanted companions managed to get to land. There they "all ate and drank rum and water together—officers as well as men; and for a change, water and rum." By nightfall, Pausch's relieved content was completed by salt meat, toasted zwieback biscuits, and the knowledge that he was safely out of range of the remnants of Arnold's fleet, which was surrounded.

But during the night, a fog built up. Under that cover and paddling with muffled oars, Arnold's boats stole through the British line. Dawn on October 12 revealed an empty bay. The chase was on again.

Ranging around the lake, several British vessels went the wrong way; but unlike at sea, complete escape was impossible. Arnold's boats were hunted down; the battle recommenced; and on October 15 American generals knew the result—"the defeat and almost total ruin of our fleet."[30] The "terraqueous warfare," as the British commander, Capt. Charles Douglas, called it, was over.[31]

From Canada, Governor Carleton informed General Howe: "We have defeated the rebel fleet upon Lake Champlain, three sail only out of 15 having escaped. The rest we have taken or destroyed."[32] And finally, the young British lieutenant John Starke wrote a neat thumbnail sketch of "the war in Canada":

The rebel fleet was attacked and destroyed in two different engagements on Lake Champlain, on the 11th and 13th of October 1776. By this victory the command of the lake was regained; the province of Quebec was secured from future invasions; and the Army, whose operations had been impeded until this object was attained, had now scope to act.[33]

In theory, Carleton's army could now join Howe's in New York. New England could then be cut off, and the rebellion would crumble. But there was one weakness in the plan. The delay caused by Arnold's gondolas had lasted past the end of the best campaigning season. The weather was growing cold, tracks and rivers icy, food and forage scarce. The British forces were obliged to return to Canada for the duration of the winter, and when, under General Burgoyne's command, they moved south again in 1777, General Howe was no longer in New York. Faulty orders were sent from London, with all the delays the Admiralty and the Atlantic could devise; and on October 17, 1777 (almost exactly one year after Arnold's defeat), surrounded at Saratoga by an American army more than twice as large as his, Burgoyne had to surrender.

In Canada, Governor Carleton received the news with dismay and wrote an angry letter to London—a letter which, two hundred years later, American naval commanders in Vietnam would be able to recognize and understand with sympathy:

> This unfortunate event, it is to be hoped, will in future prevent Ministers from pretending to direct operations of war in a country at three thousand miles distance, of which they have so little knowledge as not to be able to distinguish between good, bad, or interested advices, or to give positive orders upon matters which, from their very nature, are ever on the change.[34]

From the American point of view, the naval battle of Lake Champlain was a tactical defeat. But strategically, it was a victory without which the American cause might have been lost in 1776. For its period, it was a kind of Dunkirk: Even in defeat, the toylike fleet gave a chance for the rest of the country to endure its most critical year, until help could arrive from allies across the Atlantic. And after commerce raiding and combined operations, finding that help was the third function of the Continental Navy.

3

★

WITHOUT A
RESPECTABLE NAVY

On October 29, 1776, in the wake of Arnold's bittersweet defeat on Lake Champlain, Capt. Lambert Wickes, commander of the Continental Navy's frigate *Reprisal,* received orders to take Benjamin Franklin to France. "It is of more importance," Wickes was told, "that you get safe and soon to France than any prizes you could take, therefore you are not to delay time on this outward passage." Moreover, utter secrecy was deemed essential when landing the distinguished passenger in France; but after that, his orders said: "You had best proceed directly on the coast of England, up the Channel, before they can have any notice of you."[1]

Franklin had his own orders from the Congressional Committee of Secret Correspondence. "You will readily discern," they said, "how all-important it is to the security of American independence that France should enter the war as soon as may be, and how necessary it is if it be possible to procure from her the line-of-battle ships you were desired in your instructions to obtain for us, the speedy arrival of which here (in the present state of things) might decide the contest at one stroke."[2]

Intrigued by the prospect of revenge for the Seven Years' War, the French were ready to listen to Franklin. But they were ready for little more, until Burgoyne's defeat at Saratoga convinced them that the Americans had a chance of success. Then, as we shall see, they joined in with a will.

The Continental Navy's transatlantic ferrying of diplomatic agents to and from France continued for most of the war, but because it had to be secretive and discreet, people said little about it in public. As a consequence it is largely forgotten today, yet at the time it was a vital service. It could not have succeeded without Arnold's delaying action on Lake Champlain, and together these were the Navy's most important contributions to the American campaign, of far greater military value than any naval "annoyance."

Perhaps, apart from its secrecy, the ferrying also seemed faintly demeaning to those who performed it, for sailors have rarely taken kindly to such duties. After bidding Franklin *au revoir,* Lambert Wickes was certainly glad to commence the second half of his orders—to "proceed directly on the coast of England." This was not only more like real naval duty, but also was a more imaginative and exciting prospect: He would be the first Continental sailor to take the war into enemy home waters.

Reprisal left St. Nazaire to cruise in the Channel in January 1777—a miserable time of year in those waters, and consequently an excellent time for raiding. Wickes quickly took five prizes (three brigs, a snow, and a ship), which for him made it "a tolerable successful cruise."[3] The snow, *Swallow,* was a mail packet from Falmouth bound for Lisbon, and fought for an hour before striking her flag. Men on both sides were wounded, but none killed. In *Reprisal,* the first lieutenant's left arm was shot off above the elbow, "and the Lieut. of Marines had a musket ball lodged in his wrist."[4] Benedict Arnold may have found the marines to be "the refuse of every regiment"; to others, they were an essential adjunct to operations, and Wickes's crew included a detachment of two of their officers and thirty men.

After selling his prizes in France to pay his crew and maintain his ship, Wickes was joined in April by the Continental brig *Lexington* (a name that would grace many American warships) and the cutter *Dolphin.* (She, incidentally, was an English boat, secretly sold to the American service from her home port of Dover.) In May the three vessels set off to try their luck, standing out across the Channel for the Irish Sea. In essence such raiding was identical to privateering; the only difference was that it was done by naval ships under official orders. But to a young naval officer, that probably made it close to ideal. It was daring, exciting, novel, and, when successful, profitable too. Few captains would ask for more in wartime.

Before they left the Bay of Biscay, the squadron encountered a British ship of the line, too powerful for them to challenge. Escaping, they were blown west of Ireland by a gale and took no prizes until three weeks after leaving port. By then they were back in the north side of the Channel; and in a single week they captured eighteen vessels. Satisfied with that, they headed for base and again met a British ship. *Reprisal* had eighteen guns; her opponent had seventy-four. In the chase that followed, Wickes scattered his squadron, and to lighten *Reprisal* threw all her guns over, until finally, believing it would increase her flexibility and speed, he sawed through some of her beams. It was a common idea at the time; but it was probably that which brought about his death. Though he escaped from the British once more, he was never able to tell his adventures to his grandchildren. Returning home in September, *Reprisal* foundered in a gale and was lost with her captain.

Wickes had been a brave man, and his death was a blow to the Continental Navy. Had he lived, he might well have outshone his more celebrated colleague John Paul Jones; and of the two, it could well be argued that Wickes was the more courageous, for when he conducted his pioneering raids, he (unlike Jones) had no guaranteed safe port in France. Wickes paved the way for Jones.

Today Jones is far more widely remembered, and in the context of the U.S. Navy's whole history, that is right, as will shortly be seen. But at the time, Wickes's contribution to the immediate cause of American independence was far greater. This is not simply because he captured more prizes; they paid for his voyage, but little more. Instead, the true value of his voyage lay in its political consequences. Thinking of modern reactions to terrorist hijacks at sea and in the air, it is easy to imagine the reactions of eighteenth-century Britain to the Wickes raids: scandal, horror, and diplomatic protests to France.

By helping to heat up Anglo-French antagonism, simmering since France's defeat in the Seven Years' War, Wickes brought vital French support for America that much closer. This was exactly what the American commissioners in Paris wanted, and the French were indeed growing visibly keener. During the summer of 1777, in the French port of Brest, an American privateer (*General Mifflin,* flying the "Grand Union flag") was saluted with nine guns by Admiral du Chauffault—the traditional signal of the navy of one sovereign state to another.

There was still no formal Franco-American alliance, and if the friendship of France in Europe was important, in the western Atlantic it was more important still. There, said Robert Morris, "the enemies' cruisers are too numerous on our coasts for anything to escape in the summer months"; and in October 1777, America and its navy suffered a major disaster.[5]

Writing to Admiral Howe about it, Commodore William Hotham reported that on the sixth, at daybreak, "the general debarkation took place. All the troops except about 400, who were left to secure Verplank's Neck, were soon landed at Stony Point upon the opposite shore, from whence they had about twelve miles to march through a mountainous and rugged road, to Fort Clinton and Montgomery."[6]

On September 26 General Howe (the admiral's brother) had occupied Philadelphia, capital of the rebellious colonies. Now, under Hotham, the admiral's ships were securing the British army's communication with the sea—the Delaware River. Americans had been aware of this risk for some time: In 1775, Lewis Nicola had written a pessimistic assessment to the Pennsylvania Committee of Safety, in which he explained that any effective defense of the river "so as to protect this city from an insult by water, appears to me very difficult."[7] He added that it was not impossible, but that doing it well would probably be thought too costly. However, they tried, and in 1776 John Adams eagerly listed the preparations made for the Delaware's defense—fire ships, fire rafts, floating gun batteries, row galleys, and staked underwater barriers. Altogether, he reckoned, these would "spread destruction through any British fleet that should attempt to come up here."[8]

Actually, they were puny efforts, and as Hotham's report showed, none made much difference when his attack began. After landing troops, "the ships and transports then moved high up, and anchored opposite Peek's Hill Landing. In the afternoon the advanced squadron and the two Frigates got under sail and opened Fort Montgomery, with a view only to make an appearance and thereby to cause a diversion in favour of the attack, which we observed had now begun. Sir James [Wallace], by the help of his oars, got near enough in with his galleys to throw some shot into the Fort. The cannonading and fire of musketry continued until night, when by a most spirited exertion, a general and vigorous assault was made, and the two important Forts of Clinton and Montgomery fell by storm to His Majesty's arms. . . . The rebel frigates are both burnt, with a galley; and a sloop of ten guns is taken."[9]

Hotham then returned to New York, while 1,600 troops proceeded upriver. Conveniently for the British ships, the wind stayed southerly for some days, helping them up the stream; but on the evening of October 20, it veered to the northwest. Because of this, Hotham anticipated either news or the return of ships and troops; and a letter from Wallace on October 17 told him what had been going on.

During the advance upriver, a number of American vessels had been destroyed. At Ezopus Creek, Wallace found two gun batteries, mounting five pieces between them, "and an armed galley at the mouth of the creek, who endeavoured to prevent our passing by their cannonade. General Vaughan was of opinion such a force should not be left behind. It was determined to land and destroy them, and immediately executed without retarding our proceeding up the river. The General marched for the town and fired it; the boats from the armed vessels went up the creek and burnt two brigs, several large sloops and other craft, with all their apparatus that was in store upon the shore."[10]

Wallace observed with satisfaction that "the officers and men upon this occasion behaved with the greatest spirit." This is not surprising, because what they were doing was destroying the Continental Navy in its own base—a kind of eighteenth-century Taranto or Truk. But the letter ended with more ominous news: "By all our information I am afraid General Burgoyne is retreated—*if not worse.* "

As we know, that is just what had happened; and the surrender at Saratoga outweighed even the occupation of Philadelphia and the destruction of a large part of the Continental fleet. For one of the many consequences of Burgoyne's defeat was the French decision to join in at last and fight alongside America against Great Britain.

"Until I arrived in France and became acquainted with that great tactician Count D'Orvilliers, and his judicious assistant the Chevalier du Pavillon, who each of them honoured me with instructions respecting the science of governing the operations, etc., of a fleet, I confess I was not sensible how ignorant I had been, before that time, of naval tactics."[11]

Modesty is not often associated with John Paul Jones, but it was he who, in 1782, wrote that modest disclaimer. He has been the subject of many biographies—fittingly for the man who, of all the Continental captains, is remembered and admired by today's U.S. Navy as the epitome of the naval spirit: courageous, disciplined, loyal, capable of severity, but usually fair. Yet of all the biographies, none worthy of the man was written until over a hundred and sixty years after his death; and when Samuel Eliot Morison published his masterly *John Paul Jones: A Sailor's Biography* in 1959, it became clear that Jones was a character of more than usual complexity, and in many ways an odd man to choose as a navy's prime hero. But paradoxically, he is also the very best man to fill that niche.

Today his body lies in a sumptuous (though very ugly) sarcophagus in the crypt of the chapel of the Naval Academy at Annapolis, and in the Officers' Academy of the Japanese Navy at Etajima, his portrait and that of Lord Nelson flank the portrait of Admiral Heihachiro Togo. Of course, it is no accident they all hang side by side: In imperial Japan they were ranked as the exemplars of what were then the world's three greatest navies. Anyone who knows Togo's career would readily place him in the highest level of naval leaders. In Britain, however, Jones has never enjoyed much official popularity, and it would be astonishing to see such a trio of portraits on display there. But perhaps there should be. Certainly a British writer must acknowledge bias, and it seems fair to say that even the most generous historical comparison must place Jones third, rather than equal first, of the three. But if the accidents of history had been a little different (in particular, if Jones had been born an Englishman rather

than a Scot) it is just as fair to guess that he would have joined the King's
fleet. There he might have become an admiral, for he had the ability; he
could certainly have become a captain; and in either capacity he would
have been a great ornament to the Royal Navy. To see why, it is worth
comparing him, Nelson, and Togo in character, in achievements, and in
naval ability.

The three men all displayed remarkable dedication to the service of the
sea. Their characters, however, could not have been more different. Nelson was a man of such charm and sparkling vivacity, such consideration
for and inspiration to all under his command, that his officers and men
quite openly adored him. Deliberately and in many ways, Admiral Togo
modeled himself on Nelson; and he was a great commander, sometimes
suitably cautious, yet willing to take extraordinary risks when necessary.
Men responded to him with deep respect and even affection, but he never
inspired the unquestioning personal devotion that Nelson conjured. He
lacked the spontaneity and warmth which made Nelson—in the words
of one of his close associates—"a funny, affectionate, fascinating little
fellow." Togo was described by one of his own contemporaries as "a
quiet, silent man, with a rather melancholy face, lighted up, as the spirit
moves him, by one of the sweetest of smiles"; and he was assessed by one
of his tutors as "a great plodder, slow to learn, but very sure of what he
had learnt." Thoughtful and deliberate, he won his battles in the same
way as he conducted his whole career—single-mindedly, with meticulous
preparation and confident execution. Not, perhaps, very good company;
but certainly a man to have in charge of a fleet.

John Paul Jones never had the chance to command anything like a
decent fleet—not through any fault of his own, but through the circumstances of his time. If he had had the chance, he would almost certainly
have risen to it and might have become a more pleasant person. As it was,
he deserved and won the respect of contemporary Americans interested
in naval matters; yet even that respect was mixed, as John Adams, one
of the most pronaval of eighteenth-century Americans, made clear:
"Jones has art, and secrecy, and aspires very high," he wrote in May
1779, calling him "the most ambitious and intriguing [i.e., conspiratorial]
officer in the American Navy."[12]

But Jones never won the love of the men in his command, or even their
affection. Inside and outside his naval career he was jealous, humourless,
intolerant, and of unpredictable temper. "Eccentricities and irregularities
are to be expected from him," Adams continued. "They are in his character, they are visible in his eyes . . . his eye has keenness and wildness and
softness in it."

It sounds almost as if, looking at those strange, compelling eyes,
Adams detected an echo of Jones's native land. Born a Scot with America

as his adopted nation, Jones often claimed he had joined the Continental Navy "as a free citizen of the world in defence of the violated rights of mankind";[13] yet when the War of Independence was over and the Continental Navy was no more, he became a rear admiral in the navy of Catherine the Great of Russia, one of the more notable tyrants of the past few centuries. An Englishwoman living in France described him as "the most agreeable sea-wolf one could wish to meet with,"[14] and many women confirmed the charm and attraction he could exert on them. But Benjamin Franklin reproved him for taking all and sharing none of the credit for his actions at sea:

> Hereafter, if you should observe an occasion to give your officers and friends a little more praise than is their due, and confess more fault than you can justly be charged with, you will only become the sooner for it, a great captain. Criticizing and censuring almost every one you have to do with, will diminish friends, increase enemies, and thereby hurt your affairs.[15]

The advice is still good. Self-seeking and vastly egotistic, Jones's constant naval-political intriguing was only one aspect of his character which made many native-born Americans detest him. Nevertheless, he was a brilliant sailor, with an understanding of naval needs which was occasionally close to visionary; and it is these aspects of a complex and often contradictory man which make him the rightful figurehead of America's naval tradition. Judged on achievement alone, he could not remotely compare with either Togo or Nelson, and it would seem absurd for the U.S. Navy to honor him as it does. Nelson conquered at Trafalgar and gave Britain control of the seas; a century later, Togo conquered at Tsushima and won the maritime side of the Russo-Japanese War at a stroke. In contrast, at the peak of his career, John Paul Jones had only two successes to boast of, and they were in single-ship fights: *Ranger* versus H.M.S. *Drake,* and *Bonhomme Richard* versus H.M.S. *Serapis.* But because of the way he fought them, they have never been forgotten, and they are certainly worth studying again.

It was pure coincidence, but highly symbolic: Jones's commission as a captain in the Continental Navy came on June 14, 1777—the day Congress resolved to adopt the Stars and Stripes as America's flag. The command he was given was the 318½-ton sloop of war *Ranger,* and his first voyage in her was across to France, bearing news to Franklin of Burgoyne's surrender at Saratoga. Jones fervently hoped this might bring an early end to the war. He could then fulfill his dream of buying a Virginia plantation and settling there. In the meantime, though, he had the task of imposing his own high standards of naval discipline on a competent but undisciplined crew, who regarded him, as a non-American, with some suspicion. During the voyage he "had the most agreeable proof of the active spirit" of the crew when they captured two prizes, and he began to ponder what else he might do.[16] To his disappointment (for he always loved being in the limelight), another ship brought the momentous news of Saratoga to France before him; but after some weeks of waiting, he received very satisfying orders from Franklin.

He was told that "after equipping the *Ranger* in the best manner for the cruise you propose," he should "proceed with her in the manner you shall judge best for distressing the enemies of the United States, consistent with the laws of war, and the terms of your commission."[17] It was carte blanche, freedom to act as he chose, and Jones had a plan prepared. "When an enemy thinks a design against them is improbable," he had written, "they can always be surprised and attacked with advantage."[18] Nearly 150 years later, the Japanese commander in chief, Admiral Yamamoto, used the same principle at Pearl Harbor. In 1778 Jones decided to follow the example of Lambert Wickes and go for Britain's own national waters—and even the very coast of the country.

Before proceeding on the two cruises which ensured his undying fame (or infamy, as many British people thought then), he found the opportunity for another historic first. Cruising off the Brittany coast, he anchored in Quiberon Bay, the site of the Royal Navy's victory over the French in 1759. There, on February 14, 1778, *Ranger* and a French naval squadron exchanged salutes. The year before, the privateer *General Mifflin* had been flying the Grand Union flag (the Union Jack and Stripes) when she was saluted by a French ship. The salute exchanged between Jones and the French was not a salute between equals (the French flagship fired nine guns and *Ranger,* showing respect for a superior, fired thirteen), but it was the first time the authentic Stars and Stripes had been acknowledged in that way. And just to make sure he had been the first one to receive such an honor for the nation, Jones did it again the following day.

It was April 10 when *Ranger* set sail for British waters. Jones had three objectives—to take any available prizes, as always; to raid some part of Britain's coast; and to capture as many prisoners as possible in order to exchange them for American prisoners in British jails. He succeeded in all respects.

The prizes came quickly: a brigantine and a ship captured, a sloop and a schooner sunk with prisoners taken. Then the coastal raids: first at Whitehaven in northern England, followed by St. Mary's Isle, just over the border in Scotland. Here, Jones's success must be qualified—the raids certainly took place, and by that fact alone created a furor throughout Britain. But Whitehaven was an undistinguished fishing port, humble and inoffensive, and as *Ranger*'s surgeon remarked, *"Nothing could be got* by burning poor people's property."[19] For that was what the brave captain intended to do: come in under cover of darkness and fire the boats—the means of livelihood—and, if possible, the homes of the fisherfolk of Whitehaven.

It is difficult to see this as anything other than a sordid and nasty little affair. Quite apart from the hardship Jones wished to visit upon the innocent people of the port, he was (as a London newspaper reported) "well known by many people" in Whitehaven; he had done his sailing apprenticeship there and had been born and brought up not far away. The idea that therefore he knew his way around and could be assured of finding his way in the dark does nothing to make the plan fair or worthy of his cause.

However, the episode was made somewhat more attractive by his crew's independent reaction to the project. They had still not entirely bent to his discipline, and the prospect of work without prizes left them less than lukewarm. Several remembered that even if they were at war with England, they and the English spoke the same language, so on arrival they did the obvious thing—they found the nearest pub and settled in for a good evening's drinking. At the same time one of their number, an Irishman, ran around beating on doors and shouting warnings. Jones and a few sailors tried to fire the fishing boats; most of the others felt the best thing was to leave their captain onshore and take *Ranger* on their own account. Added to the crew's reluctance, a rain shower put out the fires and further limited the intended damage to the village. It all looked like rather a flop, yet it achieved its major objective—the harassment of the British government. Britons did not care to depend on rain to defend their soil, and the total mixture meant a lot of mud was slung at the government and its navy. Why did they not capture Jones, the traitor and pirate?

To begin with, there was a great deal of public outrage, which the government tried to divert against Jones personally. But ordinary British people began to think better of him when they heard of his subsequent raid on St. Mary's Isle, the home of the fourth Earl of Selkirk. The isle lies about 20 miles northwest of Whitehaven, and *Ranger* arrived there on the morning of April 23, only a few hours after leaving the fishing port. Jones's plan was to kidnap the earl as a hostage for American prisoners, but, ill conceived and worse managed, it went about as wrong as it could. First, the earl was not at home to be kidnapped. Second, even if he had been, he was a nobleman of such obscurity that the government in London would probably not have been very interested in his fate. Third, Selkirk supported American independence (he himself wrote to Jones later, pointing out that he was "very friendly to the Constitution and Just Liberties of America").[20] And last (although in the presence of the pregnant Lady Selkirk, the crew were eminently well behaved), the only recompense Jones could offer them for their efforts was to steal the earl's collection of silver plate.

Yet this was where, in the eyes of many ordinary Britons, Jones redeemed himself; for in due course, using his own money, he paid his men for the silver and with a note of apology sent it back to the earl. Never loath to see a government embarrassed while a thief shone with gallantry of a kind, the British public began to attach a kind of Robin Hood image to Jones—something which, on the basis of Whitehaven alone, he would never have had.

For Jones himself, the most satisfactory part of this cruise took place the day after his landing at St. Mary's Isle. Moving across the North Channel of the Irish Sea, *Ranger* encountered the British sloop-of-war *Drake.* They had met before, but on that occasion bad weather had prevented them from trying conclusions. On this day, April 24, although the wind was still high in Belfast Lough, the two ships fought for over a hour; and although they were almost equally matched in arms, the British captain was killed, *Drake*'s rigging was shot to threads, the ship surrendered, and *Ranger,* evading other British vessels, returned to France with a further prize and 133 prisoners. Better still: Ten months later, in February 1779, all Jones's prisoners and others taken by the French were exchanged for Americans captured by the British. Thus John Paul Jones achieved an important precedent in the war, for before then the British had not officially allowed such exchanges; and one may assume that that success gave him more pleasure than either of his sensational but bungled raids on the coast.

Fame was already beginning to cling to him; and with one raid more, Jones was printed indelibly on the American memory. This, of course, was the celebrated cruise of the *Bonhomme Richard* squadron—a brief, spectacular, and in some ways very curious voyage which gave more to the spirit of the U.S. Navy than any other episode of those early days.

Bonhomme Richard, originally called *Le Duc du Duras,* was renamed in honor of Benjamin Franklin, who used the French "Poor Richard" as a pen name for some of his writing. It looked to be a poor compliment: At 900 tons *Richard* was twice as large as any other vessel Jones had commanded, but she was long past her best—an elderly East India merchantman, veteran of many voyages to China. Moreover, when she set sail from Lorient, on Brittany's south coast, her crew of 380 included only just over 60 Americans. The rest were of eight different nationalities, including British; and although *Richard* led a squadron of six other vessels, two of those were privateers, three were from the French navy, and only one was American—and that one was commanded by a Frenchman who turned out to be mad.

Before the voyage began, Jones gave a proverb to the American Navy:

"I intend," he said of his new endeavor, *"to go in harm's way."*[21] With the mixed bag at his command, harm might not be far to seek; so perhaps it was just as well that the squadron disintegrated almost as soon as it left France. The privateers went off privateering; one of the French vessels got lost; a second broke her tiller; and the mad French captain, Pierre Landais, told Jones he would act "where and when he thought proper," which seemed to mean as far from Jones as possible.[22]

Pallas, the frigate with the broken tiller, eventually caught up with and rejoined *Richard* and the little corvette *Vengeance* as they headed northwards. At Cape Wrath, Scotland's northwestern point, Landais put in an unwelcome and abusive appearance, only to vanish again; so it was three ships which made the voyage close to the south of Foula (one of the most remote of the Shetland Islands), back down the east coast of Scotland, and finally down England's east coast. Landais reappeared there, apparently rejoining through lack of anything better to do; and late in the afternoon of September 23, 1779, off Flamborough Head near Scarborough, the small squadron located a convoy of forty-one sail from the Baltic, escorted by two British men-of-war, *Countess of Scarborough* and *Serapis.*

The three hours of battle which ensued were among the hardest and most bitter of that century. Little *Vengeance* was left out of it: Too small to be effective, she wisely kept at a safe distance, while *Pallas* engaged *Countess of Scarborough* and *Bonhomme Richard* engaged *Serapis.* Jones badly wanted to break up the convoy with its valuable naval supplies, but Captain Richard Pearson, commanding *Serapis,* fended him off and enabled the convoy to escape intact.

Not so *Serapis* herself, nor *Bonhomme Richard.* The battle between them began just after sunset, the two ships parallel and exchanging broadsides, each attempting to pass ahead or astern of the other in order to rake the enemy's decks with unopposed fire. Coming astern of *Serapis* in an effort to board, Jones placed *Richard*'s port beam on the enemy's starboard quarter and was driven off; *Serapis* surged across *Richard*'s bow and the rigging of the two became entangled. Heavily outgunned from the beginning, Jones had already lost two of his 18-pounders, and Captain Pearson shouted over to him, "Has your ship struck?"

Surrender was the last thing Jones had in mind. He bellowed back indignantly, "I have not yet begun to fight!"—and with that, the battle began to turn into a legend.[23]

With the ships breaking away from each other and exchanging broadsides again, the scene became even more extraordinary. As the moon rose over a calm sea, watchers on the shore saw *Richard* try to cross *Serapis*'s bow; saw the British ship move forward onto the American; and saw the pair entangle again, still firing constantly. This time they did not break away from each other. Instead, out of control, they began to drift along side by side, facing opposite directions, bow to stern and stern to bow. For two hours more they pounded each other, their sides grinding together, muzzles actually touching the opposing hull. Jones's 18-pounders were already out of action; so were his 12-pounders; all he had left were three 9-pounders. But from *Richard*'s fighting tops, musketeers and sharpshooters kept *Serapis*'s deck empty of men. Pearson's main hope lay in breaking away in order to use his full battery; Jones's only hope lay in hugging as close as possible and enduring. He was not helped by mad Landais, who (after casting himself for some time as observer) began sailing around the engrappled vessels, shooting three deliberate broadsides not at *Serapis* but at *Richard*. Nor was Jones helped by the fires which kept breaking out in every part of the ship, eight or ten at a time; nor by the five feet of water rising in the hold. But Pearson too had his problems. *Serapis* was also on fire, was also taking water, and shortly before 10 P.M. was shaken by a violent explosion as an American grenade fell into bags of gunpowder stacked on deck. At the same time Jones himself was using the fairly light and maneuverable 9-pounders to batter *Serapis*'s mainmast with double-headed shot, and toward 10:30, as it began to crack, Captain Pearson's nerve cracked too.

He had already had his ensign nailed to the mast. Now, with his own hands, he tore it down in token of surrender; and as the guns fell silent and men in both ships gradually brought the flames under control, he was conducted over to *Richard* for the formal surrender of his command. At the moment he was introduced to John Paul Jones, *Serapis* gave out a long, grinding shriek, and her mainmast collapsed overboard. Ignoring the anguished sound, the two commanding officers went below to drink a ceremonial glass of wine.

In fact, *Bonhomme Richard* was in a still worse condition, and Jones swiftly transferred his flag to *Serapis*. Through the rest of the night his men worked to save *Richard;* but, he wrote, it "was impossible to prevent the good old ship from sinking. They did not abandon her till after nine o'clock; the water was then up to the lower deck, and a little after ten I saw, with inexpressible grief, the last glimpse of the *Bonhomme Richard.* "[24]

It is true there was luck in his victory, but that is no criticism: There is always some luck in victory. What is more important is that the majority of captains would have surrendered to the superior enemy, and Jones did not. His ship had gone, but the inspiration remained: The image of his willingness to do battle against the odds, and his unwavering determination simply to fight and endure, summed up in his memorable phrase, "I have not yet begun to fight!" And until recently, there was still a ship in the U.S. Navy that bore the name designed to honor Franklin:

an aircraft carrier nicknamed *Bonnie Dick.* In 1990, she was destined to be scrapped, but the name *Bonhomme Richard* will surely be used again.

When he defeated and captured H.M.S. *Serapis,* John Paul Jones was still only thirty-two years old. He would live for another thirteen years, but that moonlit night off Flamborough Head was his highest hour. Thereafter his life was a downward series of anticlimaxes and frustration. His major occupation during the rest of the War of Independence was the completion of the Continental Navy's only seventy-four-gun warship, *America,* of which he expected to become captain; but on completion (and because of her green timbers, already half rotten) she was given to the French. Jones also spent many years in France, trying to collect prize money due to his crews and himself; he then joined the Russian navy and was given the flag rank he coveted. But though he used his ships well in Russia's service, his intolerant and acerbic nature made him enemies in the Russian hierarchy, and he left the country in some disgrace after a charge (denied, but never disproved) of rape. Aged forty-five, poor, alone, and suffering from a combination of jaundice, pneumonia, and inflammation of the kidneys, he died in Paris just a few days before the arrival of a commission from President Washington appointing him American consul in Algeria.

On the whole his short life was a harsh one, full of discontent and thwarted ambition. Every navy needs heroes, whose deeds and characters serve as models for future generations. In a fighting force, a man's deeds are clearly more important than having a companionable character. No one can demand that a hero should be likable, and a good many are not likable at all; it is better to be, or be with, a thoroughly unpleasant commander who wins than a pleasant one who loses. John Paul Jones never inspired the unswerving loyalty and devotion that is the hallmark of the supremely great commander. This was in part due to the defects of his personality—selfishness, impatience, intolerance—and in part due to the defects and limitations of the American Navy itself. Joining the Russian navy largely in order to become a rear admiral indicates that when he joined the American Navy, it was more because of the personal possibilities it afforded than because of any love of democracy. Yet balanced against that is his almost visionary understanding of what the American Navy could be. Admittedly that vision included a high position for himself; but that was incidental. More significant was that, far in advance of most of his fellow Americans, he possessed the naval instinct. Evidence of this is everywhere in his letters—such as this, written in the last months of his life:

> My own opportunities in naval warfare have been but few and feeble. . . . But I do not doubt your ready agreement with me if I

say that the hostile ships and commanders that I have thus far
enjoyed the opportunity of meeting, did not give anyone much trouble thereafter. True, this has been on a small scale; but that was no
fault of mine. I did the best with the weapons given to me. The rules
of conduct, the maxims of action, and the tactical instincts that serve
to gain small victories may always be expanded into the winning of
great ones with suitable opportunity; because in human affairs the
sources of success are ever to be found in the fountains of quick
resolve and swift stroke; and it seems a law inflexible and inexorable
that he who will not risk cannot win."[25]

Jones produced this kind of writing throughout his life; and far more
than the action against *Serapis,* it is his thinking, his understanding of
and his writing on naval matters which make him the right emblem for
the U.S. Navy. He grasped the functions and possibilities of a navy
better than most of his contemporaries in America did and, as he said,
did the best he could with what he had. After the Battle of Flamborough Head, the British view of him was well expressed by an Englishman living in Holland: "One desperate action has raised him high
in the opinion of Holland and France, for a man of great courage and
abilities."[26]

It was true; the fight with *Serapis* had been a desperate action, and one
of the few active achievements of Jones's naval life. But when the same
English critic added: "He is desperate through fear, and has been successful without abilities," the critic was being unjust. In the Battle of Flamborough Head, it would have been unnatural not to have been afraid; and
as for ability, Jones had more sea ability, in almost every way, than he
was able to demonstrate in practice.

It is not usual to make a man a hero because of what he might have
done, but Jones has to be an exception. He recognized the Continental
Navy for what it was and criticised its "little proud affectations."[27] He
even said on one occasion that it had "upon the whole done nothing for
the cause and less for the flag."[28] That was not so, and the caustic tone
was typical of his sharp and negative side; one may assume that what he
meant was that it had done less than it could have had it been ten times
larger. Those he saw as fools he did not suffer gladly, and if he had
extended the same charity to the Continental Navy as he did to himself,
he would have acknowledged they did the best possible. But (and this is
the key to his status) when others could not see beyond the immediate,
he recognized that the need would continue for as long as America had
a coastline.

"In time of peace," he wrote to Robert Morris, "it is necessary to prepare, and be *always prepared,* for War by sea." As it stands, it is a good and memorable sentence; but then he went on to improve it, paraphrasing himself. With one of the lines no American sailor can forget, he expressed the essence of all his naval thinking: "Without a respectable Navy—alas America!"[29]

4

★

I HAVE BEEN FORCED . . .
TO SURRENDER

*T*he Battle of Flamborough Head caused deep emotion on both sides of the Atlantic, yet the war in America was far from finished; and however spectacular its single-ship fights and raids might be, the Continental fleet could not possibly defeat the Royal Navy. On the British side (although far weaker than it could and should have been) there were more ships, more guns, and more men; and in case their fighting spirit flagged, there were American loyalists to inspire them with patriotic verses. Joseph Stansbury, a loyalist writer living in New York, produced a typically singable ditty:

> Then Britons, *strike home*—make sure of your blow:
>> The chase is in view; never mind a lee-shore.
>> With vengeance o'ertake the confederate foe:
>> 'Tis now we may rival our heroes of yore!
>>> Brave *Anson* and *Drake*,
>>> *Hawke, Russell* and *Blake*,
>> With ardour like yours we defy France and Spain!
>>> Combining with *Treason*
>>> They're deaf to all reason:
>> Once more let them *feel* we are Lords of the Main.
>> Lords of the Main—ay, Lords of the Main
>> The first-born of Neptune are Lords of the Main.[1]

It was good, stirring, "Heart of Oak" stuff, especially the chorus, and by the summer of 1781, the British in America were still "Lords of the Main." As James Madison wrote on July 7 that year: "The great advantage the enemy have over us lies in the superiority of their navy, which enables them to continually shift the war into defenceless places, and to weary our troops by long marches."[2]

Despite Saratoga, the war on land had developed into a tiresome stalemate, during which Washington's great achievement was to keep an army in being. Irregular guerrilla-style fighting bled British troops but could not defeat them; nor, however, could the British find a definite victory. Their attempts at raising counterrevolution came closest to success in the southern colonies: After Gen. Sir Henry Clinton captured Charleston and the entire southern army in May 1780, there was no organized American force south of Virginia for several months. Yet the time when Britain might have won the war was already past, and Stansbury's song said why: In addition to the rebels, Britain now had to "defy France and Spain."

Colonial grievances, which only a few years earlier the British government might have contented and contained, had rippled out to an almost incredible extent. An enemy of Britain was more or less automatically a friend of France, so France declared war against Britain in 1778, Spain followed suit in 1779 and Holland in 1780. Simultaneously, the remainder of Europe, under Russian leadership, formed itself into the (anti-British) League of Armed Neutrality. With the inevitable involvement, east and west, of all the colonies of the various nations, the American War of Independence had effectively become a global war, with Britain against the rest of the world. Britain by itself could not win all around. Similarly, America by itself could not win even at home.

"Next to a loan of money [from France]," George Washington wrote, "a constant naval superiority on these coasts is the object most interesting. This would instantly reduce the enemy to a difficult defensive, and, by removing all prospect of extending their acquisitions, would take away the motives for prosecuting the war. Indeed, it is not to be conceived how they could subsist a large force in this country, if we had command of the seas, to interrupt the regular transmission of supplies from Europe."[3]

The letter was written on January 15, 1781, at a time when the Continental Navy had only four frigates and one sloop left in active service. In April one of the frigates, *Confederacy,* surrendered, and the sloop vanished. In August the frigate *Trumbull* was captured. Two remained, and little could be expected from them. But, convinced that no conclusive battle could be fought on land, Washington was desperate for a major naval victory; and on September 5, off the capes of the Chesapeake, it came.

Neither of the two surviving Continental frigates had anything to do with the contest, fought between French and British fleets. Nevertheless, the Battle of the Chesapeake has a place in the history of the American Navy, for like a forceps delivery when the natural impulse is not enough, it gave the last vital tug to America's birth; and, confirming General Washington's view, it showed just what could be achieved when America had control of its own seas.

In the flagships of the two fleets, the battling nations' capitals were opposed: Rear Admiral Thomas Graves commanded his fleet of nineteen from H.M.S. *London,* while Vice Adm. Comte François-Joseph Paul de Grasse led twenty-four French ships of the line from *Ville de Paris.* Both were bearing supplies to their respective armies in and around Yorktown, where a British army under Lord Cornwallis was surrounded by joint French-American forces.

De Grasse arrived first and had the larger fleet. He was, moreover, a very able commander; but he should not have won the battle. The advantages of weather, so necessary to a sailing fleet, were all with the British. The two sides identified each other about 11 A.M.—to their mutual astonishment, for neither knew the other was in the area at all. The wind was north-northeast, comfortably astern of Graves's fleet approaching from New York and very uncomfortably on the port beam when de Grasse began beating out to sea. The flood tide, entering the bay, was also opposing de Grasse and hindering his ships' movements; Graves should have been able to wait and pick off the French ships one by one as they emerged. Nelson would have done it; so would John Paul Jones. But Graves did not. Instead, sticking rigidly to the letter of his navy's *Fighting Instructions,* he formed his fleet into a line of battle parallel with those French who had emerged. The line ran east to west and became as nearly unmaneuverable as the line de Grasse was trying to create.

A few hours of firing ensued, only to break off at nightfall; and the following day Graves's second in command, Rear Adm. Sir Samuel Hood, wrote unhappily that "yesterday the British fleet had a rich and most plentiful harvest of glory in view, but the means to gather it were omitted."[4] Both he and Graves recognized the errors: "The enemy's van was not very closely attacked," said Hood. "There was a full hour and a half to have engaged it before any of the rear could have come up." And Graves, who had flown the signal for line ahead virtually all day, now said that when that signal was out "at the same time with the signal for battle, it is not to be understood that the latter signal shall be rendered ineffectual by a too strict adherence to the former."[5]

By then it was too late, and anyway he was wrong. Other British admirals, notably Rodney and Nelson, were brave enough in later battles to break the rules and win. But the *Fighting Instructions* were not intended to be broken, and in them the line ahead was paramount; Graves could not fairly expect his captains to second-guess him.

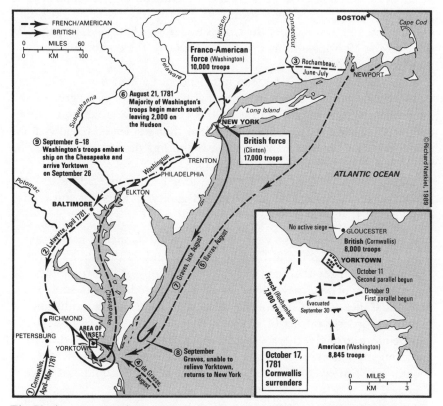

The Yorktown campaign, August–October 1981: Hampered by adhering rigidly to his navy's "Fighting Instructions," British admiral Thomas Graves could neither defeat French admiral François de Grasse nor relieve besieged British troops in Yorktown. The siege intensified (see inset) and the British surrender paved the way for American independence.

The battle continued in a desultory manner for four days, until de Grasse made for the Chesapeake again, and Graves returned to New York to repair his ships. On land, the French-American force was strengthened; the British starved; and on October 20, in direct consequence of Graves's hesitation, Lord Cornwallis wrote from Yorktown to Sir Henry Clinton in New York: "I have the mortification to inform your Excellency that I have been forced to give up the posts of York and Gloucester, and to surrender the troops under my command, by capitulation, on the 19th instant, as prisoners of war to the combined forces of America and France."[6]

A decade later, with American independence a firm fact of life, there was at least one American who thought with nostalgic regret of the unspectacular but fateful Battle of the Chesapeake. John Paul Jones correctly regarded it as a fending off rather than a splendid naval victory, a win by default rather than a conquest; and he knew very well what he would have liked to have seen that day.

"Now, my dear Kersaint," he wrote to a French vice admiral, "you know me too well to accuse me of self-vanity."[7] Kersaint must have chuckled at that. Nevertheless,

> you will not consider me vain, in view of what happened in the past off Carrickfergus, off Old Flamboro' Head and off the Liman in the Black Sea, if I say that, had I stood—fortunately or unfortunately— in the shoes of de Grasse, there would have been disaster to someone off the Capes of the Chesapeake, disaster of more lasting significance than an orderly retreat of a beaten fleet to a safe port. To put it a little more strongly, there was a moment when the chance to destroy the enemy's fleet would have driven from me all thought of the conjoint strategy of the campaign as a whole. I could not have helped it.

One would have thought that the independence of the United States had quite enough "lasting significance" for anybody. And the "conjoint strategy" was basic to that purpose; so perhaps it was just as well for America, for once, that Jones was not present. He was right to say that if he had been there and in command, "there would have been disaster to someone." But it might have been to his own side.

In fact, after the independence of 1783, unexpected disasters did come to a small but important number of Americans. The Continental Navy did not last long; there seemed no further need for it, and in 1785 its remaining ships were sold or given away. Between the end of the war and that point, trade, especially oceangoing trade, had revived rapidly. However, its pattern had changed. The British West Indies (previously a cornerstone of the Caribbean-American-European-African routes) were now barred to Americans, who by their successful rebellion had made themselves foreigners; and for the same reason, elsewhere in the world, American merchant ships were no longer protected by the Royal Navy.

This natural but unwelcome consequence of independence was most evident at the junction of Europe and Africa, where pirates prowled from bases in Morocco, Algiers, Tunis, and Tripoli—the four Barbary states of the North African Coast.

"It is not probable that the American States will have a very free trade in the Mediterranean," Lord Sheffield wrote in 1783. "It will not be the interest of any of the great maritime powers to protect them there from the Barbary States. . . . The Americans cannot protect themselves . . . they cannot pretend to a navy."[8]

The first attack came as soon as the last Continental warship was sold. The ship *Dolphin* of Philadelphia and the schooner *Maria* of Boston were captured, and their crews taken into slavery, by vessels belonging to the dey of Algiers. The pirates were the terrorists of their time, the only distinction between them and their modern counterparts being that in the eighteenth century the motive was old-fashioned greed rather than anything political. And the reaction in America was much as it is when such things happen today, though expressed somewhat differently:

> *See what dark prospect interrupts our joy!*
> *What arm presumptuous dares our trade annoy?*
> *Great God! The rovers who infest thy waves*
> *Have seized our ships, and made our freemen slaves.*[9]

John Paul Jones had already said, "Prepare, and be always prepared, for War by sea." Now, with twenty-one Americans enslaved, he wrote: "This event may, I believe, surprise some of our fellow citizens; but for my part, I am rather surprised that it did not take place sooner. It will produce a good effect if it unites the people of America in measures consistent with their national honor and interest, and rouses them from their ill-judged security which the intoxication of success has produced since the Revolution."[10]

Jones clearly had the measure of his adopted countrymen. Time and time again since then (whether through the intoxication of success, the complacency of natural security, or the innocence of good nature), they appear to have felt that no other place in the world is quite real, until the jolt of an actual attack proves otherwise. On most such occasions the nation has suddenly snapped together as one, in the way Jones hoped would happen in 1785. Yet on that occasion it did not.

The Barbary states had practiced piracy for centuries, partly as an inheritance from the Crusades, when any Christian ship was fair game to them, and partly as a useful occupation for peoples and lands unsuited to farming. For other nations, the traditional remedy was either to place a strong naval force in the Mediterranean, as the British had, or to pay ransom and tribute (protection money, in effect) as the Venetians, Dutch, Scandinavians, and Austrians did.

But America was too poor, too distant, and too busy inventing itself to do either. The ransom demanded by the Algerines worked out as $59,496; the best that Congress could offer was $4,200. In a little while Morocco (the least piratical of the states) accepted without charge a treaty of fifty years' friendship with America; but Tripoli would not accept such a thing without a flat payment of 30,000 English guineas or an annual payment of 12,500 guineas. They might just as well have said a million: Congress, without a constitution enabling it to levy taxes, could not spare a cent.

So, despite the irony that twenty-one Americans had fought for the freedom to be enslaved, the prisoners remained in Algiers, and American shipping remained vulnerable to all except the Moroccans. Probably no more than a few hundred Americans understood the strategic value of a navy; certainly, to the average landsman, defense was the distance of a rifle shot. The fate of a few of his countrymen, incarcerated thousands of miles away, was a matter of comparative indifference; and the idea that a navy invisibly distant off alien coasts could contribute to his own peace and safety at home was incomprehensible and unbelievable.

Nor could those men who understood the strategic principles agree on the best course. John Adams, for so long an ardent supporter of naval strength, now felt it best to "negotiate and pay the necessary sum without loss of time." In contrast, the normally placid Thomas Jefferson believed that a fleet of 150 guns would be cheaper, that peace "would depend on their idea of our power," and that though peace could be bought if money were available, "I should prefer the obtaining it by war."[11]

For four more years, nothing happened. The prisoners remained in chains; Jones served in Russia. Then, in the spring of 1789, key developments were made and promised. On April 30 George Washington was elected the first president of the United States. Within weeks Jones had left Russia and gone to Paris, where he began bombarding the new American administration with pleas for a post.

Simultaneously, the national constitution was adopted. Section eight of its first article specified that "Congress shall have Power to lay and collect Taxes, Duties, Imposts and Excises, to pay the Debts and provide for the common Defense and general Welfare of the United States. . . . To define and punish Piracies and Felonies committed on the high Seas, and Offences against the Law of Nations; To declare War, grant Letters of Marque and Reprisal, and make Rules concerning Captures on Land and Water"—and "to provide and maintain a Navy."[12]

At last the government would have regular funds at its disposal. James Madison, supporting Jefferson, at once proposed that a school for seamen should be established. From that, a fleet could be developed to protect U.S. shipping in the Mediterranean and perhaps release the enslaved Americans. But the Revolution had shown how long any proper navy would take to create, and when, at the end of 1790, Jefferson pointed out that "our navigation . . . into the Mediterranean, has not resumed at all," it was agreed to pay tribute and ransom.[13] The sums resolved on, in February 1791, were $40,000 for ransom, with an annual maximum of $100,000 set aside for tribute.

On June 2, 1792, John Paul Jones was appointed peace commissioner to Algiers. On July 18, before news of the longed-for appointment reached him, he died. The next appointee also died before reaching Algiers, and it was not until September 1793 that an American emissary got as far as Gibraltar. He could go no further: across the strait in Algiers, the dey would not receive him, because a truce between Algiers and Portugal meant that an unwanted number of pirates were lounging around looking for an outlet for their energies, which could easily be directed against the dey himself. The dey was more interested in finding something for them to do than in making a truce with America; and according to a prisoner in Algiers, the British consul there suggested a good use for the pirates. The allegation that this was a British idea may well have been true; and whether it was or not, in October of that year a fleet of seven or eight Algerine ships sailed past Gibraltar into the eastern Atlantic and captured eleven American vessels and over a hundred seamen.

It was a graphic demonstration of America's absolute vulnerability at sea and the contempt of other countries for American shipping. Once, acting as unofficial spokesman for the American Navy, John Paul Jones had written: "The English Nation may hate me, but *I will force them to esteem me too.*"[14] They were brave words, and they would come true; but at the end of 1793 the despairing comment of another, anonymous American was far more apt—"Our flag is about as much respected among the different nations as an old rag that's hung up in a cornfield to scare crows."[15]

PART TWO

REACHING

1794–1815

★

Under President Washington,
the authentic United States Navy begins.
In twenty-one years, it fights
the Barbary pirates, the French, and the British,
winning many famous victories.

5

★

OPEN HOSTILITIES

"*I*f we mean to have a commerce, we must have a naval force to defend it."[1]

In that single blunt sentence written in December 1793, the American minister to Spain expressed one of the fundamental aspects of any nation's naval policy. There are two halves to policies affecting a navy—the external, the question of what it should *do;* and the internal, the question of what it should *be.* In answering the external question, the minister had no doubts: Seaborne trade demanded a protective navy. In answering the internal question, the Philadelphian shipbuilder Joshua Humphreys was equally definite. He explained his views to Secretary of War Henry Knox thus:

> Ships that comprise the European navies are generally distinguished by their rates; but as the situation and depth of water of our coasts and harbors are different in some degree to those of Europe, and as our Navy for a considerable time will be inferior in numbers, we are to consider what size ships will be most formidable, and be an overmatch for those of an enemy; such frigates as in blowing weather would be an overmatch for double-deck ships, and in light winds evade coming into action.[2]

In other words, they should be superfrigates, combining the speed of a lighter vessel with the armament of a heavier one. It was a classic reply to a classic naval problem, the problem of overcoming numerical inferiority. A century later, the Japanese came to the same conclusion: A nation with limited resources should ensure that, ship for ship and class for class, its navy possessed the strongest and fastest vessels in the world. In 1907 the Royal Navy produced its version of the same theory, in the 17,000-ton battle-cruiser H.M.S. *Invincible.* Displacing 900 tons less than the revolutionary *Dreadnought* of 1906 but armed with the same 12-inch guns, *Invincible* was a new type of ship altogether; and so too, in 1794, were the "six original frigates" of the U.S. Navy.

It was not only African ships that harassed American merchant vessels at that time. As if war were the natural state of affairs between France and Britain (and many felt it was), those countries were fighting once again. A British order of November 6, 1793, to all Royal Navy ships stated that they should "stop and detain all ships laden with goods, the produce of any Colony belonging to France, or carrying provisions or other supplies for the use of such Colony, and shall bring the same, with their Cargoes, to legal adjudication in our Courts of Admiralty."[3] Of course, this did not mean just French ships, but any ship carrying French goods; and, issued without warning but with immediate effect, the order resulted in some three hundred American merchantmen being impounded in British ports. Without a respectable navy (indeed, without any fighting navy) America's only option was diplomatic protest—which made no difference at all. The ships remained impounded.

Today the answers to those early questions of external and internal naval policy seem obvious: There simply had to be a fighting navy to protect the nation's seaborne trade, and because it was bound to be small, it would have to have top-class ships. But that is to speak with the clarity of hindsight, and the United States' first-ever defense debate was a bitter affair.

Given the pressing circumstances of the time and the constitutional stipulation that Congress should "provide and maintain" a navy, this may seem surprising; but we have to remember the mental leap Congress was being asked to make. A modern defense debate is bad enough, yet the need for a permanent navy has been learned, and few now would seriously propose the fleet's complete disestablishment. However, the motion before Congress in the winter of 1793 did not simply ask for ships to be added to an existing force; it asked for a navy to be created—in modern terms, for a whole new weapons system to be adopted. If accepted, the shift in America's official view of itself and of the rest of the world (and vice versa) would be fundamental.

The closest modern parallel is not the replacement of an existing system by an improved version of the same, but the adoption of a system which is altogether new. Thus, during Ronald Reagan's presidency in the 1980s, the nearest parallel was not the expansion of the Navy but the attempted development of laser weaponry in space.

In that context it is interesting to see that many of the arguments used in 1793 against the very creation of an American Navy have quite a modern ring. Opponents of the bill maintained that it would prove to be merely the beginning of a permanent standing navy; that such an establishment would tend to involve the United States in wars, rather than keep it out of them; that the public debt would grow, the power of the federal executive would increase, taxes would become heavier, and a tax-collecting bureaucracy would have to be created. The arguments were all defeated; the same or similar arguments are still put forward, and still defeated. Nevertheless, looking back to 1793, one has to admit that every one of them turned out to be correct.

For better or worse, though, the authorization for six frigates was passed by two votes and became law on March 7, 1794; and given his initiative with *Hannah* nineteen years earlier, it was appropriate that the man who signed the birth certificate of the authentic U.S. Navy was President George Washington.

Six frigates gave the chance for six building sites, ranging from Portsmouth, New Hampshire, to Norfolk, Virginia. The benefit of employment sweetened the pill of taxation. Nominally, three of the frigates would carry forty guns each, enormous 24-pounders, while the other three would have thirty-six each. In practice, each vessel usually carried five or six extra; they were powerful indeed. They were beautiful as well—and one of them still is. The forty-four-gun *Constitution*, built in Boston, is there today. In 1828, though condemned as unseaworthy, this remarkable vessel was preserved; in 1927–31, fully restored; in 1934, returned to her original base at Boston; and now she is the oldest warship in the world that is both in commission and afloat. Nelson's *Victory*, launched in 1765, misses that honor by being in dry dock.

Constitution is an impressive sight, but not, perhaps, for the obvious reason. Displacing 2,200 tons, her hold is 14'3" deep; her beam is 43'6"; and her length overall (coincidentally identical to the height of her main-mast from peak to water level) is 204 feet. In other words, by modern standards she is only a small warship, something which is easy to forget unless one visits such old vessels regularly. Walking the decks and cabins of any one of them, one may understand something of the physical toughness, and the ship-handling skills, of the crew. The design of a warship takes account of physical comfort only inasmuch as it affects fighting efficiency; but even the roughest, least stable minesweeper of today offers more in the way of creature comforts than did *Constitution* or any of her like. Ignoring the disadvantages of hammocks, the lack of heating, electric light, and ventilation, modern noses would find one particular drawback about wooden warships: Even the cleanest soon began to stink. When, periodically, they were fumigated, rats as big as cats were regularly found; and with poor food and worse water, primitive medical aid, and no anesthetics, there are few who would put up with such a life today.

Almost as scarce are those who today could handle such a ship with confidence.[4] Skippering a yacht would be small preparation for a square-rigger. Many navies and civilian organizations still offer training in the sailing of tall ships, and in an energy-hungry world, high-technology wind-powered clippers may yet reappear on a wide scale; but no one alive could honestly claim to be able to maneuver such a vessel in battle. Nevertheless, in the eighteenth century and the first half of the nineteenth, every competent naval captain took such exploits in his stride, as part of the job. Naturally, some ships and some captains were better than others; and lean, elegant *Constitution* survives today for two reasons—she was one of the best vessels anywhere, and she had three successive captains who were among the best in America. Among them, they brought her to such fame that not only her story lives, but also the frigate herself.[5]

In 1795, however, it was touch and go whether the six original frigates would even be built. Acknowledging its opponents' arguments, a clause in the 1794 act stipulated that in the event of peace with Algiers, construction would be halted; and on Wednesday, October 14 of that year, *The Times* reported in London that "according to letters received in town on Monday from Algiers, we learn that Peace with America was announced at Algiers on the 8th of September."[6] The treaty had actually been concluded on September 5, but in March news had emerged "of the Emperor of Morocco having declared war against the Americans."[7] If not one Barbary ruler, then another; and though strictly the Algerine peace should have ended the frigates' careers before they were launched, the Moroccan declaration broke the treaty of friendship (it had a further forty-one years to run) and brought a compromise in Congress. Three of the six frigates (*United States, Constitution,* and *Constellation*) would be completed.

In these last years of the eighteenth century, apart from the pirates, America faced two far more serious transatlantic threats—threats which posed a completely insoluble dilemma.

With France and England at war, America, as a neutral, traded with both; but when it came to neutral and belligerent rights, each nation had a different view. The Americans maintained they could trade with whom they chose, but accepted the belligerent right to impound contraband cargoes. The British unilaterally extended the list of contraband goods, which led to trading ships being stopped and searched more often. This in turn seemed to the Americans to be so many infringements of neutral rights, while the French were of the opinion that American trade with

Britain violated the treaties of alliance made in 1778 between France and America. They therefore embargoed American ships in French ports and permitted their own ships in the French West Indies to pounce as privateers on American vessels over there.

No one was willing to change, so plainly there was going to be another transatlantic naval war. The only questions were when it would happen and which permutation of the possible combatants it would involve.

The decision was effectively made in 1794, when Britain and the United States signed a treaty regulating their differences. Acceptable to their governments, it was unpopular with their peoples and regarded by the French as a downright betrayal on the part of the United States. Although still preoccupied with fighting its own fallen aristocrats, the British, and most of the rest of the European monarchies, revolutionary France nevertheless intensified its erratic but stormy privateering campaign and, in 1796, broke off diplomatic relations with the United States. That December, in his final annual address to Congress, President Washington pointed out the moral: Even "the most sincere neutrality" was not proof "against the depredations of nations at war." Therefore, "so that a future war of Europe may not find our commerce in the same unprotected state in which it was found by the present," he believed that America had to "set about the gradual creation of a navy."

His choice of words was significant: The great national project stirring in his mind could not be achieved overnight, or even over several years. It would have to be very gradual, slow and steady, a patient and sustained effort of building, manning, equipping, and maintaining—even in time of peace. But he was willing to speculate that if that were done, it could "even prevent the necessity of going to war" with anyone.[8]

In his own first presidential address, Washington's successor—old pronaval John Adams—made his agreement clear:

> A naval power, next to the militia, is the natural defense of the United States. But, although the establishment of a permanent system of naval defense appears to be requisite, I am sensible it cannot be formed so speedily and extensively as the present crisis demands. . . . It remains for Congress to prescribe such regulations as will enable our sea-faring citizens to defend themselves against the violation of the law of nations, and at the same time restrain them from committing acts of hostility against the powers at war.[9]

British reaction to the speech was positive. It "breathes a very firm and spirited language," commented *The Times*, "against the depredations committed by the French on American vessels, and calls on the People to assist in forming a Naval Establishment to protect the Independence and Trade of America against such wanton insults.[10]

In the same column of the paper it was noted sympathetically that yet another American ship, valued at £100,000, had been "taken and carried into Nantes"; but if the newspaper had taken account of British behavior at sea, its comments might have been more cautious. What was sauce for the French goose could be sauce for the British gander too.

Congressional debates on the Navy lost none of their vigor during the Adams administration; yet in that time the fundamental organizational structure of the U.S. Navy was created. On April 30, 1798, the independent Navy Department was set up, freed from its previous control by the Army; on July 1 the regulations governing the Navy were put into effect; on July 11 the Marine Corps was formally instituted. Moreover, all six of the "original frigates" were authorized for completion, while funds were appropriated for the construction or purchase of another twenty-four warships, ranging from eighteen to thirty-two guns each. And although attention in London was naturally focused on the enemy across the Channel, interest in American naval developments was high, and was reported as frequently as possible:

> The House of Representatives resolved, on the 20th [April 1798], after a debate of unusual length, that the President should be authorized to employ the Naval Force of the United States as Convoys for the protection of the American Trade, without waiting until there shall exist an actual state of war between that Country and the French Republic . . .[11]
>
> On the 7th of July . . . a message was received from the President of the United States, notifying to the House, that he had approved and signed the following enrolled Bills, viz. "An Act respecting Alien Enemies;" "an Act providing Arms for the Militia throughout the United States;" and "An Act to declare the Treaties heretofore concluded with France, no longer obligatory on the United States." Thus then we see the war between France and America virtually declared . . .[12]

And finally, early in August 1798: "At length we find that OPEN HOSTILITIES have commenced between FRANCE and AMERICA."[13]

It was true; but it was difficult to put a precise date on the beginning, for war was never declared by either side. One final factor in the lead-in to hostilities was the event known to history as "the XYZ affair." The letters X, Y, and Z were code names for three French agents who tried unsuccessfully to extort bribes from their American counterparts in return for help in arranging a new treaty with France. It may sound as if the affair is remembered mainly for the benefit of indexers. Actually, it had a direct result in the increase of tension, for President Adams and Congress were so incensed at the attempted corruption that they immediately passed the Acts of July 7, which included the cancellation of all existing treaties with France.

Thereafter hostilities "just growed," and the "Quasi-War" (as it became known) officially lasted until 1800—although with the time needed for communications, fighting actually continued into 1801. All the fighting took place at sea and for the most part was similar in style to the sea fights of the War of Independence: single-ship encounters, with the majority involving privateers. But there were important differences. Strategies were more coherent; captains were more experienced; and the U.S. frigates were brand-new and built to order.

The basic U.S. strategy in this half-and-half war was put concisely by South Carolina's representative in Congress, Robert Goodloe Harper. Far away from the enemy's homeland, but close to some of its most valuable resources—the French West Indies—the whole U.S. force could attack the enemy in a weak but vital part, while only a small section of the enemy's force could retaliate at any one time.

It made good sense overall, and especially then, for the majority of France's warships were either bottled up in French harbors or otherwise preoccupied by British ships. Few French naval cruisers remained in West Indian waters, but there were several hundred (some estimates gave over a thousand) French privateers present; and these did not confine their activities to the Caribbean. As *The Times* again reported, one of them, "of 12 guns and 70 men, having been cruising off the American coast, had taken several vessels, one of them richly laden. Captain Decatur, of the *Delaware* sloop, who was also cruising in the same quarter for the protection of the trade, got information of this privateer, went in pursuit, captured her, and carried her safe into port . . ."[14]

This, the first capture of the Quasi-War, took place near Egg Island, New Jersey, on July 7, 1798—the very day Adams declared French treaties "no longer obligatory on the United States." The victim, *Croyable,* rapidly reappeared as U.S.S. *Retaliation* (typically, with a couple more guns added) and Decatur became the first of several naval names which, over the next fifteen years, would achieve celebrity. Yet though antiprivateer convoys and fights were the bread and butter of this conflict, and though Decatur's *Delaware* was a converted merchantman, the two most memorable battles of the Quasi-War were authentically naval; and one man—Thomas Truxtun—won them both.

At the end of 1798 America could muster twenty-two warships for the West Indies theater, eight of which were revenue cutters mounting fourteen guns or less. This modest force gradually grew to a total of fifty-four vessels, but its essential strategic distribution remained constant. The ships were divided into four groups, among them patrolling the arc of the Antilles from Cuba to French Guiana. Their areas of operations were:

north of Cuba; in the Windward Passage, between Cuba and Haiti; from Puerto Rico to St. Christopher; and from St. Christopher to the South American coast—the last being the largest squadron, led by two of the new frigates. And on February 12, 1799, a headline-catching report was sent to England from the island of St. Christopher:

> The American frigate *Constellation,* Capt. Truxtun, arrived here this noon, and brought in a French frigate, called *L'Insurgente,* of 44 guns, which she captured on Saturday last off the south side of, and in sight of, this island. The action commenced with a running fire south-east of Nevis, and terminated off this island, after three-quarters of an hour's close engagement. The French ship had 58 men killed and wounded; the *Constellation* had 1 killed and 2 wounded.[15]

The casualty figures and their proportion were typical of this and later American naval wars, and so was the gunnery. The French habit was to aim at the rigging, a defensive tactic: a disabled enemy could not pursue. The American tactic, like the Royal Navy's, was to shoot "between wind and water," aiming at the waterline (the most vital part) and the gun decks. American gunners were very good (as the British would find out a little later, to their great cost), and a single well-aimed cannonball, plowing murderously through a cramped and crowded gun deck, could force a ship's surrender when she still had most most of her masts and rigging intact. She could then, of course, be sailed home by the victor and used again.

Forty-four-year-old Thomas Truxtun was an outstanding officer of the sort who would have been useful to any navy at any period. He had supervised the building of *Constellation* and knew her every plank from the keel up. He had first gone to sea at the age of twelve, and in 1771, when he was sixteen, he had served for a few months in the Royal Navy. Before entering the U.S. Navy he had commanded a merchantman voyaging to China. As a naval captain, he drilled his men regularly in all aspects of ship routine and, unusually, encouraged his officers to study naval tactics; and he wrote, putting his inventions and beliefs on paper for all to see. His publications included one on an improved system of masting and rigging; one of the first American volumes on celestial navigation; and, in 1797, the first manual of signals used in the U.S. Navy. In short, he knew his business thoroughly; and so when he heard that "some evil-minded wretches" at home had been saying *L'Insurgente* was friendly, he was absolutely furious and wrote an explosive letter to the secretary of the Navy: "How such false, infamous and barefaced declarations could ever be made before a deserving public, is to me astonishing. . . . It was not for me to enquire on seeing a French frigate whether she had, or had not been successful in her pursuits after our vessels of trade."

In any case, *L'Insurgente* had been responsible for the capture of U.S.S.

Retaliation (the same *Croyable* that Decatur had taken) and her logbook and journals proved she had taken many American merchant ships as well. "And what was the conduct of her Commander on seeing the *Constellation*?" Truxtun continued. "Why, Sir, his first attempt was to deceive by a false show of colours, and when the attempt would not succeed, open hostilities were declared by the French flag being hoisted . . ."[16]

Facing criticism from fellow Americans, it might have been some consolation to Truxtun to have known that the capture of *L'Insurgente* was much admired in Britain, where anyone who fought the French was likely to be popular. In this unofficial first war of the official U.S. Navy, over eighty armed French vessels were taken. But as with fishermen's stories, one of the biggest, and the one which caused the most interest, was the one which got away—the fifty-four-gun *Vengeance*.

It was almost like a return match. *L'Insurgente* had been captured on February 9, 1799; *Vengeance* came on February 1, 1800. Despite her name and her three-to-two firepower superiority, the French ship was not at all keen to fight, and she kept as far as possible away from *Constellation* throughout the day. Truxtun did not overhaul her until 8 P.M., whereupon there began four hours of action which even the experienced American found almost too close and sharp for comfort. By midnight, both vessels were severely damaged, and when at last the French guns were silenced, Truxtun maneuvered to board her; but in doing so, *Constellation*'s weakened mainmast went overboard. *Vengeance* was able to escape. However, she was out of the war, and ran ashore at Curaçao four days later, a useless hulk.

Constellation meanwhile made for Kingston, Jamaica, for repairs, and British sailors there were very curious. One of them, Rear Adm. W. H. Dillon, "visited that ship, and, although she was powerfully armed, the impression prevailed that the Yankee had had the worst of it. The Americans did not appear to advantage."[17] Americans disputed that view and would do so now; yet there must have been a reason for it, and it is not hard to imagine what. It had been a hard battle, with twenty-five Americans dead and fourteen wounded, and at the end there had been the frustration of seeing the defeated ship slip through their fingers. Even knowing the enemy was no longer a menace, anyone would have been dispirited. And in Jamaica, *Constellation*'s officers may have had another reason to look gloomy, for at least one of their number and a few of the men had died unnecessarily. When the mainmast was lost, there were men at its top, and their commander (a young midshipman called James Jarvis) refused to let them descend, or to descend himself, without orders from the deck. All were killed; yet for "devotion to duty," Jarvis was posthumously commemorated in a formal resolution of Congress.

This seems odd. Devotion to duty is admirable, but not when it obstructs common sense; one of the least useful people in any navy is the duty hero. The training of those seamen, and Jarvis himself, had taken time and money. Surely they would have been more use to the U.S. Navy alive than dead; and a naval person might be forgiven for thinking that rather than devotion to duty, Jarvis's action, or inaction, showed a fatal lack of initiative. Nevertheless, the congressional commendation made him sound like an example to be emulated.

While making its unfortunate commemoration of Jarvis, Congress also voted a well-deserved gold medal to Thomas Truxtun. Even without that, his reputation would have been assured. Ships too can have reputations, and, not to be outdone, the converted merchantman *Delaware* turned out to be one of the most bellicose of the fleet. Under Decatur she had made the first capture of the Quasi-War; under Master Commandant J. A. Spotswood she was one of the last vessels—possibly the very last—to stop fighting. The order came to her personally from the secretary of the Navy, Benjamin Stoddert. Dated March 20, 1801 (six weeks after Congress had ratified the treaty ending the Quasi-War), it was short and sweet: "You are to cease molesting French vessels."[18]

By then the desire of the French to stop being molested was a great deal stronger than the American desire to stop molesting them. Napoleon Bonaparte had taken power from the revolutionary Directory and had no wish to dissipate his forces further than necessary, and Truxtun once wrote contemptuously of his French opponents: "Those officers plainly see that we discover all their manoeuvres, & are now (they cannot bully) ready to stoop with a degree of meanness below the character of men."[19] During the Quasi-War, the Navy had been the United States' front line, and because of the Navy, the Quasi-War was fully won. Yet much of the credit for that lay with a man far from the front line—the Navy's first secretary, Benjamin Stoddert.

"A more fortunate selection could not have been made," one of Stoddert's contemporaries wrote. "To the most ardent patriotism, he united an inflexible integrity, a discriminating mind, a great capacity for business, and the most persevering industry."[20] Stoddert himself agreed with this judgment: "You know," he wrote to his brother-in-law, "I have heretofore managed peaceable ships very well. Why should I not be able to direct as well those of war?"[21]

His self-confidence was justifiable. As a partner in the shipping company of Forrest, Stoddert and Murdock, he owned property in Georgetown (District of Columbia), London, and Bordeaux, and from practical experience knew everything that was needed for the fitting out and running of a professional merchant fleet. Construction, maintenance, repair, quality control, economy; the selection and hiring of crews and masters; the supply not only of food but also of guns for self-defense—such things were daily parts of a shipowner's routine. And since merchantmen and warships were still very similar, civilian knowledge could transfer quite easily to a naval function, and could work very well.

Stoddert had not been President Adams's first choice; that had fallen on a retired Boston shipowner, George Cabot, who had refused the honor with the honest and charming excuse of his "invincible indolence of disposition." But in refusing, Cabot conquered his laziness to the extent of describing the kind of man he thought should fill the post. This should be a man with great maritime knowledge, "including the principles of naval architecture and naval tactics. He should also possess skill to arrange systematically the means of equipping, manning, and conducting the naval force with the greatest possible despatch, and with the least possible expense; and, above all, he should possess the inestimable secret of rendering it invincible by an equal force. Thus a knowledge of the human heart will constitute an essential ingredient in the character of this officer, that he may be able to convert every incident to the elevation of the spirit of the American seaman."[22]

Adams could have been forgiven for thinking such a paragon might not exist; but Stoddert did it all—and very nearly literally all, for with only ten or so clerks to help him, he was responsible for everything from questions of strategy and policy to the procuring of nails and salt beef. He seems to have been good at everything, and perhaps best at policy. The U.S. Navy was extraordinarily fortunate in starting its life with this man at its head, for apparently instinctively, he understood just what it could do and what it should be, both in peace and in war.

Internal and external naval policies overlap in the problem of the existence and shape of a peacetime fleet. Without Stoddert (and President Adams to support him), in all likelihood the ships of the U.S. Navy would have been sold at the end of the Quasi-War, just as they were at the end of the Revolution. Stoddert tackled this question head-on, when the Quasi-War had just begun and naval opposition was comparatively muted. And he astonished everyone with a strong recommendation that, good as they were, the innovative frigates were not enough: The United States needed full-sized ships of the line, mounting seventy-four guns each. A dozen would be a start, he reckoned, with twenty or thirty cruisers to back them up. Taking a collective deep breath, Congress agreed to permit half—no doubt exactly what Stoddert expected. In fact, those six 74's had not been started by the end of the Quasi-War; but on March 3, 1801, Congress passed a "Peace Establishment Act" which included, almost word for word, another Stoddert proposal. Some of the fleet would be sold; but "six of the frigates to be retained shall be kept in constant service in time of peace [and] the residue of the frigates to be retained shall be laid up in convenient ports."[23]

Without Stoddert, without Adams, and without victories such as Truxtun's over *L'Insurgente* and *Vengeance,* this certainly would not have happened. Speaking to Congress on November 22, 1800, Adams put his finger on the central reason for its collective benevolent attitude to the fleet: "The present navy of the United States, called suddenly into existence by a great national exigency, has raised us in our esteem; and, by the protection afforded to our commerce, has effected to the extent of our expectations the objects for which it was created."[24]

Protection of commerce had indeed saved the country a great amount of money. Naval costs against France had come to $6 million, but import tariffs for the period were more than $22 million. Without the Navy, hardly any of that would have come in, and $200 million worth of exports would not have gone out. Naval appropriations for 1799 totaled $2 million; naval protection meant that marine insurance rates in the same year were slashed by $8.5 million; so clearly a navy could be good value, an expensive but sound commercial investment. But that was not all. As Adams said, the Navy "has raised us in our esteem." With the sight of the ships and the news of their victories, Americans were beginning to discover naval pride. When Truxtun beat *L'Insurgente* and *Vengeance,* Americans at home found a vicarious pleasure and excitement, and saw not one individual captain and crew and ship beating another, but the whole nation beating France. Truxtun's glory reflected on every American; Americans naturally liked the sensation; and for most of them, that newly learned naval pride was as good a reason as any commercial argument for keeping a navy in peacetime.

Not everyone saw it that way, however: Not everyone was proud that America now had an official navy, and that the Navy had brought an end to French harassment at sea; nor did everyone agree that the fleet represented value for money. Albert Gallatin (a Swiss by origin, with the financial acumen of a dozen Zurich gnomes) had no time at all for the sentimental aspect. He was, moreover, strongly opposed to the trade protection argument, convinced that "a commerce can be protected without a navy, whilst a nation preserves its neutrality"; and in 1801, with a new administration in the White House, Gallatin became secretary of the treasury.[25] Among other things, this meant he held the fleet purse strings; and hardly anyone in America then could have been more opposed to the concept of a permanent navy.

6

*

A Squadron
of Observation

"It is of the utmost importance to diminish our expenses," wrote the new president, Thomas Jefferson, to Albert Gallatin. "This may be done in the Navy Department."[1]

The words echoed well in Gallatin's parsimonious soul, and he set to work gladly. His opinion was that "if the sums to be expended to build and maintain the frigates were applied to paying a part of our national debt, the payment would make us more respectable in the eyes of foreign nations than all the frigates we can build."[2] The national debt was over $83 million, which he intended to pay off entirely within sixteen years—an admirable intention, no doubt. But in the first year, out of a total annual federal income of $10 million, he proposed to set aside $7.3 million toward payment and servicing of the debt *and* to do away with all internal taxation as well. To accomplish this miracle, every department of government would have to cut its spending by more than half.

Gallatin seems to have believed that the world was peopled with peaceful traders, and that if it were not, no harm would come to those who offered none. In this ideal view, the Navy was an obvious main target for economy: President Adams's last budget, in 1801, allocated $4.9 million for all federal expenses, out of which the Navy received $2.1 million. This was by far the largest single departmental budget; the next largest, the military, received only $1.78 million. Gallatin now said that both these departments and all others would have less than $3 million to share between them. In the Navy's case, this meant that in 1802 permitted expenditure plummeted to just over $900,000—substantially less than half of the previous year's figures. And although that was still a major share of total available funds, proportions were not the point; however one looked at it, it was a vicious attack by doctrinaire theory on pragmatic experience. At the end of the Quasi-War there had been 499 naval officers on active duty in a fleet of forty-seven vessels, ranging from gunboats to frigates. By the end of 1801 there were six frigates and one schooner active, with 195 officers retained in service on half pay, receiving full pay when on active duty. Seven further frigates had been laid up "in ordinary" (mothballed, we would say), but all the other vessels had been sold and their officers dismissed, while even the surviving half-dozen frigates were to be allowed only two thirds of their normal complement of men. Purchasing agents and civilian employees were fired wholesale; work on dry docks and harbor fortifications was stopped; all current and projected shipbuilding was canceled.

This was the biggest and harshest overnight turnaround in naval policy in the entire nineteenth century. Nevertheless, most of the assault came under the terms of the Adams-Stoddert "Peace Establishment Act," showing the strength and farsightedness of that act—for if Gallatin had been left entirely to his own devices, he would probably have been even more severe. "It would be a very economical measure," he said a while later, "for every naval nation to burn their navy at the end of a war, and to build a new one when again at war, if it was not that time was necessary to build ships of war."[3] Unfortunately (as he had learned by then) wars have an annoying habit of not providing one with enough warning to get ready from scratch.

The Peace Establishment Act had been signed on the last day of President Adams's administration, March 3, 1801. On March 4, President Jefferson took office; nine days later his secretary of state, James Madison, received a letter from Tripoli. Tripoli's ruler, the bashaw (or pasha, to give it the modern spelling—although "bashaw" seems more apt for Tripolitan rulers both then and now), demanded an immediate and substantial increase in American tribute, or else. The option was war at the end of six months; and, delayed in transit by winter storms, the threatening letter was already five months old.

Sixteen years earlier, when American merchant ships had first fallen foul of the Barbary predators, Jefferson had argued that naval force was the essential reply. Since then, he had changed his public political mind and had been swept to power by the antinaval Republican Party, agrarian literally to its roots. (Jefferson's many-sided character has often proved confusing; and to make matters worse, the "Federalists" of his time became the Republicans of today, while his adopted "Republican" party equates more or less with today's Democrats.) Now, just nine days after taking office and with the bashaw's ultimatum in hand, he was faced with the choice between his party belief and his private instinct. His party belief was that America should have no substantial naval force; his private instinct was to send someone to bash the bashaw.

By March 20 he had made up his mind. He was leader of a party, but he was also president of a nation, a nation which he had helped to form; and it had not been formed in order to pay tribute to Tripoli. In this instance, he decided, nation came above party. Because no one else would take the job of naval secretary when the navy seemed set to be dismantled perhaps for ever, Benjamin Stoddert was still in the post. No doubt he helped the president to make up his mind; and on March 24, writing to Thomas Truxtun, he gave a discreet hint of the decision: "I believe the President contemplates for you, a command in the Mediterranean."[4]

Less than a month after that, on April 19, another message arrived from across the ocean, brought by Capt. William Bainbridge. He was an unlucky man. Commissioned a lieutenant during the Quasi-War, he had been captured and imprisoned by the French. Free again and, in May 1800, commanding the twenty-four-gun ship *George Washington,* he was given the disagreeable task of carrying that year's tribute to Algiers; and once there he was ordered to carry further tribute, this time *from* the dey to the sultan of Constantinople. Commands from his own president were one thing, agreeable or not; commands from a Barbary dey were very much another, but with his ship moored under Algerine guns, he had to comply. Thereupon, he was horrified to find his new cargo included not only nearly a million dollars in cash and regalia, but also an ambassador with a suite of a hundred people, a hundred servants, and further gifts to the sultan of "4 horses, 150 sheep, 25 horned cattle, 4 lions, 4 tigers, 4 antelopes" and a dozen parrots to round things off.[5]

Algiers to Constantinople is some eighteen hundred miles. The squawking, stinking, bleating, roaring zoo could be heard and scented miles away downwind. The passengers, Bainbridge decided, were not much better: Apart from their numbers, they prayed five times a day, which made it even more difficult to move around the ship. But at least once one of the sailors got his own back, in a harmless kind of way. Since the worshipers needed to face Mecca, they always consulted the helmsman to get their spiritual bearings. It did not take much one day to turn the compass card through 180 degrees and gleefully watch the rows of backsides turned in humble supplication toward the holy city. Bainbridge probably approved.

It was only a passport from the sultan of Constantinople which prevented the dey of Algiers from using *George Washington* as a free ferryboat again. When the ship got back to Philadelphia, Captain Bainbridge,

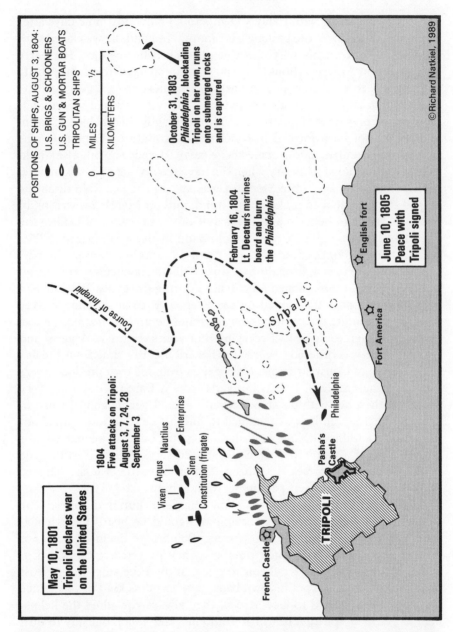

Major U.S. attacks on Tripoli, 1801–1805: Rather than pay tribute—effectively protection money—to the piratical Barbary states of North Africa, the United States ordered its youthful navy to fight. Losses included the capture and spectacular destruction of the U.S.S. *Philadelphia*, but eventually peace without tribute was won.

still fuming, declared his wish not to be sent again "to Algiers with *tribute except it be from the mouth of a cannon.*"[6] This was more than Jefferson had in mind; but it would come. The bashaw of Tripoli, forgetful or unusually forebearing, delayed his declaration of war a month over the stipulated six; it was not until May 15 that he fulfilled his threat by the traditional and graphic means of chopping down the American consulate's flagpole. By then a fundamental policy decision had been taken in America, and it would affect the U.S. Navy ever after. It was expressed in three letters written on May 20, two from the office of the secretary of the Navy and one from the secretary of state.

Thomas Truxtun, mistakenly thinking there would be no glory in the Mediterranean ("Peace can afford no field for me on the ocean"), had declined its proffered command, and in fact would not command at sea again.[7] The two letters from the naval secretary were therefore addressed to his successor, Commodore Richard Dale. "One great object of the present squadron," said the first, "is to instruct our young officers in nautical knowledge generally, but particularly in the shores and coasts where you cruise"—for it was already anticipated that they would go there again.[8] The second letter told Dale that "on your arrival at Gibraltar you will be able to ascertain whether all or any of the Barbary Powers shall have declared war against the United States."[9] If they had, he was given the appropriate orders; but "in case all are tranquil," there were detailed instructions on showing the flag all around the Mediterranean ports and convoying American merchantmen. An earlier letter to Truxtun gave further insight into the same new policy:

It is conceived also that such a squadron cruising in view of the Barbary Powers will have a tendency to prevent them from seizing on our commerce, whenever passion or a desire for plunder might incite them thereto. The intention is to divide the peace establishment into two squadrons, the second to relieve the present squadron and thus alternately to keep a force of that kind in the Mediterranean . . .[10]

The letter from Secretary of State James Madison was addressed to the consuls in both Tunis and Algiers. "The policy of exhibiting a naval force on the coast of Barbary," it said, "has long been urged by yourself and the other consuls. The present moment is peculiarly favorable for the experiment . . . "[11] It was indeed to be an experiment, but if it worked, the intention was clear: The Mediterranean would become a permanent American naval station, in peace or war. The date usually taken for the start of this policy (which would spread worldwide) is 1815, when the Mediterranean was finally clear for American ships. That would be an early date anyway, but what is really remarkable about this episode is that in 1801, with the republic only sixteen years old, Americans had already decided to try "the experiment" of permanent foreign naval stations.

At least one of the officers guessed how pleasant the Mediterranean could be: "I presume we shall have very little to do, and from what I learn of the disposition of the Commodore, he will indulge the different ships under his command with the gratification of visiting most of the ports in the Levant—Smyrna, Constantinople, Egypt &c."[12]

But possibly the most understated comment on this new, forward-looking, and active policy came from the president himself in a letter to the bashaw. Written on May 21, long before news of the truncated flag-pole in Tripoli had reached America, it was a plain statement of fact whose implication the bashaw could work out for himself: "We have found it expedient to detach a squadron of observation into the Mediter-ranean Sea, to superintend the safety of our commerce there, and to exercise the seamen in nautical duties."[13]

Perhaps it was as well that Jefferson spoke softly at that point. Whatever his private thoughts on pirates generally, and particularly on paying tribute to pirates, the circumstances of his party beliefs and the Peace Establishment Act meant that practical possibilities were limited. Com-modore Dale's squadron, composed of three frigates and a schooner, was not strong enough to do very much; his orders forbade him to take prizes; and he was not permitted to agree to peace, should the offer of it come. Under these somewhat contradictory conditions Dale was able only to make a show of force at Algiers and Tunis, followed by a temporary blockade of Tripoli. Since he was required to provide escorts for Ameri-can merchant convoys, and since the nearest source of supplies and fresh water was Malta, the blockade was largely ineffective. But *Philadelphia,* one of his frigates, managed to bottle up in Gibraltar the bashaw's two best vessels, a twenty-six-gun ship and a sixteen-gun brig; and the little twelve-gun schooner *Enterprise* captured a fourteen-gun polacca named *Tripoli.* Following orders, *Enterprise*'s commanding officer (Lt. Andrew Sterrett) had to let the polacca go again; but he took the precaution of throwing its guns and ammunition overboard, and left it with only one sail. Maybe because of the polacca's name, Congress superstitiously saw a good omen; certainly Sterrett was officially thanked for his compara-tively slight deed and given a commemorative sword. But the defeat of terrestrial Tripoli would take very much longer.

Dale's six-month tour may have been quiet, but it was a raging hurri-cane in comparison to the force sent out the following spring. In May 1802 Commodore Richard Morris reached Gibraltar with five frigates and a schooner. The efficiency of his halfhearted blockade of Tripoli may be judged by the incident of the merchant brig *Franklin.* Sailing from Marseilles after repeated assurances that the sea was safe, *Franklin* was captured in short order by Tripolitan corsairs. Their home harbor was under "blockade" by the frigate *Constellation,* which drew so much water she had to stay too far offshore even to see the harbor. But *Franklin*'s enraged captain could see her, and she could see him, when the captured brig was taken into Tripoli in broad daylight; and *Constellation* merely sat and watched.

This understanding of "a squadron of observation" was overliteral. American consuls in the region, much more belligerent than their naval partners, began to despair. "I fear that all the United States has tried to accomplish in Barbary has been in vain," wrote one of them. "Unless something drastic is done to reverse the decline in our fortunes, and I know not what it might be, the United States soon will be forced to abandon the entire Mediterranean Sea."[14]

That writer, feeling he could be of more use in the United States than in the Mediterranean, took ship for home in order to report on the situation. His name was William Eaton; and somewhere between Tripoli and Philadelphia, the idea came to him of what that "something drastic" should be.

President Jefferson was also dissatisfied. The prestige of his administration was involved, and Albert Gallatin was nagging: "I consider it a mere matter of calculation," he wrote to Jefferson, "whether the purchase of peace is not cheaper than the expense of war, which shall not even give us the free use of the Mediterranean."[15] In Gallatin's sublime universe, everything was a "mere matter of calculation"; he must have been painful to work with.

During February 1802, Congress had given the president full discretion to use the Navy for "measures of offense." The first measure (Commodore Morris and his men) had proved singularly inoffensive. Its central problem was soon perceived—wrong ships, wrong men—so in February 1803 funds were appropriated for four shallow-draft vessels suitable for inshore work. Their armament too was designed for shore bombardment: The brigs *Siren* and *Argus* carried two normal 12-pound cannon each, the so-called "long guns" for fighting ships, and sixteen stumpy 24-pound carronades capable of hurling a heavy shot high over a short distance. Similarly, the schooners *Nautilus* and *Vixen* were armed with two long guns and a dozen 18-pound carronades each.

This was more like it. Now the frigates would be able to patrol offshore while the smaller craft attacked close in—if the right commander gave them the opportunity. Morris's stalemate had to end. On June 21, 1803, he was ordered home, there to face official censure and cashiering from the service. And even before he left the Mediterranean, the new fleet, led by Edward Preble in *Constitution* and officered by "Preble's Boys," was sailing westward for a year of action—a year of legends, and the founding of many reputations.

. . .

Edward Preble, forty-two years old, had been a sailor since the age of seventeen. In the last quarter of the eighteenth century his career mirrored those of many contemporaries: two teenage years as a seaman on a privateer, followed by service as a midshipman in one of the state navies—in his case Massachusetts, although he was a native of Maine. After the Revolution he found work in merchant shipping, learning how to command on both coastal and transatlantic voyages. Building on those experiences, he was commissioned a lieutenant in the U.S. Navy during the Quasi-War. Given command of the brig *Pickering,* he operated in the West Indies under the Navy's senior officer, Commodore John Barry.

This much was not unusual for young men of the time; but Barry's tuition was good, and this pupil especially apt. By 1799 Preble had distinguished himself enough to be made a captain; the promotion brought with it a frigate, *Essex*; and under his command *Essex* became the first American warship to venture beyond the Cape of Good Hope into the Indian Ocean.

A daring man, skilled in the arts of the sea, he had yet to prove himself as a squadron commander. He was a taut disciplinarian, with a sharp temper made sharper by ulcers from his eastern voyage. This ensured unpopularity with his subordinate officers (at first) in their voyage across the Atlantic. But during the night of September 14, 1803, moving slowly toward Gibraltar, the younger men began to learn how their war would be conducted.[16] At twilight a strange sail had been sighted, too distant for identification. As darkness gathered, Preble approached warily. All that was certain was that the other ship, like his own, was a man-of-war. Her purpose, her nationality, even her size remained a mystery. It seemed possible that Preble and his boys might have their first battle before they were even over the threshold of the Mediterranean.

Constitution's decks were cleared for action. Below, gunners stood ready; above, eyes strained to make out some sign in the gloom. At last the stranger was close enough to hail. "What ship is that?" Preble called out. It was the standard international question, to which the standard answer should have been given in order: nation, rate, class, name, commander's name. Instead the question itself came back through the dark: "What ship is *that*?" Surprised at the breach of custom, Preble must have been tempted to say, "I asked first." Instead he replied, "This is the United States frigate *Constitution*," and repeated, "What ship is that?"

"What ship is that?"—the question came back again like an echo. Unless all the other crew were deaf or their captain mocking him, Preble could only assume an attack was being prepared. "I now hail you for the last time," he shouted. "If you do not give a proper answer, I will fire a shot into you."

"If you do," came the spirited but improper answer, "I will return a broadside."

"What ship is that?" Preble bellowed, his patience almost at an end.

The reply was imperious: "This is His Britannic Majesty's eighty-four-gun ship of the line *Donegal,* Sir Richard Strachan. Send a boat on board."

That did it. Although the strange vessel was nearly twice his ship's size, Preble roared at it: *"This* is the United States forty-four-gun ship *Constitution,* Captain Edward Preble, and I'll be damned if I send a boat on board any ship!" And to his gunners below he called out: "Blow your matches, boys!"

This must have been heard on the other ship. It was meant to be, but it was no bluff: *Constitution* was ready, Preble's temper was up, and with one word more from him, red-hot slow matches would be touched to powder and twenty heavy round shot would be hurled across the water.

But it did not happen. Instead, a little rowboat came paddling apologetically toward *Constitution;* an English officer came on board; and Preble discovered that the unknown craft was not an eighty-four-gun ship of the line but a frigate with twelve guns fewer than his own. Thus the incident ended amicably, though to the Englishmen's embarrassment: They had been less observant than the Americans and had had to resort to bluff and delay while their own guns were made ready. So readiness was the first of the lessons learned by Preble's boys; and the second, perhaps more important, was defiance. Whether or not the ulcers had anything to do with it, Preble's boys were impressed; and though just then they might not like him much, in later years they would all be proud to say that they had fought with him in the Barbary Wars.

Concerning the four Barbary states, Preble made his mind up fast. Within a fortnight of entering the Mediterranean, he concluded that "the Moors are a deep designing artful treacherous set of villains, and nothing will keep them so quiet as a respectable naval force near them."[17] In the same letter to Robert Smith, Jefferson's secretary of the Navy after Stoddert, he predicted: "The demands of the Barbary Powers will increase, and will be of such a nature as to make it imprudent for our Government to comply with. . . . I believe a firm and decided conduct in the first instance towards those of them who make war against us will have a good effect."

The British had held the same opinion for years. Shortly after losing their transatlantic colonies, a characteristic English article asserted that American money paid in tribute to Algeria "will be entirely thrown away" since "the other piratical states, Tripoli, Tunis, and the Emperor of Morocco, would insist upon receiving equal or even larger gratifications, and their demands would rise in proportion as they had less to dread from the American naval power." The article ended sneeringly: "How different is the case now from what it was when, under the protection of the British flag, the American vessels could sail secure, and had no other enemy to dread but the wind and waves!"[18]

It is unlikely Preble ever saw that article, but if he had, he would have felt forced to agree with it, and that would have maddened him. Yet he would also have relished its implicit challenge: to make the time come when "the Thirteen Stripes, against which the Barbarians have sworn eternal enmity," would provide as good a shield as ever the British flag had done.[19]

He began his time in the Mediterranean by making rendezvous at Gibraltar with other ships of the squadron; he continued by making a show of force at Tangiers, which brought forth instant protestations of friendship from the emperor, together with a renewal of the treaty of 1787; and he sent the frigate *Philadelphia* off, with little *Vixen* and her 18-pound carronades, to blockade Tripoli. *Philadelphia*'s captain needed no second bidding; William Bainbridge was still smarting under the memory of taking that zoo to Constantinople and was eager to repay the debt.

With the western Mediterranean thus swiftly stabilized, at least for the time being, Preble went on to Syracuse in Sicily and established his base there. Malta would have been more convenient for Tripoli, but since it was British, Preble was inclined to avoid it: The British in Gibraltar had found him peremptory, he had found them ungracious, and a distance between the two seemed desirable. In Syracuse he made the blockade of Tripoli official, and feeling things were now going well, he set sail to join Bainbridge off that unfriendly coast. Two days later, on November 24, he met a British frigate and, since the need for news overrode any other feelings, stopped to talk. The news he received was startling—*Philadelphia* was lost to the enemy, and Bainbridge and his men were imprisoned.

This is how it happened. Any sailor would agree that blockading was a dull and difficult job at the best of times—sailing to and fro, keeping station in all states of wind and weather at a given distance off the coast. If no enemy vessel emerged, at least that meant the blockade was working; but it was difficult for a naval officer in wartime to see his role as a mere prophylactic. For Bainbridge this was doubly so; where Tripoli was concerned, his personal grudge gave him an extremely itchy trigger finger. After a couple of weeks stamping crossly backwards and forwards off Tripoli harbor, he heard a report that two corsairs were cruising some hundred and fifty miles to the north. At once he sent *Vixen* hunting. For another week he remained on station, glaring and swearing at the bashaw's palace walls, but on October 29 high winds blew *Philadelphia* out to sea. On her return two days later, a sail was sighted. It was an irresistible temptation—the first prospect of action in almost a month—and suddenly the day seemed brighter. At nine in the morning Bainbridge ordered a chase. Hoisting Tripolitan colors, the quarry declared herself a legitimate target. By eleven she was within range, and Bainbridge opened fire with his bow chasers.

The coastal waters were shallow and irregular; Bainbridge must have known this in general. In detail, though, he did not know where the shoals and reefs lay. This spelled high risk at eight knots, but with fair game ahead and a fair wind astern, he rushed on. Three sailors were sent forward to cast the lead and call the depth at fifteen-second intervals. The Tripolitan dodged and squirmed, and at half past eleven the leadsmen called out rapid shoaling—from eight fathoms to six and a half in thirty seconds. Now the risk was too great. With yards braced about and helm hard over, *Philadelphia* came around as the corsair scudded on to safety. The chase was called off, the reluctant order given to beat back out to deeper open water—and then, with a harsh, grating jolt, an impact which threw men off their feet and brought her bow right up out of the water, *Philadelphia* stopped dead. She was hard aground.

They did everything they could to get her off. There was more water astern than ahead, so all sails, even the top gallants, were laid aback to try and blow her free. It did not work. To lighten her, three anchors were thrown overboard, followed by most of the guns, and water was pumped from the hold. At the same time a group of gunboats sailed out from Tripoli harbor to take their chance, nipping and annoying like terriers. In a last effort to lighten *Philadelphia,* even the foremast was cut down, bringing with it the main top gallant mast; but in the words of the report sent to the secretary of the Navy, "labour and enterprise was in vain; for our fate was directfully fixed."[20]

Preble learned most of this from the commander of H.M.S. *Amazon,* nearly a month after the event. The loss of a major warship was itself a serious enough blow to the small squadron; but what made it far worse was that the bashaw now had 307 more American prisoners and the frigate as well. With his officers' agreement, Bainbridge had surrendered. All he could have done otherwise would have been to blow the ship, himself, and all his men to kingdom come, and that, he rightly believed, "would not stand acquitted before God or Man."[21] Later, the Tripolitans had succeeded in refloating the frigate, and by the time Preble heard of the disaster, she was snugly anchored in Tripoli harbor.

Negotiation was out of the question. With a fist full of aces, the bashaw would certainly be extortionate. In Malta Preble found confirmation of the dismal news. From there he returned to Syracuse to ponder his next move, but because of winter weather, there was little he could do; storms cut short a cruise off the Tripolitan coast in mid-December. In that cruise a small ketch from Tripoli was captured. Though not much consolation for the loss of a frigate, it was better than nothing, and Preble kept it.

During the first three weeks of 1804, he stayed in Malta, establishing an excellent relationship with the British there, who proved much more friendly and understanding than those in Gibraltar. By the end of January, however, he was back in Syracuse; and there he decided what to do about his lost ship and incarcerated colleagues.

By some accounts the idea came from Bainbridge, with whom letters had been exchanged. Other accounts say the commander of *Enterprise* thought of it first, shortly before *Siren*'s commander worked out the same scheme. Equally, Preble himself may well have come to the same conclusion already. No one person can really be given the credit, for ever since they had heard of the loss, it would have been obvious to all that there were only two choices: The frigate *Philadelphia* must either be recaptured, or else destroyed at anchor.

Intelligence reports indicated an army of 25,000 in Tripoli city, with 115 cannon on the walls. In the harbor were a ten-gun brig, two eight-gun schooners, and a pair of galleys with a hundred men each, as well as nineteen gunboats, each carrying an 18- or a 26-pounder, two brass howitzers, and a crew averaging forty men. *Philadelphia* lay in the midst of all this, within range of the land batteries; and taking account of the shallowness of the harbor and the reefs, shoals, and islands which fringed it, the prospects of recapture were minimal. Destruction at anchor seemed likewise implausible: Any American vessel attempting to enter the harbor would be recognized, attacked, and probably overwhelmed long before she was near the frigate.

But then, like a sudden burst of sunshine after a storm, someone saw the answer: A Mediterranean craft was another matter. And in Syracuse, Preble had the very thing—the captured ketch *Mastico,* declared lawful prize on January 28, and as Tripolitan as the bashaw himself.

7

*

SOMETHING DRASTIC

S he cast off from the mole at Syracuse on February 3, bearing seventy-five officers and men and a very large quantity of arms and combustible materials. Leading the expedition was Lt. Stephen Decatur, Jr., commander of *Enterprise* and son of the Stephen Decatur who in 1798 had captured *Croyable,* America's first prize in the Quasi-War against France. Stephen Jr. was twenty-five in 1804. His new command was renamed *Intrepid,* very aptly: The adventure just commencing was as daring as any young man could dream of, as exciting as any could wish, and far more dangerous than most would like at all.

The plan was simplicity itself. Under cover of darkness, they were going to sail into the center of Tripoli harbor, board *Philadelphia,* overpower her guards, lay the combustibles throughout, set fire to them, jump back on board *Intrepid,* and, in modern terms, get the hell out. Of course they would be challenged, and to cover that Decatur had with him an Arabic-speaking Sicilian pilot who knew Tripoli and loathed its inhabitants. Of course they would have to fight, and to cover that they had arms, training, and nerve. And of course they would have to escape under fire. To cover that, they were relying mainly on luck.

The story has become one of the most celebrated in the early history of the U.S. Navy, told and retold to each generation since; and what remains remarkable and impressive is that Decatur and his men succeeded in every respect, without a single one of them being killed. Nelson (at that time a vice admiral commanding the British Mediterranean Fleet in its blockade of the French port of Toulon) is said to have called Decatur's deed "the most bold and daring act of the age," which sounds authentic in vocabulary and character: He never begrudged praise for professional excellence, even in another navy. And it was an excellent performance.

At the start luck seemed to be against them. From Syracuse they arrived off Tripoli in four days. There a gale kept them from entering the harbor. One of the officers, Midshipman Charles Morris, wrote about it in his autobiography when he was a commodore. *Intrepid*'s sole accommodation was one tiny cabin. Decatur and four of the other officers were crammed in there. Morris, with the other midshipmen and the pilot, had a crude shelter, so low they knocked their heads on its top when they sat up. A party of marines shared it with them, while the sailors had nothing to sleep on but the tops of barrels in the hold.

"To these inconveniences," Morris wrote, "were added the want of any room on the deck for exercise and the attack of innumerable vermin, which our predecessors, the slaves, had left behind them."[1] They had not anticipated any delay in entering Tripoli, and were not adequately victualed; their salt meat turned out to be rotten; so, in horrible conditions, they bounced around on the open sea, living on bread and water, until the gale blew itself out. It took nine days.

This may have fired their fighting urge, if any further spark were needed. At any rate, when they finally hobbled into Tripoli on the night of February 16, they were in no mood for opposition or defeat. The pilot did his job superbly: answered the Arabic challenge, explained his anchor was lost in the gale, asked to moor alongside *Philadelphia*. The guards agreed; and from the moment of contact to departure, the operation took less than twenty minutes. After a short, sharp fight in which several of the Tripolitans were killed, the rest of the guards jumped overboard and gave Decatur and his men free run of the frigate. The next main hazard was the fire and smoke they themselves started: It spread with enormous speed, nearly overcoming some of those on board and threatening to set light to *Intrepid* alongside. Thereafter, with all safely in the ketch, they came under fire not only from the shore batteries and the vessels in the harbor, but also from *Philadelphia*'s own guns. Primed and shotted, ready for action, the heat of the blaze set them off one by one; but despite the roar and rumpus on all sides, only one lucky shot hit *Intrepid,* and that passed clean through her sail without harming a soul on board.

With oars and punctured sail they escaped scot free, rejoined their escort *Siren,* and stood awhile offshore to witness—with exhilaration and a little regret—the terrible furnace they had ignited. When at last they shaped course for Syracuse, they must have known that their utterly successful mission was the single most heroic and spectacular action in the U.S. Navy since John Paul Jones had defeated *Serapis;* and they may have guessed that people would remember it, and in it would find inspiration, for as long as the United States had a navy at all.

Much less frequently remembered was *Intrepid*'s eventual tragic end. On September 14, 1804, she was made into a floating bomb to attack Tripoli once more. A hundred barrels of powder were placed in her hold, with a hundred 9-inch and fifty 13½-inch shells on her deck, packed around with shot and pigs of iron ballast. With an all-volunteer crew, she sailed into the harbor under cover of darkness and mist. It was not a suicide mission; boats were provided for the crew's escape. But it went horribly wrong—the ketch ran aground and somehow, by accident or intent, was blown to pieces with all hands on board. Not a man survived, and the few bodies that were found were unrecognizable. The sole consolation was that even in failure, they had done all they could.

Between *Intrepid*'s two voyages, the one such a conspicuous success and the other such a ghastly disaster, Preble was not idle. Blockade was reinstated—essential, but rhythmic and dull; Midshipman Morris, now in *Argus,* characterized its tedium with entries in his journal. The entire entry for August 13 read: "Moderate breezes and pleasant weather. Made and shortened sail. Tacked and wore occasionally to keep company with the squadron." Eight days later even that short note seemed too long; "standing off and on the town of Tripoli" was all that needed to be said.[2]

Negotiations with the bashaw had been attempted and dropped almost at once in the face of his continued truculence. But, using his discretionary orders to acquire more vessels, Preble borrowed six gunboats and two "bomb vessels" for shore bombardment from the Kingdom of the Two Sicilies. Added to those he had *Constitution,* three brigs, three schooners, and 1,060 men—by far the biggest American force yet assembled in the Mediterranean—and in four weeks over August and September he made five separate attacks on Tripoli. In the first of these, Stephen Decatur (now promoted to captain) jumped to prominence again when his brother James was killed in a treacherous pseudosurrender. Stephen vengefully boarded the offending vessel, sought out the killer, and dispatched in a classic, vicious, man-to-man fight.

Preble was solely responsible for bringing to the surface the latent fighting spirit of his officers and men; yet these attacks were the crescendo of U.S. naval activity in the Barbary Wars. While his second attack was actually going on, news arrived from the United States that he was to be replaced. It was not that the government felt he had done badly, far from it; but according to the rules as they stood, it was simply someone else's turn. This strict application of the rule book showed just how inexperienced the U.S. naval administration still was. By the time he was relieved, Preble was in charge of an efficient team; he knew the political and martial situation intimately; he had firsthand experience of all the constraints the Mediterranean reefs and storms could offer. Yet with all that knowledge, he had to go. In contrast, his successor, Commodore Samuel Barron, was an ill man, able to accomplish little, and Barron's successor, John Rodgers, had no time to do anything before a peace treaty was signed—a premature treaty which Americans would later regret.

Looking at how those two sailors fared, there was nevertheless one way in which the administration at the time displayed more wisdom than administrations a hundred and fifty years later, and more, would do. Barron's orders included the recognition (which in the War of Independence had not come to British minds until too late) that when the struggle was far away, the man on the spot should be free to make decisions. As his orders from home explained, "the varying aspects of our affairs in the Mediterranean—the great distance between this country and the probable places of your operation—render it improper to prescribe you any particular course of conduct. We therefore leave you unrestrained in your movements and at liberty to pursue the dictates of your own judgement, subject to the general accompanying instructions."[3] There are many living American commanders who, when fighting in Korea and Vietnam, would have appreciated such sense and trust.

With Barron ill and Preble no longer in command, the focus of the war changed. William Eaton, who had wanted "something drastic" done to bring the bashaw to terms, returned from the United States to the Mediterranean. He was a curious character. Excitable, eccentric, energetic, he had been trained to fight in the Revolutionary War and had well-developed ideas on the value of irregular forces. The plan he had hatched en route to Washington was about as irregular as it could be.

What he had dreamed up was, in plain terms, an American-led coup d'état. They should engineer events so as to throw out the existing bashaw and replace him with someone more friendly. Obviously many states had indulged in such affairs before, as the United States and others have done since, but to President Jefferson it seemed an immoral and unattractive proposition. He agreed with James Madison, secretary of state: Their country had achieved self-determination too recently to wish to remove it from others. Eaton countered with the explanation that self-determination would not be removed from Tripoli but restored, for the current bashaw had come to power in a civil war and the preceding bashaw (his brother) was alive and well and living in Egypt. By putting him back on the throne, America would be not interfering but assisting the legitimate ruler, who might reasonably be expected to be grateful.

Put like that, Jefferson's scruples diminished but did not vanish. When

Eaton talked of his project, he found no one wanted to take final responsibility. "The President," he wrote, "becomes reserved; the Secretary of War 'believes we had better pay tribute'—he said this to me in his own office. Gallatin, like a cowardly Jew, shrinks behind the counter. Mr Madison 'leaves everything to the Secretary of the Navy Department.' And I am ordered on the expedition by Secy Smith—who, by the by, is as much of a gentleman and a soldier as his relations with the Administration will suffer—without any special instructions to regulate my conduct."[4]

But this suited Eaton's character rather well. Back in the Mediterranean, he persuaded Barron to support him, and they agreed it should be a land operation, supported from the sea. At this point the endeavor began to take on some thoroughly unlikely aspects—unlikely, but real day-by-day Eaton.

First he took himself off to Egypt and located the ex-bashaw, Hamet Karamanli. Hamet turned out to be a feeble specimen, entirely unfit to rule Tripoli or anywhere else—something that had not occurred to anyone—but undaunted, Eaton proceeded to hire a mercenary army of three hundred Arabs and seventy Alexandrian Christians. Assisting him were an American lieutenant of marines, seven enlisted marines, and, from the Navy, Midshipman Pascal Paoli Peck. This young man had been named after a Corsican patriot, then fighting for his own island's freedom from French rule. In those days it was a famous name; today, "Midshipman Pascal Paoli Peck" sounds more like the first line of a limerick, perhaps to be rhymed with deck and wreck. In either case it was quite suitable for the expedition now beginning.

Eaton dressed himself up in Arab headdress and flowing robes, called himself "General," and made Hamet create him commander in chief of all land forces. That done, he set off, intending to lead his colorful band and 103 camels across some 600 miles of desert to the coastal town of Derna (now Darnah) in Tripolitania. No non-Moslem had accomplished such a feat since the days of Suleiman I nearly two hundred fifty years before; but to the surprise of his unruly followers and the consternation of the bashaw, Eaton did it. By the middle of April 1805, he was 450 miles west of Alexandria, on the shores of the Gulf of Bomba. There, contact was made with the brig *Argus* and the sloop *Hornet*. Before the end of the month, Eaton was outside the walls of Derna, while *Argus*, *Hornet*, and the schooner *Nautilus* were offshore to the north. On April 27 an ultimatum was given to and rejected by the city governor; and so the following day, at 2 P.M., a joint sea and land attack began. It was a complete success: By half past three the Stars and Stripes flew over the town—the first time it had been raised in conquest anywhere in the Old World, or indeed anywhere outside the continental United States.

With the figures of the Eaton-Hamet army suitably exaggerated, the news was communicated to the bashaw in Tripoli. He was impressed. The notion of hordes of American marines and Arab mercenaries rampaging around his landward defenses while warships battered his seawalls was not appealing, especially if it resulted in his weedy brother taking over the throne. But pugnacious as ever, he did not feel like giving up just yet. If brother Hamet wanted Tripoli that badly, he could come and get it; but he would have to fight for it. Hamet, wanting only a quiet life, had little say in the matter. Eaton was eager to carry on, as was the newly appointed commodore John Rodgers—yet all of a sudden, they were forbidden to do so.

What brought this about was that almost a year before, when Barron had been given his orders by the naval secretary, James Madison had issued another set of orders to Col. Tobias Lear, the U.S. consul general in Algiers. In the president's name, these orders gave Lear "full power and authority to negotiate a Treaty of Peace with the Bashaw of Tripoli," and in May 1805 Lear took up the option.[5] Claiming the best of motives— the prevention of further bloodshed and the rescue of the prisoners—he wanted peace, and with Eaton away in the desert, he prevailed upon the still sick Barron to turn over command to Rodgers. Then, when the change of command took place on May 22, Lear made sure that Rodgers's orders included orders to negotiate.

The treaty was signed on June 10. There would be no payment for the peace itself, or tribute; but $60,000 was paid to ransom the prisoners, Derna was evacuated, Hamet's family remained where they were—as hostages of the bashaw—and Hamet himself was left in the lurch. The American government found this sufficiently embarrassing to authorize a lump-sum payment and a pension to Hamet, and in time he was reunited with his family, so for him the United States' war with the Barbary States ended happily. However, most others were furious with Lear's arrangements.

"It is the work of a Machiavellian Commissioner into whose influence the Commodore has yielded his mind through the infirmity of bodily weakness," Eaton stormed, while Preble commented sardonically to Stephen Decatur: "That a Colonel should command our squadron, as you inform me, must be matter of surprise abroad as well as at home."[6] A special committee of Congress agreed with this, judging that though Lear had been given power to negotiate, he had far overreached himself. He had "gained a complete ascendancy over the commodore, . . . dictated every measure, . . . paralyzed every military operation" and agreed to pay the $60,000 "without displaying the fleet or squadron before Tripoli, against the opinion of all the officers of the fleet."[7] Presumably Lear had thought people would be pleased. When he discovered they were not, and that he had done very much the wrong thing, he did not last long: Shocked and demoralized, he committed suicide.

One cannot avoid feeling some sympathy for him; he meant well. But he could not have been more unhelpful if he had tried. With Eaton's extraordinary operation the war was swinging strongly in America's favor. Lear's intervention had undone much of the effort of previous years. He had hoped to avoid more bloodshed, and in the short term did so; but in the long term he probably created more than would have been necessary. Not only Tripoli but all the Barbary states could have been brought to terms at a fairly early date. Now, however, like a recurring illness, they would break out again and again, for a further twenty-five years.

For the time being, however, the Barbary Wars were over. They had been popular in America. The cause was seen to be good, and people found the Navy's exploits a source of stirring pride. Casualties in the Mediterranean were low; commerce was high. But while a war tends to unite a country, peace revives party politics; and in spite of the national benefits that Preble and his boys had brought so recently, the politics of Jefferson's party were still basically antinaval. Gallatin for one continued to chafe at naval expenditure: His 1801 budget for the Navy of under a million dollars had been forced to rise steadily to just over $1.4 million in 1805, while to cope with the loss of *Philadelphia* he had had to invent a special "Mediterranean Fund." Thus, in 1806 Jefferson faced the tricky coincidence of internal and external naval peacetime policy again: the questions of how the Navy should be composed, and what it should do, when there was no one obvious to fight.

The answer he came up with has attracted almost universal condemnation ever since. On April 21, 1806, Congress repealed the section of Stoddert's 1801 Peace Establishment Act—which stated that six frigates should be kept in constant service. Now the number was left to the president's discretion. The same repealing act limited the number of serving naval personnel to 13 captains, 9 masters commandant, 72 lieutenants, 150 midshipmen, and 925 enlisted men—a total of 1,169. (For comparison, the total in the late 1980s was in the region of six hundred thousand.) This, of course, provided an effective upper limit to the number of real warships, and while real warships were being laid up in ordinary or sold, the United States began to arm itself with vessels which any self-respecting naval nation could only regard as toys—dozens and dozens of gunboats, generally around fifty feet long, each carrying a long gun and (if they were lucky) a couple of howitzers. As an emergency measure in the Revolution Adams had hoped this kind of vessel would serve for "dodging Indian fights." In the battle of Lake Champlain,

Arnold had used similar craft; so had Preble, for inshore work in the Mediterranean; and most European navies had them for that purpose, as associates of a fleet. But now, under Jefferson, they became *the* fleet.

The gunboat navy was the physical realization of the agrarian view of a navy's function, locally based for the defense of coastal communities. This was certainly a backward move; the vessels could do no more than Adams had hoped thirty years earlier. Gun for gun they were three times more expensive than frigates. In the three years of 1805–07, purchase or construction of 263 gunboats was authorized (though fewer than two hundred were actually built); and when it came to the test, they could not even do the job they were meant for—they could not prevent enemy warships penetrating the very bays, rivers, and harbors they were supposed to protect.

Albert Gallatin, Republican and agrarian, opposed the gunboat navy; but as usual his objections were based on considerations of immediate expense rather than defense. He recognized that his ideal—burning the fleet at the end of one war and rebuilding it at the start of another—was impractical because of the time needed for shipbuilding. With gunboats, he asserted, the principle was the same, "and the objection of time does not exist," so he reckoned there was no point in building them before they were needed. "I also think," he added, "that in this as in everything connected with a navy and naval department, the annual expense of maintenance will far exceed what is estimated."[8] He was right on that, which may have given him some satisfaction in later years; but he was going against the tide of Republican opinion. Gunboats seemed to be cheap; they seemed to provide, in one single system, all that was necessary for coastal defense; and being visible and understandable, they seemed ready, like a farmer's fireside gun, to be snatched up and used at a minute's notice.

The first two of these beliefs were entirely false. Gunboats were not cheap, they were disproportionately expensive. Far from being the only thing necessary for coastal defense, without coastal forts and batteries to back them up they were about as useful as trying to put out a fire with an empty bucket. Given these mistakes, the belief in their instantaneous readiness was simply irrelevant. But more important than any of these three errors were two other misconceptions central to Republican thinking. One was that to build frigates would be seen by Britain as a threat to the Royal Navy and would invite a preemptive British attack. The other was a kind of isolationism, to the effect that if America bothered no one, no one would bother America—a naive and unrealistic hope that was not completely buried until the end of the Second World War.

But in Britain, the U.S. Navy was viewed with condescension at best and contempt at worst, tempered only by admiration of American naval gunnery and the quality of those few ships they could build. And the number of warships Jefferson's administration could have built was so few, Britain would not have remotely considered them as a threat that had to be stamped on. As for the innocent hope of minding one's own business and being left to get on with it without interruption, the world, unfortunately, did not work that way. The United States' problem lay in realizing that despite the intervening oceans, it was a part of the rest of the world.

Created in spite of the lessons of the Revolution, the Quasi-War, and the Barbary struggle, Jefferson's gunboat navy was, in short, a retrogressive and nursery conception from the start. It characterized several deep-rooted American dreams, including the wish to be able to rely on a single, simple system of defense. Nevertheless, under the political circumstances, it is difficult to see what else Jefferson could have done with the Navy short of scrapping it altogether. Much more time was needed, and much more experience, both sweet and bitter, before America would understand and accept its navy as a basic necessity of life.

8

★

MUCH SENSATION
IN AMERICA

"*P*eace and plenty! What has this world to exhibit besides?" In 1791 an anonymous British citizen, identifying himself only as "a freeholder," wrote and published a short essay on one aspect of British society.

> But while I was congratulating myself and my country with the happiness of our lot, so different from that of other nations, and so different from that of former ages in our island, my joy received an immediate check . . . for, hearing a hubbub in the street, and looking through the sash in an upper room, I saw eight or ten rough-looking fellows, armed with cudgels, marching along in a kind of hurry; in the midst of whom was an honest good-looking young man, whom they appeared to have taken into custody. Upon my enquiring into the cause, I was informed it was the press-gang . . .[1]

Most countries in the Old World operated press-gangs in time of war, to man both armies and navies. In all the principle was the same: In time of extreme national need, if volunteers were not forthcoming, men would be physically forced into service willy-nilly. Despite this universality of practice, the legendary terrors of impressment are attached today almost exclusively to the eighteenth-century Royal Navy. There are three reasons for this mistake: First, the sheer size of the Royal Navy, coupled with its hard conditions and the risk of death through disease or battle, created a constant high demand for and low supply of willing recruits. Second, the worldwide spread of the English language and the worldwide visibility of the Royal Navy meant that people connected impressment more with Britain and its navy than with any other nation or force. And third, in all the Royal Navy's global catchment area, there was one English-speaking nation which did not practice impressment and which objected volubly when its own men were pressed into the foreign naval service. That country was, of course, the United States.

Even in Britain, though, the habit was widely seen as unjust and immoral. Naturally the first person to see this was the victim, when, "imagining himself quite secure, behold he is dragged away like a ruffian, from all that is dear to him, by those whose tender mercies are cruel, and whose hearts find no pity! In vain does he reason; in vain does his broken-hearted wife intreat; in vain do the poor little infants scream, and wonder what the wild uproar means; away he is torn from them, perhaps never to see them more!" Actually the chances were that the victim was a petty villain, for since 1597 various vagrancy acts had enabled local magistrates to clear jails of their worst offenders by sending them to the navy; yet "what an idea must this give the British youth of our sea-service, while a man-of-war carries the idea of a house of correction . . . !" However, homes could be broken up and families made penniless, so the freeholder of 1791 marshaled all the arguments he could think of—moral, martial, and economic.

"It is a reflection upon the British Empire," he wrote, "whose laws, in the general, are so well calculated to defend every subject, that so cruel a method should be adopted to man our fleets; and argues a disgrace upon the naval service, that our ships of war cannot be manned without violence and opposition. Britons hurry Britons into captivity!" Acting against their will, men would be poor fighters, whereas "when men act freely, it is like a strong natural current supplied by a sufficient spring"; and as for trade, "how many ships fraught with valuable cargoes, lie under a kind of embargo, for want of hands to man them?" According to *The Times,* the answer—for January 1794 alone, and only for the Thames—was "upwards of 60."[2] A few years later, the truth of the economic argument against the press was shown more forcibly still: Impressment could take place at sea as well as on land, and in 1802 an East Indiaman, loaded with precious goods and homeward bound for England, was stopped in the Bay of Biscay by a Royal Navy ship. So many of the merchantman's crew were taken that she was unable to defend herself in the few miles back to England and was captured intact by a French privateer.

Unfortunately, the critical freeholder could offer only two solutions. One was that every freeholder like himself and every shipowner should provide, respectively, 20 percent of his income and one seaman per ship to man the fleet. Not a chance. The other was that the navy should see itself, and should be seen, not as "a punishment or a penance for every vagrant or vagabond, but rather as an honourable station, a scene of glory, in which they may distinguish their courage and capacity." In 1791 such a transformation must have seemed as distant and unlikely as the Second Coming. Yet astonishingly, exactly that transformation did occur, in a short time—not by direction, as the freeholder imagined, but as a result of Nelson's victories in the very war which made impressment a burning issue between Britain and America.

During the Napoleonic Wars of 1798–1815, the press-gang remained the one fast and certain way of getting men into ships, and the Royal Navy was not too choosy about where the men came from. By 1812 over six thousand impressed American seamen were registered in Washington. According to the British government, the figure was more modest: On February 18, 1811, Lord Castlereagh told Parliament that out of 145,000 seamen in the Royal Navy during the previous month, "the whole number claiming to be American subjects amounted to no more than three thousand three hundred."[3] The word "claiming" was relevant since Britain did not recognize the possibility of changing nationality: British-born meant British for life, even if the man became a naturalized American citizen. From this view, the Royal Navy was only taking back its own, and expected mistakes here and there. But few people in Britain seemed to consider how they would react if the same thing happened the other way around. This calm one-sidedness was shown vividly in a *Times* report of 1799: "We find that the stopping and searching for British sailors off the Havannah [Cuba] . . . has caused much sensation in America."[4] There would have been much sensation in Britain, too, if the U.S. Navy had stopped and searched British ships and taken men from them.

It was in 1807 that the American view of Britain began to be truly jaundiced. One of the six original frigates, the thirty-six-gun U.S.S. *Chesapeake,* was brought back into commission in January, in order to take over command of the Mediterranean squadron from *Constitution*. By summer she was ready to go, her refit completed and a new crew on board. Among the crew were John Strachan and William Ware, both white, and Daniel Martin, a black man, helping to ready the ship in Washington Navy Yard. Even before *Chesapeake* weighed anchor these three were the focus of considerable attention, for they had all deserted from the British frigate *Melampus* and the Royal Navy wanted them back. A formal request for their return had been rejected on the basis (spurious, in the mind of the vice admiral of the British North American Squadron) that all three were American citizens who had been pressed into the Royal Navy. This was true for at least two of the men, and probably for the third; but when the U.S. Navy refused to give them up, Vice Admiral Berkeley ordered any vessel in his squadron which encountered *Chesapeake* to stop her, by force if necessary, and to remove the trio. And as *Chesapeake* sailed down her namesake bay, the fifty-gun ship H.M.S. *Leopard* lay waiting for her.

Chesapeake's captain was James Barron, brother of the sickly Samuel Barron who had "relieved" Preble in the Mediterranean. James, as the afternoon of June 22, 1807, showed, was as ineffectual a commander as Samuel; and the only good result of his encounter with *Leopard* was that the U.S. Mediterranean squadron was spared from having a second Barron in charge of it. At the beginning of June, James Barron had reported *Chesapeake* as ready for sea. Three weeks later, when a British rowboat pulled toward her and H.M.S. *Leopard*'s guns were unmasked, *Chesapeake*'s decks were still littered with all manner of stores, including furniture and chicken coops. None of the gun had its firing mechanism fitted; most of the guns were not even secure on their carriages. The frigate was far from ready for sea, and absolutely unready to give battle; but when Barron refused to muster his men for inspection by *Leopard*'s boarding officers, battle began.

Yet "battle" is not the right word: In fifteen minutes *Leopard* fired three full broadsides, while *Chesapeake* fired only one shot, and that merely to retain a scrap of honor. Far too late, Barron attempted to make his crew defend the frigate, then ordered them to take cover and save their lives. But three died; seventeen or eighteen were wounded; all the masts were hit, and the sails shredded by grapeshot, while twenty-one round-shot hit the hull.

Barron capitulated, and in an effort to make the insult a formal, intergovernmental affair, he offered his frigate as a prize. The British captain was not interested; all he wanted was the three men. He got them (and a fourth as well) and sailed away, leaving Barron and *Chesapeake* to totter back to Hampton Roads, dazed and disgraced. When they arrived, an almighty rumpus began. There were riots in Hampton and Norfolk. British naval stores were destroyed, and up and down the length of the coast a cry arose for reparation or revenge. But hanging over from the days of the Revolution was the old fear of provoking an uncontrollable British reaction. A report from the Connecticut Committee of Safety, written in 1775, was still valid in 1807:

> The people are differently minded about the measure [of building armed vessels], many thinking that as it is impossible for us to compare by sea with the British ships etc., it will but provoke insult and expose our sea coasts and vessels inward bound to greater dangers, etc.,—others, that it will be of advantage and a protection, etc.[5]

President Jefferson's reaction to the *Chesapeake-Leopard* affair showed the set of his mind in the second half of 1807: His answer was passive defense. He forbade British warships to enter American waters, ordered those already there to leave, brought home the Mediterranean squadron (an ironic move, since Barron had been meant to command it), and approved the purchase or construction of 188 gunboats. The only immediate consequence of these moves was the capture of three U.S. merchant ships by Algerian corsairs. The British government did eventually apologize, but not because of Jefferson; rather, it was because Vice Admiral Berkeley had visibly exceeded his orders. He was removed from his post, and after some two years, two of the impressed men were returned. The other two, by then, were dead. As for Barron, a naval court of inquiry ruled him guilty of neglecting to clear for action when an engagement was probable. He was suspended from the service for five years and promptly went to work for the French navy; but in time he would be back and would do further injury to the U.S. fleet.

Meanwhile the U.S. Navy was becoming the plaything of France and England, a pawn between the two powers in their war. France, defeated at sea in the Battle of Trafalgar, was still paramount on the continent of Europe. Britain, with its trade under European boycott and its Scandinavian grain supplies cut off, issued Orders-in-Council prohibiting any direct trade between the United States and Europe: All American vessels were now required to clear their cargoes through England. From Milan, Napoleon decreed that American ships were free to obey the British order; but if they did so, France would consider that they had lost their neutral rights and had become lawful targets.

Like a person with two jealous suitors, Jefferson was being forced to choose. It was not much of a choice, for if he sided with either, war with the other would definitely follow. But in love affairs, there is always a third option—reject them both. Hoping this might work in international affairs as well, that is what the president did. Beginning on December 22, 1807, his notorious Embargo Act forbade the sailing of any American vessel carrying goods for foreign ports.

This hurt; and it hurt Americans far more than anyone else. Exports in 1807 had totaled $108 million; in 1808, the figure plummeted to an estimated $22 million. In theory, it should have been nearly zero, but smuggling went on everywhere. The Navy was supposed to enforce the embargo, although apart from the gunboats there was only a handful of larger craft available. Without the cooperation of traders and shipowners, the thankless task was manifestly impossible. Many of them did cooperate, as the 80 percent loss of trade showed; but others found handy loopholes to exploit. Whalers, for example, could go to sea, and did; and on their return it might be found that the expected cargo of blubber had miraculously changed into bales of English cloth. Similarly, coastal trading was allowed with any goods, and in emergency the coasters were allowed to put into a foreign port. Suddenly and mysteriously, there was a vast increase in the number of emergencies at sea. And at Passamaquoddy Bay in Maine and Amelia Island off the Florida coast, where the frontiers with British and Spanish territory respectively were ill defined, there were somehow far more vessels than usual; for with the hazy boundaries, it was difficult to prove that anyone was actually smuggling. It was at this time, and in such operations, that several great family fortunes were founded, including that of the Astors.

In the international arena, the effects of the embargo were completely different than what Jefferson intended. To be sure, Britain received its lowest American grain importation of the nineteenth century, but British merchant ships scooped the vacated trade lanes. Simultaneously, Napoleon seized all possible American merchantmen on the basis that since all Americans should have been at home, they must be disguised British ships. And as French grain prices were low, the emperor allowed his people to export their surplus to Britain (an odd form of warfare) in the hope that the British treasury would be bankrupted. It looked rather as if, despite their differences, the jilted suitors were ganging up.

With his attempt at peaceful coercion a palpable failure, Jefferson's second and last term as president came to a muted end. In January 1809, his and Gallatin's policy of laying up frigates in ordinary was narrowly overruled by Congress. Now all vessels were to be brought back into commission, fitted out, and placed in active service; and on March 1, three days before James Madison was inaugurated as the fourth president, the Embargo Act was repealed. In its place came the Non-Intercourse Act: Trade was resumed with all nations except Britain and France and would be resumed with either or both when they stopped troubling American commerce. This made not a jot of difference to the official attitudes of the two belligerents. But the following year, on May 1, 1810, the principle of nonintercourse was reversed by an act known as "Macon's Bill No. 2," and now Napoleon became interested.

This time the Americans offered open trade all around, including with France and England, and promised that if either country respected America's neutral rights, trade with the other would be stopped. It was a weird solution: It put America in an even worse position than that which prompted the embargo. In effect, it was as if, after rejecting both suitors, America was now promising to marry whichever would propose first; and in short order, Napoleon whipped out a glittering ring. With effect from November 1, 1810, his decrees against the neutrality of American shipping were revoked; and on November 2, with satisfaction, President Madison announced the fact, giving Britain three months' notice of the reimposition of nonintercourse if the anti-American Orders-in-Council were not rescinded by then.

Madison's minister to Russia was more perceptive than was the president. In 1825 John Quincy Adams, eldest son of America's second president, would become the republic's sixth president. In 1810 he warned President Madison that the French connection was "a trap to catch us into a war with England," and he was absolutely right.[6] Without control of the sea, Napoleon was aiming at the defeat of Britain through the economic blockade of his "Continental System." Of all the countries in Europe, only Portugal still traded with Britain. By appearing to accept the conditions of Macon's Bill No. 2, Napoleon not only cut off the United States, Britain's last major market and supplier, but also acquired a little influence on the sea through the U.S. Navy. The United States would become his creature, of its own free will and the president's honesty—for Madison was an honest man. American merchantmen continued to be impounded by French ports and ensnared by French privateers, but Madison did not change his mind or break his word to France.

Had he been less honest or less innocent, his country might have avoided a second war with England. But the Orders-in-Council were not rescinded; nonintercourse was imposed again; and on May 16, 1811, an American frigate and a British corvette opened fire on each other.

At the beginning of the month a British frigate, H.M.S. *Guerrière,* had impressed a New York seaman from the American brig *Spitfire*. The U.S. frigate *President* was now searching for *Guerrière,* intent on repatriating the unfortunate New Yorker. Just after midday on the sixteenth, a strange sail was sighted in the distance, and *President,* commanded by Captain John Rodgers, turned toward it.

Rodgers, veteran of the Quasi-War (when he had fought under Truxtun) and of the Barbary War (when he had been forced to negotiate that humiliating peace), loathed impressment. After one such incident in 1805, he had ordered that his officers should "not under any pretence whatever suffer your Vessel to be detained unless you are compelled to do so by superior force; in which case, after having resisted to the utmost of your power, you are directed to surrender your Vessel as you would to any other common enemy."[7] He saw impressment as an act of war; yet he was not popular in the service, for he was one of the hardest and proudest of American naval officers. His fighting reputation, according to one colleague, came from "his black looks, his insufferable arrogance, and the frequent and unmerited assaults he has made on poor and inoffensive citizens."[8]

The combination of these factors did not bode well for the sail he was chasing, whether it was *Guerrière* or not; and it was not. Instead of the thirty-eight-gun British frigate, it was a twenty-gun corvette named *Little Belt*. Her commander recognized the commodore's broad pendant on *President* and continued on his course; as far as he was concerned, there was no reason to stop. Rodgers thought otherwise. Throughout the afternoon and early evening he followed the corvette, slowly gaining on her until at dusk she was within hailing distance. By then (and it does seem rather convenient for Rodgers) he could see her flag but could not make it out. An exchange of hails brought no identification from either side, and someone fired a gun. That, ever since, has been the sticking point, for each said it was the other. Rodgers certainly had cautioned his men against firing without orders, and it would fit the Royal Navy's attitude to engage a superior opponent—*President*, with forty-four guns, was over twice as strong as *Little Belt*. Against that, a British court of inquiry heard evidence from a seaman in *President* that one of her guns had been fired accidentally. But in the end it matters little who actually started it, for Rodgers was evidently spoiling for a fight, and once it had begun he saw it through to the end. The end was thirteen British dead and nineteen wounded. In *President* one boy was slightly wounded, and that was all.

The following morning, incongruously, both commanding officers were models of courtesy. Rodgers, whether through gallantry or embarrassment, offered assistance to the British captain, who as politely declined and went on repairing his battered corvette while Rodgers sailed home to an ecstatic welcome. Ashore, people felt the *Chesapeake* affair was avenged; but the impressed New Yorker remained where he was in H.M.S. *Guerrière*.

The drift toward war was plainly visible, for things could not continue the way they were. During the winter of 1811–12 Paul Hamilton, secretary of the Navy, suggested that twenty further frigates should be acquired, along with a dozen seventy-four-gun ships of the line. Predictably, the House Naval Affairs Committee turned it down, recommending only ten frigates. However, the committee's chairman (Langdon Cheves of South Carolina) spoke vigorously in favor of naval expansion, saying truly that "the experience of modern naval warfare has proved that no fortifications can prevent the passage of ships of war." Instead of land batteries, he believed that "a better defence would be furnished by such a naval force as would give you mastery of the American seas," which was also true.[9]

But the annals of this, the Twelfth Congress, show a strange pattern of voting: Those who spoke most strongly for war were those who opposed naval growth, while those who wanted a stronger navy were generally opposed to war. New York and the New England states, with their strong maritime tradition, voted 31 to 6 in favor of expansion and 30 to 12 against war. Pennsylvania voted 17 to 1 against expansion and 16 to

2 for war, while the western frontier states (Vermont, Ohio, Kentucky, and Tennessee) had an exact interchange of 12 to 1 against the Navy and 12 to 1 in favor of war.

The coastal states favored naval growth partly on principle and partly because they could see that if a war developed and the Navy did not, their trade and homes would be only half defended, vulnerable in a way the inland states were not. As for the bellicose inland states, one may wonder how on earth they thought a war against Britain could be conducted without a navy. The answer is in the question: It was on the earth, not the sea, that they envisaged a war—an invasion and conquest of British-held Canada.

But what neither side knew was the mood and condition of Great Britain that winter. The weather was exceptionally hard, and with the United States linked to the Continental System, Napoleon's economic blockade was biting just as hard. Merchants everywhere urged the government to rescind the Orders-in-Council against America, and on June 16, 1812, it was done at last. Today such timing would have been lucky, but perfect, for the glad news would reach America almost at once. But at the beginning of the nineteenth century people did well to get a message across the Atlantic in less than a month; and it is one of the saddest coincidences in Anglo-American history that just two days after the odious Orders-in-Council were repealed, the United States declared war on Great Britain.

Nobody in Britain wanted the war, and nobody in the United States was ready for it—least of all the Navy. But the United States had two initial advantages: time (it would take at least a month before Britain knew war had begun) and Britain's existing deep involvement in Europe. If we add in the distance of the United States from Britain, then in retrospect the pattern of the War of 1812 seems almost inevitable. But the same could be said about many wars in retrospect, and it is never so when they start. No one then knows quite what to expect; and very few people in the summer of 1812 would have predicted that, for the U.S. Navy, it was going to be a wonderful year.

Even Secretary Hamilton rated the Navy's chances poorly. "In our navy men I have the utmost confidence that in equal combat they will be superior," he wrote in July, ". . . but when I reflect on the overwhelming force of our enemy, my heart swells almost to bursting, and all the consolation I have is that in falling, they will fall nobly."[10]

Apart from the pathetic gunboats, with their very limited capabilities, the seagoing U.S. Navy consisted of a cutter, a schooner, a pair of sloops, three brigs, and nine frigates—sixteen vessels all told, mounting about five hundred guns altogether. Two further frigates were so rotten they were not worth repairing and were condemned just after the declaration of war;

and the only other vessel in the U.S. fleet was a single brig, far away on Lake Ontario.

Much has been made of the colossal size of the Royal Navy at the same time—over six hundred vessels, a quarter of them ships of the line mounting sixty guns each, giving a total of nine thousand guns for them alone. But the vast majority of these were preoccupied in Europe or elsewhere and would never fight in American waters. A more relevant comparison is with the Royal Navy squadron which patrolled from Halifax to Bermuda. From the American point of view, though, this was bad enough, for the British squadron contained one sixty-gun ship, seven thirty-six-gun frigates, and sundry smaller craft which altogether made its gunpower roughly equal to that of the entire U.S. fleet. And in addition there were three further British squadrons based in Newfoundland and the West Indies.

This was the legitimately frightening thought for maritime Americans. The loss of even a single vessel would be proportionately far more damaging to the United States than a similar loss would be to Britain. No U.S. ships were being built; designs had not even been drawn up. All that had been done in preparation was to stockpile timber. It seemed a comparatively easy thing for the British squadrons to grow larger, or to replace lost vessels; for the U.S. Navy, growth, and even replacement, would have to depend on captures.

Meditating these points, Secretary Hamilton found them so depressing that in February 1812 he suggested that the entire U.S. fleet should be kept in harbor, either as floating batteries or as accommodation for gunboat crews. This weak-minded notion was quickly scotched by President Madison; but Secretary Hamilton had very little idea of what to do with the Navy. In May, "as war appears now inevitable," he asked John Rodgers and Stephen Decatur (now the Navy's senior officers) how they thought their small resources might best be used. Their answers have engaged naval analysts ever since, for both had strengths, but they were entirely different: Rodgers favored squadron cruising, while Decatur believed every vessel should operate independently or with one other at most. However, the two officers agreed on one thing: In order to avoid being caught in harbor and to do the maximum damage while it still had the chance, the fleet should sail as soon as possible.

Secretary Hamilton was a cautious man, and Decatur was junior to Rodgers; so although the secretary admired both captains extremely, he accepted Rodgers's plan. On June 21, three days after the declaration of war, the frigates *President, United States,* and *Congress*, the sloop *Hornet,* and the brig *Argus* sailed from New York under Rodgers's command. This represented one third of the U.S. Navy. Acting as commodore (which was still an honorary, unofficial rank), Rodgers sailed in *President,*

while Decatur captained *United States*. Two days out, the first hostile sail
was seen—the thirty-six-gun frigate H.M.S. *Belvidera*—and the first
chase of the war was on.

It took more than ten hours to close within range. As the firing began,
Rodgers personally supervised his weapons. Both sides gave and received
several hits, until one of Rodgers's guns exploded. His leg was broken;
a dozen other men were injured; and one was killed. In the confusion
Belvidera was heaving barrels, boats, and anchors over—anything to
lighten the ship—and the range drew out again. As the Americans said
later, the Briton was an expert ship handler; but he should not have
escaped, for some of Rodgers's frigates were faster, and Rodgers himself
was no novice. The Americans failed simply through lack of fleet experience, and over the next sixty-eight days of the cruise, they fared little
better. Rodgers had hoped to encounter a British convoy homeward
bound from Jamaica via Newfoundland. It was at sea, but their paths
never crossed; and in the ten-week voyage, from New York to within one
day of the Channel, on to Madeira and back to Boston, all they managed
to catch were eight merchant ships and scurvy.

Rodgers consoled himself with the belief that fear of the squadron had
"obliged the enemy to concentrate a considerable portion of his most
active force, and thereby prevented his capturing an incalculable amount
of American property that would otherwise have fallen sacrifice."[11] That
belief was echoed in most accounts of the war for over a hundred and fifty
years; but it was not entirely true. It persisted mainly because Alfred
Thayer Mahan, writing in 1905, preferred Rodgers's strategy of concentration to Decatur's of single ships; and by 1905 Mahan was a writer of
unchallengeable eminence. The strategy was right for Mahan and his
time, partly because by then the Navy had changed, and partly because
Mahan was lobbying for naval growth. But for its own time, Rodgers's
strategy was wrong. While he was away on what he admitted turned out
to be a "barren cruise," two American vessels working independently had
begun the stunning series of victories that would characterize 1812.

Ironically, both were on their way to join Rodgers's squadron when they
found their own successes. The frigate *Essex* under Capt. David Porter
left New York on July 3; nine days later, Isaac Hull in *Constitution* put
out from Chesapeake Bay. Porter found neither the squadron nor a
reported treasure ship, but in the early hours of July 11 he came across
a British troop convoy close to Bermuda. Fourteen hundred soldiers were
being taken from Barbados to Quebec, and in a very daring moonlight
raid Porter nabbed one of the transports. Two hundred soldiers and
$14,000 worth of ship never reached Quebec.

Meanwhile, the first British warships were approaching Sandy Hook, off New York. So was Isaac Hull. When he saw them on the afternoon of July 16, he thought they might be Rodgers and company. Winds were so light that he was not close enough to hoist a recognition signal until dusk; and when the signal was unanswered, Hull knew he was in the presence of the enemy.

They turned toward him, and throughout that night, the following day, the second night, and the second day as well, there was an extraordinary slow-motion chase. During the first night the ships scarcely moved. *Constitution*'s sails were soaked, the better to catch any breeze; guns were moved to the stern and the rail cut away; freshwater barrels were drained to lighten the frigate. Through the morning of the next day there was the strangest scene, as *Constitution* kedged laboriously away (in kedging, an anchor is carried ahead and dropped; the vessel hauls up to it, and the process is repeated) while the British launched rowboats to tow their ships in pursuit. It was like a slug being chased by a malevolent tortoise: ludicrously slow to an observer, but supremely tense and deadly serious to those involved. As light airs helped one side or the other, the distance between shrank and grew again; then on the evening of the second day a squall blew over. Hull made ready as it approached: Taking the wind, sails were set until the last minute, furled as the squall hit, reset the moment it passed. The British astern reacted more slowly, and *Constitution* gained the advantage. By dawn on the third day she had a lead of twelve miles, and the chase was given up.

Hull escaped through determination and superior seamanship. This was not the victory it has sometimes been called, but it was an important avoidance of defeat; if the frigate had been captured so early on, it would have been a considerable moral and physical blow. Instead (exactly one month later, on August 19, 1812) it was Hull and *Constitution* together that gave the U.S. Navy an uplift it has never forgotten.

In the intervening weeks, the frigate *Essex*—already the first American warship to have entered the Indian Ocean—increased her reputation further. After seizing the troopship near Bermuda, Captain Porter continued his cruise for two months, ranging between Bermuda and Newfoundland. Nine more prizes were bagged, worth over $300,000; and on August 13, in a battle lasting only eight minutes, *Essex* became the first American warship ever to capture a Royal Navy warship. H.M.S. *Alert* did not live up to her name, for she was entirely deceived when *Essex* disguised herself as a merchant ship; and the fact that the American had twice as many guns did not, in American eyes, diminish the victory. What was far more important than sizes or armament was the proof that a British ship was not always guaranteed to win. And hard on the heels of that first-ever capture came news of the second: the victory of *Constitution* over *Guerrière*.

. . .

According to *Constitution*'s log, the day "commenced with fresh breezes from the Northward and Westward and cloudy. At 2 P.M. discovered a sail to the Southward. Made all sail in chase."[12]

At the same time, Captain Dacres in H.M.S. *Guerrière* "saw a sail on our weather beam, bearing down on us. . . . Made her out to be a man of war, beat to quarters and prepared for action."[13]

Hull's orders were brisk: "Took in our top gallant sails, sky sails, flying jib, hauled the cannon up, took the 2nd reef in the topsails, and sent down the royal yards and got all away, and ready for action and beat to quarters, at which our crew gave three cheers. . . . Bore more up, bringing the chase to bear rather off the starboard bow, she at that time revealing herself to be an enemy by hoisting three English ensigns . . . ."

"Wore [turned by bringing the wind around the stern] several times to avoid being raked," Dacres noted, "exchanging broadsides."

"She discharged her starboard broadside at us without effect," Hull wrote then, "her shot falling short. She immediately went about and discharged her larboard [port] broadside, two shot of which hulled us, and the remainder flying over and through our rigging. . . ."

From *Guerrière,* Dacres saw Hull closing "on our starboard beam, both keeping up a heavy fire and steering free, his intention being evidently to cross our bow," while from across the water Hull watched "the enemy still manoeuvring to rake us, firing alternately his broadsides, we returning his fire with as many of our bow guns from the main gun deck as we could bring to bear. . . . The enemy, finding his attempts to rake us fruitless, bore up with the wind. . . . We then set our main top gallant sail and steered down on his beam in order to bring him to close action. . . . Hauled down the jib and lay the main top sail shivering, and opened on him a heavy fire from all our capital guns. . . ."

"Our mizzen mast," said Dacres, "went over the starboard quarter and brought the ship up in the wind. The enemy then placed himself on our larboard bow, raking us, only a few of our guns bearing and his grape and riflemen sweeping our deck. . . ."

"He," wrote Hull, "immediately attempted raking of our stern, but failed, having his bowsprit entangled in our mizzen rigging, our marines during that time keeping up a very brisk and galling fire on him. . . ."

"The Master was at this time shot through the knee," said Dacres. "Lieutenant Ready fell leading the men from the main deck and I received a severe wound in the back." Simultaneously in *Constitution* Lt. Charles Morris (a veteran of the *Intrepid* raid in Tripoli harbor) and a marine lieutenant "fell from the taffrail, the former severely wounded and the latter killed. . . ."

After that, disaster came quickly to the British. *Guerrière* broke free, and with one mast gone "had got clear of our opponent when at 6:20 our fore and main mast went over the side, leaving the ship a perfect, unmanageable wreck."

But even then Dacres was not ready to give up: "I was in hopes to . . . get the ship under command to renew the action, but just as we had cleared the wreckage, our spritsail yard went." Now, with the ship "laying in the trough of the sea, rolling her main deck guns under water," he summoned his "few remaining officers," and when all agreed that "any further resistance would be a needless waste of lives, I ordered, though reluctantly, the Colours to be struck."

Ship for ship, this had been a much more balanced battle than the one between *Essex* and *Alert*. Both captains had shown great ship-handling skill, but the better captain and better gunners won; and as the story spread that British shot simply bounced off her, *Constitution* acquired her nickname of "Old Ironsides."

In overall strength, the losses made little difference to the Royal Navy, and since *Guerrière*'s damage was so great that she had to be burned, her capture made no material contribution to the U.S. Navy. But the moral prestige was incalculable; and the tally continued for the rest of the year. On October 15 the U.S. sloop *Wasp* defeated H.M. brig *Frolic;* on October 25 Stephen Decatur, in the frigate *United States,* beat H.M. frigate *Macedonian* and won the honor of being the first captain to bring a captured British warship into an American harbor; and on December 29, now captained by William Bainbridge, *Constitution* triumphed again, reducing the Royal Navy frigate *Java* to a hulk in rather less than two hours. In the same year there were only two American losses—the brig *Nautilus* on July 17, the first vessel on either side to fall, and *Wasp,* immediately after her victory in October. But neither side felt these smaller losses mattered much, for they were almost to be expected. The frigates mattered far more. In London, said *The Times*,

> anyone who had predicted such a result of an American war this time last year would have been treated as a madman or a traitor. He would have been told, if his opponents had condescended to argue with him, that long ere seven months had elapsed, the American flag would be swept from the seas, the contemptible navy of the United States annihilated, and their maritime arsenals rendered a heap of ruin.[14]

Decatur and Bainbridge were elated; their single-ship strategy had proved far more valuable than Rodgers's squadron approach, and they won the glory that would have been denied them as members of a squadron. All three captains believed sincerely that their different approaches were best for the country, yet their personal ambitions were deeply involved as well. Thus, for the first time, American naval policy decisions contained an element (perhaps undesirable, but almost inevitable) which would continue at least until World War II. Nevertheless, as news of the frigate victories filtered through the United States, a great exultant wave of patriotism swept over the nation; and much later on, remembering his time in *Constitution,* Charles Morris described that feeling in a pleasantly understated way: "Our hopes began to overcome apprehension, and cheerfulness was more apparent among us."[15]

The declaration of war had not been received in Britain until July 26. Thereafter, for a while, the British hoped the United States would reconsider, since the Orders-in-Council had been rescinded. But when it became clear that the war was definitely on, the organization began of all ships and men that could be spared from Europe, and on December 26, 1812, official notification arrived in Washington saying that the coast would be placed under British blockade. Cheerfulness in America was at a peak; it seemed that little could go wrong, even under blockade. But 1812 was over, and all too soon it would only be a proud memory. The stunning American victories were finished.

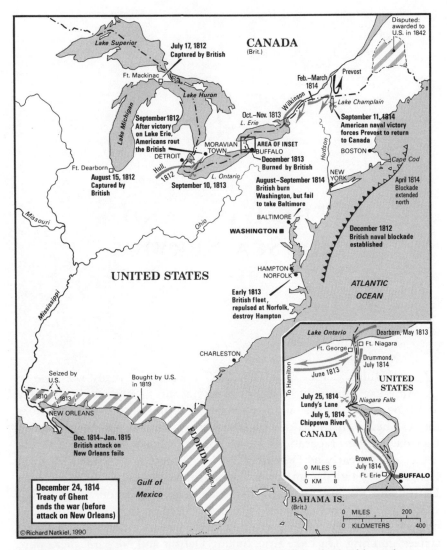

The War of 1812 demonstrated the U.S. Navy's skill in single-ship actions, yet these did not bring lasting victory. The war's indecisive end was due neither to the British nor U.S. seapower but to France's defeat in Europe.

9

★

THE LAKE AND
THE SEA SERVICE

*I*saac Hull's victory over H.M.S. *Guerrière* was triply welcome in
America: It brought honor to his service, his family, and his country
at a time when all three needed a strong infusion of self-respect. Before
the war began, the eyes of congressional war hawks had been fixed on
Canada. In the preparations for conflict, the Navy had been absurdly
neglected. As early as December 1811, the secretary of war had given
Congress a detailed plan for a double-fronted invasion of Canada, via
Detroit and Niagara; but (echoing the neglect of the seagoing navy in that
crucial prewar year) the need for a naval force on the Great Lakes was
not considered. On the easternmost lake, Ontario, there was a single
sixteen-gun brig. On Lake Erie, linking Detroit and Niagara, there were
no American naval vessels at all. As it happened, command of the army
at Detroit was given to Brig. Gen. William Hull, Isaac's uncle; and—
partly because he was not a brave man, partly because he had no naval
support—General Hull surrendered his army to the British on August 16,
1812. Three days later his nephew defeated *Guerrière*—a timely success
which rescued the family from disgrace, the Navy from neglect, and the
nation from faulty planning.

On October 7 President Madison wrote, "the command of the Lake by
a superior force on the water ought to have been a fundamental part in
the national policy."[1] By then the process was under way, and later that
same month Gen. Isaac Brock (the man who had defeated General Hull)

reported to Gov. Gen. Prevost that "the enemy is making every exertion to gain a naval superiority on both lakes; which, if they accomplish, I do not see how we can retain the country."[2] Americans had discovered they could not simply walk into Canada. But now—if it was not already too late—both they and the British felt there was a good chance they might sail in.

Suddenly the Navy was the darling of Congress. Secretary Hamilton, well-intentioned but drunk and incompetent, was asked to resign, and did so on December 29. On January 2, 1813, appropriations totaling $2.5 million were made to allow for six more forty-four-gun frigates and four seventy-four-gun ships of the line, vessels which ex-President Jefferson described ruefully as "a sacrifice we must make, heavy as it is, to the prejudices of a part of our citizens."[3] A new secretary, William Jones, was appointed on January 19, 1813; and as the British blockade began to grip the coast from the Delaware to the Chesapeake, Secretary Jones directed the Navy into new regions. Over the next two years, some action would continue in the Atlantic and on the American East Coast, and even in British home waters; but there would be far more in the Pacific, in the Far East, and on the Great Lakes.

Strategically, the Lakes would turn out to be America's most important single area of conflict. But weeks before any engagement took place there, two important events occurred on one day, thousands of miles away and thousands of miles apart. On February 24, 1813, off the coast of British Guiana, U.S.S. *Hornet* encountered and in eleven minutes defeated H.M.S. *Peacock*. It was a smart little battle, of which a Halifax (that is, a British-view) newspaper said, "A vessel moored for the purpose of experiment could not have been sunk sooner. It will not do for our vessels to fight theirs single-handed."[4] But it was also the last battle for eighteen months between American and British naval ships in the Atlantic. Nevertheless, as if by design, on that same February 24 Capt. David Peacock was able to note with considerable relief that his ship was "fairly in the Pacific." After rounding Cape Horn, which released onto her "a fury we little expected . . . that threatened to jerk away our masts at every roll of the ship," U.S.S. *Essex,* the first U.S. warship into the Indian Ocean, and first to take a R.N. warship, became the first U.S. warship to enter the Pacific as well; and there, as we shall see, while the Royal Navy controlled the Atlantic, she raised merry hell for one joyous, rumbustious year.[5]

Meanwhile, back on the East Coast of North America, *Constitution* arrived in Boston on February 27, 1813. She stayed there for ten months, held in by blockade. On March 6, Congress approved the construction of six further sloops and at the same time decided to start selling the useless Jeffersonian gunboats. By the middle of the month, Britain's blockade stretched from New York to the Mississippi. From then on, any U.S. vessel in port was going to find it extremely difficult to get out at all; but if the Atlantic was closed, hundreds of miles inland the Lakes were open. And on March 27 an energetic twenty-eight-year-old lieutenant arrived on Lake Erie's southern shore, determined to make things hum.

Oliver Hazard Perry, born in 1785, was one of those men almost tailor-made to be an American naval hero. Raised in Rhode Island, with a father who had commanded a frigate in the Quasi-War, he was part of the first generation actually born into independence. Yet the background of his childhood was one of almost constant war at sea, and while little more than a child he was commissioned as a midshipman, serving under his father. He served in the Mediterranean as well; then from 1807 he had the dull but very instructive job of commanding gunboats at Newport, Rhode Island, close to his family home. Thus he was naval to the core; he regarded war as virtually a natural state of affairs; and he knew how little his country was respected by others. He also had knowledge of building and using a company of small boats; and perhaps above all he had style, courage, and a clear eye for opportunity. In the right circumstances he was bound to make history.

His commanding officer, on the other hand, was not. Isaac Chauncey had talents which he put to good use on the shores of Lake Ontario: He could organize and he could build, and over the winter of 1812–13 he bought and built a handy fleet. But he was a cautious man, unwilling to risk his creation unless victory was assured. By the end of November 1812 he already had control of the lake, and before long Secretary Jones told him "to consider the absolute superiority on all the Lakes the only limit to your authority."[6] So in the spring of 1813, on April 27, Chauncey took thirteen vessels and 1,800 troops to the town of York (modern-day Toronto), burned and plundered the buildings, and destroyed one British vessel and captured another. In mid-May he took both fleet and Army to the Niagara River, forcing the British to retreat the whole length of the river; but simultaneously, a British attack destroyed most of his base at Sackett's Harbor.

By the beginning of June, the net result of all this was an approximate equality between the rival forces on Lake Ontario. This could have led to some ghastly, battering battle of attrition. But as luck would have it, there was also an approximate equality between the two commanders. Sir James Yeo was as cautious as Chauncey when victory was not guaranteed. Each side's fleet had taken so much time and effort to assemble that neither side was willing to risk it when, without further trouble, they could hold each other at bay; and so for the rest of the War of 1812 Lake Ontario was a stalemate. There were obvious virtues in this, the first of which was an absence of killing. But by the same token, it could have gone on indefinitely if people elsewhere had not been willing to force the issue. Before coming to how that happened, and to Oliver Perry's part in it, let us glance back across the continent to the Pacific; for there, while there was stalemate on the Lakes and blockade on the East Coast, David Porter was being very active indeed.

More than two centuries earlier, in the same ocean, Francis Drake had indulged a liking for Elizabethan England's favorite sport, "the sport of baiting Spaniards."[7] As the strength of the Spanish Empire waned and that of the British Empire grew, the sport fell out of fashion. If it had ever had rules, they would have stated that the game had to be played by an upstart naval power against a ponderous, established one. Ideally there would also have been a rule saying that no one should be hurt unless it was absolutely inevitable, and that the established power should be made to look as foolish as possible, as often as possible. That was generally the way it had worked with Drake and his contemporaries; and it was the same when Porter hit the Pacific, with the difference that now the upstart navy was American and the established one was British.

Porter took upon himself a double role. The United States and Britain both maintained substantial whaling fleets in that part of the world, and Porter knew there was at least one British privateer roaming around. He therefore determined to protect his own country's whalers while catching as many as possible of the British ones—perhaps the privateer, too, if he was lucky. He had no particular orders for this; even coming round the Horn had been his own initiative, prompted by finding himself alone on the east coast of South America in December 1812 with (as far as he knew) no other American ships and an indefinite number of British ships between him and home. The Pacific was the only way out, and there he would be able to raid for as long as it took the Royal Navy to catch up with him.

It took them a little over a year from the day he made his first catch. After stopping at Valparaiso in Chile, he snared his first whaler on March 28, 1813. It turned out to be a recapture, an American vessel previously trapped by the British, but a welcome reinforcement for all that. A month later (April 29) he located the British at last and in a single day snapped up three whalers, followed after another month by another whaler and a privateer—though not the one he expected. Manning one of the prizes, *Georgiana,* with men from *Essex,* he sent them on an independent cruise. On June 18 they met up again, and by then *Georgiana* had three more prizes with her. Overall, in a mere ten weeks and starting with one vessel, Porter had created a fleet of eight: profitable hunting indeed.

Elsewhere, however, during the same period, the U.S. Navy sustained a tragic loss—and gained an enduring legend. Thirty-two-year-old James Lawrence had commanded U.S.S. *Hornet* in her memorable eleven-minute encounter with H.M.S. *Peacock*. On his return to the United States he discovered he had been promoted to captain and allotted U.S.S. *Chesapeake,* a command he did not want. The frigate was almost ready to sail, and Lawrence's wife was seriously ill. Naturally he did not want to leave at such a time, so he asked for the command of *Constitution* instead, since she was unready for sea. But *Chesapeake* it was to be; and on May 30, 1813, he sailed in that vessel to his death.

H.M.S. *Shannon,* Capt. Philip Vere Broke, was standing off Boston with H.M.S. *Tenedos* in company, impatiently awaiting *Chesapeake*. Broke knew she was due to sail—New England held many spies. But *Shannon,* short of water, would soon have to return to Halifax, at which time *Chesapeake* would have every chance of escaping to sea. Eager to precipitate an action in the short time he had available, Broke sent a personal challenge to Lawrence, inviting him to come out and fight; and to make it both fairer and more tempting, he dismissed *Tenedos*. Today the gesture brings over some of the flavor of that naval war: of men deliberately courting death in a mutual test of skill and nerve—certainly seeking victory, but seeking almost more urgently to demonstrate their own gallantry and to be recognized, whether victorious or not, as honorable men. There was no sensible or practical reason for Lawrence to accept Broke's challenge; he needed only to wait, and by escaping to sea he would serve his country better than by dueling. Yet even before the challenge came, he had already decided to go out and fight. He had more in common with Philip Vere Broke than the English language alone.

On the morning of May 30, 1813, James Lawrence dressed (as was correct for the occasion) in his full captain's uniform. Its style, similar to Broke's uniform, would still be recognized as naval. Black calf-length boots covered his white breeches; a white waistcoat covered a white shirt, with a stock around his neck; a sword, gilded and tasseled, was buckled onto his left hip; and over it all was a wonderfully ostentatious blue and gold coat. With tails at the back and cut short to the waist in front, it had long, wide lapels and a high standing collar. There were nine gold buttons on each lapel, and four on each of the captain's cuffs—a lieutenant had three. Gold lace edged the collar, the lapels, the pocket flaps, and the skirts of the coat, and on each of the shoulders was a tasseled gold epaulette. Its splendor all marked a man out as both an officer and a target; Nelson at Trafalgar had been all too recognizable. But it also made a man feel prouder and braver than he might have done otherwise, and suited the concept of war as an occupation for civilized people; and so Lawrence wore it, not only because it was his prescribed uniform but also because it was eminently correct for a captain and a gentleman going out to duel.

After his short, sharp fight with H.M.S. *Peacock*, Lawrence had concluded that neither Royal Navy vessels nor their captains were up to much—that their reputation was founded only on past achievements, easily beaten individually by the rising skill of the U.S. Navy. Many Americans shared the opinion; many Britons suspected uncomfortably that it might be true. It would have been more true to say that no country ever had a monopoly of skill at sea; some people simply had more opportunity than others to gain experience and the accompanying skill. And whatever the level of skill on *Chesapeake,* it did not match the level on *Shannon:* the battle between them was scarcely longer than the one with *Peacock*. Less than fifteen minutes after the first gun was fired, 146 men lay killed or wounded in *Chesapeake,* 85 in *Shannon*, and Lawrence was dying. If he had survived, he would probably have been court-martialed. In that case, he would have been censured at least, and his behavior today would be remembered as shabby and discreditable, for Broke captured *Chesapeake*—one of the six original frigates—and took her as a prize first to Halifax and then on to Britain. But instead Lawrence is remembered as a hero because, as he lay bleeding to death, he gasped out again and again: *"Don't give up the ship."* The phrase was as vain, in every way, as the glorious blue and gold coats those captains wore; but it was also just as appropriate, and just as inspiring. Legends do not have to be logical to work their power, and the legend surrounding Lawrence's death became one of the most famous stories of the frigate fleet. Broke played his part in creating that legend: Subscribing to the same code of honor, he had Lawrence's body buried with full naval ceremony. Even today, other navies still recall the battle and the phrase with admiration; and perhaps, in the U.S. Navy, the story can still make men feel a little prouder, a little braver, than they might feel otherwise.

Whether it should is another matter. Another sailing, two weeks after Lawrence's death, showed what practical things the U.S. Navy could achieve in spite of the blockade. The brig *Argus* escaped from New York on June 18, 1813, carried a new minister over to France, and proceeded to a month of rampant raiding in British home waters. In thirty-one days she took nineteen prizes, a record unmatched by any other American vessel in the whole war, until on August 14 she herself was defeated off the coast of Wales by the British brig *Pelican*. Lt. William H. Allen, her captain, died, and like Lawrence was buried by the British with full naval honors. In the short term at least, Lieutenant Allen was more useful to his country than Captain Lawrence; and given, in any age, the awfulness of war on land or sea, logically Allen should be remembered with greater credit than Lawrence, for as a businesslike, efficient warrior he may have brought the war's end a little closer, in a way that Lawrence did not.

But few people can approach war as a matter of accountancy. Albert Gallatin was an exception in that respect, and since (in 1813) he sailed to Europe to negotiate a speedy end to the conflict by accepting Russian mediation, in a sense he should be seen as one of the war's real heroes. Yet the passionate illogicality attached to war denies that. Peacemakers may be blessed, but they tend not to be seen as heroic; and after a naval war, in the peace won by efficient, unromantic fighters and skillful diplomats, it is not war's flagrant horror which is recalled so readily as "the beauty and mystery of the ships, and the magic of the sea."

> *I remember the sea-fight far away,*
> *How it thundered o'er the tide!*
> *And the dead captains, as they lay*
> *In their graves o'erlooking the tranquil bay*
> *Where they in battle died. . . .*
>
> *And the sound of that mournful song*
> *Goes through me with a thrill . . .*[8]

These "dead captains" (in Longfellow's poem "My Lost Youth") were Lt. William Burrows, U.S.N., commander of the brig *Enterprise*, and Capt. Samuel Blyth, R.N., commander of the brig *Boxer*. Blyth had been one of Lawrence's pallbearers and was an experienced officer; Burrows had never been in battle before their meeting off the coast of Maine on September 5. Soon after, in London, *The Times* declared that "the fact seems to be but too clearly established that the Americans have some superior mode of firing; and we cannot be too anxiously employed in discovering to what circumstances that superiority is owing."[9] For "*Boxer* was literally cut to pieces," and so was Captain Blyth, struck in the stomach by an 18-pound ball, while Lieutenant Burrows was killed by a musket shot. Nasty as it was, the fight would have been unmemorable, except that Burrows and Blyth were buried side by side in Portland, Maine. Another layer of gallant legend covered the reality of conflict— and the dead captains would probably have approved.

Some of these legends took hold at once and inspired further legends in turn. James Lawrence was scarcely cold before a twenty-gun brig was named after him and sent into battle under a special flag bearing his dying words. In her first fight, the brig fared no better than her namesake had in his last. Even so, her commander won fame as immediate and enduring as Lawrence's; and what is more, he lived to enjoy it as well. This is where, in a hectic, action-filled year, we return to the Lakes and Oliver Hazard Perry.

On August 4, 1813, Perry wrote to Secretary Jones: "I have great pleasure in informing you that I have succeeded after almost incredible labor and fatigue to the men, in getting all the vessels I have been able to man over the bar, viz., *Lawrence, Niagara, Caledonia, Ariel, Scorpion, Somers, Tigress,* and *Porcupine*."[10] Perry's way with ships and men was as direct as his way with words. *Somers*, a merchant schooner, had been bought; *Caledonia,* a three-gun brig, had been captured from the British; but all the others (even *Lawrence* and *Niagara*, both twenty-gun, 500-ton brigs) had been chiseled out of the forest in the preceding five months. In addition to those vessels, fourteen boats had been made (as well as all the necessary gun carriages) and on shore six separate buildings had been constructed, ranging in size from 324 to 2,000 square feet. It was a prodigious effort, and Perry was lucky in having a large team of carpenters led by a New York shipwright of rare ability. The shipwright may have felt he had a precedent to match: His name was Noah Brown.

The bay in which the vessels were built had only one narrow entrance, and across that was a sandbar which left only six feet of water—hence the "almost incredible labor and fatigue" of getting the fleet onto the lake. Once over the bar, the ships were rapidly fitted out and their crews drilled; and on August 12 they sailed in search of the British.

It is worth remembering the size of the Great Lakes: Erie, second smallest of the five, is two hundred fifty miles long, and on it the American base at Presqu'île (the present-day Erie) was some hundred and seventy-five miles from the British base at Malden (the present-day Amherstburg). By the standards of any other part of the world, these are more like inland seas than lakes, but even so, they are finite. The strategy of single-ship raiding and fighting, successful on the oceans, could not be used on the lakes. Secretary Jones was correct when he said to the president that "the difference between the Lake and the sea service is that in the former we are compelled to fight them man to man and gun to gun, whilst on the ocean five British frigates cannot counteract the depredations of one sloop of war."[11] To win on the lakes, one side had to smash or outbuild the other. On Lake Ontario, equality of building and of command temperament had brought stalemate; but on Erie, a similar equality of temperament made a decision inevitable, for both Perry and his British counterpart, Capt. Robert Barclay, were fighters.

Having said that, Barclay accepted battle only when there was no option, because his fleet was inferior to Perry's in almost every way. Perry anchored at Put-in-Bay, about 35 miles from Barclay's base at Malden, and waited; he knew Barclay would emerge in due course. On September 9 the day came. By then a second British ship was finished in Malden and (just as important for Barclay's decision) food was running out. Control of the lake for the following winter had to be decided without delay.

The fleets saw each other early on the morning of September 10. The winds were light and variable. All morning the vessels closed and tried to maneuver for advantage. There were nine under Perry's command, six under Barclay's. Most serious for Barclay was the difference in firepower: For every 850 pounds of shot he could fire, Perry could fire over 1,500. And in the end it was that which made the difference, for most of the battle was fought between Perry's two brigs and Barclay's two ships. The brigs held almost all Perry's power; they alone could hurl 1,200 pounds of metal to the ships' 600 pounds. But it was hard fought and by no means decided from the start; Barclay's one superiority was in long guns, and with their greater range he used these so accurately that *Lawrence* was utterly wrecked and had to surrender, in sad contradiction of the defiant slogan at her masthead. After three hours of pummeling, though, with one third of his total crews dead or wounded, Barclay gave up. Almost a quarter of Perry's men had fallen as well (the hard casualty figures were 123 Americans killed, 145 British) yet at four in the afternoon, Perry was able to write a famous line to Gen. William Harrison, governor of Indiana: "Dear General—We have met the enemy and they are ours. Two ships, two brigs, one schooner and one sloop."

Wounded, exhausted, and exhilarated, he got it slightly wrong: Barclay's fleet had included two ships, one brig, two schooners, and a sloop. But no one was going to quibble; this was victory and defeat, pure and plain. And no one on either side who heard it was going to forget that grand, simple sentence: "We have met the enemy and they are ours." In nine quite ordinary words, Perry had written the dream and goal of every nation that ever went to war.

As 1813 drew to a close, officers of the Royal Navy assessed their enemy candidly and saw how they could benefit from his example. In December, Rear Adm. W. H. Dillon wrote, "our principal conversation at Portsmouth turned upon the war with America. Our large frigates were in no shape upon a par with theirs. . . . The American frigates were far superior in every respect: the hulls were larger, and they had heavier metal, with crews of at least 500 picked men—no boys—whereas the crew of one of our 46-gun frigates never exceeded 285, including boys."[12]

At that moment, as Admiral Dillon and his colleagues shivered in England, Capt. David Porter and the crew of U.S.S. *Essex* were relaxing—and having the time of their lives—in the Marquesas Islands. They had been at sea, an all-male company, for more than a year. Now, in addition to the simple pleasure of walking on dry land, they were supplied with everything they could want: plenty of fresh food, wood, water, alcohol, and more.

"With the common sailors and their girls," Porter wrote of this fabulous interlude, "all was helter skelter, and promiscuous intercourse, every girl the wife of every man in the mess, and frequently of every man in the ship. . . . The girls, from twelve to eighteen years of age, rove at will. . . . They give free scope to the indulgence of their passions, living in the most pleasurable licentiousness."[13]

In Porter's view the islands were ideal: a safe haven for the fleet (now increased by four more British whalers) and an earthly heaven for the crews. It is surprising that when the time came to leave, in mid-December, only three sailors attempted to desert: Perhaps Porter's own lack of moralizing on "the most pleasurable licentiousness" was part of his ability as a leader. Inevitably, though, the American sailors left their mark on the Pacific islanders: first in novel diseases (which Porter obviously could not control), and also by intervening in a local war, from which Porter could have stayed aloof. In any event, after seven weeks of having Paradise handed them on a plate, the sailors left for their own world and its war; and the islands, had they ever returned there, would not have been the same.

But they never did return. There are few chances of heaven on earth, and in December 1813, the Marquesas were the last such chance for David Porter and his crews, a sweetness they were fortunate to taste while they could; for the sailors' downfall was only a few weeks away.

10

★

THE AMERICANS
TAUGHT US A LESSON

S trange occurrences took place in North America at the beginning of
1814, as novel and irrevocable as venereal disease in the Marquesas
Islands. In 1802 the world's first mechanically successful steamboat,
Charlotte Dundas, had been tested in Scotland. In 1807, powered by
British-built engines, the 100-ton *Clermont* introduced commercially successful steam navigation to the world, servicing the Hudson River. Then
in 1814, with New York under blockade and fearful of actual invasion,
Clermont's designer, Robert Fulton, put two and two together and suggested that steam power should be applied to warships as well. Secretary
Jones hailed the idea: steam, he said, was "an agent with which we are
now so familiar in navigation, that it is a matter of surprise how skepti-
cism could have continued so long."[1] With only seven years' experience
of steam in America, he was exaggerating, but it is greatly to Jones's
credit that he recognized a good idea when he saw it. What was more,
so did everyone else. In an exuberant display of the quick action possible
when professionals and politicians agree, Jones asked for a quarter million dollars to develop the project; the Senate gave him double; the House
of Representatives passed the bill's final reading unopposed; and on
March 9, 1814, less than ten weeks after the first formal proposal, President Madison approved it all. America would have the world's first steam
warship.

In fact, that distinction was almost won without any government involvement at all. With Lake Erie secured and Lake Ontario stalemated, the focus of inland naval action came once again to Lake Champlain, where Benedict Arnold's cockleshells had performed that vital delaying action in the War of Independence. In the War of 1812, seen by many as America's second war of independence, Champlain was once more a wide-open gate to north or south.

The man with the duty of either closing it against Britain or keeping it open for America was Lt. Thomas Macdonough, thirty years old and a veteran of both the Quasi-War and the Barbary War. (In the latter, as one of Preble's boys, he had taken part in the storming of *Philadelphia.*) Like Chauncey and Perry on the other lakes, Macdonough had been beavering away since the autumn of 1812, assembling some kind of a fleet with the materials at hand. By spring 1813 (with a short winter break in order to get married) he had three armed sloops ready, based in Burlington, halfway down the lake's eastern shore. In the summer of that year two of them were lost to the British, who once again were sawing and hammering at the lake's northern end, building their own fleet.

Macdonough moved further south to the town of Vergennes. This was located some eight miles from the lake proper, up Otter Creek, but it was a superb naval base: Its prewar industries included a blast furnace, a rolling mill, and forges using local iron, while the creek provided energy for every kind of watermill. And in Vergennes (coincidentally, at the same time as Secretary Jones in Washington was promoting the concept of steam warships) Macdonough bought a steamboat, *Vermont,* from the local transport company. But he took her engines out.

He might have left them in, of course, if he had known what was happening in the capital. Taking them out may look like a failure of imagination on his part; yet in the middle of a war, in such a key location, it was on balance the sensible thing to do. He was already on the defensive. *Vermont,* which he renamed *Ticonderoga,* could have given him an unanswerable advantage—if he had been sure how to work her *and* if he had been sure she would work. But steam vessels were notoriously unreliable; so choosing to deal with the devil he knew, Macdonough turned *Ticonderoga* into an armed schooner, powered by sail alone.

By a further coincidence, it was at this time that—without much choice in the matter—David Porter in the Pacific was making ready to face a devil he knew all too well. From the heavenly Marquesas he had shaped course for Valparaiso, arriving there on February 3. It was a rash decision, for by then he knew that a British squadron was looking for him, and since Valparaiso was the only major port on four thousand miles of South American coast, they and he were very likely to put in there sometime. Perhaps he hoped they would; the fun of catching whalers was limited, after all, and he may have wanted the old challenge of a more worthy enemy. If so, the name of the enemy must have been a shock. On March 8, 1813, the British frigate *Phoebe* and sloop *Cherub* entered Valparaiso. *Phoebe* was commanded by Capt. James Hillyar; and once upon a time in Gibraltar, when their countries had been at peace with each other, he and Porter had known each other well.

Though they had had a warm relationship then, both captains had to forget it now. After a week of swapping insults in the neutral harbor, Hillyar put to sea, hoping to tempt Porter out to fight. Porter personally wanted to fight very much, but *Essex* was at a disadvantage compared with *Phoebe*. The weight of metal each frigate could fire was about equal, but forty of *Essex*'s forty-six guns were carronades, the very heavy short-range guns. *Phoebe* likewise had forty-six guns, but thirty of them were long guns. Their shot was comparatively light, yet their range was long; they would be able to hit *Essex* well before she could hit back.

Porter had had a lot of luck in the Pacific. Now he would need a lot more if he were merely to survive an encounter with *Phoebe,* let alone defeat her. But in Valparaiso his luck ran out completely. When he decided to leave, on March 28, *Essex* quickly lost her main topmast in a sudden squall. From the open sea he scurried back to Chilean coastal waters, hoping their neutrality would protect him while repairs were made. It did not. Out of range of *Essex*'s carronades, Hillyar opened fire with his long guns in a macabre kind of target practice. After three hours' bombardment, 155 of the American crew of 225 were dead and Porter surrendered.

It was not a gallant victory, and it caused a lot of fuss at the time; but sooner or later, in fair fight or not, the defeat of *Essex* was more or less inevitable—there were simply too many British ships looking for Porter and his men. And at least by baiting the British like mad, Porter and the seventy men who survived with him had had a year of wonderful sport.

Elsewhere, in varying degrees, a few American ships were still striking lucky. After being blockaded in Boston for ten months, *Constitution* slipped out, captured a Royal Navy schooner and three merchantmen, and then by the skin of her teeth got back into Marblehead again at the beginning of April 1814. On April 29 the newly built sloop *Peacock* (one of Noah Brown's New York products) took the British brig *Epervier,* which was carrying $118,000 in cash. An apt omen: This *Peacock* was going to be a lucky ship.

The name *Wasp,* however, seemed to be one that brought good luck followed by disaster. By 1814 there had been three vessels of that name in the American Navy. The first, an eight-gun schooner built in 1775, was blown up in 1777; the second, an eighteen-gun sloop built in 1806, was a fast, good sailer and in 1812 captured H.M.S. *Frolic;* but no sooner was that done than she herself was captured. In 1813 she was taken into the Royal Navy under the somewhat confusing name of H.M.S. *Peacock,* to replace the one sunk by James Lawrence; and finally she was lost with all hands off the Virginia Capes. The third American *Wasp,* another eighteen-gun sloop, was built in Massachusetts in 1813 and from there set sail for the English Channel on May 1, 1814, arriving one month later. In the first three weeks of June she took seven prizes and on June 28 sank a Royal Navy brig. After a lengthy refit in Lorient, she caught another three prizes, including an R.N. sloop, then headed south for Portugal, caught another prize there—and was never heard from again. Like her predecessor, she was lost at sea with all hands; no one has ever known exactly where.

Despite her eventual ill fortune, such exploits as these, in or near British home waters, caused outrage there. "They have literally swept our seas," said the *Naval Chronicle,* "blockaded our ports, and cut up our Irish and coasting trade. . . . The insurance between Bristol and Water-ford or Cork is now *three times higher* than it was when we were at war with all Europe!"[2]

The Admiralty was inundated with letters demanding protection, and public meetings were held in Liverpool and Bristol to get the point over. At this point a historical curiosity intrudes. It was easy enough for an island trading nation like Britain to appreciate the threat to its existence posed by an efficient trade war, but at the beginning of the War of 1812 no one in Britain had seriously considered that the United States could carry out an efficient trade war. At the same time, very few people in the United States properly understood what a potent threat against Britain their navy could be—if it were given the right ships and men. But by the summer of 1814, just when British merchants were starting to get badly worried by the possibilities and Americans were starting to understand the same, their time was already virtually over.

Most of America's important vessels were often locked in harbor; the exploits of *Essex* and *Wasp,* even of *Constitution* and others in 1813 and 1814, were notable because they were exceptions. If they had been the rule from the start, when Britain was still heavily committed in Europe; if Secretary Jones had been in office then; or if Napoleon had had a greater understanding of sea power; then the U.S. Navy—acting as Napoleon's transatlantic sea arm—might have affected the war in Europe far more drastically than it did. Conceivably, European history might have been very different, with incalculable implications.

However, none of those "if's" was the case, and in April 1814, with Napoleon's abdication, thousands of experienced British soldiers became available to fight for Britain across the ocean, in Canada, and on the East Coast of the United States. Thus, on September 3, 1814, Adm. Sir Alexander Cochrane was able to send a satisfied letter to the Duke of Gloucester, describing events of the previous week, when his men had paid a visit to Washington, D.C. He wrote:

Sir,

I will not take up Your Royal Highness's time with a detail of our adventures, farther than to say that within the short space of eight days, the enemy flotilla has been destroyed, his Army defeated, the capital taken, all the public buildings including the Capitol, President's Palace, a Naval dockyard and ships of war reduced to ashes; and the Army, unmolested, allowed to return fifty miles to the place they landed without a shot being fired. In their action and during our advance we sustained a loss not exceeding three hundred men, which is astonishingly few considering what the troops had to perform.[3]

The burning of Washington, D.C., and the sequel to that action form part of America's naval history for at least two reasons. First, the sole effective defense of the capital was provided by a U.S. naval contingent. Seven thousand American militia turned and ran when faced with veteran British troops, while Commodore Joshua Barney, U.S.N., with five guns and five hundred sailors, put up a spirited resistance against vast odds, showing that trained fighters were better than amateurs—even when fighting out of their element. Second, it was during this war that Americans began to gain a true national awareness, which included the understanding that the Navy was a national instrument.

The burning of Washington was done partly in revenge for the burning of York in Canada, and partly to instill terror and to show the uselessness of further fighting. If Americans were so impotent that they could not defend their own capital, they could not defend much. On these counts it was a short-term success; yet in the long term, and completely unintentionally, the British helped created one of the cornerstones of America's national identity. Hardly anyone now thinks of the burning of York (although if the place had not changed its name, the action might well be remembered, for Toronto is not small). But most Americans have at least a vague idea that at some time the dirty Britishers burned Washington; and an uncountable number of times each year, Americans sing about the sequel to Washington's destruction, when in mid-September British forces made a similar hit-and-run raid on Baltimore. It was expected that a land attack combined with a naval bombardment of Fort McHenry (Baltimore's key seaward defense) would bring another quick and easy victory. But this time it did not.

Instead, after a nightlong assault, the dawn's early light of September 14, 1814, showed the Stars and Stripes still flying over the fort; and, inspired by the sight, a Maryland lawyer took the tune of an old drinking song and wrote for it a new and more dignified set of words.

A national anthem and the memory of a burnt capital are powerful rallying points. Whatever else they intended in the autumn of 1814, the British did America a backhanded favor, providing the country with two lasting symbols of its own survival.

When the attack on Baltimore began, another battle of equal importance was taking place four hundred miles to the north. From his base in the iron-working town of Vergennes, Thomas Macdonough had moved his vessels to Plattsburg Bay, halfway up Lake Champlain's western shore.

His fleet now included four 10-ton row galleys; half a dozen gunboats, scarcely larger than the galleys; a sloop; a schooner (*Ticonderoga,* the ex-steamboat); a brig; and a ship. Altogether they displaced less than 1,800 tons. The British fleet which would oppose them aggregated over 2,400 tons, and the prevailing northerly wind favored a British advance.

But Macdonough was no fool. Like Valcour Bay, where Arnold had hidden, Plattsburg Bay was protected to the north. If the British wanted to give battle, they would have to sail past and beat back; and although they had an overall advantage in long guns (fifty-seven against thirty-seven) Macdonough made further clever use of the lake's natural conditions by anchoring his craft in positions which would oblige the British either to come within range of his heavy carronades, or else run aground. In carronades he had a slight advantage: thirty-six, including one massive 50-pounder, against thirty-three. But the main advantage he had was the British governor general, Sir George Prevost, who insisted that the British fleet should attack—even though it was obviously unready.

Among shipbuilders, there used to be a tradition that the best ships were built in a year and a day. Sunday, September 11, 1814, was a year and a day after Perry's victory on Lake Erie. Macdonough had a strong belief in God and did not like to do battle on a Sunday, but when the British masts were seen approaching, he and his men were prepared. The only thing he considered necessary for complete readiness was a short prayer for victory, and the officers were gathered on the quarterdeck for that purpose. That afternoon, when the battle was over, Macdonough wrote to Secretary Jones: "Sir: the Almighty has been pleased to grant us a signal victory on Lake Champlain, in the capture of one frigate, one brig, and two sloops of war of the enemy."[4]

His pious disclaimer of credit was not merely a conventional humility; people did not expect a victor to be humble, and Perry's proud note of the previous year showed how different the two men were. But if there was any divine intervention, it had been at the stage when a leader as competent as Macdonough was placed against one as incompetent as

Prevost, who had given no assistance to his naval forces and who, after their defeat, promptly retreated to Canada. He was court-martialed no less promptly, but died with the case unfinished.

However, with that British defeat, the war on the Lakes was finished, and no less a leader than the Duke of Wellington said so at once. When asked to take over from Prevost, he refused, saying: "That which appears to me to be wanting in America is not a general, or general officers and troops, but a naval superiority on the Lakes. The question is, whether we can acquire this. If we can't, I shall do you but little good now, and I shall go there only . . . to sign a peace which may as well be signed now."[5]

Peace was indeed close. But other momentous events were still in store, emerging before and after the war's official end. On October 29, 1814, *Demologos*—"the Voice of the People"—was launched in New York harbor. Robert Fulton's steam-powered warship, the first of her kind in the world, was a strange and mighty vessel. He had recognized that paddle wheels on the outside would be excessively vulnerable: A single well-placed hit would instantly disable the ship. So *Demologos* was built somewhat like a catamaran, with two parallel hulls joined by a solid bow and a solid stern, and the paddles were placed in the gap in the middle.

Her sides were nearly five feet thick; her boiler (placed on one side of the central paddles) and her engines (placed on the other) were low down for stability and security, and she was armed with thirty long 32-pounders. She was also armed underwater with two massive short guns, designed to fire a submarine shot of 100 pounds at very close range; and although her best speed was only 6½ knots, this was better than the average speed of the best sailing warships. Moreover, at 2,475 tons she was approaching the size of a line-of-battle ship; but while she operated well in harbor, her seagoing qualities were slight. And since she was not completed until after the war and her inventor's life were over, in the end this remarkable, advanced vessel came to nothing, and was used only as a receiving hulk, temporary accommodation for sailors in transit.

In the weeks following the launch of *Demologos,* the British force which had burned Washington and tried to burn Baltimore was being reinforced in Jamaica. It became the largest single British expedition of that war: 7,450 troops, fourteen frigates, and six ships of the line, as well as many smaller craft. On December 8, 1814, this force arrived off the Mississippi, and six days later overwhelmed the first opposition, a handful of gunboats commanded by Lt. Thomas ap Catesby Jones. On December 23 the British army was only eight miles short of New Orleans, their objective being to capture the city and as much else as possible to use in bargaining for peace. And in this whole unnecessary war, begun solely because of delays in communications, the Battle of New Orleans was, for the same reason, the least necessary conflict of all.

The war had begun because the United States had made its declaration at the very moment when its argument with Britain (the Orders-in-Council prohibiting direct American-European trade) was ended by the repeal of the prohibition. If that information could have been transmitted to the United States in time, there would have been no fighting. Likewise, on Christmas Eve 1814, the peace treaty between the two nations was signed in the Belgian town of Ghent and transmitted with all speed to Washington. It took seven weeks to get there, arriving in the charred capital on February 11, 1815. Only five days later it was ratified by a unanimous vote of Congress; but by then at least two thousand men had been killed, men who would have lived if the news could have come more quickly. They were the British victims of the Battle of New Orleans, fought two weeks after the treaty was signed. There were American victims too, but where as over two thousand Britons lost their lives in a stupid frontal assault on well-established defenses, only thirteen Americans died. The Battle of New Orleans is scarcely heard of in Britain. In the United States (although it did not affect the war, since that was already over) it is remembered as a considerable victory which erased all the defeats, blockades, and burnings of the war.

Even so, it remained a self-inflicted war. When the Americans heard, back in 1812, that the British Orders-in-Council had been canceled, they could have called off the conflict there and then, without loss of face—in fact, it could have been presented as a bloodless national victory, with Britain apparently backing down rather than fight. Why they did not call it off remains a mystery.

New Orleans was not the only place where fighting continued after peace was agreed. In mid-December 1814, only days before the treaty was signed, *Constitution* escaped from Boston to go hunting in the Atlantic. On January 14, 1815, *President* slipped out of New York, followed on January 20 by *Hornet, Tom Bowline, Macedonia,* and *Peacock. President,* commanded by Stephen Decatur, was captured almost at once—a severe misfortune for that officer, although later he could truthfully say he had not surrendered in wartime. The frigate was taken to England, arriving at Spithead in March, where Rear Adm. Dillon reported that she "caused a sensation among the naval officers. I went with many other captains to examine the Prize. She was of a much more superior scantling than ours: in fact, the Americans taught us a lesson for the improvement of our frigates."[6]

The other American vessels had better luck. On February 20, off Madeira, *Constitution* captured not one but two Royal Navy craft simultaneously, the thirty-four-gun frigate *Cyane* and the twenty-two-gun corvette *Levant.* Both were smaller than she but jointly were stronger and much more flexible—had they been able to cooperate completely. They were not and so were beaten fair and square, even if they should not have been fighting at all. Meanwhile *Hornet* and her companions were heading for Tristan da Cunha, far down in the south Atlantic; and off that remote island, on March 23, *Hornet* made the final Royal Navy capture of the war, when in a brief and bloody action—blood was running from the British scuppers inside five minutes—she took H.M. sloop-of-war *Penguin.*

One might have thought that by then the United States had had enough of war at sea in the previous forty years. There had been the War of Independence, the Quasi-War, and the Barbary adventures, as well as the War of 1812. But barely a fortnight after the ratification of the peace treaty with Britain, war was declared against Algiers.

This really came under the heading of unfinished business, picking up where things had left off some years before. This time, however, the chastising of Barbary was designed to be swift and lasting. Two squadrons totaling nineteen vessels were organized, one led by William Bainbridge in *Independence,* the first seventy-four-gun ship of the line to sail under the American flag. Preparing her meant that the second squadron, led by Stephen Decatur in *Guerrière* (a brand-new frigate named after the British *Guerrière*) got under way first, on May 20, 1815. And as things turned out, this squadron was all that was needed.

On June 17, off Cabo de Gata, a promontory in southeast Spain, they met and defeated the forty-six-gun Algerine flagship *Mashuda.* The fight was short and was the only important one of the war, for on June 30—with a hostile force he could not possibly match anchored in sight of his palace—the dey of Algiers signed a treaty of equality with America. He demanded no tribute; he gave up his American slaves. Of course, he would have been rash to have done anything else.

Reminders were needed from time to time over the next fifteen years, and once again the Mediterranean became the base for a permanent American naval squadron; but Decatur's return to that sea, twelve years after he burned *Philadelphia* in Tripoli harbor, marked the effective end of the Barbary Wars.

And by chance, the very next day (July 1, 1815) marked the effective end of the War of 1812—the moment when the news of peace got through to the last American warship still fighting. While the dey of Algiers was reluctantly signing his treaty some eight thousand miles away, U.S.S. *Peacock* was just entering the Strait of Sunda, between Java and Sumatra. From Tristan da Cunha she had had a fruitful voyage across the Indian Ocean, taking several prizes, but by now rumors of peace were beginning to circulate: Twice in the previous five days, British merchantmen had told them the war between their countries was over. After the first occasion, one of the young midshipmen, William Tennent Rodgers, noted in his journal: " 'Tis rather doubtful," and they kept the merchant ship until they could be sure.[7] After the second one, young Rodgers wrote, "hostilities were not to cease until ratified by our President which from the terms never will or ever ought to be the case. Terms, no fishing off Grand Banks, no trade east of Cape of Good Hope!!! If such is the case, we are the last ship east of the Cape and so we will make the most of our time."

In the Sunda Strait on July 1, *Peacock* encountered an English brig. Believing her to be English too, the brig approached, and "on discovering his error, the captain of the brig sang out, 'There is peace with America'; but on being ordered to haul down his flag (as a token) he refused, on which we fired a broadside into him which he returned and struck his colors. She proved to be the honorable East India Company's cruiser *Nautilus,* sixteen guns, bound from Batavia to Calcutta with dispatches and 30,000 dollars in specie, and copper to the value of 100,000 dollars!!"

This time, however, the British captain managed to prove beyond doubt that peace had actually been made. With enormous regret at the loss of such a fine prize cargo, the Americans allowed him to proceed upon his way. "Thus are our bright prospects blighted," Rodgers wrote despondently. Yet he and his colleagues got some satisfaction from finding "in this brig an American called John Deane alias John Crow . . . and for fighting against his country, he was brought on board to be taken to America for trial."

Rodgers did not notice the great irony of the situation: that in this, the last belligerent meeting of the War of 1812, *Peacock* had stopped and searched a peaceful ship and from her, on the grounds of alleged nationality, had taken a seaman against his will. Precisely such behavior on the part of the Royal Navy had enraged Americans for years.

Nevertheless, the war really was over, and *Peacock* turned for home. It was a war which need never have been fought, and which won few obvious benefits; the Treaty of Ghent returned both sides to their prewar positions, not even mentioning the question of impressment.

But some good came out of it. Americans understood that Canada was never going to be a part of their country; Britons understood that the United States really was a country in its own right; and between them, bit by bit, they agreed upon the American-Canadian frontier and established stable treaties of lasting disarmament along that border. And the U.S. Navy garnered much: Its frigate victories gained it huge public esteem, for it had shown it could fight superbly, while the frigates themselves had attracted considerable British professional admiration. In the War of 1812, the use of single frigates had proved more effective than squadron cruising; the time for that would come later, as the Navy evolved. Something else was that Secretary Jones (who resigned in December 1814, feeling his job was done) proposed a permanent academy for training naval officers. The fleet came out of the war stronger not only in experience, but also in ships, than when the conflict began; and as an unusual case, under Jones's direction much of that strength was retained, with only slight postwar congressional cuts.

All the same, forty years is a long time to be fighting in one way or another, almost without remission; so with all told, it is pleasant to be able to conclude these years from 1775 to 1815 with a note from the personal journal of Midshipman William Tennent Rodgers. On October 30, 1815, U.S.S. *Peacock* arrived home at last. She anchored at five in the afternoon; Rodgers went ashore; and there—in such delight that he had to use capital letters—the young man "FOUND ALL FRIENDS WELL!"

PART THREE

RESPECTABILITY

1816 – 1865

★

Thirty years of peace give way to
war with Mexico,
planting the seeds of the Civil War.
In both conflicts,
the power of the U.S. Navy
is crucial.

11

★

OUR PEACEFUL
CONFEDERACY

*W*ith the conclusion of the War of 1812, the United States entered upon three full decades of peace. Only once in its entire existence has the nation improved upon that record: There were thirty-three peaceful years between the end of the Civil War and the beginning of the Spanish-American War in 1898.

This meant that an entire generation born in 1816 grew to full maturity without having to fire a single shot in war; and since there was now little question of the U.S. Navy's being other than a permanent part of American life, the fleet was able—for the first time in its brief, pugnacious history—to enjoy the mixed blessings of a permanent peacetime establishment.

It began its new role with two optimistic, forward-looking innovations. First, in February 1815, a suggestion made by outgoing Secretary of the Navy William Jones was put into effect: His successors would not have to struggle alone with all the minutiae of naval organization as he had, but would be assisted by a three-man Board of Navy Commissioners. Its members were to be senior captains (John Rodgers, David Porter, and Stephen Decatur formed the first board), and thus an important new concept was introduced: Professional officers were going to have a say in the administration of the Navy Department.

But they were not going to rule it. Secretary Jones's immediate successor, Benjamin W. Crowninshield, put the captains firmly in their place when they tried to tell him how to organize squadrons and assign personnel, and President Madison backed him up, saying that if the Board of Navy Commissioners were independent of the secretary they would be independent of the president as well, which would never do. The three captains were limited to looking after "civil, material and logistical functions," and this and other limitations made the board a clumsy instrument; but it was a step in the right direction, at least.

The second innovation was an act passed in April 1816 for the "gradual increase of the Navy." At the end of previous wars the fleet had generally been sold off as quickly as possible; but this act, far from disposing of the United States' small sea arm, allocated a million dollars annually for six consecutive years of naval construction.

The Navy's mood at that time, a feeling of genial pride, was caught neatly in the journal of one officer, a chaplain with the inappropriate name of Philander Chase. In the summer of 1818 he joined the frigate *Guerrière* for a cruise to Europe and the Mediterranean. On Friday, August 21, "early in the morning," he wrote, "we discovered at the same time both the English and French coast—Cap la Hague and the Casquettes on the French and Portland Bill and St Alban's Head on the English. . . ."[1] Seeing the English coast for the first time brought on a fit of sentimentality for Britain: "The land of my ancestors, our forefathers, that country which first gave spring to the liberties of the world—that land—the first to elicit genius and the first to encourage it. . . ." But then he pulled himself together; he was American, not British, and Reverend Chase reminded himself that Britain was also "that land which stoops only to America—and then stoops as if she wondered how she could be moved to stoop to anyone." Later, with the glow of pleasure heightened by his reception in Britain and elsewhere, he wrote to a friend:

> Dear Frank . . . Our little American navy is gradually growing in importance. . . . Its history now gratifies the feelings and flatters the pride of any true son of Yankeeland. Could you but see the respect which in all foreign countries is paid to the American Navy and its officers, you would immediately say with me that it is to our Navy, and will always be so, that we shall be indebted for whatever honors we may receive among the nations on the continent of Europe.

Backed by the security of six years' funding, the Navy now planned to build twelve new forty-four-gun frigates, along with nine seventy-four-gun ships of the line and three steam vessels for harbor defense. This was not only novel, but a sound answer to the perennial question of internal policy, namely what a navy should include. The Navy Board gave enthusiastic support to the building of more big sailing ships, which is not surprising. They gave no recorded support to the idea of steam vessels (which is not surprising either) and the vessels were never completed. Yet what is almost incredible is the slow speed at which the seventy-four-gun liners were built. The first, *Delaware,* was laid down in Norfolk in 1817 and launched in 1820—not a bad rate for peacetime. *North Carolina* was also launched in 1820, at Philadelphia, but of four 74's laid down in 1818, the earliest to be launched was *Vermont*—in 1845. *New York* was still on the stocks at Norfolk when she was burnt in 1861; *Alabama* was finally launched at Portsmouth, New Hampshire, in 1864, by which time she was so outdated she could be used only as a storeship; and as for *Virginia,* commenced in Boston in 1818, she was never launched at all but was eventually broken up on the stocks in 1874, fifty-six years after the laying of her keel.

The ignorance of steam's potential power and the snail's-pace construction of big sailing warships came from various combinations of policies and personalities. On the one hand, the three captains of the Navy Board had learned their skills, and found their fame, in sailing frigates. Steam to them was as alien (and nearly as incomprehensible) as it was to American Indians. Steam engines were noisy, dirty, smelly, inefficient, and heavy, and burned so much coal that refueling was needed every few dozen miles. None of these drawbacks counted for much with riverboats; but in the Navy Board's view, almost any one of them was a good practical reason for keeping the fighting fleet well clear of steam.

On the other hand, there were the twin questions of cost and use of the big ships. Any sailing captain might yearn to command a seventy-four-gun liner, yet at sea such a ship cost a fortune to support. Its proper opponent was another liner. However, if other liners came to be fought, they would come not in ones but (obviously) in lines, and skilled as the U.S. Navy was in single-frigate fighting, it had little knowledge of and no skill in fleet actions. Thus, the value of 74's was a moot point, even to those who would have their command. Some were built in time to be used before they were totally outdated; indeed, one 120-gun ship, *Pennsylvania,* was completed in those decades of peace. But a degree of conservatism from leading officers and a close control of the Navy's budget in Congress meant that frigates, not ships of the line, always remained the backbone of the United States' sailing navy.

Looking back, it is easy to see the implications. In technological terms, the fleet was only marking time, and consequently was likely to become outdated. But that did not appear to matter then; from the Navy's point of view overall, the important things were, first, that it had not been disbanded, and, second, that it had found a useful peacetime job: the promotion and protection of foreign trade.

U.S. overseas trade did not merely expand with the return of peace, it boomed to record-breaking levels. The southern states benefited especially—by 1818 New Orleans was the nation's second largest exporting center, and by 1834 it led all other ports in the United States. China was a firm favorite with the merchants: By 1820 U.S. trade with China was second only to Britain's. But in the South China Sea, in the Sunda Strait, off the coasts of revolutionary South America, and through the Caribbean, pirates prospered at merchants' expense. In the Caribbean alone, it was alleged that between 1816 and 1822 there were 3,002 cases of piratical seizure (nine a week on average), usually accompanied by torture and rape; real piracy was not a romantic business.

So in October 1817 the naval sloop *Ontario* under Capt. James Biddle left New York to police the east coast of South America; in May 1819 the frigate *Congress,* Capt. J. B. Henley, left Hampton Roads for the seas near China—the first American warship to do so and in 1820 the first such vessel to arrive in the Philippines. In 1821 the U.S. Navy ships present off Chile and Peru were organized into the Pacific Squadron; the idea born in the Mediterranean was being extended. The following year the idea was extended further with the establishment (under Biddle) of the West Indies Squadron—a handsome group of nineteen vessels, including two frigates, five sloops, two brigs, four schooners, two gunboats, and four "barges." The barges were similar to the gunboats, but while the gunboats had only numbers to identify them, the barges had pungent names: *Galinipper, Midge, Mosquito,* and *Sandfly*—the four most annoying and voracious insects of the region.

To modern ears, however, the term "squadron" (as it was used then) is rather misleading, and the term "West Indies Squadron" particularly so. Today a squadron suggests a group of ships operating together under one command, and the existence of several squadrons suggests a substantial active navy. Yet though each of these early "squadrons" had one officer in overall control, and though he was given the honorary title of commodore, it would be more accurate to think of him as an area commander; for with a large section of the globe to patrol and only a few ships to do it, the vessels were usually dispersed far and wide, working alone, and only on rare occasion in company.

At the same time, within the Navy as a whole, there were almost as many ships being built as were on active service; but the building was dreadfully slow, and almost as many ships again were laid up in dry dock. The Mediterranean Squadron had been reduced to one frigate, one sloop, and one schooner, leaving a handful of vessels for all other duties; and so one way and another, far from being merely one of several subgroups making up the total fleet, in 1822–23 the "West Indies Squadron" was very nearly the entire active navy. And the reason for this was that in 1821 Congress stepped in, having decided that if the Navy was going to be a permanent establishment in peace or in war, it had better be economical.

What happened was that in 1821, with the act of 1816 for the Navy's "gradual increase" due to expire, a bill was put forward to retire half the vessels on active service and slow down current construction. Another bill (defeated by 67 votes to 66) proposed that no new vessels should be brought into service; and though a third, which was passed, allowed construction to continue for a further six years, the money available was cut in half, from $1 million to $500,000 annually.

Similarly, in 1816 there had been 5,500 naval personnel; in 1822 the number permitted had dropped to 4,000; and while annual average appropriations for all naval needs were $3.7 million in 1817–21, in 1822–25 the figure slid to $2.9 million. In short, the Navy was being allowed to exist, but little more.

Much less easily measurable was the damage done to the fleet by the loss of three outstanding leaders—Perry, Decatur, and Porter. In 1819 Oliver Hazard Perry, the hero of Lake Erie, was sent to Venezuela to act the diplomat. (Many governments used their naval officers this way, though the officers usually disliked it, feeling a good bombardment was the best diplomacy.) Perry's mission was to negotiate peacefully for the security of American sea trade in Venezuelan waters, and he succeeded; but it cost him his life, for he contracted yellow fever and died during the return journey down the Orinoco.

The following year Stephen Decatur was killed without even the redeeming feature of dying in the course of duty. James Barron, commanding officer in the humiliating encounter of *Chesapeake* and *Leopard,* had returned from ten years in Europe in 1818. Decatur had always been openly contemptuous of Barron for the *Chesapeake* affair. He had also been a constant champion of Perry's claim to the victory at Erie against the counterclaim of a fellow officer, Jesse D. Elliott; and in March 1820, unwilling to do the deed himself, Elliott contrived to make Decatur and Barron face each other in a duel at eight paces. Barron was wounded painfully in the thigh, but he lived; his own bullet wounded Decatur mortally from thigh to stomach and killed him slowly.

It was not a good way for an illustrious career to end, and the ending of David Porter's naval career was as bad, or worse. In 1824 he was court-martialed for doing more than was required of him. He was an unusual officer—not only a man of daring, as his foray into the Pacific had shown, but also open-minded, farsighted, and pragmatic. After taking command of the West Indies antipirate squadron, he decided that deep-draft wind-powered vessels were of limited use against the pirates' boats. These, with oars and shallow drafts, could escape into shoal waters, even in a flat calm; so in 1823 Porter sent his frigates home, persuaded the Navy to buy a little 100-ton steamer, *Seagull,* and used her both as a tug and as a weapon. In the same year, as it happened, the Royal Navy acquired its first two steam vessels; but more than a decade ahead of the rest of his navy, Porter became the first naval officer in the world to use steam in combat.

This did not count for much in 1824, though, when his downfall came. Hearing that an American naval officer had been imprisoned in Puerto Rico, he used the Navy's preferred diplomatic tactic and landed two hundred men on the island. The officer was released and a swift apology gained; but then came the court-martial. Sentenced to six months' suspension from the Navy, Porter left in disgust at the end of that time; and so, in five years, the Navy lost three of its most celebrated and respected officers.

Stepping aside from the flow of history for a moment, Porter's court-martial gives a sidelight on one curious American trait, a seemingly traditional preference for the Army over the Navy. The justification for Porter's sentence was that the previous year (1823), President Monroe had enunciated his famous doctrine. This said, in effect, that if European nations did not interfere with the parts of the Americas which did not belong to them, the United States would not interfere in European matters. But Puerto Rico belonged to Spain; Porter's landing was viewed as unwarranted interference; and so he was carpeted. What really annoyed Porter about this and the reason he left the Navy as soon as he could, was that in 1817 Gen. Andrew Jackson had invaded Spanish Florida, created an international incident by hanging one British gunrunner and shooting another, and seized Spanish Pensacola. Yet far from being punished, Jackson was fêted, and in short order Florida became part of the United States.

Of course, the law had changed in the meantime, but there would appear to have been more than that between the difference of treatment. The implications of the Monroe Doctrine were by no means fully understood, and if the Navy had had more self-confidence it could have found another way to deal with Porter; court-martial was not essential. Yet it looks as though, perhaps subconsciously, even the officers of the naval court were affected by a widespread prejudice in the Army's favor. As a separate entity, the Navy Department existed for 149 years, from 1798, when it was hived off from the Department of War, to 1947, when with the Army and Air Force it was unified into the Department of Defense. In those 149 years, there were only twenty-seven years when Congress allocated more money to the Navy than it did to the Army. Moreover, several career soldiers have become president; George Washington was of course the first (not only the first president, but also the first soldier-president), and General Jackson was another, becoming the seventh president in 1829. It is true that several presidents have been deeply interested in the Navy, and some (such as John F. Kennedy, Jimmy Carter, and

George Bush) have served in the Navy; but not one has been a career naval officer. It seems to be a matter of fact in American history that generals get votes, admirals do not.

If this is so, the early U.S. Navy may itself have been partly to blame. In 1824 President Monroe and his secretary of the Navy, Samuel L. Southard, presented a report to Congress on the state and philosophy of the fleet. "It were better," said Monroe, "to have no ships than to have them filled with incompetent and unskilled officers." No one would argue with the statement, and few argued with another of the president's assertions, that "the great object in the event of war is to stop the enemy at the coast."[2]

With the change of a single word, the sentence would still be seen as an ideal objective—"to stop the enemy at *his* coast." It would then imply that the best defense from seaborne attack is control of the seas; but that was not at all what Monroe and Southard meant. There was a lot of sense in their report. It recognized that neither neutrality nor distance had kept the United States safe, and that its coastal defenses had been thoroughly inadequate. Yet it also contained one central blind spot. Everything about it was based on the premise that the best defense was defense—that if one succeeded in keeping an enemy out of one's own vital areas, eventually the enemy would get bored and go away. This completely ignored the sea-controlling, coast-blockading pattern set by the Royal Navy against both France and the United States itself. The report went on to recommend that the rank of admiral should be introduced to the U.S. Navy; but it contained no recommendations as to the size of the Navy, its strategies, or the fleet tactics such an introduction would suggest.

The report's main weakness (evident even in the best professional American naval thinking at the time) was that practicality, so often a virtue in war, blinkered the development of naval theory in peace. Because no one could foresee the need for, far less the possibility of, the United States' blockading another nation—especially one across the Atlantic—no one thought about it, or about fleet tactics.

Certainly one should never use hindsight to criticize, and certainly the daily business of getting on with their jobs prevented naval officers from giving much time to the development of theories. (The same would be true today if it were not for staff courses giving officers time to think.) But in the early nineteenth century, this lack of analytic reflection on the part of supporters of the Navy was their opponents' best weapon. A navy of some sort was generally, though not universally, accepted as a new and permanent necessity; but cogent arguments would have to be produced if it was going to change in character or even to grow by very much, and as yet no one in the United States was able to frame such arguments. The recommendation for admirals typified this. Despite repeated suggestions, the rank was not introduced until 1862. Before then it seemed a good idea for the dignity of the service and of the nation; but nobody—not even naval officers—could really say why there should be admirals, or what they should do. As one officer wrote in a letter to a newspaper in 1823, "What do we want of admirals?"[3] But everyone understood the value of a general.

John Quincy Adams, the eldest son of the second president of the United States, became the republic's fourth president in 1825, and proved to be just as stauch a naval man as his father had been. During his time in office the Brazil (or South Atlantic) Squadron was established as a protection for U.S. shipping when Brazil and Argentina went to war in 1826; and in December of that year, he expressed his conviction to Congress that "it was the destiny and the duty of these confederated States to become, in regular process of time and by no petty advances, a great naval power."[4]

The act of 1816, modified in 1821, was once again due for renewal or revision, and the debate which surrounded this in 1827 was perhaps the best thing to happen to the Navy while Adams was president. It was not apparent at once, and any contemporary naval officer would probably have felt the Navy did badly: No new ships were authorized, merely the stockpiling of timber. Furthermore, the annual expenditure for improvements remained at half a million dollars for another six years (the bill itself was described as being for the "gradual improvement of the Navy," unlike the 1816 "gradual increase") and much of the money went on building the Navy's first two dry docks. The establishment of a naval officers' academy was proposed again and defeated again on the grounds that it was undemocratic and that merchant ships provided the best possible training. But—and this was the real benefit to the Navy—the argument led to a spirited debate on naval readiness.

"The moment we get through one war, we prepare for another," complained Sen. Nathaniel Macon of North Carolina, not very accurately.[5] He saw navies as useful only for conquering other countries, which he did not want to do. Opposing him, Sen. Robert Y. Hayne of South Carolina believed "a Navy was not only the safest, but the cheapest defense of this nation," and argued that the fleet should be nurtured "not upon irregular and varying acts of legislation, but . . . on some regular plan, from which there ought to be no departure, except in some great emergency."[6]

The two senators' comments represented differing contemporary views, one that in an emergency, an ad hoc fleet could be created at short notice, and the other that it could not. Since the bill that sparked the debate was neither passed nor defeated entirely, neither side could be said to have "won"; but while anti-Navy debating points remained much the same as ever, those of the pro-Navy lobby were slowly—very slowly—evolving. And therein lay the difference that in the end would count.

When General Jackson took up the reins as president in 1829, he was helped into the saddle by a very distinct antinavalism. In his first speech, on March 4, he announced, "the bulwark of our defense is the national militia, which in the present state of our intelligence and population must render us invincible."[7] He was lucky the assertion was not put to the test.

By the year's end he had decided that only those ships necessary for protection of commerce should be kept in commission—which, since the local scourge of piracy had been effectively stamped out by then, meant the Navy was suffering from its own success. Jackson was not an irrational man. He did not want to scrap the Navy altogether, because he could see uses for it; but these uses were simply not as extensive as the Navy would have liked. Nevertheless, it was on his order that the sloop *Vincennes* set off in 1829 to perform the U.S. Navy's first circumnavigation of the world—a two-year voyage of diplomacy, flag-showing, and the occasional act of rescue and reprisal. It was also due directly to him that David Porter came back from Mexico, where in high dudgeon he had accepted a commission as a rear admiral. Porter was given the job of chargé d'affaires in Constantinople, and in 1831 secured ratification of America's first commercial treaty with Turkey and the Ottoman Empire. Jackson had made not only a generous gesture, but a good judgment as well.

Again, it was at Jackson's instigation that the frigate *Potomac* sailed in 1832 to Kuala Batu in Sumatra to investigate the murder there of some American merchant seamen. Unfortunately, the commanding officer, Capt. John Downes, far overreached his orders. Deciding to shoot first and ask questions later, he conducted the United States' first armed intervention in Asia, and for his pains (though he secured promises of future good conduct from the Sumatrans) he was never given command of another warship.

A similar project the same year, once more originating with Jackson and his secretary of the Navy, Levi Woodbury, had less immediate but far graver consequences. The Falkland Islands, ceded by Spain to Britain in 1771, were claimed some fifty years later by Argentina, independent since 1816. Nobody lived there, so nobody bothered much about it: U.S. sealers continued to come and hunt there, and when cattle and cowboys were imported from Argentina, the sealers hunted cattle by way of variety. This led to two of their ships being impounded and taken to Buenos Aires, which in turn led to the dispatch to the Falklands of the U.S. sloop-of-war *Lexington* to sort matters out. Capt. Silas Duncan settled the affair by taking the forty gauchos living there back to Argentina, whereupon Britain, awakened to the reality of that distant scrap of sovereign territory, took formal possession of the islands in 1833. Argentinian protests cut little ice in Washington; the view there was that the Monroe Doctrine had not been violated, for the islands were already legally British, and that Duncan's action has been to suppress piracy. "But," wrote Samuel Eliot Morison in 1965, "the Duncan incident has never been forgotten or forgiven at Buenos Aires";[8] and of course, seventeen years after that observation, in the British-Argentinian Falklands War of 1982, "the Duncan incident" required further bloody clarification and placed the United States on a diplomatic tightrope.

But to return to the nineteenth century—at the end of 1832 Secretary Woodbury observed that the United States' "greatest exposure and danger are on the water." To this perfectly correct remark he added, "our means of attack and defense there . . . will probably always prove equal to sustain us with credit in any hostilities into which the convulsions of the world may hereafter plunge this peaceful confederacy."[9] The longwinded, shortsighted assertion was open to considerable question, for after *Demologos* and Porter's use of *Seagull,* the U.S. Navy had literally run out of steam. Not a single vessel in the fleet was powered by anything other than wind, water, or muscle.

Elsewhere, however, the situation was becoming markedly different. The Royal Navy had used an unarmed steamer in Burma in 1824 and had started collecting armed steamers in 1828; the French navy had used half a dozen armed steamers against Algeria in 1830; and in 1827—during their war of independence against Turkey—the Greeks had become (somewhat surprisingly) the first people to use an armed steamer in actual warfare, as distinct from Porter's peacetime activity against pirates.

In this technological advance the U.S. Navy was being left far behind, not least because the advisory Board of Navy Commissioners was still composed of veterans of the War of 1812—men of distinction and influence, but sixteen years older than when the board was established and growing steadily more conservative, more opposed to steam. So although Woodbury's time as secretary ended on a good diplomatic note (the sloop U.S.S. *Peacock* carried emissaries to Bangkok, where, on March 20, 1833, America's first treaty with an Oriental power was signed) it was his successor, Mahlon Dickerson, who initiated the serious use of steam in the U.S. fleet. And this notable progress, the most important single step since the Navy was begun, marked the start of Jackson's second term as president.

Simply getting the money for the project was an achievement in itself. In the previous six years, making do with limited cash had brought some odd bookkeeping into naval practice. The *Peacock* which carried the diplomatic party to Bangkok was nominally the same *Peacock* which, built in 1813, was immediately sent to war against the British and performed so well. Legally speaking, she was renovated in 1828, which meant that funds could be appropriated without question from the repairs account. Certainly a *Peacock* went into the New York navy yard, and a *Peacock* came out; and since each time the ship had the same number of masts and the same number of guns, it would have taken a sharp-eyed member of Congress to notice that the ship which came out was a foot shorter than the one which went in. Except for the account books, this was no renovation; the old sloop had gone for firewood, and without anyone officially knowing about it, an entirely new vessel had been built. Two years later, in 1830, an even more audacious "renovation" took place when *John Adams,* built in 1799 as a twenty-eight-gun frigate, miraculously came out of Norfolk navy yard as an eighteen-gun sloop; again, no one seemed to notice. The members of the Navy Board may have been old and conservative, but they were canny as well.

However much respect they commanded individually, as a body the Board of Navy Commissioners was an obstacle to an adventurous naval secretary such as Mahlon Dickerson. He could see that the mid-1830s were a period of changed naval circumstances—there was money which could be made available, there were more naval stations around the world, and there was a local enemy. Dickerson had a good idea of what he wanted to do about all this, but he needed the elderly commissioners' agreement; so, giving them to understand his desires, he asked them to write him a report.

They had to consider the three new factors he had noted. First and most unusual was that in 1835, for once in their lives, members of Congress found themselves with surplus funds floating around; the national debt had actually been paid off, and taxes were still flowing in. Second, a temporary diplomatic crisis with France prompted the creation of the East Indies Squadron, under which grand name *Peacock* and *Enterprise* sailed. The West Indies Squadron, at the same time, had diminished to a frigate, three sloops, and a schooner, with the same on the Pacific station and two sloops on the Brazil–South Atlantic patrol. How loosely the term "squadron" was used is underlined by the voyage of the sloop *Vincennes.* After her successful circumnavigation of the globe in 1829–31, she was sent off in 1835 to do it again; yet all the time she was nominally in the Pacific Squadron.

Before coming to the third factor Dickerson presented to the board, let us pause to look more closely at *Vincennes*'s voyage of 1835. It is not in itself an essential part of the argument, but one of her officers, Robert Lewright Browning, recorded the voyage in a detailed journal which today rests in the Library of Congress; it makes such delightful reading that a trip to the Pacific sounds irresistible.

· · ·

From the evidence of his diary, Browning was a wise, tolerant, and good-humored man with a ready pen. Voyaging to the Marquesas and on to Tahiti, the Friendly Islands, Guam, and China before returning via Singapore, Cape Town, and St. Helena, he was able to visit many places which had been discovered by Western explorers only in the previous sixty years or so; and in much of his writing, the feeling not of mere novelty but of real newness comes over vividly.

Approaching the Marquesas, "everyone," he said, "was on deck enjoying the new and beautiful scenery of towering mountains, high rocky cliffs and deep narrow verdant valleys"; and when an English sailor who had married a native girl came paddling out to act as a pilot, bringing with him a local chief, Browning encountered a phenomenon which would spread to most navies: tattooing. The chief, Obuiya, appeared to be fully dressed; but when he came on board, Browning saw that his only garment was "a narrow strip of native cloth passed between the legs and made fast around the loins—an economical dress, that! In lieu of other clothing he was tattooed all over—even to the eyelids—in fanciful figures, which are indelible." The newness of it all was a mutual experience: When poor Obuiya came on deck ("exceedingly stout," with "a fine face and a tremendously bushy head"), he seemed terrified; "and the captain, to give him confidence, slapped him familiarly on the shoulder, which so increased his fright that he would have jumped overboard . . ."

Browning was the best kind of visitor such islanders could have. He loved the climate and the vegetation, he was charmed by the islands, and, like Porter before him, he did not criticize the people for their different habits of religion and morality.

"When bread and fruit grow upon trees without cultivation," he said, "and hogs and fowls increase and fatten without care—where the climate has never dictated the necessity of clothing, it is not surprising that they take the world easy, and prefer singing and dancing away a lifetime, to adopting the customs and cares of civilization. Civilization would multiply their wants, cares, necessities, and troubles; and in their remote situation give them but few advantages. But they are of such fine specimens of mankind, I should like to see them living after some civilized fashion. The women with such symmetrical and delicate forms, such classic features, such tapered arms and fingers, and such delicate skin that they seem designed for ladies of the first order. And the men are tall, strait, athletic and muscular—averaging larger than any other race I have ever seen."

He believed firmly that arms should be kept from them, "as they would only use them in war against other tribes. But our whale fishermen are not so scrupulous . . ." Islanders lacked scruples in a different way, as David Porter had found in 1813:

"When in our ramble," Browning noted, "we go into any of their huts, they offer us anything they have. If there are any women, they are the first thing offered. Often, indeed, they offer themselves; and being refused, they will recommend another for a 'motaky vaheena'—a nice woman— without exhibiting the least jealousy. The women being refused, bread-fruit, coconuts, and water are offered."

Of course this was not prostitution, but a different morality entirely; and Browning recounted with some relish a story of three American missionaries who had come to the islands with their wives "to make Christians of these thoughtless, idle, merry, ignorant, lascivious peo-ple"—as the missionaries no doubt saw them. Unfortunately, the island-ers "would only listen to their preaching as a subject of laughter." Worse, "the missionary ladies excited great curiosity among the men, to know if they were made like their women"—for the missionary ladies were covered from head to foot in strange garments. "Frequent attempts at examination were made, and one time they were so resolved on gratifying their curiosity by examination, that they were only restrained by the husband of the lady presenting a musket at the most determined one. After this the missionaries thought it advisable to leave."[10]

We too must leave Browning on his fascinating voyage and return to a sadder encounter with native people which was beginning simultaneously in Florida. In brief, this—the third factor the Navy Commissioners had to consider—was something which old John Adams would have called "a kind of dodging Indian fight." Starting with an uprising by the Semi-nole tribe, it extended rapidly to include the Creek tribes of Georgia and south Alabama—a local naval guerrilla war which would continue for eight years. On March 2, 1836, the Navy Board's reaction to the new conditions (the influx of funds, the spread of permanent stations, and the proximity of an enemy) was given in their report to the secretary of the Navy.

The signature on the report was that of John Rodgers—a war veteran since 1798, now sixty-three years old and in the last two years of his life. His recommendation, and the board's, for "the naval force which is 'necessary to place the naval defenses of the United States upon the footing of strength and respectability which is due to the security and welfare of the Union' " was a combination which cost him much mental sacrifice.[11]

Basically it was more of the same as he had always known—more sloops, more frigates, and fifteen more ships of the line, with a further ten kept ready for completion. But these traditional items were followed by a reluctant recommendation for twenty-five steamers. If such a suggestion had been made and accepted twelve years earlier, the United States would have led the world in naval technology. But David Porter, one of the board's original members, had left it when he went off to the Caribbean with *Seagull,* and after he quit the Navy altogether, *Seagull* had been laid up in Philadelphia. By 1836 she was completely unserviceable; and so, it could be said, was John Rodgers. With only one break for sea duty, he had been a member of the board since its inception twenty-one years before, and for eighteen of those years had been its president. Coming around to steam after all that time did not exactly make him an evangelist of naval progress; and when Secretary Dickerson ordered him to have a steamer designed and built, Rodgers was obliged to admit complete ignorance of the subject. So a 142-ton tug named *Engineer* was bought for naval use in New York harbor, and a New Yorker, Charles H. Haswell, was engaged to work on her. One year later, the result of his labors was seen when the 180-foot *Fulton II* made 12 knots on her trials.

Martin Van Buren had won the presidential election of 1836, but on taking office on March 4, 1837, he retained Naval Secretary Dickerson, who was thus able to see *Fulton II* through from an idea to a reality; and in his remarkable final speech as president, General Jackson revealed how Dickerson had managed to push the project so hard. In the past few years, the general's opinions on national defense had altered dramatically. He still held that coastal fortifications were essential, yet now he stated it would be "impossible by any line of fortification to guard every point from attack against a hostile force advancing from the ocean."[12] His answer to the problem was to urge naval increase without delay: "Now is the time, in a season of peace and with an overflowing revenue . . . without increasing the burdens of the people. It is your true policy, for your Navy will not only protect your rich and flourishing commerce in distant seas, but it will enable you to reach and annoy the enemy, and will give to defense its greatest efficiency by meeting danger at a distance from home."

At the time Jackson made those remarks, the sixty-four-year-old professional naval officer John Rodgers was ill and preparing to retire from the presidency of the Navy Board. Yet the remarks from the aged general (Jackson was seventy years old in 1837) showed he understood the Navy's role better than Rodgers did. Jackson was simply more open to new thinking and did not oppose a navy per se as Rodgers opposed steam. And—though the general had been elected on an agrarian, antinaval ticket—when one looks again at the imaginative and creative use he made of the Navy, his record leaves a sneaking feeling that in fact he had been a closet navalist all along.

12

★

DISPUTES AND
COLLISIONS

*A*fter asking how anyone could "consent to let our old ships perish, and transform our navy into a fleet of sea monsters," James Paulding gasped: "I am being steamed to death!"[1]

As a popular writer, he could turn some neat phrases; yet had he been only a writer, most of them would have been forgotten long ago. His naval phrases are remembered today because, at the age of sixty, a lifelong interest in naval matters brought him to a position of some political clout: In June 1838 he replaced Mahlon Dickerson as President Van Buren's secretary of the Navy. And Van Buren had given him a clear lead; in the new president's words, America needed "no navy at all, much less a steam navy."[2]

Paulding's ability as a writer had been given official recognition of a sort back in 1815, when he was awarded the post of first secretary to the Navy Board, at an annual salary of $2,000. Since his principal clerk did most of the work, Paulding (who, like many a writer, had been "fettered by poverty") found the job gave him "leisure, respect, and independence, which last is peculiarly gratifying from its novelty. . . . My spirits are good, my prospects fair, and the treatment I receive from all around is marked with respectful consideration." He noted, with engaging naïveté, that Benjamin Crowninshield (then secretary of the Navy) "smokes my segars in the politest manner imaginable"; and he became thoroughly steeped in the board's prevailing attitude.[3]

The year before he became naval secretary, the board gave its riposte to *Fulton II* by laying down the keel of *Pennsylvania*. Displacing over three thousand tons, measuring 210 feet between perpendiculars and carrying 120 guns, she was the largest sailing man-of-war ever built for the U.S. Navy. She was also the Navy Board's last grand fling, a splendid gesture of defiance against creeping modernity—and a huge waste of money. As her hull took shape and *Fulton II* rumbled around on trials, the Royal Navy counted twenty-one steam warships in its fleet, while the French navy had twenty-three. Paulding, the standard-bearer for sailing-ship sentimentalists, put himself firmly with the Canutes of the Navy Board; but though he was by inclination reactionary, within days of taking office he was involved, by chance, in one of the U.S. Navy's most progressive peacetime achievements. For in July 1838, the time came to sign the orders dispatching the Wilkes Exploring Expedition to the Pacific Ocean and points north and south.

The Exploring Expedition had a dauntingly wide range of objectives to fulfill, as paragraph 11 of the orders indicated:

> All the duties pertaining to astronomy, surveying, hydrography, geography, geodesy, magnetism, meteorology, and physics generally to be exclusively confined to the Navy officers—these are deemed the great objects of the Expedition and it is confidently believed that there are none who are so well qualified to perform them.[4]

There were also zoological, botanical, geological, mineralogical, and conchological studies to be undertaken, if possible by the medical officers—wonderful blanket instructions which convey vividly the contemporary state of knowledge. But this was the heyday of Baron Alexander von Humboldt, perhaps the last man to be acknowledged as a universal genius, a man who knew almost everything there was to know on every subject. At the turn of the eighteenth century the baron had made a five-year journey through South America; he had then spent twenty-one years writing thirty-three books about it, and even as the Wilkes Expedition was getting under way, he was preparing a modest five-volume description of the physical universe entitled *Kosmos*. If one man could accomplish so much, four ships of American naval officers could have a fair go at Paulding's wide orders.

Not that they were really Paulding's orders; he was simply the man who happened to be in office when they came to be signed. The origins of the expedition went back to 1816, when an ex–U.S. Army captain, John C. Symmes, announced that the North and South poles focused on holes large enough to accommodate sailing ships. Voyaging through these, he predicted, would prove that the planet was composed of concentric, habitable spheres.

This superbly daft theory was adopted by a civilian "scientist" named Jeremiah N. Reynolds, who stuck to it for eight years. After he eventually lost faith in the polar holes, the bee of Antarctic exploration remained in Reynolds's bonnet, and in 1828 John Quincy Adams's naval secretary, Samuel Southard, became interested too. Exploration had long been a recognized peacetime function in both the British and French navies, best exemplified by Captain Cook's voyages between 1768 and 1779, and Southard felt rightly that the U.S. Navy could and should play a part. But one way and another, obstacles came up, the main one being expense, and those who had been keen cooled off. However, Lt. Charles Wilkes, a recognized expert in scientific navigation, was associated with the project from the first stirrings of official interest, and when at last the expedition became possible, he was made its leader. His success in that role came not only in the expedition itself, but in his own best-selling narrative of the voyage, and in having something like a million square miles of Antarctica named after him—not a bad reward for a naval lieutenant.

"Sir," wrote Wilkes to Secretary Paulding on August 22, 1838, "I have the honor to inform you of the sailing of the exploring expedition. It was left at 9 a.m. of the 19th by the pilot; Cape Henry bearing west by north twenty-five miles distant, the wind at east-north-east, blowing a pleasant breeze."[5]

On January 6, 1839, he sent further news—"U.S. Ship *Vincennes,* off the harbor of Rio de Janeiro. . . . Sir, I have the honor to advise you that we are under way, the *Peacock, Porpoise* and tenders *Seagull* and *Flying Fish* in company."[6]

Seagull, incidentally, was not the steamer David Porter had used, but a 100-ton pilot schooner, armed with two guns; she was lost off Cape Horn later in 1839. *Flying Fish* was a similar vessel, and remained with the explorers until 1842, when she was condemned and sold in Singapore, there to begin a career of great notoriety as an opium smuggler. *Peacock* was the "renovated" *Peacock* of 1828; she made it as far as the Columbia River in Oregon, where she was wrecked on July 18, 1841. *Porpoise,* a ten-gun brigantine built in Boston in 1836, survived the voyage, only to be lost in the China Sea in 1854; but *Vincennes* came triumphantly through everything.

In her, Wilkes sailed via Madeira to Rio, and south around the Horn to survey and explore in the Tuamotu and Society islands before proceeding to Samoa and (in December 1839) to Sydney. From Australia he headed south, and on January 19, 1840, identified land at roughly 160 degrees east, 67 degrees south. Today one may readily locate the point on a map; and part of the readiness of location is, of course, because Wilkes went there. It is easy to remember that he and his companions sailed without any of the modern aids to navigation—radio, satellite navigation, good food and medical help, airlifts. But it is equally easy to forget that they sailed without even a decent chart of their destination, with nothing but their ships, their skill, their sense, and their courage. A person setting out on such a voyage today would be thought a fool not to take advantage of every available aid; yet Cook and Wilkes and all the other great explorers had no choice, if they were to go at all. Arthur Hugh Clough, a poet living at that time, put it prettily in one of his verses:

> *Where lies the land to which the ship must go?*
> *Far, far ahead, is all her seamen know.*
> *And where the land she travels from? Away,*
> *Far, far behind, is all that they can say.*[7]

If wars are fought not only to protect or acquire trade but also so that the next generation may live in greater security, the same may be said about those early explorers, risking, even losing their lives so that the next traveler could journey in greater safety. With Wilkes the comparison is especially apt: Many of his Pacific charts were used over a century later in the United States' war with Japan.

He covered nearly a thousand miles of Antarctic coastline, edging along the glaciers until he came to the area now known as the Shackleton Ice Shelf; and after five weeks of gales, snowstorms, icebergs, frozen decks, and frozen rigging, he turned northward to the warmth. From Sydney again he went to New Zealand, and on for four months (May–August 1840) of surveying in the Fiji Islands. At sea, fifty reefs and 154 islands were marked out, and on shore there was bloodshed—islanders killed two officers, and in a disproportionate reprisal fifty-seven islanders died. From there the squadron wintered in Honolulu, surveying islands to the south before moving on in April 1841 to the northwest U.S. coast. Puget Sound, part of the northern California coastline, and sections of the Columbia, Williamette, and Sacramento rivers were surveyed, an effort which took the whole of that summer. Surveying is a slow, tedious, invaluable business; and again, it is easy to forget that every figure of depth on a chart is there because someone took the trouble to actually go and measure it.

Wilkes was able to help not only his inheritors but also contemporary explorers, such as James Ross of the British Royal Navy. In 1818 Ross had been a member of the first expedition trying to locate the Northwest Passage, and at the same time as Wilkes sailed south, Ross was preparing to do the same. After his Antarctic voyage Wilkes gave Ross a copy of his new chart, because Ross "had himself afforded me all the assistance in his power while I was engaged in preparing the instruments for this expedition."[8] In Antarctica, Ross, of course, discovered Victoria Land and the Ross Barrier, had an enormous dependency named after him, and was knighted—a very beneficial scratching of backs, all in all.

From Sacramento, Wilkes returned to Honolulu, and thence via the Carolinas to Manila, surveying all the way. From Manila he went to Sulu in the Philippines, and at last turned *Vincennes* homeward by way of Singapore and the Cape of Good Hope. Very nearly four years had passed. On June 9, 1842, he arrived back at New York, bearing a wealth of new knowledge with him. This, for the U.S. Navy, was a new kind of heroism: proof that a navy at peace could be beneficial in ways that a navy at war could never be. A navy at war helps shape the world; a navy at peace can extend it.

Yet Wilkes, the bringer of knowledge, found more awaiting him at home. The Navy had not marked time in his absence. Great changes had been put into motion, and were culminating even as *Vincennes* dropped anchor in New York harbor. Indeed, the successful return of the Wilkes Exploring Expedition was only one of the events which together made 1842 a banner year for the U.S. Navy.

Not one of the vessels used in the Wilkes expedition was a steamer: When the flotilla departed in 1838 *Fulton II* was still the only steamer the U.S. Navy possessed. Her commander was a younger brother of Oliver Hazard Perry. Born in 1794, nine years after Oliver, Matthew Calbraith Perry outlived Oliver by thirty-nine years. They joined the identical Navy; on their deaths, they left behind them virtually entirely different fleets. Oliver had won his fame in a 500-ton sailing brig on a lake; Matthew would find his in a 3,220-ton steam frigate many thousands of miles away across the ocean, in Japan.

Matthew himself was one of the reasons for the transformation that took place in the U.S. Navy. His attitude, roughly, was that anything which had been good enough in the War of 1812 was almost certainly not good enough any longer. In 1833, with the establishment of an officers' academy deferred yet again, he set up the Naval Lyceum in the Brooklyn navy yard. It was a place for self-directed study rather than formal education, but it had a lecture room, a library, and a reading room, which was more than anyone else had managed to organize. And in 1839, when the secretary of the British Admiralty referred to *Fulton II* in Parliament, Perry shared the Englishman's opinion entirely: Sir Charles Wood found it "not a little curious, that in that country, the mother of steam navigation, this steam vessel should be the only one belonging to the government."[9]

Considering that there were over seven hundred commercial steamships in America by then, the U.S. Navy's lack of steam was not just a little curious, it was absurd. Perry had been traveling in Europe the year before; and back home, he applied such influence, imagination, and energy to what he had learned abroad that in March 1839 Congress passed a bill authorizing the construction of two steam frigates, *Mississippi* and

Missouri. These sister ships were each to be 229 feet long, displacing 3,220 tons, with four guns and twin paddle wheels amidships; and the Navy Board and Secretary Paulding were infuriated.

Another progressive move in 1840 succeeded in establishing naval schools in Philadelphia and Norfolk—even though many members of Congress still agreed with a splendid remark by John Reynolds, representative for Illinois. "What?" he exclaimed. "Educate a sailor in a cloister? Set a man down in a dark retreat of a college cell to learn how to manage a ship in a storm? No Sir!"[10]

The changes gathered pace. In 1841, ahead of all other navies, authorization came to construct a steam warship with an underwater propeller instead of paddle wheels; and under a sudden scare of possible war with Great Britain, the number of naval officers' billets was increased by almost as much as the total increase in the previous twenty years. With changes of administration in both Britain and America, the war scare (which started with the arrest for murder of a Briton in America) passed off as quickly as it had come; but by 1842, when Wilkes returned in triumph, this increase in manpower was one of the major alterations the explorer found. But even that was not the last, or the most important.

In 1841, three men held the title of president of the United States: Van Buren, who departed office on March 4; William Harrison (like Jackson another successful general of the War of 1812), who took office on March 4 and departed life a month later; and his vice president, John Tyler. Indeed, in the twelve years from 1841 to 1853, there were no less than seven different presidents and ten different secretaries of the Navy. Five of those ten served under President Tyler, and of those, the most effective was Abel P. Upshur of Virginia.

"Wars," said Upshur in his report to President Tyler for 1841, "often arise from a rivalry in trade, and from the conflicts of interests which belong to it. The presence of an adequate naval force, to protect commerce, by promptly redressing the injuries which are done to it, is one of the best means of preventing those disputes and collisions."[11]

The Democratic Party's traditional support by the farming community gave it an equally traditional dislike of the Navy; and in a period dominated by Democratic congresses, Upshur stood out in the Navy's executive leadership. While he was secretary, a permanent Home Squadron was established: Keeping all ships on distant stations meant that in emergency they would take a dangerously long time to recall. His estimates of naval costs for 1842, over $8.5 million, were more than half as much again as for the previous year; and he based this increase on a useful calculation. For its commercial and territorial protection, he reckoned that the United States could not "safely stop short of half the naval power of the strongest maritime Power in the world." For the first time, he was using the concept of international relative standards of naval strength—the concept which would become, later in the nineteenth century, the touchstone of the Royal Navy's "Two-Power Standard" and, in the early twentieth century, the basis of all naval construction races and limitation conferences.

A quarter million dollars from the 1842 estimates went for the construction of something which should have been a milestone in naval development: the Stevens Battery. This vessel was called a "battery," meaning a gun emplacement, because of the firm belief that a steamship could not be more than a floating adjunct to land defenses. Yet the Stevens Battery was a proper ship, and had she been completed, she would have been the world's first ironclad seagoing warship. Instead that distinction went to the French *Gloire,* launched in 1859, and the Stevens Battery (abandoned through congressional unwillingness to pay for her full development) became another great might-have-been of American naval history.

Secretary Upshur's main strength was a good sense of direction in naval planning. Unfortunately, most people in America's naval administration lacked that sense of direction—a failing characterized in 1842 by the completion of *Mississippi* and *Missouri* and the simultaneous launch of *Cumberland* and *Savannah*. The paddle steamers were advanced vessels; but *Cumberland* and *Savannah* were two of the frigates laid down after the War of 1812, frigates which the paddle steamers made obsolescent. Not obsolete—a technological development does not usually render everything before it completely and utterly useless at once; for a transitional time, the older form is less effective, but not immediately ineffective. Yet to produce these four ships in the same year, with two of them based on plans devised a quarter of a century before, showed just how confused the midcentury Navy had become.

Responsibility for much of the confusion could be placed corporately with the Board of Navy Commissioners; but one of the system's weaknesses was that none of the commissioners, now aged and gray, had to accept individual responsibility for any maladministration. This was an area where, with little opposition (except from the commissioners), Upshur's clear view took effect. In August 1842, he abolished the board and replaced it with a workable system which, for more than a century, would form the basis of all U.S. naval administration: the naval bureaus.

To begin with there were five bureaus: Provisions and Clothing, headed by either an officer or a civilian; Medicine and Surgery, headed by a naval surgeon; Ordnance and Hydrography, and Navy Docks and Yards, both headed by naval captains; and finally, led by a constructor, the Bureau of Construction, Equipment and Repair. This one's nickname (the Bureau of Destruction and Despair) reflected the maddening inefficiency of the new system in its early days; but it was a vast improvement over the Navy Board.

Although the introduction of the bureau system was Upshur's major contribution to the Navy, of course it was not his own personal invention. Junior officers had long been clamoring for change of that sort. Prominent among them was a Virginia-born lieutenant, Matthew Fontaine Maury. Using a pseudonym, he had filled the columns of the *Southern Literary Messenger* for four years with stinging critiques of the old Navy Board, articles which had impressed Secretary Upshur. In the same year the board was abolished, Maury was made director of the Depot of Charts and Instruments (later to become the Naval Observatory) in Washington, D.C. And resting awhile at that very useful vantage point, we may observe how over the next few years the Navy, national policy, and physical geography all wove together and affected one another.

Geographically, the focal points were scattered far and wide: Maine, Oregon, Texas, Mexico, the Pacific islands, and China. Politically, one thread united them: a bold, barefaced expansionism looking clear-eyed and confident into the distant future. And the naval strand in the network was a collection of individual officers with shared attitudes: Charles Wilkes, Thomas ap Catesby Jones, Lawrence Kearney, and Robert Stockton.

The first knot in the geopolitical web was Maine and the Webster-Ashburton Treaty of 1842. Some twelve thousand square miles along the border of Maine and Canada were still contested by Great Britain, and the treaty (negotiated between Secretary of State Daniel Webster and the British minister, Lord Ashburton) settled the boundary somewhat in favor of the United States, giving it seven thousand square miles of the disputed area. But over on the northwest side of the continent, a similar dispute was brewing about the boundary between Canada and Oregon; because of this, one of the results of Charles Wilkes's expedition was kept carefully secret. Apart from his best-selling *Narrative,* he published two dozen books with colleagues over twenty years (evidently bitten by the von Humboldt bug) and, for the government, wrote a special report, which was not published until 1911. Some of the things it said were said in the *Narrative* too—the high quality of San Francisco harbor, the commercial possibilities of Puget Sound and the Juan de Fuca Strait—but it also recommended that the government claim all of the so-called "Oregon Territory." This area, far larger than present-day Oregon, stretched from 42 degrees north to 54 degrees 40 minutes north, bounded by the Pacific to the west and the Rockies to the east—around half a million square miles, all told, offering incalculable riches in fish, furs, and timber—quite apart from whatever unknown minerals might be found underground.

The report was kept secret for fear that its grand recommendation would damage negotiations in both Maine and Oregon. When the final division of the territory was agreed on by treaty in 1846, it was more logical and equitable: The frontier was drawn along latitude 49 degrees north, leaving Vancouver Island in Canada and providing the United States with about 285,000 extra square miles. So in the event, Wilkes's secret recommendation did not directly affect the negotiations; but his published work, with its topography and descriptions of the West Coast, created a nationwide interest in the possibilities of the West as a whole, including the Pacific Ocean. Wilkes anticipated the absorption into the United States not only of Oregon but also of California and Hawaii, and he pointed out how U.S. possession of the continent's Pacific coast would simplify communication with the west coast of South America, the entire Pacific Ocean, and all of Asia. These were heady proposals, suggesting a truly global view of America's possible size and influence; to realize and exploit them, the Navy would be essential, and would have a genuine reason for growth.

In 1815 Thomas ap Catesby Jones had been a lieutenant, fighting in the prelude to the unnecessary Battle of New Orleans. By 1842 he was a commodore in charge of the U.S. Navy's Pacific Squadron; and on October 20 of that year (again unnecessarily) he captured Monterey, then the Spanish capital of Upper California. Two days later he handed the town back to its owners, who were not in the least resentful; in his position, they said sympathetically, they would probably have done much the same.

This odd event was just part of the gradual decay of the Spanish Empire. Jones's position was that of the man on the ground, obliged to take a risk without full, reliable information. All he knew for certain was that California had seceded from Mexico and that, while still claiming the land, Mexico recognized the new government. He also knew that six years earlier, in 1836, Mexican-owned Texas had declared itself an independent republic; that diplomatic tension over Texas existed between Mexico and the United States; that both France and England were involved in that tension; that the Oregon boundary dispute with England had not yet been resolved; that France had taken possession of the Marquesas; and that a British squadron had recently sailed from Callao in Peru, destination unknown.

All that was accurate and reliable. The inaccuracy that prompted his capture of Monterey was a report in a Mexican newspaper saying that Mexico and the United States were at war. They were not, but Jones deduced that the British squadron was on its way to claim Upper California, possibly through a secret treaty with Mexico. If that were the case, he was not going to let them get away with it.

The deduction was plausible, and had it been correct the initiative

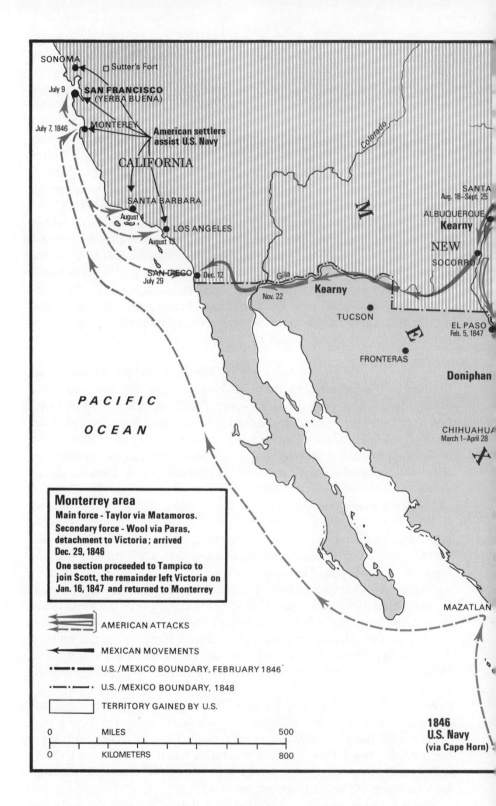

SONOMA ☐ Sutter's Fort

July 9

SAN FRANCISCO
(YERBA BUENA)

July 7, 1846 • MONTEREY

American settlers
assist U.S. Navy

CALIFORNIA

SANTA BARBARA

August 4

• LOS ANGELES

August 13

SAN DIEGO • Dec. 12
July 29

Colorado

SANTA
Aug. 18–Sept. 25

ALBUQUERQUE
Kearny

NEW

SOCORRO

M

Gila

Kearny

Nov. 22

TUCSON

EL PASO
Feb. 5, 1847

FRONTERAS

E

Doniphan

CHIHUAHUA
March 1–April 28

PACIFIC

OCEAN

MAZATLAN

Monterrey area

Main force - Taylor via Matamoros.

Secondary force - Wool via Paras,
detachment to Victoria; arrived
Dec. 29, 1846

One section proceeded to Tampico to
join Scott, the remainder left Victoria on
Jan. 16, 1847 and returned to Monterrey

◄══ AMERICAN ATTACKS

◄── MEXICAN MOVEMENTS

•─■─•─■ U.S./MEXICO BOUNDARY, FEBRUARY 1846

•─│─•─│ U.S./MEXICO BOUNDARY, 1848

☐ TERRITORY GAINED BY U.S.

0   MILES   500
0   KILOMETERS   800

**1846
U.S. Navy
(via Cape Horn)**

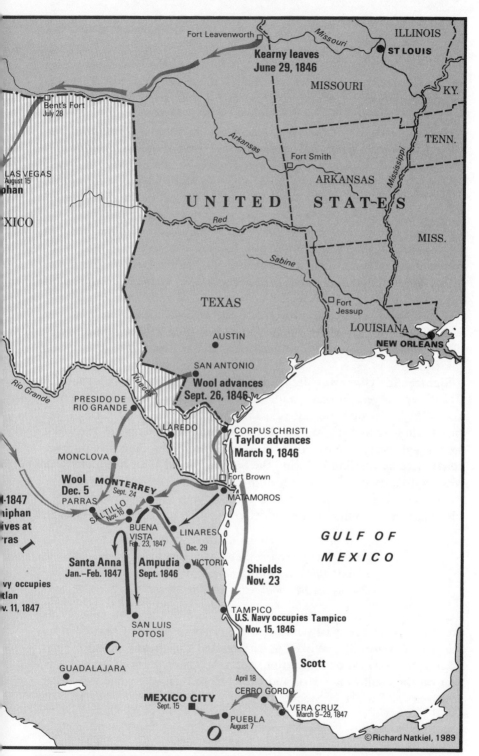

The war with Mexico involved two distinct and critical naval campaigns as well as many land battles. Defeated Mexico lost 40 percent of its territory, and the United States became a Continental nation.

would have been laudable. Unfortunately for Jones, the newspaper report was baseless; and though Mexican officials made light of the affair, it was not the sort of thing from which Jones could walk away whistling. If his guess had been right, he would have been a hero; instead, he was relieved of his command. But this was only temporary, more a matter of form than a disgrace: He was quickly given another command, and if his action had been premature, he was not going against naval hopes or national hopes.

Wilkes's expedition was designed to be "useful to the Navy, honorable to the Country, and highly advantageous to the commercial interests." It had succeeded in every respect, and its message was underlined by a further naval initiative. Shortly before Jones volunteered his own form of diplomacy in California, Commodore Lawrence Kearney, in *Constellation,* learned in Hong Kong that Britain had just obtained trading rights with China. Like Jones, Kearney felt disinclined to let them get away with it. Unlike Jones, he used a skillful combination of conciliation, boldness, and an already good relationship with the local Chinese viceroy to put the U.S. case for equal treatment. When Kearney left for home late in 1842, he knew the treaty was assured, and its ratification followed quickly.

Eighteen forty-two was altogether a bonanza year for the still youthful U.S. Navy—a year of many and varied achievements of which the fleet would long be proud. In that year the English poet Arthur Clough was only twenty-three years old and had not yet written his poem "Say Not the Struggle Naught Availeth." Winston Churchill brought it to international fame by quoting it during the Second World War; but in 1842 in Washington, as people thought and dreamed of Texas, California, the Pacific, and beyond, the men of the U.S. Navy—indeed, probably the whole nation—would have responded powerfully to the poem's last lines:

> *And not by eastern windows only,*
> *When daylight comes, comes in the light;*
> *In front the sun climbs slow, how slowly—*
> *But westward, look: the land is bright.*[12]

There was a continent of promise out there to the west—if only its existing owners could be persuaded to part with it—and beyond it an ocean of opportunity. Wilkes had suggested the dream; Kearney had taken a step toward its realization. Soon, ap Catesby Jones would reappear on the California coast; and even before then, the stage was being prepared for Robert F. Stockton.

13

*

WE WILL GREET YOU WITH BLOODY HANDS

*I*n 1825, on behalf of the United States, John Quincy Adams offered
to buy from Mexico that part of its territory lying between the Sabine
River and the Rio Grande: an area known as Texas. The offer was
refused, and refused once again when President Jackson repeated it. But
Mexico encouraged Americans to settle the land, and by 1834 twenty
thousand lived there with two thousand black slaves. Altogether there
were four times as many Americans in the region as there were native
Mexicans; but in 1831 Mexico abolished slavery in all its provinces. The
institution was allowed to continue de facto in Texas until 1835, when
President Antonio López de Santa Anna abolished it outright—and
thereupon the resident Americans, following the example of their forebears with regard to Britain, proclaimed themselves independent. Defending that independence, two hundred of them died in the Battle of the
Alamo, but many hundreds more, attracted by the new government's
land grants, flocked over the border from the States.

On his last day in office (March 3, 1837), at the same time as he publicly
recognized the United States' need for a navy, President Jackson gave
political recognition to the new republic. So did France and Britain.
Nobody was surprised that Mexico did not.

The Texans would have accepted immediate annexation into the
United States. For the time being, however, that option was precluded by
the United States themselves, where slavery was beginning to be a conten-

tious political issue. In 1820 a balance of slave and free states had been
struck within the Union. In the late 1830s, the possible annexation of
Texas, which was large enough to be divided into several states, threatened to upset the balance. Existing free states feared the new lands might
remain slave-owning but hoped they might renounce slavery, while existing slave states hoped and feared the exact opposite. And so matters
stood, in very simplified form, when in October 1843 U.S.S. *Princeton*
completed her first trials under the command of Commodore Robert F.
Stockton.

Remembered today as the conqueror of California, where the town of
Stockton is named after him, Robert F. Stockton described himself as "an
American—a straight-out American," and the description was good.[1] A
painting and a daguerreotype of him exist, both done about 1845. As one
would expect, the painting is rather more flattering, but both images show
a man recognizably of the Victorian period. He wears a dark double-
breasted coat with high collar, a shirt with a standing collar, and a dark
cravat tied around the neck; but it is the head and face which convey the
period more. His face is long and rectangular, his nose aristocratically
aquiline, his jaw very firm. In the painting his eyes look mild and his
mouth is gentle; in the daguerreotype, his lips are firmly pressed together
and his eyes stare sternly at the photographer. And in both he has a
magnificent set of muttonchop whiskers—all told, the very image of a
high-minded gentleman of the Victorian era, possessed of a sure knowledge of himself, his world, and his place in it.

No less should have been expected of him. His grandfather had been
a signatory to the Declaration of Independence; his father, known as the
"Old Duke," had been a friend of George Washington and of "god-like"
Daniel Webster; his family was one of the wealthiest and most influential
in New Jersey.

Robert himself contributed materially to the family fortune by establishing, with the Stevens family (the originators of the Stevens Battery),
a monopoly on canal and railroad transport in New Jersey. While doing
this he showed great interest in steam power, and it was he who arranged
the construction of the world's first screw-propelled steam warship,
Princeton. The ship was experimental, of course, and Stockton was careful to absolve her designer, the Swede John Ericsson, of any credit:
Stockton believed such vessels would change history, and he saw clearly
his own place in that process. Equally clearly he saw his countrymen's
place: "a distinctive element of their nationality," he maintained, was that
they formed "one CHRISTIAN NATION."

This, he said, was the reason why "the only country which enjoys
Republican Government, and whose people adequately appreciate free

institutions, is the United States. . . . In our hands alone is the precious deposit. Before God and the world, we are responsible for the legacy. Not for our benefit only, but for the benefit of the whole family of man."[2] It followed that where other countries were concerned, the United States had "an indisputable and perfect right to interfere whenever, by such interference, she can promote her own interests and advance the cause of liberty."[3]

Wealthy, influential, pious, ambitious, and nationalistic, Robert Stockton was indeed a man of his time, his class, and his country, a man who wished to cast history in his own mold and who was sure that everyone would benefit thereby, whether they wanted to or not. But it is unlikely he ever imagined he would have quite such a direct effect as he did on February 28, 1844, when he managed to blow up the secretary of the Navy and the secretary of State.

Stockton had invited President Tyler on board *Princeton* for a demonstration river trip, to show off both the vessel and her 12-inch smoothbore guns named "Oregon" and "Peacemaker." "The big guns of the *Princeton* can be fired with an effect terrible and almost incredible," he had written to Naval Secretary David Henshaw, adding that "the improvements in the art of war adopted on board *Princeton* may be productive of more important results than anything that has occurred since the invention of gunpowder."[4]

Stockton's assessment was not far wrong. But having accepted the invitation, Henshaw had a lucky escape, for nine days before the demonstration trip, he was replaced as naval secretary by Thomas W. Gilmer. Thus it was Gilmer who died when (after several successful firings) one of the big guns exploded. The dead secretary of state was Abel P. Upshur, ex–naval secretary; before he was blown up in the accident, the last official business he had been involved in was negotiating for the annexation of Texas.

Replacing Upshur as secretary of state, John C. Calhoun was told by ex-President Jackson that "Texas must not be lost." If it were, Jackson believed that "of necessity" it would be lost to Britain and that American emigration to California would then be stopped.[5] On April 12, 1844, barely six weeks after the deaths in *Princeton*, Calhoun signed a treaty of annexation with the Texans. Three days later the new naval secretary, John Y. Mason, ordered the Home Squadron under Commodore David Conner to concentrate in the Gulf of Mexico as a deterrent to any Mexican attack against the new member of the Union; but on June 8, by a vote of 35 to 16, the Senate refused to ratify the treaty, precisely because it feared a war with Mexico might result. The campaign for the next presidential election was just beginning, and at once the annexation question became a central issue.

President Tyler decided to place the matter before Congress again, this time requiring only a joint resolution for its ratification. The difference meant that instead of the two-thirds majority he had already failed to win, he now needed only a simple majority. On February 28, 1845, it was obtained, and on March 1, Tyler signed the resolution. But considering that most voters in the subsequent presidential election favored annexation, it was ironic that Tyler was not reelected. In his political career he had already switched parties twice, with the net result that now neither party wanted him; and the man who came in as president on March 4, strongly in favor of annexation, was James K. Polk.

Thus, although many people did not realize it, the background was set for a new round of U.S. expansion. "Who *is* James K. Polk?" his opponents would ask with mingled contempt and confusion. It was a good question, for he was the first "dark horse" president of the United States, someone risen from obscurity to occupy the White House. Just under fifty years of age when he came to power, he was a man with a thin, sad, serious face and an ambitious, sly, secretive character; and more than most presidents, he was a man for the moment.

Many years later, his secretary of the Navy, George Bancroft (a prominent historian) recorded Polk's four "great measures," the objectives of his administration. They were: "one, a reduction in the tariff; another, the independent treasury; a third, the settlement of the Oregon boundary question; and, lastly, the acquisition of California."[6] Polk achieved all four, the first three coming in 1846 through normal legal congressional procedures. California was more tricky. Mexico would not sell the land, and after Texas accepted annexation on July 4, 1845, Mexico cut off diplomatic connections with the United States. But if California could not be bought, it could be won in war. The question was how to start a war that could be made to look legitimate.

On the day Tyler won his joint resolution to annex Texas (February 28, 1845), his last naval secretary, John Mason, ordered Commodore Robert Stockton to take *Princeton* and three other vessels on a transatlantic cruise. Stockton did not refuse, but he did not go. Throughout the presidential campaign, he had actively supported Polk's candidacy, naturally sharing the territorial wishes of the president-elect. It did not take much to delay departure until the new president could provide more interesting orders, and on April 2 they came: The commodore was to take his squadron to the Gulf of Mexico.

On May 12, he arrived at Galveston, where he contacted Maj. Gen. Sidney Sherman, chief officer of the Texas militia, and Anson Jones. The acceptance of annexation was still a few weeks away, and for the time being Jones was still president of the republic. Stockton had an unusual proposition, which he made in a suitably roundabout way. Rather than visit Jones personally, he sent his secretary, Dr. Wright, who "took three days," the Texan president wrote later, "in unfolding to me the object of their visit."[7] It could be stated in three sentences: First, Jones should authorize Sherman to raise an army of at least two thousand men; second, they should attack, capture, and hold the Mexican town of Matamoros; third, Stockton and his ships would provide protection, provisions, arms, munitions, transport, and pay for the Army.

Dr. Wright added that President Polk "did not want to be known in the matter, but approved Com. Stockton's plan." Without pussyfooting, President Jones said to the doctor and General Sherman: "So, gentlemen, the Commodore, on the part of the United States, wishes me *to manufacture a war* for them," and the object of the war would be to gain control of California. Exactly, replied his guests; whereupon Jones stalled. A few days later he recieved another visitor with news he had expected: Britain's minister to Texas, Charles Elliot, returned from Mexico with Mexican acknowledgement of Texan independence. With that information, said Jones, *"One word* settled Com. Stockton's business, and I assured him I never had the least idea of *manufacturing a war for the United States.* Soon after which he left our waters and sailed for the Pacific in search of the same *un*pacific object which brought him to Texas."

Stockton's part in this attempted subterfuge is a matter of record, but President Polk's is not, except for circumstantial evidence. To this day historians are still divided into those who see Stockton's action as an independent initiative, quite in character with the man, and those who see it as one half of a conspiracy with Polk. But whichever is true, it makes little difference. The two men were of like mind. If a war could not be manufactured with the help of Anson Jones, there were other ways.

Simultaneously a plot of another sort altogether was in progress on the East Coast. While Stockton was down in Texas attempting to make Jones into an agent provocateur, Naval Secretary George Bancroft was completing a very neat, and much more constructive, sleight of hand. To avoid the steamy heat of the Washington summer, Congress was in recess. Among many other politicians the secretary of war left the capital; but Bancroft stayed and temporarily took over the secretary of war's duties in addition to his own. As mentioned earlier, Bancroft was a historian. Perhaps because of that, he valued education highly and for a long time had been very bothered by the limited schooling on offer to young naval officers. He knew what he wanted to do about it; the problem was that he needed the agreement of the secretary of war. The solution presented itself in the summer of 1845—a simple, brilliant idea, which only required him to move fast.

The (acting) secretary of war and the naval secretary—both Bancroft—

were in complete agreement with each other. In the absence of Congress, Acting Secretary of War Bancroft gave Naval Secretary Bancroft control of a group of Army buildings in the small riverside town of Annapolis, Maryland. Thanking the acting secretary of war, Naval Secretary Bancroft then shifted the temporary, ill-equipped Philadelphia Naval School to Annapolis, directed returning midshipmen to report there, and installed five instructors. To soften the shock for Congress's return, he also fired most of the Philadelphian instructors, thereby saving $30,000 a year. On its return, Congress blinked a little at the changes, saw that they were good, and voted that the thirty thousand dollars saved should be used to improve the new school.

As simply as that, the decades of argument over a permanent school for naval officers were resolved; and of course, the U.S. Naval Academy is still there, still producing the young officers of the future, as it has done for a century and a half. Navies the world over seem to have a knack of choosing lovely places in which to train their aspiring leaders (Etajima in Japan, Dartmouth in England), and Annapolis does not fall short. The town, compact and charming with its brick-paved streets and brick and timber houses, leads to a small, attractive harbor and on to the campus of the academy itself. There, on the banks of the River Severn, the shaded lawns, the paths, and the elegant buildings, both old and modern, seem to a visitor to complement perfectly the training activities on the water; while in the library one may work indefinitely without running short of resources. Indoors and outdoors it hums with life and action; or if one needs a spell of peaceful reflection, then in the crypt of the chapel lies the body of John Paul Jones; and beyond the playing fields, across the water in the quiet, well-tended cemetery, there are other famous names. For anyone interested in navies past or future, it is altogether a most agreeable place to be—small wonder, then, that the famous dead choose to be brought back there, and the less famous young still compete to enter.

Bancroft's act of swift legerdemain was a great blessing to the U.S. Navy, and though very constructive was, in its deviousness, typical of the Polk administration. The president always maintained that his intentions toward Mexico were peaceable. But even his apologists, taking his words at face value, acknowledge that deviousness was James K. Polk's main characteristic; and naturally, after thirty years of peace, Polk would not suggest a deliberate intention to start a war. Nevertheless, the immediate cause of the Mexican-American War of 1846–47 was President Polk's order to Gen. Zachary Taylor to enter Mexican territory.

On January 13, 1846, Taylor was ordered to cross the Nueces River— which for a hundred years had been accepted as the southern boundary of Texas—and advance to the north bank of the Rio Grande, which was definitely in Mexico. He did so and blockaded the town of Matamoros on the Rio Grande's south bank; so it was scarcely surprising when on April 25 a skirmish took place between his forces and those of Matamoros, with some casualties. American blood had been spilled, which was all that was needed for the United States to declare war against Mexico on May 11.

"In going to war," wrote Secretary of State James Buchanan that day, "we did not do so with a view to acquire either California or New Mexico or any other portion of the Mexican territory."[8] This was in a draft letter to American ministers and consuls; but before Polk allowed the letter to be sent, he made Buchanan delete the reference to California. He wanted the place.

By virtue of geography, Polk's Central American war was mainly a land war. But on both geographical sides of the land war, naval wars took place in the Gulf of Mexico and off the coasts of California and western Mexico. The battles in those opposing waters were as different in their conduct as in their locations.

In the Gulf of Mexico, Commodore David Conner was in charge of everything except his face—he had a facial neuralgia, causing him intermittent but intense pain. Having fought in the War of 1812, he knew there would be no memorable sea battles in the war he now had to lead, because Mexico had only two warships of any worth, and at the start of hostilities, both had been transferred to the British merchant fleet. "The Navy in this war will I fear have few opportunities for distinction," he wrote to his wife. "Mexico presents scarcely anything assailable but the castle of San Juan D'Ulloa, and that would be as little affected by our shot as Mount Ararat."[9] His instructions from Bancroft confirmed this: The squadron would "blockade the principal Mexican ports, protect our commerce from the depredations of privateers, assist the operations of our army, and lead to the earliest adjustment of our difficulties with Mexico."[10]

During the first nine months of the war, the only part of this not very exciting program that Conner was able to put into effect was the blockade. Although the Mexican government offered letters of marque to its own and foreign merchantmen, few were taken up, and privateers were never a problem. Many months also passed before the U.S. Army was in a position to need naval assistance; but securing and maintaining the blockade was far from easy. The still inexperienced bureaus in Washington (especially the bureau of "destruction and despair") had no idea of how to keep a constant flow of food, water, ammunition, and medicine to the ships. Apart from his own ailment, Conner had to try and cope with outbreaks in the squadron of scurvy, malaria, and yellow fever—the last sickness known to the Mexicans by the vivid name of "black vomit."

Added to that, when the fever season passed in October, the storm season began. From then until April, shipping in the Gulf could be hit at any time by a "norther," a full gale blowing from the Texas coast, with driving rain, waves over 20 feet high, and winds approaching 50 miles an hour. The signs foretelling a norther were so variable and indefinite that there was, in practice, no warning.

Merely keeping ships on station was, in short, an achievement in itself. The squadron exercised the same kind of sea control as the Royal Navy had done off the American coasts during the Revolution and the War of 1812, and off the French coasts during the Napoleonic Wars; and they were discovering that a great part of naval power involved tedious, arduous, and unspectacular duties. This was not the sort of work which could easily sustain morale; nor, to a public expecting flair and dash, did it appear particularly useful, especially in contrast to the Army's more thrilling exploits. "The Navy should do something," said one of Conner's colleagues, "which will answer to make newspaper noise."[11]

In November 1846 plans for that something were put into motion: an amphibious landing operation in which the Army and Navy would cooperate to capture the coastal town and castle of Veracruz, 220 miles east of Mexico City. Once that was done, the Army would march on the capital. The whole idea was proposed by Gen. Winfield Scott. Working out that 14,000 men would need to be put ashore, Scott soon realized that landing such a force would be no slight thing. Nothing of that magnitude had ever been attempted by U.S. forces before—indeed, until Gallipoli in 1915, no country tried such a large invasion again, and Americans did not take part in a larger one until the invasion of North Africa in 1942. Thus, when Scott and Conner got together in early March 1847, they set a precedent, a world record that would last for sixty-eight years and an American one unbeaten for ninety-five years.

A key part of the operation were the craft devised for the landings, the first ever made in the United States for such a purpose. Scott called them surfboats; averaging thirty-seven feet long, they were designed to fit inside one another when loaded in transports. Quickly built, of light construction, they were wide, flat-bottomed, and double-ended. Each had a crew of eight and carried about forty men; using sixty-four of these little vessels, Scott and Conner landed approximately nine thousand soldiers near Veracruz in one day (March 9, 1847) without a single boat or a single life being lost.

Landings of supplies and further troops continued for the next ten days. "Everything," the general wrote, "of course must be landed in surfboats, and from an average distance of more than a mile, on the open beach of the sea. Commodore Conner's squadron is indefatigable in assisting us."[12] But on March 20, halfway through the one visible success of his command in the Gulf, the squadron was Conner's no longer. That afternoon the steamer *Mississippi* arrived with fresh orders and a fresher man than the sick commodore; and at eight the following morning, Conner made a signal to his fleet: COMMODORE PERRY COMMANDS THE SQUADRON.

Conner had overstayed the time allotted for his job, and just before *Mississippi* arrived he had written to his wife saying he would soon apply for a relief; but all the same, he was disappointed not to be able to see the attack through. However, Perry did bring extra vigor to the operation, and was welcomed: "Cheer after cheer went up," a junior officer remembered in later years. "Under the energetic chief who succeeded to the command . . . the navy of the United States sustained its old prestige."[13]

Within a couple more days the army onshore had risen to 13,000. Big shell-firing guns were removed from the warships, ferried ashore (a delicate and risky operation), and remounted in a combined battery. On March 24 they opened fire; at 5 P.M. next day a flag of truce flew over Veracruz; two days later the city surrendered; and at 1 P.M. on March 29—only ten days after his arrival—Perry penned a message to the secretary of the Navy. "I write this from within the castle," he said. "The batteries in the city are now saluting the American flags already hoisted on the forts of the city."[14]

With the possible exception of Conner, it was an exhilarating moment for all Americans concerned. Only fourteen of their number had died, with fifty-nine wounded. Mexican military casualties were about the same; unfortunately, the civilians suffered more, with a hundred deaths. But Veracruz was Mexico's second city, and its capture opened the way to the capture of Mexico City itself, six months later; and General Scott happily acknowledged his indebtedness to "the entire Home Squadron, under the successive orders of Commodores Conner and Perry, for prompt, cheerful and able assistance from the arrival of the army off this coast."[15]

The capture of Veracruz was not the end of the war in the Gulf, but it was the most important single event there—not least because, in an army and navy that lacked a unified command or any close coordination in Washington, it was an example of Army-Navy cooperation of which any country would have been proud. And it made all the more noticeable the lack of cooperation between the forces in California.

Like Conner, Commodore John D. Sloat of the Pacific Squadron was a sick man. He was also an extremely cautious man, and although he had orders dating from June 1845 to take San Francisco and blockade other ports as soon as he knew war had begun, he remembered the precipitate action of Thomas ap Catesby Jones. Communication between Washington and California was, naturally, even more difficult than between Washington and the Gulf. Thus it was not until June 8, 1846, over three weeks after he first learned of the skirmish on the Rio Grande, that Sloat decided he ought to do something; and it was a further month before he made up his mind what to do. On July 7, without opposition, he took Monterey, which was within his orders, and announced the annexation of California, which was not. Two days later, again without opposition, his ships seized San Francisco. It was all much easier than he had expected, but he was still not convinced he was meant to be doing it; so when the forty-four-gun frigate *Congress* arrived at Monterey on July 15, Sloat breathed a sigh of relief. The frigate contained Commodore Robert F. Stockton, and Sloat was determined to hand over command as soon as possible.

He did so in two stages, transferring shore operations to Stockton on July 23, and six days later the entire command. And with the transfer, the period of peaceful conquest ended. Mexican Californians began organized resistance; Stockton countered willingly, and in his public pronouncements overturned Sloat's earlier conciliatory approach. On August 13 he occupied Los Angeles, an undefended town of fifteen hundred people. By then Mexican governance of California had ceased. Stockton set about establishing a civilian government, with elections arranged for September 15, and prepared to seize Acapulco as a springboard for an attack on Mexico City. However, before the end of the month, his Los Angeles garrison of less than fifty men was thrown out of town. Fighting continued in a variety of locations up and down the coast over the next few weeks, led partly by Stockton and partly by a lieutenant of the U.S. Army Topographical Corps, John C. Frémont. Already well known as an explorer, Frémont was named governor of California by Stockton; and then early in December, after a march of six hundred miles from Santa Fe in New Mexico, Brig. Gen. Stephen W. Kearny entered California from the east.

Individually, and in their own ways, the three officers were effective warriors. Collectively they were a disgrace, and if there had been any continuing resistance in California, they would have been a disaster as well. Kearny insisted that only he had the authority to establish a civilian government; Stockton refused to accept this, announcing that he would request Kearny's recall; and Frémont (an Army lieutenant) informed General Kearny that he would obey only the naval commodore's orders. The degrading quarrel was resolved only by the arrival on January 22, 1847, of Commodore Branford Shubrick at Monterey. Senior to all of them, he banged heads together sufficiently to bring an end to the unseemly dispute.

Despite it, though, California had been conquered and subdued in a little over six months. During March 1847 (just as Conner, Scott, and Perry were battering Veracruz), Shubrick divided the Army and Navy areas of responsibility in California and its gulf in the obvious way: The Army took shore control, which placed the problem of government squarely in Kearny's lap, while the Navy organized customs and port regulations. Having sorted that out, Shubrick conducted a steady, businesslike campaign of blockade (from July 1847 to May 1848) down lower California and the west coast of Mexico.

Meanwhile, through the summer of 1847, General Scott advanced on Mexico City from Veracruz, and on September 17 accepted the capital's surrender. Autumn and winter passed before negotiations between the warring republics were concluded, and in both the Gulf of Mexico and the Pacific, ships of the U.S. Navy remained on station. At last, on February 2, 1848, the Treaty of Guadalupe Hidalgo brought the end of the war in sight. On March 10 the treaty was ratified in Washington, and fifteen days later in Mexico. It took two full months for official confirmation of the end of hostilities to reach Commodore Perry, and a further fortnight for the same news to reach the Pacific coast. And when it did, an ironic episode took place. Before Thomas ap Catesby Jones's premature capture of Monterey in 1842, there had been a distant possibility that California might be sold to the United States, as Louisiana had been in 1803. Though politely shrugged off by local officials, Jones's precipitate action made the distant possibility a definite impossibility; and that, coupled with President Polk's determination to possess the state, was one of the root causes of the war. Jones, of course, had been relieved of his command. But on May 6, 1848, he returned to take it up again; and so it fell to him to bring the war in California to an official end.

Even in the victorious nation, the war in all its aspects—its beginning, its conduct, and its effects—was far from universally popular. While it was still in progress, the House of Representatives voted that it had been started unconstitutionally. Thomas Corwin of Ohio declared: "If I were a Mexican, I would tell you, 'Have you not room in your own country to bury your dead men? If you come into mine we will greet you with bloody hands, and welcome you to hospitable graves.' "[16]

The representative from Illinois, a young man named Abraham Lincoln, said of Polk: "He is deeply conscious of being in the wrong. . . . The President is in no wise satisfied with his own positions. . . . He is a bewildered, confounded and miserably perplexed man."[17]

And many years after it was all over, a young lieutenant of the Mexican war wrote that "even if the annexation itself [of Texas] could be justified, the manner in which the subsequent war was forced upon Mexico cannot."[18] It was, he added, "one of the most unjust ever waged by a stronger against a weaker nation"; and although he was writing thirty-seven years after the event, the comments are worth noting, for the writer was Ulysses S. Grant, eighteenth president of the United States.

As for the cost of the war, rather less than two thousand Americans had died in action or from their wounds. There had been over eleven thousand deaths from disease and over nine thousand desertions. In financial terms, direct costs amounted to about $58 million; decades later, a further $64 million went in pensions; and under the peace treaty, America paid Mexico $15 million for ceded lands. From that point of view it was a bargain. American possession of Texas was confirmed down to the Rio Grande; Upper California, including San Diego, was confirmed; and joining the two together, New Mexico (which covered today's Arizona as well) also became U.S. territory. Altogether the war added over half a million square miles to the United States, at a total cost of 48 cents an acre; and on January 22, 1848, eleven days before the peace treaty was signed, gold was found in California. No thought was given to any oil or gas; those riches would come later. But in the first decade of the forty-niners, over $550 million worth of gold came from their mines.

When thinking of the California gold rush, one should not imagine a tidal wave of pent-up population gratefully released to new, essential lands: the total U.S. population was only 20 million, and with the Oregon boundary settlement added in, Polk's administration extended the nation's area by 750,000 square miles. Overall, therefore, it was hardly crowded, but some people did not want to stop—Robert Stockton for one advocated the annexation of all Mexico, a call which Polk's vice president, George M. Dallas, echoed when he imagined "a more perfect Union, embracing the entire North American continent."[19] Of course, it did not go that far in the end; but the incredibly rapid physical expansion produced a profound double-edged effect on the American psyche, the foundation of all American dreams.

One effect was the new and enormous freedom open to all. The nation covered the continent from one ocean to the other, "from sea to shining sea"; it was immense, untrammelled, beautiful. The great truths justified and made real the legends: Nowhere else on the globe could a man find such liberty. In the new, half-lawless lands of the West he could challenge opportunity as nowhere else, without hindrance of inheritance. With the exception of Alaska (purchased from Russia in 1867 for $7.2 million), Polk's administration brought the continental United States to its present-day area, with a population less than a tenth the size of today's. Putting it simply, between one shining sea and the other there was an awful lot of land and not many people.

The other effect (obvious when one thinks of it) was that finding themselves possessed of more land than they knew what to do with—finding also that those lands were richly productive and infinitely varied—Americans turned their energies toward the land and away from the sea. Except for those living on the coastal fringes (the fringes which, only seventy-five years before, had been the whole of the nation) the sea became a backdrop—to some, a thing viewed only for beauty; to many, a thing only imagined or remembered; and to most, a thing neither seen nor thought of at all. Only to a very small proportion was the sea still a daily part of their working lives.

At the same time, although the Navy had worked more than adequately in the recent war and had done all the things a navy should, it had had so little direct opposition that it had missed out on glamour, publicity, and popular successes. In those areas the Army had scooped the pool to the extent that President Polk's successor was Gen. Zachary Taylor, who first led troops onto Mexican soil. And when writers like Richard Henry Dana and Herman Melville wrote of life at sea, even the most romantic landsman learned that under the graceful sails of a great ship, life was hard, tough, and completely unromantic. Dana's *Two Years Before the Mast* came out in 1840, Melville's *White Jacket* in 1850 and *Moby Dick* in 1851. Dana's book contained one brief, self-censored but particularly lively picture of a captain whose crew asked for larger bread rations:

> He clenched his fist, stamped and swore, and ordered us all forward, saying, with oaths enough interspersed to send the words home, "Away with you! Go forward every one of you! I'll *haze* you! I'll work you up! You don't have enough to do! If you a'n't careful I'll make a hell of heaven! . . . You've mistaken your man! I'm Frank Thompson, all the way from 'down east.' I've been through the mill, ground and bolted, and come out a 'regular-built down-east johnnycake'—when it's hot, it's d———d good, but when it's cold, it's d———d sour and indigestible, and you'll find me so!"[20]

Melville hardly improved the picture: "When I go to sea," he wrote, "I go as a simple sailor, right before the mast, plumb down into the forecastle, aloft there to the royal masthead. True, they rather order me about, and make me jump from spar to spar, like a grasshopper in a May meadow. And at first, this sort of thing is unpleasant enough. It touches one's sense of honor . . ."

A sense of honor was something every American could feel, and the implication of Melville's words seemed clear: At sea, you sacrificed free will. But in the woods, mountains, plains, and deserts, you were your own man, able to rise or fall according to your own strength and effort.

Merchant sea life paled in comparison, and the Navy was dull hand-maiden to the more glamorous forces on and of the land.

This antipathy to the sea was not what Melville meant to convey. "What of it," he asked, "if some old hunks of a sea-captain orders me to get a broom and sweep down the decks? What does that indignity amount to, weighed, I mean, in the scales of the New Testament? Who is not a slave? Tell me that."[21]

From any but the most philosophical reader, the answer would have been: Not me, for one. Personal freedom, the touchstone of all things American, was given its greatest single boost by the U.S. victory in the war against Mexico. And curiously, Melville's backhanded praise of a seaman's way of life touched on the most sensitive legacy of that war—the question of what *kind* of society should be permitted in the newly won lands. Should they be slave states or free? *We will welcome you with bloody hands. . . .* In settling that question, more blood than anyone could imagine would be spilled, and the navies of both North and South would adventure in ways undreamed of.

14

*

SHOCKS, AND THROES, AND CONVULSIONS

*D*uring the first half of the nineteenth century, slavery and slaving were issues which bore directly upon the U.S. Navy in several ways. In 1808 Congress outlawed the transatlantic slave trade with Africa. In 1817 the American Colonization Society was formed to promote the repatriation of free blacks to Africa. Working with the society, both Robert Stockton and Matthew Perry had been instrumental in the creation of Liberia, the land of free slaves—indeed, Perry chose the site of its capital, Monrovia, named after President Monroe. In 1820 Congress declared transatlantic slaving to be piracy, punishable by death, and in the same year the Missouri Compromise gave a temporary solution to what already promised to become an intractable problem.

This "compromise" accepted that a line at latitude 36 degrees 30 minutes north (that is, the northern borders of North Carolina, Tennessee, and Arkansas) should be the dividing line between thirteen slave states to the south and thirteen free states to the north. Before then, when confronted with the question, the southern states had usually defended their "peculiar institution" (as they themselves called it) with an air of apology, describing it as an arrangement essential for their economic well-being. But through the 1820s and '30s, after the Compromise, that attitude gradually gave way to an ever more vigorous and muscular defiance; and since illegal transatlantic slaving still continued, the U.S. Navy's African Squadron was formed in 1843, to protect ordinary American trade there and to suppress the trade in humans. Matthew Perry was the squadron's first commodore.

It was not only off the coasts of Africa that the Navy encountered slavery. In Rio de Janeiro, a young New Yorker came ashore from the seventy-four-gun liner *Delaware,* active in the Brazil–South Atlantic Squadron, and recorded his impressions. "Upon landing, a stranger from a non-slave-owning country is struck with the singular appearance of the negro population," he wrote.[1] "The whole labour of bearing and moving burdens is performed by these people, and the state in which they appear is revolting to humanity. Here was a number of beings entirely naked, with the exception of a covering of dirty rags, tied about their waists; their skins from constant exposure to the weather had become hard, crusty and seamed. . . . Some were chained by the necks and legs, and moved with loads thus encumbered. Some followed each other in ranks, with heavy weights on their heads, chattering the most inarticulate and dismal cadence as they moved along."

But the same young man noted that there was one very big difference in South American slavery, compared with that of his homeland. In Brazil, though a black slave "was far lower than other animals of burden" he noticed that in Rio there were also black soldiers, citizens, and priests. A typical soldier was "clean and neat in appearance, amenable to discipline, expert in exercise"; a typical citizen was "remarkable for the respectability of his appearance, and the perfect decorum of his manners," while a typical priest "seemed in a certain degree superior to, and more devout in his impressions, than his white associates."

This nineteen-year-old with the sharp eye and active pen was called Daniel Noble Johnson. His position in *Delaware* was special, with some privileges: He was a clerk, and he wrote a bright, lively, entertaining journal of his three years "on the Brazils." He was writing in the early 1840s, but a decade later life at sea had not changed very much; and it is worth leaving behind the expansive, potentially explosive land of the early 1850s for a short voyage through his journal: It shows much of life and death and attitudes in a peacetime sailing navy.

Monday, Novr. 1st 1841—At 8 a.m. all hands were called to up anchor, and at 11 a.m. we got underweigh and stood out of the Roads on our destined station. Our ship's company mounted the rigging and gave three hearty cheers as we passed the *Constitution,* which was returned by the crew of that ship, but with what different feelings must they have regarded this interchange of good wishes. They had just returned, while we were departing to undergo the same deprivation of the society of our nearest and dearest friends for perhaps three long years, and how many of our shipmates may during our ensuing cruise be laid low . . .[2]

To any modern sailor, that moment at the start of a long voyage is still recognizable—a mixture of excitement, some foreboding, and a little homesickness. And then as now, it was not confined to the junior crew members—Stephen C. Rowan, who took possession of San Diego in the Mexican War, was first lieutenant in the eighteen-gun sloop *Cyane* when he wrote:

> At sundown discharged the Pilot and took one last look at the shores of the Old Dominion. . . . This separating from home—from the dearest object of our affections; the uprooting of every enduring domestic tie is terrible beyond description. . . . Trusting in that Divine Providence that guards the fall of a Sparrow, I humbly hope to be restored to my country, to my family and friends, and to the dear partner of my joys, with honor to myself and credit to the corps of which I am a member.[3]

But junior or senior, such open and poignant expression of emotion stayed where it belonged—in the pages of a private journal, to be read and recognized only by later eyes. Once at sea, there were other priorities; and for most people, the first of these was getting one's sea legs. Two days out, young Johnson noted that "our quarter deck and mizzen chains made a ludicrous appearance today, having been crowded since we left the capes with sea-sick reefers [midshipmen], clerks, secretaries, &c." Two days after that, when "a smart gale" hit these young men, "there was considerable confusion in getting aloft." From the officer of the deck came a stream of furious orders: " 'Stand by to furl the Royals and top gallant sails.' 'Stand by the royal and top gallant halyards—Man the top gallant clue lines! Lay aloft there, you haymaking lubbers! Haul taut! In royals and top gallant sails! Move quick there, you lazy rascals, or I'll flog every soul of ye! Lay out and furl!' "

The threat of flogging was real in the U.S. Navy of the 1840s and earlier; the punishment was not abolished until 1850, and when it was, not only many officers but also many older seamen believed discipline would become impossible. Johnson watched flogging as a matter of course: "This morning all hands were called to witness punishment, and the culprits were brought up from the brig, and arranged, as usual in the starboard gangway, under the charge of the master at arms. There were two men who had been guilty of desertion, two for stealing, and one man who had been guilty of the revolting and degrading crime of sodomy." It seems a little odd that only one man was involved in the last "crime"; perhaps it was a homosexual rape. Whatever the case, Johnson believed the punishments were justified, since "our service has become so degraded." But flogging was not the worst risk sailors ran in peacetime.

"Among our merry, reckless host of apprentice boys, was one quiet, gentle boy of fifteen," Johnson wrote. Ordered one morning to his usual station at the top of a mast, the boy "left the deck and was seen to gain the top. A moment after, was heard one piercing shriek—a crash—and the mangled and bloody corpse of our young and beloved shipmate was stretched upon the deck—his brains literally besprinkling his fond associates. . . . He had broken his back in two different places, his neck was broken, and his skull shattered to atoms."

Death by accident or disease was frequent. In harbor, the body would be buried ashore; but

> there is something peculiarly melancholy and impressive in a burial at sea. There is no coffin or hearse, procession or tolling bell; nothing that gradually prepares us for the final separation. The body is wound in the drapery of its couch, much as if the deceased were only in a quiet and temporary sleep. In these habiliments it is dropped into the wave, the deep waters close over it, the vessel passes quickly on, and not a solitary trace is left to mark the spot. . . . There is nothing that can point to the deep, unvisited resting place of the departed Mariner.

Yet there were happier times as well, especially runs ashore in the extravagantly beautiful harbor of Rio; there Johnson and his friends "made a straight wake for the hospitable mansion of Monsieur Pharaux, where we partook of a splendid supper on what might be called the anti-temperate principle" and found company to sustain them in their bouts of homesickness. There were occasions ashore or afloat for music and dancing too; and before bidding farewell to Daniel Johnson, it is worth quoting in full one of his most vivid descriptions of life at sea—his entry for July 9, 1842, ending with something of the strange joy and poetry the ocean can inspire.

> We are getting along, towards our destined port, we have a good breeze and fine weather, which tends very much to make us light-hearted. For the last two or three evenings, the weather being fine, and the wind steady, our band have been stationed on the forecastle, and the men amused themselves by dancing. This elegant accomplishment, as it is generally termed, belongs of right; for without the least instruction, without ever having been taught a single figure, or step, or even told that he must stand upright and turn out his toes, he goes ahead, and keeps time with a precision and emphasis seldom met with in a saloon. There are with him, no studied bows, no mincing airs, nor simpering looks, no rivalries nor jealousies, significant nods, nor quarrels about positions, nor even partners; for if Lucy is engaged, Mary is not, and that is sufficient for him. He unships his tarpaulin, dashes into the ranks and bounds to the music

with an exulting life and heart. Nor is the presence of the tender sex, however desirable, indispensable to the sailor in his dances; for on the deck of his ship, and far away at sea, where woman may never have been, if a lip, or a lute, or a string make the music, he is ever ready to move to it with his quick step and vigorous limb. And he may sometimes be seen, when the winds are piping and frolicking through the shroud, keeping fantastic time to their wild notes.[4]

The frequency of flogging depended very much on the individual ship's commander. With some it was rare, although everyone used it from time to time; but rarest of all punishments for indiscipline was the ultimate— hanging from the yardarm.

During the 1840s there were two particularly important hangings. On September 17, 1846, in the early months of the Mexican War, Seaman Samuel Jackson was executed on Commodore Conner's order. His offense was twice knocking down an officer and using "mutinous and seditious words," and his death was designed to keep order by example in the morale-eroding blockade. Conner's decision was legitimate and caused little public criticism, but the cause of Jackson's offense was pathetic in the extreme: He had left a pair of shoes on deck and knocked the officer down after that gentleman kicked the shoes overboard.

The other case was, in its own way, even more unfortunate. This was the infamous mutiny in the brig *Somers,* late in 1842. Commanded by Master Commandant Alexander Slidell Mackenzie, finished, equipped and manned by Commodore Matthew Perry, the brand-new brig was to be used experimentally as a school ship for naval apprentices, and was on her maiden voyage from New York to West Africa when a conspiracy to mutiny was uncovered. The plot was to murder the officers and any crew who would not collaborate, after which the brig would be turned into a pirate ship and sailed to the Caribbean. Bearing in mind that the ringleader was only nineteen and that almost three quarters of the crew were younger, the plot sounded to the American public like an adolescent fantasy bred from reading too many novels. In part, it was just that; but it was also a deadly serious affair, carefully thought through, with a very fair chance of success: *Somers* was fast, and enough older, skilled sailors were involved to make the risks practicable. And because Mackenzie and his officers were sure there had been a "full and determined intention to commit a mutiny," on December 1 he sentenced the three prime conspirators to death.[5]

The executions were carried out the same day, and there the matter might well have ended, for by an act of Congress passed in 1800, "if any person in the navy shall make or attempt to make any mutinous assembly, he shall on pain of conviction thereof by a Court Martial, suffer death."[6]

But instead of ending there, it became a cause célèbre in America. One reason was that technically Mackenzie, though commanding officer, did not have the power to call a court-martial, and the council formed by his officers was therefore not a court-martial. The other reason was that the ringleader, Philip Spencer, was the son of the secretary of war.

On the return of *Somers* to New York, a naval court of inquiry was convened, and shortly afterward (at Mackenzie's request) a court-martial, to try him on charges of cruelty, illegal punishment, conduct unbecoming an officer, oppression, and murder. The news had created such a stir that this was the only way he felt he could clear his name; and suffice it here to say that, in a long and sorry business, he was cleared—acquitted of all charges. Yet though he was exonerated, it was not an affair of which he or his service could ever feel proud. Apart from Mackenzie himself, one of the officers most affected was Matthew Perry. He had been the one to assign *Somers* as a school ship; he had appointed Spencer to the crew. He had also appointed two of his own sons, one of his nephews, and Mackenzie, who was his brother-in-law. Such apparent nepotism was not unique; from the "family business" days of John Glover, Washington's first naval shipowner, the fleet had become a tradition in various families, which frequently intermarried—a factor which could be a great strength but on this occasion seemed a severe flaw. With Mackenzie, Perry's career and public image were dented—but not permanently. Happily, one can turn from these critical but exceptional episodes, leave them behind as a bad memory, and join Perry ten years later in the achievement which crowned both his long naval career and the history of the Navy in the 1850s.

He had never really wanted to go to Japan; he would have preferred the command of the Mediterranean Squadron. But the plain fact was that he was the best-qualified person available for this job—"Certainly the man for the navy," a fellow captain had written a few years before. "In many respects he is an astonishing man, the most industrious, hard working, persevering, enterprising officer of his rank in our navy. . . . His great powers of endurance astonish everyone; all know that he is by no means a brilliant man, but . . . respected and esteemed."[7] Another officer condensed this paean into an abstract but even more telling phrase—a ship "seemed to have a sense of importance because he was aboard."[8]

Nonetheless, the most important reason for choosing Perry was his formidable record as a naval diplomat. He had negotiated successfully in Turkey, Naples, Africa, and Mexico—as he himself wrote of the latter two, by "conciliating the good will and confidence of the conquered people, by administering the unrestricted power I held rather to their comfort and protection than to their annoyance."[9] In Japan, he believed the people "if treated with strict justice and gentle kindness, will render confidence for confidence, and . . . will learn to consider us their friends."[10]

Very well: He was setting out with an excellent attitude, giving a motto which modern diplomats could still hang above their desks and carve above their doors and take benefit thereby. But the magnitude of his task is more difficult for a modern mind to grasp. With the exception of the tiny island of Deshima off Nagasaki, where an enclave of Dutchmen were abasing themselves for the privilege of limited trade, the borders of Japan had been closed to the outside world since 1638. To foreigners, the country was simultaneously known and unknown: Except for the most ignorant in the West, most people were at least aware of its existence, but outside the most educated, few had any knowledge of its life or culture. In this way, although Perry's mission was primarily diplomatic, it was also an exploring expedition like the Wilkes voyage. The great difference was that whereas nobody lived in Antarctica, Perry knew well that Japan had had a civilized society centuries before his own country was even settled.

In the first half of the nineteenth century the number of Western contacts with Japan could be counted on two hands. From 1804 there was a series of heavy-handed Russian attempts to establish trade; in 1808 H.M.S. *Phaeton* extracted supplies by threat of bombardment; in 1832 an envoy en route for Siam and Muscat in U.S.S. *Peacock* died before reaching Japan; in 1837 an Anglo-American merchant ship was repelled by shore fire; in 1845 an American whaler managed to repatriate some shipwrecked Japanese fishermen; in 1846 U.S.S. *Columbus* under Commodore James Biddle anchored at the entrance to Tokyo Bay, achieving nothing but the status of a temporary tourist attraction; and in 1848, again by threat of bombardment, U.S.S. *Preble* managed to take some shipwrecked Americans off the islands.

The record of contact was therefore brief and discouraging, but from the available reports Perry learned as much as possible about Japan. One of the things he learned (from Comdr. James Glynn of *Preble*) was that the Japanese themselves had followed the progress of the Mexican War and had been deeply impressed by the Scott-Conner-Perry capture of Veracruz. At the same time some Japanese were learning of advances in Western weaponry, medicine, and other sciences. Smuggled books were the only source of such knowledge, and when looking for a modern parallel, smuggled Bibles and samizdat literature suggest the USSR. But in spite of the restrictions and rivalries between the USSR and the United States, there have been plenty of shared history, trade, and diplomatic exchange, so that parallel does not altogether work. Nor does the idea of comparing Perry's voyage to an interplanetary contact; that goes too far the other way to be exact.

In Perry's own day, the nearest comparison was with China, forced by the recent opium war with Great Britain to extend trading privileges to Western nations. There too an ancient civilization had been unwillingly joined to the modern world; but even that comparison was incomplete, for China had never closed itself off utterly—and unlike China, Japan was not going to be opened by direct force. It could have been, of course, but Perry's orders (mainly written by himself) included this paragraph:

> His mission is necessarily of a pacific character, and will not resort to force unless in self-defense in the protection of the vessels and crews under his command, or to resist an act of personal violence offered to himself or one of his officers.[11]

In short, there was and is no parallel to Perry's Japanese journey—it was unique. And that much-abused term is justified on three grounds: The approach was peaceful; the country approached contained an ancient civilization; and for over two hundred years that civilization had been formally and voluntarily sealed off from all others, although it and the rest of the world were well aware of each other's existence.

Although a situation like that has never happened anywhere else in the world, clearly a change in the status quo was inevitable sooner or later. This makes it tempting to see Perry as a mere agent of change. But he was much more than that, for (as he wrote before setting out) he was embarking on "an enterprise which, if unsuccessful, saying nothing of my own mortification, would fatally retard the ultimate accomplishment of the desired end: the opening of a friendly intercourse with Japan."[12]

With a fleet of four ships (*Mississippi, Susquehanna, Plymouth,* and *Saratoga*) he arrived in Tokyo Bay on July 14, 1853. Anyone with enough ships and guns could have smashed his way into Japan. Anyone prepared to humiliate himself enough could have wheedled his way in. The former would have caused terror, resentment, and the probable destruction of Japanese independence; the latter, like the Dutch at Deshima, would have existed only as objects of contempt. But very few people could have done what Perry did, opening the country for trade at the same time as gaining its respect and avoiding any compromise of its independence.

He succeeded because he looked right, he sounded right, and above all because he treated the Japanese as he expected to be treated by them: with respect but without deference, as honored equals. His impressive physique, his deep voice, his air of command—the "sense of importance" he created—joined with his scrupulous behavior and the obvious latent power of his warships, and all worked to the same end. The system of government under the shogun was called *bakufu,* literally meaning "government behind a curtain." Perry used the idea, keeping himself concealed from public view until an official with a rank comparable to his own came forward. He overawed, but he did not threaten. Since all speech

John Paul Jones, exemplar of America's first navy, the Continental Fleet: "The most agreeable sea-wolf one could wish to meet with," said one English lady.

Other Britons, branding the Scottish-born Jones a pirate, circulated suitably villainous propaganda drawings "from the Life" to discredit him.

"I have not yet begun to fight!": In *Bonhomme Richard* (center), Jones grapples with H.M.S. *Serapis* (left) during the legendary moonlit action off Flamborough Head, while his insane French colleague Landais fires indiscriminately at both ships.

A radically different concept: A 1776 attack by *Turtle,* the world's first semisubmersible to be used in war, failed only because the detachable explosive charge (behind the operator) could not be fixed to the target's hull. With no opposing force to support it, *Turtle*'s drill merely pushed it away.

The Anglo-French Battle of Virginia Capes (September 5–10, 1781), shown here, was actually not nearly as well organized as the painting suggests; yet its outcome altered the whole world, for it effectively gave the United States its independence.

One of the "six original frigates," U.S.S. *Constitution* (launched 1797) is still a commissioned warship and still afloat—the oldest such vessel in the world.

"We have met the enemy and they are ours": With his fleet of bargelike brigs—broad, shallow, and heavily armed—Oliver Hazard Perry defeated comparable British forces on Lake Erie (September 10, 1813).

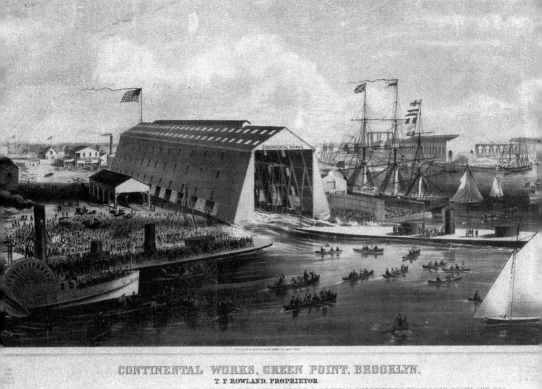

"Vessels of every description": As a monitor is launched in 1862, rowboats, sloops, three-masted ships, and paddle steamers crowd around a Brooklyn yard.

History's first battle between ironclads: The inconclusive duel of C.S.S. *Virginia* (left) and U.S.S. *Monitor* at Hampton Roads (March 9, 1862).

By such men is history made: Before the battle, some extremely relaxed officers pose on the undamaged *Monitor*'s deck.

"The forts," said Farragut, *"should be run."* When they were, on April 24, 1862, "they opened upon us a tremendous fire," said one of his officers, "...and then all sorts of things happened."

Gideon Welles described the commerce raider C.S.S. *Alabama* as a "roving wolf, which has no country, no home, no resting place." On June 19, 1864, in battle with U.S.S. *Kearsage,* she found her final resting place (rediscovered in 1990) off the French port of Cherbourg.

"A volcano of fire": Prompting instant suspicions of Spanish sabotage, the destruction of U.S.S. *Maine* in Havana harbor (February 15, 1898) precipitated the Spanish-American War. Research decades later indicated that the explosion was more probably caused by an internal design fault.

With the New Navy, the republican United States became an imperial power. Following the Battle of Manila Bay (May 1, 1898) the Philippines were colonized —hostages to fortune 7,000 miles from California and only 1,000 from Japan.

After Manila, victorious Commodore George Dewey was rapidly promoted to admiral of the Navy, a rank awarded only twice before. Posing on his flagship *Olympia,* he ignores a gaping, highly vulnerable gun port.

"They came at us like mad bulls": In a gallant last gesture of defiance, Admiral Cervera's tin-pot fleet charged from Santiago to destruction (July 3, 1898).

Ships of the New Navy: The battleship U.S.S. *Kearsage*...

...the cruiser U.S.S. *Atlanta*...

...and U.S.S. *Holland*, its first submarine.

Popping up like a proud jack-in-the-box from his submarine's conning tower, inventor John P. Holland shows her small size—54 feet in length, 10-foot beam, capable of 8 knots surfaced and 5 submerged.

"Did you ever see such a fleet on such a day?": In 1907 Theodore Roosevelt's "Great White Fleet" stretches to the horizon in its hugely successful world tour.

Taking the twentieth-century Navy somewhat precariously to the air, Eugene P. Ely flies from the adapted deck of U.S.S. *Pennsylvania* to the nearby shore of San Francisco Bay (January 18, 1911).

In March 1922 the two-year conversion of *Jupiter* was completed, giving the U.S. Navy its first aircraft carrier, U.S.S. *Langley,* here seen in San Diego in 1934. Note the funnels—by folding them down, one of the many hazards of deck landing was removed.

had to be interpreted, visual appearances were more important than usual, and the effect of lavish ceremonial was heightened by being used sparingly. In his diplomatic experience Perry had noted that with a proud people, a "people of forms, it is necessary either to set all ceremony aside, or to out-Herod Herod in assumed personal consequence and ostentation. I have adopted the two extremes—by an exhibition of great pomp, when it could properly be displayed, and by avoiding it, when such pomp would be inconsistent with our institutions."[13]

Put so baldly, it may sound as Perry duped the Japanese into a treaty through sham and confidence trickery. He did not; he was wise enough not to judge the Japanese by the level of their technology, but to recognize that they were an intelligent people, perfectly able to assess for themselves whether or not his motives were genuine. He used form because form matters; but he could not have carried it off if he had not been true behind the form. As the official report of the mission said:

> He felt that it was well to teach the Japanese, in the mode most intelligible to them, by stately and dignified reserve, joined to perfect equity in all he asked or did, to respect the country from which he came, and to suspend for a time their accustomed arrogance and incivility toward strangers. The Japanese so well understood him that they learned the lesson at once.[14]

Thus, in 1854, on behalf of their respective nations, Perry and representatives of the Emperor of Japan signed a treaty of "commerce and amity." Once again a peacetime navy had extended the world; and on September 19 of that year, Secretary of the Navy James C. Dobbin wrote to Perry:

> You have won additional fame for yourself, reflected new honor upon the very honorable service to which you belong, and, we all hope, have secured for your country, for commerce, and for civilization, a triumph the blessings of which may be enjoyed by generations yet unborn.[15]

Looking back, there is much sad irony in reading the secretary's words; generations then unborn have enjoyed some blessings from that triumph, but have endured many heavy curses as well. And at the time, Japan itself had much to endure. Although Perry personally had gained Japanese respect, he did not—probably could not—fully comprehend the turmoil his presence produced in Japanese minds. However, he and everyone else could see the physical turmoil which followed. Japan's de facto ruler, the shogun (the most powerful of the daimyos, the regional military lords), had signed the treaty in the interests of national safety. But Japan's emperor was a conservative, xenophobic man. Hardly believing the tales of steam-powered ships bearing great guns from across the sea, he refused to credit the fear that unbeatable force might be brought against Japan, and would not ratify the treaty. Though he was ruler only in name, his ratification was essential, and he was supported by daimyos as insular as himself. Civil disturbances broke out, gradually building to full-scale civil war; and so—unintentionally but directly—the first gift of the West to Japan was fifteen years of conflict.

It ended in 1868, with the Imperial party victorious; but the old emperor was dead. The name the new emperor adopted to symbolize his reign was "Meiji," meaning "enlightened rule"; and he did rule, for not only the old emperor but the entire shogunate system was gone.

The most important part of Emperor Meiji's new enlightened rule was summed up in the maxim *fukoku-kyohei*—"Enrich the country, strengthen the army." The phrase was old, but was seen in a new way, because, from examples all over Asia, the leaders of the new Japan saw that two paths lay ahead. Either their homeland could become a Western colony, economically, politically, or both; or it could remain independent—*if* it could be as strong as its new potential enemies.

Considering the magnitude of their recent national trauma, it is still astonishing how clearly the Japanese saw the road to their own future and how unitedly they embarked upon it. They understood that the sea was no longer the shield it had been for centuries, but instead a channel of potential danger. So they not only strengthened their army; in next to no time they created a throughly modern navy as well. During the civil war, every party had acquired a ship or two; immediately the war was over, the surviving vessels were taken under imperial control; six years later, in 1872, the Imperial Japanese Navy was made a department of state. Because the Japanese were as yet unable to build ships themselves, there was good business here for Western shipyards, and it was eagerly snapped up by British and American companies. At least one American, however, had serious misgivings. In 1864, during the United States' own Civil War, a Union yard was building a ship for Japan which Secretary of the Navy Gideon Welles wanted to take over for the Union fleet. Asking advice from Secretary of State William H. Seward, he received an unequivocal reply—take it over immediately. For two reasons, in Seward's opinion, the Japanese should not have it. First, the ship could provide real aid for the Union. Second, he said, "if they ever got such a vessel, they would begin to play the pirate and raise the devil." Only ten years had passed since Secretary Dobbin's letter of optimistic congratulation to Perry. In harsh contrast, Seward's words planted an ominous signpost to the future.

At the same time as Matthew Perry was preparing for and making his epochal voyage to Japan, Lt. Matthew Maury (still in charge of the Naval

Observatory in Washington) was setting in motion a remarkable plan of his own. Born in Virginia in 1806, he was a full son of the South, yet disapproved of slavery. Stronger than his disapproval, though, was his concern that the southern way of life might be destroyed by the more powerful northern economy. The solution he came up with took shape in 1851–52, when a naval expedition under Lt. William L. Herndon and Passed Midshipman Lardner Gibbon investigated the Amazon. Officially, their objective was to assess the river's navigability and to work out how easily Brazilian trade could come to the United States; but privately instructed by Maury, they were also going to find out if land could be acquired for southern planters. If suitably large areas were available, Maury's idea was to shift thousands of slaves out of the United States and reestablish the southern economy in a place unthreatened by the northern one.

Nothing came of it, of course, but the fantastic scheme was symptomatic of the growing urgency and divisiveness of the slavery question. And very soon afterwards, a lawyer in Illinois made a speech which became famous. For his opposition to the Mexican war, Abraham Lincoln had lost his place in Congress and had returned to his legal practice. Now, trying for office again, he spoke in the town of Peoria, 125 miles southwest of Chicago. There he declared:

> Slavery is founded in the selfishness of man's nature—opposition to it, in his love of justice. These principles are in eternal antagonism; and when brought into collision so fiercely, as slavery extension brings them, shocks, and throes, and convulsions must ceaselessly follow.[16]

Slowly it was becoming clear to every American that the Missouri Compromise was breaking down and would not be repeated. In 1858, standing as a candidate for the Senate four years after his Peoria speech, Lincoln announced: "I believe this government cannot endure, permanently half *slave* and half *free*. . . . It will become *all* one thing, or *all* the other."[17] And with many emphases, he made a terrible prophecy:

> We are now far into the *fifth* year, since a policy was initiated, with the *avowed* object, and *confident* promise, of putting an end to slavery agitation. Under the operation of that policy, that agitation has not only, *not ceased,* but has *constantly augmented.* In my opinion, it *will* not cease, until a crisis shall have been reached, and passed.

What that crisis might be, he did not and could not specify; but it was close. In November 1860, Senator Lincoln was elected sixteenth President of the United States. In December of that year, Senator John J. Crittenden of Kentucky (a southerner, but strongly supportive of the

Union as a whole) made a hopeless attempt at compromise between the
free and slave states, proposing that their dividing line should be extended
westward to the Pacific. It was an honest attempt to preserve the Union,
but it was impossible: Lincoln and the party he now led had sworn to
prevent any further extension of slavery at all. With the failure of the
Crittenden compromise, a crisis was imminent. And on December 20,
1860, the state legislature of South Carolina convened in Charleston and
made a unanimous declaration:

> The union now subsisting between South Carolina and other States,
> under the name of "The United States of America," is hereby dis-
> solved.[18]

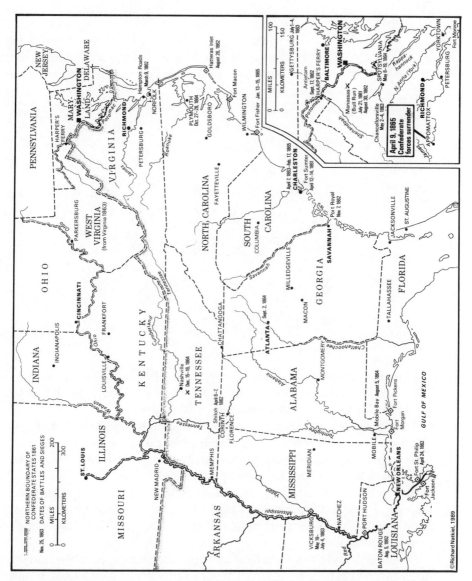

The Civil War permanently changed the face of naval conflict through the effective introduction of mines, submarines, and ironclad ships. The Confederate States Navy inflicted much damage on northern commercial shipping, but the Unionists' "Anaconda" naval strategy surrounded the South.

15

★

MANY EXCITING
SUNDAYS

*T*o his "dissatisfied fellow-countrymen," President Abraham Lincoln's inaugural speech was explicit—it was they, not he, who would decide on "the momentous issue of civil war."

"The government will not assail you," he stated on March 4, 1861. "You can have no conflict without yourselves being the aggressors. You have no oath registered in heaven to destroy the government, while I have the most solemn one to 'preserve, protect and defend' it."[1]

But on February 8, 1861, representatives of six states (South Carolina, Georgia, Florida, Alabama, Mississippi, and Louisiana) met in Alabama, elected Jefferson Davis as their president, and created the Confederate States of America.

Nine weeks and a day went by. Four miles east-southeast of the Battery in the lovely coastal town of Charleston, South Carolina, on a small island in Charleston harbor, the stone and brick building of Fort Sumter had only recently been completed. It had taken thirty years to build; and it was at that Union target, at 4:30 on the morning of April 12, 1861, that the first shots of the Civil War were fired from Confederate guns on shore. Over the next four years more than half a million Americans were killed.

During the twelfth, the citizens of Charleston were able to watch from the shore; on the thirteenth, they were able to see the fort surrender and the Stars and Stripes hauled down. And over thirty years later, writing of that first day of civil war, an officer of the Confederate States Navy said,

"The object of Mr. Lincoln and his party was accomplished: *the first gun was fired by the Confederates.* In the excitement which followed, men did not remember that between nations the aggressor is not he who first uses force, but he who first makes force necessary."[2]

The point of view is well worth remembering, but not as an indictment of Lincoln. Fifteen years before the shots at Charleston, and eighty years after, Mexicans and Japanese would have known just what the Confederate officer meant, for without reference to each other, they felt exactly the same. Certainly in each of those three wars there were firebrands— Mexican, Confederate, or Japanese—who were delighted their side was the first to open fire; yet just as certainly in each case, there were intelligent people who honestly believed, then and always, that their hands had been forced by the United States.

However, the decision at Charleston made all other matters irrelevant. The national agony had begun. And if hearth, home, and family represented all that was best and most desirable, civil war was their absolute antithesis, the worst of all possible worlds. For most people, the question of allegiance was answered by their birthplace; yet deep convictions could and did split families, giving the conflict one of its cruelest aspects and making it truly a civil war. Robert E. Lee, general in the Confederate States Army, was a cousin of Samuel P. Lee, commander of the Union naval forces on the James River. Two brothers of the Crittenden family were major generals in the opposing armies. Three of President Lincoln's brothers-in-law died for the Confederacy. One of the greatest of the Union naval officers, David G. Farragut, was a native of Alabama, where the Confederacy's first capital was established at Montgomery. David Porter, son of the commodore of the same name, fought for the Union, while two of his own sons joined the southern army under Stonewall Jackson. Blood divided; the nation fractured; and the U.S. Navy fragmented. One fifth of its officers resigned and went south to their own states within seven weeks of the surrender of Fort Sumter.

Yet they took no ships with them, and a slightly greater proportion of southern officers remained with the North. Moreover, those who went south went knowing (as one of them wrote) that in the South "until the organization of the Confederate States, there was not a ship owned by any State, nor the least effort made to procure one; that there was not a piece of ordnance of any kind; not a yard in which a yawl-boat could be built; not a machine-shop capable, without material alterations, of constructing the simplest piece of naval machinery; not a rope-yard, not a percussion-cap machine; only one powder mill, no supply of nitre, or sulphur, or lead." So they knew the handicaps they would face—but they went south all the same.[3] In Washington, the condition of the Union Navy hardly offered greater encouragement. Gideon Welles, coming to office as Lincoln's secretary of the navy on March 7, quickly learned that there were ninety vessels in the fleet. Forty-eight of them, though, were laid up and out of commission, while thirty more were scattered around the world at the various squadron stations. The most distant were several months' voyage from home, while close at hand in the Home Squadron, there were only a dozen ships.

Following the surrender of Fort Sumter, the two new presidents rapidly disclosed their attitudes. Loath to believe that the conflict would be long, yet seeing it was "too powerful to be suppressed" by normal means, Lincoln called for an army of 75,000 volunteers. He could have had many more: Men were turned away when the limit was reached. Even conscription would have been accepted readily: Shooting at the flag was unforgivable. If he had acted more decisively at once, the war might have been shorter; but the effect of swift suppression by brute force would have probably been like capping a volcano. Even the threat of coercion implied by Lincoln's call to arms was enough to send Virginia into the Confederacy, and it may be that the atrocious bloodletting was actually psychologically vital to the Union's reunion.

Jefferson Davis, elected president of the Confederacy, did not hesitate. Two days after the northern appeal for volunteers, he announced that letters of marque were available for any vessel wishing to hunt Union merchantmen or warships. Two days after that, on April 19, Lincoln proclaimed a blockade of the southern coastline from South Carolina to Texas. But the very next day the Union Navy suffered a severe blow: The large navy yard at Norfolk, Virginia, was lost to the south.

As they retreated from it, soldiers of the northern force set fire to the yard, and later, Thomas Scharf of the Confederate States Navy commented drily that "the burning of the navy yard at Norfolk is almost a matter of inheritance. Our forefathers, in the Revolution, burned the first navy yard, to prevent it from falling into the hands of the British; the United States again burned it, in 1861, to deprive the State of Virginia of its use; and the following year, for the third time, the yard was committed to the flames by the Confederate army."[4]

The yard was burned in the Revolution because, for fear of provoking insurrection, it had not been reinforced until too late; but when it was burned in 1861, the job was only half done. Vessels in the harbor were scuttled first and set alight afterwards. Of course, the fires did not penetrate below the waterline, and since after the ships' scuttling that level was unnaturally high, some of the hulls could be raised and rebuilt. The huge dry dock was not touched. Nearly two thousand naval guns were left intact; foundries, machine shops, smiths' shops, and stores of timber were likewise almost unharmed, and in a short time all were being operated by Confederate hands.

Further compounding his own difficulties, just a week after the burning, Lincoln extended the area of blockade to include the whole coastline from Texas through Virginia. This meant that a total of some 3,500 miles—much of it "double" coastline with chains of outer islands protecting inner sounds before the coast proper—was theoretically under blockade by the North; yet they still had only a handful of vessels to patrol it all.

The secretaries of the two navies (Gideon Welles in the North and Stephen Russell Mallory in the South) faced almost impossible demands. Both proved to be as effective as circumstances allowed, and although President Davis was not at all sea-minded (despite the early issue of letters of marque), Mallory had two advantages over his northern counterpart. For eight years preceding the secession, he had been chairman of the Senate's committee on naval affairs and in that position had learned a lot about the current state of foreign navies; and he had the flair to put that knowledge to immediate effect.

Welles, in contrast, was comparatively out of touch with naval matters when he came to office. He had been chief of the Bureau of Provisions and Clothing in the Mexican War, but since then had been a journalist. Fifty-nine years old in 1861, massively bearded, cautious and deliberate in character, he was lampooned in the northern press as the old man of the sea sitting on Sinbad Lincoln's neck. This was because he had strongly opposed the imposition of blockade, yet the lampoons were unfair, for few people grasped the policy's international implications.

Welles argued (correctly) that in international law a blockade would be illegal. To be legal, it would have to be effective, and with next to no ships available, this one quite obviously could not be. A still more serious implication was that instituting a blockade, effective or not, would put a completely different international political complexion on the rising struggle. A nation containing rebellion within its own frontiers should declare its ports closed. In practical terms this would certainly be ignored in the South, but it would have the formal effect of keeping the rebellion a domestic affair. Blockades, on the other hand, were used against other nations, not against one's own. To blockade the South was not only close to de facto recognition of the Confederacy as a separate political entity, it also indicated that the South could ask other countries to respect it as a full belligerent—possibly even to the extent of finding foreign allies.

These were cogent arguments, but they were overruled. As for the South, Stephen Mallory would have been delighted if his main difficulties had been points of law. He had to cope with being naval secretary for an as yet unrecognized country which had no ships, no means or skills to build them quickly or in worthwhile numbers, and no organized economy. Yet something he did have was enough knowledge and imagination to see a way through, and on May 8, 1861, he spelled it out:

"I regard the possession of an iron-armored ship as a matter of the first

necessity. Such a vessel at this time could traverse the entire coast of the
United States, prevent all blockades, and encounter, with a fair prospect
of success, their entire navy."[5]

The same idea had occurred to at least one person in the North, an
ironmaster from New Jersey named Abram S. Hewitt, who wrote to
Welles asking if the Navy would require iron plates and beams. On May
9, Welles said it would not: No iron vessels were planned by his department. Yet on May 10 the Confederate Congress authorized Mallory to
go ahead with that very plan, and at once he arranged for an agent to
travel to England "charged with the duty of purchasing vessels." Here
was a man of foresight indeed.

On July 20, less than 30 miles from the White House, the first terrible
indication of the way the land war would develop appeared at Bull Run.
Thirteen thousand Union troops met 11,000 Confederates. Against the
odds, Confederate Thomas J. Jackson refused to retreat, thereby earning
his nickname of Stonewall; around him, the combined casualties were 20
percent; and the Union force was routed.

Two days earlier, Secretary Mallory had reported to the Confederate
Congress on progress in the charred Norfolk navy yard. He had good
news: "The frigate *Merrimack* has been raised and docked."[6]

Merrimack had been a handsome, forty-gun steamer-sailer. Three-
masted and square-rigged, she had also had a funnel amidships and a
screw propeller—a typical midcentury frigate, her hybrid design enabling
her to cruise economically under sail and fight efficiently under steam. In
the panic at the yard she had been scuttled first and fired next, leaving
most of her hull and machinery comparatively undamaged. She was
practically a gift to the Confederacy, and Mallory knew just what to do
with her.

If she were restored to her original condition, she would be trapped in
the river by the Union blockade. "It has therefore been determined," he
explained to his colleagues, "to shield her completely with three-inch
iron, placed at such angles as to render her ball-proof, to complete her
at the earliest moment, to arm her with the heaviest ordnance, and to send
her at once against the enemy's fleet. It is believed that thus prepared she
will be able to contend successfully against the heaviest of the enemy's
ships, and to drive them from Hampton Roads and the ports of Virginia."

The resuscitated vessel would be called *Virginia,* after the land of her
rebirth. As the project took shape, local people became extremely interested; no one in the United States or anywhere else had seen anything
quite like *Virginia* before. Her design was largely a matter of trial and
error, and as her constructor remembered later, he "received but little
encouragement from any one while the *Virginia* was progressing. Hun-

dreds—I may say thousands—asserted she would never float. Some said she would turn bottom-side up; others said the crew would suffocate; and the most wise said the concussion and report from the guns would deafen the men. Some said she would not steer; and public opinion generally about here said she would never come out of the dock. You have no idea what I have suffered in mind since I commenced her; but," he added proudly, "I knew what I was about, and persevered."[7]

In Washington, Secretary Welles now knew what he was about as well. A copy of Mallory's ironclad recommendation had come into his hands, followed by repeated reports of the activity at Norfolk—reports strong enough to convince him that the Union Navy needed an ironclad to match. At once he thought of the Stevens Battery, languishing in Hoboken, New Jersey, where it had been begun nineteen years before. Inspection soon showed the battery to be completely unsuitable, and a public invitation for new designs was issued. Fifteen came up, of which two (a gunboat and a frigate) were thought to have some future; but no one remembered the Swedish inventor of *Princeton* fame, John Ericsson.

Since 1844, when Naval Secretary Gilmer and ex–Naval Secretary Upshur had been killed in the explosion on *Princeton,* Ericsson had been out of government employment, though the deaths were not his fault. It was by complete chance, an accidental meeting, that he came once again to the U.S. Navy's attention in 1861; and he had the answer to their problem. Actually, he had had it for years, but nobody had been interested before. When he showed a model of his invention to Welles's adjudicating committee, there were no cries of thunderstruck revelation (one of the committee even said it looked like "nothing in the heaven above or on the earth below or in the waters under the earth," and he was right) but it seemed to have possibilities.[8] Along with the gunboat and frigate designs, Ericsson's was approved, and he thought of a good name for it. Because the new vessel (if it worked) would keep a close, constant watch on and admonish Confederate naval actions, he decided to call it U.S.S. *Monitor.*

Welles had also begun other measures to augment the diminutive Home Squadron. Almost all ships on foreign stations were recalled; construction started on eight new sloops, twenty-three gunboats, and a dozen double-ended paddle steamers. These unusual craft had their paddles amidships, a rudder at each end, and two engines pointing in opposite directions. The plan was to use them in the narrow creeks and rivers of the South, where they would have no space to turn; a captain would be able to stop one engine and start the other when he wanted to reverse course.

Simultaneously with this construction, Welles organized the purchase or charter of as many available merchant ships as were suitable for conversion to a war role. There were plenty of merchantmen on the market—the U.S. merchant navy was second in size only to the British, 90 percent of it belonged to the northern states, and with the southern threat of privateering, rocketing insurance rates had forced the rapid transfer of cargoes to neutral hulls. But if the merchant ships were there, a comment made by Matthew Perry many years before still applied:

"Under no circumstances . . . can a steam vessel, built expressly for the transportation of freight or passengers, be made, in any manner, equal in convenience or efficiency to a vessel originally intended for war purposes."[9]

However, a fleet was taking shape; and on August 26, with a handy amphibious operation, a southern base for the northern blockaders was secured at Hatteras Inlet off the coast of North Carolina.

If one wanted to look for omens, the capture could be read whichever way one chose. The inlet separates Ocracoke Island and Pea Island in the strange, desolate, wild, attractive chain called the Outer Banks, a narrow line protecting half the North Carolina coast from the Atlantic. Inside the Banks, in 1584, Raleigh established the first English colony in the New World, so perhaps one could take that as a good sign. On the other hand, in 1587, the colony vanished without a trace. Perhaps better not look for omens after all.

As ever, blockading seemed dull; as ever, young naval men longed for something else and learned slowly while they longed. U.S.S. *Pocahontas* may have been "one of the prettiest gunboats in the United States Navy," as her first lieutenant wrote to a friend, but, he added, "We of the Navy have the poorest show, nothing but blockading." The time would come when Alfred T. Mahan would understand that a local base for sortie and return was worth more than prettiness, or an oracle.[10]

On November 7 a second southern base was taken: Port Royal in South Carolina, only 60 miles from Charleston, by now thought of as the seat of the rebellion. On the sea at least, the Union could feel heartened. But the very next day, Charles Wilkes, the explorer, created a chilling threat of war on a second front—against Great Britain.

In their new roles as Confederate commissioners to Europe, John M. Mason and John Slidell (both former members of the national Senate) were traveling from Havana to Southampton in the British mail steamer *Trent* when Wilkes (commanding U.S.S. *San Jacinto*) overhauled the steamer and ordered it to stop. A boarding party came over to *Trent*, removed the commissioners, and allowed the steamer to go on her way, while the two men were taken ashore to prison.

Memories of international incidents at sea are long. At home Wilkes was hailed as a hero, turning about the insult of the *Chesapeake-Leopard* affair fifty-six years earlier. U.S. outrage then had been met by British incomprehension; British outrage now was met by chortling glee in the United States, and Wilkes was promoted. But the British were deadly serious: An insult to the flag required an apology—or war. Inadvertently, Gideon Welles heightened the already fraught situation by writing publicly that his department gave "emphatic approval" to Wilkes's action, which the British government took to be an accurate reflection of the presidential attitude. It was not; Lincoln did not object to the commissioners' imprisonment, but he would have preferred Wilkes to go about it legally by taking *Trent* into port and letting the courts decide the case. Most of all, Lincoln absolutely did not want any transatlantic complications just then; life in America was sufficiently complicated already. Yet with Wilkes the man of the moment, the domestic political embarrassment of an apology to Britain was unacceptable as well.

It was Secretary of State William H. Seward who found a way out of the impasse, on Christmas Day, 1861. All that was needed, he believed, was a public announcement that the Confederate cause was failing rapidly. That would mean the Union government had no further use for the prisoners, who could be set free. The proposal was sent to Britain, arriving when the country was in mourning: On December 14, Queen Victoria's husband, Prince Albert, had died. Under the circumstances the British decided it was hardly the time to go to war or even to insist on diplomatic niceties. The release of the commissioners was acknowledged; the demand for an apology was waived; and with considerable relief, the United States was able to concentrate once more on the unpalatable truth that the Confederacy was still very far from failing.

On November 20, while the *Trent* affair was distracting Lincoln's cabinet, Secretary Mallory reported to his own president again on the condition of the Confederate Navy. In a prophetic mood, he stated that "iron-clad steamships capable of resisting the crushing weight of projectiles from heavy ordnance must, at an early day, constitute the principal part of the fighting vessels of all naval powers."[11] Contracts had been issued at home for the construction of gunboats, and abroad (through Mallory's assistant James D. Bulloch) for rams and cruisers. Early in June the first commerce-raiding cruiser, bought in New Orleans, was ready for action. C.S.S. *Sumter* (a barquentine-rigged screw steamer) would become infamous in the North; and as she set out to hunt, C.S.S. *Virginia,* ex–U.S.S. *Merrimack,* was simultaneously taking on her improbable new form.

No one who had seen *Merrimack* would have recognized her now. The masts were gone, burnt away; the upper deck was cut down almost to the waterline. Only that part of the vessel which would be underwater was retained, and a fish or a diver would have seen an apparently standard vessel. Anyone above water, however, saw something resembling the roof of a house 170 feet long. Sloping sides tapered to a flat top some 20 feet wide, with a large central funnel. At regular intervals along the sloping sides, as well as fore and aft, gun ports were pierced through—ten in all. Six of the guns were smooth-bored with a 9-inch caliber; two, which completed the broadside, were 6-inch rifles; and at bow and stern, a 7-inch, reinforced, rifled gun protruded.

The roof of this strange creation was made of pitch pine and oak, two feet thick; the flat top was a grating, to give light and air to those inside; the sides were armored with two layers of iron plating, the inner layer laid horizontally, the outer layer vertically, and both two inches thick; and finally, on the underwater bow, there was a ram weighing two thirds of a ton. All in all, Mallory was right when he said, on February 24, 1862, that "the *Virginia* is a novelty in naval construction, is untried, and her powers unknown; and hence the department will not give specific orders as to her attack upon the enemy." But he was confident "that the opportunity and the means for striking a decisive blow for our navy are now, for the first time, presented" and concluded that "action, prompt and successful just now, would be of serious importance to our cause."[12]

At the same time, Ericsson's *Monitor* was also taking shape. Similar in concept to *Virginia,* she was very different in design and just as odd in appearance. "Cheesebox on a raft" was the term most used to describe her: The cheesebox was an armored revolving turret, centrally placed and housing two heavy guns; the raft was an iron-plated water-level deck. Underwater, as with *Virginia,* was a standard hull.

Ericsson was no less confident than Mallory—he set about rolling the iron for *Monitor*'s keel even as the contract was being drawn up, and construction, he said, would take ninety days. Accidents, alterations, and adjustments stretched the three months to four: She was launched on January 30, 1862, given over to the Navy on February 19, and commissioned on March 4. Five days later, at 10:30 in the morning, Comdr. John A. Dahlgren (commandant of the Washington navy yard) was called from his office. The president's carriage was at the gate with the president in it. Dahlgren, inventor of the bottle-shaped gun which bore his name, was the U.S. Navy's foremost expert on naval ordnance and was told that Lincoln needed to consult him on a professional matter. Hurrying down to the carriage, Dahlgren was shocked when he saw the president—"Poor gentleman," he thought, "how thin and wasted he is." The carriage turned away from the yard, and Lincoln looked at the commandant. "I have frightful news," he said.[13]

The intelligence had just arrived—a handful of telegrams, a sensational newspaper report, scanty, confused, and frightening. C.S.S. *Virginia* had steamed out of her dock at Norfolk navy yard. She had not turned turtle. Her crew had not suffocated. Under the command of Franklin Buchanan (who, six years before, had been the first superintendent of the Annapolis

Naval Academy), she had steered perfectly well. In every way she had confounded her critics.

At the mouth of the James River, where it enters Chesapeake Bay, five Union vessels (two forty-gun steam frigates, two fifty-gun sailing frigates, and a twenty-four-gun sailing sloop, *Cumberland*) were standing on blockade. The weird and monstrous shape advanced toward them and opened fire, exchanging broadsides with one of the larger frigates. Shots hit both vessels; the frigate was badly damaged; *Virginia* steamed on unscathed. The sailing sloop *Cumberland,* at anchor, could not move. With the tide on the turn, she could not even be pulled around to bring her broadside to bear on the ironclad, whose first heavy shot killed nine of the sloop's crew. The firing continued for fifteen minutes as the Confederate vessel maneuvered into a ramming position—then, with her whole weight behind it, she crashed her 1,500-pound ram into *Cumberland*'s bow. For some minutes she clung there, the ram so deeply embedded she could not move away; then, swinging around on the tide, she broke off the ram and *Cumberland,* already sinking, sent three swift broadsides at her. *Virginia* had five companions—a twelve-gun steamer, a two-gun steamer, and three single-weapon gunboats. Leaving the doomed sloop, they all converged on the fifty-gun sailing frigate *Congress,* as she sailed in desperation to shallower waters. Running aground, she could not sink, but she could not escape. Soon she was ablaze from *Virginia*'s heated shot and incendiary shell; 120 of her men died; and in Norfolk, the ironclad's constructor admitted that even he was "astonished at the success of the *Virginia.* "[14]

When Lincoln and Dahlgren arrived at the White House, they found "general excitement and alarm." Members of the Cabinet turned thankfully to Dahlgren for advice. When he could give none, the panic increased. "But the most frightened man on that gloomy day," Gideon Welles remarked, "was the Secretary of War." Edwin Stanton "was at times almost frantic," literally running from room to room, terrified at what the new weapon could do. "The *Merrimack,* he said, would destroy every vessel in the service—could lay every city on the coast under contribution—could take Fortress Monroe . . . come up the Potomac and disperse Congress, destroy the Capitol and public buildings . . . go to New York and Boston and destroy those cities . . ."

Stanton seemed to hold Welles personally responsible, and "asked what vessel or means we had to resist or prevent her from doing whatever she pleased." Welles told him about *Monitor.* "Stanton asked about her armament, and when I mentioned she had two guns, his mingled look of incredulity and contempt cannot be described; and the tone of his voice, as he asked if my reliance was on that craft with her two guns, is equally indescribable."[15]

But against an ironclad with rifled guns, *Monitor* was all they had—

and in fact, she was already in action. Strange to say (given that northern command of the sea now depended on her) the Union Navy had taken no interest in her construction, beyond providing an inspector; and she had been built in New York. During the long voyage south she had had to be towed for much of the way, with waves washing all over her low freeboard and down her smokestack, extinguishing her fires. By mid-afternoon on March 8, sheer coincidence brought her to within earshot of *Virginia*'s first battle, but she could not get to the site until after dark. By then *Virginia* had long gone. In the darkness, *Monitor* rescued some of the survivors, who, with her crew, worked through the night to put her in fighting trim. At midnight (according to her log) the beginning of Sunday, March 9, was "fine weather and calm." It remained so all night, and "at sunrise saw 3 steamers lying under Sewell's Point. Made one out to be the Rebel steamer Merrimack. At 7:20 got under weigh & stood towards her & piped all hands to quarters."[16]

At least *Monitor*'s crew knew beforehand that they would be facing another ironclad steamer. *Virginia*'s crew had no inkling of such opposition and were astonished to see a metal enemy. Nothing daunted, they got up steam and headed out to meet the challenge. *Monitor*'s log notes that at 8:20 she "opened fire on the Merrimack" and dismisses the next four hours with a splendidly laconic sentence: "From that time until 12, constantly engaged with the Merrimack." The historic battle—the world's first engagement between ironclads—was in progress at the very time Secretary Stanton was emitting "wailings and woeful predictions" and going "repeatedly to the window . . . to see if the *Merrimack* was not coming to Washington."[17]

His terror was needless. "At 1 P.M.," says *Monitor*'s log, "the Merrimack hauled off in a disabled condition." The Confederate view was rather different: As far as they could tell, *Monitor* was the first to withdraw.

Whichever went first, after fighting for four hours—sometimes less than 50 yards apart—with the smoke clouds from their guns so dense the ships almost vanished from each other's sight, they separated (battered, but with their flags still flying) to the sound of "the cheers of their respective friends . . . to indicate that no victory had been won by either side."[18]

And that was the verdict: a draw, in which both had been damaged but neither defeated. *Monitor*'s log shows no awareness of the historic nature of the battle, but its writer certainly knew; even before the firing had finished, men were on deck gathering souvenir pieces of shrapnel. As soon as the battle was over, Gideon Welles's very able assistant Gustavus Vasa Fox came on board. With other politicians and foreign diplomats, he had been on hand to witness the event and could thoroughly corroborate Welles's final downbeat but accurate comment on the day: "It was one of the many exciting Sundays we had during the Civil War."[19]

16

*

VICKSBURG MUST OF NECESSITY FALL

*I*n other naval nations, interest in the Battle of Hampton Roads was
high, partly because both *Monitor* and *Virginia* were of such unusual
design and partly because of the technical information derived from the
fight. Other ironclads had been used in battle, but none had ever fought
each other directly. Stephen Mallory had called C.S.S. *Virginia* "a novelty in naval construction," and inconclusive novelty was the keynote of
Hampton Roads. But as the U.S. Navy grew to meet the needs of civil
war (by its end, the Texas-Virginia blockade alone included nine hundred
vessels), ships were manned by crews to whom not only ironclads, but
everything about a navy was novel.

"To a mind just about as familiar with practical navigation as it is with
the geological formation of the mountains in the moon, and no more so,
the first part of the first voyage is an astounding experience," one young
greenhorn admitted.[1] His name was Samuel F. Train, and in early 1862
his rank, which he filled with pride and good humor, was acting assistant
paymaster in U.S.S. *Ino.* She was a new eight-gun 895-ton clipper ship,
commissioned only a few months before Train joined her, and from the
moment of getting on board (or trying to get on board), he kept a journal
recording a frankly landsman's-eye view of events.

It is no joke, to start with, for one who has always been accustomed
to going up and down stairs on a slant, to be rowed in a small boat
to a ship's side, and suddenly find himself under the necessity of

making a perpendicular ascent, and that too, in great peril of having the first step jerked several feet into the air, just as he gets ready to put his foot on it.

He had read of ships, but had never actually considered what being on a ship really involved. Apart from the mysterious orders ("a string of technicalities which would puzzle St. Paul") he was bothered by the lack of carpets, and even more so by the seemingly incredible movement of the ship, even when moored:

> So you stay where you are, and keep your eyes and ears open, and very likely your mouth too, while the ship is being got under way. Then the Officers bawl at the sailors as if they were all deaf, and had done something wrong, and the sailors have the impudence to repeat after the officers just what they say, which sounds very much like mocking them.

Down below, as the ship lurched unpredictably from side to side, he could not even undress; so he wrapped himself in a blanket, "and lay down to anything but quick dreams. It is surprising how little motion of the vessel is exceedingly annoying to a landlubber." Yet these troubles paled to insignificance when the ship was fully out at sea. He had never believed it when books spoke of mountain-high waves, but:

> Seeing is believing. I have stood on the "Quarter Deck," holding firmly by a rope, when we were speeding onward at the rate of 16 knots per hour, and looked ahead way down the steep inclined plane at the dark "blue water," which has all the appearance of a lofty, impassable wall directly in our pathway; and as our noble ship has lifted her head majestically above the threatening barrier, I have turned to view the track so lately passed, and had my vision greeted by a scene more terribly sublime . . . wave piled on wave you see, till literally mountain-high, and then you see a perfect avalanche of liquid mountains, rushing after you & threatening with one fell swoop to bury everything beneath them, and as you gaze on the restless surging billows stretching far away on every side of you and see no sign of life . . . and then call back your thoughts and fix them on the *paltry foothold* which you style your "noble ship," you wonder that a human being ever dared to trust himself in such a place.

He was not exaggerating the ship's speed: 16 knots took *Ino* from Boston to Cadiz in less than fourteen days. The main purpose of voyaging across the Atlantic when there was a war at home was "to seek the 'Sumpter,' that notorious 'pirate and privateer,' whose depredations have struck such terror to our merchant men."

In the seven months since she had escaped from New Orleans, C.S.S. *Sumter* (Train always spelled her name wrong) had captured eighteen Union vessels. Greater than the direct damage to the North was the indirect damage done by the ship and her sister privateers—increased insurance and a loss of confidence among traders. Although militarily she was a negligible threat, political pressures forced the U.S. Navy to detach ships from blockading to catch her; and at dawn on the day after *Ino*'s arrival at Cadiz,

> We discerned the *Tuscarora* lying only a little way off, and the "Rebel Steamer" *Sumpter,* about five miles distant, defiantly flying the "Confederate flag." But we were in *Spanish waters,* & *she* was in *English,* so all we could do toward keeping her "out of mischief" was to lye still & watch the *old Rat* through the "bars of her cage."

This miniature blockade continued for several weeks, but its issue was never really in doubt; the Confederate could not escape. At length her captain, Raphael Semmes, decided to pay off his crew, sell the ship, and live to privateer another day. In the weeks of watching and waiting, Samuel Train, fresh from his wide-eyed journey across the Atlantic, felt he had confirmed that worse things happen at sea than on land. But while he and his colleagues rocked quietly at anchor in a Spanish harbor, twenty-four thousand men were dying in one small part of America.

Over two early spring days (April 6–7, 1862) at Pittsburgh Landing in Tennessee, the Battle of Shiloh was fought by 55,000 Union troops against 42,000 Confederates, and one man in every four was killed—more than 13,000 Northerners and about 11,000 Southerners. It was a Union victory at a horrible price; but it opened the way to further victories in the West. Simultaneously, the Union's naval campaign continued in the Gulf of Mexico, building to another hard-won—and ultimately decisive—naval encounter, very far from the sea.

The Union's basic naval strategy had been devised, surprisingly, by Gen. Winfield Scott. From the experience of Veracruz, he knew how usefully Army and Navy could cooperate, and early in the Civil War he perceived that the Confederacy could not be beaten on land if it were not beaten on the water as well. His plan (derisively nicknamed "the Anaconda" by its critics) was to constrict and strangle the Confederacy and split it in two. The coastal blockade was part of this process. The other part was to gain control of the most important inland waters: the Mississippi and Missouri rivers.

"Keep your lips closed and burn my letters, for perfect silence is to be observed," David Farragut warned his wife late in 1861.[2] She kept silent, but she did not burn his letters; she feared they might be all she had to remember him by. For as he told her, "I am to have a flag in the Gulf, and the rest depends upon myself. Keep calm and silent. I shall sail in three weeks."

On February 21, 1862, Farragut took over command of the area centered on Ship Island, halfway between New Orleans and Mobile. His flagship was *Hartford,* a steamer-sailer sloop with twenty-two 9-inch Dahlgren guns. With her, "when you are completely ready," said his orders, "you will collect such vessels as can be spared from the blockade, and proceed up the Mississippi River and reduce the defenses which guard the approaches to New Orleans, when you will appear off that city and take possession of it under the guns of your squadron."[3]

The vessels that could be spared were another seven steamers, fifteen gunboats, and a flotilla of mortar schooners. The defenses on the approach to New Orleans were Fort Jackson on the right bank; a battery on the left; between the two, a chain-linked barrier of hulks, their masts and rigging cut down and trailing in the river to entangle propellers; and, further up the left bank, Fort St. Philip. Farragut's orders told him to "reduce the defenses" first, but land fortifications are notoriously difficult to defeat by waterborne forces alone, and Farragut had no army support. On April 29 he issued his own general order.

"Whatever is to be done will have to be done quickly," he wrote. *"The forts should be run.* "[4] Break through the barrier, run the gauntlet of the forts, then isolate them from the city—today it reminds one of the island leapfrogging strategy of the Pacific War, and it was just as effective. After the war a Confederate general admitted: "When the obstruction existed, the city was safe; when it was swept away, as the defenses then existed, the city was in the enemy's power."[5]

On the night of April 20 the chain-linked barrier was literally swept away by the gunboat *Itasca.* With the river running at 4 to 5 knots, the gunboat's progress upstream was slow. A small breach was made by slipping part of the chain, but with the hulks securely anchored, the gap was small; so *Itasca* crept through, continued upstream, then turned and charged the chain at full speed, with the strength of the current to help her. On impact she rose four feet out of the water, riding on the chain and pulling the hulks with her—then the chain snapped; she was through; and one third of the river's width was open.

The full attack came four nights later. "Although it was a starlight night," wrote one of Farragut's officers, "we were not discovered until well under the forts; then they opened upon us a tremendous fire . . . and then all sorts of things happened."[6]

At a loss to describe in detail the shooting, bombing, burning, and ramming as Farragut's vessels encountered forts, hulks, and Confederate steamers, the officer felt his phrase "all sorts of things happened" was pretty lame, but actually it conveys brilliantly the confusion and chaos of that rapid night action. Once New Orleans was taken on April 25, Baton Rouge, far up the river, fell too, followed by Natchez, still further up; and on July 1, Farragut's forces advancing from the south and Union gunboats advancing from the north joined together at Vicksburg, Mississippi—the geographical crossroads of the Confederacy. The river there runs north to south; the railroad ran east and west. To the east lay Mississippi; to the west, Louisiana; northwest, Arkansas; and in the distant northeast, Tennessee—every one a Confederate state. If town, river, and railroad all fell to the Union, the southern states would be sliced into four quarters, scarcely able to communicate with one another at all.

But it did not happen. Vicksburg held on. Union crews were ill, supply lines long and tenuous, ships worn and damaged. On July 25 a partial retreat began northward and southward. The river was not completely evacuated; for hundreds of miles, in its northern and southern reaches, it remained in Union control. The center was still firmly Confederate, yet Farragut had achieved much. Fifteen years earlier, as a commander in the Gulf under Commodore Conner, he had deplored the apparently cautious attitude adopted by Conner "and the old officers at home." The reward, he said then, would be that "not one of them will wear an admiral's flag."[7] However, for his deeds on the Mississippi, he did. On July 16, 1862, eighty-seven years after the birth of the U.S. Navy, the rank of rear admiral was created, and David Farragut was the first to be given it.

On August 29, 1862, the Union strayed for the second time onto the battlefield of Bull Run. Over the next two days another 15,000 Northerners added their lifeblood to the mud, and some 8,000 Southerners died as well; the savagery of these battles would not be matched anywhere until the First World War. From his victory at Bull Run, the Confederates' General Lee crossed the Potomac into Maryland. On September 17 the armies clashed again at Antietam, less than sixty miles from the center of Washington. Again thousands were slaughtered. But this time the Union won—although not in the decisive way it could have, had Gen. George McLellan used his potentially overwhelming reserve. Nevertheless, the battle had two important political consequences: The Confederacy was now on the defensive on land, and when the British learned this, they decided to withhold political recognition from the southern states—a recognition which had long been pondered, and which, if granted, would certainly have altered the whole nature of the war.

The second political consequence was local, direct, and with enormous implications for all of American society. On September 22, just five days after Antietam, Lincoln issued his Emancipation Proclamation. With effect from January 1, 1863, slaves in areas "in rebellion against the

United States" would be free men and women. Unenforceable without southern acquiescence or defeat, the proclamation was no more than a declaration of intent; but it put matters on the line, winning the Union much moral support abroad and hardening attitudes on each side at home.

Far from being ready to acquiesce, the Confederates could still count at least three major ports among their advantages—Wilmington, North Carolina; Savannah, Georgia; and Mobile, Alabama. And it was from Alabama, on January 15, 1863, that C.S.S. *Florida* escaped to range the seas as a privateer.

Through the course of the war, nineteen vessels of various kinds sailed as Confederate privateers. Some were prizes themselves; some were bought, built, or seized in America; several were bought or built in France and England. Not all the vessels intended as privateers actually made it to sea: Tightening up on neutrality laws prevented a few of the foreign-built ones getting away, while the Union blockade kept others in southern ports for the whole war (including the yacht *America,* after which the America's Cup was named). But between them, the nineteen that did get to sea captured 258 vessels of all sorts. Of the prizes whose values were recorded, the least was worth $1,500 and the most valuable, $1.5 million. The most successful raiders captured or destroyed many times their own value in northern shipping. In terms of vessels, the "notorious pirate" *Sumter* took eighteen, yet she was not the most rapacious: *Tallahassee* took twenty-nine; *Shenandoah* took thirty-six; *Florida* took thirty-seven; and *Alabama* took sixty-nine.

Alabama's captain was Raphael Semmes, who had captained *Sumter.* With his two ships, he alone was responsible for one third of all Confederate captures. In the North his name became an object of loathing and terror; to those merchants who still sent goods in nonneutral hulls, he seemed like a malevolent ghost, able to appear and disappear at will, leaving nothing but the report of another loss.

Yet for all their style and dash, the privateers had no more long-term military effect than their predecessors in the Revolution or even the glamorous frigates of the War of 1812. There were not enough of them, nor could there ever be. The American carrying trade fell away badly and did not return to its antebellum levels for three generations. But northern imports and exports continued to be carried in other countries' ships, whereas in the South, as the blockade grew ever tighter, overseas trade evaporated.

During 1861 Jefferson Davis emulated President Jefferson's embargo at the beginning of the century and placed an embargo on cotton exports, expecting to encourage foreign recognition and further blockade running. The policy was no more successful than it had been before. Recognition never came; with northern encouragement Egypt's cotton trade boomed to fill the gap, and blockade runners made fabulous profits for themselves, not for the Confederacy. (Sometimes, of course, the runners did not get through. In the Shipwreck Heritage Centre in Hastings, on England's south coast, there is a poignant little memento to a mother and baby who died in a wreck in the Danish Virgin Islands in the early 1860s. In the same wreck—believed to have been a runner for the Confederacy—were found dozens of guns, rusted together in a corrugated mass.) By the time President Davis relaxed the embargo, the blockade was a reality; the chance to create a solid economic base for the southern war effort was gone; and through the first half of 1863, the anaconda clutched more firmly as northern vessels divided the South.

The stake at the beginning of 1863 was the two-hundred-mile section of the Mississippi between Vicksburg and Port Hudson. The Mississippi Squadron (under Rear Adm. David Porter, the Union's second flag officer) controlled the mighty waterway to the north of Vicksburg. South of Port Hudson and down to the Gulf, Farragut had control. In between the two crucial towns, the Red River joined the Mississippi and brought supplies to the Confederate forces in both. A blockade of the Red River would cut that line and seriously weaken the two towns; but to get to it, Farragut would have to go up the Mississippi past the high bluffs and guns of Port Hudson. Like Vicksburg, Port Hudson had been strongly reinforced since the Union's naval retreat from the river the year before. The whole Union operation would therefore have to be a joint military-naval action by their northerly and southerly forces simultaneously. The Navy would establish and protect water communications, while the Army would take and hold the land; in the northerly force, Gen. Ulysses S. Grant would work with Porter, while on the southerly side Gen. Nathaniel P. Banks would cooperate with Farragut.

Vicksburg and Port Hudson were both on the Mississippi's left bank, and both, from clifftops, commanded the river at points where it bends sharply, the natural flow making the opposite, right bank shallow. The navigable channel in each place ran close in to the cliffs, making any vessel very vulnerable to attack from above. Moreover, the natural land defenses to the north of Vicksburg were strong; between the town and the confluence of the Yazoo River and the Mississippi, the land was cut by miles of twisting creeks and bayous, while the Yazoo itself was overlooked by Hayne's Bluff. All in all, nature and the Confederacy in 1863 had made a seemingly impregnable fortress.

With Admiral Porter, General Grant spent the first months of the year trying to approach Vicksburg from the north, working down the Mississippi's right bank, across the bayous. The attempt did not work, for reasons Dr. Ninian Pinckney, a naval surgeon, made clear:

> The object of the admiral is to pass to the Yazoo above Hayne's Bluff. Here there is a heavily fortified point to pass. This bluff is seven miles from Vicksburg & in its rear. This once taken, Vicksburg must of necessity fall. In order therefore to take this fortification, the admiral has devised a plan by which he can get above the battery, without having to pass in front of it and thereby be exposed to its galling fire.

Porter hoped to squeeze his ironclads through a series of bayous, but

> the water is very shallow and heretofore nothing but small vessels of very light draft have passed them. The Confederates never dreamed of an attack in this way. The admiral runs this risk. . . . If the river falls before he can reduce the fort, he will be caught in a complete net. No supplies could reach him. . . . If this fails, there is no probability of the fall of Vicksburg.[8]

With Ulysses Grant around, there was plenty of action, difficult as it was; but in the South, General Banks was cautious to the point of inertia. Writing to his wife on February 1, 1863, Farragut said: "You will no doubt hear more of 'Why don't Farragut's fleet move up the river?' Tell them, because the army is not ready. Farragut waits upon Banks as to when or where he will go."[9]

Twice in the following two weeks, before committing himself to the arduous and perilous slog down through the bayous, Admiral Porter tried to simplify his task by securing the river south of Vicksburg. On each occasion an ironclad ran successfully past the town, only to be captured in the stretch below; and when he heard this, Farragut told one of his captains: "The time has come. I must go—army or no army."[10]

There was more to his decision than professional frustration and impatience with Banks's army; more too than the wish to overcome the previous year's retreat. Farragut, twelve years older than David Porter, had served with Porter's father in the Pacific in the War of 1812. From Porter Senior he had received his first command, a prize ship, before he was thirteen years old; and Porter Senior had adopted him. Thus the two admirals converging on Vicksburg were adoptive brothers—a strange slant. Farragut issued a general order echoing his attack on New Orleans: "The captains will bear in mind that the object is to run the batteries [at Port Hudson] at the least possible damage to our ships."[11] This was correct, navally speaking, but no one would have complained if he had added that there was a personal object as well.

On March 14 he made the dash with seven ships, including the steamer

Mississippi. Once Commodore Perry had called her a paragon; now she was feeling her age, and the advance was almost a disaster. Indeed, Farragut actually called it a disaster, for only two of the seven vessels got past, and *Mississippi* was blown up in the attempt. But the two that made it (one of them Farragut's flagship, *Hartford*) blockaded the Red River.

When Porter learned this news, he did not call it a disaster, but "a godsend. . . . It is worth to us the loss of the *Mississippi,* and is at this moment the severest blow that could struck at the South."[12] Grant agreed: "I look upon it as of vast importance."[13] And Gen. John C. Pemberton, commander of the Confederate forces at Vicksburg, wrote in dismay: "The Mississippi is again cut off. Neither subsistence nor ordnance can come or go."[14] A few months later, when he saw the results he had helped bring about, Farragut accepted their verdict on his "disaster"—"My last dash past Port Hudson was the best thing I ever did, except taking New Orleans."[15]

It was the most successful Union action on the river that month. Two days later, on March 16, 1863, Porter began his probing through the bayous; but five days after that, he had to retreat. As Dr. Pinckney marveled:

> He actually carried his ironclads through passes so narrow that the sides of the vessels cut into the trees. He penetrated a hundred and twenty miles through lakes, bayous and creeks, some of which were not fifty feet wide, and at the time when he was compelled to abandon the project he was within sight of the Yazoo. The army failed to keep up with the boats, and the enemy had 400 negroes employed in felling trees in his front and rear so as to impede his progress. Porter's retreat was not the result of a defeat—it was a masterly conducted affair and he succeeded in rejoining his squadron. For 100 miles he had to steam backwards, there not being sufficient room to turn his vessels.[16]

And these were not the double-enders designed for that sort of work, but ordinary steamers, bouncing from the trees on one side to those on the other. But masterly as the retreat may have been, it was a retreat nonetheless; and on the East Coast, April opened with a naval retreat that was the result of a definite Union defeat.

The northern assistant naval secretary, Gustavus Fox, had been thrilled at the spectacle of the Battle of Hampton Roads, declaring *Monitor* "absolutely invulnerable." An improved second generation was already under construction, mounting one 11-inch and one huge 15-inch gun, and both Fox and Welles reckoned that they should be used to capture Charleston at the first opportunity. However, there were problems attached to this: Charleston's whole harbor was mined, and marked with ranging buoys. Not only forts Sumter and Moultrie but the entire shoreline bristled with guns, and if a ship passed any given buoy, the gunners knew exactly how far away it was. Not surprisingly, Adm. Samuel F. Du Pont (in charge of the Charleston blockade) did not want to enter the harbor, but on April 7, against his better judgment, he tried.

His fleet included eight improved monitors and one ironclad frigate. It did not take long for the buoys to prove their usefulness. In two hours the nine vessels managed to fire a paltry 139 shots, while the shore guns replied with 2,200, hitting Du Pont's ships an average of fifty-six times each. Yet Du Pont was luckier than he knew; during the two hours of combat, his flagship was sitting on top of a mine which could not be electrically fired only because the wires connecting it to the shore were broken. In the battle, just one of his men was killed (the sole victim of gunfire in a monitor during the war) but one of the vessels limped out of the harbor to sink and the other eight, dented and battered, slunk away in humiliation.

The Union had been beaten off again. Yet if the lights of Charleston were bright that night, outside the harbor the northern blockade was still in place. By then, on the banks of the Mississippi, Grant and Porter had developed a new plan. "I am happy to say," wrote Grant to Farragut, who was still blockading the Red River, "the admiral and myself have never disagreed upon any policy."[17] Their current idea was simple, but very bold. Grant would march 45 miles down the right bank of the Mississippi. This would bring him to an easy crossing point 25 miles south of Vicksburg. Once he had reached the left bank, he would advance on the town and attack it, or if necessary besiege it. So far, so good; but three further factors were involved. First, to effect the crossing, Porter would have to send at least some vessels south through the gauntlet of Vicksburg bluffs. Second, because of the bluffs, Grant would not be able to advance directly on Vicksburg from the south. Third, Grant would have to cut himself off from his supply base during his advance, and no one could predict how long that would take.

Porter rushed the river at Vicksburg's hairpin bend on the night of April 16–17, 1863. Gunboats, river steamers, and rams fled past under a torrent of fire from the looming bluffs. Astonishingly, only one vessel failed the passage, which was repeated a week later with equal success by the fleet of transports which would carry Grant's army over the river. By the end of April, as a feint was made against Hayne's Bluff, Porter's seven ironclads bombarded and crushed Confederate shore batteries at Grand Gulf, and General Grant led a vanguard of 20,000 troops across the Mississippi. On May 1, Grant defeated the Confederate forces at Grand Gulf. Four days later, Porter himself was at Red River, and Farragut was able to return to New Orleans. By mid-May, Grant's Army of the Tennessee had covered a hundred miles doglegging east and west, had won five battles, and was hammering at the gates of Vicksburg.

"Mighty events, which I have already predicted, are coming to pass," wrote Dr. Pinckney. "The contest at Vicksburg . . . will be a bloody affair." On May 22, Grant attacked the town, was repulsed, and settled in for a siege. "Vicksburg holds out beyond precedent," Pinckney wrote on May 30. "And yet I cannot see how we can fail to take it. . . . Grant is a bold fighter and was never known to give up. He is the most desperate fighter we have, and I think will prove a good general. . . . The Confederates have about thirty days' half rations for their soldiers. . . . They are determined to fight it out at all hazards. It is wonderful how they hold out against such odds." And as Grant pounded the city from the land, Porter bombarded it from the river: "The admiral flies around in a little tug," Pinckney added admiringly, "while the bullets are falling like hail around him. He is a splendid man, and I think when you see him, you will agree with me."[18]

It was impossible for either Vicksburg or Port Hudson to last forever. Yet if they did not, the Confederacy would be split in two halves, east and west. The defenders endured for the whole month of June. Then on July 1, in distant Pennsylvania, at a place called Gettysburg, 70,000 of their comrades clashed with 93,000 Union men. That battle lasted three days, in which a total of *forty-three thousand* men died; and on July 4, 1863 (the eighty-seventh anniversary of the Declaration of Independence), Union generals and admirals knew that both at Gettysburg and at Vicksburg, they had won.

In Washington, on July 7, Gideon Welles was receiving a delegation from Maine concerned about the protection of fishermen when he was handed a dispatch from Admiral Porter, "communicating the fall of Vicksburg on the fourth of July. Excusing myself to the delegation, I immediately returned to the Executive Mansion."[19] There, with a map spread out before him, President Lincoln was pondering Grant's movements at Vicksburg when Welles rushed in and gave him the news.

He seized his hat, but suddenly stopped, his countenance beaming with joy—he caught my hand, and, throwing his arm around me, exclaimed: "What can we do for the Secretary of the Navy for this glorious intelligence? He is always giving us good news. I cannot, in words, tell you my joy over this result. It is great, Mr. Welles, it is great!"

Filled with delight and excitement, the two men left the mansion together; and side by side, they walked away across the sunny lawn.

17

★

THE REBS . . . HAVE GOT
GOOD COURAGE

*T*he U.S. Civil War has been called the first "modern" war, and though every war echoes the one before and presages the next, in many ways the Civil War predicted more than it repeated. On land, with rifled artillery, trench warfare, vast slaughter, and the exploitation of the air by the use (albeit limited) of observation balloons, it foreshadowed the First World War. At sea, one of the most remarkable characteristics of the conflict was the use made by both sides of advanced and experimental naval technology. The all-metal monitors with their rotating turrets, and the odd, rooflike construction of C.S.S. *Virginia* and other similar vessels, were the most celebrated. The Dahlgren gun, with its peculiar external bottle shape following the ratio curve of internal pressure, was the most consistently effective. But this war also saw the widespread use of mines and the first fatal use of a submarine.

In those days mines were known as torpedoes after the torpedo eel, which gives an electric shock. Coming in a variety of shapes and sizes, they were all basically quite simple weapons, detonated either by contact or by an electrical impulse through a wire connected to an observation post on shore. It was one of the latter type (fortunately with broken wires) above which Du Pont sat for two hours when he attacked Charleston.

Most commonly, the contact mines were made of old beer barrels caulked at the seams and stuffed with up to 120 pounds of gunpowder. Moored to float horizontally underwater, their ends were capped with conical projections to give a smooth flow of water over them, and contact fuses were built into their upper sides. Simple as they were, they worked: In one three-week period over March and April 1865, this type of mine blew up seven Union vessels in Mobile Bay. But they were undiscriminating, and two that drifted from their moorings in Charleston destroyed a pair of Confederate steamers.

More selective, though highly perilous to all concerned, were spar torpedoes, the rudimentary ancestors of today's underwater torpedoes. These were cylindrical or egg-shaped mines mounted on the end of a long spar, mounted in turn on the bow of a small vessel, and driven as rapidly as possible by whatever means available against the target vessel. On the rare occasions these were used, the attackers were just as likely to get blown up as the target. But on the night of October 5, 1863, what turned out to be perhaps the most adventurous use of underwater weaponry was introduced to naval warfare.

John Dahlgren (by then a rear admiral) had relieved Du Pont at Charleston, and Du Pont's ex-flagship *New Ironsides* was the target, with Dahlgren in it. As Daniel Angell Smith (paymaster on the nearby monitor *Nahant*) wrote to his sister, the Confederates "came down about 10 o'clock at night on some kind of an infernal machine with a torpedo attached, and run square into her bows where it exploded. It did not damage the vessel, but gave them a good ducking."[1]

Smith used a phrase that future generations would repeat for the same weapon: The "infernal machine" was a submersible, forerunner of the true submarine. C.S.S. *David,* attacking the Goliath of the U.S. Navy, had a submarine's instantly recognizable cigar shape. She was about 7 feet wide and 50 long; attached to her bow were a spar and a "torpedo" adding a further 10 or 12 feet to her length. Steam-powered (with her boiler placed forward, leading back to a two-bladed propeller astern), she carried a crew of four, and when she was in fighting trim, only her smokestack and tiny central cockpit projected above the water. In fact, she was so nearly invisible that her captain (Lt. W. T. Glassel, C.S.N.), thought she might well be deemed an illegal weapon—so he carried a shotgun to reply to any challenge. Secret weapons seemed somehow unfair, and he wished to give fair and unmistakable warning.

In her attack on *New Ironsides,* the target was slightly damaged (Paymaster Smith was wrong) but *David* herself was put out of action: In the "good ducking," the geyser of water sent up by the explosion cascaded down her funnel and put out her fires. Two of the crew abandoned ship and were captured; the other two managed to restart the fires, and the ship hobbled back to Charleston; and everyone, Confederate or Unionist, was deeply shaken. "Since the torpedo came down," Smith wrote nearly three weeks later, "our men have slept at quarters every night. We have all had to go to quarters from one to three times in the night, but the rebs are as frightened as we are . . ."

Dahlgren laid Fort Sumter under siege, striking daily at its defenses and those of the rest of the harbor. Beginning on October 26, 1863, the visible effects were terrific: "Sumter cannot stand this kind of pounding long," Smith told his sister. "You would be surprised to see the quantity of bricks and dust that a fifteen-inch shell will throw up." The fort seemed to disintegrate day by day in front of Union eyes, but digging in ever deeper, the defenders made shelters in the ruins and refused to give up. Early in December Smith noted that "the Rebs put up a new flag staff in Sumter last night. It is about fifty feet high. They have got good courage . . ."

They certainly had, for in the face of Dahlgren's monitors with their 15-inch guns, they held on for a full eighteen months, until February 17, 1865; and when they gave up, it was only because by then Charleston was surrounded on land as well as by sea.

In some ways the fort was actually less vulnerable than the besieging squadron. Fox had called monitors "absolutely invulnerable" when he saw the original in action at Hampton Roads. In his excitement, of course, he had exaggerated—as was clearly proved by the fate of the monitor *Weehawken,* one of the Charleston squadron. In June 1863, operating with *Nahant* off Savannah, Georgia, she captured the Confederate ironclad ram *Atlanta.* The victory was purely a matter of superior technology: *Weehawken*'s guns could fire further than *Atlanta*'s, and shooting at will out of Confederate range, the monitor had to fire a mere five times. Badly damaged by four hits, *Atlanta* ran aground, which was just the kind of result Fox liked. But as time went by, *Weehawken*'s men grew careless. "Dear Sis" heard from brother Daniel all about the tragedy of December 6.

> The monitor *Weehawken* sunk at her buoy yesterday afternoon at half past two o'clock. Twenty-eight men and four officers were drowned. The wind was blowing strong from the north-east and it was rougher than it has been at any time since I have been aboard. The vessel went down so sudden that I had just time enough to see her men washed off the top of her pilot house when she went down. . . . She went down with her colors flying, they could be seen clear of the water.

Perhaps suddenly realizing the effect his words might have on his sister, Smith continued: "Don't think that the *Nahant* is going that way for it was carelessness that lost the *Weehawken.* They had open their fore and berth deck hatch since morning, and a heavy sea swept them away, and nothing could prevent the water from running in. . . . They had taken in a large quantity of ammunition four days previous, which made her down to the head, and caused the water to run forward instead of aft and the pumps were no use." And then he concluded, rather weakly, "Don't get frightened"—as if the thought of a loved one being trapped in a metal box under water could be anything but frightening. Given that, it is pleasant to add that Smith survived the war, and that he and "dear Sis" were safely reunited.

The families of the crew of C.S.S. *H. L. Hunley,* though, saw only bodies. This was the original underwater killing vessel, and although she resembled *David* in appearance, she was somewhat nearer a true submarine than a submersible. Lateral fins enabled her to dive and surface, and though there were no air tanks, she had water tanks to assist diving. Because she was meant for actual underwater movement, she was not steam-powered—instead, eight men hand-cranked her propeller around—and instead of a spar torpedo, her mine was trailed astern. The idea was that she would dive beneath and pass under her target; the mine would follow, contact, and explode, while *Hunley* escaped on the other side.

It was ingenious, but it did not work. In experiments the vessel sank on five separate occasions, killing a total of forty-one men, including her inventor, H. L. Hunley. Even this did not prevent a sixth crew from volunteering, and on February 17, 1864 (exactly a year before Charleston's surrender) Lt. G. E. Dixon, C.S.N., took her out on her last voyage. After the fatal experiments, he had decided to abandon the trailing mine idea, to use a spar torpedo like *David*'s, and to approach barely submerged. The chosen target was U.S.S. *Housatonic,* a new steam sloop. *H. L. Hunley* was a hundred yards away when *Housatonic*'s officer of the deck spotted her. The sloop already had steam up, and backed at once, but the mine still struck. *Housatonic* sank in five minutes, and five of her crew died while the rest clambered into the rigging to await rescue. Meanwhile, *H. L. Hunley* vanished. Swamped or sucked down, she sank as well; and after the war, when the harbor was being cleared of wrecks, she was found a hundred feet from *Housatonic,* the corpses of her crew still inside.

When returning to their place of their birth, salmon jump dams. Generally speaking, warships do not jump dams at all; but that is what happened on the Red River in May 1864. West of the Mississippi, the Union's cause had been made more complicated by a French connection: Just before the fall of Vicksburg, troops of Emperor Napoleon III invaded and took over Mexico, installing an Austrian archduke as emperor there. Napoleon III had hopes of persuading Texas to become independent once more and, through the influence of his Mexican-Austrian puppet, of making himself a power within the North American continent.

In opposition to this and the Texan Confederates as well, the feeble

Gen. Nathaniel Banks was ordered to advance along the Red River as far as Shreveport, the main Confederate arsenal in the area. Admiral Porter was ordered to provide maritime support, using some of his gunboats (still busily patrolling the Mississippi and blockading the Red River) as transports and protection for the troops.

Progress up the Red River was tricky: It was narrow, winding, and shallow, the water level was dropping further, and there were rapids. Despite these handicaps, Porter managed to get six gunboats three quarters of the way to the joint Army-Navy destination. But on April 10 General Banks bumped into a southern army, disliked the experience, and turned back—leaving Porter unescorted, high, and almost literally dry. Hampered all the way downstream by the river's natural barriers, the gunboats were constantly harassed by Confederate sharpshooters as well, until they were back at the rapids. And there they stopped. Going upstream, they had been hauled over the rapids by brute force. Returning down, there was not enough water to allow hauling—in fact, the boats were not even afloat any longer; drawing seven feet, they were sitting on the mud in only 40 inches of water.

The problem was solved in an unorthodox but resourceful way. With trees, rocks, and sunken barges, a dam was built across the river. Gradually the water rose; the gunboats floated free; and then on May 9 the center of the dam burst. Taking fortune literally at the flood, Porter ordered the boats to race the rapids at once. Thumping, bouncing, and rolling, they did so; and they survived, only one being holed and as swiftly repaired. A little dazed, but very pleased with themselves, they returned to the Mississippi to tell their patrolling colleagues of the spectacular adventure, and in Washington, Congress gave its official thanks. Nevertheless, it was yet another repulse for the North; and in the same period, at the battles of Chancellorsville and Spottsylvania, the Union lost a further 30,000 men.

Altogether the brightest star for the Union in this unhappy first half of 1864 was an event which took place far from America: the sinking of C.S.S. *Alabama* by U.S.S. *Kearsage* on June 19 outside the French port of Cherbourg. Over sixty U.S. merchantmen had fallen victim to this raider as she ranged from the Atlantic to the Indian Ocean. Built in Laird's yard at Birkenhead in England and known there as Hull No. 290, she had left the River Mersey late in July 1862, bare hours before the arrival of governmental orders for her detention under the rules of neutrality. Captained by Raphael Semmes with Confederate officers and a British crew, she terrorized northern traders, who (as always) demanded naval protection.

"There is no little censure," Gideon Welles had written just after Christmas 1863, "because fast vessels are not sent off after the *Alabama,* and yet it would be an act of folly to detach vessels from the blockade and send them off scouring the ocean for this roving wolf, which has no country, no home, no resting-place."[2]

But with reluctance, ships were eventually detached. They searched for Semmes from the West Indies to the East Indies, off the coast of Brazil and off the Cape of Good Hope. He always managed to keep one jump ahead, making the most of neutrality laws wherever a safe haven was found, and stretching those laws when local conditions permitted. But two years' roaming took its toll of the ship and forced a prolonged stay for refit and repair in a good harbor. Semmes chose Cherbourg; and while he was awaiting permission for *Alabama* to be overhauled, U.S.S. *Kearsage* steamed in.

Once before, in Martinique, the Confederate vessel had been trapped by a U.S. Navy ship. On that occasion she slipped away at night. This time, *Kearsage* waited four days and nights. She was faster than *Alabama*, better armed (among her seven guns were two 11-inchers, while *Alabama*'s largest was 8 inches) and partially armored, with vertical chains over her hull. *Alabama* was of unarmored oak. Nevertheless, as Semmes reported later to Secretary Mallory, "I steamed out of the harbor of Cherbourg between nine and ten o'clock on the morning of the 19th of June, for the purpose of engaging the enemy's steamer."[3]

As a French warship escorted *Alabama* to the edge of the 3-mile limit, the townsfolk of Cherbourg flocked out to watch from the shore. *Kearsage* lay 4 miles further out. On a clear summer's day, with telescopes in hand, even 7 miles was not too distant for the excited citizens to be able to see, but one daring and impudent yachtsman (an Englishman, as it happened) actually followed *Alabama* out for a better view.

The steamers took three quarters of an hour to come up to each other, a slow-motion preamble of rising tension onshore and on board. They were a mile apart when watchers on the land saw the first puff of smoke from *Alabama,* followed by the first gun's rumble and the sight and sound of *Kearsage*'s reply. And then, for an hour and a quarter, the spectators watched one of the oddest sights they could ever have seen—a mobile, but entirely localized, battle at sea. It was something that could scarcely have happened in the age of sail, for as Semmes reported, "to keep our respective broadsides bearing, it became necessary to fight in a circle; the two ships steaming around in a common center, and preserving a distance from each other of from three-quarters to half a mile."

The vessels used a combination of solid shot and explosive shell. With *Kearsage*'s extra range and partial armor, it was pretty much a foregone conclusion. When *Alabama* began to sink, Semmes tried to make for the shore, but inrushing water extinguished his furnace fires. He struck his colors in surrender, but *Kearsage,* thinking the flag had only been shot away, fired five times more, stopping when the Confederate began to settle in the water and men were seen jumping overboard. Nine in *Alabama* had been killed, and ten more were drowned.

When the news came to the United States, a popular comment there was that *Alabama* had been built of English oak, crewed by English seamen, and sunk by an American in the English Channel. This was all true; and perhaps, had Semmes not been Confederate, the commentators would have added that he and forty of his men were also rescued by an English yacht, for after his front-row view of events, the yachtsman sailed in and took on board as many as he could.

Seven weeks later, the name "Alabama" sprang once again to prominence. In Mobile, Alabama, the Confederate Navy had built its single most powerful ship. The iron-plated ram *Tennessee,* with a casemate roof like *Virginia,* had two 7-inch and four 6-inch rifled guns, was 209 feet long, and carried 6 inches of armor. The entrance to Mobile Bay's 400 square miles was further defended by three gunboats, two forts, and numerous mines. Outside, Admiral Farragut had long wished to attack, but the Red River and Mississippi had taken ships from his squadron time after time. However, on August 4, 1864, he had all the vessels he could want: four monitors, seven wooden sloops, and seven gunboats. All he lacked for ideal conditions was a westerly wind and a flood tide—the tide to speed his fleet in, the wind to blow their smoke toward the main defending fort.

The next day at dawn the wind was right and the tide was right. At 5:30 A.M. the fleet began moving in, with sloops and gunboats lashed together in pairs. (The idea was that if one was disabled, the partner could try to power both.) At 6:30, accompanied by her three gunboats, the Confederate ram *Tennessee* started a lumbering approach—her best speed anyway was 6 knots, and the tide was setting against her.

At the same time, Farragut's leading monitor, *Tecumseh,* opened fire on the fort—just two shots, and they would be her only ones. As she fired, Farragut's leading sloop sighted a minefield, backed, and came close to colliding with the flagship, next in line. The sloops crowded together, blocking one another's lines of fire and caught in a crossfire from the Confederate fort and squadron. *Tecumseh* continued to press forward as the Union sloops swarmed around each other; then in the middle of the cramped waters, 500 yards from the flagship and only 200 yards from the Confederate ram, she struck a mine.

Those old "torpedoes" may have been primitive and unreliable, but when they worked they were savage. Gunsmoke already settling over the ships was briefly blown away by the explosion, and *Tecumseh* was seen to rear up and plunge, her propellers coming clear of the water; then she was gone. To get a view above the smoke, Farragut had already climbed into his flagship's rigging, and from there, as *Tecumseh* vanished and the leading sloop's captain dithered, he bellowed: "Damn the torpedoes, full speed ahead!"

Hartford, his flagship, surged out of the confused line of sloops. Mines were heard thumping on her hull, but none exploded. The way was clear and the fleet followed, curving around the slow Confederate *Tennessee* as she tried to ram and chasing the three rebel gunboats into shallow water. Watching *Hartford* race up the bay, Franklin Buchanan (commander of the Confederate squadron) turned to the captain of *Tennessee* and said: "Follow them up, Johnston; we can't let them off that way."[4]

Buchanan had been *Virginia*'s captain in the first fight with the original *Monitor,* and after that had been promoted to rear admiral—an empty title in a navy that did not have the strength to fight large actions and one for which, in any case, he did not really have the skill. Out of all the options open to him, pursuing Farragut's vessels into deep water was the instinctive one, but the worst. The opportunity he offered was taken at once: Half of Farragut's fleet converged on his ship. The sloop *Monongahela* rammed her squarely but succeeded only in crushing her own bow against the enemy hull, while her shot bounced uselessly off *Tennessee*'s casemated top. Two more sloops, *Lackawanna* and the flagship *Hartford,* struck the Confederate hard, then collided with each other as three monitors came up and opened fire. One of these, the double-turreted *Chickasaw,* maintained a steady fire for thirty minutes with 11-inch shells, ripping great holes in *Tennessee*'s hull and disabling four of her six guns. Inside the Confederate, her rudder chains were shot away; Buchanan's leg was broken in an explosion; and as three of the sloops lined up to ram again, Captain Johnston asked the admiral what he should do. "Do the best you can, Johnston," Buchanan replied, "and when all is done, surrender."

All had been done. Johnston tugged in the boathook, which had held the flag since its staff had been shot away, and tied a white flag to it.

"I shall at any time be pleased to receive proposals for peace," said Jefferson Davis two weeks later, "on the basis of our Independence. It will be useless to approach me with any other."[5]

An air of unreality was creeping into the southern president's statements. Atlanta was on the point of evacuation: On September 2, 1864, Gen. William T. Sherman took the city for the Union. Another of the last Confederate raiders was lost five weeks later when U.S.S. *Wachusett,* in the neutral Brazilian port of Bahia, rammed and captured C.S.S. *Florida.* Seven days after that, Sherman began marching through Georgia, burning, looting, and with brutal efficiency destroying everything in a sweep

60 miles wide and 240 miles long to the coast at Savannah. And during the night of October 27–28, at Plymouth, North Carolina, C.S.S. *Albemarle* (another casemated ram along the lines of *Virginia*) was blown up and sunk.

"Torpedoes are not so agreeable when used on both sides," Admiral Farragut had said in March: The United States objected vigorously to their use by the South. Farragut spoke for the North when he added, "I have always deemed it unworthy of a chivalrous nation; but it does not do to give your enemy such a decided superiority over you."[6] Quite so—and chivalry is always the second casualty of war.

In November 1864 Lincoln was reelected president of the United States. In December Gen. George H. Thomas thrashed a Confederate army at Nashville, taking 10,000 prisoners; and as Tennessee emptied of organized Confederate resistance, the siege of Fort Fisher, at Wilmington on the coast of North Carolina, began.

Guarding the mouth of Cape Fear River, Fort Fisher was one of the largest Confederate earthworks, its faces running a quarter mile one way and three quarters of a mile the other. Upriver, 20 miles to the north, Wilmington (still North Carolina's main deepwater port) was by then the only remaining port where small, swift Confederate vessels regularly ran the blockade. Everything from saltpeter to shoes came in, and though the quantities were small, the supplies were vital to the forces under Gen. Robert E. Lee. (Ironically, the Unionist admiral commanding the North Atlantic Blockading Squadron for much of that time was Robert's cousin Samuel P. Lee.) When it was decided that Fort Fisher must fall, Porter was brought back from the Red River to do the job; and, after a preliminary bombardment, he started the full attack on Christmas Eve.

Five ironclads and over forty other vessels, mounting more than six hundred guns between them, delivered two shots a second at the fort, waiting for a Union army of 6,500 men to rush in and take it. The Army did not turn up. On Christmas Day, when the overdue soldiers arrived, the bombardment recommenced; then, after advancing to within a hundred yards of the fort, the troops turned back. Their generals had decided the fort was not sufficiently damaged to justify an assault. General Butler in particular assessed it as impregnable and went back to Washington to say so; and when he was in the very act of making his report, news arrived of the fort's surrender. On January 13, 1865, Farragut had bombarded it for the third time. Another Union army of 8,000 was ready and—this time—eager. For good measure the admiral sent in 2,000 sailors and marines. The fort's garrison was only 2,100. They capitulated on January 14; the Confederacy's last blockade-running port was gone; Sherman, finished with Georgia, was tearing through the Carolinas; and on January 30 Gideon Welles noted in his diary: "Great talk and many rumors from all quarters of peace."[7]

The final famous names came tumbling down. February 17, 1865: Charleston fell at last. April 2: General Lee evacuated Richmond. Washington was in an uproar of jubilation—Welles wrote that the city "appeared patriotic beyond anything ever before witnessed."[8] And at last, on April 9, 1865, in the courthouse at Appomattox, the final scene of four years of death and hope and terror took place. Generals Lee and Grant met, and Grant accepted Lee's surrender of the Confederate Army of North Virginia to the Union Army of the Potomac.

Passing his men, General Grant announced: "The war is over," and let them bellow out their victors' delight. Then he silenced them and added: "The rebels are our countrymen again."[9]

For Abraham Lincoln, they had never been anything other. "The tidings were spread over the country during the night," wrote Welles, "and the nation seems delirious with joy. . . . This surrender of the great Rebel captain and the most formidable and reliable army of the Secessionists virtually terminates the Rebellion. There may be some marauding, and robbing and murder by desperadoes, but no great battles, no conflict of armies."[10]

The great parts played by the land armies of both sides were universally apparent. But if others in the North ignored the contribution of their fleet, Lincoln recognized it, and just after the fall of Vicksburg in 1863—that crucial time in the Union's campaign—he paid tribute to the ships and men of the U.S. Navy. "At all the watery margins they have been present," he said.[11] "Not only on the deep sea, the broad bay, the rapid river, but also up the narrow muddy bayou, and wherever the ground was a little damp, they have made their tracks."

Despite its very considerable efforts, the same could not be said of the Confederate Navy; in 1884, its ex–assistant secretary, James D. Bulloch, observed sadly that "the whole that could be accomplished was not sufficient to turn the scale, or to greatly delay the final result of the war."[12]

On November 6, 1865, the last Confederate flag to fly in war was hauled down when the one remaining commerce-raiding cruiser of the Confederate Navy sailed into a British port and gave herself up. By then Lincoln was five months dead, victim of an assassin in the most dramatic event ever seen in Ford's Theater. If he had lived, the peace might have been real; the reconstruction he had planned might, perhaps, have been as generous and painless as he had hoped; it might not have gone with the wind. Yet a generation later, even a Southerner could see that the true victory lay with neither North nor South alone, but with the restored nation as a whole. In 1894 J. Thomas Scharf, ex-midshipman in the Confederate Navy, pondered his youthful experience and looked to the future of South and North together:

If the United States surprised the nations of the world by the development of its war power during that war, a careful examination of
what was accomplished in the Confederate States will be found to
have greatly exceeded the results in the United States when the
conditions and circumstances of the two parties to the war are
considered and contrasted. If, while fighting each other and each
party destroying everything that could not be removed, these grand
results were respectively accomplished—what limit shall be set to
the capabilities of such a people united and excited by the same
determination in their defense of their common country?[13]

PART FOUR

REACTION

1 8 6 5 – 1 8 8 1

★

*As the nation grows in peacetime
and older officers oppose change,
the fleet decays.*

18

*

SO NEGLECTED OF
LATE YEARS

*O*n July 4, 1866, ninety years had passed since the Declaration of
Independence. In those nine decades, the United States had fought
at sea in six separate conflicts—the Revolution, the Barbary Wars, the
Quasi-War, the War of 1812, the Mexican War, and the Civil War. The
U.S. Navy had gained experience in blockading and being blockaded; in
diplomacy and distant patrols; in sail and steam. It had firsthand knowledge of armored and unarmored vessels, of mine warfare and of submarines—not only from the attacks of C.S.S. *David* and *Hunley,* but also
through the construction, late in the Civil War, of its own *Intelligent
Whale,* a hand-cranked machine never used in combat. Gideon Welles,
by adding three extra bureaus, had refined the Navy's administration to
a form which remained essentially unchanged until after the Second
World War. The accuracy of its gunners was well known; it had dry
docks, navy yards, foundries, and rolling mills; and it had contributed
materially to world exploration.

One of its few notable weaknesses was a lack of experience in fleet
action, although its leaders knew all there was to know about single-ship
fights and commerce raiding. Its nine decades of adventures had given it
the legends and traditions essential to a great navy, and at the end of the
Civil War, in simple terms of numbers of vessels, it rivaled the Royal
Navy. In Britain its monitors were apprehensively admired: The U.S. fleet
had proved it could affect and implement foreign policy. To those outside

the United States it seemed evident that with its navy as a political instrument, the country could begin to play with confidence against the Great Powers, and, if it played with skill, could be sure of joining that select group.

And yet in 1876, the centenary of the Declaration of Independence, a world survey of "Naval Powers and their Policy," published in Great Britain, did not include the United States. Fifteen nations were described, including some which one might not think of as obvious today—Brazil, Turkey, Peru, Austria. But of the American fleet, all that was said was that its guns were "condemned all over the world and superseded," and that its "system of armor plating is also unsound."[1] The survey concluded: "It is surprising that the Navy of the United States has been so neglected of late years."

Five more years went by. Then, in 1881, another survey (entitled "Warships and Navies of the World") added five more fleets to the list of those worth describing—the Portuguese, Greek, Egyptian, Chinese, and Japanese. Only twenty-seven years earlier, Perry had signed the first treaty with Japan, and already that country's navy was important; but as far as the United States was concerned, a detailed examination of the Navy was deemed pointless because of its "present degenerate condition."[2]

At that time, when the British Empire was at its height, most Britons accepted as a matter of course that a big navy was, of itself, a good thing: It was both an emblem and agent of power. So they were astonished when, after the Civil War, Americans virtually destroyed the U.S. fleet—and not only did so with apparent alacrity, but also, it seemed, deliberately neglected what was left. For some reason, the United States appeared to be willfully throwing away the chance of power abroad. To imperial Britons, such perverse behavior was mystifying.

Thirty years later, in 1911, the British Royal Navy was still supreme on the seas. The Imperial German Navy had developed into the world's second most powerful fleet. The Imperial Japanese Navy had catapulted itself to the rank of third-strongest fleet in the world, amazing everyone by defeating both China and Russia. And among these changes, there had been such positive changes in the U.S. Navy too that Alfred Thayer Mahan felt able to hope "that our Navy will be brought at least equal to that of Germany."[3]

In 1912 he was confident enough to increase the target: "The U.S. Navy should be second only to that of Great Britain."[4] By then there was a phrase to describe the years of America's naval neglect—the dark ages. Mahan's first and most famous published work, *The Influence of Sea Power upon History, 1660–1783,* came out in 1890. Since then his influence on American naval thinking has been so dominant—and the U.S.

Navy has itself been so influential—that the dark ages of the U.S. Navy, from 1865 to 1898, are still often remembered in the United States as an embarrassment, almost as something to be hidden from posterity.

But to dismiss those years out of hand is as much a mistake as it is to think that a big navy is, by definition, meritorious and useful. Mahan advocated a large navy, but not for its own sake—as he said in a postscript to one of his letters, "It should always be remembered that the question of increase is not primarily naval, but one of national external policy."[5] And it is in those terms that the "dark" years should be seen.

"November 24th at sea. Ugh! What thundering *big* seas! Cold too as Greenland! Howling like sixty!"[6] U.S.S. *Hartford,* Farragut's old flagship, was heading east in the winter of 1865, and one of her officers was not enjoying the voyage. "What on earth induced Mr. Vasco da Gama to call this cape by the sweet name of La Buena Esperanza (Good Hope) I don't know," he complained. "I am sure *I* never wish to see again these immense masses of water rolling and tumbling and roaring about you."

Hartford's mission reflected the two main aspects of the United States' limited external naval policy after the Civil War: diplomacy and the defense of merchant shipping. To put it in the key phrase of the day, she had to show the flag. "The commerce and the navy of a people have a common identity and are inseparable companions," Gideon Welles said when the Civil War was over. "Each is necessary to the other, and both are essential to national prosperity and strength. Wherever our merchant ships may be employed, there should be within convenient proximity a naval force to protect them and make known our national power."[7] To that end, Welles reinstated the policy of distant stations and sent *Hartford* out to be flagship of the East India Squadron, operating from the Strait of Sunda to Japan. Antebellum trade with the region had been brisk; but when *Hartford* arrived off Macao in February 1866, her commanding officer, Henry H. Bell, had disappointing news. "I regret to say," he reported to Welles, "that we have seen but one merchant vessel under United States colors, between the Cape of Good Hope and Macao, although we have encountered many of them under the flags of other nations."[8]

It was one of the first postwar signs of the continuing effects of Confederate raiders. American trade was there, but it was mostly in ships which, though perhaps American-owned, were foreign-registered. Almost a million tons of American merchant shipping had transferred to foreign flags during the war, and the victorious government did not permit those ships to reflag under the Stars and Stripes. Just before the war, 66 percent of U.S. foreign trade was carried in 2.5 million tons of American shipping; by 1900 less than 10 percent of the trade was still carried in American vessels, and they totaled little more than 800,000 tons' displacement. Overall, trade blossomed: From the end of the war to the end of the century imports tripled in value, while exports went up eightfold. But it was not in American hulls; and the U.S. Navy could scarcely pretend to be defending ships which simply were not there.

American hearts had ceased to beat to the rhythm of the sea. For merchants, ships under foreign flags did the job of carrying goods to and fro perfectly well. For most of the rest, worn out by four years of bloodshed and having no wish or need for national colonies, activity at sea implied foreign complications, while the land had more than enough to offer both native-born Americans and immigrants—gold, railways, industry and agriculture, and, in theory, freedom for all. With its physical area and its political system finally established, the consolidation and exploitation of the continent could gather pace, and people saw little need for a navy.

Central government, representing the people, shared their view; yet though everyone expected postwar naval reductions, few would have predicted their dramatic scale and speed. In 1865 there were 671 commissioned ships of war in the U.S. Navy, with 7,000 officers and 51,500 enlisted men. Two years later, 433 of the ships had been decommissioned, and most of those sold; the officer corps had shrunk by 5,000 and the body of enlisted men by nearly 40,000. This gave a disproportionate number of officers, but they were more difficult to get rid of than the enlisted men; and now some of them put themselves firmly in the way of any advance or alteration for the Navy.

In general, a rivalry developed over the question of relative status between line officers (those who filled executive billets traditional in a sailing navy) and the new caste of engineer officers essential to a steam navy, with line officers determinedly resisting moves toward equality. Based on prejudice, jealousy, or both, this resistance was sustained by a selfish (but natural) desire to avoid losing or diminishing the pay and perks of office. And line officers fought encroaching equality so effectively that the two corps were not merged until 1890.

Line officers also fought change in another, more reactionary way. In the Civil War, everyone had seen the use of steam power. After the war, however, even those who had used it well and gained much from it relinquished steam altogether; and among these men, Vice Adm. David D. Porter was infamously foremost. On March 11, 1869 (as if his steam-powered attack on Fort Fisher and his campaigns on the Mississippi and Red rivers had never taken place), he ordered "a return to the old custom," the use of sail. Another of his decisions, three months later, was that "constant exercise shall take place with sails and spars." Twelve days after that, he ordered "commanders of fleets, squadrons, and of vessels

... to do all their cruising under sail alone," adding that "they must not be surprised, if they fail to carry out this order, if the coal consumed is charged to their account."[9] Threatening to make a captain pay for any coal his ship used was a sure way to prevent the use of steam and to concentrate the mind on sailing at all times.

Porter's opinions would have had no effect if he had been one of the 5,000 retired officers; but he had come to a position of wide power. When Gen. Ulysses S. Grant took office as president in 1869, he appointed as naval secretary a nonentity named Adolph E. Borie, with Porter as his adviser. Nominally, Borie remained in office for three months, when George M. Robeson took over; but for those hundred days, David Porter—a professional officer—was effectively civilian head of the Navy too. If he said sail, men sailed. And they kept on doing it long after Robeson came in, because Porter was promoted to admiral—a move not calculated to reduce his influence—and Robeson, who maintained Porter's orders intact, concluded eight years of office with a public self-congratulation at having avoided the national expense of building an armored fleet.

When Robeson's successor, Richard W. Thompson, took office, he knew next to nothing about ships and had never been in one. It is said that the first time he ventured on board a vessel and looked down below, he exclaimed: "Why, the durned thing's hollow!" The story seems too absurd to be true, but it does give a measure of the ability of naval secretaries in the "dark ages": they were an ignorant and ineffective lot. Yet they did the job the government and the country wanted them to do.

"We all know that the Navy, since the necessity of maintaining the blockade and chasing pirates has been over, have only had a holiday season," said one senator in 1868. "I think we can indulge in a little less gala parade on the oceans and lay up more of our vessels."[10] The degradation of the Navy in public esteem became a self-fulfilling prophecy. The Navy was not seen to be needed, so funds for construction and repair were withheld and ships sold; because there were no funds to keep them in shape, the remaining ships became more and more bedraggled; looking useless confirmed the belief that they were useless; and the vicious circle began again. In a foreign port it was especially noticeable, as letters home showed:

"The harbor here has ten immense ships of war," an officer wrote from France, "and we with our unpainted sides make a sorry figure. . . . It makes me sorry to think we are such small potatoes compared to them."

From Gibraltar, an ensign wrote: "I cannot tell you how disappointed I am in the *Trenton*. I had hoped to get at least on board a ship of war which might at least not be sneered at in the comparison of our ships with those of foreign navies—but alas! The *Trenton* is a failure comparatively." And yet, as the first U.S. warship to have electric light, she was one of the best ships of the fleet. "If I can respectably do it," the ensign concluded, "I am not going to sea in a United States man of war until one is built fit to be called such."

In distant Asia the same dismay was felt: "A North German frigate came in today," said an American naval engineer. "It is a very nice looking vessel, in fact she looks more like a Man of war than any vessel we have on this station."[11]

Reacting to their demoralizing conditions, naval men often made the situation worse by their behavior in public places, particularly in French ports. In 1870 Villefranche (a small port on France's south coast, not far from Nice and set against the magnificent backdrop of the Maritime Alps) was adopted as a point of stores and rendezvous for the Mediterranean Squadron, now renamed the European Squadron; and whenever a ramshackle, embittered ship sailed in, officers and men had a thoroughly good time gambling, dancing, drinking, going to the theater and opera, falling in love, and entertaining visitors on board.

"We have had such a nice time in Nice it is a bore to be anywhere else," one officer wrote.[12] "This place is given up to gaieties," another agreed. "There is nothing like it in our fashionable places, nor in fact anywhere else in the world." Everyone present thought it was wonderful—"Although I haven't sought it," a third protested, "I see a great deal of Nice people, and dine out several times a week. Offers of seats at operas, rooms at two houses, dinners. . . . I am having a splendid time." Carnival at Mardi Gras in February was a special highlight: "I assure you I never had a jollier time," said a Marine officer, revealing that he joined in the procession "dressed as an old worm." It could be nearly too much of a good thing: "You can go to a breakfast, an afternoon reception, a dinner and a ball, all in the same day," a commander told his father, "and you can do it every day of the week almost, if one's constitution will stand it. . . . I am rather glad we are going away."

Senior officers stuck in America disapproved. "The custom of 'wintering' and especially at Villefranche is believed to be very injurious to the morale of the service," Rear Adm. Daniel Ammen wrote to the secretary of the Navy. "Vessels should not be permitted to visit Villefranche at all except en route."

Ammen was only half right. A few days' letting off steam in a welcoming port after a long, rigorous voyage never hurt anyone. On the other hand, if riotous debauchery became the main object of the exercise (and so it seemed to Ammen) something was wrong; but he missed the point. If sailors in Villefranche "let the side down," as he saw it, they did so because they no longer felt the side was worth keeping up. With their worn-out ships the butt of foreign jokes, knowing their service was disdained at home and aware that their own authorities did not support improvements, they found little reason to be grateful and less to be proud; and Ammen himself was part of the problem. Stuffy and very old-fashioned, he believed that "the time is not distant when the marine ram will take the place of the enormously expensive armor-plated gun-bearing ships of today."[13] Even as late as the 1890s he was still deprecating the concept of a steam navy, while back in the 1870s, when agitation from junior officers might have stemmed the rot, he was chief of the Bureau of Navigation, controlling all officers' assignments. Any young critic at that time could easily find himself taken from a reasonable billet and sent off to Asia, Africa, or the South Atlantic.

It made no difference whether one thought the U.S. Navy should be steam or sail, modern or archaic; either way, the decline was evident. Depending on one's view, the fleet was either not as good as in the old days, or else it was not keeping up with modern developments. Or, as many felt, it was still too big. There is only one thing to put on the credit side for government and nation—at least the navy was not *dis*established. To cite that as a plus really is scraping the barrel for virtue, but there was hardly anything else. Otherwise, a single bright point was the establishment in 1873 of the U.S. Naval Institute, providing in its monthly *Proceedings* a forum of professional debate. Apart from that very worthwhile creation, there was for the Navy as a whole—with its size and role suddenly and drastically circumscribed—one sole defense: the dogged perseverance displayed by some of its officers and men. And with that to combat national disdain and neglect, it hobbled on.

Among the Navy's diplomatic activities in the "dark ages" was the voyage to Europe and Russia (in 1866) of Assistant Naval Secretary Gustavus Fox. This created quite a stir on both sides of the Atlantic, because for the first time the journey was done in a monitor. "Did you cross the Atlantic in that thing?" an amazed British admiral asked Fox. Certainly, replied the assistant secretary. "I doubt if I would," the admiral grunted. But the fact that it was possible gave the British food for thought, and in Russia, Fox was feted for six weeks.[14]

From the middle of 1867 to the end of 1868, Admiral Farragut was commander of the European Squadron. For those seventeen months, he was effectively a diplomatic activity in his own right. Everyone from St. Petersburg to Constantinople, including royalty, wanted to meet the hero of New Orleans and Mobile Bay. It was more of a triumphal progress than a tour of duty; and while it was going on, a member of the House of Representatives observed sardonically: "Our people can rest assured that their European Squadron is naught else but a picnic for which they must pay the bills."

But there was little else to do in the Mediterranean. With few merchant ships to protect, few marauders to protect them from, and no war to fight, active duties were limited to little more than giving security to expatriate American citizens—including those whom Louis Goldsborough, first commander of the squadron, called "turbulent, disturbful, dirty Missionaries!!!"

Since the beginning days of the republic, American missionaries had been traveling to most parts of the unenlightened world, spreading the Gospel. Members of the U.S. Navy frequently wished they would not, for they tended to go to places that only the Navy could reach; and as Comdr. Robert W. Shufeldt of the Asiatic Squadron said, it was "a matter of regret that these missionaries, preachers of a gospel of peace, should seem so often to need the interpretations of a Gunboat, in order to make the heathen understand them."[15] Other officers recorded similar cynicism: In Turkey, Lt. Charles Sperry said, "I believe that the wayward Turks are accused of having roasted either a stray missionary or possibly boiled a stray consul over his rosy kitchen fire, and we are supposed . . . to wring satisfaction from the Sultan,"[16] while in 1870 Adm. Stephen C. Rowan observed that "peace and quietness now appear to be the rule, with an occasional exception, such as . . . the murder of a missionary now and then."[17]

In 1867 new links were thrown across the Pacific to Asia: The island of Midway was taken as a coaling station, and the Pacific Mail Steamship Company commenced a monthly service between San Francisco and Hong Kong. Four years later an attempt was made to open Korea to trade. Like the Japan of old, the "Hermit Kingdom" cherished its lack of contact with other countries. Unlike Perry, though, Rear Adm. John Rodgers left several hundred dead and came away suggesting that 5,000 soldiers should be sent to occupy Seoul. It was not an auspicious start to American-Korean relations, and eighty years later American soldiers would see more than enough of Seoul.

More successful, at least in the short term, was a treaty contracted in 1872 with Samoa for an American naval base at Pago Pago. But in 1879, shortly after the treaty had been ratified in Washington, British and German warships began to intrude, and soon war notes were being sounded by all. Such scares (and there were two others in the "dark ages") made Congress turn repentant eyes on the fleet—at any rate, until the scare blew over.

The first of these episodes was the *Virginius* affair of October 1873. For five years revolutionaries in Cuba had been fighting against Spain's continued rule of the island. *Virginius,* a steamer flying the American flag, was captured with a cargo of arms and a number of insurgents on board. Taken to Cuba by her Spanish captor, the steamer was impounded and fifty-three passengers and crew, including Americans and Britons, were shot after a summary trial. Vessels from the Royal Navy and the U.S.

Navy were swiftly on the scene, demanding an end to the executions until the case had been properly investigated. While American newspapers clamored for war, Secretary Robeson recalled the European Squadron and announced that the fleet was ready for anything. But in something of an anticlimax, it was discovered that the *Virginius* had been flying the Stars and Stripes illegally. The prisoners were returned; the Spanish paid indemnities to the families of those who had been shot; and Robeson took the opportunity to exercise the fleet off Key West. Five frigates, six monitors, fourteen small wooden vessels, and sundry auxiliaries took part, and it was pathetic. Not one of the vessels could do better than 4½ knots. Deterioration was embarrassingly obvious: As one newspaper said with caustic honesty, the combined squadrons were "almost useless for military purposes. They belong to a class of ships which other governments have sold or are selling for firewood."[18]

But it was not until the 1880s that the Navy's ruling conditions began to change. In 1879 Chile went to war against Peru and Bolivia, winning a string of naval victories. The United States had economic interests in Peru and, when it became clear that Peru was losing, sent a naval mission to Valparaiso in order to try to persuade Chile to stop fighting. The American Pacific Squadron contained only a few old wooden vessels; the Chilean navy was one of the most up-to-date in the world and included two new English-built battleships with 12-inch armor and breech-loading guns. Naturally the Chileans felt the Americans were being both intrusive and impertinent, and according to a member of Congress they "simply told the American admiral, and the American Government, through him, that if he did not mind his own business they would send him and his fleet to the bottom of the ocean."[19] One of the American captains, deeply offended, said how amazed he was "that Chile, elated and made overconfident by her easy victory over her neighbors, means to fight even so formidable a power as the United States." It was as well for his bruised pride that the two countries did not go to war; the feeble remnants of the U.S. Navy would have been trounced, and an overland campaign would have been out of the question.

Nevertheless, it was about that time that moves began that would eventually result in the United States becoming an acknowledged world power, with its navy a prime instrument of foreign policy. On June 29, 1881, the new secretary of the Navy, William H. Hunt, wrote a letter to Rear Adm. John Rodgers, namesake and son of the first head of the Navy Commissioners. "In order to meet the exigencies of the Navy," he said, "it is highly important, in the opinion of the department, to present in the report of the Secretary at the next session of Congress a practical and plain statement of the pressing need of appropriate vessels in the service at the present time."

A board would be set up to advise the department under seven headings—the number of vessels to be built; their class, size, and displacement; the materials and form of construction; the nature and size of their engines and machinery; the necessary ordnance and armament for each; the appropriate equipment and rigging; and the internal arrangements, any other details, and final likely costs of each. Two of the headings were particularly noticeable: materials of construction, and nature and size of engines and machinery. It was clear what the secretary had in mind, and on November 8 the board reported back.

"The unarmored vessels now in service are altogether inadequate in number and efficiency for the work that they are constantly called upon to perform," they declared. Pondering construction materials, they explained they had thought about iron and rejected it, deciding that "notwithstanding the greater cost of steel as a shipbuilding material, the lack of experience in the manufacture of steel frames in this country, and the experimental stage that steel shipbuilding is passing through in Europe, it should be recommended as the material of construction." As for armament, "it is imperatively necessary that a reliable type of high-powered, rifled, breech-loading gun should be introduced into the service." And they concluded with emphasis: "*Such vessels are absolutely necessary* for the defense of the country in time of war."

Twenty-nine million dollars, they said, should be allocated for the immediate construction of sixty-eight vessels, including eighteen unarmored steel cruisers, twenty wooden cruisers capable of doing 10 knots, five steel rams, five torpedo gunboats, and twenty torpedo boats. Moreover, they recommended that within eight years, in addition to the foregoing, the Navy should include twenty-one ironclad battleships and seventy unarmored cruisers.

The fifteen men of the advisory board were all professional naval officers. The previous year one of them (Lt. Edward W. Very) had been the gold medalist in the U.S. Naval Institute's third essay competition, writing on "The Type of (I) Armored Vessel, (II) Cruiser, Best Suited to the Present Needs of the United States." Thus the institute was already intimately involved in the field of formal advice to the government; and the length, detail, sweep, and clarity of the board's report, submitted three days before its deadline, showed that despite the dark years, its members had kept their knowledge of developments and modern naval theory up to date. It showed too a sound basis for negotiation with Congress: Not everything was completely unfamiliar to a layman (for example, "all classes of vessels should have full sail power" as well as steam), and after a decade and a half of stagnation, more was recommended than Congress could be possibly expected to approve in one go. But if the mere *principle* of steam, steel, and rifled guns was accepted as a basis for the fleet, the U.S. Navy would be on the brink of transfiguration, reconstruction from the keel upwards.

To say that the dark ages were drawing to a close and that a new American naval dawn was about to break suggests an inevitable cyclical rhythm. Such was not the case, nor has it ever been; the only obvious times anyone can confidently predict expansion and contraction are at the beginning and end of a war. To lay the blame for the dark years entirely on ignorant naval secretaries and reactionary naval officers is likewise a mistake, although some secretaries of the period were incredibly ignorant and some officers abnormally reactionary. Certainly the U.S. Navy had been "neglected of late years"; seemingly, to foreign eyes, America had thrown away its advantageous international potential after the Civil War and had dropped out of the game. Following the reconstruction of the Navy in the 1880s and '90s, and until very recently, the prevailing view in the United States has echoed the foreign view of a century ago. This (which might be called the imperial interpretation) viewed the dark years as an incomprehensible error, a blind alley in the United States' journey to world power. But that hundred-year-old view from other countries (particularly Great Britain and France) was based on the assumption that everyone wanted world power. To see a nation capable of the challenge rejecting it voluntarily was mystifying. Guardians of empire saw empire as the thing most to be desired. The only plausible explanation for not wanting an empire and its essential partner, a great navy, had to be folly, ignorance, or reaction.

Because the United States' acquisition of world power in the twentieth century has coincided with the blossoming of its new navy, the imperial interpretation of the "dark ages" has been widely adopted there as well. That interpretation assumes that in the twenty-five years from 1865 to 1890, Americans thought the same and had the same values as British and French people then and Americans today. On the whole, though, they did not, which is why their twentieth-century descendants (and nineteenth-century Europeans) called the dark ages dark. Actually, that period may have been the brightest in U.S. history. After the terrible slaughter of the Civil War, with half a million dead, no one wanted another war; and with millions of square miles having been added to the nation, no one needed another war. Without having to look further, there was more than enough empire available within the nation's coasts and frontiers; and beyond those coasts and frontiers there was absolutely no plausible threat. As Alfred T. Mahan wrote in 1890:

> Except Alaska, the United States has no outlying possession—no foot of ground inaccessible by land. . . . The weakest frontier, the Pacific, is far removed from the most dangerous of possible enemies. The internal resources are boundless as compared with our present needs; we can live off ourselves indefinitely in "our little corner" . . .[20]

In those words he neatly paraphrased the real American mood of the preceding quarter century. Any country bordering the sea always faces the same questions—whether or not to have a navy; if so, what it will be expected to do; and how, therefore, it should be composed. All of these come down to the question of perceived necessity.

For example: In 1865, just after the Civil War ended, Gideon Welles was criticized for the apparently unnecessary launch of a new iron ram vessel. To his critics, he said: "I engaged in this work and made this contract with great caution. At the time this decision was made, a foreign war was feared. We had a large defensive force, but not as many and formidable vessels as we should need in the event of a war with a maritime power."[21]

Again: In 1870 a member of the House Committee on Naval Affairs gave a tidy definition of the terms which governed his country's naval thinking: "I have but one desire in the discharge of my official duties as connected with the Navy, and that is to render it respectable, powerful, and efficient. I use these terms in their American, and not in their British sense. I do not speak of a British navy or a French navy; I speak of an American Navy such as it has been to our fathers, and such as it should be to us in time of peace."[22]

And though he was answering yet another criticism on his handling of the naval side of the Civil War, a remark from Secretary Welles aptly sums up the whole reason for the U.S. Navy's "dark age." In 1865, he wrote: "I was accused of not having a navy of formidable vessels. *I had vessels for the purposes then wanted.*"[23]

By the end of its first hundred years, the nation had allowed its navy to decline into a shoddy and disreputable pretense, no longer "respectable, powerful and efficient" in any sense, British, French, or American; and there were perfectly good reasons for this. In their first hundred years, Americans had achieved much more than had ever been dreamed of when the Declaration of Independence was written down, and eventually had neither the need nor the wish to go further. Hawaii did not belong to the United States then; nor did Puerto Rico. The Imperial Japanese Navy was not a tangible threat to the Pacific frontier; the Panama Canal did not exist. All those factors justified the Navy's decline. But while it was going on, the happy security of "our little corner" was twice shaken by war scares; and, as Mahan pointed out, U.S. independence could be compromised not only by war, but by peaceful competition as well.

"Should that little corner be invaded by a new commercial route through the Isthmus," he said, "the United States in her turn may have the rude awakening of those who have abandoned their share in the common birthright of all people, the sea."[24]

But then the United States' second hundred years began—and the fleet and the nation were transformed together.

BOOK TWO

STEAM AND STEEL

1881 – 1991

1

★

APPROACHING UNDER
STEAM

"The American Republic has no more need for its burlesque of a Navy than a peaceable giant would have for a stuffed club or a tin sword."[1]

That, in 1882, was the opinion of an American social commentator named Henry George. The Navy then possessed fourteen ironclads (most of them Civil War monitors) and a handful of wooden vessels. None had any armament more powerful than a 5-inch smooth-bore gun, most were crumbling to pieces, and all were outdated. But only fifteen years later, in 1897, Theodore Roosevelt stated that "ultimately those who wish to see this country at peace with foreign nations will be wise if they place reliance upon a first-class fleet of first-class battleships," adding the somewhat worrying remark that "all the great masterful races have been fighting races."[2] And in that year the U.S. Navy's North Atlantic Squadron alone included two armored cruisers, two second-class battleships, and three first-class battleships. Secretary of the Navy John D. Long was certainly justified in noting that "our naval power has more than doubled within the last few years."[3]

The change in both quantity and quality was so rapid and so radical that even while it was happening, a phrase was invented to describe the process: the New Navy. "Reconstruction," the other word most often used then and now to label that decade and a half, hardly goes far enough. The ships that were built were not more of the same as always; nor was the strategic thinking which provided their theoretical justification. The New Navy was the result of a new view of the nation and the rest of the world. It was also, in part, the trigger of that new view—at first only a small and scattered group of men had the imagination to see the possibilities a re-created navy would provide for the nation, but once its re-creation was under way, the possibilities became more and more apparent.

For the nation, the last twenty years of the nineteenth century were a time of transition; for the Navy, they were more than a time of reconstruction—they were years of renaissance. Looking back today over two centuries of American naval history, those twenty years separate the first and second centuries with astonishing sharpness. In its first hundred years, the U.S. Navy was built of wood, powered by wind, and governed essentially by a coastal defense, commerce-raiding, single-ship strategy. Then came the dividing years, the birth of the New Navy; and in their second hundred years America's warships have been built of steel, powered by steam, and governed by a strategy of oceanic fleets.

Of the world's other three major navies in the first half of the twentieth century (the German, Japanese, and British), the British Royal Navy had, by comparison, a long and leisurely transition to modernity. The German and Japanese navies (beginning just after the American Civil War, when the reunited states were withdrawing from the sea) started in modernity and stayed modern until their defeats in 1945. Only the U.S. Navy has this distinctive wood-and-canvas, steam-and-steel division, and the twenty years of its laborious rebirth are made still more remarkable by the events which bracketed them: the assassinations of two presidents. In 1881 President Garfield was murdered, an event which happened to coincide with the beginning of the end of the Old Navy—it was Garfield's secretary of the Navy, William H. Hunt, who sought the initial recommendations that eventually did away with the old fleet. A similar unfortunate coincidence marked the end of the New Navy's beginning: In 1901 President McKinley was shot dead, and his successor, Theodore Roosevelt, was one of the new fleet's strongest advocates.

The change from old to new was far from easy. At the same time, Japan was speedily creating its own navy from scratch, strengthened in the endeavor by an undivided national opinion. Yet though America was virtually starting from scratch as well, debate and controversy were to be expected there. In the end, the reconstruction process was very American; beginning with contention and diversity, it moved to consensus and action, and ended with achievement and enormous national pride.

No one can have been very surprised when, in 1882, the chairman of the House Naval Affairs Committee dismissed outright the recommendations of Secretary Hunt's advisory board. Quite apart from the nature of the recommendations, revolutionary to America (ironclad battleships, steel cruisers, rifled breech-loading guns), the price tag of $29 million was enough to put anyone off. Foreign relations were generally stable, and in places notably good—in 1882, for example, Capt. Robert W. Shufeldt successfully concluded a trade treaty with Korea. Under these circumstances, the need for naval renovation was unclear; yet for some people, Hunt's shopping list, costly as it was, did not go far enough.

Benjamin F. Isherwood (when chief of the Bureau of Steam Engineering under Gideon Welles toward the end of the Civil War) had developed fast steam cruisers. Admiral Porter, in his strange postwar reaction against steam, had fired Isherwood, but since then Isherwood's views had not changed. With three other members of Hunt's committee, he submitted a minority report, maintaining that the unarmored cruisers of the majority recommendation could not be "properly considered as fighting machines, although they carry a respectable armament" because "all foreign ironclads, even those of the least dimensions and thinnest armor" could defeat them.[4]

From H.M.S. *Warrior,* its first ironclad, the Royal Navy had progressed between 1860 and 1876 to a massively protected ironclad (the seventh H.M.S. *Dreadnought*) which sported iron armor plating 24 inches thick, while France in 1881 had vessels with 20 inches of *steel* armor. Protected cruisers, with plating on the deck alone and no added protection on the hull, were small beer in comparison.

As early as 1868, some American naval officers, such as Stephen Rowan, had perceived the inevitable trend. In Hong Kong, Rowan observed H.M.S. *Rodney,* the flagship of Vice Admiral Keppel, and remarked: "This is the only old-style ship of the line now in commission—it will likely be the last. I grieve that we are compelled to give up this class of ship; they were treasures in the days of wooden walls and small calibers, but won't do now."[5]

Nevertheless, even in the 1880s there was still a prevailing belief that increased coastal defenses would be enough for the United States: mines, rams, torpedo boats, gunboats, and monitors, which in 1882 an ex–naval secretary declared were the most efficient vessels for the purpose. In 1883 Hunt's successor, William E. Chandler, repeated that the United States' physical isolation remained its best defense; a little later, Robert Shufeldt testified that the United States would never take a war into European home waters; and in 1887 Admiral Porter reiterated that monitors could resist "the heaviest European ironclad that could reach our shores."[6]

Over forty years on, after World War I, another admiral wrote of the 1880s, putting their mood in a nutshell: "Our Navy was maintained simply as a measure of precaution against the wholly improbable danger of our coast being attacked."[7]

However, in the 1880s it was at least recognized that if the coast were attacked, its defenders would have to be metal ships of some sort, and that wooden ones should be phased out. In 1882 and '83, repairs on wooden vessels were limited first to 30 percent and then to 20 percent of the cost of building a new one, and in the 1883 construction debate, appropriations were authorized for three small steel cruisers and a dispatch boat. But in the same year, midterm elections produced a Democratic majority in the House of Representatives. Three small cruisers were enough for them, and hesitant Republican steps toward a new navy were stopped. Unless a substantial section of public opinion began to see a navy as something more than a coastal defense force, nothing would happen without being imposed from the outside.

Those first three small cruisers (*Chicago, Boston,* and *Atlanta*) were hybrid vessels combining steam with sail power. One of the obvious and oft-repeated arguments against all-steam ships was America's lack of a worldwide network of coaling stations, such as that provided for the Royal Navy by the British Empire.

Admiral Porter, who had threatened to bill commanding officers for every scrap of coal used by their ships, still asserted that the new cruisers should be able "to go around the world without touching their coal."[8] At the same time, in direct opposition, the Navy Department's advisory board (all of them professional officers like Porter) said categorically that "the use of sails as a means of propulsion should be entirely abandoned . . . for there is hardly a doubt, but that the *Chicago,* at sea under sail alone, would be a prey to an antagonist of one-third her size, approaching under steam." And they added that if "it would be argued that sails should be retained to extend a warship's range since we lacked convenient coaling stations," then the answer was straightforward: "Coaling stations must be provided."

When men of such standing disagreed on fundamentals, it was not surprising that most others were confused and opted for the seeming stability of the status quo. However, the new navalists' central thesis was that the existing stability was unlikely to last forever. Through the U.S. Naval Institute's *Proceedings,* a limited audience of professionals read in 1879 that "an untroubled assurance of peace is no guarantee that war will not come."[9] Even that plain statement failed to affect everyone who read it, and it affected the general public not at all; but only a few years later, its author, Alfred T. Mahan, would be known and quoted throughout the naval world. And the forum which brought him to global eminence was "a college . . . for an advanced course of professional study, to be known as the Naval War College."[10]

Soon to be widely imitated abroad, the new college would become the main voice of the New Navy, the foundry of thought for the U.S. Navy's second (and third) century; and there was something very appropriate about its location. Its originator, Commodore Stephen B. Luce, chose the site for practical reasons. He wanted a deep-water harbor in a northern climate, away from the unhealthy summertime humidity of Washington and Annapolis, and he wanted a powerful senatorial supporter. He found both in Rhode Island—the very place where, 109 years earlier, in 1775, members of the Rhode Island General Assembly had made the first-ever proposal for "an American fleet . . . for the protection of these colonies."[11]

Located at Newport, the college has become one of the most highly respected institutions of its kind in the world. When it began, however, there was grave doubt whether it would survive more than a few years. Its first building was a half-ruined poorhouse; at the end of its first year its equipment totaled one chart of the Battle of Trafalgar, four borrowed desks, and twelve borrowed chairs. It had no official funding; in the subjects it was intended to investigate ("all that related to naval tactics, naval strategy and the naval policy of a state"), Luce noted that "not only were there no instructors but there were no textbooks"; and since he was obliged to lobby, discreetly but strongly, for support, Secretary of the Navy William C. Whitney soon took against the project: "I finally awoke to the fact that the whole thing was being set up and worked in Congress behind me," Whitney wrote to his wife, promising to "wipe the whole thing out shortly."[12]

Part of the problem facing this novel venture was its very novelty—not only in the United States, but worldwide. In 1810 an Army War College (the *Kriegsakademie*) was established in Berlin, followed by the British Military Staff School in 1873 and the French *École Militaire Supérieure* in 1878; but the nearest thing to a naval parallel anywhere was the Royal Naval College at Greenwich, and that provided only technical courses. What Luce had in mind was "no less a task . . . than to apply modern scientific methods to the study and raise naval warfare from the empirical stage to the dignity of a science."[13]

Leadership of eighteenth-century wars had been regarded as the exclusive province of gentlemen; the favorite leaders of the nineteenth century, particularly in the United States, were inspired charismatic amateurs. Luce was moving toward a twentieth-century concept of warfare as a scientific struggle, based on unchanging fundamental principles and led by professionals trained in the comparative analysis of previous naval wars. Both in the United States and abroad such training existed for armies, but nowhere for navies; even in Britain the rise of sea power had been a matter of trial and error, of individual skill and intelligence, rather than a fulfillment of systematic knowledge.

When he was a young officer in the Civil War, Luce had taken part in the siege of Charleston, hoping like his colleagues that with sufficient battering the town would submit. One day General Sherman said to him:

"You Navy fellows have been hammering away at Charleston for three years, but just wait until I get into South Carolina; I will cut her communications and Charleston will fall into your hands like a ripe pear."

That was exactly what happened, and later Luce remembered how "after hearing General Sherman's clear exposition of the situation, the scales seemed to fall from my eyes. It dawned upon me that there were certain fundamental principles underlying military operations—principles of general application whether the operations were conducted on land or at sea."[14]

If, today, the statement seems naive, it is partly because of the very effectiveness of the U.S. Naval War College in working out and teaching those general principles. Certainly the first major publication, in 1890, by a Naval War College lecturer was highly influential, and not only in America; indeed, even though it is now in many ways outdated, Alfred T. Mahan's book *The Influence of Sea Power upon History, 1660–1783* remains one of the best known of all American naval textbooks.

In 1887 Mahan had realized that "there is nothing in the range of naval literature to place alongside the many and elaborate treatises on the art of war on land in its various branches. Much indeed has been written. But what has thus far been produced is for the most part fragmentary, representative of special views, partial and unsystematic in treatment. No attempt has been made to bring the whole subject under review in an orderly well-considered method."[15]

The daunting task of correcting that situation became Mahan's personal challenge at the college. Noticing that "there is an entire lack of textbooks upon which to base a course of instruction," he did the only thing that could be done—he wrote the book himself.[16] It began as a series of lectures to unwilling, bored lieutenants; it ended as a standard reference, guide, and provoker of thought in admiralties and navies all around the world. Drawn from his close study of "the many and various treatises," it was not a work of original thought; but it was completely original in its philosophical, analytical synthesis of others' thoughts. It was far from the last word on the subject, but it pulled together all the threads into a single coherent volume. As such it was a masterpiece, and the lieutenants left the college feeling, much as Luce had, that they had experienced a revelation. Mahan's revelation was that he had shown them how to think: Success for him lay "rather in forming correct habits of thought than in supplying models for close imitation."[17]

The lessons he taught had been learned in Britain, Japan, and Germany, as well as in the United States. But they took time to be accepted at home, and there is an almost unbelievably narrow stuffiness in a remark made by Commodore Francis M. Ramsay three years after the book's publication. Ramsay was chief of the Bureau of Navigation, in charge of officers' assignments. Mahan asked to be excused from sea duty in order to carry on studying, teaching, and writing—and Ramsay turned him down. The reason was plain to any right-thinking naval man: As Ramsay said, "It is not the business of naval officers to write books."[18]

Nor, it seemed, was it any longer the business of naval officers to go exploring. The heyday of American naval exploration had passed with the Civil War—a bad state of affairs from almost any point of view, for greater knowledge of the physical world could benefit almost everyone, and the U.S. Navy had built itself a respectable pedigree of explorers. In the late 1830s there had been the Wilkes Expedition to the Pacific and Antarctica; in the 1850s a veritable fountain of global curiosity had sprung up in the fleet, with William Lynch investigating the Dead Sea, James Gilliss conducting astronomical observations in Chile, the Rodgers-Ringgold survey of the western Pacific, Thomas Page charting the River Plate, several searches for the lost British explorer Sir John Franklin, Perry's journey to Japan, surveys of the west coast of Africa, and attempts to determine the best route for a canal or railroad across the Isthmus of Panama.

But the fountain dried up after the Civil War. Exploration was expensive. The Army still mounted occasional expeditions, but the Navy was unable to—even though it showed it could still voyage successfully in naturally hostile waters, as in 1884, when three naval vessels rescued the seven survivors of an Army expedition to the west of Greenland. Yet despite official discouragement, there were two important expeditions by naval personnel during the 1880s: one a tragedy, the other the first step to a triumph.

The first was the voyage of the steamer-sailer *Jeannette,* commanded by Lt. George Washington De Long, "to that unknown part of the world lying North of Behring's Strait."[19] Because of naval disapproval, the ship was supplied and the journey financed by a New York newspaper magnate; and when *Jeannette* left San Francisco in July 1879, De Long noted in his journal that "not a sign of a Naval Officer was seen in the departing ovation." Delayed for a while by searching for a Norwegian explorer who had in fact made his way to safety, *Jeannette* was frozen in the icepack barely two months after her departure from San Francisco—"and that at a point which a sailing ship, the 'Vincennes,' reached in 1855 without any difficulty," De Long wrote gloomily.

Late in November the ship broke free briefly into a "canal" through the ice, "and we were pushed, forced, squeezed and driven through this mile of canal amid a grinding and groaning of timbers, and a crashing and tumbling of ice that was fearful to look at"—all by moonlight, before being frozen in again. Sinister omens were seen: a bloodred halo around the moon; a black aurora which blotted out the stars as it moved. The thermometers froze solid; and for a total of nineteen months the ship remained beset in the pack, until on June 12, 1881, she was crushed. The explorers then took to the boats. Where possible, they rowed or sailed; otherwise, when the floes closed in, they hauled their craft across the ice, always heading for the nearest coast—Siberia.

In a gale, one boat and all its crew vanished forever. The other two boats made it to land but were widely separated. Thirty-four men had set out from the banners, bells, and bunting of San Francisco; twenty-two of them died in the Arctic, drowned, frozen, or starved to death. De Long was one of the victims, dying of hunger and exposure; the commander of the second boat, Chief Engineer Charles Melville, was one of the fortunates who survived, and he returned to the Arctic in 1882 to locate and bring back the bodies.

But perhaps the most poignant part of the heroic tragedy was on a private level. De Long had been married only a few years, and he and his wife were still deeply in love with each other. Fifty years later, when she was an old woman, Mrs. De Long was persuaded to write of the ordeal and, through reliving it, found she fell in love with her dead husband all over again. By then Melville (who was also married) had become an admiral, and might have been expected to have had the happier life; he had survived and succeeded. Yet his wife, an alcoholic, a spendthrift, and a good shot, had gone mad. If one were forced to choose Melville's fate or De Long's, one might well feel De Long had the better side of it.

No such tragedy attended the journey to Greenland in 1886 of Robert E. Peary, the other important expedition of this period. In a letter to his mother he wrote: "Remember. . . . I *must* have fame, and I cannot reconcile myself to years of commonplace drudgery and a name late in life when I see an opportunity to gain it now, and to sip the delicious draught while yet I have youth and strength and capacity to enjoy it to the utmost."[20]

He was then thirty years old; he had been attracted by the Arctic since the age of six; and he had an overwhelming desire for celebrity. In an earlier letter he had said: "I don't want to live and die without accomplishing anything. . . . I would like to acquire a name which would be an 'open sesame' to circles of culture and refinement anywhere, a name . . . which would make me feel I was the peer of anyone I might meet."

Before his thirtieth birthday he had completed a detailed plan of attack on the Arctic which included two wholly new ideas, "an entire change in the expeditionary organization of Arctic research parties." Instead of using several ships, the party should be as small as possible, and should live as much as possible in the Eskimo manner. Eskimos could survive in that inhospitable region, so it seemed logical to follow their habits—but no previous explorer had thought of that.

Equally logically, the culmination of Arctic exploration had to be the discovery of the North Pole. Peary's first step into "that northern region which holds my future name" was in the summer of 1886. Approaching Greenland, he was thrilled by the continuous daylight ("Truly this midnight sun, this Arctic circle has given me a glorious reception") and by luck he found a companion, Christian Maigaard, who was every bit as daring as himself. Following the principle of keeping the expedition as small as possible (and also because of lack of funds), Peary had been going to explore the icecap alone. Had he done so, he probably would not have come back.

The Greenland icecap has an area of 1.35 million square miles, and the ice can be anything from 1,000 to 5,000 feet thick. There is nothing to see but sky, sun, and ice—and sometimes not even those: "Many a time I have found myself traveling in gray space," Peary wrote, "feeling the snow beneath my snowshoes, but unable to see it. No sun, no sky, no snow, no horizon—absolutely nothing that the eye could rest upon . . ." Moving through such dense fog, indistinguishable from the snow underfoot, gave the uncanny sensation of "walking upon nothing," when he "would be obliged to stop until the passing of the fog, or formation of higher clouds, gave me something to keep the course by."

Apart from fog blindness ("blindness with wide-open eyes"), there was the danger of snow blindness; there were hidden crevasses and fragile snow bridges, glacial streams and pools; and when Peary and his companion finally turned back, there was a hair-raising "dash down the slope of the eternal ice." For that labor-saving but risky adventure, they tied their sledges together like a catamaran, and with an improvised sail and using a hatchet for a rudder, they sped "down the frozen slope with a breathless rush," arcing over chasms fifty feet wide. Amazingly, they got back to their coastal base in one piece, completely undeterred by all the hazards they had encountered.

Peary and Maigaard had penetrated about a hundred miles inland from Baffin Bay, to a height of over 7,500 feet above sea level—further than anyone else had ever gone into Greenland. To his mother, Peary wrote: "My last trip has brought my name before the world; my next will give me a standing in the world." And the achievement was completely his own. He had tried to go on an official naval basis, arguing that exploration should be viewed as "special duty with the Geographical Society." But like Commodore Ramsay telling Mahan he had no business writing books, Secretary Whitney took a dim view of Peary's proposal. If he went anywhere, it would be as a civilian, said Whitney—"the service upon which you are about to engage can in no sense be considered naval duty."[21]

Naval duty meant protecting recognized American interests, and that was all. But while Peary plodded happily over the icecap and Mahan wrote his mental revolution (both diligently ignoring official discouragement), events in distant places taught others that the United States had interests beyond its coasts.

Early in 1885, a coup in Panama threatened to cut the United States' substantial import and export trade across the isthmus; in 1889, ten years of rivalry with Germany over coaling facilities at Pago Pago in Samoa (which had already brought scares of war) came to a natural climax in a terrific hurricane. The United States' so-called warships out there, with their "old-fashioned engines and defective steam power," were wrecked, leaving the Pacific Ocean almost bare of American naval shipping.

This was not all. From 1879 to 1888, Count Ferdinand de Lesseps (known, for his construction of the Suez Canal, simply as "the Great Frenchman") was busily trying to dig a sea-level canal through Panama. The project foundered in fever, mud, and rain, but it was obvious that sooner or later a canal would be built, and as one American naval officer pointed out: "When any two nations become involved in war, the one that has the most powerful navy will attack the commerce of the other where it converges on the canal." Asking if the United States would be prepared to defend the canal's neutrality, he declared that no European nation would be deterred by the mere disapproval of the United States and concluded that "the Monroe Doctrine is therefore a right that we must maintain by force."[22] To this Mahan added that "militarily speaking, the piercing of the Isthmus is nothing but a disaster to the United States in the present state of her military and naval preparedness."[23]

Such considerations gave weight to arguments for a larger navy but did not define its composition. A single seagoing armored vessel was authorized after the 1885 Panamanian revolution, and in the wake of the Samoan hurricane, Secretary Benjamin F. Tracy reported that if the United States were to fight even a defensive war with any hope of success, armored battleships were essential. He recommended the construction, over twelve or fifteen years, of twenty coastal defense vessels, sixty cruisers, and twenty battleships. Many thought battleships an unnecessary extravagance; a common belief existed that cruisers, even unarmored ones, were like an army's cavalry and could reduce a hostile battleship force long before it reached U.S. shores. Stephen Luce brusquely dismissed this: "One of the functions of light cavalry is to protect the flanks of the army," he wrote in 1889. "Our cruisers are to protect the flanks of what? Nothing! There is no main body, no line of battle, no battleships, no navy, nothing but accessories." And he added, still more bluntly, "The battleship is the foundation of the Navy. The United States has no battleships, therefore she has no Navy."[24]

Though disputed by some Americans to this day, Darwin's theory of evolution found swift general acceptance in the United States; but it was open to two contrary interpretations. On one side, social reformers like Henry George (who called the U.S. Navy a needless "burlesque") believed that humanity had evolved beyond war, at least in the New World. The archaic practice might continue to afflict the Old World, but war would not touch the United States again. Working from the same basis, others (like Luce and Mahan) did not accept that physical evolution was bound to bring moral evolution with it. Instead, they maintained that the principle of survival of the fittest still applied in the United States as elsewhere; and the Navy had its own version of evolution.

In martial terminology, the word "evolution" signifies the coordinated movement of a body of men or group of ships; and in his report for 1889, Secretary Tracy established a "squadron of evolution," to be composed entirely of new vessels and to be kept together as a unit. In 1801, early in the Barbary Wars, the Old Navy had had a "squadron of observation" in the Mediterranean. With the squadron of evolution, the New Navy marked its newness and moved visibly toward the goal of being a cohesive fighting fleet.

Congress made a wise decree in 1886: Any new American warships should be made of American steel and iron. As the fleet took on its new shape, domestic industries burgeoned to match its needs, and more people understood that a Navy could provide the direct benefit of employment, even for civilians.

Other external goads increased the momentum. In 1891 Chile was in the throes of revolution, and, as a neutral site, the American Legation in Valparaiso became a place of refuge for the overthrown government. A vengeful mob hunted down a group of American sailors, wounding eighteen and killing two of them. For four months, until a peaceful settlement was effected, the two countries again hung on the edge of war. The following year, turmoil in Hawaii brought a request from those islands for annexation by the United States. The offer was not taken up, but many American naval officers felt that sooner or later possession of the islands would be essential for America. Back in 1867, Admiral Porter had said as much: "Honolulu is bound to be the principal stopping place between China and California and a point of great importance to American commerce. . . . We could not afford to let so important an outpost fall into the hands of any European power."[25]

In 1893 the new secretary of the Navy, Hilary A. Herbert, firmly endorsed the Navy's political utility, stating in his annual report: "We must make and keep our Navy in such a condition of efficiency as to give weight and power to whatever policy it may be thought wise on the part of our government to assume."[26]

In 1894 the cauldron of Latin American politics brought revolution to Brazil, and an American squadron of five new cruisers and one old gunboat was sent to Rio to protect U.S. merchantmen. Though still not large, it was difficult to remember when the U.S. Navy had last mustered such a show of strength, and with a good deal of nerve (but not much difficulty) they managed to release the merchant ships held in Rio's harbor.

In the following year, 1895, there was still more Latin American trouble, this time precipitated by the United States. Venezuela had a long-standing claim on a part of neighboring British Guiana. Deciding that this could be a test case for the Monroe Doctrine, a note was sent from Washington to London demanding that the dispute should be put to arbitration. Not surprisingly, the British thought this a considerable cheek. Nevertheless, at the end of the year, President Cleveland began talking tough, telling Congress that America "would resist by every means in its power the appropriation by Great Britain of any land which, after investigation, we have determined of right belongs to Venezuela."[27]

But when the Naval War College prepared plans for a possible conflict with Britain, it began to look as though the president might have gone too far. The United States had a first-class battleship completed, two second-class ones building, and a newly launched armored cruiser. Against these, the cutting edge of U.S. "power" abroad, Britain possessed sixteen armored cruisers of the most modern type, and over three dozen battleships. Even allowing for British commitments elsewhere, the Royal Navy would still find the U.S. Navy little competition, unless a third navy joined in on the American side. As Americans began to grasp the possible consequences of President Cleveland's bluster, the British, confident in their claim, accepted arbitration; and when the arbitrators found in Britain's favor, Americans and their president learned with some relief that his posturing would not be tested.

But fifteen years earlier, with hardly a seaworthy ship to call its own, America would not have dared even to posture. Since then, the general mood in the country had changed again. The erratic but large modernization and expansion of the fleet since 1881, the series of war scares coming rapidly one after another, and the gradual fading of Civil War memories as a generation reached adulthood after growing up in peace—all these (added to the evidence that the United States' national interests went beyond its continental borders) created a new national assertiveness. Requiring an outlet, the assertive energy made the idea of war nationally acceptable once more—particularly if a war could be found which could be fought in a good cause, which would benefit U.S. interests, and which could be won.

Sooner or later it was bound to happen. Something would offend the country: a murder, an arrest, an interference. It could have happened almost anywhere, for the United States was by now ready for a fight, confident, tough, and touchy. It could have been in Hawaii; public opinion now favored annexing the islands, although that was likely to bring protests from Japan. It could have been in Central or South America, over some more or less artificial argument like the Venezuela boundary dispute. But closer to home than any of these was another flashpoint— one of the last unwilling members of Spain's decaying empire in the Americas: the island of Cuba.

PART TWO

REVEILLE

1898 – 1918

★

*Sudden victory far away
brings sudden responsibility;
the new century brings
a new alignment of naval power.
In a world at war,
using great minefields and convoys,
the United States tips the balance
to Allied victory.*

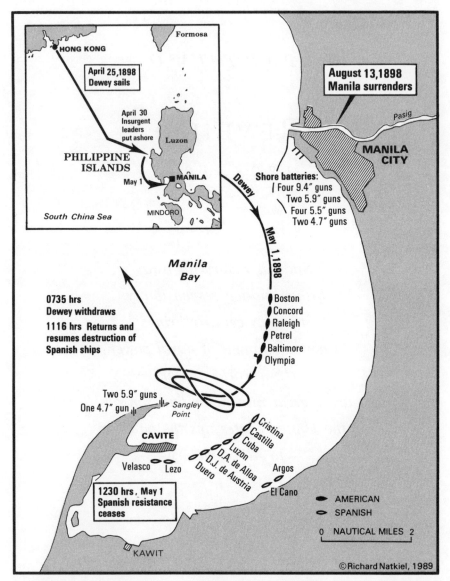

The Spanish-American War in the Philippines: Manila Bay—scene of Dewey's most famous victory and source of subsequent enormous complications as the United States became an imperial power.

2

★

A FEELING OF
UNEASY EXCITEMENT

*I*t was a good cause. No one except the Spaniards would deny that,
and people paid less and less attention to what the Spaniards thought.
The cause was to liberate a colonial island from its unwanted imperial
rulers, a situation which the United States, once an unwilling colony,
understood very well. Cuba's location put it distinctly within the U.S.
sphere of interest even then. When a canal was built through Central
America, which few doubted would happen, that interest would be doubly underlined. Moreover, on the island, Americans already owned property to the value of some $50 million, and between Cuba and the United
States there was an annual trade of $100 million.

Because of its commercial and strategic interests, the U.S. had already
offered to buy Cuba from Spain on three occasions, only to be rejected
each time. As early as 1823 John Adams had feared Spain might cede the
island to Britain—still too recent an enemy, then, to be thought of as a
potential good neighbor; and until the end of the Civil War, there had
been a constant nagging worry that slaves in Cuba might revolt, establish
a black republic (as had happened in Haiti), and spread revolution to the
southern states. Yet when revolution came to Cuba in the 1880s, it was
not blacks against whites but Cubans against Spaniards; and its consequences on the island gave the United States' interest in the place something of the feeling of a crusade, for the Spanish solution was brutal
repression—fire, starvation, concentration camps, and the deaths of
scores of thousands of Cubans.

"The struggle for existence among the nations is ceaseless, vigorous and relentless," said Lt. Comdr. Richard Wainwright, lecturing at the Naval War College in 1897. "The law of the survival of the fittest is as true for the political aggregation as for the individual."[1]

Reading in their newspapers of the Spaniards' atrocities, ordinary Americans sympathized with the islanders' wish for independence; resented an imperial dominance so close to their own shores; and bred a deep, righteous anger. An offer to settle matters for Spain was rebuffed— the condition for the offer, Cuban independence, was not on Spain's list of practical options. But while common Americans seethed with indignation, officialdom neither wanted a war anywhere nor was sure, if one began, who would most likely be the enemy—in July 1897, addressing the Naval War College, Adm. Reginald R. Belknap assessed war with Spain, Japan, or Great Britain to be equal possibilities.

However, one man in officialdom shared the common view of Spain and Cuba and was in a position to do something about it. In December 1897 Assistant Secretary of the Navy Theodore Roosevelt arranged for Commodore George Dewey to become commander of the Asiatic Squadron. If a conflict with Spain came, the Spanish empire would be vulnerable in more places than Cuba alone; and Roosevelt assessed Dewey as a man unafraid of responsibility, one "who meets the needs of the situation in whatever way is necessary."[2] Common Americans loaded the gun; Roosevelt readied it for firing. The trigger needed only to be pulled.

The New Year of 1898 opened with riots in Havana as Spanish reprisals against the insurgents took the island's death toll to more than two hundred thousand. America's consul general, Fitzhugh Lee, cabled Washington for protection for American citizens and property, and on January 25 the second-class battleship U.S.S. *Maine* arrived in Havana harbor.

Authorized in 1886 as an armored cruiser, *Maine*'s keel had been laid in 1888 and she had been launched in 1890. Before her commissioning in 1895, she had been redesignated from a cruiser to a battleship: 6,650 tons of displacement, with four 10-inch guns, six 6-inch guns, seven 6-pounders, eight 1-pounders, two Gatling guns, and four torpedo tubes. One of the young men who knew a great deal about her (certainly more than most people) was Edward H. Watson. As a naval cadet, he had taken part in a cruise in *Maine* ending in April 1897, and in learning about the ship had written down all her technical particulars:

> Between perpendiculars, 310 feet. Length overall, 324′ 4″; extreme beam, 57′; normal mean draught, 21′ 6″. Amidships for a length of 180′ there is a waterline belt of vertical Harveyized steel, extending from 3′ above to 4′ below the waterline. It is 12″ in thickness from

the top to 1' below the waterline, whence it tapers to 7" at the bottom.[3]

With good armament, good armor, and two vertical triple-expansion engines providing a trial speed of 16 knots, *Maine* was the respectable equivalent of ships in many navies around the world, including the British *Royal Sovereign* class and the Spanish class of *Almirante Oquendo.* But she had one weakness which a young cadet like Watson could not be expected to know, and which he did not write down.

"There are some bunkers," said a report to the naval secretary, "in which a fire would involve great danger; namely, those adjacent to magazines." Two American naval vessels of similar internal layout had had fires which caused the charring of woodwork in the magazine, "and if they had not, fortunately, been discovered in time, there might have been in each case a terrible disaster."[4]

For twenty days *Maine* lay quietly at her mooring buoy in Havana harbor; and then, during the night of February 15, without any warning, she exploded. Two hundred and sixty-six of her company died. The next morning the New York *World* reported that "as yet the cause of the explosion is not apparent," and Naval Secretary John D. Long wrote in his diary: "There is an intense difference of opinion as to the cause of the blowing up of the *Maine.* In this, as in everything else, the opinion of the individual is determined by his original bias."

Today, both comments are scarcely less valid than when they were first written. The Spaniards expressed regret but said it was nothing to do with them, even if it had occurred in their harbor; they supposed it was the work of Cuban insurgents trying to provoke a confrontation with the United States. Since then, three separate U.S. inquiries into the cause of the tragedy have been conducted. The third, by a team of experts led by Rear Adm. Hyman G. Rickover, found in 1976 "no technical evidence in the records examined that an external explosion initiated the destruction of the *Maine.* The available evidence is consistent with an internal explosion alone. . . . The most likely source was heat from a fire in the coal bunker adjacent to the 6-inch reserve magazine."[5]

This turned on their heads the two previous inquiries of 1898 and 1911, conducted, respectively, just after the sinking and just after the eventual raising of the ship. Perhaps, coming so comparatively soon after the event and its consequences, no one could have expected the 1911 inquiry to disagree with that of 1898; and the original inquiry, as diligent and conscientious as possible, was the important one, for that gave Americans a guide and justification for action. By 1976 action had become long-gone history, and the Rickover inquiry, confirming what other nations had believed for three quarters of a century, was of some historical interest but no vital importance. In 1898 the question of who or what blew up the *Maine* was of overwhelming interest, and crucially important; for, while in Havana shops and theaters were closed and Spanish flags flew at half mast, in the United States (as William Randolph Hearst's *Evening Journal* announced) there was a "Growing Belief in *Spanish Treachery.*"[6]

On February 21, six days after the explosion, the inquiry opened in a vessel moored close by the twisted wreck, still protruding from the harbor waters. Four days later in Washington, Secretary Long took an afternoon off from the worries of the Navy Department and left it in the control of his assistant, Theodore Roosevelt. At once Roosevelt snatched the chance of his temporary authority and fired off an astounding battery of orders to the U.S. Navy in every part of the world. Guns were shipped from the navy yard in Washington to New York, to be fitted into merchantmen; squadron commanders everywhere were told to be ready to sail at a moment's notice; and in the Far East, Commodore Dewey was instructed to gather his ships in Hong Kong and keep their bunkers full of coal. For "in the event of war Spain," said the cable, "your duty will be to see that the Spanish squadron does not leave the Asiatic coast, and then offensive operations in Philippine Islands."[7]

Dewey had no hopeful illusions of the future. He had finished writing his notes for the day when he received the cable, but he opened his notebook again and wrote one more line: "War with Spain imminent."[8]

By the middle of March the court had reached its verdict: U.S.S. *Maine* had been sunk by a mine. They came to their conclusion honestly, and they believed it; but if they had said anything else, they would have had a hard time convincing the public at home. Americans wanted Spain guilty, and not only to justify a revengeful fight. There was a strong moral element in the national indictment: "the spectacle," as one senator said after going to see for himself, "of a million and a half people, the entire native population of Cuba, struggling for freedom and deliverance."[9] Yet it was not the verdict the president wanted: McKinley did his best to defer a decision and to preserve peace. Nor was it the verdict Queen María Cristina of Spain wanted: "The Americans intend to provoke us and bring about a war, and this I would avoid at all costs," she wrote. "But," she added, "there are limits to everything, and I cannot let my country be humbled by America."[10]

At the end of the month, Dewey wrote from Hong Kong: "I believe I am not over-confident in stating that with the squadron now under my command, the [Spanish] vessels could be taken and the defenses of Manila reduced in one day."[11] What he did not say in this official report (because his government already knew it) was that he would have only one chance. If he were defeated in the Philippines, or even if he were forced to withdraw, he would be 7,000 miles from any possible help, probably with damaged ships and diminished crews, almost certainly without enough ammunition to defend himself further, and quite certainly without enough coal to return to friendly waters. And he underestimated the Spanish force which could be ranged against him.

In the last two weeks of March and the first three weeks of April 1898, Spanish and American warships were on the move all over the world. As Dewey planned and prepared in Hong Kong, the battleship U.S.S. *Oregon* thundered southward from San Francisco, the city where she had been built and, less than two years earlier, commissioned as BB-3. Over 350 feet long, with a main armament of four 13-inch guns, she was ill suited to her present journey. She had a limited coal capacity; she tended to roll badly; a low freeboard meant that in heavy seas, her decks were often awash. But she was undertaking an epic voyage which no American warship would ever be obliged to do again in time of war. She was heading around the Horn to join her sisters *Indiana* (BB-1) and *Massachusetts* (BB-2) in the Caribbean, 16,000 miles from San Francisco.

These three, with *Iowa* (a battleship in a class of her own, mounting four 12-inch guns), were the backbone of the new U.S. fleet, the final fruits of the years of reconstruction. Gathering with them on the East Coast were a second-class battleship, *Texas;* half a dozen modernized monitors; eight torpedo boats; a pair of armored cruisers; eleven protected cruisers; and twenty-one unprotected cruisers and gunboats. When war began (and as a Spanish army officer in Cuba wrote later, "Anyone who had not seen the war coming must have been blind"), their numbers would be effectively enhanced by fighting close to home waters and places of safety, supply, and repair.[12]

Segismundo Bermejo, Spain's minister of marine, was not blind; but he had the blithe confidence of a proud and ignorant man. Scanning the lists of Spain's navy, he could tell it was powerful enough to see off the Americans. The fact that its main ports were 3,500 miles from the Caribbean bothered him very little. Spanish sailors, he knew, were well trained and disciplined, while the American fleet was manned by mercenaries from many nations. And partly because of that belief, he felt *Oregon* could be discounted for a start: She would almost certainly remain on the West Coast.

Bermejo was wrong on just about every point, and so were most people outside the United States. In British ships in Hong Kong, large bets were made on the fate awaiting Dewey's squadron. Dewey himself noted that "the odds were all laid heavily against its success," and not one person "dared to wager that our squadron would be victorious."[13] Personally, he was optimistic: He had four cruisers, two gunboats, and a Revenue Service cutter, with two colliers. To the best of his knowledge, Spanish forces in the Philippines were limited to two cruisers, two gunboats, a dozen armed tugs, and a few small land batteries. He was wrong. In Manila, Admiral Patricio Montojo y Pasarón had seven large fighting ships and nearly sixty shore-mounted heavy rifled guns, with at least twenty gunboats scattered through the islands.

Nevertheless, Montojo was perturbed and nervous: "I am without resources, or time," he wrote on April 11.[14] And his counterpart in the Atlantic was even more unhappy. On April 20, Adm. Pascual Cervera y Topete made rendezvous in the Cape Verde islands with four cruisers, three destroyers, and three torpedo boats, under orders to proceed to the defense of the Caribbean. But two of the torpedo boats were in such bad condition they could not raise steam and had to be towed; one of the cruisers had not yet had its main battery of 10-inch guns mounted; another's keel was so heavily barnacled she could proceed at only a fraction of her nominal speed; ammunition for the secondary 5-inch batteries was unreliable; other guns on three of the four cruisers had defective breech mechanisms; and not one of the ships' coal bunkers was more than half full.

For weeks President McKinley had tried to prevent war. But on April 20 (as, for the first time, Admiral Cervera was glumly inspecting his gathered ships) the president signed a joint resolution of House and Senate. It called "for the recognition of the independence of the people of Cuba, demanding that the government of Spain relinquish its authority and government in the island of Cuba and Cuban waters, and directing the President of the United States to use the land and naval forces of the United States to carry these resolutions into effect."[15]

Largely due to the efforts of men like Theodore Roosevelt, the U.S. Navy was in a fair state of readiness and, fighting close to home, could even have had a reasonable chance of success against an equally prepared but rather larger navy far from its bases. In theory, the distantly based Spanish navy *was* equally prepared and rather larger. But in practice it was neither, and the Spanish government had little excuse. Two years earlier, Admiral Cervera had written prophetically of "the sad disappointment prepared for us by the stupidity of some, the cupidity of others, and the incapacity of all, even of those with the best of intentions."[16]

Cervera saw three reasons for this state of affairs: lack of money, lack of skills, and a frantically inefficient bureaucracy. "We are reduced, absolutely penniless, and they [the Americans] are very rich," he said. "If the [armored cruiser] *Carlos V* is not a dead failure, she is not what she should be; everything has been sacrificed to speed, and she lacks power. And remember her construction is purely Spanish." And "as for the administration and its difficulties, let us not speak of that; its slow procedure is killing us. . . . My purpose is not to accuse, but to explain why we may and must expect a disaster," he concluded. "I am sure that we will all do our duty, for the spirit of the navy is excellent; but I pray God that the troubles may be arranged without coming to a conflict, which, in any way, I believe would be disastrous to us."

Replying to the admiral, Minister of Marine Bermejo believed that Cervera "and all of us will fulfill the sacred duty which our country imposes upon us," and that battles were coming "in which it will be decided who is to hold empire of the sea."[17] They were the only two points on which he and the admiral agreed.

As wars go, the U.S. war with Spain had two virtues: It was short and it was decisive. Once it began there was little waiting around, and once it was over there was no doubt about who had won, and how, and why. And for the purpose of popular memory, it had the further virtue of extreme simplicity—in its 113 days, there were only three major battles. Even so, the popular memory of one of those is usually wrong: In the sole major land battle of the entire war, Theodore Roosevelt and his horseless "Rough Riders" did not charge up San Juan Hill, as many people think they did, but up the neighboring Kettle Hill, part of the San Juan ridge. The assistant naval secretary had not been prepared to sit the war out in Washington; as he said, it was too easy to be an armchair war hawk, "a parlor jingo." "My power for good, whatever it may be," he explained to a friend, "would be gone if I didn't try to live up to the doctrines I have tried to preach."[18] Gaining a lieutenant colonel's commission in the First Volunteer Cavalry, he lived up to his own doctrines in style. And the common mistake about San Juan Hill was easily made: The blockhouse on that hill was the target of a general charge, in which the Rough Riders took a flanking part, 400 yards away on the next hill.

With his war activity in both Army and Navy, as assistant secretary and lieutenant colonel in charge of a half-amateur troop, the charismatic and colorful Roosevelt was a high-profile leader ready-cast in the mold of an American hero. Imagining him a quarter mile away from his real location during that critical charge put him where the Americans wanted, and where he would have preferred to have been—at the crucial center of things; and after the war, it earned him the governorship of New York State.

However, in contrast to the muddle about San Juan, popular memories of the war's other two major battles are generally accurate: Manila Bay and Santiago were two swift, confident American naval victories which between them forever changed the map of the world and America's part in it.

When it left Hong Kong on April 25, 1898, Dewey's squadron consisted of four protected cruisers (his flagship *Olympia, Raleigh, Baltimore,* and

Boston), two gunboats, a Revenue Service cutter, and two recently purchased colliers. With "the prospect of an adventurous cruise" ahead of
them, the colliers' British officers and men all elected to remain with their
ships and accompany Dewey. Despite Britain's official neutrality, the
mood between the two countries was good—when the governor of Hong
Kong formally requested Dewey to leave, he added: "God knows, my
dear Commodore, it breaks my heart to send you this notification." And
"on our way out," wrote Dudley Carpenter, the surgeon in *Raleigh*, "the
British seamen and soldiers cheered us. . . . It was very spirited."[19]

From their first stopping point at Mirs Bay (35 miles up the Chinese
coast), Carpenter remembered that "the squadron sailed very auspi-
ciously, and a gorgeous trip of three days was made; moonlight nights,
calm seas, and all that sort of thing."

"The weather is intense heat, burns the pitch out of the seams of the
deck," wrote Charles Julian, one of the officers in *Baltimore*. For him,
as for most of his colleagues (children of the post–Civil War generation),
war was a complete novelty, a heroic dream from stories and newspapers,
and now an imminent, frightening reality: "You cannot imagine the
suspense we are in."[20]

Eight weeks later and many thousands of miles away, Theodore Roosevelt felt the same sensation and echoed Julian's words: "I suppose," he
said, "that, excepting among hardened veterans, there is always a certain
feeling of uneasy excitement the night before the battle."[21]

With their three-day crossing complete, Dewey's vessels reconnoitered
Subic Bay, 25 miles from Manila. They half expected to find Admiral
Montojo lying in wait; it was a good defensive herald for the greater bay
of Manila. Montojo had indeed been there just two days before, with five
cruisers and a dispatch boat. However, after two unpleasant discoveries,
he had returned to Manila. The first was that Subic's defenses had been
entirely neglected; the second was that (in his own words) one of his
cruisers (the wooden *Castilla*) "could merely be considered as a floating
battery, incapable of maneuvring, on account of the bad condition of her
hull."[22] Worse still, her propeller shaft leaked so badly that it had to be
plugged with cement. That stopped the leaks, but it stopped the engine
as well. So all he could do was to leave Subic defenseless, line his ships
at anchor in Manila Bay—with their masts, yards, and boats removed to
reduce casualties from flying splinters—and hope: hope that the shore
batteries would keep Dewey out, or even that the mines which were
reputed to block Manila's entrance might put the American off altogether. But Dewey did not believe in the mines, and if they were there,
he was ready to risk them.

"We arrived at the harbor entrance of Manila Bay at 11 o'clock p.m.,"
Charles Julian noted in his diary. "We were going in under cover of

darkness and right below in range of their guns. . . . No lights were shown on our ships except the stern light on each ship, all hands were at quarters and all the guns were loaded with extra charges at hand. . . . Every eye was strained, every ear was on the alert to catch the slightest sound."

"It was not until the *Raleigh* got well inside and near a small black rock that we were discovered," Dudley Carpenter the surgeon recalled, "and then we saw a clear light set off from the same black rock, followed by a whirr and a report . . ."

". . . that peculiar striking hissing sound of a flying projectile," said Julian. "The first shot had been fired and the game was on."

But for several more hours, very little happened. They had passed the gate of the bay with scarcely any opposition. If there were any effective mines, none was hit. Slowly and cautiously the squadron proceeded across the bay, until (in the words of Dewey's aide, Comdr. Nathan Sargent) "as the daylight of Sunday, the 1st of May, shot up from the East with the suddenness common to the tropics, the Spanish vessels at last were sighted."[23]

In *Baltimore,* Julian realized that "the most critical moments of our lives were drawing near." As he watched, "the Stars and Stripes were broken at every masthead and every peak," and his captain remarked: "There it goes, men. . . . Let us see what we can do under the flag." The ships were finally readied, and "when every man sadly took his station, there was nothing but a grim determination to do or die to be seen written on every face. . . . Those minutes I'll never forget, they seemed like hours."

The colliers and the Revenue cutter were left at a safe distance offshore. Onshore, a local Spanish newspaper reporter scribbled his notes: "In perfect and majestic order—why should we deny this?—the Yankee ships advanced in battle array."[24]

"At 5:15 a.m.," Admiral Montojo recorded, "I made signal that our squadron open fire." This must be correct; reports from both sides agree. But Montojo continued: "The enemy answered immediately."[25] Perhaps at the time it seemed like that; or perhaps he felt afterwards that it placed him in a better light. Actually, though, it was not until twenty-five minutes later, at 5:40 A.M., that Commodore Dewey felt he was at the optimum range. It was then that he turned to his flagship's captain and gave the order by which everyone remembers the ensuing battle—"You may fire when you are ready, Gridley."[26]

Many weeks passed before the full details were known at home in the United States, but just a few days after that shattering first of May, the central facts were known all over the world, conveyed in an exuberant cable to the offices of the *Herald* in Paris. William Freeland Fullam, an American naval officer and newspaper columnist, wrote:

Not one Spanish Flag flies in Manila Bay today. Not one Spanish warship floats except as our prize. More than 200 Spanish dead, 500–700 wounded attest accuracy American fire. Commodore Dewey last Sunday attacked Spanish position at Cavite. Swept five times along line. Secured one most brilliant successes modern times. Fact that our loss was trifling adds pleasure victory without detracting from its value. Number times our ships were hit proves how brave stubborn was Spanish defense. Almost miraculous none of our men killed. Only seven wounded.[27]

It was correct in almost every respect. "The Americans fired most rapidly," Montojo recorded. "There came upon us numberless projectiles, as the three cruisers at the head of the line devoted themselves almost entirely to fight the *Christina,* my flagship. A short time after the action commenced, one shell exploded in the forecastle and put out of action all those who served the four rapid-fire cannon. . . . Another shell exploded in the orlop. . . . At 7.30 one shell destroyed completely the steering gear. . . . Another shell exploded on the poop and put out of action nine men. Another destroyed the mizzen masthead, bringing down the flag and my ensign. . . . A fresh shell exploded in the officers' cabins, covering the hospital with blood, destroying the wounded who were being treated there. Another exploded in the ammunition room astern, filling the quarters with smoke. . . . It was impossible to control the fire. . . . Amidships several shells of smaller caliber went through the smokestack . . ."

The catalogue of destruction continued, and that was only for the flagship. It was similar for all the other Spanish vessels as well, yet none of the American ships was seriously damaged, and few American sailors were injured. However, Fullam's newspaper report was wrong in one detail: One American died, far out in the bay. He was the chief engineer in the Revenue cutter *McCulloch,* and as Surgeon Carpenter noted, he was killed by the heat in the engine room.

"It was terrible below," wrote the surgeon. "I had a small taste of it when I went below to get four collapsed firemen to the sick bay. This was about all I had to do in the whole fight"—perhaps a good thing, with a name like his—"so it gave me a fine chance to see the fight, and also an opportunity to whack the *Christina* several times."

Admiral Montojo surrendered at 12:30, a little less than seven hours after Dewey's memorable order. The Spanish commander concluded his official report of the disastrous morning with an accurate analysis of its causes: They were "the inefficiency of the vessels which composed my little squadron, the lack of all classes of the personnel, especially master gunners and seaman gunners; the ineptitude of some of the professional machinists, the scarcity of rapid-fire cannon, the strong crews of the enemy, and the unprotected character of the greater part of our vessels." Yet he stood by his men too, adding that "all the chiefs, officers, engineers, quartermasters, gunners, sailors, and soldiers, rivalled one another in sustaining with honor the good name of the Navy on this sad day." This praise seems to have been more than a simple platitude, for the Americans agreed with it. The Spaniards had fought well—simply not well enough. And in the satisfaction of victory, Surgeon Carpenter rounded off his account of the battle with a neat assessment of the enemy's strength and weakness: "To give the devil their due, I must say the Spaniards fought bravely. But they could not shoot straight."

3

★

To Cheer the Spanish

On February 13, 1898, the *New York Herald* predicted that a war with Spain "would from the beginning be of a naval character and the fight would be concluded in a short time."[1] Between the war's first action and Admiral Montojo's surrender, ten days elapsed. The defeat of the fleet in Cuba, Cervera's fleet, took a little longer—largely because, for some time, no one except Cervera knew where his fleet was.

Commencing at 3 P.M. on April 22, the first action of the war was the blockade of Havana by ships of the U.S. Navy's North Atlantic Squadron under Acting Rear Adm. William T. Sampson. It was a more substantial force than Dewey's, including two battleships, an armored cruiser, three further cruisers, five gunboats, seven torpedo boats, and three monitors.

According to Gov. Gen. Ramón Blanco, his people in Havana were very little dismayed by this. "But," he cabled to Madrid, "if people should become convinced that [Cervera's] squadron is not coming, disappointment will be great, and an unpleasant reaction is possible"—by which he meant a coup, his own murder, and a probable speedy surrender of the island.[2]

Meanwhile, in the Cape Verde Islands, Admiral Cervera and his captains were of the opinion that they would be more useful to Spain if they defended the Canaries, which could become an advance base for American attacks on Spain itself. Minister Bermejo disagreed and ordered Cervera off to Puerto Rico, Spain's nearest island in the Caribbean.

"I shall do all I can to hasten our departure," Cervera answered gloomily, "disclaiming all responsibility for the consequences."[3] He would have been less gloomy, and Bermejo even more complacent, if they had known of the reaction in America when news of Cervera's westward sailing came through. All along the East Coast there was panic and terror—which showed how little thought the good citizens had given, even yet, to the concept of an oceangoing navy. With proud cheers they had sent their own ships away to the Cuban blockade, and now suddenly they felt naked and defenseless, realizing (or at least believing) that Spanish ships could attack the coast where and when they chose. The best solution, it appeared, was to demand that individual ports and harbors should be defended by individual ships, strung out over hundreds of miles. This in turn showed how completely the naval strategists had failed to get their message across to the public; grand theories of distant power did not seem to relate very closely to the imminent prospect of an enemy shell demolishing one's own front porch. Again and again it had to be explained that individual ships could be picked off one by one, and that a squadron a hundred miles away offered more protection than a lone vessel outside the harbor walls.

Yet if it was misguided, it was also natural to want some visible defense close at hand; and Cervera's squadron caused the U.S. Navy much more trouble when it was a spectral bogey than when the ships actually came face to face. For however unlikely a Spanish raid on the East Coast might be, it remained an outside possibility; and although it might be militarily insignificant, the moral chaos and confusion it would engender in a population already half hysterical would be out of all proportion. Furthermore, of greater military significance was the chance that, unless he was caught on the high seas or in some port, Cervera could actually relieve Havana, perhaps trapping the blockading American ships between his own and the Spanish shore batteries. Thus several interlinking objectives had to be pursued simultaneously by the U.S. Navy—the East Coast had to be calmed; the blockade had to be maintained; Cervera had to be located; and all this had to be done without spreading the fleet around too thinly.

A patrol squadron of eight auxiliary cruisers was detailed to patrol the East Coast from Maine to the Delaware. Under Commodore Winfield Schley (whose name, incidentally, does not rhyme with hay, but with high), a "Flying Squadron" was created, consisting of two battleships (one the sister of the defunct *Maine*), an armored cruiser, and a protected cruiser. Based at Hampton Roads, these four would be able to dash north or to the Caribbean, depending on where the need arose. The Havana blockade was given over to lighter vessels, still tolerably capable of preventing blockade runners from the harbor and the adjacent coast; and Admiral Sampson, with ten ships, went hunting for Cervera.

At that time, Admiral Cervera and the "Cape Verde fleet" (as Washington planners now called it) were struggling despondently over the Atlantic at an average 6½ knots, in the general direction of Martinique. Looking at his half-gunned cruiser, watching the torpedo boats being towed (all three of them now), thinking of his coal bunkers as they neared empty, and pondering Bermejo's refusal (because of the situation's complexity) to formulate any war plans, Cervera would have been astonished if he had known of the fear and fuss his ragbag fleet was inspiring in the United States.

Fifty-nine years old, with a full white beard, Cervera was a career naval officer with much active experience, and he assumed that, ramshackle or not, his fleet would be brought to battle at the earliest opportunity. Hence the objective of Martinique: Naval logic told him American scouts would be out, and on this route—more southerly than the obvious one—he hoped to slip past them. The stratagem came within a whisker of success. Even today, with satellites and radar, the ocean is still a good place to hide ships. In 1898 the very large expanses of water meant that Cervera's protections were the limits of the human eye and the distance between a successful scout and the nearest cable station.

For his part, Admiral Sampson decided Cervera would head for Puerto Rico; it was Spain's nearest island, and unblockaded. Directing his ships that way, butting into the trade winds and contrary seas, the thousand-mile voyage from Havana took Sampson four days more than he expected. Arriving outside the harbor of San Juan on May 12, he found nothing and contented himself with bombarding the port for 3½ hours. But that same day, two reports came in to Washington, both saying the same thing: Cervera had been seen.

One report (from a terrified New Yorker) placed him off Sandy Hook at the mouth of New York bay. The second said he was in Martinique. There was no doubt which was right: Apart from anything else, the Martinique sighting had been made two days earlier by the auxiliary cruiser U.S.S. *Harvard*. It really was a stroke of luck, good or bad; *Harvard*'s patrol area covered almost 400 miles, from St. Thomas in the Virgin Islands down to Martinique. But no sooner had Cervera been seen than he vanished again, into the wide Caribbean.

It is easy to forget how large the Caribbean is. From Martinique to Puerto Rico is 400 miles; from Puerto Rico to Jamaica, 800; from Jamaica to Havana, another 700. Given (on a clear day) a horizon of 25 miles in every direction, at any one moment a single vessel could visually cover an area of less than 2,000 square miles. And the central Caribbean alone, from Nicaragua to Martinique and from Venezuela to Haiti, covers more than a third of a million square miles.

But to keep the sea, a fleet must fuel, and Cervera's stock was desperately low. Destination: Curaçao, off the northern coast of Venezuela.

There, according to Minister Bermejo, he would find a collier waiting with 5,000 tons of coal. On May 14 the admiral cabled the minister: "Collier has not arrived." It can hardly have been a surprise; Bermejo had not often been right before. To make matters worse, Curaçao, a Dutch property, was neutral, so the maximum permitted stay for belligerent ships was forty-eight hours. Only two vessels were allowed in, and those two were able to buy only 400 tons of coal for the whole squadron. With that very small consolation, Cervera assumed correctly that his presence would have been reported to the U.S. Navy; so on the evening of May 15 he slipped away and disappeared once again.

It took Admiral Sampson's fleet a further three days to return to Key West. Commodore Schley's Flying Squadron was already there, responding to the Martinique sighting of Cervera. Early the next morning (May 19) Schley set off for the south side of Cuba, to blockade the port of Cienfuegos. That, or Havana on the north side, had to be Cervera's goal; and with Sampson moving down to interdict Havana again, U.S. ships would be ready and waiting in either location. It did not occur to either of the American commanders that their enemy would go anywhere else; but just as Schley was leaving Key West, Admiral Cervera was entering the Cuban harbor of Santiago, 360 sea miles from Cienfuegos and 500 miles by land from Havana.

None of the three commanders, Spanish or American, was stupid. Just as Cervera assumed that he would need to evade American scouts, so Sampson and Schley assumed that he would be carrying supplies for the Spanish army in Cuba and that his ships would be fully coaled. They consequently reasoned that he would wish to avoid the problems of overland transport of supplies and would go for the port nearest the army, either Cienfuegos or Havana. But Cervera's assumption was right, and the others' were not. Sampson and Schley would have found it very difficult to believe; but then, they did not have to deal with Minister Bermejo. So it took them another ten days to find the "Cape Verde fleet"—even though, on the day Cervera arrived in Santiago, a message saying so was received at Key West.

Long before the war began, a small and highly secret U.S. intelligence network had been established in Cuba. Its focus was the Havana cable office, which in turn was in the governor general's palace—a first-class place for gathering and sending information. So far, messages out had been accurate and reliable, but the one revealing Cervera's presence in Santiago seemed so illogical, it was almost incredible. The Americans assessed it as a ruse to tempt ships away from blockading the other, more sensible ports: The spy must have been found out and replaced, with intent to confuse and deceive.

In fact, he had not been found out, but the U.S. naval command was very confused, not knowing what to believe and trying to cover all possibilities at once. Sampson stationed a force 200 miles east of Havana, watching distant approaches to both that harbor and Key West. Schley was ordered to leave Cienfuegos when he was sure it was empty and proceed to Santiago, just in case the spy's message was true. This he did; but he had never been told that the spy in Havana even existed, so he was extremely skeptical about Santiago. Logic and instinct told him it was the wrong place. The feeling was so strong that when he was actually outside its harbor, with the view of the interior blocked by high hills, Schley turned away, unable to resist the conviction that Cervera was anywhere but there.

Twenty-seven hours later he changed his mind. Whatever his feelings, he realized he had not carried out his orders to check Santiago fully. But though he had already sent a message announcing his course for Key West, he did not now send one announcing his return to Santiago. In Washington, therefore, Naval Secretary Long knew only that Schley had turned back from the brink of possible success, and that if Cervera *were* in Santiago, he could be landing supplies, replenishing stores, repairing his ships. For Secretary Long, it was "the most anxious day in the naval history of the war . . . the only instance in which the Department had to whistle to keep its courage up." He had no fast, certain method of communicating with Schley, and as he remarked later: "To deal with [the Spanish squadron] was not difficult when its whereabouts were known, but to feel that it might leave the Cuban coast, that its movements might be lost track of, and that it might appear at any time on the coast of the United States, was depressing beyond measure."[4]

With his fastest ships, Sampson in turn was now speeding toward Santiago, hoping not to be too late. At the same moment, irritated and uncertain, Schley approached the port for the second time; and inside the port, Cervera and his captains could not decide what was going on outside.

Schley's Flying Squadron had been augmented by the battleship *Iowa*, commanded by Capt. Robley D. Evans—"Fighting Bob," as he was known. It was from the bridge of his ship, at dawn on May 28, 1898, that Cervera's squadron was identified at last. From that moment, inside and outside the harbor, in Spanish and U.S. ships alike, everyone knew that the defeat of the "Cape Verde fleet" was only a matter of time.

A single incident which had taken place in Europe some weeks earlier characterized the differing approaches to war of the Spanish and U.S. authorities. The story was told in a letter dated April 19 from Lawrence

Benet, a Paris-based arms dealer, to Edward W. Very, vice president of the American Ordnance Company in Washington.

"Dear Very," Benet wrote, "I have just cabled you to the effect that our stock of guns has been completely exhausted with the exception of mountain artillery. This is due to a very pretty piece of work on the part of Lieut. Colwell, which is well worth repeating." (John C. Colwell was the American naval attaché in London, on temporary, but effective, duty in Paris.) "Early last week," the letter explained, "the Spanish government purchased the *Normania* and *Columbia,* and rushed them into a Spanish port, where they could be armed and fitted out. Then the Hamburg agents of Spain in this purchase proceeded to order from us everything suited for their batteries that we had for instant delivery. This order was given us on Friday, and the one-third advance payment was to be made by noon on Saturday, and the balance on Monday. . . . On Friday night I remarked that it was a pity that Spain should be able to arm these ships. Colwell then offered to try and raise the money if we would sell to him, and I told him to go ahead, for I felt certain that the Spaniards would be a little late in their payments. Sure enough they were late, and five minutes after noon on Saturday, their time being up, Colwell paid cash in full and secured everything."

And Benet concluded wryly: "Since then my time has been principally taken up in expressing sympathy with the Spaniards, who hardly seem to realize that the guns are gone. In fact their Naval Commission appeared today to carry out the inspection and proof, and apparently they are still somewhat dazed."[5]

One can indeed feel some sympathy for the Spanish in their plight. To be five minutes overdue may have seemed like abnormal punctuality to them; yet evidently they had not grasped that in a modern naval war, there would be no place for *mañana,* and that a delay of five minutes could be the difference between victory and defeat.

On June 1, a month after Montojo's defeat in Manila and five days after Cervera's discovery in Santiago, a third Spanish fleet was being prepared in Cádiz under Adm. Manuel de la Cámara. Its objective would be the relief of the Philippines; its route there would be through the Suez Canal. But that day Secretary Long sent a cable to Lt. William S. Sims, the regular naval attaché in Paris:

GIVE OUT THE FOLLOWING INFORMATION: PROBABLY FALSE, POSSIBLY TRUE. AS SOON AS CERVERA'S SQUADRON IS DESTROYED, AN AMERICAN FLEET OF ARMORED VESSELS AND CRUISERS WILL BE DETACHED AGAINST SPANISH PORTS AND THE COAST OF SPAIN GENERALLY. THE

AMERICANS SEEM TO BE ESPECIALLY INCENSED AGAINST CADIZ, AND
DOUBTLESS THAT PLACE WILL COME IN FOR A TASTE OF ACTUAL WAR.[6]

Long had seen for himself the panic on the East Coast when Cervera's
ships were thought to be a threat. There was no reason why Spanish
civilians should not react similarly to a similar threat.

That same day, Admiral Sampson arrived outside Santiago. In addition
to his flagship *New York,* he brought the battleship *Oregon,* now 16,000
miles from her home base in San Francisco. Minister Bermejo had told
Admiral Cervera that the warship would never undertake such a long
voyage. Because of that, Cervera half expected to see her, and was not
much surprised when he did; but he wished the minister could occasionally be right.

To the combatants at least, this sea war was obviously one-sided.
Perhaps it was because of that that sailors on each side felt able, from time
to time, to applaud the bravery of their opponents, as Surgeon Carpenter
had done at Manila. One of the few Spanish opportunities to return a
chivalrous compliment—one of the few occasions when a brave American
endeavor went visibly wrong—was outside Santiago on the morning of
June 3. On his way to Santiago, although confident that he could beat
Cervera, Admiral Sampson had thought of a quicker alternative. Rather
than wait for the Spanish ships to come out, he could block them in. If
done properly, it would remove them from the war just as effectively, and
could save much time and many lives. The channel into Santiago bay was
narrow, twisting, and shallow; a single heavily laden wreck in the right
place could block it entirely. The only drawback was that whoever took
the vessel in and wrecked it, under the fire of shore guns, would have little
prospect of survival. Volunteers were requested for probable suicide, and
almost every man in the squadron stepped forward.

Eight men were chosen, but nine went: The ninth, refusing to be left
out, stowed away and was not found until too late. Their vessel was a
333-foot, 7,000-ton collier, to be sunk at a point where the channel was
little more than 350 feet wide. Her bow would be run ashore, underwater
charges would blow out her hull, and the flood tide would sweep her stern
around to ground on the opposite bank—or so it was hoped.

It was simple, and it very nearly worked. But coming in before dawn
under heavy fire, the collier's steering gear was shot away; eight of the
ten underwater charges failed to explode; and, drifting aimlessly beyond
the narrows, she sank in a place where she offered no obstruction. However, all the volunteers survived unhurt and in the morning were picked
up by a Spanish motor launch. As guards drew guns, the volunteers
thought they were about to be shot; then, to their surprise and relief, the
white-bearded officer commanding the launch looked at them in clear

admiration, praised them for their valor, and ordered his men to take every care of the prisoners. They did not realize for some time who their unexpectedly courteous captor was. They all knew his name, but none of them had seen Pascual Cervera before.

For one month more the decision was deferred. In that time, Sampson bombarded Santiago; the island was invaded by 16,000 U.S. troops (one man, coincidentally, for every mile that U.S.S. *Oregon* had steamed); the battle of San Juan Heights was fought; and in France, Lieutenant Sims continued his campaign of disinformation and intelligence gathering.

One item he gleaned from his network of agents came from a very human indiscretion: The executive officer of the armored cruiser *Carlos V* ("not what she should be," Cervera had said) had a mistress in Madrid. When the Cámara fleet left Cádiz, the officer could not resist telling his lady where he was going. She in turn could not resist writing to him, and one of Sims's agents intercepted the letter. It was addressed to Port Said; so on June 25 Sims was able to confirm to Washington that the fleet was heading for the relief of Manila, where Dewey, juggling diplomacy with Spaniards, Britons, Japanese, and extremely intrusive Germans, still held the city under blockade while the wrecks of Montojo's ships rotted and rusted in the bay. Eight weeks after his historic morning of battle, Dewey was still mainly dependent on his own resources, still largely out of touch with home; and as Sims reported, the third Spanish fleet sailed "enthusiastically expecting victory."[7]

But they were wrong again. Again, naval victory, for the second and final time in the war, went to the Americans. On July 3, while the fleet under Cámara was broiling in the Red Sea, the climactic Battle of Santiago was fought.

It began with an astonishing and touching display. Outside the port, the men in Sampson's squadron saw a sight unlike anything they had ever seen before, or would ever see again. From the narrow entrance of Santiago harbor, very slowly and carefully and deliberately, four cruisers and two destroyers emerged one by one—the only remaining movable vessels in Admiral Cervera's squadron. There was no haste, no rash charge: instead, simply a scrupulous attention to tricky navigation and an extraordinary air of defiant pride. For though it was clear to everyone that Cervera's ships could not escape or survive, yet they came out with all their flags flying, "dressed as for a regal parade or a festal day."[8] From the moment they had left the Cape Verde Islands, they had known they were Spain's blood sacrifice for the national honor, bound to die, if only to justify the incompetent political administration of a bankrupt country. Nevertheless, Spain was their country, and despite its ludicrous politicians, they loved it; and so they submitted to their fate and duty with despair, and grace, and gallant style.

The weather was beautiful that Sunday morning. "The air was so pure," said "Fighting Bob" Evans in the battleship *Iowa,* "that the outlines of the distant mountains were clearly visible with the Spanish blockhouses picturesquely perched on the loftiest peaks. There was no indication of haze, and the blue of the mountains blended with the blue of the sky." He was in his cabin when the alarm went, and before he had reached the spar deck, the first gun had fired. When he came to the bridge he could see Cervera's flagship, *Infanta María Teresa,* with "her magnificent battleflag showing just clear of the land"; and on the decks below him, Evans's men paused in their hasty preparations and began "to cheer the Spanish ship as she stood boldly out."

A moment later, "they came at us like mad bulls."[9] Defeat might seem inevitable, but there was no meek acquiescence or simple surrender. The battle flag meant what it said: The Spaniards would fight for as long as they could.

It was a little less than four hours—not a long time in which to see the death of 324 men, the overwhelming of six ships, the loss of a colony, and the crumbling of an empire. "There was no doubt in my mind as to the outcome," Admiral Cervera wrote to Governor General Blanco in Cuba, "although I did not think that our destruction would be so sudden."[10]

When the signal for battle was given, Victor Concas, captain of Cervera's flagship, had foreseen something more: "It was the signal that four centuries of grandeur was at an end, and that Spain was becoming a nation of the fourth class."[11]

He was right, and his observation recorded the single most notable aspect of the naval battle off Santiago. For by the same token, the battle signaled that America was becoming a nation of the first class: As one empire decayed, another was rising in its place. It signaled, moreover, the approaching end of Britain's century of maritime world dominance, won in 1805 at the battle of Trafalgar. An editorial in the *Madrid Herald* had stated categorically that "as soon as fire is opened, the crews of the American ships will commence to desert, since we all know that among them are people of all nationalities." When he saw the editorial, Cervera remarked that though he did not know the crews, "I may say that the crews that defeated our predecessors at Trafalgar were recruited in the same way."[12]

He did not pursue the comparison, but he could have pointed out other similarities. Like Cervera, the French Admiral Villeneuve at Trafalgar had seen he would have little chance of success if ordered out to fight. Both admirals had attempted to convince their political masters of naval facts which to them were plain. Both were controlled by men who had no idea of the nature of sea power, yet both continued to obey. And each, in his self-predicted defeat, heralded the end of empire, the shifting of worlds.

In the sea fight off Santiago, a Spanish defeat was inevitable. The best they could possibly hope for was the escape of one of their ships, and maybe for one of the U.S. ships to be put out of action. But the Spanish ships were harried and herded, some exploding on the water, others running aground in flames, until all were destroyed. None of the U.S. vessels was seriously harmed, and only one U.S. sailor died.

But to some in the U.S. Navy the total victory carried a sour aftertaste, because later there was a long public wrangle between the two U.S. commanders, Commodore Schley and Acting Rear Admiral Sampson.

Though his job was the most important sea command of the war, Sampson was only an acting flag officer; his substantive or confirmed rank was that of captain. Both he and Schley were very good sea officers— Sampson has been described as the paragon of his time—but Schley was already a substantive commodore and naturally enough felt that he, not Sampson, should have been given the promotion, acting or otherwise. Sampson was a reticent man; Schley, in contrast, was affable and always maintained good relations with the press. Thus there was fertile ground for mutual jealousy, and after the battle this mushroomed into open mutual antagonism, centering on who should get the credit for the victory.

As admiral commanding the blockade, Sampson had so little expected Cervera's ships to come out that—as chance would have it—shortly before they did emerge, he had left the immediate area. When he saw what was happening, he returned as quickly as possible, but in the meantime Schley had given the actual order to commence firing. Before his departure, Sampson's last order had been "Disregard the movements of the flagship," and on his return he did not actively rescind that order. Consequently, among the other U.S. ships, there followed a good deal of confusion about who was in charge, if anyone. Neither admiral nor commodore issued any orders except to their own ships; the captains simply got on with it. With someone like Nelson, that would have been because they were all so thoroughly versed in what the admiral expected them to do that they needed no orders. Among the U.S. fleet off Santiago, it was because no orders were given.

Immediately after the battle, Commodore Schley fired off a couple of exuberant signals ("glorious victory," "great day for our country") which were somewhat overdone but entirely natural. Perhaps suspecting a preempting of credit, Sampson gave these a very frosty reception. Subsequent newspaper reports did, in fact, shower praise on Schley—which he was quick to refuse, sending the secretary of the Navy a cable for publication, specifically saying that the honor was due to Sampson, not to himself. He showed this to Sampson, who gratefully authorized its transmission; but before it was sent, Sampson added a secret message forcefully complaining about Schley's conduct of the blockade—something he had never done while the blockade was going on.

If this sounds like a hypocritical and mean action, it was; and it was that which sparked the public controversy that poisoned the rest of the lives of both men. There were other strange and unpleasant actions on Sampson's part, including a public accusation against Schley for cowardice. Yet to be hypocritical, or even mean, was weirdly out of character for Sampson, who was a reserved man, to be sure, but always honest and correct.

What no one knew at the time was that, even before the war had begun, he was badly ill. A dark-haired man, he was also bearded, with a positively enormous flowing walrus mustache; yet in the space of one year, between late 1897 and late 1898, first the beard and then the mustache as well turned completely white. He lost weight; it was noted too that he appeared to become hesitant in action, confused in speech, and progressively more likely to be struck literally dumb by the need to make any decision. He died in May 1902, almost exactly four years after the battle; and though he was only sixty-two at the time of his death, he had become utterly senile. "Softening of the brain" was what they called it then; more recently (in Ned Beach's excellent book *The United States Navy: 200 Years*) the symptoms have been diagnosed as matching those of that dreadful ailment Alzheimer's Disease.

It was a demeaning and pathetic end to a life and career that had promised much, and to a battle that had gained much. The final moments of the Spanish defeat off Santiago were conducted in an altogether more appropriate manner—appropriate both in terms of naval custom, and also as part of the signal for the future. It used to be accepted that ships fought ships, and not the men within them, and that once an enemy was defeated, the victor should try to save the lives of as many of his erstwhile opponents as possible. With rare exceptions, the high-speed, high-technology sea warfare of the twentieth century has sadly put paid to that ancient custom, and the afternoon of Sunday, July 3, 1898, was one of the last occasions when a victorious fleet was able to enjoy the luxury of gallantry.

Watching as the cruiser *Vizcaya* ran aground, Capt. Robley Evans of *Iowa* saw Spanish survivors up to their chests in water, as Cuban insurgents fired on them from the shore and as sharks, attracted by the blood, lunged at them. "It was an awful sight," he wrote, "and one long to be remembered by those who witnessed it."[13] But the defeated men struggling in the water were not abandoned; Evans ordered boats to the rescue, and "the alacrity with which our men manned the boats showed plainly their sympathy for their prisoners." The wounds of the injured were treated, and the dead were buried from *Iowa*'s deck, "the burial service conducted by their own padre in the presence of their own commanding officer and their own shipmates, and their bodies launched overboard from under the folds of their own flag." And then came the most important survivor of all.

"All preparations were made to receive the Admiral with the honors due his rank," Evans recorded. "The full marine guard of eighty men was paraded, officers mustered on the starboard side of the quarterdeck, the officers and crew of the *Vizcaya* were arranged on the port side of the quarterdeck, and the crew of the *Iowa,* dressed as they came out of battle, clustered over the turrets and superstructure. . . . The guard presented arms, the officers uncovered, the bugles rang out their flourishes; and as the distinguished officer stepped onto the quarterdeck, the crew of the *Iowa* broke out into cheers, and for fully a minute Admiral Cervera stood bowing his thanks. It was the recognition of gallantry by brave men, and the recipient was fully aware of its meaning. Though he was scantily clad, bareheaded, and without shoes, he was an Admiral every inch of him."

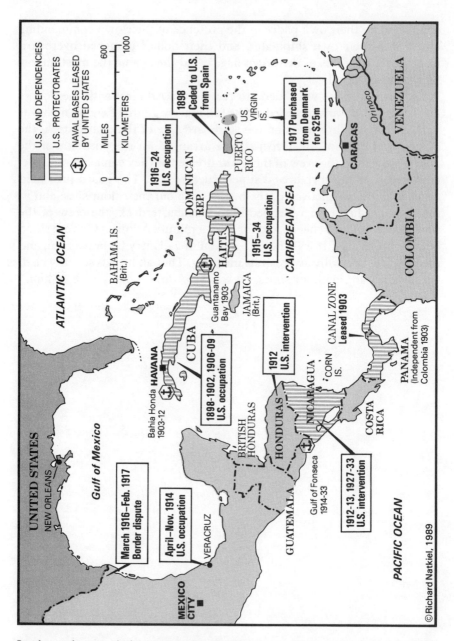

In the early twentieth century the Caribbean was the proving ground of the Monroe Doctrine. By all possible means—war, occupation, intervention, and the fomenting of insurrection—Americans made it clear they would tolerate neither European nor Latin misrule in their hemisphere.

4

*

SUCH A FLEET . . . SUCH A DAY

" "*U*nless all signs deceive," said an editorial article in Blackwood's *Edinburgh Magazine,* "the American Republic breaks from her old moorings, and sails out to be a world power."[1]

"No illusion is possible," wrote a member of the Institut de France in Paris. "The equilibrium of the world is moving westwards."[2]

After Cervera's defeat on July 3, the end of the Spanish War came quickly. On July 16 Santiago surrendered, and the U.S. Army moved on from Cuba to an unopposed promenade through Puerto Rico. In the Red Sea, Admiral Cámara's ships did an about-turn, left Manila to stew, and headed back to protect the Spanish coast from the threat (carefully leaked by Lieutenant Sims) that Sampson would cross the Atlantic.

Sampson did not have to go to the trouble. On August 12, 1898, peace was signed. No one in distant Manila knew about the peace until much later; but the Spanish governor general had already concluded correctly that he would receive no help from Spain, and on August 13, after a prearranged mock battle to preserve his official honor, he surrendered to the newly promoted Rear Admiral Dewey.

In the United States, where his brave and chivalrous behavior was universally admired, Admiral Cervera discovered (much to his own surprise) that he was a hero. "If Spain were as well served by her statesmen and public officials as she is by her sailors," said one commentator, "she might yet be a great country."[3] In America's own navy, the stars of

Admiral Sampson and Commodore Schley were somewhat dimmed by their grubby dispute; but the nation scarcely knew how to express its admiration for George Dewey. A commodore when he left home to go to war, he returned in 1899 not merely a rear admiral (which many people felt he should have been made before ever setting off) but admiral of the Navy, an honor which had been granted only twice before.

Nevertheless, his very success brought difficulties, both then and later. "If only old Dewey had just sailed away when he smashed the Spanish fleet," said President McKinley, "what a lot of trouble he would have saved."[4] At the time (except for the 11,000 Army officers and troops who joined Dewey in June and July 1898), few ordinary Americans had any clear idea of the location of Manila, or even of the Philippines. If, when passing the main island in Manila Bay's entrance, the soldiers had been asked how to spell its name, most of them would have been considerably puzzled; and not even their general, Arthur MacArthur, would have guessed how familiar Corregidor would become to their sons, and his.

The war was so widely supported at home that every man who lived through it or died in it was a hero, at least to those at home; and among the national heroes, one bespectacled, middle-aged, middle-sized man was head and shoulders above all the rest. "Such a small war" was how Theodore Roosevelt described it; but it made him, and gave him power and dominance in America and beyond for a full ten years after it was over. "I have worked hard all my life, and have never been particularly lucky," he said in 1898, "but this summer I *was* lucky, and I am enjoying it to the full." In that one year he had been assistant secretary of the Navy, lieutenant colonel of the Rough Riders, and governor of New York State as well—enough distinction to satisfy any three average men for a lifetime—and he declared, "if I never hold another office," he would not care.[5]

But from the first day of the twentieth century, the world's new equilibrium was confirmed. On January 1, 1900, the last Spanish governor left Cuba—the "ever-faithful isle," the only Caribbean island to have remained Spanish since its discovery. Reversing Columbus's course of four hundred years before, that last governor's voyage acknowledged the end of direct Spanish rule in the Caribbean, the final curtain on Spain's West Indian empire. In the United States it was an election year; McKinley was returned for a second term; on March 4, 1901 he was inaugurated; and his vice president, who would not have cared if he never held another office, was Theodore Roosevelt. Six months later came the bullet that killed McKinley, and Roosevelt (still only forty-two years old) became America's twenty-sixth and youngest-ever president.

Thus, the completion of the U.S. Navy's rebirth was marked in macabre fashion, as its beginning had been marked twenty years before by the assassination of President Garfield. "It is a dreadful thing to come into the presidency this way," said Roosevelt, "but it would be a far worse thing to be morbid about it. Here is the task, and I have got to do it to the best of my ability; and that is all there is about it."[6]

Some years later, assessing Theodore Roosevelt's presidency, a senior naval officer wrote that Roosevelt "took his duties as commander in chief of the army and navy more conscientiously than any other President except George Washington." Others have equaled or surpassed him since—most notably his distant cousin Franklin—but at the time, though it may seem a little unfair to Abraham Lincoln, the judgment was broadly correct. The man who made it was Bradley A. Fiske, and he, and other officers of like mind, had every reason to be grateful to Roosevelt. Any navy has its quota of conservative minds, unwilling to alter existing systems, often to the point of active opposition. Balancing them, most navies contain at least a sprinkling of forward-thinking individuals; and, at the end of the nineteenth and start of the twentieth centuries, Fiske was one of the U.S. Navy's forward thinkers.

William S. Sims—who, as naval attaché in Paris, had directed its secret service operations during the Spanish War—was another. When they eventually retired, both men held the rank of rear admiral and between them were ultimately responsible for changes in the Navy's systems which can reasonably be said to have culminated in the victories of the Pacific war. Of course, they were not alone within the Navy, but before Roosevelt became president, neither had had an easy ride. Not that his presidency suddenly made life simple for forward-thinking officers; it never happens like that. Nevertheless, throughout his presidency, Roosevelt gave Fiske, Sims, and like-minded colleagues every support he could.

Bradley Allen Fiske would have been remarkable in any fleet. Of all the many facets of his legacy to the Navy, possibly the most valuable and certainly the most enduring was a fundamental administrative change: the creation in 1915 of the office of the Chief of Naval Operations, a post which he himself would have been ideally suited to fill. He never did, largely because (as will be seen later) the then–secretary of the Navy found the idea of getting ready for war particularly unpalatable. Fiske died in 1942, close on eighty-eight years old, and in his long life he fought at sea during the Spanish War and the Philippine Insurrection; wrote five books; was president of the U.S. Naval Institute for a record twelve years; and patented over sixty naval inventions, including a revolutionary telescopic gun sight. Being also (in 1911) the first admiral to leave and return to a ship by airplane, he was, in short, anything but a stick-in-the-mud.

Although four years younger than Fiske (and, in 1901, still only a lieutenant) William Sowden Sims was the acknowledged spokesman of the U.S. Navy's radical officers. This was mainly because despite his lowly rank, he knew how to express his plentiful ideas of reform so that people far senior would listen. Of all the radicals, he was also the most daring, perfectly willing, if he decided it was necessary, to write directly to the president; which is exactly what happened barely a month after Roosevelt took office.

The problem then exercising Sims's mind was naval gunnery. Analyses of the Battle of Manila Bay had shown that Surgeon Carpenter's smugness (no more than typical of the fleet as a whole) had been misplaced. To say that the Spanish "could not shoot straight" was no doubt true, but it suggested that the Americans could—that U.S. naval gunnery was still as good as it had been in the days of the Revolution and the War of 1812, when even Britain's Royal Navy paid tribute to its accuracy. In fact, it was dire. At Manila, all but one of the Spanish ships had remained at their moorings, the weather was good, and Dewey's captains were able to choose their times and places of firing, almost as if they were at target practice. Between them the U.S. ships fired about six thousand rounds; yet between them, they scored only 141 definite hits, only 2.3 percent of the total fired off. Reversing that, it meant that more than ninety-seven of every hundred shells they fired were a sheer waste of time and money, contributing nothing to the outcome but noise and smoke.

The Americans won their victory at Manila not because they were outstandingly efficient, but because their Spanish opponents were even more stupefyingly inefficient. The potential consequences of carrying on in the same way were clear. Imagining a U.S. fleet of any given size in battle against an enemy the same size, the enemy would need a success ratio of less than 5 percent in order to inflict twice as much damage as it received. Again reversing that, it meant that if an American fleet met an enemy capable of only 5 percent successful hits, then in order to have any likelihood of victory, the American fleet would have to be twice as numerous as the enemy. The British Royal Navy's fleet average was 30 percent; it followed that if a single R.N. vessel fought a dozen similar U.S. vessels, it could have a chance of beating them all.

At the moment it was painfully clear to some of the more thoughtful U.S. commanders that, if the fleet had been ranged against anyone more competent than the Spanish, the result of Manila Bay could have been very different. Sims was especially aware of this, for while carrying out his duties in the Far East, he had met a similarly maverick British naval officer, Capt. Percy Scott. In his ship, H.M.S. *Terrible,* Scott gave Sims a thorough demonstration of a gunnery system of his own, which he called "continuous aim." Leaving out the technical details, suffice it to say here that the system achieved results of 80 percent successful hits. The theory Sims derived from this was that H.M.S. *Terrible*'s firepower was as effective as any three dozen similar American ships put together—that H.M.S. *Terrible,* all alone, could outfire most of the U.S. Navy combined.

For Sims, this was at best an embarrassing thought. At worst, it could be highly dangerous. It was true that even within the Royal Navy, Scott's results were exceptional; but having seen them, the R.N. authorities were taking his methods on for use throughout the fleet. Not so the U.S. naval authorities: When Roosevelt had become president, Lieutenant Sims had been hammering at the U.S. Navy establishment for some time, trying to get the new system adopted; but he had had no success at all. Roosevelt's accession to the presidency gave him a chance he might not have again, and, though it was attended by considerable risk to his own career, he took it. A single accurate shot was worth more to any commander than an exuberant fusillade of a hundred misses; results were all that mattered. So, after considerable thought, Sims accepted the risk and wrote a letter. It transfigured his career and the entire U.S. Navy.

The information he supplied was something Roosevelt already suspected. Almost at once Sims was made inspector of target practice for the Asiatic Squadron. Within a year, while he was still a lieutenant, Roosevelt appointed him to the same post for the whole U.S. Navy, and fleet intelligence officer as well. The fleet never looked back.

Polymath that he was, Theodore Roosevelt was equally at ease talking of their professions with bankers or boxers, and talking to anyone about the Navy. Since the publication (when he was only twenty-four) of his book called *The Naval War of 1812,* naval matters had been second nature to him; and two of his phrases encapsulate his view of the U.S. fleet.

"I have a great horror," he said on one occasion, "of words that cannot be backed, or will not be backed, by deeds." The United States could not claim or pretend to power and influence without also accepting the price, which, on another occasion, he specified: "The American people must either build and maintain an adequate navy, or else make up their minds definitely to accept a secondary position in international affairs."[7]

These were the keynotes of his presidency, and he put them together in one of his best-remembered presidential phrases: "Speak softly, and carry a big stick." Everywhere he looked he could see the need to make that stick as big as possible; for apart from the many issues at home, his inherited "task" had two great aspects beyond the U.S. coasts—the duties of the Monroe Doctrine and the spoils of the Spanish War.

The spoils of war were Cuba, Puerto Rico, and the Philippines—Cuba as an American protectorate; Puerto Rico as an annexed possession; and the Philippines (after much heart searching on McKinley's part) as the nation's most distant colony, 7,000 miles from San Francisco. Fifteen hundred miles closer there was also the small, isolated staging post of Guam; and roughly halfway between Guam and San Francisco, Hawaii had at last been annexed while the war was going on. Hawaii was a popular acquisition, the Philippines much less so. Taking them (one Democratic senator predicted) would "make necessary a navy equal to [that of the] largest of powers; a greatly increased military establishment; immense sums for fortifications and harbors; multiply occasions for dangerous complications with other countries, and increase burdens of taxation."[8] The senator, George Gray of Delaware, turned out to be right on every point, but McKinley countered his arguments. It would be cowardly and dishonorable, he believed, to give the islands back to Spain. To give them to the United States' commercial rivals in the east (France, Germany, or Britain) would be bad business, while leaving them to themselves would bring anarchy and misrule; so "there was nothing left for us to do but to take them all, and educate the Filipinos, and uplift and civilize and Christianize them."[9]

Unfortunately (and apart from the fact that most Filipinos, being Roman Catholics, were already "Christianized"), many of the islanders had fought expecting the end of Spanish rule to bring independence. When it did not, and they found they had merely exchanged one imperial master for another, their disillusion was severe; and in the United States' first experiment in overseas empire, Americans and Filipinos fought one another as savagely as Spaniards and Cubans had done. Between December 10, 1898 (when Spain accepted $20 million for the islands), and July 4, 1902 (when President Roosevelt declared the "Philippine Insurrection" over), 4,200 Americans and 20,000 or so Filipinos killed one another, while a further 200,000 Filipinos were estimated to have been indirect victims. The education, uplifting, and civilization of a colony had a higher price for all concerned than even Senator Gray had imagined, and soon President Roosevelt feared the price might never be paid in full.

At the same time, the Monroe Doctrine gave him headaches and opportunities in plenty. The republics fringing the Caribbean were permanently unstable in their politics, as well as financially reckless, borrowing large sums from foreign financiers and then refusing to pay them back. It seemed to Roosevelt that the Latins' irresponsibility stemmed in part from the Doctrine itself: They appeared to believe they could misbehave as much as they liked, knowing the United States would not tolerate any European incursions into the Americas. Therefore, in his first annual message to Congress in December 1901, Roosevelt explained that this was not quite so—the Doctrine did "not guarantee any state against punishment if it misconducts itself, provided that punishment does not take the form of acquisition of territory by any non-American power."[10] In Latin America, the message was not clearly understood at first. In Europe it was; and one year later the Venezuelan Crisis filled the headlines as German, Italian, and British warships blockaded that country's ports pending the repayment of $12.5 million of bonds.

Coincidentally, the U.S. battle fleet (commanded by Admiral Dewey) was then in Puerto Rican waters on exercises. The admiral had very little time for Germans or the German navy—during his blockade of Manila, by breaking the blockade repeatedly, they had caused him far more trouble than the Spaniards had ever done. Now, off Venezuela, his aide noted that "the Germans seem to be running things rather high-handedly. The Venezuelans deserve it. Still, we can *not* allow them [the Germans] to go too *far.*"[11]

With the president's approval, Admiral Dewey made his presence in the region clear, to the eventual satisfaction of everyone except Venezuela's president, Cipriano Castro. There was no invasion by European forces, but Venezuelan forts were bombarded and vessels seized by the blockading Europeans until President Castro offered to accept arbitration from the Hague; and with the crisis successfully passed, Roosevelt claimed his fleet had been sent to force the Germans to accept arbitration. This was not so: The ships had been scheduled for their Puerto Rican exercises long before the crisis. But the Navy's presence did limit German high-handedness, and no president was going to pass up such an obvious chance to promote his own favorite policy.

In the seven and a half years of Roosevelt's presidency, the Monroe Doctrine and the Caribbean came together repeatedly. Each demanding occasion underlined his basic attitude. He put it plainly in his annual message for 1904, in what became known as the "Roosevelt Corollary" to the doctrine:

> If we are willing to let Germany or England act as the policeman of the Caribbean, then we can afford not to intervene when gross wrongdoing occurs. But if we intend to say "Hands off" to the powers of Europe, then sooner or later we must keep order ourselves.[12]

The practical demands of the theoretical doctrine needed to be drummed in over and over if people were to grasp its implications fully. In 1901, and again in 1902, American naval forces were sent to the Isthmus of Panama to protect transisthmian communications; in 1905 a direct involvement with Dominica began, which ten years later would result in the island becoming a U.S. protectorate. But Roosevelt's most striking and notorious naval intervention was in 1903, again in Panama, when he backed that country's successful revolution.

This was how it happened. Since 1846, a treaty had existed between Colombia and the United States which guaranteed to U.S. nationals the right to trade across Colombia's northern province of Panama. The Colombian government had often asked the U.S. Navy to assist in putting down small insurrections in the area, but in 1901 and '02, the ships arrived before they were asked. Roosevelt agreed with Admiral Mahan's assessment of the isthmus: Although the French attempt had failed, a canal was bound to be built there sooner or later. And the president was determined that his country would not lose out.

In January 1903 Secretary of State John Hay negotiated a treaty with his Colombian counterpart for a hundred-year lease to be granted to America on a 10-mile-wide strip of land across the isthmus, at a cost of $10 million. Nominally, sovereignty would remain with Colombia, but in practice it would rest with America; and for that reason, on August 12 the Colombian government refused to ratify the treaty. Roosevelt believed they were simply stalling for more money. At the same time, another insurrection was brewing in Panama, supported by French businessmen who stood to make a great deal of money if the American lease was agreed to before their own expired and became worthless; and now, unofficially, U.S. Army officers began to assist in the planning of the Panamanian revolution.

On October 19 three American warships set off for the Panamanian coast, receiving orders on November 2 that if by any chance an insurrection should start, they were to take over the transisthmian railway and stop Colombian government troops from coming into the province. The revolution started the next day, as planned; the naval commanders obeyed orders and prevented the legitimate government from reestablishing control; the following day, a provisional Panamanian government was announced; a further two days later, it was accorded recognition by the United States; and only twelve days after that, on November 18, 1903, the new Republic of Panama accepted a treaty identical to the one rejected by Colombia.

If soft speech was not enough, this all showed that Roosevelt was quite willing to use the big stick; and although only Colombia was directly affected, the shock ran through the whole of Latin America. In North America there was wide criticism of the operation's unseemly haste, as well as its basic illegality and immorality; but few people seriously thought it ought to be reversed. In any nation on the road to world power, pragmatism and moral idealism have rarely been easy partners, and it was an uncomfortable period for sensitive American consciences. Yet an American-controlled isthmian canal was made essential not only by intimations of possible world power, nor even by the promise of national commercial benefit. The first and final imperative was safety: securing the nation's defensive ring against growing forces—possible enemies—on opposite sides of the world.

· · ·

A half century earlier, when the U.S. Navy was of little international consequence, Germany's navy had been even less so and Japan's navy had been nonexistent. Simultaneously all three had grown, and in 1894–95 (just three years before the Spanish-American War) Japan had astonished the world by defeating the huge, ancient Chinese Empire in a war over Korea. Immediately afterwards, Japan's main strategic prize (Port Arthur) was lost through the diplomatic intervention of Russia, France, and Germany; but in 1902, after nine months of secret talks, Japan and Great Britain announced that they had become allies. The move affected the world's naval equilibrium at least as much as the Spanish-American War had: By checkmating the Russo-Franco-German "Triple Intervention" it enabled Britain to reduce the Royal Navy's commitment in the Far East and created a powerful additional lever in keeping open the West's "Open Door" policy of Chinese trade, which the Russians were attempting to monopolize. But it also enabled Japan to think once more about overseas expansion; and so, seeing both possible benefits and possible threats, Americans' reaction to the alliance was ambivalent.

At the same time in Germany, under the professional guidance of Adm. Alfred von Tirpitz (secretary of state of the Ministry of Marine) and the direction of Kaiser Wilhelm II, another major navy was rapidly taking shape. Among them, all over the world, the influences of these four fleets—British, U.S., Japanese, and German—would dominate the first half of the twentieth century.

In anticipation of the bloody events to come, Great Britain prepared war plans against Germany; the United States also plotted against Germany and (despite the Anglo-Japanese Alliance) against Japan; Japan plotted against the United States; and Germany plotted against both Britain and the United States. In Germany the Büchsel plan (named after Vice Adm. Wilhelm Büchsel) was formally adopted by the Imperial Navy in November 1903, just at the time when President Roosevelt was acting as unofficial long-distance midwife to the new Republic of Panama. The Büchsel plan focused on the Caribbean and possible German expansion into South America: Early in a war, it said, Puerto Rico should be seized and made into a German fortress, and at war's end the United States should be made to renounce its iniquitous Monroe Doctrine.

A few months earlier, U.S. warships had steamed to the already troubled city of Beirut, acting on reports that one of their diplomats there had been assassinated. It turned out he was actually alive and well, but the hair-trigger reaction of Roosevelt's navy did not appeal in Germany, where the action was viewed as an excuse for the United States to become involved in the eastern Mediterranean. It seemed the United States could interfere wherever it liked, while other nations were expected not to interfere in the United States. As the *Neueste Nachrichten* newspaper commented, "These are the same American chauvinists who want to forbid European intervention in American affairs on the grounds of the Monroe Doctrine."[13] A Viennese publication agreed that although the doctrine was "still regarded as of binding force in the sense of excluding European influence from America, it does not appear in any way to prevent the Americans from establishing themselves in other continents."[14] They did have a point; and for any competitor to see the doctrine as an arbitrary, unilateral measure designed for the United States' sole benefit was reasonable.

In that fluid situation—with war fleets being created around a globe which had few internationally agreed spheres of influence; with ambitious nations building in the name of security and eyeing one another in grave suspicion—perhaps the only point on which all would have agreed was that sooner or later, somewhere or other, an explosion was probable. Yet such things rarely happen where and when imagined, and every nation except Japan was taken aback when, on the night of February 8–9, 1904, the Imperial Japanese Navy attacked the Russian navy's squadron at anchor in Port Arthur.

Forty years earlier, in 1864, when the Civil War was at its height, Secretary of the Navy Gideon Welles had pondered what to do with a ship which was being built by the Union for the Japanese navy. Secretary of State William H. Seward had been in no doubt: The Japanese should not have it. "If they ever got such a vessel," he said, "they would begin to play the pirate and raise the devil."[15]

From its surprise opening to its naval climax at the Battle of Tsushima and the subsequent peace treaty of September 5, 1905, the Russo-Japanese War was in many ways novel, and in every way phenomenal. It was the first time the world saw a real test of nineteenth-century developments in naval theory and material; compared with the sea battles of the Yellow Sea (August 10, 1904) and Tsushima (May 27–28, 1905), the Spanish-American battles of Manila and Santiago were mere coastal melees. In the way the Japanese massed their ships, rather than scattering them far and wide; in the way they took and kept control of the crucial sea lanes from the very beginning; and in the way they refused to be diverted into any commerce-raiding sideshow, their conduct of the sea war seemed to be a complete confirmation of Admiral Mahan's theories for the United States.

As a navalist, Roosevelt loved it and could scarcely believe the news of Japan's victory at Tsushima. Out of a fleet of thirty-eight Russian vessels, only four escaped, and the president wrote: "I grew so excited that I myself became almost like a Japanese, and I could not attend to official duties. I spent the whole day talking with visitors about the battle."[16] But as a strategist, he had already recognized the war's possible implications: In the summer of 1904 he remarked, "I am well aware that if they [the Japanese] win out, it may possibly mean a struggle between them and us in the future; but I hope and believe not."[17] And one year later, describing Japan, he also defined the nature and place of that potential struggle: Japan and its navy were a "formidable new power—a power jealous, sensitive and war-like, and which if irritated could at once take both the Philippines and Hawaii from us, if she obtained the upper hand on the seas."[18]

Roosevelt liked and respected the Japanese, with their bullish, challenging attitude to the world's established power chain; and he understood them a good deal better than did most of his countrymen. Nevertheless, it has been asserted that his sole direct involvement in the Russo-Japanese War bred anti-American feeling in Japan, fostering a resentment which climaxed at Pearl Harbor, thirty-six years later. Actually the basis for this rather extravagant assertion lies not so much in historical fact as in the World War II stereotype of the Japanese people as cunning, devious, sly, and revengeful; yet Roosevelt himself did do quite a lot, unintentionally, to build the stereotype and make the assertion sound credible. The circumstances behind it were these.

Despite the speed with which they won control of the seas, the efficiency with which they prosecuted the war on land and sea, and the total national dedication to the cause of war, Japanese resources were much more limited than those of Russia. Estimating correctly that Russia could lumber on indefinitely, eventually beating Japan by sheer weight of numbers, the Japanese government decided after Tsushima to quit while they were ahead. Knowing Roosevelt's sympathy for them, they asked him to mediate for peace. This he did in the navy yard of Portsmouth, New Hampshire, coaxing the Russian representative (Count Sergei Witte) and the Japanese representative (Jutaro Komura) to an agreement which gave Japan all the territorial recognition it had fought for ten years before in Manchuria and Korea. The one thing the treaty did not give to Japan was a $600 million indemnity for the costs of the war, and ordinary Japanese people, still unversed in Western diplomacy, felt they had been sold down the river. Rather than achieving the main objectives with a little give-and-take, they felt simply that the winner should take all. Not realizing that Tsar Nicholas would have preferred to carry on fighting rather than pay cash as well as territory, they rioted. The "revenge" interpretation takes this as the first step (or an early step) toward Pearl Harbor. In fact, the focus of the Japanese anger was not Roosevelt but their own government, which fell four months later.

Internationally the treaty was seen as fair, and for his efforts the president was awarded the 1906 Nobel Peace Prize. Nevertheless, in his second term as president, he again contributed unwittingly to the later legend of revengeful Japan by using his countrymen's prejudices about the Orient to get himself out of a trap he had made for himself, and to further his own domestic naval policies.

In the election of 1904, he romped home with over 56 percent of the popular vote, and by the end of 1905 (his fourth full year as president) he was well satisfied with the country's naval progress. Congress's annual appropriations for the Navy had risen from $85 million when he had first come to office to $118 million; ships displacing a total of more than a quarter million tons had been authorized or added to the fleet, including, most prominently, ten first-class battleships. By December 1905 he believed (and said in his annual message to Congress) that thenceforth it would be necessary to add only one battleship a year to maintain the fleet's strength. But in the same annual message he paradoxically supported the Navy Department's request for an annual replacement and growth program of two battleships.

The Navy's own estimate of what would constitute adequate strength was even greater than his, and the department was trying to create a fleet centered on no less than forty-eight first-class battleships. To this the president's reaction more or less, was, why not? Forty-eight battleships would be still better than the twenty-eight he had in mind, although he felt that twenty-eight, with one annual replacement, would be quite enough to be going on with. However (as predicted by his friend the Republican senator Henry Cabot Lodge), if the president said one would be enough, he would find it difficult if he changed his mind and asked for more.

Too late, Roosevelt realized he had painted himself into a corner; opponents of further naval expansion would be sure to remind him that he himself had said one was enough. And they did, for two years (1906 and '07), while the president kicked himself and looked for a way to dry the paint.

It was this impatience and annoyance with himself, rather than any real external threat, which made him exploit the Japanese crisis of 1906. For some years before the war with Russia, there had been a steady stream of Japanese immigration to the U.S. West Coast. In California it seemed that the nation's projection of itself as the land of opportunity was becoming, if anything, too successful, and the California legislature built an increasingly tangled set of restrictions around Japanese immigration. This, in turn, created resentment in Japan—not because of the principle of exclusion, as George Kennan (a friend of Roosevelt's) explained, but because Japanese were placed "below Hungarians, Italians, Syrians, Polish Jews, and degraded nondescripts from all parts of Europe and Western Asia."[19] On October 11, 1906, the discrimination culminated in a decision by the San Francisco school board to segregate Japanese students; and at that point it appeared a crisis had been reached.

"The whole world knows that the poorly equipped army and navy of the United States are no match for our efficient army and navy," growled a Japanese newspaper, the *Mainichi Shimbun.* "It will be an easy work to awake the United States from her dreams of obstinacy when one of our great Admirals appears on the other side of the Pacific. . . . Why do we not insist on sending ships?"[20]

More than any other nation in the world at the time, Japan was justified in calling its admirals great, and earlier in the year President Roosevelt had published a speech made by the greatest of them, Admiral Togo, the victor of Tsushima. In his speech, Togo called for perpetual Japanese war readiness, and Roosevelt had published it as a model for America to follow. But now people remembered that Togo had also said that by "adding our actual experiences in the war to the training that we have already received," the Imperial Navy "must plan future developments."[21] Altogether, it sounded uncomfortably threatening.

The West Coast attitude had bothered Roosevelt for a long time. In May 1905 he said angrily: "The Senators and Congressmen from these very states were lukewarm about the navy last year. It gives me a feeling of contempt to see them challenge Japanese hostility and justify by their actions any feeling the Japanese may have towards us, while at the same time refusing to take steps to defend themselves against the formidable foe, which they are ready with such careless insolence to antagonize."[22] Yet with the school crisis, Californians began to feel uneasily that they might have gone too far. Like their cousins on the East Coast in the Spanish-American War and their forebears in the War of Independence and the War of 1812, they apprehensively imagined an enemy fleet advancing across the ocean. Now, therefore, when the president spoke of making the U.S. Navy even larger, they listened with greater eagerness than before. Naturally Roosevelt used the opportunity; and he also used an opportunity provided by the British.

In the ten years between the end of Japan's war against China and the beginning of its war against Russia (that is, from 1895 to 1904), typical first-class U.S. battleships had carried four large guns (11-inch to 13-inch caliber) and a larger number of medium-caliber guns. Such vessels were the backbone of the U.S. Navy, as of all other important fighting fleets; until suddenly (in December 1906) they all became outdated. The name *Dreadnought* was already old in the Royal Navy—the first ship to bear it had fought against the Spanish Armada in 1588. But the eighth H.M.S. *Dreadnought* (launched in February 1906 and completed the following December) is justifiably the most famous, for at a stroke she brought naval architecture to a peak which other nations would ignore at their peril. Her name came to signify a particular kind of vessel: From her completion until aircraft carriers dethroned the battleship, capital ships were simply either pre- or post-dreadnought—and if they were pre-dreadnought, they were well advised to keep out of the way.

The concept was easy to grasp, but revolutionary. Instead of a mixed-caliber battery, H.M.S. *Dreadnought* mounted ten 12-inch guns. Theoreticians had worked out, and the Russo-Japanese War had proved, that mixing large and small guns wasted weight and space. The big guns could fire before the smaller ones were within range, and the smaller ones took up room which could be filled with more big guns. H.M.S. *Dreadnought* was longer, wider, faster, heavier, and of higher freeboard than any previous battleship, and Adm. Sir John Fisher (the First Sea Lord who prompted her creation) suggested with tongue-in-cheek delight that she should be called "The Hard-Boiled Egg"—"Why? Because she can't be beat!"[23]

This was why Roosevelt insisted that the United States had to have the same kind of ship as well—though not through any fear of Anglo-American conflict; the long hangover of suspicion between the two nations had finally been dissipated by the Spanish-American War, and since then a remarkable rapprochement had grown. Just after that war, Joseph Chamberlain (then Britain's colonial secretary) had looked prophetically forward to "that close union [of Britain and the United States] which, if accomplished, will be the most important event that the coming century has in store for us"; and speaking for the Admiralty just before *Dreadnought*'s completion, Admiral Fisher referred to the United States as "a kindred state with whom we shall never have a parricidal war." No cause for alarm, then, across the Anglo-American North Atlantic, but if Japan or Germany or both followed the British lead, the United States would start to slip again.

Hence Roosevelt's determination to keep up with the neighbors; and the United States was already quite well placed in the all-big-gun lists. The dreadnought concept was not originally British, but Italian, and had been published in the 1903 edition of Fred T. Jane's annual *Fighting Ships*. The Royal Navy stole a march on everyone else by being the first to turn the idea into reality, but Japan had almost taken that honor by ordering the construction in 1903 (as soon as the Italian plan was published) of a 20,000-ton, all-big-gun battleship to be named *Aki*. It would have been an absolute sensation if the baby navy of the East had been first with such a weapon, but the war with Russia (quite sufficiently sensational anyway) interrupted both building and the supply of big guns; so *Aki* was not completed until 1911 and then was only a semi-dreadnought, with a heavy but mixed main battery of four 12-inch and twelve 10-inch guns.

The Germans, meanwhile, got going on their own biggest battleship to date, *Nassau,* just after *Dreadnought*'s launch. At 18,900 tons she displaced a thousand tons more than *Dreadnought,* but in spite of her large size *Nassau* was intended to be a traditional mixed-battery ship. When *Dreadnought*'s implications were worked out in Germany, *Nassau*'s construction came to an abrupt halt as the designers hastened back to their drawing boards, and it was not until July 1909 that the vessel finally appeared to public gaze. Even then, she was still not a real dreadnought. True, she had a main battery of twelve 11-inch guns, but two of the turrets masked each other, reducing her broadside to no more than that of *Dreadnought.* Worse, her designers had missed the point of uniformity and crowded her with an additional twenty-eight 3.4- and 5.9-inch guns, which not only wasted weight and space but also demanded 180 more men than *Dreadnought.* Finally, while the British ship was powered by steam turbines (the first major warship to be so powered), the German vessel had old-fashioned, unreliable reciprocating engines. In short, with too many guns, too many men, and not enough power, she was a rushed job and a missed opportunity.

The U.S. Navy, however, was ready to take an edge on its German and Japanese rivals. The designs for its first all-big-gun battleships were prepared before the Royal Navy set this new spiral in naval building spinning. At 16,000 tons displacement, with a waterline length of 450 feet and a speed of 18.5 knots, *South Carolina* and *Michigan* were going to be smaller, shorter, and slower than *Dreadnought* herself and would have only eight rather than ten 12-inch guns. But the concept was correct: The uniform large-caliber guns would give them an uncomplicated, accurate, long-range attack capability—the whole purpose of the all-big-gun ship.

Nevertheless, though the designs were ready and accepted in 1905, Congress prevented the beginning of their construction until 1906 and at the same time authorized only one battleship for 1907. This ship, *Delaware,* would be the United States' first full dreadnought, and Roosevelt was convinced that more were not only advisable but essential if the United States were to maintain its political power aboard. In January 1907 he warned the House Naval Committee of the situation as he saw it. During the summer Congress threw back at him his own words of 1905 ("One is enough") and refused to budge. Somehow the president needed to regain the initiative, and in December 1907 he did so.

On the third day of the month he put his annual message to Congress in the plainest possible terms: "To build one battleship of the best and most advanced type a year would barely keep our fleet up to its present force. *This is not enough.* In my judgment, we should this year provide for four battleships."[24]

Even the most diehard antinavalist could see he meant business; and thirteen days later, as opponents prepared their arguments for the coming

debates, he stood on the deck of the presidential yacht *Mayflower* to set
in motion the biggest naval public relations show he could possibly devise—the Great White Fleet. Close to *Mayflower* were the United States'
sixteen best battleships, all painted a brilliant, peaceful, celebration white,
gleaming in the pale sunshine of the Chesapeake winter's day and weighing anchor for a fourteen-month cruise around the world. Naval bands
played; the great guns thundered in salute; and the president (a slightly
comical sight, returning the salute with one hand and holding his top hat
on with the other) exclaimed to everyone and no one: "Did you ever see
such a fleet on such a day?"[25]

The answer had to be: Never in the United States. Like *Dreadnought,*
this magnificent publicity stunt was a brainwave, and retrospectively the
obvious thing to do. Japan had celebrated its victory over Russia with an
imperial naval review; Great Britain frequently used naval reviews to
boost and maintain national pride. It was about time the United States
had one—after all, the nation was the world's third largest naval power
and needed to realize it. The fleet had other national and international
purposes as well: to boost the United States' prestige abroad, to train the
crews, to help calm the crisis with Japan—and to confirm various aspects
of the Naval War College's new "Plan Orange," the recently developed
war plan against Japan.

The cruise of the Great White Fleet achieved all its objectives. Showing
the flag en masse across 46,000 nautical miles produced infinitely more
publicity than could have been gained by the same number of ships
patrolling singly or in small groups here and there. During the fourteen
months of voyaging, the fleet stopped at Trinidad and four ports around
South America; then, proceeding from San Francisco, it visited New
Zealand, Australia, and Japan before moving via China and the Red Sea
to the Mediterranean. In all the South American, Southern Pacific, and
European ports of call it was received enthusiastically. South Americans
saw it as a renewal of Monroe's doctrinal vows for their protection against
Europe; to the chagrin of the British Admiralty, Australians and New
Zealanders saw it as a protection against Japan; Europeans saw it as an
opportunity to jockey for American favor in their own knotty politics;
and everyone, wherever the fleet anchored, saw it as a wonderful excuse
for public holidays and festivities.

All that had been hoped for; and to the surprise of many Americans,
the fleet was warmly welcomed in Japan too. As one diplomat in Tokyo
noted, it had "great political significance. . . . Far from giving umbrage
or inspiring any fear in Japan, this deployment of forces is regarded as
a guarantee of peace."[26]

The ships, officers, and men were greeted in a most friendly manner
"not only by the Emperor and his staff but by the entire nation," and
celebrations continued for a whole week.[27] In the carnival atmosphere,

Admiral Togo (sixty-one years old and the world's most respected living admiral) even permitted the visiting ensigns to toss him into the air from a blanket. Many years later, when some of those ensigns were admirals themselves, one of them—William F. Halsey—remembered the occasion and said bitterly: "If we had known what the future held, we wouldn't have caught him the third time!"[28]

But in 1908 it seemed the Pacific Ocean would remain as peaceful as its name. In Washington, Japan's Ambassador Takahira signed an agreement with Secretary of State Elihu Root to maintain the status quo on the ocean, and the fleet proceeded contentedly from Tokyo, confident that its presence had done much to restore Japanese-U.S. relations. It certainly had; but the curious thing was that it was not in quite the way they thought. It had been not the Japanese who needed calming down, but the Americans.

Even before the Great White Fleet had been thought of, the London *Times* correspondent in Tokyo reported that "in this country there is absolutely no talk of war. All the excitement, all the bellicose rumors emanate from the American side."[29] This was largely true: Belligerent grumbles in Japan, such as those of the *Mainichi Shimbun,* were minority vaporings.

Roosevelt knew that practically speaking, the notion of Japan attacking the U.S. West Coast was an impossibility; the problems of distance and supply would have been insuperable. He knew too that in the Philippines the United States was vulnerable to Japan; that when it was completed, the Panama Canal would also require defense; and that the United States could not afford to let slip its favorable position relative to Japan and Germany simply because shortsighted politicians could not see the chance of future danger. So he used the spook of Japan and the spectacle of the Great White Fleet to diminish opposition to his dreadnought program and began developing a pleasant place in the Hawaiian Islands as the U.S. Navy's main Pacific base. In a short time Pearl Harbor would be able to give distant defense to both the Panama Canal and the Philippines, and it was far enough from Japan to be safe itself.

Before his much-regretted judgment in 1905 that one new ship a year would be enough, Roosevelt had made another mistake. In 1904 he had said that under no circumstances would he run for reelection in 1908; so in the last year of his presidency he visibly lost his personal sway over Congress and the Senate. Cross-party opposition to the dreadnought program was strong and vocal, with Republican and Democrat representatives from at least a dozen states promising that it would bring higher taxation, more bureaucracy, a greater likelihood of war, and a growing international arms race.

These were old arguments; with the exception of the last, they had all been trotted out repeatedly since the first suggestion of an American fleet was made in 1775. Still, age had not wearied them, and with the new warning of an arms race they remained as correct as ever. Even so, they were less likely than ever to succeed. Americans had won the right to be consulted in international affairs; and whether or not they were sure they wanted that right, they were not going to back off altogether. After a strong debate, two of the four dreadnoughts were authorized, and (although at that stage no funds were appropriated for their building) the straitjacket of one a year was broken.

When Roosevelt had become president in 1901, he had immediately begun a policy of radical naval reform, aiming to lessen the shore establishment, to increase the number of personnel and commissioned ships, to provide constant training, and thus to win higher efficiency all round. When he left office on March 3, 1909, he had moved close to all those goals. In 1901 the U.S. Navy had had 883 officers and 25,050 men; in 1909 the figures were 1,096 and 44,500, respectively, while over the same period annual naval appropriations rose from $85 million to $140 million. Technologically, the fleet was being kept up to date, and (although they were regarded as little more than modern monitors, cheap instruments of coastal defense) twenty-seven submarines had been authorized. The old practice of scattering ships in distant stations had been abandoned in favor of one fleet concentrated on each coast. And less than two weeks before he once again became a private citizen, President Roosevelt was on hand to witness the conclusion of his last big naval fling: the Great White Fleet's return home, on February 22, 1909.

At the beginning of the century, the U.S. Navy had been sixth largest in the world; by 1909, it was second only to the Royal Navy. From the British perspective, Lord Lansdowne (then First Lord of the Admiralty, equivalent of secretary of the Navy) remarked: "It has not dawned on our countrymen yet . . . that, if the Americans choose to pay for what they can easily afford, they can gradually build up a navy, fully as large and then larger than ours." Roosevelt knew that was true. "And," Lansdowne had concluded, "I am not sure they will not do it."[30]

In contrast, Roosevelt was not sure they *would* do it. As outgoing president, he was fully aware that he personally could take the main credit for placing the United States' fighting ships in their new high position. Whether that would continue was quite another question. The fleet's future depended not on him, but on his successors.

5

*

HOW TO TELL SHIPS
FROM AUTOMOBILES

W hen he left office in 1909, President Roosevelt had been involved
with, and directly influential in, U.S. naval affairs for eleven full
years. In that period, the U.S. Navy's doctrine and demands had been
through a revolution. Alfred Mahan's basic principle (that fighting ships
should operate as a coherent fleet rather than as a scattered police or
guerrilla band) had been shown to work, both in the United States' own
war with Spain and in Japan's war with Russia. As a result the U.S. battle
fleet, based on the Atlantic coast, had become the world's most powerful
single fighting unit; yet its very success in war had brought potentially
insuperable problems as well. For the United States' territorial interests
had expanded from the confines of the continent to include Puerto Rico
to the east and the Philippines to the west—islands more than ten thousand miles apart in a straight line and with over twice that distance of
sea separating them in the route around Cape Horn.

On the West Coast the Pacific Fleet, established in 1907, contained
eight armored and eight auxiliary cruisers (vessels fast enough to get away
from a hostile battleship fleet but too weak to engage with any hope of
victory) while the so-called Asiatic Fleet, also established in 1907, had
only three cruisers and a handful of destroyers and gunboats for patrol.
Looking warily at Japan in 1910, Maj. Gen. William P. Duvall (then
commanding general in the Philippines) wrote that "so long as the battleship fleet is not in these waters we have no hope here."[1] Yet powerful as

it was, the single battle fleet could not be in two places at once and would take a very long time to get from one side of the new U.S. empire to the other; and the crux of the problem was the possibility that the fleet might be needed in both places at the same time.

Naval planners could not ignore the Japanese fleet: With its proximity to the Philippines, it had to be viewed as a potential threat, even if relations between the countries were completely cordial, which they still were not. Nor could the planners ignore the threat from across the Atlantic as Great Britain and Germany jostled each other in their ac- celerating naval race. Germany, moreover, posed a double-sided threat, for apart from having designs on the Caribbean, it had acquired the Pacific island groups of the Carolinas and Marianas, which formed a hurdle between the Philippines and the United States. Not one but two new empires were growing from the grave of the empire of Spain. If he chose, it seemed that Kaiser Wilhelm could strike the U.S. empire in the Pacific as readily as the one in the Caribbean; and if he chose to hit the Caribbean, not even the Anglo-Japanese Alliance could guarantee that Japan would not take the opportunity of distraction to jump on the Philippines.

On his last day in office, President Roosevelt gave his successor, Wil- liam Howard Taft, a sound piece of Mahanian advice: "Under no circum- stances divide the battleship fleet between the Atlantic and Pacific Oceans prior to the finishing of the Panama Canal."[2] After the failure of de Lesseps's attempt and the success of the U.S.-backed revolution in Pan- ama, work on a U.S. canal across the isthmus had begun in 1904. In Cuba, American doctors had eradicated yellow fever. In Panama (after an initial epidemic and panic) their experience was applied and by 1905 the disease had gone from there as well, along with malaria; and since the French had already dug out a fair amount of earth and made most of the possible mistakes, construction got into full swing in 1907. However, the canal would not be complete until 1914; so Mr. Roosevelt was pleased to hear President Taft's inaugural address, for it included the judgment "that the strength of our navy is the union of all the fighting material at one point, and that when we need it in the East we will send it all there."[3] But to Roosevelt's consternation, the new president at once set about policies in the Far East which seemed likely to *result* in a need for American warships there.

Since 1902, when the Anglo-Japanese Alliance had been signed, Roose- velt had pursued a delicate balancing act between Europe and the Orient. Though he never joined the alliance, he associated closely with it; but after Japan's victory over Russia on one side of the world, and as the German fleet grew on the other side, he found he had to rely more and more on Britain as a shield against Germany, while at the same time he himself had to cope with Japan—Britain's ally—in the Pacific. The Root-Takahira agreement of 1908 stabilized the ocean's territorial status quo and guaranteed that Japan would uphold the Open Door principle in China; yet it also gave tacit American support to Japanese adventures in Manchuria. This was far from ideal, but Roosevelt saw that it was the best that could be done under the circumstances. In his view, the two salient facts of the matter were, first, that in varying degrees the other Great Powers recognized the Open Door principle, although they all stood more or less in its way in practice; and second, that until America had real naval muscle in the area, not much could be done to improve matters through diplomacy alone. At any rate, support in principle was better than outright opposition.

However, with no more ships than before, Taft set out to make the Open Door a reality, most notably through one scheme to neutralize the Russian- and Japanese-owned railways in Manchuria, and another to create an international banking consortium. These and other plans trod heavily on Russian and Japanese toes, infringing those countries' spheres of interest. It was obvious to Roosevelt that without strength to enforce the treading, no good would come of it. "Never draw," he cautioned Taft, "unless you mean to shoot," to which Taft replied that he was only doing the morally correct thing in trying to promote the national interest.[4] The attempt not only failed, but backfired—none of the Great Powers except Germany was willing to support it, while Japan and Russia reacted by defining more exactly their overlapping spheres of interest. Each thus enabled the other to get on with exploiting southeast Asia more busily than before; but Taft never believed he should have let well alone. He and Roosevelt represented a classic division of American thinking: Roosevelt the pragmatist, willing to turn a blind eye to the misdeeds of others in exchange for security in his own patch; and Taft the idealist, unwilling to compromise his ideals even when he had no way of enforcing them.

The Taft years (1909–1913) were filled with naval thought, much of it focused on the Far East and most of it ineffective. Apart from the unrealistic approach to the Open Door, which set U.S. interests back more than it promoted them, a similar inept high-mindedness showed again how useless moral suasion was without force behind it. Starting in 1909, the Bethlehem Steel Company made a determined effort to sell ships and naval guns to China. Arguing that a successful deal would be equivalent to an unofficial alliance, the company gained governmental assurance that American officers would be sent to command and train the new fleet—new, because since its defeat by the Japanese in 1894 China had had no navy of international consequence. William J. Calhoun (the U.S. minister in China) took a dim view of the affair, reckoning that Prince Tsai Hun (the man in charge of Chinese naval purchases) was not only corrupt but gullible:

> Our shipyard people may be able to give him such gastronomic exhibitions, illuminated with plenty of fireworks, as will impress him with the superiority of our naval constructions. . . . The Vickers and Maxim people made quite an impression on him by a display of fireworks, in which his portrait appeared, dressed in the glittering and emblazoned uniform of an Admiral.[5]

Calhoun went on to say that tempting the prince to spend what little money his country had would make the United States a betrayer of the Chinese people: The money would be far better used for internal reforms. Nevertheless, on October 21, 1911, the bargain was concluded—China would spend $15 million on U.S. naval supplies. But only ten days earlier, riots had started in Hangkow, 500 miles up the Yangtze River; and with them the Chinese revolution began.

In December, Sun Yat-sen established a revolutionary government in Nanking. On February 12, 1912, China's boy emperor—the last of the Manchu dynasty—abdicated. In the intervening weeks, other countries remembered the murders of foreigners during the Boxer Rebellion of 1901 and made ready for the mutual defense of their nationals in China. President Taft gave particularly loud support to the idea of "concerted action": one for all and all for one, without any single nation taking the opportunity to extend its sphere of influence in the sprawling Middle Kingdom. Yet to the surprise of all foreigners concerned, there was no need for mutual defense. In Chinese eyes, the revolution was a purely internal affair, with no antiforeign element whatever, and both imperial and revolutionary forces were scrupulous in their treatment of outsiders. Moreover, discontent with the imperial regime was so widespread that even among Chinese there was comparatively little bloodshed; and once other nations understood this, Taft suddenly found himself on the sidelines, still calling for concerted action as Russia claimed special rights in Mongolia, Turkestan, and northern Manchuria, while Japan did the same in Inner Mongolia and southern Manchuria, and Britain followed suit in Tibet.

By the middle of 1912, Taft's would-be moral leadership had diminished to plaintive suggestions that the new Chinese republic should be internationally recognized. The other western nations may have agreed that morally Taft was in the right; but their consciences were troubled very little, because they had found that once inside the Open Door, Americans were as ready as anyone else to try to close it behind them.

Just before the revolution, Taft's administration had learned that China's navy would have U.S.-made hulls, but British guns, and that U.S.

officers would lead only one squadron, while other foreign officers would lead the remainder. Since the United States had hoped to supply all necessary ships, guns, and officers as well, their protests at this were strong, but unavailing. In the Great Power politics of the Orient, Taft had become like the leader of a temperance evangelist band in a brewery on New Year's Eve, unable either to convert the sinners or join in the party himself. (Pursuing the metaphor, it did not help that one of his friends had slipped a very visible hip flask—the would-be all-American Chinese fleet—into his back pocket.) Sniggering at the apparent double standard, the other countries declined to recognize the Chinese republic, saying that it had not yet fulfilled the necessary conditions. What they actually meant was that they had not completed their dominance of the various outlying regions; so they got on with that, leaving poor Taft at the back of the room to bang his tambourine unheard.

Throughout Taft's administration, U.S. defense of the Philippines was consistently and illogically neglected. No one in a position of power was willing to recognize the implications of the president's Far Eastern policies. One reason for this was a running argument among the U.S. armed forces on the best site to develop for Philippine defense; but that was only one symptom of the surprising weaknesses under the Navy's strong surface. In many respects the existing fleet (created so largely by Roosevelt's muscular acceptance of Mahan's theories) resembled a plant bred in darkness and then force-grown: a pale, weak, attenuated stalk held up an impressive, oversized head. The fleet had fallen badly out of balance.

In 1889 Stephen Luce had declared that "the United States has no battleships, therefore she has no Navy"; but twenty years later the Navy had (compared to the rest of its force) far too many battleships, which was not much better than having none. Replacing the old Board of Commissioners, the Navy's General Board (established in 1900 under Admiral Dewey) performed some of the functions of a general staff, and in 1911 it produced a worryingly clear statement of the fleet's imbalance. There were altogether 173 commissioned vessels, of which 33 were battleships. There were no battle-cruisers, no ammunition ships; there were fifty destroyers, but only one destroyer tender; a dozen armored cruisers and seventeen protected cruisers, but only three scout cruisers; thirty-eight submarines, but only two submarine tenders. To serve them all there was a single hospital ship and a single repair ship. To meet the demands of the existing battleship force and without adding any further battleships, the General Board said the fleet as a whole should include 346 commissioned vessels—exactly double the existing number of units, but in a very different proportion of types.

There were also severe technical deficiencies. A characteristic affecting the majority of ships was poor ventilation, which meant that in hot weather the crew could not sleep belowdecks at night, and could only work in the engine rooms for short periods before being exhausted. Another frequent weakness was the location of the armor plating: When a vessel was at full load, the armor-plated section of its hull would be so low that only a foot or two remained above water, minimizing the protection it could give against shell fire. Some of the worst design faults actually endangered the crews.

Many vessels had too little freeboard, which meant that in a heavy sea they were unable to fight: The gun turrets became flooded and unworkable. U.S.S. *Kearsage* carried no less than fourteen guns in one compartment protected only by 6-inch armor. Between the individual guns were nothing but 2-inch wood screens, and one well-placed enemy shell could knock out all fourteen guns at once. Some of the ships' gun turrets (in particular in the *Kearsage* class) had excessively large gun ports of 9 square feet or more in area—more than enough for an enemy shell to come hurtling straight in. Or if it was not an enemy shell, it could be flareback from the gun's breech as hot gases left behind after firing exploded when the breech was opened to reload. In either of those cases— an enemy shell or flareback—the explosion could communicate directly through the powder hoist to the powder handling room. Nor were these just theoretical problems: In a single flareback on U.S.S. *Missouri,* eighteen men in her No. 2 turret and a further twelve in her handling room died.

Mirroring the fleet's imbalance and technical weaknesses, the U.S. Navy was oversupplied with dockyards on the East Coast, where there were nine, and drastically undersupplied on the West Coast, where there were only two. Among them, the eleven had fewer dry docks than the single largest British yard; yet domestic political pressures usually prevented the closure or relocation of any but the most overtly useless.

President Taft's secretary of the Navy, George von Lengerke Meyer, worked hard to correct the worst of these deficiencies and tackled the growing inadequacy of the Navy's administration as well. Much of the blame was placed on the bureau system and its personnel: The system was no longer up to the task it was meant to fulfill, and the personnel were often the old, the conservative, the overcautious. Roosevelt had tried to develop the General Board into an authentic general staff coordinating all aspects of the currently discordant system. Secretary Meyer tried again, appointing aides in each bureau to report to him; but the establishment of a proper general staff was still stopped by congressional fears that civilians would lose control of the military.

January 1908 brought publication (in *McClure's Magazine*) of a blisteringly critical article by Henry Reuterdahl, a civilian marine artist. Writing from information supplied by discontented officers, he listed many of the Navy's flaws: no naval range finders, no battle signals, no general staff, no means of steering a compass course in battle, no means of handling a fleet in a fog. Above all, said Reuterdahl, the source of all the weaknesses was that the United States was still "only beginning to have a definite naval policy."[6]

No matter that Meyer tried hard; no matter that President Taft's intentions were good. When they both left office in March 1913, national naval policy was still undefined—except, perhaps, as spasmodic opportunism governed by vested interest.

Just eight years earlier, the philosopher George Santayana had written his most famous (and usually misquoted) sentence: "Those who cannot remember the past are condemned to fulfill it." Politicians might not be expected to know much about philosophy, but in 1913 it seemed that some U.S. politicians hardly remembered their national past at all. As long ago as 1827 the point had been made (by Senator Robert Hayne of South Carolina) that "a Navy was not only the safest but the cheapest defense of this nation" and should be built "on some regular plan." But it still was not; and in February 1913, only a few weeks before Woodrow Wilson took office as president, a report of the House Naval Committee showed the same sort of collective amnesia.

"For the purpose of defending our country against attacks from any nation on earth," they said, "we confidently believe that our Navy is amply sufficient and fully adequate, and for any other purpose we need no navy at all."[7]

But had this not been heard in America before? It sounded as though they had decided to repeat Secretary Woodbury's report for 1832—on the sea, he had asserted, "our means of attack and defense. . .will probably always prove equal to sustain us with credit in any hostilities."

There was one change, and a good one: The 1913 report implicitly renounced aggressive unilateral actions. But otherwise it showed a naive and disquieting complacency, for the United States was once again slipping in the ranks of naval nations. At the beginning of the century, the U.S. Navy had been sixth largest in the world, after those of England, France, Russia, Germany, and Italy. By knocking Russia out in 1905, the Japanese promoted the United States to fifth place. In 1907 no less than thirteen armored cruisers and battleships were completed for and delivered to the U.S. fleet, which suddenly jumped to second place. Now a little larger than either the French or German navy, it was still only about one third the power of the Royal Navy. A further large delivery of six capital ships in 1908 confirmed the new ranking, and in 1912 a German general, Friedrich von Bernhardi, asserted that "the American navy is at the present moment stronger than the German, and will henceforth maintain this precedence."[8]

He was wrong: In that year, Germany's brisk building overtook the United States. "I am persuaded," Alfred Mahan wrote in 1913 to Carter H. Fitz-Hugh, a member of a peace society, "that at this present moment and for many years to come the great preparations for war now sustained are the surest guarantee for the continuance of actual peace."[9] He was wrong too, and, perhaps surprisingly, the Naval Committee's comment that the U.S. Navy was big enough was substantially correct. There were four reasons for this.

First, the Anglo-Japanese Alliance of 1902 had been renewed and revised, to U.S. advantage. Originally, England and Japan had promised to support each other in the event of war with any two other nations. The revised treaty specifically excluded the United States from the list of potential Anglo-Japanese enemies, so now, if Japan and the United States fought, Britain would not have to join the Japanese side. Since there was no likelihood of Japan fighting the United States without British help, in practical terms this meant the Pacific was now a stable ocean.

Second and simultaneously, the United States' new stability in the Pacific was mirrored in the western Atlantic, when Guantanamo Bay in Cuba was developed as a U.S. naval base, affording protection to the eastern approaches of the almost-completed Panama Canal.

Third, the only serious threats the U.S. Navy could face were from the superior British and German navies; but their race with each other had canceled both out of the equation. And finally, for all their greater mobility, the steam navies of the modern age had lost one strength of the days of sail. Dependent not only on food supplies but now on fuel supplies as well, there was no navy in the world which could feasibly attack the United States without first seizing a strong offshore base, and the U.S. fleet could prevent that happening. In short, in 1913 the United States was strategically invulnerable.

It would have been an enviable situation for the new president and his secretary of the Navy—if there had been no other complications. Thomas Woodrow Wilson, fifty-seven years old, was the son of a Presbyterian minister and had inherited a strongly moral and missionary attitude to life. Highly intellectual as well, he had trained as a lawyer and after teaching jurisprudence at Princeton had become president of the university and then governor of New Jersey. Josephus Daniels, six years younger, had been a newspaper editor before being made chief publicist of Wilson's presidential campaign, and his appointment as naval secretary was simply a reward for the successful campaign. His knowledge of naval affairs was slight, but with the president he shared a passion for education. From the Navy's point of view, he was not the most obvious person to be their civilian head, especially in a year like 1913; one did not have to be clairvoyant to see that a war in Europe was becoming more and more probable and that somehow the United States would certainly be affected. However, it was much harder to predict what Secretary Daniels would do, and throughout the summer and autumn of 1913 U.S. naval officers waited anxiously.

December 1913 arrived, and with it the secretary's first report to Congress. His construction proposals were modest and unexciting: two battleships, eight destroyers, and three submarines. Considerably more surprising were his plans for the Navy's shore establishment: The yards which had been closed would be reopened; all would be expanded; and government-owned factories for guns, armor, and powder would be created along with coal mines and oil refineries. But in his general discussion on naval building, he drifted into fine unreality. In Britain, Winston Churchill had recently suggested an international one-year naval building holiday. Airily dismissing stark European truths, Daniels took up the idea and stretched it: "It ought not to be difficult," he said, "to secure an agreement by which navies will be adequate without being overgrown," and he proposed an international arms limitation conference. President Wilson agreed profoundly with this ideal; others ignored it, and instead narrowed their eyes at Daniels's favorite proposal—that the Navy would become a "great university," with all personnel being taught English, arithmetic, and religion.[10]

On June 28, 1914, Archduke Franz Ferdinand, heir presumptive to the Austrian throne, was assassinated at Sarajevo in Austria-Hungary, shivering the alliances of Europe toward the last edge of peace. Two days later President Wilson signed the December 1913 Navy bill into law, and at midnight that night, Secretary Daniels's General Order No. 99 came into effect. For some time past, enlisted men had been forbidden to have alcohol, but the officers' wine mess continued. Disliking the anomaly, Daniels decreed that as from July 1 the U.S. Navy would be completely dry. Officers in every American warship made sure they were ready for it. The stocks of alcohol had to be disposed of somehow; and there were some magnificent parties in the fleet that night.

By the end of the first week of August 1914 all Europe was at war, and President Wilson announced the United States' official reaction: strict neutrality. "The United States must be neutral in fact as well as in name," he told the Senate on August 19: no entangling alliances with the Old World—not least because the New World was composed of so many groups of different ethnic origin that it seemed that involvement in Europe could split Americans apart. The largest single ethnic group of non-English-speaking origin were people of German descent, and whatever politics said, inevitably emotions divided into pro-German, pro-Allied, and pro-neutrality. Only two years earlier, Admiral Mahan had said privately: "The position of Germany as regards expansion is one that commands much sympathy—so to say, her ambitions are natural and laudable."[11] Now that war had begun, many Americans still held to that view.

In keeping with his neutral stance, the president wanted the nation's arms program to remain exactly as it was; but others who equally advocated neutrality disagreed strongly. In November 1914, one voice, growing steadily louder, recommended "An Easy Solution for Securing Peace on Earth." Only two things needed to be done: "Abolish: Kings, Oligarchs, Race Antipathies, Unfair Competition, Land Grabbing, Injustice and Sin. Establish: The Rule of the People, A Satisfactory World Tribunal, Justice, Charity, and A Changed Human Nature." And in case of difficulty in achieving those goals: "Ad Interim: MAINTAIN A STRONG NAVY."[12]

These were the unmistakable tones of the Navy League of the United States. The league had come into being during the winter of 1902–03, following the creation of similar groups in Britain, Germany, France, Belgium, Portugal, and Spain. Over 2,100 years earlier there had been comparable organizations in ancient Greece and Rome; but where the ancient leagues actually built ships and trained sailors, the modern ones saw themselves as educators, telling other citizens "what a navy means to the country and what it ought to mean to them."[13] Theodore Roosevelt gave the U.S. Navy League unequivocal encouragement, yet ordinary Americans showed a spectacular lack of interest in it: By the end of 1913 it had only seven thousand members and an annual income of under $15,000. At the same time, the German Navy League had a membership of over one million and an annual income of $250,000.

From its beginning, the U.S. Navy League had issued warnings that sooner or later the United States and Germany would clash, and now that the warnings seemed close to becoming true, the league tackled its self-imposed task of national alert with vigor. Members took courage from the president's own writing: In 1908, Wilson had published a five-volume *History of the American People* in which he dismissed President Jefferson's anti–naval embargo policy of a hundred years earlier, saying that the War of 1812 was a "war of arms brought on by a program of peace."[14] And in his second annual message to Congress, Wilson heartened the league further by declaring that "a powerful navy, we have always regarded as our proper and natural means of defense. . . . We shall take leave to be strong upon the seas, in the future as in the past."[15]

The declaration (partly in response to a congressional criticism that the Navy was weak, undermanned, and inefficient) seemed to promise well; but when Secretary Daniels followed it with the assertion that "the Navy is always ready. . . . It lives in a state of preparedness," then it became clear that explosive naval growth was not part of the administration's plan.[16]

Under the leadership of Admiral Dewey (eighty-seven years old, but still with an undimmed view of the United States' need for sea power), the General Board recommended that sixty-three vessels should be added to the fleet, including four battleships and sixteen destroyers, and alleged that the existing force was already under strength by nearly 20,000 men. Refusing to accept this, Daniels prohibited publication of the board's report until its estimate of the manpower shortfall had been removed. His own report recommended the building of only eighteen vessels, including two battleships, six destroyers, and seven submarines. This was almost exactly the form taken by the final bill, except that seventeen submarines were authorized. Yet of that unusually large number, all but one were going to be small coastal craft—nothing more than the modern equivalent of John Adams's "row gallies," Jefferson's gunboats, or the monitors of the Civil War.

"Mr. Daniels's crime is not that he has let an efficient Navy deteriorate," said one sharp-tongued critic. "It is that with our defenseless condition exposed in all its nakedness, with an aroused public sentiment demanding instant action and willing to pay the cost, he sits back, his face bathed in perpetual sunshine, and tells us what a fine Navy we have, gives out misleading information concerning its condition, cuts to the quick the recommendations made for its improvement by his experienced advisers, postpones the building of ships which are already authorized, wastes his time fussing with Government armor-plate factories and ship-building plants, and goes before Congress not to advocate a Navy commensurate with our needs, but to persuade that august body to do as little as it possibly can toward satisfying the popular clamor." Cartoons lampooning Daniels as a tightfisted, complacent, ignorant, meddlesome old woman appeared: He was seen in bonnet and bodice reading books with titles such as *Gunnery at a Glance* and *How to Tell Ships from Automobiles,* while beside him a wastebasket overflowed with papers headed "Expert Suggestions," "Competent Advice," "Intelligent Criticisms," and so on. Throughout the summer of 1915, battle was joined in the United States between advocates of peace and those of war, or at least of readiness for war. Across the ocean, equally ancient naval strategies were adopted: blockade by the British and retaliatory commerce raiding by the Germans. Both violated traditional American principles of freedom of the seas and neutral rights; both risked American ill-will at best and active U.S. opposition at worst. With the United States now the most powerful of the neutral nations, this was perhaps the gravest risk the warring opponents could take; yet neither could afford not to take it.

"We would as soon fight the British as the Germans," said Adm. William S. Benson to his colleague Rear Adm. William S. Sims.[17] Sims (the same man who, as naval attaché in Paris during the Spanish-American War, had run an effective intelligence campaign) was emerging as one of the most able officers in the fleet and was very pro-British. Benson, on the other hand, deeply disliked the British, and in 1915, as the navy's most senior officer, he became the first Chief of Naval Operations (CNO). At long last, after the General Board of 1900 and the aid system of 1909–13, the Navy was acquiring something like a general staff, giving coordinated professional advice to the civilian secretary. Daniels did not want it and managed to curtail the new CNO's powers. But whatever the prejudices of Daniels or Benson, President Wilson remained commander in chief, and it was his message to Germany on February 10, 1915, which made the United States almost certain not only to join the war, but to do so on the British side.

The difference between British and German violations of neutral rights at sea was literally a matter of life and death. The British seized neutral cargoes, but they did not kill anyone in the process and they paid for the cargoes. In the years of U.S. neutrality, German submarines killed some two hundred Americans and many more neutrals of other nations; and when, early in February 1915, Kaiser Wilhelm announced unrestricted submarine warfare against all vessels approaching the British coast, President Wilson responded (on the tenth of the month) with a warning that Germany would face "a strict accountability" for lives or property endangered or lost. From that moment it could be assumed that the United States would not back off—and it was certain that Germany could not. An exact date could not be foreseen, but a clash between them had become inevitable.

6

★

WOW! BUT IT
WAS GREAT WORK

*U*S. neutrality had not been under such severe threat from outside for over a hundred years, since the end of the War of 1812. Now the debate began to spread nationwide: Should neutrality be maintained, and if so, how? Or should preparations be made for war, and if so, what? The Navy League had one answer for both questions—"Battleships are cheaper than battles." Stating that the Navy was "our main defense" and "cannot be improvised," league literature added pointedly that "the weight of a powerful navy gives force to diplomacy."[1]

Seventy-nine days after President Wilson's diplomatic announcement of Germany's "strict accountability," *Gulflight* was sunk—an American tanker torpedoed without warning by a U-boat. The date was unpleasantly apt: May Day.

On that same day a 31,500-ton Cunard liner departed New York for Liverpool on her regular monthly voyage, taking mail and passengers across the Atlantic. In 1907, when she was only a year old, R.M.S. *Lusitania* had won the blue riband for crossing the ocean at nearly 23 knots. Six days out from New York, in the early afternoon of May 7, 1915, she was approaching the Old Head of Kinsale, 18 miles from Cork harbor's entrance, when *U-20* hit her twice on the starboard side. In all, 1,198 passengers and crew drowned, including 128 Americans. Theodore Roosevelt pronounced it "piracy on a vaster scale than the worst pirates of history"; murmurings in the United States grew into a concerted baying for war. But Wilson would not be forced. Diplomacy must work; or if it did not, then "first," he said, "we must have professional advice."

"I would be very much obliged if you would get the best minds in the Department to work on the subject," he told Secretary Daniels, and added: "I want their advice, a program by them formulated in the most definite terms. Whether we can reasonably propose the whole of it to Congress immediately or not, we can determine when we have studied it. The important thing now is to know fully what we need."[2]

That same day (July 21) he sent a third diplomatic note to Germany concerning *Lusitania*. The first (sent on May 13) had demanded disavowal, reparation, and a guarantee it would not happen again. The German reply stalled. The second note (June 9) came close to being an ultimatum by stating the absolute illegality of the sinking. Rather than sign what he considered to be a rash and dangerous note, Wilson's secretary of state resigned. Again the German reply was unsatisfactory. In the third note Wilson informed the kaiser that any further similar aggression would be construed as deliberately unfriendly. It was no coincidence that that note and the letter to Daniels were written in one day: Those in the United States who clamored for war could not see through the White House doors, but behind them the president made haste slowly. Realizing painfully that neutrality and diplomacy might become impossible, he began to prepare with sober realism.

Never slow to offer advice (even if unsolicited), the Navy League published "A Brief Outline of Legislation Advocated." Its five points were the establishment of a Council of National Defense, a naval reserve of 50,000 men, an increase in the merchant marine to supply combat vessels, a new personnel law to provide younger commanders, and a five-year building program to provide a fleet able to defeat any possible aggressor. The General Board's recommendations to Daniels echoed much of this, and one November evening in New York, Wilson showed he was listening:

"I would not feel that I was discharging the solemn obligation I owe the country," he announced in a speech to the Manhattan Club, "were I not to speak in terms of the deepest solemnity of the urgency and necessity of preparing ourselves to guard and protect the rights and privileges of our people."[3]

He chose his words carefully, still hoping that preparation for conflict might prevent conflict and that he might be supported both by those who demanded continued neutrality and those who demanded immediate entry into the European war. In December the Navy bill was put to Congress, and it was massive—a scarcely modified form of the General Board's recommendations, calling for 186 vessels to be added to the fleet by 1921.

The debate that followed was sharp and bitter, with country and Congress divided: The coastal states to the east and west gave vigorous support, while many of the states of the South and Midwest (hitherto simply indifferent) became actively hostile to any preparation whatever. Putting the idea to them of a larger navy as a shield or deterrent cut no ice; their fear (which had brought the Democrat Wilson to office against a split Republican vote) remained unchanged. Their fear was that possessing weapons creates the will to use them: Arm a man and he will fight; give a boy a hammer, and "he will find that everything that he encounters needs pounding."[4] The analogy was amusing when applied to a child. Applied to nations and humanity, it was depressing in the extreme.

Secretary Daniels hated even talking about the notion of war. "The words 'war' or 'preparedness for war' were practically never used by the Secretary," Admiral Sims wrote in later years.[5] The preparedness press sketched Daniels steering the U.S. Navy over a waterfall, his compass ignorance, his wheel complacency, and his ship's flag emblazoned with the motto "Vacillation forever."[6]

Faster than his Democratic supporters or his secretary of the Navy, Wilson was changing—not in his fundamental view of the world and its wars, but in his assessment of realistic action. He wanted to alter the world, to give it a moral humanity led by the United States. Diplomacy alone was ineffective, and in one week (January 27 to February 3, 1916), starting from New York, he toured eight Midwest cities, taking his new message to the people, using all the missionary zeal he had inherited from his father and the rhetoric he had learned as a lawyer. He ended in St. Louis, and there, speaking without notes, he described how no other navy had to defend so great an area as the U.S. Navy. Because of that, according to the authorized version of his speech, he told his audience that the U.S. Navy "ought, in my judgment, to be incomparably the most adequate Navy in the world."

The phrase has become famous, but it still sounds odd. The president was a highly educated and literate man, yet to talk of "incomparably the most adequate Navy" sounds half literate at best. Happily, he did not say it; a weaker mind in his office changed his more robust, off-the-cuff words. Blunt, bold, and frightening to some, Wilson had said in St. Louis that the U.S. Navy should be "the greatest Navy in the world."[7]

Not even Theodore Roosevelt or Admiral Mahan had asked for that much. Through the wintry first months of 1916 the battle in Congress heated up to a degree not seen in those halls before; at the same time, far across the cold Atlantic, a similar policy battle was taking place in Germany. After *Lusitania,* another British liner, *Arabic,* had been sunk by *U-24* off Ireland, with three Americans among the forty passengers who died. Wilson's powerful protest brought (on September 18, 1915) a temporary halt to unrestricted submarine warfare. But the Imperial German Navy still regarded the U-boat as "the only effective weapon against England," and on December 30 of that year Admiral von Holtzendorff asserted that if it were used again, 600,000 tons of British shipping could be sunk each month, and the war would be won in 1916. On February 23, 1916, unrestricted submarine warfare was resumed, with the kaiser's order that only armed vessels were to be attacked without warning. Yet Wilhelm was not optimistic—on March 10 he said confidentially to one of his admirals: "One must never utter it nor shall I admit it . . . but this war will not end with a great victory."[8]

A fortnight passed, and then the unarmed steamer *Sussex* was torpedoed in the English Channel. Again Americans died; one more time, said Wilson, and diplomatic relations with Germany would be broken; and as unrestricted U-boat warfare was again suspended, the president turned his attention to Congress. Democrats were divided, while Republicans supported the Democratic president. The bill could not be passed as it stood, but by May a compromise had been reached, reducing the number of battleships and substituting five battle-cruisers. It was curious that the bill's opponents should agree to this; perhaps "battle-cruisers" did not have the emotive overtones of "battleships." Anyway, their introduction would help to balance the fleet, for with light armor and heavy armament, they had the speed of cruisers and the firepower of battleships. But each one was going to cost more than any U.S. battleship ever had, and on June 2 (the very day the bill passed both House and Senate) the first reports came into Washington of the Battle of Jutland.

The German and British fleets that fought there had had, between them, fourteen battle-cruisers—five German and nine British. Two of the Germans had been severely damaged, two others were close to sinking, and one had been sunk. Of the nine British, three had been barely able to return home and three had been sunk. And this was the kind of ship Congress had just agreed to build.

There was a brief turmoil in the capital and the country—and then a rare unity. The conventions of both parties were just beginning, and in a few days both parties called for massive naval increases. At the end of the month a new bill was presented. On July 21 (by a 71 to 8 vote) it passed the Senate. In August one of its last opponents underlined the paradox that, with both Germany and Britain about a hundred thousand tons weaker than before Jutland, the United States was about to be "in dollars and cents the greatest military-naval nation the world has ever seen."[9] With only fifty others, he registered his negative vote. Ninety-nine abstained, and 283 voted in favor of the biggest naval act in American history. It provided exactly what the General Board had originally recommended—ten battleships, six battle cruisers, ten scout cruisers, fifty destroyers, nine fleet submarines, and fifty-eight coast submarines—and went still further, telescoping the board's five-year plan to only three years. And all the representatives who took part in the vote left the House knowing that whatever else happened, the United States would never be the same.

At once a strange thing happened: that is, almost nothing. After the hectic summer, the fall of 1916 was dominated by the new presidential election. Campaigning for Wilson, the Democratic party used the slogan "He kept us out of war." It was true, and however nervous Germany might be of American involvement, however resentful the United States might be of German submarines, the two countries were still at peace with each other. In the campaign, Wilson never said he would definitely take the United States to war; but he was equally careful to avoid committing himself to eternal neutrality. If he became president again, he had in mind a more radical plan than either.

The popular vote was narrowly in his favor: 49.3 percent against 46 percent for the Republican candidate, Charles Evans Hughes. One month later the German chancellor, Theobald von Bethmann Hollweg, preempted the American president and proposed peace with Britain. Grabbing the chance, Wilson requested Germany and Britain to specify the terms on which peace could be made. "Complete restitution, full reparation, and effectual guarantees" was the British response—vindictive and uncompromising, but also straightforward and natural. To Wilson, Germany temporized again; Bethmann Hollweg knew that an open statement of his own government's minimum terms (an Allied indemnity, German possession of German-occupied lands in France, Russia, and Luxembourg, plus a protectorate over Belgium and Poland) would end any negotiation instantly. On January 22, 1917, Wilson addressed the Senate with a speech which became known for its key phrase, "Peace without Victory." In it he presented the concept of a postwar international league of peace, suggesting that it could work if the European war ended promptly, with compromise and without rancor.

There was never the slightest chance that such an advanced and civilized notion could prevail; the destruction had been too great already for any combatant to want anything short of peace with total victory. On January 31, Bethmann Hollweg announced a version of his government's terms, knowing they would be unacceptable. On the same day, in room 40 of the British Admiralty's Old Building in Whitehall, cryptographers were at work deciphering a telegram from Germany's foreign secretary, Arthur Zimmerman, to Ambassador Count von Bernstorff in Washington. It contained the condition under which the German war leaders had allowed Bethmann Hollweg to make the peace terms known: namely, that if they were unacceptable, unrestricted U-boat warfare would begin again on February 1 and would not cease until Germany was victorious. In addition, the telegram instructed von Bernstorff to persuade Mexico to join with Germany in war against the United States.

When he learned the contents of the telegram, Wilson had no peaceful option left. Von Bernstorff was ordered home; diplomatic links with Germany were cut. A couple of weeks later, Mayall W. Beech, a clerk in the Navy Department Telegraph Office, Washington, found time to describe the frantic activity and confused emotions of that day:

> At about eleven in the morning of February 3rd, Oliver, Watts and myself were languidly cussing the ill luck that condemns us to sit around doing nothing instead of following our hearts' desires by filtering through the crowds on F or 9th streets, when a fellow at the Western Union flashed us the news that Count Burnstel [*sic*] had been given his "g'wan home." Came then the deluge. Until midnight we handled over nine hundred messages WITHOUT A DELAY. How we did it, I am at a loss to say. . . . We worked—by god, we worked. Wow! But it was great work—interesting work, fortified by a nervous push that seemed to permeate our whole souls; and if anyone had waved Old Glory before us [during] those hours, we'd have alternately yelled like fools and cried like swaddling babies.[10]

But if on February 3 Beech felt alarmed, excited, and confused, he could have spared a sympathetic thought for his president on April 6. Wilson's presidency had already been studded with paradox—winning office with a minority vote against divided Republicans; remaining neutral while assisting Britain; signing into law the United States' largest-ever naval act while calling it a normal increase. The sixth day of April 1917 must have brought the worst paradox of his upright life, for that day Woodrow Wilson—the great humanitarian, the son of a preacher—sent the United States to war against Germany; and it was Good Friday.

"It is a fearful thing to lead this great peaceful people into war, into the most terrible and disastrous of all wars, civilization itself seeming to hang in the balance," he said. But fearful and painful as it was, there was a saving consistency in his mind: "We shall fight for the things which we have always carried nearest our hearts," he continued. "For democracy, for the right of those who submit to authority to have a voice in their own government, for the rights and liberties of small nations, for a universal dominion of right by such a concert of free peoples as shall bring peace and safety to all nations and make the world itself at last free."[11]

A League of Nations—it was a brave and distant vision, and the first step toward it was to find out exactly the situation with the Allies. Respecting the traditional American fear of foreign alliances, Wilson never made the United States more than an "Associated Power" along-side Great Britain and France. One of his first representatives in London was Rear Admiral Sims, who arrived there on April 9, 1917. At once he began to confer with the First Sea Lord, Adm. Sir John Jellicoe, and learned shocking facts. Since the reopening of unrestricted submarine warfare just two months before, almost a million tons of British merchant shipping had been sunk. By the end of April, it was predicted, the total would rise to 2 million tons.

With disturbing calmness, Jellicoe told Sims: "It is impossible for us to go on with the war if losses like this continue." He added that all available vessels were being used against submarines, and when Sims remarked, "It looks as though the Germans were winning the war," Jellicoe replied: "They *will* win, unless we can stop these losses and stop them soon."

Surely there was a solution, Sims said. No, Jellicoe answered—"absolutely none that we can see now."[12] "Everything, indeed, combined to show that the allies were really within sight of disaster," wrote Sir Henry Newbolt, Britain's official naval historian. "Admiral von Holtzendorff's prophecy of victory was apparently verging toward fulfilment, and only a change in our system of defence could turn the tide."[13]

Sims's report arrived in Washington on April 14. In it he urged that as many destroyers as possible should be sent over as soon as possible: The Royal Navy had nearly three hundred, but at least a hundred were always protecting the Grand Fleet in Scapa Flow, a further fifty protected the Channel Fleet, others were positioned in the Mediterranean, and only three dozen or so were available to patrol all the coasts of France, England, and Ireland.

The report raised serious problems. The appalling destruction of merchant ships was a revelation. The General Board's war plan, geared to a defensive conflict in the western Atlantic, was completely unsuited to the war that actually needed fighting, and so was the gigantic Naval Act of 1916. Capital ships (battleships and battle cruisers) were scarcely necessary in European waters: The British Grand Fleet offset Germany's High Seas Fleet completely. But that was not the heart of the problem. What worried both the General Board and Admiral Benson, the Chief of Naval Operations, was that they did not believe the war in Europe (the Great War, the "war to end wars") would be the last war for the United States. If Britain fell, which seemed all too likely, they feared a coalition of Germany, Austria, and Japan against the United States on its own. In such a war, capital ships would be vital. They also distrusted Britain: Turning the United States' marine construction entirely over to small naval ships and to merchant vessels (thus replacing and protecting the lost merchant stock) could defeat Germany; but simultaneously it would permit the Royal Navy's continued world dominance. That was not the point of the 1916 act, from either the board's point of view or the president's. Both wanted a very large, well-balanced fleet—the president, candidly, because he would be able to negotiate from strength for a just and perpetual world peace; the General Board, less candidly, because for the first time ever, their program had total national support, and they were dreaming of much bigger things yet.

In any case, it did not seem the British had exhausted every possibility in the fight against submarines. Certainly their limited number of available small vessels (destroyers and the like) were being worked to death; certainly mines were being produced in large numbers and merchantmen were being armed. But what of convoy, the traditional method of protecting merchant ships? As commander in chief of the Grand Fleet, Jellicoe had held convoy to be impossible for steamships. Now as First Sea Lord he stuck to that view and was supported by merchant masters, who believed they would be unable to handle groups of ships safely, especially zigzagging without lights at night or in fog.

Capt. William V. Pratt, U.S.N., put the prejudices of both sides in a suitable light. As a firm friend of the pro-British Admiral Sims and a faithful assistant to the anti-British Admiral Benson, he pointed out that the essential goal for everyone was to "win THIS WAR."[14] An Allied victory would ensure Japanese loyalty, and as for the British, he said that whatever difficulties might arise after joint victory, "their cause is our cause now."[15]

By the time he made those comments (in May and June 1917), the problems of prejudice were in fact on their way to solution. Since February coal had been successfully convoyed from the south of England to France. Dutch convoys had also been successful, and by April 21 Jellicoe authorized experimental Scandinavian convoys—although he still recorded his doubts of the concept's value. Three days later (April 24), the first six American destroyers to assist the Allies left Boston under Comdr. Joseph K. Taussig, arriving in Queenstown (now Cobh) near Cork on May 4. On April 26, Adm. Sir Alexander Duff (head of Jellicoe's Anti-Submarine Warfare division) wrote to Jellicoe: "It seems to me evident that the time has arrived when we must be ready to introduce a comprehensive scheme of convoy at any moment. . . . We can accept the many disadvantages of large convoys with the certainty of a great reduction in our present losses."[16]

It was not entirely coincidental that the previous day, Prime Minister Lloyd George had told the Admiralty he would visit them shortly. They knew well that he wanted convoy started at once. Later, the prime minister and the Admiralty disagreed on who had made the decision and why, but after reading Duff's comments and before seeing the prime minister,

Jellicoe authorized an experimental convoy from Gibraltar. It sailed on May 10, followed two weeks later by another, equally experimental, from Hampton Roads, Virginia. Both convoys arrived in Britain *without loss.* By August 1, ten thousand ships had been convoyed into Britain with a loss of only half of 1 percent.

When Commander Taussig arrived in Queenstown on May 4 with that first batch of U.S. Navy destroyers, more or less the first thing the local British admiral, Vice Adm. Sir Lewis Bayly, wanted to know was at what date and time Taussig's ships would be ready to start patrol. "We are ready now," Taussig said, "as soon as fueled."

It was a classic reply, fully in the spirit of John Paul Jones and Oliver Hazard Perry; yet political and military circumstances dictated that for the remainder of the war the U.S. Navy could be, in most senses, only the Royal Navy's junior partner. The overwhelmingly greater part of the U.S. contribution was in the land campaign on the continent of Europe, and it was there that the gore and glamour and glory were to be found. Today, imagining Americans in World War I, the doughboys spring at once to mind—young soldiers in their tens of thousands, singing and fighting through the muddy fields of France. Sailors serving under the Stars and Stripes seem scarcely to figure at all.

This is hardly fair. Popular opinion today says that without the United States, Britain would have lost the war, and there, popular opinion is right. But popular opinion is very wrong in relegating the U.S. Navy to a role of small importance. There can be no doubt that even with its empire's support, Britain would have been defeated, probably in the winter of 1917–18, had the United States not joined in. There can be little doubt that, if it had had the chance, the U.S. Navy would have joined in any battle going; however, after the Battle of Jutland in the middle of 1916, there simply were no more big fights at sea. But the doubts are huge and obvious when we wonder just how those doughboys would have been transported to France safely—or how they would have been transported there at all—without the U.S. fleet.

As far as World War I is concerned, there was, for the U.S. Navy, a certain similarity with the Mexican War of sixty years earlier. In both, the Army fought all the headline actions, while the Navy performed essential functions, dangerous but unglamorous. In both wars, those functions included superlatives—during the Mexican War, the biggest landing of troops ever undertaken; during World War I, the biggest convoy of troops. That was the U.S. Navy's primary contribution, and the vital one; but there was more, for in mine laying, antisubmarine warfare, and naval aviation, the fleet took contemporary technology to the limit, pointing the way to the future. No one would deny that in

fighting, the doughboys were preeminent; but it is worthwhile remembering who enabled them to fight, and how.

Describing the hazards and difficulties of convoy, Americans' diaries
bring over some of the nervous tension permeating those groups of darkened ships. Entering the submarine danger zone, the convoy would be
met and escorted into port by destroyers, but throughout the ocean
crossing, forty ships or more would be protected by a single cruiser. Their
major guardian was the wide ocean itself.

At all times they had to face the urgent needs of keeping position
relative to the other vessels; of keeping lights to a minimum and preventing sparks from the funnels at night; of zigzagging even during fog; and
of depending for repairs and the treatment of sick and wounded only on
themselves. Keeping the destination rendezvous secret until after sailing
presented the immense difficulty of communicating its latitude and longi-
tude to every ship by semaphore or Morse light; and a typical signal in
the log of Cyrus Robinson Miller, commanding U.S.S. *Cleveland,* advised
captains of their worst peril:

> In case convoy is attacked when without escort ships will disperse
> and zigzag at full speed to rendezvous. . . . [Submarines] may attempt
> to enter convoy. Prevent this by keeping closed up. Dawn is the most
> dangerous time. Stragglers must close up at full speed or they lay
> themselves and the convoy open to attacks. From warnings received
> by escort the submarines are very active today.[17]

One day, John MacGavock Grider (one of the 2 million Americans
safely convoyed to Europe during the war) noted ruefully in his diary that
he had been arrested by the guard for smoking on deck. "No lights, no
matter how faint, can be shown. . . . A British Commander told us that
one ship was torpedoed because someone carelessly struck a match on the
deck."[18]

Grider belonged to a group of 210 university students who, early in
1917, volunteered to be trained by and to fight with Britain's Royal Flying
Corps. In his ship, submarine watches were posted at five points. "Each
man had a certain arc that he was to keep his eye on," he wrote. "No
man was to take anything to drink for twelve hours before he was to go
on watch. We were supposed to look out for gulls, which they say usually
follow the wake of a sub. . . . No periscopes have been sighted yet, though
one boy got all excited over a big piece of timber that was sticking up."
Gradually approaching the Irish coast, "nervousness has been growing
for last few days about subs. . . . We have had to wear our life preservers
all the time since yesterday morning."

He added a very good description of "dazzle painting," the system

devised to camouflage ships at sea: "The Painted Lady, as we call the
camouflaged cruiser that is escorting us . . . sure is a queer-looking boat.
She's painted all different colors in lines and squares and you can't tell
which way she is going or what she is until you get close to her. Another
boat in our convoy is painted the color of the ocean and then has a smaller
ship painted over it going the other way. From any distance it is very
deceptive. Another ship has the same arrangement, except the deception
is in the angle of her course."

Hydrophones for underwater listening were a key invention in the
antisubmarine war, first used successfully in combat on April 23, 1916,
when *UC-3* was detected by this method and destroyed.[19] On the surface,
however, a more visible and so more morale-boosting addition were the
submarine chasers. The U.S. Navy built over 440 of these small, cheap
vessels during the course of the war. Close to Ireland, Grider "went up
on deck and the sea was swarming with submarine chasers. Lord, how
happy every one was at the sight of them! They are the prettiest little ships
I ever saw, about a hundred and twenty feet over all, I would say. . . .
We have three American chasers with us but we couldn't tell which they
were. Lord, those little boats are fast; they fairly fly thru the water and
cleave it so clear and clean. I would give a leg to own one."

In the single month of April 1917, Allied merchant shipping losses had
been close to 835,000 tons. In June well over half a million tons of
unconvoyed shipping was lost. Three months were needed for results to
be shown for certain, and another three before the system took full hold;
but the convoy experiments were a magnificent success. By November
1917 the monthly loss dropped to little more than a quarter million tons;
and that figure could be coped with, for as Jellicoe had dropped his
prejudice, so the U.S. Navy's General Board had been made to overcome
theirs.

By July 5 the initial force of six U.S. destroyers in Queenstown had
increased to thirty-four, remaining at approximately that level for the rest
of the war. On Secretary Daniels's order, Captain Pratt became Admiral
Duff's counterpart, heading a board to study antisubmarine possibilities.
On July 6 Pratt recommended that in addition to the sixty-six destroyers
already building, two hundred of a new standard type should be started
immediately, and that they and merchant ship construction should take
precedence over all capital shipbuilding. After the war, one vicious but
accurate critic said the secretary had been "the single greatest obstruction
of the creation of an adequate and efficient Navy until the threat of
immediate war actually hung upon the borders of our country."[20] This
was true—as Admiral Sims put it, "the Department thought that the
country did not want to go into war; and . . . therefore the Department
did not consider it wise to take any steps which might make the navy

ready for war."[21] Now, however, Daniels was trying his best to make up for lost time, and approved Pratt's recommendations on the very day they were given.

Taken aback, the General Board protested that if their plan for the fleet was altered, the United States would be unable "to meet a possible new alignment of powers at the end of the war, or the German Fleet if it takes the offensive."[22] For the same reason the Chief of Naval Operations and the board resisted merchant ship construction and the dispatch of a division of battleships to join the Grand Fleet in the North Sea. "We have got to think of the future," Admiral Benson grunted. In early November 1917, Benson visited London and Paris. He saw nothing to alter his opinion that the United States might well have to defend itself alone at a later date, but he did recognize the need to display solidarity. Accordingly, four U.S. battleships steamed to Scapa Flow, and now at last, with objections to altered construction plans overcome and the new destroyers, troop transports, and merchant ships being launched with increasing rapidity, the U.S. Navy's part in the Great War was firmly established.

"I always feel a sense of security," Capt. D. J. Munro, R.N. wrote to Rear Adm. Harold D. Cooke, U.S.N., "when I see the Stars and Stripes heave in sight."[23] How proud John Paul Jones would have been to hear that remark—"The English Nation may hate me," he said once, "but *I will force them to esteem me too.*" By the time of the armistice on November 11, 1918, there were 354 U.S. Navy vessels of all kinds in European waters, including among others eight battleships, five cruisers, sixty-eight destroyers, nine submarines, and 129 sub chasers. But to put those figures into perspective with the British and French navies, the U.S. destroyers and cruisers represented only about a third of those types of Allied warship in Europe. In more exact percentage terms, the ratios of British to American to French destroyers were 70 to 27 to 3, and of cruisers 61 to 35 to 4. In all, 927,000 men (45 percent of all U.S. troops sent to France) were transported over 3,000 Atlantic miles by U.S. Navy ships, and not a single one of those men was lost by enemy action at sea. The so-called "bridge to Europe" provided by the fleet was, more prosaically and less romantically, a glorified ferry service—tedious, dangerous, uncomfortable, repetitive. But crucial too: It was the biggest ferrying ever undertaken, and without it Britain and France would certainly have been defeated. If it had begun earlier—if the secretary had been prepared and the General Board fully committed—the war would probably have been shorter. If the Admiralty had not delayed in instituting convoy, Allied merchant losses would certainly have been less. But with both the Admiralty and the Navy Department, the great good fortune was, first, that in the end they were willing to sink their prejudices; and second, that when they did so, it was—by a matter of weeks—not too late.

. . .

Three aspects of U.S. naval involvement are particularly worth a closer look, not least because each—submarines, mines, and the addition of air power—was first properly used in the Civil War. Of submarines, a vivid story is told by one who was there. A hundred and thirty-eight years earlier, twenty-four-year-old Nathaniel Fanning had fought alongside John Paul Jones against H.M.S. *Serapis*. As captain of *Bonhomme Richard*'s main fighting top, Midshipman Fanning led the action which cleared *Serapis*'s deck and rigging of British seamen. Afterwards, recommending him for promotion, Jones said "he was one cause among the prominent in obtaining the victory."[24] On November 17, 1917, U.S.S. *Fanning* obtained both prominence and victory: That day, "bleak and cheerless, as are most winter days on the south coast of Ireland," she became the first U.S. warship to sink a U-boat and capture its crew.[25]

Eight years old, *Fanning* was long, low, and fast, her 742-ton displacement spread through 294 feet length overall, with a draft of only 8 feet 4 inches. Her oil-fired turbines gave her a maximum speed of 30 knots; she was armed with depth charges, five 3-inch guns, and six 18-inch torpedo tubes. One of her company of eighty-nine was a junior officer named Robert B. Carney. "Just to keep up interest in what might otherwise be a routine trip," he wrote, "the crew that morning was put through a new drill for the first time: prize crew and prisoner guards were stationed and instructed." They never dreamed how soon they would need the drill.

Late in the morning, *Fanning* and her five escort colleagues came out of Cork harbor, spread out fanwise, checked the approaches, and summoned their convoy to join them. It took hours for the whole convoy to emerge, pass through the possible mined areas, and form up, and the operation was still going on at 3:30 P.M., when *Fanning* sighted an oil slick in a place where no slick should have been. A short investigation brought no result; then, as they returned to the convoy, "the humdrum business of shepherding untrained merchantmen into a military formation suddenly quickened into adventure." Coxwain Loomis, a man with "a most extraordinary pair of eyes," had spotted a periscope. "The officer of the deck could not see it—never did see it—but he had good information intelligently given" and he acted on it instantly. Rushing to the estimated position, the ship dropped a single depth charge. Other destroyers hastened to them as the charge exploded, and "minute after minute passed without result—just another bit of excitement—perhaps it was a porpoise or a floating spar—or an overtaxed imagination. Perhaps just a good chance to break the monotony. But then the unbelievable happened."

At a steep angle, *U-58* burst out of the water. As she settled and began to sink, her decks were quickly crowded with surrendering men; and as

Fanning drew alongside to take off prisoners, Germans and Americans stared at each other "with the curiosity of the victor, or the stunned apprehension of the loser." The experience did young Carney no harm: Many years later, after living and fighting through another world war, he became Chief of Naval Operations.

Among the unprecedented statistics of World War I (the millions of tons of shipping sunk, the further millions of human deaths on land and sea), there is one which is frequently forgotten but which represents a technical achievement which was outstanding then and remains remarkable now. This was the great mine barrier laid by the U.S. Navy across the whole width of the North Sea.

Coming out from Germany, U-boats had only two routes to the Atlantic—the Channel, nearby and short but narrow and harassed; or the long way round, up through the North Sea and past Scotland. The Grand Fleet kept Germany's surface ships lurking in port and patrolled against submarines, but it could not be a fully effective barrier against the underwater enemy. The Admiralty had considered (and had dismissed as beyond their ability) the idea of mining the North Sea from Scotland across to Norway—230 miles. Hearing of this, Adm. Ralph Earle of the Bureau of Ordnance saw it as a challenge and persuaded Secretary Daniels that the U.S. Navy could do it; and with the Admiralty still skeptical, the U.S. Navy offered to do the entire job alone. On November 2, 1917, the offer was accepted. By agreeing, Britain had little to lose, and much to gain.

The main reason for the confidence of Admiral Earle and his colleagues was the recent development of the antenna mine, which superseded the contact mine, the only kind available in Britain. In an antenna mine, a float was linked to the mine by a 70-foot copper wire. To explode the mine, a passing ship had only to touch any part of the long wire. The touch set up an electric current which in turn blew up the mine. Since it did not have to physically hit a ship, the antenna mine had a much more extensive range: The Admiralty had estimated 400,000 contact mines would be needed for an effective North Sea barrage; the Navy Department estimated that a paltry 100,000 antenna mines would be just as good.

Not that they had them ready to lay; apart from a stock of working prototypes, the whole preposterous operation had to start from scratch—from the basic planning to making the weapons, transporting them to Scotland's east coast, and stringing them out in a swift, reliable, systematic way. But rather than being daunted by the magnitude of their self-imposed task, they relished it; and they succeeded.

Five hundred subcontractors made the parts. In Norfolk navy yard, charges of 300 pounds of TNT each were made at the rate of a thousand a day. Two dozen Great Lakes steamers manned by naval reservists transported them to Britain's west coast. From there they were taken through the Caledonian Canal (its entire length lit by the U.S. Navy for night work) parallel to an American naval oil pipeline coast to coast; and in Inverness and Invergordon they were assembled into complete weapons, two thousand a day.

Stimulated by the example, the British assisted wherever possible: They prepared the bases, and when the actual operation of laying began in March 1918, they laid more of their own. But their contribution was necessarily limited, and the task remained largely in American hands. Under Capt. Reginald R. Belknap, a fleet of ten steamers specially adapted and fitted for mine laying began work in Norwegian territorial waters. The mines were arranged to float at various depths down to 60 fathoms, and by September 20 a single line had been laid across the North Sea's entire width. Thereafter, until it was no longer necessary, the operation continued, thickening the barrage. Eventually, with 13,546 British mines and 56,571 American mines, it reached a maximum north–south thickness of 35 miles; and with an average of about a dozen mines to the square mile, moored at varying depths, it formed a nightmarish three-dimensional maze for any U-boat. At least six were sunk, nudging blindly along in the underwater darkness, and more were damaged. The psychological effect on U-boat crews was at least as important; and though some British naval officers thought the whole thing a waste of resources, the plain (though not simple) fact of the creation of the barrage remains one of the wonders of the war.

So too was the development of American naval air power. Spotting balloons had been used in the Civil War, but until very recently, heavier-than-air flight had been an absurd notion.

"The machine has worked. It seems to be worthwhile for this government to try whether it will not work on a large enough scale to be of use in the event of war."[26] On March 28, 1898, Assistant Secretary of the Navy Theodore Roosevelt reported in those words to Secretary Long. "The machine," devised by Professor Samuel Langley of the Smithsonian Institution, was an aircraft. One month later (just two days before Dewey's battle at Manila Bay) a joint Army-Navy board decided that such things could be used for three main warlike purposes: scouting and reconnaissance; communication; and bombing, "as an engine of offense with the capacity of dropping from a great height, high explosives into a camp or fortification."[27]

After that remarkably farsighted report, however, the Navy lost interest, partly because of the demands of the war against Spain. The Army gave Professor Langley $50,000 to develop the project. The Navy gave him no money—but they did lend him a chain and anchor.

For more than a decade thereafter American naval aviation remained nonexistent, while civilian and Army experimenting and experience grew. Then, on November 14, 1910, a civilian pilot, Eugene Ely, made the first ship-to-shore flight from the cruiser *Birmingham,* followed two months later by a shore-ship-shore flight, landing on the cruiser *Pennsylvania* and returning. Some of the more brilliant minds saw possibilities: Capt. Bradley A. Fiske proposed that air stations with a hundred bombers each should be established in the Philippines to defend the islands. "Why waste the time of the General Board with wildcat schemes?" an admiral asked—and turned him down.[28]

Nevertheless, by 1916 a twenty-nine-year-old American in Britain, John Lansing Callan, felt confident enough to write: "My opinion of the British Aviation Corps is that it is managed very poorly indeed and the system is terrible. At some of the stations I visited I found Captains of the R.F.C. [Royal Flying Corps] who were in charge, that didn't know why a carburettor was on a machine. No wonder they can't do anything."[29]

Callan, bounding with energy and the desire to fight, criticized anyone who seemed to feel otherwise. American convoy administrators were "really inefficient . . . in regard to the safety of men's lives. They fill the public full of bull." The English "are doing nothing at all with their seaplanes . . . far from what the people are getting in the papers." Admirals lacked pep, while even the Red Cross were "a bunch of slackers. . . . God help the wounded is all I can say." As for the opposition, Callan observed in the middle of 1917 that "the Germans have absolute control of the air over the Channel," while he and his colleagues were provided with "nothing but a load of junk." It was "a rotten crime" that they had "nothing better to war with. It is absolutely deplorable."[30]

Much of what Callan saw was (in his view) a rotten crime, and often he was right. His vitriol did his career no damage (he ended up an admiral himself), and it was, in any case, typical of that of many of the young and enthusiastic aviators of World War I. Pilots, especially naval pilots, still tend to regard themselves as a breed apart, an elite. Submariners do the same, but because the submarine service is essentially secretive and hidden, it has never had quite the same popular, glamorous public image. That image took quick hold in the First World War: Aircraft themselves were so rare, and pilots so very obviously brave, that any man with the coveted wings on his uniform was certain to be pointed out, and likely to be stopped, by enthusiastic people passing him in the street. It was, moreover, an image created by the exceptional circumstances of real danger, not by any propaganda: Before the war, official support for air power, and especially naval air power, was at least as limited in Britain as in the United States.

In Germany the contrast was great. In 1909 the government there allocated the contemporary equivalent of £40,000 to military aviation. In the same year, having spent £2,500 on aerial experiments, the British government canceled all funding on further projects. In 1910 there were twenty-six military airships in Europe. Fourteen of them were German; one was British. And though the first heavier-than-air flight had not been made until 1903, with the first cross-Channel flight following in 1909, by 1912 the German view was clear: "We must devote ourselves more energetically to the development of aviation for naval purposes." Furthermore, this supporter of naval pilots was not even an admiral but a general—Friedrich von Bernhardi. Writing in his book *Germany and the Next War,* he stressed:

> A pronounced superiority of our air-fleet over the English would contribute largely to equalize the difference in strength of the two navies more and more during the course of the war. It should be the more possible to gain a superiority in this field because our supposed enemies have not any start on us.[31]

It was this shortsighted Allied neglect (neglect of what seemed to the fliers to be a weapon of obvious potential power) which fed the fliers' spleen. "If I was running the war," John Grider, the young pilot, wrote on August 20, 1918, "the first thing I would do would be to get control of the air no matter what it cost. That's what's saved England all these centuries—control of the seas. And her fleet is big enough to keep control without fighting. The Air Force would do the same thing."[32]

The unreadiness for air war gave some of the Allied aviators a consoling sense of making history; many of their deeds were entirely new, not only to them but to everyone else. On April 23, 1917, John Callan noted that "two machines were launched from the catapult and made trips to sea about 50 miles. . . . Bartlett and Whiting made the flights. Bartlett carried a passenger in his catapult shot. This was the first time this has ever been accomplished."[33] Three months later he recorded "the first work being done on a [U.S.] naval air station," and thought with satisfaction that it was "rather an historical event."[34]

In fact, although it was erratic and sometimes too hurried even for basic safety (prototype aircraft were sometimes sent untested into battle), the air strength of both the United States and Britain escalated rapidly during the war. In September 1917 the number of operational U-boats reached a wartime peak of 139. The maximum daily average of U-boats at sea was 56, and against them, in a ratio of 21 to 1, the Royal Navy employed 2,932 patrol craft (submarines, destroyers, trawlers, and decoy ships) and 244 aircraft: 50 airships and 194 airplanes. Similarly, the little Naval Air School at Pensacola, Florida, was enlarged (and is still there); schools were established in Miami, San Francisco, Long Island, and

Hampton Roads; a naval aircraft factory was swiftly built in Philadelphia; and up in Halifax, Lt. Richard E. Byrd (later to achieve fame as an explorer) became first commanding officer of the first joint American-Canadian naval air station.

Slowly American naval aviators in Europe were supplied with good planes. At first they had to make do with bought or borrowed foreign-built machines, including reject models from France. But by the end of the war, the American Naval Flying Corps contained about 25,000 men. More than 16,000 of them were in Europe, and there (in addition to all the other air forces based on land or sea) they had over five hundred Curtiss float-planes at twenty-seven different bases, as well as fifty balloons and three airships.

But with unprecedented adventure came unprecedented stress. "I don't know which will get me first," Grider wrote on August 19, 1918, "a bullet or the nervous strain." He flew for the R.F.C., but (as one of his colleagues remarked) his diary could have been written by any of the aviators. In it he recorded the pleasures and horrors of training: the professional pleasures, such as the first sight of a Sopwith Pup ("as pretty and slick as a thoroughbred horse. Tiny little things just big enough for one man and a machine gun"), heightened by personal pleasures ("We get champagne with our meals at $2.10 a bottle. . . . This is indeed the life!"). And the horrors: "We were all out on the tarmac having our pictures taken for posterity when somebody yelled and pointed up. Two Avros collided right over the airdrome at about three thousand feet. God, it was a horrible sight. . . . They came down in a slow spin with their wings locked together and both of them in flames. Fred Stillman was in one machine and got out alive but badly burned, and Doug Ellis was in the other one and was burned to a cinder."[35]

Each week, in those fragile, unreliable machines, an average of three pilots were killed in training. The most common causes were either the aircraft spinning out of control and crashing to earth, or the wings simply falling off in midair. There were no parachutes, and in one particularly awful accident a pilot was seen to fall out of his cockpit, plummeting straight to the ground as the airplane wandered away to crash elsewhere.

After just six months' training, Grider was in France, at the front, at war. During the following three months he shot down three German planes, frequently coming close to death himself: "I'll never be able to shoot at a bird again. I know too well how they must feel."[36] And he described "real fear":

> It's something that grows on you, day by day, that eats into your constitution and undermines your sanity. . . . Here I am, twenty-four years old, I look forty and I feel ninety. I've lost all interest in life

beyond the next patrol. . . . Last week I actually got frightened in
the air and lost my head. Then I found ten Huns and took them all
on and I got one of them down out of control. I got my nerve back
by that time and came back home and slept like a baby for the first
time in two months. What a blessing sleep is! . . . I know now how
men laugh at death and welcome it.[37]

Many of his friends were killed, more than he could bring himself to
believe:

When you lunch with a man, talk to him, see him go out and get
in his plane in the prime of his youth and the next day someone tells
you he is dead—it just doesn't sink in and you can't believe it. And
the oftener it happens the harder it is to believe. I've lost over a
hundred friends, so they tell me—I've seen only seven or eight
killed—but to me they aren't dead yet. They are just around the
corner, I think, and I'm still expecting to run into them at any time.
I dream about them at night when I do sleep a little and sometimes
I dream that some one is killed who really isn't. Then I don't know
who is and who isn't. . . . Springs keeps talking about Purgatory and
Hades and the Elysian Fields. Well, we sure are close to something.[38]

Writing that entry about the end of August 1918, he was closer than he
knew to the end of everything. Stuart Farrar Smith, captain in the U.S.
Naval Construction Corps, was in Paris at 11 A.M. on November 11,
1918, and there he heard the last guns of the war, firing to announce the
armistice. "In almost an instant all the streets were ablaze with colors
. . . people yelling and singing and producing noise in every way, drays
etc full of people all driving slowly up and down, all yelling . . ."

With difficulty he and his friends pushed through the crowds to a café,
where they "drank to 'Clemenceau, the man who won the war,' to Foch
& Joffre & to France in general. I don't think we wasted much time on
the British although they truly deserve it, for they have done wonders,
& we wasted no time at all on ourselves. It's a pleasant thing to think that
no one of the allies can say 'We won the war,' while any one of them can
say 'Without us, the war would have been lost.' "[39]

Captain Smith's judgment was almost perfect. It was indeed a pleasant
thing to realize and acknowledge that victory had been a truly Allied
business—to see and say that no single ally had won the war, and that
without any single one of them, it would have been lost. The only thing
that marred his judgment was the modesty through which he and his
friends "wasted no time at all" on themselves. Perhaps they felt that since
they had not fought battles, they did not deserve praise. People in such
a situation often feel like that, and people afterwards, who may never have

been close to a war, often agree; the praise is accorded to those who fought the enemy face to face. Yet that is frequently a mistake, and certainly is in this case. The mine barrage across the North Sea was a technical marvel; hesitant as they were, antisubmarine warfare and naval aviation were at the leading edge of naval science; and above all was the protection of convoys.

U.S. soldiers and British people often seemed ungrateful—indeed, they often were ungrateful, even though the success of the convoy system was the fundamental reason for their survival, individually and nationally. Such ingratitude was natural enough. The proud British found it hard to accept that someone else had had to come to the rescue. The U.S. soldiers, like any soldiers, would have rather been on land than on the incomprehensible sea at any time.

But land folk generally forget that the first and last purpose of any armed fleet is to give protection upon the seas, for those going about their lawful pursuits; and that is what the U.S. Navy did in World War I. They may not have fought in great surface battles, but the ships and personnel of the U.S. fleet were true upholders of the tradition they inherited, and which they passed on. Smith and his friends should have drunk a toast to themselves, to the U.S. Navy; and since they did not, we can drink it for them.

John MacGavock Grider never saw the celebrations. Little more than a year before, when his convoy had left Halifax for Britain, he had written: "I don't want to be a hero—too often they are all clay from the feet up, but I am determined to die well. Thank God, I am going to have the opportunity to die as every brave man should wish to die—fighting—and fighting for my country as well." Not long before the armistice, he did die fighting. A hundred and twenty miles north of Paris, 20 miles behind their own lines, the Germans buried his body in the cemetery at Houplines, near Armentières.

John Lansing Callan did not mention the armistice. On November 8, 1918, he was dining in Rome. One day he would reflect how ironic it was that then, as the "war to end wars" came to its end, his dinner partner was one Lt. Comdr. Shigetaro Shimada of the Imperial Japanese Navy, naval attaché and aide to Japan's minister of marine. But long before that, when he arrived back in the United States at last, on February 28, 1919—with peace not yet formally signed and the Great War still a very close memory—he voiced his relief in another unconscious irony: "Have been in Europe a little over twenty months and have had a wonderful cruise. The war was great!"[40]

PART THREE

RESTRAINT

1919–1933

★

Confident in victory,
hoping for a lasting peace,
the American people hail
naval limitation.
The U.S. Navy and the Royal Navy become
acknowledged equals; but the
prophecy of a late president begins to
acquire a frightening reality.

7

★

THE BATTLES
OF THE FUTURE

*I*n the last days of fighting, in the sight of their officers, sailors of the
Imperial German Navy gathered to demand peace and to cheer
Woodrow Wilson's name.[1] On December 13, 1918, heavily escorted, the
liner *George Washington* arrived in Brest, taking Wilson to the peace
conference; and the cheers of the defeated German sailors were taken up
and echoed in Britain, France, and Italy. To the people of Europe, after
four years in an abattoir, the president's vision of perpetual peace appeared almost messianic, and they received him with faith and hope.

Early in January 1918, Wilson had announced his "Fourteen Points"
as a suitable basis for peace. Nine of the fourteen concerned national
boundaries, while the others called for open diplomacy; the freedom of
the seas for all nations; the dropping of economic barriers; disarmament;
and (the fourteenth point) a League of Nations. The people loved it; the
politicians did not. President Clemenceau of France remarked sardonically that even God Almighty had only given ten commandments; Prime
Minister Lloyd George of Great Britain wondered suspiciously just what
Wilson meant by freedom of the seas; and the "Naval Battle of Paris"
began.

Freedom of the seas, as spelled out by Woodrow Wilson, meant exactly
what it said: "absolute freedom of navigation upon the seas outside territorial waters, alike in peace and in war, except as the seas may be closed
in whole or in part by international action for the enforcement of international covenants."[2]

It well defined the U.S. interpretation of freedom of the seas, held since independence; and there was hardly a phrase in it which would not raise the hackles of either the Admiralty or the British government. During any period of war, since long before U.S. independence, Britain had claimed (as the wartime right of a belligerent) the legal ability to stop and search any ship anywhere, neutral or not. If contraband goods destined for the enemy of the day were found, the ship could be taken and held in a British port; and the list of contraband goods could be extended unilaterally, without notice. The War of 1812 had been fought because of the nations' differing interpretations of "freedom of the seas" and had ended with both views still unchanged.

To renounce belligerent rights and give them over in trust to some as yet unformed international organization would negate Britain's strategic position off continental Europe and threaten its entire imperial network. It was out of the question.

At that moment both the British and U.S. navies were larger than either had ever been before. In terms of manpower, the Royal Navy had expanded nearly threefold during the war, from less than 150,000 to almost 440,000. But the U.S. Navy had become even more numerous, with close to half a million officers and enlisted men and women—seven and a half times larger than it had been at the beginning of 1917 and in terms of human resources the largest sea force in the world. Against that, the Royal Navy maintained a vast preponderance in material terms, whichever way it was measured; for example, its forty-two first-line capital ships against America's sixteen gave Britain 136 12-inch, 144 13.5-inch, and 96 15-inch guns, against 80 12-inch and 88 14-inch American guns.[3]

Before Wilson arrived in Europe, Lloyd George told the president's representative that "Great Britain would spend her last guinea to keep a navy superior to that of the United States or any other Power."[4] The reply was just as plain—neither the United States nor any other country "would willingly submit to Great Britain's complete domination of the seas any more than to Germany's domination of the land, and the sooner the English recognized this fact, the better it would be for them."[5] And Wilson's spokesman added an explicit threat: If necessary, America could *and would* outbuild Britain in sea or land forces, or both.

Lending credibility to the threat, American yards had begun building the ships of the giant 1916 act, which had been delayed by the wartime need for destroyers and small ships; and within a month of the armistice, President Wilson proposed to Congress that the 1919 act should repeat that of 1916. To the British, physically, emotionally, and financially wrung out by the war, the continuing effort to meet such a challenge was the last thing they wanted. They had already begun a massive program of scrapping combat ships: Between November 1918 and April 1921 the Royal Navy got rid of no fewer than 38 of its battleships, two battle cruisers, 87 light cruisers, 300 destroyers and torpedo boats, and 106 submarines.[6] But if forced by American competition, the program could and would be suspended. As Winston Churchill warned his countrymen:

> Nothing in the world, nothing that you may think of, or dream of, or anyone may tell you; no arguments, however specious, no appeals however seductive, must lead you to abandon that naval supremacy on which the life of our country depends.[7]

The president's personal adviser, Col. Edward M. House, described the British and American views of each other in a telling and dramatic phrase: "The relations of the two countries are beginning to assume the same character as that of England and Germany before the war."[8]

Exhausted but once again defiant, the British were taking Wilson's proposal at face value. So was the president's team of naval experts, headed by Admiral Benson, the Chief of Naval Operations. "Unless peace is secured in accordance with the principles laid down by the President," Benson wrote to Secretary Daniels, "this war will have been fought in vain."[9] True to Mahan's precept that wars began through trade rivalry, Benson's team pointed out that "every great commercial rival of the British Empire has eventually found itself at war with Great Britain—and has been defeated."[10] The world war had been a tonic for the U.S. merchant marine, larger in 1918 than it had been since 1865, and since trade rivalry with Britain was bound to ensue, the team argued strongly for the maximum possible fighting navy.

But what neither the U.S. experts nor the British politicians realized was that, basically, Wilson was bluffing. While his naval planners fully anticipated another war (and accepted that, just as easily as Japan, Britain might become the enemy), Wilson believed he was moving close to his deepest desire: the establishment of an era of lasting global peace. Its means would be the League of Nations, whose covenant would be included in the peace treaty with Germany; and the bogey of the 1919 duplicate bill was there simply to make sure that Britain supported the League of Nations.

Publicly, however, his message to Britain was: Support the League or be outbuilt. On April 9, 1919, with ill humor and bad grace on both sides, agreement was reached—Britain would support the League, and the 1919 bill would be dropped. Even so, other disagreements remained between the victor nations over the naval terms of the peace treaty.

On November 21, 1918, British and U.S. sailors together had witnessed the surrender into internment of the major part of Germany's navy; the question thereafter was what should be done with it. The British Admiralty's view was that the German warships should all be sunk, and surprisingly (considering that a mass sinking would help keep up the Royal Navy's relative strength) this found general American agreement. Not so with either the French or Italians, though; both nations wanted a large share of the ships to add to their own fleets. But none of them imagined the eventual outcome: the simultaneous scuttling, on June 21, 1919, of sixty-six German warships interned in Scapa Flow—by the officers of the German navy. Ten battleships, five battle-cruisers, five light cruisers, and forty-six torpedo boats, among them displacing some half million tons—it was a splendid and useless gesture of pride and contempt, an appropriate epitaph to Germany's latest war, and (in the words of Adm. Sir Rosslyn Wemyss, the First Sea Lord) "a real blessing."

Seven days later the peace treaty was signed. Once again Wilson embarked in *George Washington* to fight for his dream of world peace—this time at home. Congress and the country, he knew, saw the peace treaty's difficulties as proof that alliances should be avoided. To obtain the treaty and the League of Nations covenant, the president had had to make unpleasant compromises with the Allies on his Fourteen Points. Lloyd George had won the day on the question of freedom of the seas—at least, the British and U.S. definitions remained what they had always been. Colonel House advised Wilson to be prepared and willing to compromise with Congress as well.

He was not; and that became his undoing. It is possible (though not certain) that while in Paris, when he was under exceptional strain, he had already had one minor stroke. The victorious conclusion of a bitter war, together with the seeming approach of an eternal peace on earth initiated by himself, combined in his fervent, idealistic, but vain character to produce stresses which only the most pragmatic person could override. However, it *is* certain that Admiral Benson instructed *George Washington*'s captain to afford the president "whatever seclusion he may desire" with "quarters . . . to be arranged as required by Rear Adm. Cary J. Grayson," Wilson's personal medical adviser—an abnormal level of care. Equally certainly, the president disregarded Colonel House's recommendations of compromise with Congress.

Three quarters of the Senate would have voted for American membership in the League of Nations, with either no or just a few modifications. The only staunch opponents were hard-right Republicans, for whom the Democrat Wilson had already had too much success. But when he could not find the unquestioning acceptance he wanted, the president turned to the nation in a speaking tour, as he had done when he was preparing the people for the likelihood of war. The missionary, the legal, and the visionary characters of the man all spoke together in that tour, foretelling doom: "I can predict," said the president, "with absolute certainty that within another generation there will be another world war if the nations of the world do not concert the method by which to prevent it."[11]

And to the generation which had seen the submarine at sea and the tank on land, the bombing of civilians and the gassing of armies, he prophesied that the weapons of the next war would make those seem like toys. But on the twenty-first day of the tour (September 25, 1919), he collapsed, half paralyzed. He never fully recovered; nor, inevitably, did his administration. To the world he left the League of Nations—a legacy which turned out to be of limited value. It might, perhaps, have been more valuable if the United States had been part of it; but President Wilson's own praiseworthy but obdurate moral stance—his refusal to compromise principle for the sake of politics—proved fatal not only to his health but to his political dream as well, and the United States refused to join the League.

Thus the years between the two world wars began with a great hope stillborn; and they contained many fearful portents as well. At the beginning of the Russo-Japanese War of 1904–05, a Russian admiral remarked, "War does not always start with the firing of guns," adding that, in his opinion, that conflict had begun long before. He could also have observed that war does not always end when the guns are silenced. For the Allied nations and the United States, the Great War did not completely end with the armistice, or even with the Treaty of Versailles. Before the armistice and after the treaty, all were involved in armed struggles on the fringes of revolutionary Russia: the "interventions" in the northwest Russian province of Archangelsk and in Siberia, Russia's far east. To understand these, and how they contributed to the eventual outbreak of World War II, we must go back to the state of the Pacific at the very opening of World War I.

When World War I began, Germany's government hoped the Pacific would be formally declared a neutral zone, to be untouched by conflict. Otherwise, the country's colonies (the Mariana, Marshall, and Caroline island groups, as well as Western Samoa) and its leaseheld trading areas on the Chinese coast would become immediately and excessively vulnerable to Japan, acting as Britain's Far Eastern ally. The Germans had even offered their territory at Kiaochow on China's Shantung peninsula (now Chiao-Hsien) to the United States in an attempt to keep Japan out of the war. But by the end of August 1914, the port was under Japanese blockade; on November 7 it was captured; and it remained Japanese until 1922.

The British too would have been happy to keep the war out of the Pacific, or later—once Kiaochow had been captured—to have limited Japan to the China seas. But German ships in the Pacific under Vice Adm. Maximilian von Spee made Allied action there essential, and the

Japanese were the nearest allies. While forces from New Zealand and Australia occupied Samoa and New Guinea respectively, the Imperial Japanese Navy hunted von Spee toward South America. As they did so, they occupied the previously German islands of Yap in the Carolines and Jaluit in the Marshalls. By October 20, 1914, they had gained strategic control of both those island groups and of the Marianas, straddling the midocean line of direct communication between the United States and the Philippines.

With the Marshalls only 2,000 miles from Hawaii, the United States' near-traditional fear of Japan sprang up again. The fear could verge on paranoia: In 1911 Californians had been considerably scared by newspaper reports that Magdalena Bay, in the Mexican peninsula of Lower California, was going to be sold to Japan. In November 1914 Germany "informed" the United States that both Britain and Japan were using Magdalena Bay for coaling operations (which they were not), and in the spring of 1915 the *Los Angeles Times* ran a thrilling scare story saying that Japanese warships were preparing a naval base in another bay in Lower California. Again they were not; the story was a complete fiction, although the reporter had in fact seen a Japanese cruiser, *Asama,* in Turtle Bay. What he failed to discover was that the cruiser had run aground—and that the U.S. government knew all about it.

Yet though President Wilson deplored such wildcat scaremongering ("its energy," he wrote, "is malign, its energy is not of the truth, its energy is mischief"), there always remained a seed of worry and doubt over Japan's intentions both in the Pacific and in Asia.[12] With the United States' full participation in the Great War came the removal of all U.S. Navy warships from the Pacific and, in November 1917, an agreement between Secretary of State Robert Lansing and Ambassador Viscount Ishii of Japan. Providing Japanese guarantees for the Open Door policy in China and American recognition for Japan's "special interests" in that country, it also provoked an immediate reaction from the American naval attaché there: "Ishii agreement will without question result in immediate and marked increase in Japan's aggressive actions towards China. This with view to consolidating her dominant position in Asia . . ."[13]

The government in Washington thought its attaché might well be correct: The agreement did not finally solve the problems of Japan in Asia and the Pacific; it only shelved the problems temporarily, while all energies turned toward winning the war in Europe. And like a perennial weed, the problems came back before the war was even over.

In the same month Lansing and Ishii signed their agreement, Bolsheviks in Russia mounted the October Revolution. At once the White Russians fought back, assisted by Allied forces. There were two focal points of Allied intervention—Archangelsk in north Russia and, at the other end of the continent, Vladivostok. In each place there were hundreds of thousands of tons of Allied military stores and supplies, the protection of which provided an excuse for intervention. And it was only an excuse—the Allies were desperate to avoid a separate Russian-German peace, which would release German forces from the existing two-front war.

The Allied intervention in north Russia was comparatively straightforward. It involved British, French, and some U.S. soldiers and sailors, the U.S. naval element being led by a colorful character named Rear Adm. Newton A. McCully. Many years before, in 1904, as assistant naval attaché to St. Petersburg, McCully had been in Port Arthur while it was besieged by the Japanese and had subsequently made his way back to St. Petersburg by camel across the Gobi Desert. In 1918 the "intervention" in which he and the other Allied forces fought was covertly as anti-Bolshevik as it was overtly anti-German. But with the Treaty of Versailles, it had to end or become overtly anti-Bolshevik. So, perhaps unfortunately, it ended, with the Allied evacuation of Archangelsk and Murmansk complete by mid-October 1919. Yet it also ended with a compassionate action by McCully: He took seven Russian orphans home to America and adopted them all.

The Siberian intervention was somewhat more complex. It started with the almost simultaneous arrival in Vladivostok during January 1918 of one British and three Japanese warships, responding to a call from the British Ambassador in Tokyo. It was not until early February that a U.S. warship joined them. Two years of confusion followed.

The problem was that each of the Allies involved had a different motive. The French were incensed because the new Soviet Russia had repudiated French loans to tsarist Russia. They were also frightened of the German strength which could be released against them if the Eastern Front collapsed. The British were frightened for the same reason, and anyway they opposed the Bolsheviks on principle. The Japanese feared having a revolutionary government close to their own shores; while the Americans, guessing that Japan was going to try and take over as much as possible of Manchuria and Siberia, believed Russia should be allowed to work out its own destiny.

In short, it was a mess. Uncertainty and suspicion of one another's motives not only plagued Allied relations but also hampered the counter-revolutionary efforts both of White Russians and of a Czech legion, composed of fifty or sixty thousand Czech ex-prisoners of war in the area.

The first actual landing occurred on April 6, 1918, after the murder of some Japanese citizens in Vladivostok. Five hundred Japanese and fifty British marines went ashore, while the crew of U.S.S. *Brooklyn* remained firmly on board. A second landing took place in early August. This time

Brooklyn was allowed to join in, and President Wilson also recommended that the United States and Japan should send 7,000 troops each to help maintain order. Captain Payne of H.M.S. *Suffolk* found his American counterpart (Rear Adm. Austin M. Knight) merely "obstructive." This was not really Knight's fault: He had orders from Secretary Daniels (and therefore presumably from President Wilson) to do "nothing . . . that could in any way affect the confidence of the Russian people in our sincere desire to help them establish and maintain government of their own choosing."[14]

As agent of an idealist, Knight was in a tricky and frustrating position. So was Wilson himself. In mid-October 1918, describing the Russians as "a lot of impossible folk fighting among themselves," he remarked that they would probably "wallow in anarchy for a while," during which time it would be best to leave them alone. "You cannot do business with them, so you shut them all up in a room and lock the door, and tell them that when they have settled matters among themselves you will unlock the door and do business."[15] But others intended to do business first. By the end of October the Japanese had landed not 7,000 but 70,000 troops.

This seemed to confirm the United States' worst suspicions of Japan's expansionist motives, and U.S. troops remained in Vladivostok until January 1920. The British troops were evacuated in November 1919. By then, as in north Russia, the Treaty of Versailles had removed any ability to pretend that the intervention's only purpose was to bolster the Eastern Front. Astonishingly, the Czech legion had taken control of the Trans-Siberian Railway from Vladivostok to west of the Urals, and the White Russian admiral Alexander V. Kolchak had advanced to within four hundred miles of Moscow; but with the signing of the Versailles treaty, Soviet forces compelled the Czechs and White Russians alike to retreat eastwards. In February 1920 Kolchak himself was captured and shot; during November 1920 the last of the Czech legion was evacuated from Vladivostok; and Japan remained in control not only of sections of the Siberian coast, but also of the oil-rich Russian island of Sakhalin.

One might well ask what it all achieved. Born out of a complex web of conflicting loyalties, desires, and principles, the final achievement of the Siberian intervention could be summed up in one word: distrust. Soviet distrust of the West; U.S. distrust of Japan, fully reciprocated; and perhaps worst for the coming decades, increasing distrust between Britain and the United States.

One might also ask whether it was worth it. In military and diplomatic terms, the answer has to be: emphatically not. But with the people and the principles and the world as it was, to ask whether it could have been avoided altogether is quite another question.

· · ·

Alongside these political portents came technological ones as well. When Eugene Ely made his pioneering ship-to-shore flight from U.S.S. *Birmingham* in November 1910, he had been trained for the job by Glenn H. Curtiss. Five months before that, Curtiss (one of the early geniuses of naval aviation) had played a prophetic little game. On a lake, he floated a target representing a battleship. He then flew over and dropped imitation bombs made of lead piping on it. What he saw made him announce that "the battles of the future will be fought in the air."[16] At that moment, as he knew perfectly well, the world's great navies were limbering up in the first post-dreadnought big-ship building race, and his words now sound like those of a man either obsessed, or possessed of something like second sight. The concept of aerial warfare was not new at all; but Curtiss's bold, imaginative assertion was several years ahead of most contemporaries' ideas.

In April 1917 the U.S. Naval Air Service included 43 officers and 209 men. At the time of the armistice nineteen months later, it contained some 50,000 personnel (over 3,000 officers and almost 47,000 enlisted men) and had acquired an impressive number of aircraft in its short life: 1,865 seaplanes and flying boats, 242 land-based planes, 15 airships, and more than 200 balloons. These totals were still short of the British, though, and during the war the Royal Naval Air Service had led the way in operational experience and technical improvement. In the early months of 1919, therefore, senior American naval officers visited Britain to study methods there—"So many of our ideas of naval policy have been gained from the British," wrote Capt. G. W. Steele, "that any discussion of the subject must consider their methods."[17]

The very favorable report brought back by those officers contributed to the General Board's own firm-jawed report on the United States' future naval air policy. Issued on June 23, 1919, it said that "to ensure air supremacy, to enable the United States Navy to meet on at least equal terms any possible enemy, and to put the United States in its proper place as a Naval power, fleet aviation must be developed to the fullest extent. . . . A naval air service must be established, capable of accompanying and operating with the fleet in all parts of the world."[18]

The report was soon followed by a remarkable demonstration of the airplane's progress: In May 1919 Lt. Comdr. A. C. Read of the U.S. Navy made the first flight across the Atlantic, from Newfoundland to Portugal, stopping at the Azores en route. His aircraft was numbered NC-4, and it was a naval plane built by Glenn H. Curtiss.

A decade after Curtiss's prophecy (and despite the flattering remarks made by their American colleagues) even the technical and operational advances of the Great War did not inspire the British Admiralty's "Post-War Questions Committee" when it came to consider the future of aircraft. Running their own assessment of the use of air power in war, the committee reported: "We do not consider that aircraft using any known form of weapon will render the capital ship obsolete until the capabilities of aircraft increase beyond anything that appears probable in the near future."[19]

In August 1919, only weeks after the General Board's affirmative report on air power, the Navy's first dry dock in Pearl Harbor was christened. At the same time, the area's thoughtful commandant (Rear Adm. William B. Fletcher) wrote his own disconcerting forecast:

> Sea planes brought by swift carriers . . . could rise from the lee of the nearest reefs to the northward and westward [of Hawaii], or the neighboring islands or from the sea itself, sweep down on Pearl Harbor and destroy the plant unless adequate defense is provided.[20]

And America did not have any carriers, let alone a swift one.

Aviation within the U.S. Navy had a somewhat vague status. In Britain, the Royal Naval Air Service and the Army's equivalent were unified in the Air Ministry to become the Royal Air Force; and arriving back in the United States in February 1919 after a successful wartime air command in Europe, Brig. Gen. William (Billy) Mitchell was determined to promote a unified U.S. Air Force. His main reasons were the financial independence such a service would have and the open-ended careers it would offer aviators. He therefore attacked the existing structures, such as they were, and the beliefs of both the Army and Navy air services. His favorite targets, literally and metaphorically, were ships, the bigger the better—especially battleships, those expensive, impressive pets of the traditional Navy and now, he proclaimed, outmoded, outdated, and fatally vulnerable to attack from the air. With Mitchell's input, the arguments already rumbling over aircraft versus battleships truly took off—he knew how to attract and create publicity, was always ready to testify at committees, make public speeches, write articles, or be interviewed; but his most celebrated stunt (it was not truly an experiment) came when the Navy decided that a series of gunnery, bombing, and explosives trials should be undertaken.

The first victim was the Navy's first battleship, U.S.S. *Indiana,* veteran of the Spanish-American War. On November 1, 1920, she was taken to Chesapeake Bay, where underwater charges of TNT, of varying sizes and at varying ranges, were used to simulate mine and torpedo attacks. On her decks further charges were planted and exploded, and Navy planes dropped water-filled practice bombs on her. It was not particularly surprising that she sank: The purpose of the exercise was to find out how much punishment she could take and how modern ships could be improved in the light of that knowledge.

The series continued with U.S.S. *Massachusetts,* sister to *Indiana.* She too sank—obligingly, from Mitchell's point of view. But his moment arrived in July 1921, when the Navy rashly asked him to participate in target experiments using the 22,800-ton ex-Imperial German Navy dreadnought *Ostfriesland.* This time the attack was to be by aerial bombing only, which was why Mitchell was invited. As with the previous experiments, rules were made so as to derive the maximum information from the trial: In particular, only one bomb was to be dropped at a time, and after each one observers would go on board to evaluate the damage.

Mitchell agreed to the rules; but when the time came and the 543-foot vessel was underneath him, he could not resist the temptation. He had probably never had any intention of resisting. His bombers dropped sixty-seven 2,000-pound bombs on the ship, scoring three near-misses and sixteen direct hits. Naval observers had no chance of even getting close, let alone examining the individual hits. Naturally *Ostfriesland* sank; naturally "the death of the dreadnoughts" became national headline news, as Mitchell had anticipated; and naturally the Navy was furious. They had gained no information at all, and even captured or obsolete battleships did not come a dime a dozen. The cost and effort of the trial were wasted; and worse was the sensational publicity.

Scientifically, Mitchell's exploit achieved nothing. But while both Army and Navy disliked the idea of a unified air service, both could see the value of air power, and some senior naval officers even believed Mitchell might be right when he said battleships were outdated. Admiral Fiske had championed air power for years; and now Adm. William F. Fullam took to publishing articles in the *New York Herald* under the pen name "Quarterdeck." In one typical piece, he described a postarmistice victory display of 220 aircraft in San Diego Bay. "It was a thrilling and imposing sight," he wrote with sober wonder.

> The sky was fairly obscured by buzzing planes. . . . We could not stand on the deck of a ship that day in San Diego harbor without being forced, however reluctantly, to realize that a new era had dawned in Naval Science, that a new weapon had appeared to upset all previously conceived ideas of the forces that would contribute most effectively to the maintenance of Sea Power in the years to come. . . . It was clear to me that if each of those airplanes had been supplied with bombs no bigger than an orange, my ships could not have remained at anchor in San Diego harbor.[21]

At the same time, Admiral Sims (back from London and now head of the Naval War College) pondered what would happen if two fleets, equal in everything except carriers, should fight. Even before Mitchell's stunt,

Sims was convinced that the side with more carriers would "sweep the enemy fleet clean of its airplanes, and proceed to bomb the battleships, and torpedo them with torpedo planes." Now he concluded thoughtfully: "It is all a question as to whether the airplane carrier, equipped with 80 planes, is not the capital ship of the future."[22]

8

★

SEEDS OF
MISUNDERSTANDING AND
GRAVE TROUBLE

*F*ew people cared greatly for the final version of the Treaty of Versailles. The French and Italians thought it was far too lenient; both countries wanted vast cessions of German-held territory, and though France got Alsace-Lorraine, the Italians did not receive the sections of Austria they wanted. Out of the small number of ex-German warships that had not been interned and scuttled at Scapa Flow, the British disliked having to allow France and Italy five cruisers and ten destroyers each, with ten submarines going to France as well, and very much disliked the naval realities President Wilson had forced them to recognize. Wilson himself believed the treaty was too severe on Germany, since the Allies forced him to allow an indefinite war indemnity on the defeated nation. The Germans liked it least of all, which was only to be expected—and for most others, not much to worry about.

The main problem about Germany, it seemed, was that its government was unable to control the senior officers of its armed services. The Scapa Flow scuttling was cited in support of this, yet though it was suspected that many ex-officers were active militarists (and they were), nevertheless, within five years of the treaty, Allied authorities recorded their official belief that Germany was effectively disarmed.

Whether it was true or not that the old enemy actually was disarmed, within only two years of the treaty a frightening truth had become glaringly obvious: The old Allies were all busy rearming at a stupendous rate.

Great Britain had scrapped almost 2 million tons of its world war stock of combat shipping, but had begun building again. The United States had suspended the 1919 duplicate of its 1916 Naval Act but was working on the 1916 act and successors. In 1918, even before the armistice, U.S. naval planners had stipulated that their service should be "designed to exercise, in the Pacific, a commanding superiority of naval power, and in the Atlantic, a defensive superiority against all potential enemies."[1] In 1919 (for the first time since Mahan's veto) the U.S. fleet was divided about evenly between the two oceans; and on July 7, 1920, after nine years of lobbying, the Imperial Japanese Navy won governmental approval for its "eight-eight" fleet—an entirely new fleet centered on eight battleships and eight cruisers, to be completed in ten years and to be backed up by the existing fleet.

At the same time in Japan, the 708-foot, 38,500-ton battleship *Nagato* was nearing completion, the first battleship in the world to be armed with 16-inch guns. On the last day of 1921 (when even France and Italy, comparatively low ranking in naval terms, had thirty-three and twenty-four warships, respectively, under construction) the three great naval powers had among them 227 warships under construction, including thirty-three capital ships averaging 40,000 tons' displacement each.

Something had to be done to halt the international race: Apart from the crippling financial burdens on economies whose postwar boom was fading fast, many groups and millions of individuals found it morally repugnant to be building so much armament so soon after the worst war in history.

But someone had to take the initiative. The British felt they could not: With the Royal Navy's supremacy symbolizing imperial unity, statesmen in London were unwilling to risk the psychological and actual consequences in the colonies and dominions that an offer of reduction could bring. Similarly, since they were only the world's third naval power, the Japanese felt that they could not initiate arms reduction or limitation; and neither Japan nor Britain was willing to restrict its own building while the United States insisted on continuing its own naval expansion.

Gradually it became evident that if a move was made at all, the United States would have to make it; and in mid-December 1920, with poor paralyzed Woodrow Wilson being spoon-fed through the last months of his presidency and the Republican Warren Harding getting ready for office, Senator William E. Borah from Idaho gave formal voice to the need. Noting that apparently it was only U.S. naval expansion which made Japan reluctant to reduce its "eight-eight" program (a view suspicious American naval strategists never accepted), he requested the incoming president to open negotiations with both Japan and Britain "to accomplish immediately a substantial reduction of the naval armaments of the world."[2]

In March 1921, in his inaugural address, President Harding stated the United States' readiness "to associate ourselves with the nations of the world, great and small, for conference, for counsel; to seek the expressed views of world opinion; to recommend a way to approximate disarmament and relieve the crushing burdens of military and naval establishments."[3] "Crushing" was not too strong a word—at that time, to meet the perceived U.S. threat in the Pacific, Japan was spending 48 percent of its national budget on the armed forces.

Within days the first response had come from Britain—a strong note of approval from the First Lord of the Admiralty, Lord Lee of Fareham. "Personally," he said on March 16 in a speech to the Institute of Naval Architects, "I am prepared to put aside all other business," because "there can be nothing more pressing in the affairs of this world."[4]

In Washington there was a sense of caution. The hesitation there was focused on the continuing existence of the Anglo-Japanese Alliance, due for termination or renewal in the summer. Although it had long since outlived its original purpose (the containment of Russian power in the Far East), for reasons of strategy and sentiment the governments of Britain and Japan were inclined to keep it going.

Around the world, attitudes to the alliance were somewhat like this: The British, though often stating that it held no threat to the United States, did not want to relinquish it if the United States was going to keep building warships. By the same token, the United States did not want to stop building while the alliance still existed. Australians and New Zealanders wished an end to it. They did not care for the fact that there were far more Japanese warships than British in the Pacific; they wondered openly against whom the Japanese, as allies, were supposed to be protecting them; they deplored the Japanese occupation of the ex-German Pacific islands and the consequent loss of trade; and they honestly feared that like Russia, China, Korea, and Manchuria, they too might fall victim to Japan's long-suspected expansionism.

As for the Japanese themselves, they, like everybody else, were mainly interested in their own national security. Their fear of the U.S. fleet was reasonable: There were more U.S. warships stationed in the Pacific than ever before, and though it was not known in Japan, there was the stated objective in the 1918 American plan "to exercise, in the Pacific, a commanding superiority of naval power."

A commanding superiority equals an optional ability for offensive action; power gives choice. From the Japanese viewpoint, their own continued naval building might be cripplingly expensive, but as long as the United States continued to build, it was vital. Strategically, the alliance with Britain was not vital to them, though it was useful; but in a deep-seated emotional way, it was invaluable. They knew it had been the first full-scale alliance Britain had made for a century and that it had marked

Japan's entry into the small group of modern Great Powers. And although in this last idea they were mistaken, they felt too that if the alliance were abandoned, it would mark a kind of humiliating demotion, as if they could not hold their own in the world.

But abandoned it was—on December 13, 1921, when representatives of the United States, Britain, Japan, and France signed the "Four-Power Treaty," one of nine treaties and twelve resolutions signed or adopted during the Washington Naval Conference of 1921–22. The conference was a tour de force of U.S. diplomatic control, resulting substantially in the achievement of U.S. aims; yet it would not have happened like that, and might not have happened at all, if it had not been for a secret and carefully guarded American skill.

All shades of senior U.S. opinion on the Anglo-Japanese Alliance came together in the view that it had to go. Not only did it oblige Britain to share technical and technological knowledge with Japan, it also provided a shield for Japan's expansion. Waiting to discover the alliance's future, the United States delayed convening a conference. Waiting likewise for a U.S. initiative, the British became impatient. With their Far Eastern allies, they began discussing the possibility of a "Pacific conference"; and the United States' secret skill came into play.

> The first telegram we deciphered which pointed definitely to the opening of a Pacific Conference between the Great Powers to settle disputes in the Far East was telegram No. 813, dated July 5, 1921, from the Japanese Ambassador in London to his home government in Tokio.[5]

Thus, ten years after the event, wrote Herbert O. Yardley, the first and greatest of American cryptologists of that period. By the time of writing, he was a bitter and disillusioned man, thrown out of employment in 1928 by a too-scrupulous secretary of state. Henry L. Stimson's celebrated remark that "Gentlemen do not read one another's mail" put an end to sixteen years of code breaking—a practice which had often worked to the United States' advantage, most of all (or so it seemed then) in the organization and execution of the Washington Naval Conference.

Knowledge of the proposed Anglo-Japanese Pacific Conference precipitated action in the United States. On July 8, 1921, President Harding sent out invitations to London, Paris, Rome, and Tokyo. Matters concerning the Pacific would be included in the Washington conference; but its primary purpose was naval disarmament. Through the decoding work of Yardley's "Black Chamber," the United States retained the initiative, shaped the agenda, and knew the innermost thoughts of Tokyo. In the eighty-eight days of the conference, Yardley wrote, "the Black Chamber sent to Washington . . . some five thousand deciphered Japanese messages which contained the secret instructions of the Japanese Delegates."[6]

The main U.S. objectives at the conference were threefold: first, to achieve formal parity between their navy and the Royal Navy; second, to keep the Japanese navy at the level the United States deemed suitable; and third, to bring an end to the Anglo-Japanese Alliance.

The belief in the need for and value of naval parity with Britain reflected Mahan's dictum of trade competition as the source of war, and ex-President Wilson's hope for a future free of war. To some extent the feeling was echoed in Britain; as one writer there had put it: "In competition for sea power, whether interpreted in terms of men-of-war or merchant ships, lie the seeds of misunderstanding and grave trouble between this country and the United States."[7]

And shortly before the calling of the conference, Michigan Congressman Patrick H. Kelley looked optimistically toward the early light of a new dawn: "When America and the great English-speaking empire—the British Empire—can go out upon the seas of the world as equals, there will be no disagreement which intelligent statesmanship cannot amicably adjust."[8]

The U.S. government already knew (indeed, Lord Lee, the First Lord of the Admiralty, had "emphasized the fact" to the U.S. naval attaché in London) "that Great Britain now is content with equality and not supremacy in regard to naval armament."[9] Given that, the United States could reasonably hope Japan might fall into line; not to do so would mark the Japanese as conference wreckers, open militarists, and expansionists. For Secretary of State Charles Evans Hughes, President Harding's senior delegate, the question was how best to ensure and control agreement from the outset.

The opening of a typical international conference would involve little more than mere diplomatic pleasantries, after which the delegates would disperse into committees for close study of the agenda. Such was the process expected by the foreign delegates when the Washington Naval Conference began on the morning of Saturday, November 12, 1921. But instead of the traditional, genteel, noncommittal introductory remarks they all anticipated, Hughes astounded everybody present, and everybody who read or heard about it, by opening the conference with an immediate, comprehensive proposal for global naval disarmament. Not only that, he put the U.S. cards on the table straight away, stating the limits to which the United States was ready to cut, and proposing reciprocal limits for all the other nations. In its timing and complete surprise, it was a marvelously theatrical performance, delivered for maximum effect; newspapers the world over were full of it, describing the openmouthed foreign delegates and the rapturous storms of applause which burst from the galleries after the secretary's last dramatic phrases:

> Enormous sums will be released to aid the progress of civilization. At the same time the proper demands of national defense will be adequately met and . . . preparation for offensive naval war will stop now.[10]

The conference reconvened three days later; everyone else needed the time to take in what Hughes had said and to formulate their replies. On Tuesday, November 15, both Arthur Balfour for Britain and Adm. Baron Tomosaburo Kato for Japan announced their agreement in principle. With that, the real business of the conference began—the working out of agreement in practice and detail. Based on the ratio of existing strength, Hughes had recommended the instantly famous formula of 5:5:3 for Britain, the United States, and Japan. There followed weeks of arduous, often critical negotiations on the type, tonnage, and armament of vessels to be included. Perhaps the nearest the conference came to failure was in late November, when it appeared that the Japanese would insist on a 5:5:3.5 ratio, increasing their proportion by some 50,000 tons. But with the steady stream of deciphered Japanese diplomatic messages, "the American Government," said Yardley, "could not lose. All it need do was to mark time. Stud poker is not a very difficult game after you see your opponent's hole card."[11]

By the end of November the cables showed Japan weakening—5:5:3 would be acceptable, if the other powers would agree to a maintenance of the status quo of defenses in the Pacific. At the beginning of December the cables showed Arthur Balfour working on Admiral Kato—"He was unbearably anxious for fear that . . . the whole armament limitation would be overthrown."[12] And on December 10 they showed the crucial break-through—from his political masters in Tokyo, Admiral Kato read:

> We have claimed that the ratio of 10 to 7 was absolutely necessary to guarantee the safety of the national defense of Japan, but the United States has persisted to the utmost in support of the Hughes proposal, and Great Britain also has supported it. . . . Now, therefore, in the interests of the general situation and in a spirit of harmony, there is nothing to do but accept the ratio proposed by the United States.[13]

Of course, it was not only Admiral Kato who read his political masters' secret message, but also (courtesy of Yardley's Black Chamber) the political masters of Washington as well. And now they knew they would gain all they desired.

Three days later (December 13, 1921) came the signing of the Four-

Power Treaty, by which the United States, Britain, France, and Japan agreed to respect the status quo of islands in the Pacific. As the American delegates reported to President Harding, this "terminated the Anglo-Japanese Alliance," and they were particularly optimistic about the arrangement. Back in 1914 the Navy League had asserted that the only real alternative to maintaining a strong navy was to establish "a changed human nature," something the league believed manifestly impossible. Although when they reported to the president on February 9, 1922, the delegates were not thinking of the league's sardonic admonition, nevertheless they virtually paraphrased it: "To stop competition," they said, "it is necessary to deal with the state of mind from which it results." The difference was that, far from being sardonic, they sincerely believed the conference had brought about a basic change in international attitudes:

> The negotiations which led to the Four-Power Treaty were the process of attaining that new state of mind, and the Treaty itself was the expression of a new state of mind. It . . . substituted friendly conference in place of war as the first reaction from any controversies which might arise in the region of the Pacific.[14]

That, at any rate, was their belief, and it made them happy men. Their contentment was increased by the other treaties arising from the conference—the Nine-Power Treaty between the United States, Belgium, the British Empire, China, France, Italy, Japan, the Netherlands, and Portugal to respect the integrity of China and the Open Door; the treaty between the United States, the British Empire, France, Italy, and Japan on the use of submarines and poison gas in warfare; and, above all, the Treaty for the Limitation of Naval Armament, signed by the same five nations on February 6, 1922, and effective (after ratification by all the governments concerned) from August 17, 1923.

This, the major diplomatic achievement of President Harding's short administration, was an appropriately lengthy document. It contained three chapters, with twenty articles in the first, rules and definitions of terms in the second, and four articles of miscellaneous provision in the third.

In summary, it fulfilled Secretary Hughes's recommended ratio. This has been known ever since as "5:5:3"—its full, more tongue-twisting form was 5:5:3:1.67:1.67, the two 1.67's being allocated to France and Italy. The formula set the maximum displacement for any ship at 35,000 tons, with maximum gun caliber at 16 inches for capital ships and 8 inches for all others. Aircraft carriers were not to exceed 27,000 tons, with the total British and U.S. allocations each being 135,000 tons. Britain would retain twenty-two existing capital ships, the United States eighteen, Japan ten. Those figures were to be stabilized by 1931 at fifteen each for Britain and

the United States and nine for Japan. Britain would scrap nineteen old
ships and four which were being built; the United States, fifteen of each;
and Japan, ten and six respectively. With certain specified exceptions, all
the contracting nations would build no capital ships for ten years from
the date of signature; similarly, with certain specified exceptions, the
United States, Britain, and Japan agreed not to add to the existing fortifications of their Pacific islands; and finally (unless two years' notice to
terminate had been given) the treaty as a whole would remain in force
until December 31, 1936.

It seemed pretty comprehensive, especially to non-naval people, and
around the world reaction to the treaty fell into two broad categories:
wholehearted non-naval approval (not least because of the tax reductions
it made possible) and profound naval chagrin. In every navy there were
individuals who praised the treaty, but in general, U.S. navalists concluded that their diplomats had been outsmarted by the British, because
more U.S. than British warships previously authorized or being built had
been scrapped, and because in their estimate the lack of limitation on
cruisers gave Britain a continuing actual naval superiority. Their British
counterparts believed that, on the contrary, British diplomacy had been
outsmarted by the United States, since Britain had scrapped the most
existing ships in return for the United States' scrapping ones which were
unfinished or only planned. Navalists of both nations agreed that Japan
had scored a coup with the treaty's Article XIX, forbidding further
fortification of Pacific islands: This, they said in dismay, gave the Imperial
Japanese Navy an unbreakable hold over the western Pacific. But Japanese navalists were no happier: In their view, the 5:5:3 ratio was too small
for national defense, while any formalized inferiority at all suggested the
humiliating idea that Japan was a second-class nation; and underlining
that, in their view, was the fact that the old alliance had gone. Japan, they
said, had been "cast off like an old shoe" as the result of an Anglo-
American conspiracy.

But to anyone outside the fleets, such criticism (whether from British,
Japanese, or U.S. naval men) seemed only to be expected, and for most,
the early 1920s held every reason for great hope. Since the Versailles
Treaty of 1919, the world had been at peace, and now a radical move had
been made to restrict armaments. But under the surface, in the minds of
powerful men around the globe, resentment fueled distrust. It took more
than a treaty, fair or unfair, to alter human nature; and if Mahan was
right in saying that trade rivalries led to war, the very treaties designed
to establish and maintain peace actually extended the risks by planting
more "seeds of misunderstanding."

Only sixteen months after those much-applauded, much-reviled five signatures, one senior U.S. naval officer published his own view of the

outcome: "In truth, the Washington Conference saved the Navy from the consummation of an out-of-date, wasteful, futile naval race. The American delegates proved to be the best naval strategists the United States has ever known!" At first reading, this sounded very like one of those heavily sarcastic remarks made in deep frustration; yet there was truth behind it, and the writer's next sentence appeared frank and exultant, even sinister. The U.S. delegates, he asserted, "freed us from a ten-year-old naval plan for a war in the past and permitted us to build up our navy for a war in the future!"[15]

The author was Adm. W. F. ("Quarterdeck") Fullam, one of the main protagonists of air power, enthusiastically realizing that because the treaty had not done away with navies altogether, it offered the chance of reshaping the fleets of the future. The only real limitations had been placed on battleships and aircraft carriers (France never ratified the treaty on poison gas and submarines, so that one never became effective). Since battleships and carriers alike were inordinately expensive, and since the argument on their relative values still continued, they would probably have found a natural limitation anyway. What Fullam saw was that a formal limitation on battleships could make it easier to lobby for the maximum number of carriers allowed—and the aircraft to go with them.

If he assumed that there would be more wars, he also asserted that "intercontinental wars will be well-nigh impossible in the future." Not every U.S. service commander was so sanguine. Just before the conference was called, Maj. Gen. Charles T. Menoher (chief of the U.S. Army Air Service) had submitted another startlingly prescient report on the situation of Pearl Harbor in the island of Oahu:

"Without control of the air," he stated, "our entire force at Oahu will be practically helpless. . . . The defenses of Oahu are concentrated in a rather small area and thereby are rendered vulnerable to well directed aerial attack. Having gained superiority of the air, the enemy might bomb at will the vulnerable points essential to the defense of Oahu such as coast defenses, wharves, navy yards, store houses, oil and gasoline tanks, etc."[16]

Though General Menoher did not specify Japan, there was no other possible enemy in that region; and Admiral Fullam was far from being the only naval officer to realize the expansive possibilities of limitation. Every nation which signed the treaty swiftly saw that, up to a unit limit of 10,000 tons' displacement, they could build as many smaller warships as they liked; and within two years of the signatures, they were all doing exactly that. Not only with cruisers, but with submarines, destroyers, and every class of vessel large or small, methods were eagerly sought to modernize, to reduce weight, and to improve fighting qualities.

One U.S. naval officer, Dudley W. Knox, wondered what other outcome anyone could have imagined. "The inevitable result of any international restrictions upon the size of the Navy," he pointed out, "will be competition in naval efficiency, keener than ever."[17] Under the water, on the water, above the water, and through it, there were ways of massaging the treaty.

For one thing, electronics were not mentioned at all, and both the U.S. Navy and the Royal Navy pushed ahead with submarine detectors. The Royal Navy's Asdic (an acronym taken from the Allied Submarine Detection Investigation Committee) was ahead of the U.S. equivalent, sonar; Asdic's first successful trials took place in 1919 and 1920, and by 1932 it had been installed in all postwar British destroyers. By the same time, the U.S. Navy had only just managed to produce a version of comparable quality. But the U.S. fleet soon overtook in an area of at least equal importance, for the Washington treaty was shot full of holes, and one (no doubt to Admiral Fullam's delight) was big enough to accommodate even aircraft carriers.

Following the United States' first carrier (a converted collier renamed U.S.S. *Langley* and commissioned in 1922), the battle cruisers *Lexington* and *Saratoga* were slated for conversion. This caused a slight problem: The treaty allowed 33,000 tons as a carrier's maximum size, and there was no way the two ships could end up at less than 34,000 tons each. On completion each displaced almost 36,000 tons; but the way out was simple. The standard displacement of 33,000 tons "does not include weight allowance," said a contemporary data publication, "for providing means against air and submarine attack."[18] Both Britain and Japan similarly converted battle-cruisers into carriers, but given the United States' early breach of the treaty's spirit and letter, that navy's later protests at breaches in other navies seem somewhat disingenuous.

In June 1921 Rear Adm. William A. Moffett was appointed first head of a brand-new Bureau of Aeronautics. His success was steady rather than spectacular; but by the end of 1924, while the British Admiralty was still struggling toward a decision, the U.S. Navy had a place reserved for air power. In that year a special Board of Inquiry under Adm. Edward W. Eberle made four powerful recommendations, all of which were acted on. The first was that a "progressive and adequate airplane building program" should start, with a budget of $20 million in its first year; second, another carrier should be built, of 23,000 tons; third, Naval Academy students should receive aeronautical training; and finally, there should be "a definite policy to govern the assignment of naval personnel to aviation duty."[19]

A quick jump back in time now, to the day when Robert Peary (who had craved fame all his thirty-six years) finally found it. The date was April 6, 1909, and he wrote ecstatically: "The Pole at last!!! The prize of three centuries, my dream and ambition . . ." In that last, successful haul, he had needed six weeks to reach "the point where north and south and east and west blend into one"; and in the same year the Wright brothers' plane was accepted into U.S. military service.[20] On May 9, 1926, taking off from Spitzbergen, Comdr. Richard E. Byrd, U.S.N., in a flight whose outward leg took only nine hours and three minutes, became the first man to fly over the North Pole.

A comment made that December by the secretary of the Navy (Curtis D. Wilbur) was fully justified. Since 1919, he pointed out, "the principal effort of the Navy Department has been directed toward the application of aircraft to fleet operation and development of suitable aircraft for that use."[21] A navy that could fly across the North Pole could fly pretty much anywhere, and on November 28, 1928 (three weeks before the twenty-fifth anniversary of the first heavier-than-air flight), Richard Byrd became the first person to fly over the South Pole as well. Only twenty-five years from Kitty Hawk to the Antarctic Pole—it was a vivid indicator of the speed with which the United States had grasped, developed, and exploited the possibilities of flight.

By 1929 the U.S. Navy owned carriers totaling 78,700 tons' displacement, yet this still looked like a poor proportional comparison with the Royal Navy's 107,550 carrier tons or the Japanese navy's 67,000 tons; and a British government document of March 1928 stated that in aviation the Royal Navy "already possessed a marked lead" over the U.S. Navy. However, it depended on whether one took carriers or their aircraft as the important measure; for as another benchmark of change, over 250 carrier-borne aircraft took an active part in the U.S. fleet exercises of 1929. At the same time, the Royal Navy had only about 150 carrier aircraft altogether. It was already getting hard to remember that only ten years previously, American naval aviators had had to come to Britain to learn.[22]

The streamlining and modernizing of the U.S. Navy, and the new international cruiser-building race, took place against a background of burgeoning economic prosperity in the United States and apparent political stability in Europe. In 1924 Italy and Yugoslavia confirmed by treaty the status quo of the Adriatic, one of the troublesome questions left by the war. In 1925 the Locarno treaties between Britain, Belgium, France, Italy, and Germany guaranteed Europe's western frontiers; and with Poland and Czechoslovakia, France made treaties of mutual assistance in the event of German aggression. In 1926 (though the United States and the USSR still remained outside the League of Nations, and in spite of the strong legacy of distrust), Germany joined the League—an event which was perhaps one of the best signs that the era of peace was becoming real and secure.

Meanwhile, in the Far East (though China was still fragmented by civil war between communists, independent warlords, and the Kuomintang [Nationalist] Party under Chiang Kai-shek), Japan seemed as stable as many nations in the West. Japanese troops left the Chinese province of Shantung in 1922, and in 1925 (in return for the Soviets' recognition of Japan's 1905 peace treaty with the tsar), the island of Sakhalin reverted to the USSR. Although the emperor of Japan was not only head of state but head of government as well, parliamentary democracy ruled in his name; and his name could not have been more optimistic. On December 25, 1926, when after years of decline his physically and mentally ill father died, Prince Hirohito became emperor and chose the reign name by which he himself would be known after his death. It was "Showa," and it meant "Shining Peace."

But in spite of these happy omens, relationships across the two oceans could be difficult and ambiguous too. On September 1, 1923, the Great Kanto Earthquake demolished most of Tokyo, Yokohama, and Yokosuka, slaughtering 140,000 people and destroying the Imperial Navy's 120-acre base at Yokosuka. Foreign aid poured in to repair, to rebuild, and to replace, and the first vessels to arrive with assistance were U.S. Navy warships. Deeply grateful for the gesture as much as for the actual vital help, the Japanese were equally deeply disconcerted when (in 1924) Congress passed new immigration laws, leading to the effective total exclusion of Japanese immigrants, and followed that in 1926 with a major battle fleet exercise in the Pacific.

At the same time as sending such contradictory signals across the Pacific, U.S. naval views of Britain were chillier than at any time in the previous thirty years. The rivalry was obvious not only in building plans, but in resources. The modernization of the fleets included conversion from coal- to oil-fired boilers, and wherever the U.S. Navy looked for oil it seemed the Royal Navy had gotten there first. If they had not gone through the world war together, the two nations could have found ideal Mahanian conditions for war with each other, and both often felt they would have embarked on it cheerfully.

Though a British-American war was never a real option, by the second half of the 1920s the time was clearly approaching for all the naval nations to confer again and fill in some of the holes left by the Washington treaty. On June 20, 1927, therefore, they came together in Geneva—and they completely failed to agree. With astonished and futile attempts to reconcile the Westerners, the Japanese delegates looked on as their British and U.S. counterparts found, with rage and frustration, that each was as intransigent as the other.

The Japanese proposal was the simplest of all. It suggested, in effect, that everyone should just stop building warships. Even if unrealistic, it was an honest proposal (at that time, the Japanese government did hope for real limitation), but it was ignored by the big two, who stuck fast on the question of cruisers.

For Britain, the Admiralty proposed a reduction in the vessels' maximum size from 10,000 to 7,500 tons, and reckoned they would need seventy to protect the fleet and British Empire trade routes. On the same basis they estimated the U.S. Navy would need forty-seven such vessels, and the Japanese twenty-one. For the United States, the General Board proposed that total U.S. or British cruiser tonnage should be in the region of 250,000 to 300,000 tons. That would mean a British allocation of only twenty-five to thirty cruisers of the Washington treaty size, or between thirty-three and forty of their suggested new reduced size—in either case far short of the seventy deemed necessary by the Admiralty. The board also demanded "equality with Great Britain" as "the sole basis on which a just treaty limitation can be imposed."[23]

While the British had no objection to the U.S. Navy's building up to match the Royal Navy's proposed cruiser tonnage, they refused to come down to the Americans' proposed overall cruiser ceiling. "We cannot help it if they build up to our required standard," said Adm. Lord Jellicoe, "but we can avoid lowering our standard to suit them."[24] Against that, the U.S. admiral Hilary P. Jones, chief naval adviser at the conference, knew that Congress would not remotely consider building to the British ceiling; and distrusting and disliking the British as much as his predecessor Admiral Benson had done in the war, he refused to accept anything other than parity on his figures.

Neither side would shift, and on August 24, 1927, after nine weeks of recrimination and depression, the conference came to its inevitable end of complete failure. It had achieved nothing but transatlantic antagonism—eagerly assisted toward that undesirable end by the domineering, anglophobic Admiral Jones and the efforts of one William B. Shearer, a professional lobbyist employed by the largest American shipbuilding firms and the newspaper magnate William Randolph Hearst. Both east and west of the Atlantic, hostile newspapers accused the other side of deliberate destructiveness and lamented the decline of international cooperation toward continued peace.

Barely a year later, though, the drive for peace seemed to have revived and become stronger than ever before. On August 27, 1928, in Paris, Secretary of State Frank B. Kellogg and French Premier Aristide Briand signed the "International Treaty for the Renunciation of War," otherwise known as the Kellogg-Briand Pact. Representatives of thirteen other nations signed the treaty that day, and eventually sixty-two nations accepted its resolve. Italy, Germany, and Japan were among the countries which agreed to "renounce war as an instrument of national policy."

On the assumption that only aggressors start wars, the pact allowed signatories to go to war in self-defense. But self-defense is a slippery, elusive concept, depending on viewpoint; and within months of the first signatures, which were hailed everywhere else as a great advance for mankind, the German navy began building *Deutschland,* later renamed *Lützow.* The Versailles Treaty permitted Germany to retain six old battle-ships with an age limit of twenty years, and forbade their replacement with anything larger than 10,000 tons. Such was the announced tonnage of *Deutschland* and her sisters *Graf Spee* and *Scheer;* but each in fact displaced 12,500 tons and was armed with six 11-inch guns. Diesel en-gines gave them a maximum speed of 28 knots; eight 5-inch and six 4.1-inch guns as secondary armament meant that these nominal heavy cruisers were actually a new kind of ship altogether. Other nations called them pocket battleships and pondered how they fitted into the pact to renounce war.

Between 1924 and 1928 the Japanese had also laid down cruisers exceeding the limits of the Washington treaty. Moreover, they too had claimed these as 10,000-ton vessels, though four each of the *Nachi* and *Atago* classes displaced up to 30 percent more than was admitted. Some U.S. naval officers, such as William H. Sebald (later U.S. ambassador to Japan) suspected this; as early as 1927 "circumstantial evidence" con-vinced him "that the Japanese Navy, even then, was violating the strict limitations."[25]

But suddenly (on October 24, 1929) even the few Americans who felt certain the treaty was being breached found more immediate cause for worry. Beginning on that day, the Wall Street crash was the republic's tenth financial crisis, and by far the worst—never before had prices fallen so fast or so far. As the shock waves spread around the world, each nation had to find its own way of coping with the crisis.

After the Great War, the enormous reparations forced on Germany by the Versailles Treaty (vigorously but ineffectively opposed by President Wilson) had brought the "great inflation." Over ten years the exchange rate of U.S. dollars and German marks gave a staggering statistic: In 1914 one dollar was worth 4.2 marks; in 1923 the same dollar was worth 4.2 *million* marks. Germany's decline worked down from the top. The war demolished its monarchy; the postwar great inflation struck at its middle class; the 1929 crash hit its working class. In that year 1.89 million Germans were unemployed; by 1930 the figure was over three million.

The United States, vastly more prosperous before the crash than Ger-many, suffered even more. One of its millions of unemployed was Herbert Yardley, who was making gainful use of his unwanted free time. Stimson would not let him break codes, but that was all he knew about; so now, filled with resentment, Yardley was busy writing a book about codes—and how to break them, American-style.

In both Britain and America, new political administrations had the misfortune to face the world financial crisis within months of taking office: in Whitehall, the Labour Government of Ramsay MacDonald, a lifelong pacifist, and in Washington, the Republican government of Herbert Hoover, a Quaker. Despite the differences of their political outlooks, the two leaders shared many basic moral beliefs and jointly paved the way for a new attempt at limitation. On January 21, 1930, the London Naval Conference opened—a five-power conference with Britain, the United States, Japan, Italy, and France represented. Mindful of the 1927 fiasco, the British and U.S. delegations came with the full intention of reaching agreement this time; and when the conference was over, MacDonald wrote that "from beginning to end the two delegations worked in complete harmony. To all intents and purposes they were one team."[26] It was an exaggeration, but in comparison to the other delegations, true: the French and Italians, eyeing each other's interests in the western Mediterranean, were uncooperative, and the Japanese came demanding an increase in the Washington ratios from 5:5:3 to 10:10:7.

In February the conference was interrupted twice: On the seventeenth, pressed by the financial crisis, the French government fell, while on the twentieth elections took place in Japan. In both countries the existing authorities were returned to power; the respective delegates returned to the conference; and on April 22 the Five-Power Treaty was signed.

The cruiser problem was solved by Britain's reducing the number it demanded; by all powers agreeing to divide the vessels into two types, those with 8-inch guns and those with 6-inch guns, with a percentage of tonnage transferable from one group to the other; and by Japan's accepting a 5:3 ratio of the larger cruisers and a 10:7 ratio of the smaller. Each of the big three reduced its capital-ship stock (Britain by five ships, the United States by three, and Japan by one) and extended the big-ship building holiday by six years. The Japanese also gained parity (at 52,700 tons) with Britain and the United States in submarines. The French, as always, had adamantly opposed the abolition of a weapon they claimed to be purely defensive, and suitable for smaller navies; but under the terms of the treaty, submarines became subject to the same international laws as surface vessels. It appeared a welcome move, but it was unrealistic: The very nature of the submarine gave it belligerent opportunities which no surface ship could have, and which in war would be quite irresistible—whatever the law said.

The agreements that came out of the conference were not very far reaching, nor were they its most important features. Those, instead, were purely political: first, the improved Anglo-American relationship, now distant but friendly instead of distant and frigid; and second, the fact that in the Japanese elections, Prime Minister Hamaguchi had been returned to power—for he represented parliamentary democracy, still a weak infant in Japan. Throughout the 1920s, since the Washington treaty, Japan's Imperial Navy had divided slowly but surely into two factions, for and against that treaty. Those in favor tended to be either men of the older generation, originally trained by Britain's Royal Navy and retaining its Western ideal of fairness; or else the more intelligent members of the middle generation who had worked abroad—men such as Capt. Isoroku Yamamoto, a Harvard graduate, ex–naval attaché in Washington and a member of the delegation to London. Those who opposed the Washington treaty did so through a misplaced romantic idealism mixed with a plain old-fashioned desire for immense power. For both reasons, they saw the treaty's ratio as a national humiliation; felt sympathy for defeated Germany; and found a spiritual challenge in the belligerent attitude of the Imperial Army—originally trained by Prussian officers.

By 1930 the Japanese naval officers who opposed the treaty had become a vocal and puissant group. They claimed to represent the authentic spirit of Japan, undiluted by foreign influence, and deployed emotional arguments of unreasoning patriotism to press for a navy at least as big as the United States' or Britain's. But the reelection of Prime Minister Hamaguchi seemed to indicate that the militants had not yet prevailed completely; and like peaceable Britons and peaceable Americans, peaceable Japanese welcomed the belief that their nations could still agree.

However, the London conference of 1930 was the last time all the naval nations agreed: The seeds of misunderstanding were growing to full, livid bloom. That same year, the Imperial Japanese Navy conducted a fleet exercise to test the U.S. defenses of the Philippines, and from Washington the Office of Naval Intelligence reported that if it had been a real attack, the U.S. fleet would have been "completely destroyed."[27] On November 14 Prime Minister Hamaguchi was shot and fatally wounded by a militant assassin. In 1931 Yardley's book *The American Black Chamber* was published. In the United States, where its admissions were officially denied, it was an immediate popular success and sold well; in Japan, it sold twice as many copies.

Japanese democracy was dying; German democracy was already dead. From 1930, as apocalypse echoed out of Wall Street, the democratic Reichstag remained technically sovereign in Germany, while the country was actually ruled by emergency decree. It remained so until 1945. During the early thirties, the democratic parties accepted the state of affairs, asserting that the alternative—civil war in defense of democracy—was worse, and believing that time would improve matters if they bore with events; but they deluded themselves. The old monarchy was gone; the democrats had not acquired the stamp of true, accepted authority; and with the army symbolizing raw yet disciplined power, the throne lay free for dictatorship, and the vision took shape of revenge for the Versailles Treaty. In Japan too grew dreams of revenge for the government's seemingly craven withdrawals from Siberia and Sakhalin, their submission, and the Americans' deception at Washington. On September 18, 1931, the "Manchurian incident" began, as the Japanese army began to take its own foreign policy decisions, invading Manchuria on its own authority. In the United States nine days later, facing a government income more than halved from $4.1 billion to $2 billion since the crash of 1929, President Hoover halved the Navy's destroyer construction for 1932 and canceled all naval building for 1933. "At every turn," shrieked the horrified Navy League, he was trying "to restrict, to reduce, to starve the Navy." They were right; his profound Quaker beliefs could hardly allow him to do otherwise.[28]

The next month (October 1931) a report came to London from the Royal Navy's Commander-in-Chief China, Adm. W. H. Kelly. In a combined exercise, "attackers" had successfully landed on Singapore Island without the "enemy" vessels even being seen. Three months later (the end of January 1932), on a pretext as spurious as the army's in Manchuria, Japan's Imperial Navy began the "Shanghai incident," bombing the Chinese city; and in the U.S. Navy's spring Pacific exercise, Adm. Harry E. Yarnell took two aircraft carriers and a few destroyers to the north of Oahu, launching from them an entirely unexpected and entirely successful "attack" on Pearl Harbor. A League of Nations commission, inquiring into the rights and wrongs of the Shanghai and Manchurian incidents, had absolutely no useful effect whatsoever and produced only scathing self-criticism. The Finnish representative demanded:

> Is the League a reality or not? Is it a debating club, or, at the best, merely an instrument of mediation? Nothing has been done for fear of doing too much. It would be much better to recognize the inadequacy of the League than to pretend the Covenant can do what it cannot do.

The Norwegian representative was still more despondent: "If the League does not secure peace and justice," he predicted, "then the whole system by which right was meant to replace might will collapse."[29]

Grey, the League's vice president, wrung his hands in despair: "There are people who will ask, could not the League of Nations have done more?" he lamented. "I will ask, what more could it have done? . . . I do not like the idea of resorting to war to prevent war."[30]

The day before Lord Grey's lament, Rear Adm. Montgomery M. Taylor (commander in chief of the American Asiatic Fleet) sent Admiral

Pratt (now Chief of Naval Operations) his assessment of East–West relations. "The only thing we have gotten," he wrote, "is an increase in Japanese enmity and, I fear, some loss of regard by the Chinese for, as they think, letting them down. . . . The failure of the powers to make their protests good will I fear trouble us all in the future."[31]

On May 4, less fainthearted than the League of Nations, the U.S. Navy's General Board instituted an immediate revision of its War Plan Orange, bringing the plan aimed against Japan up to date. Eleven days later the "May 15 incident" took place in Tokyo: Forty-one conspirators, including ten young naval officers, attacked various parts of the capital and slew, among others, the seventy-eight-year-old prime minister. Their punishments were minimal: "When we consider what caused these pure-hearted youths to make this mistake," the navy minister remarked, "reverent reflection is proper."[32] In the same month, Germany's first postcrash government fell. During the course of 1932 the country had three different administrations, ending with an army general (Kurt von Schliecher) as chancellor. And all the time (a sad irony in that hectic and turbulent year) delegates of the Five Powers were meeting in Geneva, trying to work out extensive plans for general disarmament, including the abolition of bombing.

Eleven years previously—in 1921, the year of the Washington conference—the United States' wartime assistant secretary of the Navy had been struck by polio and paralyzed from the waist down. Despite that handicap, Franklin Delano Roosevelt was elected governor of New York State in 1928, and reelected in 1930 with an increased majority. As 1932 drew to a close, with deepening economic depression throughout the industrialized world and over 12 million unemployed in the United States alone, a decisive majority of Americans chose the crippled governor for their next president.

Just before his own paralyzing stroke in 1919, President Wilson had predicted "with absolute certainty that within another generation there will be another world war if the nations of the world do not concert the method by which to prevent it." Taking a generation as twenty-five years, that gave the world until 1944; and already the prophecy was taking on a frightening air of reality. On January 30, 1933, despite a slip in the movement's standing in the November elections, the senile octogenarian President Hindenburg of Germany appointed an ex-corporal of the Austrian army, the National Socialist leader Adolf Hitler, as the nation's fourth chancellor in eight months. On February 27, 1933, the Reichstag building in Berlin burned down; the following day (by emergency decree as "a protection against communist acts of violence endangering the state") certain articles of the German constitution were canceled. Telecommunications and the mail were no longer to be private. Along with personal freedom, the freedoms of speech, of the press, and of association were curtailed. On March 4, President Roosevelt took office; in Germany, on March 23, new elections were held, and the next day (though the Nazis were still a minority in the Reichstag) the notorious "Enabling Act" was passed. It stated:

> The laws passed by the Reich government do not have to adhere to the constitution. . . . The laws passed by the government of the Reich will be drafted by the Chancellor. . . . Treaties agreed by the Reich with foreign states, which concern the constitutional affairs of the Reich, do not require the consent of the legislative institutions.[33]

In March 1933 the Japanese announced their intention of leaving the League of Nations, and on April 18 Admiral Taylor wrote dryly from Shanghai:

> One cannot but admire the way the Japanese have been thumbing their nose at the rest of the world. The diplomatic corps of the nations seems to have gotten itself in something of a box with their high-sounding treaties which, in this part of the world, mean nothing. It seems to me we have been caught bluffing.[34]

In the twelve years since the first Naval Limitation Conference had begun in Washington, the United States had had three Republican presidents, all either opposed to or not interested in the Navy. With secrecy and bribery, Harding's secretary of the interior (Albert B. Fall) had leased naval oil reserves in Wyoming and California to private concerns; neither Harding nor his successor, Coolidge, permitted the Navy to grow to the size allowed by the treaty; and in his four years in office, Hoover did not authorize the construction of one single naval vessel.

Especially when set against the increasingly disturbing international background, it was a dismal record, and it looked as though it were going to continue. Before taking office, President Roosevelt had spoken of a still smaller but highly efficient navy, and within a week of his inauguration Congress had authorized him to make further wide-ranging financial cuts. Nevertheless, just before leaving office at the end of June, the Chief of Naval Operations (Adm. William Veazie Pratt) wrote a warm letter to the new president, emphasizing "what a pleasure it is to me to know that the fate of the Navy lies in the hands of a man who loves it as you do."[35]

It was true that Franklin Roosevelt had loved the Navy for many years, as his distant relative Teddy had done, but the outgoing CNO's praise was based on much more than sentiment. After twelve years of naval neglect, and in spite of the country's being in the midst of an economic depression, the president had pulled off a marvelous coup for the Navy's benefit, without having to increase its normal funding and without seriously offending Congress or anyone else. Financial advisers of the "New Deal" believed that spending rather than saving would help end unemployment, so on June 16, 1933, the National Industrial Recovery Act was passed; and from it (by Executive Order No. 6174) the president promptly extracted $238 million for the Navy to build thirty-two ships over three years.

Roosevelt had not been certain the order would go completely unchallenged, but it did, and in private he showed his own satisfaction and surprise. "Claude," he said to his naval secretary, Claude Swanson, "we got away with murder that time."[36]

PART FOUR

RELUCTANCE

1933 – 1941

★

As international agreements expire,
nationalism grows throughout the world.
An undeclared conflict disrupts the Far East
and Europe explodes into war;
but though the president prepares his fleet,
his country sees neutrality and the oceans
as protection enough
and is unwilling to fight.

9

★

OUR CITIZENS
DO NOT WANT WAR

*A*s the early years of the 1930s shuffled past, grim and humiliated by the darkening depression, the U.S. Navy—like some chrysalis twisting in the darkness—began to grow again. In the summer of 1933 Roosevelt's initiative under the National Industrial Recovery Act provided for the completion in three years of four cruisers, two carriers, four flotilla leaders, sixteen destroyers, four submarines, and two gunboats. It was the Navy's most vigorous growth since World War I and the subsequent twelve years of Republican neglect.

Meanwhile, around the world, openly or secretly, unhappy events occurred which seem in retrospect like milestones in an inevitable decline from a fragile peace. In October 1933 Germany withdrew from the Geneva Disarmament Conference and followed Japan out of the League of Nations; the next month Gen. Sadao Araki (Japan's minister of the army) put it to his government that "in order to have enough of the raw materials . . . which will be lacking in wartime, we should plan to acquire and use foreign resources existing in our expected sphere of influence, such as Sakhalin, China, and the Southern Pacific."[1]

On March 27, 1934, the Vinson-Trammell Act was passed by Congress, giving the U.S. Navy its first systematic program of ship replacement: a carrier, two cruisers, fourteen destroyers, and six submarines for 1935; fifteen destroyers and another six submarines for 1936; two battleships, twelve destroyers, and a further six submarines for 1937; and for

1938 and '39, two battleships, eight destroyers, and four submarines per year.

It sounded good, and it was good; but all it would do was to bring the fleet up to treaty limits. By consistently building up to its own limit, the Japanese navy already had 80 percent of the U.S. Navy's strength; and in Japan, during the autumn of 1934, two domestic events of fundamental global importance took place. The first was private; the second, very public.

Privately, at a conference of Japan's admirals and field marshals, Prince Hiroyasu Fushimi (chief of the Imperial Navy General Staff) outlined the navy's basic strategy. The United States, he said, "occupies the most important position in the strategies of the Imperial Navy." At the start of a war, the Japanese fleet would aim "to clear out the enemy's seaborne military power in the Orient and at the same time, in cooperation with the army, attack their bases, thereby controlling the western Pacific; then, while protecting the empire's trade, to harass the operations of the enemy's fleet, and thereafter await the assault of the enemy's home fleet and defeat it through surprise attack."[2]

Taken by itself, the outline was no more than the equivalent of the U.S. Navy's War Plan Orange against Japan—simply a theoretical answer to the question of how to act if a war began. But at the same time as Fushimi spoke secretly in Tokyo, Vice Adm. Isoroku Yamamoto was speaking openly in London. Preliminary talks were under way for a further naval disarmament conference, to take place before the current treaties expired at the end of 1936. Admiral Yamamoto's instructions were to press for a revised treaty in which all signatory navies would have a common upper limit of tonnage, being free within that limit to construct the most appropriate vessels for their needs. Since the proposal implied either a very large Japanese navy or fairly small British and American navies, there was little chance it would be accepted, and it was not; so on December 29, 1934, the admiral followed his next instruction from Tokyo. Giving the necessary two years' notice, he announced that from the end of 1936, Japan would no longer be bound by treaty and would build whatever warships it chose.

In the spring of 1935, President Roosevelt began receiving a very large number of letters, all saying more or less the same thing. "At the present critical time when Japan is seeking a larger navy," wrote someone from Baldwinsville, New York, "it doesn't seem very clever for *you* to *flaunt* our navy in Japan's face."[3]

From schools, churches, institutions, and individuals all over the nation the criticisms flowed in. From California came "a suggestion that the naval maneuvers proposed to take place in the Western Pacific this sum-

mer be transferred to some other quarter where they cannot be miscon-
strued by our Japanese neighbors as an unfriendly gesture." From Wis-
consin: "The proposed maneuvers are likely to be misinterpreted by the
people of the Far East, and are likely to plunge us into another world
war." From a mortuary boss, who might have been expected to feel
differently: "Whether intended or not, this would be a most provocative
act and only increase the tension between the United States and Japan."
From Michigan, Connecticut, Washington, Ohio, and Illinois, the message on the maneuvers was the same: "Kindly have them in some other
place less provocative of war." And from a mother of three in New
York: "Why send our navy to the Pacific? . . . Do you call that 'keeping
the forces within one's own borders'? . . . Our citizens do not want
war. . . . Don't forget that every peace treaty contains an unwritten clause,
setting the date for the next war."

Back in 1919, President Wilson had said that within a generation,
"with absolute certainty . . . there will be another world war." Eight years
to go—or less.

Despite the protests, the Pacific maneuvers of February–May 1935
went ahead as planned, at a location very close to the International Date
Line. Whether they acted as a deterrence or a provocation depended on
one's point of view. But though the protests were, in a large measure,
organized rather than spontaneous, they were not simply the incantations
of dogmatic antinavalists. Instead, as each nation struggled with the
depression, and as the world outside the United States grew more and
more worrying, the traditional U.S. response was emerging once again:
the isolationist instinct to bar the windows, lock the gates and doors, and,
above all, avoid getting involved—there were problems enough at home.
And on June 24, 1935, shortly after the end of the maneuvers, one of those
problems was thrust into the face of a disgusted U.S. public by the Nye
Report.

Summarizing thousands of pages of testimony and evidence, the preliminary report revealed corruption, conspiracy, and profiteering
throughout the munitions industry, often actively assisted or connived at
by the Navy Department. According to the report, munitions and shipbuilding companies had periodically created war scares to boost their own
trade; during World War I, when a profit of about 5 percent was regarded
as acceptable, they had taken typical profits of 22 to 39 percent, even
ranging up to 90 percent; and "the committee finds no assurance in the
wartime history of these companies to lead it to believe that they would
suddenly change their spots in the case of another war."[4]

The scandalous revelations intensified isolationism; the idea of businesses making vast amounts of money from war was too repugnant for
most people to take. Not for a century and a quarter, since the time of

Thomas Jefferson, had the American people been so inclined to withdraw from the world. Simultaneously in Britain, a world of worries brought out the policy of appeasement, fobbing off dictators, daring to trust them; and so the two great Anglo-Saxon nations stood back in 1934 as Hitler organized a Nazi revolt in Vienna. They stood back in 1935 as (contrary to the Versailles Treaty) he reintroduced conscription in Germany, ordered the construction of submarines, and reclaimed the Saarland bordering France and Luxembourg. And in 1936 they stood back as he remilitarized the Rhineland; as General Franco began a civil war in Spain; as Mussolini annexed Ethiopia; and as Japan abrogated the Washington and London naval treaties.

"Japan has no intention of constructing a Navy which will be a menace to other nations," the American naval attaché in Tokyo reported on March 1, 1937. The optimistic words were not his own, but quoted from a radio speech made by Vice Admiral Yamamoto, now vice minister of the navy as well. Japan, the admiral continued,

> believes that they [the other naval nations of the world] should not take any steps towards instigating a naval construction race. However, Japan cannot but equip herself with a naval strength sufficient to defend herself, in the event that other powers plan to expand to the extent of becoming a menace to her.[5]

In other words, Japan was going to build and to threaten, but was not going to accept the responsibility for it.

Eighty days later, the New York Times' correspondent Hugh Byas interviewed Adm. Mitsumasa Yonai, Japan's navy minister. "The Japanese Navy declares without reserve that it contemplates no armament programs whatever that might menace other countries," Yonai stated. "The Navy adheres to the fundamental principle of non-menace and non-aggression."[6]

Whether Yonai and Yamamoto were lying or misinformed is a complex question, probably beyond answer: Both were honorable men, and, while they could, they honestly and adamantly opposed a Japanese-American war. But even before the limitation treaties had expired, Japan—in great secrecy—was building midget submarines and the mighty Yamato class of superbattleships, with their 18.1-inch guns. The maximum gun size permitted under treaty was 16 inches. Adding 2 inches to the diameter may not sound much; but an 18-inch shell possessed 30 percent more hitting power than the legal 16-inch shell. With the passing in the United States of the 1934 Vinson-Trammell Act, the Japanese navy had decided that since it could not outbuild the United States in quantity, it would build ships of incomparable quality.

If the two admirals' remarks revived any sense of trust or hope abroad, it was soon shattered. On July 7, 1937 (less than three months after Yamamoto's speech, and less than three weeks after Yonai's interview), the "China incident" began as Japan commenced seven years of undeclared war against its giant, disorganized, and primitive neighbor. For the United States, there was one reassuring figure to remember. Despite its relative slip in surface and submarine vessels after the treaties, the U.S. Navy had become very well off in carrier-borne aircraft. Great Britain had 204; Japan had 461; but America had 709. Preparation in naval air and distance from the enemy were factors which, it seemed, had to give *some* security. Less optimistic or more realistic, the French ministries of the navy and of the air had already had bombproof underground quarters prepared "into which," as the U.S. naval attaché in Paris reported, "they can move at a moment's notice." Giving lunch on September 20, 1937, to Commandant Batet (chief of the military cabinet of Admiral Darlan, who was in turn chief of staff of the French navy), the attaché noted too that "Batet is convinced that France will be at war inside of two years, and wagered a luncheon with the writer to that effect."[7]

As Japan's undeclared war in China became more intense, focusing especially on Shanghai with its international business settlement, Roosevelt warned Americans in China that they should leave for their own safety. If anything happened to them or their property, he said, "the United States has no intention of going to war either with China or Japan . . . but instead would demand redress and indemnities through orthodox friendly, diplomatic channels."[8] The man on the spot (the U.S. Navy's new Commander in Chief, Asiatic Fleet) was Adm. Harry E. Yarnell. Just five years earlier he had successfully "attacked" Pearl Harbor. Now the fleet under his command was small (only two cruisers, thirteen destroyers, six submarines, and ten gunboats to show the flag through the whole western Pacific), but on September 27 he sent an order to all his vessels contradicting the president's "friendly, diplomatic" policy:

"Most American citizens now in China are engaged in businesses or professions which are their only means of livelihood," said Yarnell. "These persons are unwilling to leave until their businesses have been destroyed or they are forced to leave due to actual physical danger. Until such time comes our naval forces cannot be withdrawn without failure in our duty and without bringing great discredit on the United States Navy."[9]

What was this? Americans living in China had been warned by the president to leave, or take the risk on their own responsibility; yet here was a senior naval officer giving them, in effect, a promise of active naval protection in the event of trouble. He was also, of course, giving a challenge to those Americans at home who would have left their countrymen to stew. Quite properly, Yarnell reported his order to Washington; and he may have been surprised when he was not countermanded by the president. The reason was simple. In the United States, public reaction to Yarnell's initiative was good, and Roosevelt used it. On October 5 he inserted a celebrated extemporaneous remark into a prepared speech: "When an epidemic of physical disease starts to spread, the community approves and joins in a quarantine of the patients in order to protect the health of the community." Listeners swiftly understood who he meant.

Since October 21, 1936, Italy and Germany had been joined by a secret protocol outlining their common foreign policy—a link which Mussolini soon publicly referred to as the Axis. Since November 25, 1936, Japan and Germany had been joined publicly by the Anti-Comintern Pact, ostensibly aimed at containing international communism. Then, on November 6, 1937, Italy joined the Anti-Comintern Pact. Hitler triumphantly announced the creation of the Tripartite Alliance, and the consequences of Yarnell's defiant order came quickly. On December 12, 1937, in a 60-mile stretch of river far up the Yangtze, Japanese shore batteries and military aircraft bombed and fired on a British merchant ship, four British gunboats, and a U.S. gunboat from Yarnell's small fleet. The British vessels were hit by fire, and one enlisted man was killed; but the American gunboat *Panay* was sunk, and many of her crew were wounded as they struggled ashore through aerial machine-gun fire. Following an investigation led by Adm. Yamamoto, the Japanese government was quick to apologize. Joseph C. Grew, the American ambassador in Japan, was intensely relieved, "yet," he wrote in his diary, "I cannot look into the future with any feeling of serenity."[10]

His forebodings were well founded. Already reports were coming from China of appalling Japanese atrocities in the city of Nanking. That was where the British merchant ships had been bombed, and *Panay* had been only 30 miles or so further upstream. Two days after those events, the sack of the city began, and it was so horrible that many people could not believe what they heard. But on February 9, 1938, Admiral Yarnell had a lunchtime visitor—George Fitch, an American born in China and perfectly fluent in Chinese. In his diary, Yarnell noted how Fitch told him what had begun in Nanking on December 14, 1937:

> The reports of atrocities were not exaggerated, but on the other hand, were understated. Slaughter of men, ex-soldiers and others, by the thousands. Innumerable cases of rape, and in many cases, murder and mutilation of the women afterwards. Wholesale looting indulged in by the officers and men alike. Little control exercised over the men by the officers. Men were rounded up and machine-gunned in droves, then gasoline poured over dead & wounded & set

on fire. Other prisoners used for bayonet practice. Mr. Fitch said that he never dreamed that any so-called civilized race of people could show the inhumanity and sadism shown by the Jap. troops in Nanking.[11]

Even today, Japanese school history books skate around this subject, but in the War Crimes Trials, it was all proved to be true. Before World War II, the Rape of Nanking was the worst single documented episode of atrocity in history. It was also a mere rehearsal.

In January 1938 Britain and the United States came to a secret agreement to the effect that if the Japanese made any southward move, the U.S. fleet would concentrate at Pearl Harbor while a British battle fleet would be based at Singapore. In March, Representative Carl Vinson of Georgia (originator of the act to bring the Navy up to treaty strength) brought forward a bill to increase it by a further 20 percent over ten years. And in the same month, Adolf Hitler annexed his own native country, Austria, to Germany. A plebiscite in early April gave the operation a veneer of legality; but the Nazis' achievements, and their mood of demented pride, were more accurately sketched by a poster for the plebiscite. It said:

Step by step
  Adolf Hitler
    is tearing apart the dictated Treaty of Versailles!

1933 Germany leaves the League of Nations of Versailles.
1934 Reconstruction of the Wehrmacht, the Navy and the Luftwaffe begun!
1935 Saarland brought back home! Armed power of the Reich regained!
1936 Rhineland completely liberated!
1937 The myth of war guilt ceremoniously extinguished!
1938 Germany and Austria united in the Reich! Greater Germany achieved!

Therefore on 10 April the whole of Germany will acknowledge their liberator
Adolf Hitler
                    All say: YES![12]

Throughout the summer of 1938 information flowed into the Washington-based Office of Naval Intelligence from the attachés in Tokyo and Berlin. From each capital came the same message: The Axis nations were arming, but did not want a war with the United States. Some reports, or sections of reports, stand out.

Tokyo, 13 April: "The [Japanese] Navy is not building any superdread-nought and has at present no intention of doing so." Although it came from the navy minister, the statement was simply untrue: *Yamato,* the biggest battleship ever built, displacing nearly 72,000 tons at full load, was commenced in 1937, and her sister *Musashi* in 1938.

In the same report, a retired Japanese naval officer "in conversation . . . with a reliable source stated that a Japanese-American war is now out of the question." But further on, the same officer remarked that "the present world situation may lead to a war between democratic and totalitarian states, and in this Japan would oppose America in the Pacific . . . and felt no doubt of the ultimate victory of the Japanese Navy."[13]

Berlin, 22 June: "It is not believed that Germany, government or people, want war. The building up of the armed forces is primarily for a show of German strength at diplomatic conferences . . ."[14]

Against this optimism, there was pessimistic caution as well.

Tokyo, June: "The Japanese are going places. For the present the United States has not much to fear. But when Japan has consolidated her gains in China several years hence, a clash with her is inevitable."[15]

In April 1938, as part of Fleet Problem XIX, Vice Adm. Ernest J. King (Commander Aircraft, Battle Force) repeated Yarnell's exploit of 1932, with a second and equally successful mock attack against Pearl Harbor, launched from unnoticed vessels north of Oahu. On both occasions, the judgment was that if the attack had been real, it would have succeeded; yet the "if" was so large that few people considered it worth taking seriously. It was an interesting exercise, and that was all.

"Throughout the last war," wrote Capt. D. J. Munro, R.N., to his friend Rear Adm. Harold D. Cooke, U.S.N., "the two navies co-operated with each other in a perfectly charming manner; to our mutual benefit and instruction."[16] With optimistic implications of future cooperation, that was written in August 1938. In September of that year, some truly believed their fears of war had been dissolved; British Prime Minister Neville Chamberlain visited Hitler three times, returning on the last occasion (September 28–29) with a heartening faith that "peace in our time" would continue.

But at once the German dictator's troops entered the Sudetenland, the German-speaking area of north Czechoslovakia; and within two months, the U.S. naval attaché in Tokyo reported (on November 28):

> . . . the aftermath of that Conference [between Chamberlain and Hitler] gave Japan added confidence in its ability to see the China War through to the desired end. Where first she stepped rather gingerly, fearing at almost any moment intervention or some other

action by Third Powers, the results of the Munich Conference confirmed her belief that England, whom she most feared, was for the time being impotent. . . . Nevertheless, that intangible, uncertain power, the United States, still remained.

And then the attaché described in detail a benefit Japan was finding in China. "The Japanese Navy has been engaged in a quasi-naval war for the past sixteen months," he pointed out. "While her battle fleet has not been in actual fleet combat, nevertheless it cannot but have profited insofar as efficiency is concerned . . ."

As far as he could learn, Japanese warships had been operating fully manned, ammunitioned, and supplied, cruising at high speed during daylight and darkened at night; performing blockade duty, sometimes in actual combat; cooperating with the army; developing convoy work; and conducting minesweeping, antiaircraft defense, escort duty, and landing operations. The naval establishment as a whole had benefited too, increasing every year; and "last, and most important of all factors tending towards the developing of the efficiency of the navy, has been the opportunity given to Japan for employing in actual combat that newest weapon of all, naval aircraft."

The attaché felt very strongly about this. "Consider," he wrote, "the position of the Japanese Navy in this respect: from August 12th 1937 her naval aircraft have been continuously employed in combat operations." Detailing the many types of operation, he pointed out that "while aircraft losses have been heavy, the experience gained must have been invaluable. This applies not only to operational experience but also to the development of material."

In personnel, experience, and equipment, he reckoned that Japanese naval aircraft probably led the world. Finally, assessing "Japan's Naval Strategy in a War with a Major Power," he declared:

> She undoubtedly would not hesitate to undertake offensive operations but not beyond supporting distance of her strategically excellent geographical position. By this is meant that Hong Kong, Singapore, Dutch East Indies, Philippines, Borneo, Guam, Aleutian Islands and possibly the Hawaiian Islands would be in jeopardy . . .[17]

The report was passed on for official assessment. And the official assessment said that, while Hong Kong and all the others would be probable targets in the event of a war with Japan, the Hawaiian Islands were indeed possible; but not very plausible. Today one can only marvel at the attaché's thorough professionalism and regret that the authorities at home did not recognize what an intelligent man he was.

· · ·

Following the Nye Report, with its revelations of profiteering by munitions manufacturers, Congress had passed a series of Neutrality Acts intended to keep America out of anyone else's wars. Over the winter of 1938–39, in the same mood of fearful defensiveness, the House and Senate debated a series of measures designed to improve the safety of various air, submarine, and naval bases. One of these was the island of Guam, in the otherwise Japanese-held Mariana group about 1,400 miles south of Tokyo. Japanese press reaction was swift: "If such a plan is adopted," said the influential newspaper *Asahi Shimbun,* "it would be done only with a hostile move against Japan in mind."[18]

"Typically Japanese," the American naval attaché snorted. "The bill for the construction of bases is held as a measure of 'fortification' (while Japan's huge expenditures at Saipan, Palan and elsewhere are ignored). . . . In their coloring of the news by distorted presentation of it, facts are blandly ignored. . . . Sketches of maps are even distorted to place Guam practically off Tokyo Bay."[19]

Nevertheless, concerned about provoking the Japanese, Congress whittled the money for Guam down and down and eventually struck it off the bill altogether.

"We have learned," said President Roosevelt on January 4, 1939, "that when we deliberately try to legislate neutrality, our neutrality laws may operate unevenly and unfairly—may actually give aid to an aggressor and deny it to the victim."[20] He had realized that, from the best of motives, the initiative in an unstable world could easily be thrown away; and at the end of March 1939, on behalf of Great Britain, Prime Minister Neville Chamberlain did just that. On the fifteenth of that month, German armies entered the Czech capital of Prague, finally goading Chamberlain too far. In an abrupt turnaround of policy he gave up appeasement. On March 31 both Britain and France guaranteed Poland against aggression—thus leaving the ultimate decision entirely in German hands.

On the same day, Japan annexed the small but strategically important Spratly Islands in the South China Sea—only 700 miles from Singapore, the keystone of Britain's Far Eastern defense system. However, within ten days, the U.S. naval attaché in Tokyo felt able to report that "it is within the realm of possibility that the Navy, headed by Admiral Yonai, will be the stumbling block to the Army's militaristic plans."[21] The attaché was being optimistic, but not unduly so, for while Japan's army rampaged through China and Manchuria, its navy was sharply split, with many officers uncritically supporting almost any war plan and a small but influential group remaining in determined opposition.

On April 7 Italian forces invaded Albania. In these chaotic weeks— with Germans in Austria and Czechoslovakia, Italians in Albania and Ethiopia, Japanese in China and Manchuria, and British policy turned

A Japanese eye view of Pearl Harbor as a torpedo hits U.S.S. *West Virginia* (December 7, 1941). "We had considered an air raid…as a very remote possibility," Admiral Kimmel wrote five days later, "…but the first attack wave was practically unopposed."

"Those splendid ships—lost…": With decks awash and superstructure ablaze, *West Virginia* was one of three battleships completely disabled at Pearl Harbor. The U.S. Navy was thus forced to adopt a carrier-centered strategy.

Despite the instinctive urge to direct every effort against Japan alone, the United States remained true to the promise of "Germany first." Across an unusually (and deceptively) tranquil Atlantic, a convoy heads for Britain.

History's first carrier-versus-carrier battle was fought in the Coral Sea (May 7–8, 1942). Strategically it was an American victory, tactically a draw. As U.S.S. *Lexington* burns uncontrollably, sailors scramble down ropes to waiting destroyers. Not a man was lost from her crew.

Made possible by superlative intelligence work, the critical Battle of Midway (June 4, 1942) was an overwhelming U.S. victory: Japan lost four heavy carriers, one heavy cruiser, 322 planes, and 3,500 men, against an American loss of one heavy carrier (*Yorktown,* pictured here), 150 planes, and 307 men.

During the Battle for Leyte Gulf, U.S.S. *Suwannee*'s wardroom was converted to an emergency sick bay—a scene repeated in almost every naval encounter. And these men were the lucky ones.

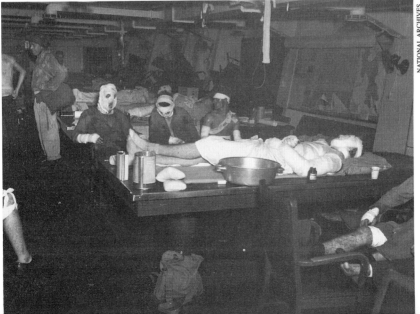

The instant before a kamikaze hits U.S.S. *Missouri* (April 11, 1945), sailors duck or stare in horrified fascination. The attack had only limited success: five months later the same ship was used to receive Japan's surrender.

With her antiaircraft armament bristling, U.S.S. *Pennsylvania* leads *Colorado, Louisville, Portland,* and *Columbia* into Lingayen Gulf in the Philippines (January 1945). All but *Colorado* had fought in the Battle for Surigayo Strait, where *Louisville* was Oldendorf's flagship.

Landing craft carry troops toward Iwo Jima, the "island fortress" (February 19, 1945). In the ensuing five-week shore battle, U.S. forces endured nearly 30 percent casualties (6,812 dead, 19,189 wounded), while of the 23,000 Japanese defenders, only 1,083 were taken alive.

Iwo Jima's unexpectedly tough resistance delayed the assault on Okinawa by a month. Taking part in the blistering preinvasion bombardment (March 31, 1945), this LCI (Landing Craft, Infantry) was one of 1,450 vessels deployed against the island. Lasting from April 1 to June 21, the shore battle claimed the lives of nearly 8,000 Americans, at least 24,000 Okinawan civilians, and perhaps 131,000 Japanese.

After Japan's surrender, carrier task groups of the victorious Third Fleet steam unmolested toward Tokyo, seeming to cover the entire ocean.

In the last moments before the formalities of national surrender, Japan's delegates, led by Foreign Minister Mamoru Shigemitsu, wait by U.S.S. *Missouri*'s 16-inch guns (September 2, 1945).

As the United States' representative, and marking the U.S. Navy's greatest victory, Adm. Chester W. Nimitz—promoted three months later to the rank of fleet admiral—signs the instrument of Japanese surrender.

Korea: Going in. Four months after Soviet-equipped North Korean troops opened the war with their invasion of South Korea, 50,000 U.N. troops were landed at Wonsan by over a hundred ships (October 26, 1950).

Korea: Getting out. 105,000 U.N. troops and 91,000 Korean civilian refugees were evacuated from Hungnam under U.S.S. *Missouri*'s protective fire. As witnessed by this U.S. Navy patrol frigate, all supplies remaining in the dock area were destroyed by naval demolition teams (December 28, 1950). The war was to end in a stalemate.

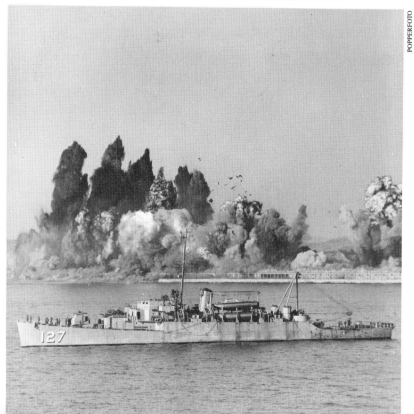

Cuba, 1962: Taken by a U-2 reconnaissance plane and analytically labeled by photographic intelligence, this picture of a medium-range ballistic missile base at Sagua La Grande was typical of many placed before a shocked and frightened American public.

Introduced in the mid-1960s and capable of 30 knots, small, light PCFs (Patrol Craft, Fast) soon became known as "swift boats." Ranging South Vietnam's myriad waterways—not only around Saigon, as pictured, but far up rivers into the jungles as well—they helped prevent the entry of Viet Cong military supplies from Cambodia.

Meanwhile, in more familiar waters, the Cold War continued. Here in the Mediterranean (January 1968), a Soviet *Kynda*-class cruiser shadows the U.S. aircraft carrier *Franklin D. Roosevelt.*

In the Gulf of Tonking (October 1968), discharge from the steam catapult on U.S.S. *Coral Sea*'s flight deck marks the launch of an A-3 Skywarrior on a bombing mission over North Vietnam.

A U.S. Army UH-1E Iroquois medical evacuation helicopter prepares to lift a wounded soldier from the banks of the Vietnamese Vam Co Tay River (February 1969), while U.S. Navy ATCs (armored troop carriers) provide security.

With the Vietnam War lurching to its end, many South Vietnamese naval vessels fled, bearing refugees. Tied together in Subic Bay Naval Base in Manila, this flotilla was among thirty-three such vessels appropriated in international waters by the U.S. Navy in the first three weeks of May 1975.

Vietnam marked the United States' first national military defeat; but in the summer of 1975, under grandstands emblazoned with the names of past U.S. naval conquests, there was no sense of irony when officer cadets at Annapolis celebrated graduation with a traditional gesture of joyous abandon.

"Under way on nuclear power": Capable of over 20 knots and with a submerged displacement of 4,640 tons, the 292-foot U.S.S. *Parche* (SSN 683) goes through initial sea trials in the Gulf of Mexico.

Seen here off the coast of California in 1981, U.S.S. *Constellation* (CV 64) is one of the largest warships in the world: length, 1,046 feet; full load displacement, 80,800 tons; top speed, over 30 knots; total crew, 5,300; approximately 85 aircraft; flight deck area, 4½ acres.

After twenty-nine years in reserve, U.S.S. *Missouri* (BB 63)—site of Japan's surrender in 1945—was renovated and, in May 1986, recommissioned. Here she marks the seventy-fifth anniversary of the Royal Australian Navy (1987) with a broadside salute from her nine 16-inch guns.

"An era of violent peace": On January 6, 1988, with a U.S. Navy helicopter overhead and an escort of three U.S. Navy frigates (*Gallery, McClusky,* and, in the foreground, *Elrod*), three reflagged Kuwaiti tankers approach the Strait of Hormuz—the United States' twenty-third convoy in the southern Arabian Gulf.

upside down—the U.S. Navy was working through Fleet Problem XX, based this time east of the Panama Canal, in the Caribbean. The ships were scheduled thereafter to go to New York for the World's Fair; yet on April 14, several weeks ahead of schedule and without warning or explanation, President Roosevelt ordered them back to their normal bases, mostly in the Pacific.

"He doesn't need to say anything," ex–Secretary of State Henry L. Stimson observed to his successor, Cordell Hull. "The movement of the fleet is a language which the Axis powers well understand."[22]

The prominent Japanese newspaper *Hochi Shimbun* was in no doubt: "It is nothing short of a demonstration or threat against Japan." And the same article added defiantly: "If the United States thinks that by sending a fleet to the Pacific it can to any extent restrain Japan's actions, nothing could be more mistaken."[23]

In fact, at that very time U.S. naval policy was undergoing a radical change. If the worst possibility became reality, the traditional color-coded plans for coping with individual aggressor nations would not be enough. For the first time since the U.S. conquest of the Philippines in 1898, planners were facing the possibility of simultaneous war in two oceans. Preparing to resist a multiple threat, the original single-color codes had to be blended; and after five months of review, the aptly named "Rainbow" recommendations were produced. There were five Rainbow plans in all, covering different permutations of enemy and attack. Rainbows 2 and 3 assumed no U.S. involvement in the Atlantic. The other three assumed the U.S. Navy would have to "carry out the operations of an Atlantic War," Rainbow 5 going so far as to recommend that the main weight of the fleet's offensive power should be in the Atlantic.[24]

With this plan, the Pacific force would be held at three quarters the size of Japan's navy and would play a defensive role—even if it meant the loss of Guam and the Philippines. Meanwhile, the Atlantic force would protect the Panama Canal, the Caribbean, the transatlantic shipping lanes, and the Atlantic seaboard, and fight in the eastern Atlantic, Europe, and Africa.

Rainbow 5 was prepared not a moment too soon. Shortly before dawn on Friday, September 1, 1939, one and a half million German soldiers began Hitler's invasion of Poland. Two days later, Admiral Yarnell noted in his diary that the weather in Washington on Sunday, September 3, was fair and warm. He also noted that, honoring its promise to Poland, "England declared war on Germany." France did so as well; and there was another matter of close concern for the admiral—"SS *Athenia* of Donald Line reported torpedoed and sinking 200 miles off NW coast of Ireland. Bound from Liverpool for Montreal with 1,400 Americans on board."[25] He was not quite right: There were 1,400 passengers, of whom only 316 were American. But twenty-eight of those, and ninety other passengers, were drowned.

War in Europe and the deaths of American citizens—they must have a consequence. Yet all of it was so far away it scarcely seemed real. And for a while, even some of those far closer to the scene managed not to realize that anything much had happened. Capt. Stuart Smith, U.S.N., was sixty-five years old at the time; he had been retired for seventeen years and in September 1939 happened to be visiting friends in England. Spending a few days and a lot of dollars in the Ritz Hotel in the middle of London, he wrote in his daily diary: "Sunday September 3rd—Up late. Did not go out. Believe there was an air raid alarm about 11.30 but did nothing about it."

Ten minutes before that alarm, the prime minister had declared war against Germany. Smith clearly did not read any newspapers that morning or listen to the wireless, and the staff of the hotel presumably saw no reason to alarm their guest unduly. Without further comment, his diary continues: "Lunched and dined in grill. Monday September 4th—Air raid alarm about 2.30 A.M. Went down to shelter (the grill room lounge)—only about a score or so of guests in the hotel. Back to bed. Up about noon & saw in the Times that *war had been declared about 24 hours earlier!* War begins!"[26]

At the same time as Captain Smith was getting up to read the paper in London, the U.S. naval attaché in Rome called on his German counterpart, Capt. Werner Lovich, "to ask him what information he had on the reported torpedoing" of S.S. *Athenia.*[27] Lovich, the attaché reported, "was very much surprised and said he did not think it could possibly be true." Genuinely agitated, the German said that "the sinking of this ship without warning in the first few days of the war would be too horrible to contemplate."

"Probably just another rumor or false alarm," the American remarked, "like the false air alarms that London has been having." The German attaché had been prepared to believe that the London air alarms, sounded only minutes after the declaration of war, heralded real raids. He commented sardonically that "that is just the sort of show that Göring might put on. . . . Have the whole air force take off at the same time just to show what a large force he has." The U.S. attaché said again that he was glad the reported torpedoing was false—"That sort of thing," he pointed out, "would bring the United States into the war."

"Of course," said Lovich, and they parted company. Back in his own office, the U.S. officer found that the rumored sinking had been confirmed. Both he and Lovich had agreed that war with the United States must surely follow; but the next day, to overwhelming public support, President Roosevelt confirmed that the United States would remain neutral.

In Europe the decision was a surprise to many, and a shock to some; but Roosevelt could not really lead Americans to war when a very large section of them did not want to participate. However, at the same time, he began organizing an operation without precedent and without status in international law: an oceangoing "neutrality patrol."

Initially this covered the western Atlantic up to 300 miles from the coasts between Canada and the Guianas in South America. Despite its name, its function was unneutral, for if a U.S. warship sighted a belligerent vessel apparently intending to attack a European possession in the Western hemisphere, it would not only track the vessel but report its sighting in plain English. Formalized on October 2 by the Congress of American Republics in Panama, it placed the U.S. Navy in the unwelcome position of patrolling a very large area of sea under increasingly severe weather conditions, and without being able to do anything very active if a belligerent was sighted. On that day too, a warning came from Germany that all merchant ships in international waters could be stopped and searched—a move hardly calculated to please the United States. It had gone to war over that exact issue in 1812, and over a century later "Freedom of the Seas" had been the second of President Wilson's Fourteen Points.

In 1939 the German warning swung American public opinion toward a partial repeal of the Neutrality Acts, which among other things placed an embargo on arms trade with belligerents. Prime Minister Chamberlain had already told Roosevelt, "If the embargo is repealed . . . I am sure the effect on German morale will be devastating."[28] On November 4 the embargo went; France and Britain promptly placed large orders; but German morale, publicly at least, was entirely untouched.

"America is still not dangerous to us," Hitler declared. "The strengthening of our opponents by America is still not important."[29] From Berlin, the American naval attaché reported that "the present U.S. neutrality law . . . is being hailed by the German press as a model for all neutral nations to copy."[30]

There was, in fact, little reason for German morale to be shaken. After Poland had been crushed by the Nazi blitzkrieg, warlike activity in Europe through the winter of 1939–40 was so limited that isolationist Congressman William E. Borah coined the phrase "phony war"—or *Sitzkrieg,* as the wits had it. In private, President Roosevelt commented that his nation was "patting itself on the back every morning (and thanking God for the Atlantic Ocean and the Pacific Ocean)." He could see that for America, it was all fine and dandy. But would it continue like that? "My problem," the president concluded, "is to get the American people to think of conceivable consequences without scaring them into thinking they are going to be dragged into the war."[31]

10

*

IF YOU ATTACK US . . . WE
SHALL CRUSH YOU

As 1940 began, the British naval captain Donald Munro wrote to his American friend Adm. Cooke: "I gather a great many people think we are anxious to get the USA into the war, but this is not so. We don't want anyone to fight our battles, but they can keep the Japs in order and this is all we want."[1]

There were some British people—Winston Churchill among them—who wanted nothing more than to see the United States in the war on Britain's side; but Munro's view was, as always, a fair reflection of the current majority view. A little later he was writing again: "I expect there are a great many in the US Navy who would like to come over to continue the good work you did in the last war—but we don't want another Wilson, of that the nation is tired. No more Fourteen Points: we have had enough of that."[2]

Throughout 1940 Munro's letters (informal and unofficial as they were) reflected Britain's official attitude as the European war grew more desperate and the Pacific implications more urgent: an attitude of increasing hope and need for the direct involvement of the United States, offset by a deep reluctance to permit complete U.S. control. And certainly, as Munro guessed, some U.S. naval men did want to "continue the good work" at the first opportunity. For example, working the Neutrality Patrol, with most of the physical and mental stresses but none of the releases of war, U.S.S. *Broome* reported a German freighter, tracked it until a British warship arrived, and stood by while the freighter was sunk.

Shortly before then, the Office of Naval Intelligence (ONI) completed an estimate of the size of the world's seven major navies. This provided some intriguing comparisons. The Royal Navy, including the navies of the British Empire, still possessed the greatest tonnage overall (more than 1.3 million tons) and had a further 970,000 tons being built or authorized. The German navy included 204,000 tons, with over 250,000 tons being built or authorized. The U.S. Navy had just under 1.12 million tons, with a further 430,000 tons in preparation; and the Japanese navy (so the ONI estimated) had a little under 860,000 tons and was preparing 40,000 tons more.[3]

Assuming the figures for Japan and the United States were roughly correct, completion of the ships under construction and authorized would give Japan 900,000 tons and the United States 1.55 million—a 50,000-ton American advantage over the defunct 5:3 ratio. Adm. Harold R. Stark (Chief of Naval Operations since August 1, 1939) had announced that the United States would keep to the ratio system, and intelligence indicated that the speed and amount of construction was about right.

Naturally the Japanese thought otherwise, as an editorial in the *Osaka Mainichi* indicated:

> The fact that [the United States] adheres to the ratio plainly shows its intention to conduct overseas operations against Japan. The fundamental strategy of the Japanese Navy is based on non-menace and non-aggression. . . . It is doubtful whether provocative naval expansion by America will contribute towards the promotion of peace in the Pacific.[4]

Many other newspapers expressed a similar conviction, and "from the foregoing," the observant U.S. naval attaché in Tokyo reported, "it is clear that the Japanese are really concerned over this latest aspect of the naval problems. The Japanese people have been made to feel that the United States is building a strong aggressive navy for the sole purpose of attacking Japan in her home waters . . ."

In fact, the figures were wildly out—in Japan's favor. For eighteen months the Imperial Navy had maintained absolute silence about its building works, and the ONI estimates for Japan stopped at May 18, 1938. Thus, quite apart from smaller vessels, they said that at a time when the U.S. Navy had fifteen battleships in existence and a further half dozen in preparation, Japan had ten complete and none either being built or authorized. Actually, the superbattleships *Yamato* and *Musashi* (which would displace almost 72,000 tons each) were already under construction and, before the end of 1941, would be launched and working toward completion.

". . . and," the U.S. naval attaché concluded, "the Japanese Navy can be expected to use this public feeling to the utmost to obtain more appropriation for building up the Japanese fleet."[5]

On April 2, 1940, in the neighborhood of Hawaii, the American fleet's Pacific maneuvers began. One week later the "phony war" in Europe came to a sudden end with the German invasion of Denmark and Norway; Denmark capitulated within four hours. On May 1, as Japanese forces launched wider offensive operations in China, Roosevelt appealed to still-neutral Italy not to enter the war, and Mussolini told the U.S. ambassador in Rome, William Philips, that Germany could not be defeated militarily. "Fifteen countries can now be called upon by Germany for every kind of supplies," the Duce said. "The blockade of the Allies is therefore completely ineffective."[6]

On May 9 the Pacific Fleet was scheduled to return to the West Coast; but two days before that, the president took a fateful decision. Until further notice, the fleet would remain at Pearl Harbor—"because of the deterrent effect," its commanding officer was later told by Admiral Stark, "which it is thought your presence may have on the Japs going into the East Indies."[7]

On May 10 the industrious naval attaché in Rome reported again: "The German Naval Attaché called at 1150 this morning by appointment. Germany invaded Belgium, Holland and Luxembourg this morning at 0300 . . ."

As befitted diplomats, the meeting between the two attachés was (according to the American's report) courteous, even downbeat: "I said that it was too bad that countries like these should have to bear the brunt of war; they had not in any way been connected with the causes which led to the war. . . . I said that the invasion of these neutral countries would make a very bad impression in America." Lovich (the German attaché) had thought of that and "wondered if it would bring America into the war." The American carefully did not say no; instead he replied that "America definitely did not want to go to war or to get mixed up in European politics, if it could be avoided." He then allowed himself to show his disapproval with a taunt, couched in appropriate language: "I said to Lovich that he was a sailorman of the old school and that I could not believe that he approved of the invasion of these small neutral countries. For a moment he appeared not to have understood. When I repeated the statement, he flushed slightly, appeared confused and said that he had hoped neutrals would not be involved."[8]

In Great Britain that same day, Neville Chamberlain resigned as prime minister, to be succeeded by Winston Churchill. Eleven days later (May 21), the German army was on the shores of the English Channel. So far, the government in Washington had assumed that whatever else happened, France and Britain would hold out. Now, suddenly and shockingly, it seemed they might both fall beneath the unstoppable lightning war—they, and their navies. Many of the ships would doubtless be lost (bombed, torpedoed, even scuttled in defiance) but much of the 2 million tons of Allied naval shipping would be sure to survive—possibly to be turned against America.

"The U.S. is at last profoundly moved and frightened," wrote Lord Lothian, Britain's ambassador in Washington, to a friend. "The old isolationism is dead. Nobody is against a vast armament programme. . . . We shall doubtless get what help we want, short of war. But USA won't enter the war, unless and until its own vital interests are affected."[9]

In Washington decisions were made rapidly: First priority should be given to Rainbow 4, the defense of both North and South America, with the main part of the fleet based in the Caribbean, a holding force left in the Pacific, and no Pacific involvement beyond the 180th meridian.

In that month's issue of the magazine *Contemporary Japan,* Masanori Ito, an important naval writer, published an article summarized by the all-seeing U.S. naval attaché in Tokyo:

1. The United States Navy is too big for "legitimate" defensive purposes. 2. The latest US vessels have "unusual cruising power" in contrast to Japanese vessels. 3. This shows that the US fleet is aggressive, the Japanese fleet defensive in general character. 4. The United States should revise her naval policy and maintain a "defensive" navy.[10]

"We are very glad," Captain Munro wrote to Admiral Cooke, "that your fleet is keeping the other 'mad dog' quiet in the East. . . . If your fleet was not in the Pacific the Far East would be in an uproar."[11]

The United States was even then on the brink of an enormous revision of naval policy—but not of the nature Ito wanted. On June 1 the keel of U.S.S. *Washington* was laid down, the first U.S. battleship to be commenced since 1921. Nine days later, Mussolini declared war on France and Britain; Italian troops invaded France; and in a speech to the graduating class of the University of Virginia, President Roosevelt announced:

We will extend to the opponents of force the material resources of this nation, and, at the same time, we will harness and speed up the use of those resources in order that we ourselves in America may have equipment and training equal to the task of any emergency, and every defense.[12]

The next few days showed what he meant and the dread now felt in American hearts; for as Paris fell on June 14 the president signed an act to expand the Navy by 11 percent, then, on June 17, the Chief of Naval

Operations, Admiral Stark, asked Congress for a further 70 percent expansion of the Navy at a cost of $4 billion. This—the largest procurement in American naval history—would add 200 ships to the 488 existing or under construction, meeting the likely demands of war in two oceans. At any other time such a bill would have been impossible; now, however, it shot through to authorization on July 20 and appropriation on September 9. But construction of the ships would not be completed until 1946.

"Japan is getting out of hand," Munro wrote to Cooke, "and we look to you to put a 'brake on' their activities. . . . If the Japs were finally convinced you would not come in, they would join the Hun."[13]

Thus, while France surrendered to Germany and Italy and Britain fought alone, the "short of war" policy predicted by Lord Lothian took shape, designed to aid Britain, deter Japan, and gain time for U.S. rearmament. On June 27, 1940, Roosevelt declared a state of national emergency; on July 2 Congress gave him the discretionary ability to prohibit the export of any war material in the interest of national defense; and on July 5 he banned the unlicensed shipment of strategic minerals, chemicals, aircraft parts, and engines to Japan, extending the embargo on July 31 to include aviation fuel. At the same time U.S. liaison with the British began to grow closer. As a young officer during the First World War, the current CNO (Admiral Stark) had worked with the redoubtable Admiral Sims in London, and now neither Stark nor the president wanted to repeat the handicaps created in those days by delays in planning. So, with orders dated July 30, Rear Adm. Robert L. Ghormley left for Britain early in August to be a "Special Naval Observer." In August came an agreement between the president and Prime Minister Mackenzie King of Canada, whereby each country was able to use the other's naval facilities, and on September 5 *The New York Times* carried banner headlines:

ROOSEVELT TRADES DESTROYERS FOR SEA BASES;
TELLS CONGRESS HE ACTED ON HIS OWN AUTHORITY;
BRITAIN PLEDGES NEVER TO YIELD OR SINK FLEET

British people were thrilled. "It would be impossible," reported the newspaper's London correspondent, "to overstate the jubilation in official and unofficial circles caused today by President Roosevelt's announcement that fifty United States destroyers were coming to help Great Britain in her hour of peril."[14]

The bases (leased for ninety-nine years) were in Bermuda, the West Indies, and Newfoundland, and the destroyers were overage vessels from the First World War. "For this old iron we have had to pay with several very important bases on our territory," Lloyd George grumbled, ". . . but what could we do? There was no other way out."[15]

Despite such complaints, the elderly ships were a vital short-term plug, replacing victims of the U-boats commanded by Vice Adm. Karl Dönitz. More important, the exchange signaled a growing transatlantic closeness; but the month's most important event for the long term took place carefully shaded from the glare of publicity.

Although the ace code breaker Herbert O. Yardley had ended his career in disgrace, and although his "Black Chamber" had been closed, the study and application of signal intelligence had never fully halted. Likewise, the creation and development of ever more sophisticated codes had continued. Germany had its Enigma encoding and decoding machine, shared for a while by Japan and known to American code busters as the Red machine. Then, on February 20, 1939, the Japanese introduced an entirely new machine of their own invention, working between Tokyo and their embassy in Washington. They called it Type 97; the Americans called it Purple. For eighteen months it defied analysis—eighteen months of dedicated slogging at a task which would, to most people, be unimaginably intricate. The first breakthrough came in August 1940, and with that there soon followed (on September 25) the first complete decryption of a Purple message. After so much labor, all concerned found it an event of such breathtaking gratification that the process was instantly nicknamed "Magic."

The interception, decryption, and translation of worldwide secret Japanese diplomatic messages then began and would continue uninterrupted for many years. Each of the diplomatic messages was called a magic, with a small *m*; and one of the first and most sinister came on September 27. It revealed that Japan, Italy, and Germany had entered into the Tripartite Pact—a military and economic agreement "to establish and maintain a new order."[16]

"When Japan is convinced that America is going to declare war," the U.S. naval attaché in Rome reported on October 14, 1940, "Japan will capture the Dutch East Indies by a lightning stroke before America can send ships or forces there. When they get these islands"—and their vast oil reserves—"Japan will not be afraid of America or any combination of powers."[17]

November opened with a presidential break with tradition: Roosevelt was running for a third term in office, and won it on the fifth day of the month. Three days later S.S. *City of Rayville* hit a mine and sank in Australia's Bass Strait (the first U.S. merchant ship to be lost in the war and a savage indicator of how far the war could range from Europe) and as the New Year began, critical days and events tumbled past.

In January 1941 Congress reconvened to hear the president call for the United States to support the nations which defended the "Four Freedoms"—freedom of speech and religion, freedom from want and fear—

and to debate fiercely his proposed "Lend-Lease" program of arms credits "to those nations which are now in actual war with aggressor nations." In the last days of the month, following Admiral Ghormley's visit to London, conversations wrapped in profound secrecy began in Washington between senior staff officers of the armies and navies of the United States and Britain; and three letters were written in Pearl Harbor.

With effect from February 1, Adm. Husband E. Kimmel was appointed commander in chief of the U.S. fleet. On January 29, writing from the U.S.S. *Honolulu* to a friend, his first letter said: "I realize the great responsibility that accompanies the command." From the same ship to another friend, his second letter said: "I am sensible of the responsibility of the job, and hope that I can measure up to it." His third letter was written from the flagship *Pennsylvania* the day before he took up his command, and in it he said:

I am convinced that nothing should be left undone to provide for the most effective possible use, when needed, of all our aviation components in this area. . . . The objective of the Fleet will be to direct every effort towards realistic and practical joint air readiness.

Of those hopeful early letters, however, the one which now seems saddest was written to the CNO, Admiral Stark, concerning U.S. bases in the western Pacific, from Hawaii to Midway. "These bases," said Kimmel, "have much exceeded the initially contemplated developments and, on the whole, they are excellent, well designed for their intended purposes, represent a good job done under difficult circumstances, and will withstand a substantial enemy effort."[18]

"Swedish military attaché, in conversation with German Party member, was told that following conquest of England, Africa would be taken, followed by German exploitation of South America."

So reported the U.S. naval attaché in Berlin on February 15, 1941, adding that according to the party member, Germany's war was "now not only against England but also against US which is only strong force left against the New Order."[19]

In those months—as the United States continued to arm and the number of men registered for the draft passed 16.4 million; as the Neutrality Patrol continued its irksome, exhausting, and stressful work; and as the Atlantic Fleet was formally reconstituted—the diplomats continued to work. On January 27, 1941, the U.S. ambassador to Japan, Joseph C. Grew, noted in his diary: "There is a lot of talk around town to the effect that the Japanese, in case of a break with the United States, are planning to go all out in a surprise mass attack on Pearl Harbor. Of course I informed the government."[20]

In February Admiral Kichisaburo Nomura ("a man of high personal character," wrote Grew, "who through long association had my esteem and respect") presented his credentials as Japan's new ambassador to the United States and within days informed Roosevelt that there would be no war between their countries unless the United States wished it.[21] Simultaneously, the Germans and Italians prepared for a visit from Japan's foreign minister, Yosuke Matsuoka.

Through his colleague in Rome, the U.S. naval attaché in Berlin sent further information. Nazi party members might feel that the United States and Germany were effectively at war, but the Führer did not: "Hitler determined keep US out of the war. Japan assigned role of 'menace.' Hitler said worried over possibility action in Pacific by Japanese extremist group may involve US. . . . The Germans will attempt to explain to Matsuoka that after England's collapse, Germany will extend effective political and if necessary military aid to support Japan's claims."[22]

Within three days of that report, the secret staff discussions in Washington concluded with an agreement known as ABC-1 (American-British Conversations) which stated that if the United States came into the war, the Pacific would be defended while all forces would combine to defeat Hitler. "The question as to our entry into the war," wrote Admiral Stark to Admiral Kimmel, "now seems to be *when,* not *whether.*"[23]

Adm. Ernest J. King had been given charge of the reactivated Atlantic Fleet. His command included ships which were often overaged, crewed by men who were usually underexperienced, for operations which stretched them all. His Fleet Order of March 24, 1941, entitled "Making the Best of What We Have," gave his characteristic solution: "The difficulties and discomforts—personnel, material, operations, waiting—shall be dealt with as 'enemies' to be overcome—by our own efforts."[24]

The quality of their potential human enemies became horribly vivid on the night of April 3–4, when a convoy of twenty-two slow merchantmen carrying Lend-Lease equipment to Britain was ambushed by U-boats. Out of the twenty-two merchant ships, ten were sunk. "The situation is obviously critical in the Atlantic," Stark wrote to King. "In my opinion, it is hopeless except as we take strong measures to save it."[25] The CNO immediately arranged to transfer three battleships, one carrier, four cruisers, and two squadrons of destroyers from the Pacific to the Atlantic, for King was going to have to carry out the ABC-1 agreement in the Atlantic. But in spite of having that duty, he was not allowed to see its plans.

On April 9 his area of responsibility suddenly expanded further, when, on the invitation of the Danish minister in Washington, Greenland came under U.S. protection; the following day, for the first time in World War II, the U.S. Navy fired a shot in anger. The destroyer U.S.S. *Niblack,* rescuing survivors from a torpedoed Dutch freighter south of Iceland, detected a U-boat apparently preparing to attack, and dropped depth charges. They missed; but King approved the destroyer captain's action. On April 18, though Germany and the United States were still officially at peace, he ordered all ships and aircraft in his command to attack any Axis vessel within 25 miles of the U.S. East Coast.

Meanwhile, Hawaii—the center of Admiral Kimmel's area of command—contained many first- and second-generation Japanese immigrants. "From the American standpoint" (according to "a semi-official magazine supported by the Japanese Army"), "the most serious defect of Japanese immigrants is that they never forget that they are Japanese. . . . Hawaiian-born Japanese will never become Americanized. . . . On the surface, however, peace prevails."[26]

But not for long. On May 27 the president declared a state of unlimited national emergency. "The war," he said, "is approaching the brink of the Western Hemisphere. It is coming very close to home." One month later, as Hitler launched his gigantic and treacherous attack against the USSR, the cabinet of the Japanese government changed. "Japan will probably follow an increasingly independent course," the naval attaché in Tokyo predicted, "in order to settle the China Incident and consolidate her position on the continent before the European war is ended."[27] On July 8 further disturbing intelligence reports indicated that Japan's expansion into Southeast Asia would proceed, even if it brought war with Britain and America; and on July 21 Japanese troops occupied French Indochina. Five days later, U.S. policy in the Far East changed drastically: The former Army chief of staff, Gen. Douglas MacArthur, was named commander of U.S. forces in the Far East; the reinforcement of the Philippines was given first priority; and Japanese assets in the United States were frozen. From then on, unless the government in Tokyo compromised, war was certain to come.

Had any U-boat commander been in the vicinity of Newfoundland on Sunday, August 10, 1941, and had he managed to penetrate unobserved into Placentia Bay, he might have witnessed through the uncertain circle of his periscope a target that could have been disastrously tempting, a sight never seen before—the president of the United States, a neutral nation, being taken from the cruiser U.S.S. *Augusta* to the battleship H.M.S. *Prince of Wales* in order to join the prime minister of Great Britain, a nation at war, in worship. The Atlantic Conference began formally the following day, and on Tuesday the Atlantic Charter was concluded. It announced to the world, and to the still powerful isolationist forces in America, that Britain and the United States shared common principles of freedom and self-determination.

Still the possible enemy remained unconvinced. Masanori Ito contemplated Roosevelt's proposed "Two-Ocean Navy" and found little to fear. "The program is an improvised and hastily continued plan," he wrote in the August 1941 issue of *Contemporary Japan*. "It is problematical whether it can be carried out, the difficulties being a probable shortage of building materials and equipment . . . for here the question of preparedness comes in . . . [Overnight] no industrial country, however advanced, can convert peacetime industry to the production of such [essential arms-and armor-making] equipment."[28] Simultaneously, the magazine *Shufu-No-Tomo* publicized excerpts from a roundtable conference of Japanese naval flying officers. The U.S. naval attaché in Tokyo was particularly struck by "their emphasis on the importance of torpedo planes" and listed some of their remarks:

"The arms have been fully studied and experimented with since we were still cadets. . . . It takes only a little over ten seconds to dive aiming at an enemy ship and to release a hit, so that the enemy has scarcely time to respond to our assault. . . . The principle of the Navy is 'a decisive battle under air supremacy.' "

And, most ominously of all: "If an American warship is sunk by a submarine this very night, Japan and America will open fire against each other at once. *The time is already past when we can be considering whether a Japanese-American war will break out.* This must be fully recognized."[29]

The U.S. Marine Corps had been in occupation of Iceland since early July, and since the middle of that month U.S. warships had escorted ships of all non-Axis nations to and from the island. On September 1, 1941, this voluntary responsibility was extended to cover the whole western Atlantic. With U.S. destroyers already actively aiding the Royal Navy in the hunt for submarines, some incident between the United States and Germany was bound to occur; and on September 4 it came. The destroyer U.S.S. *Greer* located *U-652* about 125 miles southwest of Reykjavik. For more than nine hours, until ordered to cease, *Greer* tracked the submarine on sonar, guiding British aircraft to the scene. In that time each vessel attacked the other—*U-652* first, firing a torpedo shortly before 1 P.M., rapidly answered by a spread of depth charges from the destroyer. Neither vessel was damaged, but three days later in the distant Gulf of Suez *Steel Seafarer* (an American merchant ship) was sunk by German aircraft. Following these incidents President Roosevelt spelled out—to those of his countrymen who still doubted it—the "reality of relations with Germany."

"To be ultimately successful in world-mastery," he explained on September 11, "Hitler knows that he must get control of the seas. He must first destroy the bridge of ships which we are building across the

Atlantic. . . . He must wipe out our patrol." The president continued: "We have sought no shooting war with Hitler. We do not seek it now. But neither do we want peace so much that we are willing to pay for it by permitting him to attack our naval and merchant ships. . . . Let this warning be clear. From now on, if German or Italian vessels of war enter the waters the protection of which is necessary for American defense, they do so at their own peril."[30]

Was this, or was it not, war? In every way but the final, formal declaration, it was war, and from the day of the speech, U.S.S. *Belknap* kept a war diary. Every naval ship keeps such a diary when hostilities are officially declared, but *Belknap* was the only American warship to write a war diary before December 7, 1941. "United States declares war on Axis," one of the first entries noted. "Declaration made not in the obsolete formal exchange of diplomatic notes, but by the President's declaration of a 'shooting war' in his speech."[31] Roosevelt had indeed ordered his ships to shoot Axis vessels on sight; and as the CNO remarked: "So far as the Atlantic is concerned, we are all but, if not actually, in it. . . . Contacts are almost certain to occur. The rest requires little imagination."[32]

It seems now as if more and more U.S. attention was, understandably, being directed toward the Atlantic. But what of the Pacific? Captain Munro could imagine what might transpire, if not exactly how. "On the face of it," he wrote to the American Admiral Cooke late in September, "it is suicidal for Japan to challenge the might of the U.S. As I see it, Japan is beaten in China, her army has paid a heavy price without real result, her treasury is bankrupt, her economic situation is very bad, but her navy having done nothing has suffered not at all. In view of all this it is my guess there will be war, and the navy will be called upon to Save the Empire. Make no mistake about it, it is a highly efficient navy."[33]

Yet the distraction of the German navy could not be ignored. Ten minutes after midnight on the night of October 16–17, 1941, while steaming southwest of Iceland, the destroyer U.S.S. *Kearny* was torpedoed amidships by *U-568*. By exemplary use of damage control techniques, the destroyer's crew managed to get her to Reykjavik, but eleven men died— the first Americans to be killed in action in World War II. Later that same day, Gen. Hideki Tojo became prime minister of Japan; and on the last day of the month (Halloween, while children at home were threatening their neighbors with trick or treat) the U.S. Navy lost its first ship in this undeclared quasi-war. The twenty-one-year-old destroyer *Reuben James* was hit amidships, like *Kearny,* but the old ship's thinner plates barely protected her at all. She split in half, her bow section sinking instantly; and as Kapitänleutnant Erich Topp of *U-552* observed, the stern section was "atomized by powerful detonation of her own depth charges."[34] One hundred and fifteen officers and men died, blown to pieces, drowned, burned, or suffocated by oil as they swam.

"The Navy is already at war in the Atlantic," Stark wrote, then added gloomily: "But the country doesn't seem to realize it. Apathy, to the point of open opposition, is evident in a considerable section of the press." Secretary of the Interior Harold L. Ickes could not understand Roosevelt's reaction and noted: "Apparently the President is going to wait— God knows for how long or what." Yet a member of the German embassy in Washington had already realized exactly what was happening and reported to Berlin:

> The American Government, in contrast with Wilson in 1917, does not make the question of war or peace dependent upon incidents on the high seas, but uses these incidents, which by its policies have become unavoidable, to dramatize its propaganda in order to break down public opposition to its present course of action.[35]

On November 20, 1941, Admiral Kimmel received a letter from the CNO. "The next few days hold much for us," Stark wrote. Negotiations with Japan were becoming progressively more difficult, with proposals and counterproposals being made and rejected by both sides. A new diplomat, Saburo Kurusu, was expected to assist in a new round of talks. But Admiral Stark continued, "I am not hopeful that anything in the way of better understanding between the United States and Japan will come of his visit."[36]

Kusuru brought two new proposals for Ambassador Nomura. The first would bring about a limited withdrawal of Japanese troops from China in return for a comprehensive settlement of the Sino-Japanese conflict. It was rejected. In the second fallback proposal, Japan offered to cease military operations if the United States would supply a million gallons of aviation fuel. That was rejected too, and Admiral Stark said bluntly to Ambassador Nomura: "If you attack us, we will break your empire before we are through with you . . . we shall crush you."[37]

On November 26 came intelligence reports of Japanese troop convoys heading for Indochina. On the same day, the Imperial Japanese Navy's Strike Force sailed from its rendezvous in the Kurile Islands northeast of Japan. It seems astonishing, but discord between the Imperial Army and the Imperial Navy was so great, and communication between the forces and civilian authorities so poor, that in Tokyo neither the prime minister (who was also the minister of war) nor the foreign minister knew this event was taking place. The force (under Adm. Chuichi Nagumo) included twenty warships—nine destroyers, a light cruiser, two heavy cruisers, two battleships, and six of Japan's ten aircraft carriers. Bearing a total of 493 aircraft, they shaped course for Pearl Harbor.

Six days later (December 2), Kimmel wrote again from his command offices in Oahu to Stark. "I have frequently called to your attention," he said, "the inadequacy of the Army anti-aircraft defense in the Pearl Harbor area with particular reference to the shortage of anti-aircraft guns. So far, very little has been done to improve the situation." This contrasted markedly with the tone of his letters from the beginning of the year. "I have issued orders to the Pacific Fleet," Kimmel added in a postscript, "to depth bomb all submarine contacts in the Oahu operating area."

This letter crossed with one coming from Stark: Dated November 25, Kimmel received it on December 3. Its subject was the *Reuben James* sinking, which Stark estimated had "set recruiting back about 15%." Then he too added a postscript, an afterthought: Neither the president nor Secretary of State Cordell Hull "would be surprised over a Japanese surprise attack."[38] It was also on December 3 that another senior U.S. naval officer, Adm. Charles H. McMorris, asserted cheerfully: "Pearl Harbor will never be attacked from the air."

Two years earlier, on August 2, 1939 (less than a month before the war in Europe had begun), Albert Einstein had written from his holiday home at Nassau Point in Long Island to Roosevelt, describing to him the theoretical potential of an atomic bomb and his fear that Nazi Germany might be trying to build one. Now, on December 6, 1941, the president approved research funds to create such a bomb.

During the morning of December 7, 1941, as scheduled, the *Annual Report* of the secretary of the Navy was issued. In it, Secretary Knox declared: "I am proud to report that the American people may feel fully confident in their navy."[39] At the very moment the report was issued, Admiral Nagumo's task force was approaching a critical point in its voyage. At six-thirty in the morning, Hawaiian time (11:30 A.M. Washington time), the task force reached that point: an area of unmarked ocean 300 miles north of Oahu. It was a moment of great satisfaction, and of mounting tension, for in complete safety and apparently undetected by anyone, the fleet had come within flying range of Pearl Harbor. Now the next stage of the operation could begin. Outwardly calm, the admiral turned his carriers into the wind and prepared to launch his aircraft.

PART FIVE

RENOWN

1941–1945

★

With the greatest single shock
in its history, the challenge
to the United States becomes unavoidable.
The nation sends out
the greatest navy it has ever created,
and wins its greatest victory.

11

★

THOSE SPLENDID
SHIPS—LOST

*W*hen Admiral Nagumo's aircraft left his sight, he must have
known the world was about to change forever. There is no record
of his thoughts at that time; but ever since those same aircraft streaked
in above Oahu and war burst like a thunderclap through the Pacific and
the United States, events at Pearl Harbor on December 7, 1941, have
never ceased being described and analyzed in words and pictures. Even
in 1950, Winston Churchill said of that day, "the story has now been
exhaustively recorded." In 1963 Samuel Eliot Morison went further. "No
military event in our or any other country's history," he wrote, "not even
the Battles of Gettysburg and Jutland, has been the subject of such
exhaustive research as the air assault on Pearl Harbor."

For these reasons the action will not be described in great detail here.
Although it lasted only two hours (a blink of time in U.S. history) the
attack on Pearl Harbor was, and probably still remains, the greatest single
shock ever received by the American nation—to such an extent that even
those who were born after the event, including people who have never
seen Pearl Harbor, have a vivid impression of the destruction wrought
that Sunday morning. Those alive at the time but living elsewhere recall
with great clarity their emotions on hearing the appalling news; and for
those who were present and survived, the memory is unerasable. In this
outline, three of them (a Navy pilot, an Army pilot, and a civilian engineer) stand for the thousands who also endured the battle.

There were close on two hundred aircraft in the first attack—high-level bombers, dive-bombers, torpedo bombers, and fighters. Their route from the carriers was direct, and, flying at 200 miles an hour, their launch area was only an hour and forty minutes from the coastline of Oahu. From Kahuku Point (the island's northernmost part) to its southernmost end at Diamond Head, Oahu is only 35 miles long: mere minutes of flying time. Emblazoned with the rising sun, the aircraft crossed the coast at 7:40 A.M.; arcing around the western half of the island, at 7:55 they were above Pearl Harbor, tranquil and sleepy. Below them, set out in neat lines, they could see nine battleships and an uncountable number of cruisers, destroyers, submarines, and auxiliaries. On shore and afloat, peacetime routine prevailed—then, roaring and screaming overhead, the aircraft dropped their bombs, released their torpedoes, fired their guns; and below them, surprise was absolute.

Twenty-nine-year-old Lt. Thomas E. Moorer had just returned from two months of air patrol over the Pacific. Now in retirement from the highest professional post, Chief of Naval Operations, Admiral Moorer can instantly recall the last months of 1941. His flying orders had been strict: Under no circumstances should he and his colleagues overfly Kwajalein "or do anything that would be considered provocative by the Japanese."[1] His patrols had been based on Midway, radiating 600 or 700 miles to the north and in pie-shaped arcs around. He had escorted marines to Wake Island (all by celestial navigation, there being no radar and little or no other navigational equipment in the fighter aircraft), and for the eight weeks of patrol he had flown every day. At last, on Friday, December 5, his squadron was ordered back to Hawaii for a blessedly free weekend.

On December 6, Lee Benbrooks, a twenty-two-year-old Army Air Force radio operator, was promoted to sergeant.[2] With his friends and colleagues at Hickam Air Field, a few miles southeast of Pearl Harbor, he celebrated promotion and Saturday night with a beer party in one of the hangars.

Rudy Peterson was working that weekend. An ex-Navy man with eight years' experience in submarines, he was watch engineer in charge of the day watch in Building 149 at the Pearl Harbor Naval Shipyard.[3] The building housed Power Plant No. 2. A routine duty there was to check the efficiency of operations by means of circular recording charts, most of which were mounted on instrument panels. One of them was not: A chart recording boiler feed water was mounted on a structural column, a part of the building. Theoretically, this meant that vibration in the building could be transmitted onto the chart, possibly distorting it; but no one was much worried—it would have to be an incredibly powerful vibration.

All three men were indoors at the moment of the attack. Moorer, a married man, had chosen to live outside the confines of the naval base. His house was on a hill overlooking Pearl Harbor, and it was from there that he heard the aircraft shrieking over. Benbrooks, up early despite the previous night's party, was in his barracks, happily sewing his new chevron onto his uniform; and Peterson was at work in Building 149. Then the first explosions rocked the harbor. Running to a window near his control station, Peterson "saw the hangar fires and saw one plane dive low to launch a torpedo close to the minelayer *Oglala.*" Instinctively he threw himself onto a whistle cord, sounding a superfluous alarm as the building shuddered around him.

At Hickam Field, Benbrooks and his colleagues could not see the actual harbor, and at first "neither myself nor anyone else standing at the window had any thought that there was a hostile action under way." Moments later three planes screamed directly over the barracks. "I can remember right now, to this day, distinctly, the sort of feeling of revulsion that I felt when I saw those big red emblems—and we knew immediately what we were doing."

Closer to the harbor, Moorer did not have even a temporary illusion that it might be a training exercise: "I knew exactly what it was. . . . The first thing that I saw was the planes attacking Hickam, then right after that I picked up these large formations of horizontal bombers coming in to attack the battleships." The future CNO leaped into his car, raced to the harbor, and commandeered a boat. In minutes, as the first wave of attackers struck, he was with his squadron. In the pandemonium he saw an enlisted man desperately firing a dismounted machine gun "with the heat of the barrel burning the flesh off his hands—but he still held it." As the battleships blazed, "the harbor was about five inches deep in oil," and as Moorer motored seaward in a flying boat, the oil came up over the aircraft's windshield. Maneuvering blind, he could see nothing more until he was outside the harbor, when a crewman took a bucket of gasoline from the tank and washed the filth away.

Coming very low, very fast, with scarcely any opposition, the first run of Kate torpedo bombers hit three battleships—*California, Oklahoma,* and *West Virginia.* The second run struck a cruiser and capsized a minelayer; the third hit another cruiser and a fourth battleship, *Utah.* Simultaneously the dive-bombers launched eight separate assaults from different directions. Under their attack, four more battleships caught fire (*Nevada, Maryland, Tennessee,* and *Pennsylvania*), while *Arizona*—the ninth and last—was struck in the forward magazine and boilers. In moments she exploded and capsized, and four hundred sailors were buried alive in her sinking hull.

By now the opposition was frantic, fierce, and brave—but inevitably uncoordinated, and almost completely ineffective. Onshore, scattered through the island's airfields, only about a dozen American aircraft were able to take off; 188 were destroyed, mostly on the ground. On the waters of Pearl Harbor, the turgid black oil gushing from the ruptured ships scorched out the lungs of those who sought safety by diving overboard. Into the air above, vast dark clouds of smoke plumed upward, pierced by flames and the flashes of huge explosions: Then, after forty minutes of sustained assault, the first attack wave was gone. But there was no respite, for behind them, arcing around the island's eastern side, came a second wave—another 168 aircraft plunging with the same devastating accuracy into the cauldron that had been Pearl. Between them, the attack waves were over the island for less than two hours and lost only thirty aircraft from their number. But for that small price in those two hours of unremitting savagery, in addition to destroying 188 American planes, they killed or wounded over 3,600 people and wrecked or immobilized some 300,000 tons of U.S. naval shipping: eight auxiliaries, three destroyers, three cruisers, and eight battleships.

"Remember Pearl!"—the words became a national war cry: a plea, a challenge, and a demand, with a power still unmatched in U.S. history.

The rest of that appalling Sunday ticked away: ghostly, frightened, angry hours, with a renewed attack expected every moment. As the smoke continued to roll and as shock and panic began slowly to subside, the time came to rescue what was left and plan what to do next. Sometimes the most unexpected little objects survived. At Hickam Air Field, after manning a gun all day, Lee Benbrooks discovered that his barracks and all his personal possessions had burned to ashes—with one tiny exception. On the ground near the smoking ruin he found the shirt he had been sewing that morning, his new sergeant's chevron still securely in place.

In Building 149, Power Plant No. 2 was still functioning, and as he checked what was damaged and what was intact, Rudy Peterson found another small, unique memento of the morning's devastation. The boiler feed water record chart, secured to the structural pillar, looked as if it had recorded an earthquake: The shuddering building had made the chart's single steady line leap and jerk like a seismograph recording, and it marked the exact times of both attack waves.

But of course neither of them, nor anyone else, needed a physical memento to remember that awful morning; none of them could ever forget it, even if he wanted to. And Admiral Moorer probably speaks for all Americans who lived through the trauma of December 7, 1941:

The thing that impressed me the most about Pearl Harbor was the psychological impact of being told, every minute, "Now, don't do

anything to provoke the Japanese; whatever you do, don't do anything to provoke the Japanese—*Commence firing!*"

At once the question arose of who was to blame—a controversy which
rumbled furiously for years and which still occasionally resurfaces. Five
days after the attack, Admiral Kimmel wrote to Admiral Stark: "We had
considered an air raid on Pearl Harbor as a very remote possibility,
particularly at the time that it occurred. . . . The ships in harbor opened
fire very promptly but the first attack wave was practically unopposed.
The fact that all ships were able to open fire so promptly during the
breakfast hour indicates that the ships in harbor were alert and prepared."[4]

It is scarcely a pleasant experience to be on the receiving end of history,
yet up to a point Kimmel was right; after the initial shock the harbor's
defense was heroic and extremely brave. But with four battleships, a
minelayer, and a target ship sunk; with serious damage inflicted on four
more battleships, three light cruisers, three destroyers, a seaplane tender,
and a repair ship; and with thousands of deaths, it was obvious to all that
the ordered level of preparation and alertness was horribly inadequate.
Someone had to take the blame, and to most people Kimmel was the
natural and legitimate scapegoat. Strangers wrote to him suggesting he
should commit suicide—"You are certainly of no use to yourself, nor to
the American people."[5] Senior naval officers felt equally vengeful—
"Where was Kimmel?" Capt. Charles Lockwood, U.S. naval attaché in
London, wrote to his wife. "Resting at the sub base, no doubt. If we lose
him as well . . . we actually gain quite a lot."[6]

Kimmel was swiftly relieved of his command and did not serve with
honor again. Today his mortal remains lie under an unornamented tomb-
stone in a peaceful corner of the naval cemetery at Annapolis; and today
Admiral Moorer quietly dismisses the vitriolic passions that followed
Pearl Harbor—"It wasn't really his fault at all."

Kimmel had many personal friends who stood by him, but such a view
was not fashionable at Christmas 1941. "Someone should burn for this,"
growled Charles Lockwood, and many Americans would have agreed
with him, mentally placing Kimmel on top of the pyre. "Those splendid
ships—lost in the first scrap . . . and after all the warnings that have gone
out!! We just stand around in groups and mourn." Lamenting in London,
Lockwood half echoed lines from one of John Masefield's poems:

> *These splendid ships, each with her grace, her glory,*
> *Her memory of old song or comrade's story,*
> *Still in my mind the image of life's need,*
> *Beauty in hardest action, beauty indeed.*[7]

He probably gave no thought to the poem, yet it would have been an apt echo—both of the ships that had gone and of the years of war to come: years of hardest action for the U.S. Navy. And Lockwood's lament ignored three other factors that would prove crucial.

The first was that in spite of the devastation in Pearl Harbor itself, its shore facilities had escaped almost untouched—docks, workshops, and oil farms. The base as a whole could have been utterly wrecked; the loss of life could have been far greater than it actually was; and the relaunch of the U.S. Navy into the Pacific could have been delayed incalculably longer than in fact it was.

Second, though it was a horrible demonstration, the assault at last put an end to the question of whether battleships unsupported by aircraft were superior to aircraft unsupported by battleships. They obviously were not—a conclusion underlined three days later when two unsupported British warships, *Prince of Wales* and *Repulse,* were sunk by air attack alone. So when the shipping sunk in Pearl began to be replaced, it was not with battleships but with carriers. The lesson had been dreadful but was quickly learned: The naval war in the Pacific would be, to a very large extent, an air war.

Connected with this was the third factor which Lockwood (and most people) overlooked at the time: namely, that by great good fortune the U.S. Pacific Fleet's three existing carriers were not in Pearl at the time of the attack. *Enterprise* was on her way back from Wake Island, having delivered aircraft there; *Lexington* was going to Midway on the same errand; and *Saratoga* was undergoing scheduled refit on the West Coast.

Occasionally it has been suggested that this was because of prior warning, and it is true to say that at least a fortnight before the attack took place, both the British and the Americans were aware a Japanese strike must be imminent. The British FECB (Far Eastern Combined Bureau) had worked out (by the simple means of a graph with Japanese merchant ships returning home on one axis and dates on the other) that Japan would launch an attack by the end of the first week of December 1941 in either Malaya or Hawaii. This information was passed to the United States, and between U.S. and British code breakers much further information was exchanged. In retrospect—shorn of the thousands of other messages and now, of course, completely readable—these make it look as though the Western powers must have known beforehand not only that the attack was imminent, but that Pearl Harbor was definitely the target. But they did not, and the late William Casey (chief of London OSS—the forerunner of the CIA—during World War II) put the reasons well:

Among those not reading the intercepts was [William] Donovan, President Roosevelt's Co-ordinator of Information. The military had confined the priceless intercepts to a handful of people too busy to interpret them. Small wonder that [William J.] Friedman [who had broken the Japanese diplomatic cipher before the assault] cried out in despair on hearing of the attack on Pearl Harbor, "But they knew. They knew." The fact is that Friedman knew, but those with the responsibility and power to act had received only an accumulation of raw intercepts. No one had put the pieces together for them and told them of their momentous implications. . . . All the pieces of information were available in Washington, but no one put them together in a mosaic that might have cushioned, if not avoided, the blow against Pearl Harbor.[8]

But at least the United States was truly united again. The president's immediate declaration of war against Japan was received with vast enthusiasm, a national urge for revenge which never waned until, almost four years later, the representatives of the emperor stood in surrender on the decks of U.S.S. *Missouri.*

Declaring war against Japan, Roosevelt made no mention of Germany or Italy. Yet on December 11, thrilled and astonished by the Japanese attack (whose target he had not known of beforehand) Adolf Hitler declared war against the United States. So did Mussolini; and with grim sarcasm, Charles Lockwood wrote: "Isn't that just too mean of them! Now we can really get down to business."[9]

On Christmas Eve 1941, the Arcadia conference began as Roosevelt, Churchill, and their top military and naval men met in Washington to plan Allied strategy. But while the new Allies were far from ready for actual joint fighting, the Axis was poised for plunder. In the seventeen days since Pearl Harbor, Japanese forces had attacked the Philippines, Malaya, Thailand, Singapore, Hong Kong, Guam, Midway, Wake, Shanghai, the Gilbert Islands, Palmyra, Jolo, Burma, and Borneo. The British battleship *Prince of Wales,* the battle-cruiser *Repulse,* and the cruiser *Galatea* had been sunk; the American garrisons at Guam and (after heroic resistance) at Wake had surrendered; and Japan had achieved total air and naval superiority in the Philippines. Moreover, in the Atlantic (even before Hitler's declaration of war) Vice Adm. Karl Dönitz, commander of all of Germany's U-boats, had seen that America's east coast offered "an opportunity of getting at enemy merchant ships in conditions which elsewhere have ceased almost completely. . . . There can hardly be any question of an efficient patrol, at least a patrol used to U-boats."[10]

Arcadia ended on January 14, 1942. By then Hong Kong had surrendered, Bataan was besieged, and Corregidor was under daily attack. In the Dutch East Indies, the Celebes had been invaded; and on January 13, 1942, six of Germany's large Type IX U-boats arrived at their new stations to begin *Paukenschlag*—Operation Drumbeat. "The conditions," Dönitz noted with delight, "have to be described as almost of peacetime standards. . . . The Commander found such an abundance of opportunities for attack in the sea area south of New York to Cape Hatteras that he could not possibly use them all. At times up to ten ships were in sight sailing with lights on peacetime courses."[11]

The Battle of the Atlantic had started as soon as Britain declared war on Germany, and because the United States came to make the Pacific War so especially and spectacularly its own, the U.S. Navy's great part in ultimate victory in the Atlantic is often half forgotten. Yet Arcadia endorsed Rainbow 5 and ABC-1: the "Germany first" doctrine, projecting U.S. power primarily across the Atlantic. As the senior Army and Navy officers (Gen. George Marshall and Adm. Harold Stark) said: "Our view remains that Germany is still the prime enemy and her defeat is the key to victory. Once Germany is defeated, the collapse of Italy and the defeat of Japan must follow."[12] Yet though the fundamental approach was agreed on immediately, it began extremely badly.

For Admiral Dönitz and his U-boats, 1940 had been a "happy time"; pickings in the Atlantic had been rich and easy until the British brought a primitive form of radar into use. In 1942 the happy time returned: In American coastal waters, between the middle of January and the end of April, Paukenschlag claimed eighty-seven ships totaling 515,000 tons. In March alone, twenty-eight ships totaling 160,000 tons were sunk off the U.S. Atlantic coast, and Admiral Ernest King (newly created CNO as well as Commander in Chief, U.S. Fleet) acknowledged that the "situation approaches the 'desperate.' " The humiliating fact was that, despite all the naval contacts there had been with embattled Britain, America was completely unprepared to face submarines off its own shores. There were no coastal convoys: Ships sailed independently, and even when the ships were no longer lit, cities on the coast remained brilliantly illuminated, turning the ships into easily targeted silhouettes. There were no escort vessels and hardly any patrol planes—instead, as Dönitz chortled, "much single-ship traffic, clumsy handling of ships, few and unpracticed sea and air patrols and defences." The U-boat admiral was clear about the value of Paukenschlag:

> The enemy powers' shipping is one large whole. It is therefore immaterial where a ship is sunk—in the end it must be replaced by a new ship. The decisive question for the long term lies in the race between sinking and new construction. . . . The center of the enemy's new construction and armaments is in the United States. . . . I am therefore grasping the evil at the root.[13]

In the last days of 1940, Roosevelt had determined that the United States should be the "arsenal of democracy" ("The people of Europe . . . do not ask us to do their fighting. They ask us for the implements of war"), but now that the United States was fighting too, the demands for implements of war curved upwards. Amid the universal clamor for ships, tanks, trucks, aircraft, and weapons of every kind (a clamor made worse by confusion over what form of production should be given priority), the arsenal was being rapidly depleted. The need for steel could not be met; and on May 14, 1942, as the Allies' crisis of supply worsened, Admiral Dönitz confidently reported the latest figures of maritime destruction to his Führer at the Wolf's Lair, Hitler's headquarters in east Prussia. In the four months since Paukenschlag had begun, 112 tankers totaling 927,000 tons had been sunk in U.S. coastal waters alone. In the same period worldwide, 303 Allied ships totaling over 2 million tons had fallen to Axis submarines, aircraft, and mines.

"There is, therefore," said Dönitz, "already now an absolute decline taking place in the enemy tonnage. . . . Merely 4–500,000 tons per month need to be sunk in order to prevent any increase. Anything above that cuts into the tonnage."[14]

By then a partial convoy system had come into effect off the eastern United States, and at last the coastal cities were persuaded to accept a nightly blackout. But the U-boats had become so daring that they would cruise openly on the surface during daylight; and despite the ice and gales of the far North Atlantic, others took their toll of supply convoys to Russia. Admiral Sir Dudley Pound (chief of the British naval staff) wrote to Admiral King: "These Russian Convoys are becoming a regular millstone round our necks and cause a steady attrition in both cruisers and destroyers."[15]

Nevertheless, there were some words of reassurance too—from a Royal Naval Volunteer Reserve commander, Roger Wynn. In peacetime he had been a barrister; now he was in charge of the submarine tracking room at Bletchley Park, the British secret intelligence center. His assessment was that "with an adequate and efficient air escort, wolf pack tactics on a convoy should be impossible. We hope to achieve this beyond the reach of land-based aircraft by auxiliary carriers with the convoys."[16] Admiral King agreed, but, as he wrote in a press release, "only time will bring into service the adequate numbers of sea-going escort vessels which are essential to the extension of the use of convoys."[17] It was a slim hope, but there was little else to cling to.

Back in September 1940, trying to prevent Japan's entry into the war, Admiral Yamamoto had given his more bellicose colleagues a frank warning. "If I am told to fight regardless of the consequences," he said, "I shall run wild considerably for the first six months or a year; but I have utterly no confidence in the second and third years." On January 18,

1942, representatives of the three Axis nations signed a military convention in Rome laying down "guidelines for common operations against the common enemies," and agreeing on a division of the world into areas of influence for each. Japan's section lay from 70 degrees east to the West Coast of America, including the Dutch East Indies, New Zealand, and Australia; and as the wolf packs howled in the Atlantic, Yamamoto, true to his word, continued to run wild in the Pacific. Mussau Island, north of New Ireland, was occupied; landings were made at Rabaul, Kavieng, and Balikpapan; and as the war came within a thousand miles of Australia, New Britain, New Ireland, Dutch Borneo, and the Solomons were invaded. The invasion of Amboina Island in the Dutch East Indies gave Japan control of the southern approaches to the Molucca passage; attacks were made on Port Moresby and the Dutch naval base of Surabaya in Java; Samarai Island, only 380 miles north of Australia, was bombed; and on February 15, 1942, after 9,000 British, Indian, and Australian deaths in combat, Singapore surrendered at last.

Four days later, the port of Darwin in northern Australia was bombed, more thoroughly than Pearl Harbor had been; not only shipping but most of the port installations were destroyed. The town was evacuated and left empty as, less than eleven weeks after the strike on Pearl Harbor, the possibility of a Japanese invasion of Australia appeared horribly close to reality. Three days after that, to the west of Santa Barbara in California, the Elwood oil field was shelled by a Japanese submarine (the first direct attack on the U.S. mainland by Japan), and February 1942 ended with the Battle of the Java Sea. Fifteen Allied warships from the Dutch, Australian, British, and American fleets opposed an invasion force of eighteen Japanese warships and ninety-seven transports heading for Java. It was the biggest surface battle since Jutland, a generation earlier. But while both opponents at Jutland had claimed a victory, there was no doubt who won and lost in the Java Sea: Eleven of the fifteen Allied ships were sunk, Java was invaded, and three months and a day after Pearl Harbor, Japan's grip on the oil-rich Dutch East Indies was complete.

In 1898, when bringing an army to assist Admiral Dewey in the conquest of the Philippines, Gen. Arthur MacArthur had entered Manila Bay past the island fortress of Corregidor. In 1904, accompanied by his son Douglas, he had been an official American observer of the war between Russia and Japan. On March 11, 1942—much against his will and swearing that he would return—Gen. Douglas MacArthur was evacuated from the same island fortress as Japanese guns and aircraft pounded it remorselessly.

But five weeks later (April 28, 1942) came the United States' first slight chance of direct retaliation against Japan. Back in 1908, as a member of the Great White Cruise, Ens. William F. Halsey had visited Tokyo and been one of those young Americans privileged to toss the great Admiral Togo in a blanket. It had been fun, and the young man had enjoyed it; but now, returning toward Tokyo, the grim-faced, square-jawed Admiral Halsey was in command of a small task force, focused on the carriers *Enterprise* and *Hornet* and bearing a flight of sixteen specially modified B-25 bombers. These normally land-based aircraft had been given extra fuel tanks for their mission—which was to bomb Tokyo and other major cities of Japan.

Crewed by U.S. Army Air Force personnel under the leadership of the USAAF's best pilot (Lt. Col. James Doolittle, one-time holder of the world air-speed record), they were spectacularly successful. The raid—as daring and impudent as Stephen Decatur's raid on Tripoli in 1804— achieved its main purpose: a vigorous psychological kick at Japan and an equally vigorous boost to American morale.

In immediate military terms, it was only a kick. There still seemed no way to stop the Japanese: Timor, Bali, and Mandalay came under attack, while the ensign of the rising sun burst into the Indian Ocean, assaulting Colombo and Trincomalee and sinking some 135,000 tons of Allied warships and merchantmen in the Bay of Bengal. Luzon surrendered, and Corregidor finally fell. But in this continuing tide of Japanese victory, the Doolittle raid began to produce a real military benefit for the Allies.

Furious and ashamed that the U.S. air raiders had bypassed them, virtually all of Japan's available warships pounded off in search of Halsey's long-vanished carriers. As they did so, they generated a huge amount of radio traffic, carefully monitored by eavesdropping U.S. cryptanalysts, for whom it was a potential windfall: The more examples of code they had, the better their chances of breaking it. At the same time, the Imperial Navy realized that if it could not control the central Pacific and eliminate the enemy carriers, the fortunate survivors of Pearl Harbor, they themselves might be obliged to spend much time and effort safeguarding the homeland.

Thus, two crucial elements developed side by side: Japan's naval strategy for the next phase of the war and America's ability to read that strategy in secret. And over four days in early May, on the waters northeast of Australia, ships of the U.S. Navy fought ships of the Imperial Japanese Navy in a battle unlike any other in previous history: for in the Battle of the Coral Sea, the opposing vessels never actually saw one another at all.

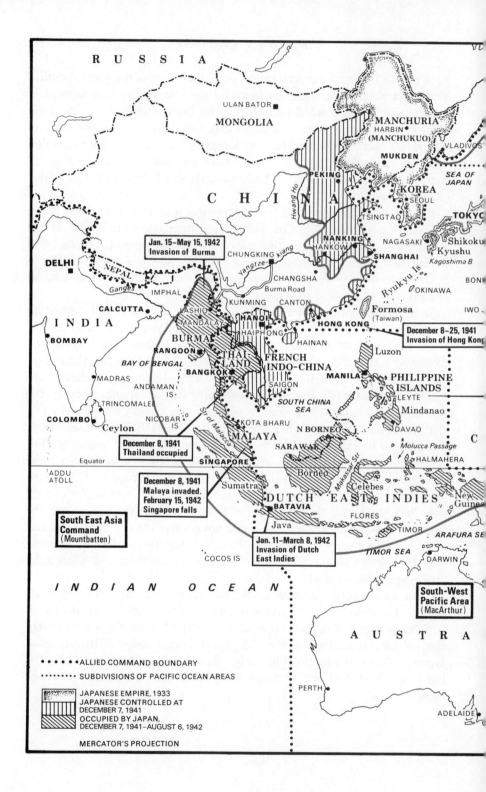

RUSSIA

MONGOLIA
ULAN BATOR ■

MANCHURIA
(MANCHUKUO)
HARBIN ●
MUKDEN ●
VLADIVOS

SEA OF
JAPAN

C H I N A
PEKING

KOREA
SEOUL ●
SINGTAO ●

TOKYO
Shikoku
NAGASAKI ● Kyushu
Kagoshima B
BON

**Jan. 15–May 15, 1942
Invasion of Burma**

CHUNGKING
Yangtze-kiang
Hwang Ho

NANKING
HANKOW
SHANGHAI

DELHI ■

NEPAL
Ganges
IMPHAL

CHANGSHA
Burma Road
KUNMING
CANTON

Ryukyu Is
● OKINAWA
Formosa
(Taiwan)
IWO

CALCUTTA ●

I N D I A
BOMBAY ●

LASHIO
MANDALAY
BURMA
RANGOON ■

HANOI
HAIPHONG

HAINAN

HONG KONG

Luzon

**December 8–25, 1941
Invasion of Hong Kong**

BAY OF BENGAL
MADRAS ●
ANDAMAN
IS

THAI-
LAND
BANGKOK ●

FRENCH
INDO-CHINA
SAIGON

MANILA ●

PHILIPPINE
ISLANDS
LEYTE

●TRINCOMALEE

NICOBAR
IS

SOUTH CHINA
SEA

Mindanao
DAVAO ●

COLOMBO ●
Ceylon

Str of Malacca

KOTA BHARU
MALAYA

N BORNEO
SARAWAK

● Molucca Passage
HALMAHERA

Equator

**December 8, 1941
Thailand occupied**

SINGAPORE ●

Borneo

Makassar Str
Celebes

ADDU
ATOLL

**December 8, 1941
Malaya invaded.
February 15, 1942
Singapore falls**

Sumatra

DUTCH   EAST   INDIES
BATAVIA ●
FLORES

New
Guinea

**South East Asia
Command**
(Mountbatten)

Java

TIMOR
ARAFURA SE

**Jan. 11–March 8, 1942
Invasion of Dutch
East Indies**

TIMOR SEA
DARWIN ●

COCOS IS

I N D I A N   O C E A N

**South-West
Pacific Area**
(MacArthur)

A U S T R A

PERTH ●

ADELAIDE ●

● ● ● ● ● ALLIED COMMAND BOUNDARY

·········· SUBDIVISIONS OF PACIFIC OCEAN AREAS

JAPANESE EMPIRE, 1933
JAPANESE CONTROLLED AT
DECEMBER 7, 1941
OCCUPIED BY JAPAN,
DECEMBER 7, 1941–AUGUST 6, 1942

MERCATOR'S PROJECTION

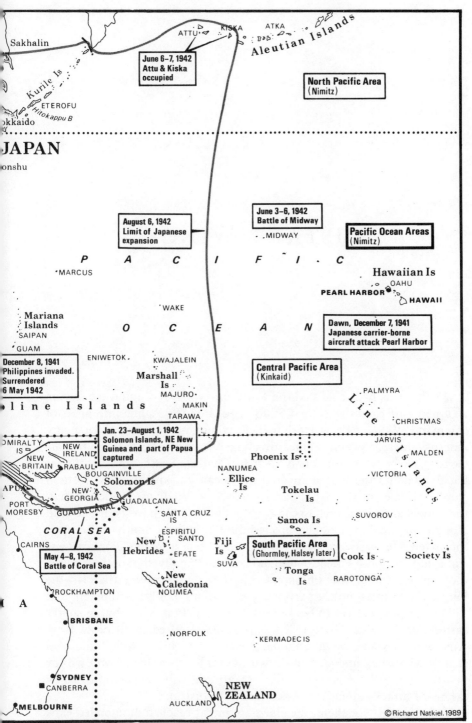

Sakhalin

Kurile Is
ETEROFU
Hitokappu B
okkaido

**JUNE 6–7, 1942
Attu & Kiska
occupied**

ATTU
KISKA
ATKA
Aleutian Islands

North Pacific Area
(Nimitz)

JAPAN
onshu

**August 6, 1942
Limit of Japanese
expansion**

**June 3–6, 1942
Battle of Midway**

MIDWAY

Pacific Ocean Areas
(Nimitz)

P A C I F I C

MARCUS

Hawaiian Is

OAHU
PEARL HARBOR
HAWAII

Mariana
Islands
SAIPAN

WAKE

O C E A N

**Dawn, December 7, 1941
Japanese carrier-borne
aircraft attack Pearl Harbor**

GUAM

ENIWETOK
KWAJALEIN

**December 8, 1941
Philippines invaded.
Surrendered
6 May 1942**

Marshall
Is
MAJURO

Central Pacific Area
(Kinkaid)

PALMYRA

line Islands

MAKIN
TARAWA

CHRISTMAS

L
i
n
e

**Jan. 23–August 1, 1942
Solomon Islands, NE New
Guinea and part of Papua
captured**

Phoenix Is

JARVIS
MALDEN

DMIRALTY
IS
NEW
IRELAND
NEW
BRITAIN
RABAUL
BOUGAINVILLE
Solomon Is
NEW
GEORGIA
GUADALCANAL

NANUMEA
Ellice
Is

VICTORIA

I
s

APU
PORT
MORESBY
GUADALCANAL

SANTA CRUZ
IS
ESPIRITU
SANTO

Tokelau
Is

SUVOROV

CORAL SEA
CAIRNS

New
Hebrides
EFATE

Fiji
Is
SUVA

Samoa Is

South Pacific Area
(Ghormley, Halsey later)

Cook Is

Society Is

**May 4–8, 1942
Battle of Coral Sea**

New
Caledonia
NOUMEA

Tonga
Is
RAROTONGA

ROCKHAMPTON

A
BRISBANE

NORFOLK

KERMADEC IS

SYDNEY
CANBERRA
MELBOURNE

AUCKLAND

**NEW
ZEALAND**

©Richard Natkiel. 1989

With the vast Pacific divided into four Allied command areas, aircraft carriers
displaced battleships as the instruments of naval power: For the first time, in the
Battle of Coral Sea, ships fought without sighting each other.

12

★

DISTANT WINGS

*A*s the Axis had separated the world into spheres of influence for the new order, so the United States separated the Pacific into areas of command. West of Pearl Harbor, U.S. command was unreal for many months—merely penciled lines dividing bits of paper, with names attached. There were four areas: North, Central, South, and Southwest Pacific. The northern area covered the ocean upward from the fortieth parallel, a line roughly from San Francisco to Vladivostok. Below that, the central area descended to the equator and stretched westward beyond Hong Kong, making a dogleg around the Philippines. South of the equator, extending westward over New Zealand but stopping short of Australia, lay the South Pacific command area; and finally, the southwest area took in Australia, the Philippines, and the intervening islands—the Dutch East Indies, now a part of Japan's triumphantly swelling empire.

That empire was set to burgeon still further. Port Moresby, in southeastern Papua New Guinea, lies only three hundred miles or so from Australia. Japanese naval command referred to it as "MO," and said clearly what they intended to do with it: "The objective of MO will be first to restrict the enemy fleet movements and will be accomplished by means of attacks along the north coast of Australia."[1]

Unfortunately for them, the clarity of intent reached unintended ears: On March 28, 1942, that message was decoded by a small team of brilliant U.S. naval cryptanalysts based in Pearl Harbor and led by one of the greatest of American code crackers, Comdr. Joseph J. Rochefort.

The new incumbent of Admiral Kimmel's position was Adm. Chester Nimitz, an ex-submariner and, until Kimmel's disgrace, chief of the Bureau of Navigation. With a ruddy complexion, snow-white hair, and piercingly blue eyes, Nimitz looked like the Stars and Stripes come to life. From Pearl Harbor he controlled the North, Central, and South Pacific areas, and as he worked to make that control something more real than lines on a chart, he used Rochefort's invaluable code-breaking skills to the utmost. Gradually it became clear that, around May 3, 1942, Japanese landings would be attempted somewhere in New Guinea, New Britain, or the Solomons. On April 30 the fleet carriers *Zuikaku* and *Shokaku* (veterans of the raid on Pearl Harbor) weighed anchor and began steaming south toward the Coral Sea, 2,000 miles away. On the same day, almost 4,000 miles east of them, the carriers *Enterprise* and *Hornet* left Pearl Harbor and headed for the same destination.

The Japanese objective was threefold: the invasion of Port Moresby; the establishment of a seaplane base 800 miles further east, in the central Solomons; and, halfway between the two and 200 miles south, the establishment of a similar base in the Louisiade archipelago. The inverted triangle formed by those three pointed firmly south to Australia.

A formidable power was sent to take possession of that triangle. Its major units included eleven troop transports, seven destroyers, two light and six heavy cruisers, and three carriers—*Zuikaku, Shokaku,* and the light carrier *Shoho.* Jointly they bore 147 aircraft, and the force's overall commander (Vice Adm. Shigeyoshi Inouye) was optimistic: "It is not likely," he informed his officers, "that powerful enemy forces are in the area."[2]

Over the next three days the forces converged. With the great handicap of distance, the two carriers from Pearl Harbor could not possibly intercept their opponents. Instead, it was hoped that they would be in time to assist two further U.S. carriers, *Yorktown* and *Lexington,* bearing a total of 143 aircraft and commanded respectively by rear admirals Frank Fletcher and Aubrey Fitch. Unknown to the Japanese, these were already close to position, as was another smaller force (commanded by a Royal Navy officer, Rear Admiral Crace) of cruisers and destroyers.

By the evening of May 3, soldiers of the Imperial Army were busy disembarking on Tulagi, site of their proposed seaplane base in the central Solomons. The conventional dates for the Battle of the Coral Sea are May 4–8, for at dawn on May 4 a U.S. air strike against Tulagi sank one Japanese destroyer, three minesweepers, and five seaplanes. But that episode is far removed from the battle's main characteristic; nor was there any further contact between the opponents over the next two days, for the simple reason that neither had any clear idea of the size or position of his enemy's fleet.

At last, early on the morning of May 7, 1942, they found each other—

or thought they had. At 0736, the first sighting went to a Japanese scout, who reported a cruiser and a carrier. The Japanese believed this to be the only U.S. carrier in the southwest Pacific, and a major strike of seventy-eight aircraft was launched against it. A second sighting was claimed at 0815 by U.S. scouts reporting four heavy cruisers and two carriers. The U.S. forces similarly assessed this as the main Japanese force and launched ninety-three aircraft in attack.

But instead of a cruiser and a carrier, the Japanese had seen a fuel ship and a destroyer; and instead of the enemy's main force, the Americans had seen two destroyers and two heavy cruisers. Both sides had launched major attacks against minor targets; and had it not been that both made the same error at about the same time, either would have been wide open and vulnerable.

Inevitably, the fuel ship and destroyer were sunk; but luck favored the Americans more than the Japanese, for in the same broad vicinity as the reported "main body" was the light carrier *Shoho.* At 1100 she was sighted and attacked. With so many aircraft assaulting her, the result was never in doubt; and minutes later, when Lt. Comdr. R. E. Dixon radioed the result to *Yorktown,* the U.S. Navy gained its newest epigram:

"Scratch one flattop. Dixon to carrier, scratch one flattop." It was the first Japanese carrier to be sunk in the Pacific war.

Misidentifications continued to plague both sides through the afternoon and evening and into the night. Without damage to themselves, the cruisers and destroyers under Rear Admiral Crace successfully fought off an attack by thirty-one Japanese land-based bombers, who reported two battleships and a heavy cruiser sunk—only to be jumped on by three U.S. Army aircraft which had flown up from Australia.

"Fortunately," Crace wrote later, "their bombing, in comparison with that of the Japanese formation minutes earlier, was disgraceful."[3]

A search party of twenty-seven Japanese aircraft sent out in the afternoon found nothing, jettisoned their bombs and torpedoes, and on their return flight passed close to the U.S. force. Spotted on U.S. radar, ten of the airplanes were shot down, and at dusk another half dozen, thinking they had found their own ships, attempted to land on the two U.S. carriers. So taken aback were the Americans—naturally assuming the aircraft must be friendly—that five of those rash Japanese escaped; but out of the original twenty-seven, only seven made it safely back to their carriers.

Early next morning (May 8) came the crisis. By then the two forces were very closely matched: six destroyers, four heavy cruisers, two carriers, and 121 Japanese aircraft opposed seven destroyers, five heavy cruisers, two carriers, and 122 U.S. aircraft. Dawn searches through heavy rain squalls revealed the enemies to each other. Their ships were still almost two hundred miles apart. To give battle at such a distance would have been inconceivable in any previous era of sea warfare. In the days of sailing navies, battles were frequently fought at "half pistol-shot" range—a hundred yards. *Yamato*'s 18.1-inch main armament—the largest naval guns ever built, and still unsurpassed—could fire 40 miles, but even those gigantic weapons were crude, inflexible, and limited in comparison to the aircraft now launched by both admirals.

On May 7 luck had favored the United States; on May 8 experience favored Japan. In attacks which were close to simultaneous, *Zuikaku* found protection under a heavy rain squall and remained unharmed; *Shokaku* was hit on her flight deck, which made her unable to launch further aircraft; *Yorktown* likewise was hit on her flight deck, which nevertheless remained usable; and *Lexington* was hit twice by torpedoes and twice by bombs.

The latter hits proved fatal, although neither directly nor immediately so. By 1245, though still listing 7 degrees to port, *Lexington*'s damage had been shored up, the fires extinguished, and the flooding brought under control; but at 1247, sparks in her generator room ignited gasoline fumes from fuel tanks ruptured by the first torpedo. Under the force of the internal explosion, the entire ship shuddered, and fires burst out anew in every part. For an hour more, blazing inside and outside, she was able to make 25 knots. But gradually she slowed; gradually the firefighters were beaten back; at 1707, when all hope was lost, the order was given to abandon ship; and hours later, when she still refused to sink, the destroyer *Phelps* was sent in with torpedoes to end the awful sight and deliver "Lady Lex" from her torture.

For the first time in history, carriers had challenged carriers as aircraft were proved to be the new artillery of the sea; and also for the first time, the Allies were able to list a naval victory against Japan. The Japanese navy also claimed the victory, and tactically they were right: They inflicted greater physical losses than they sustained. Seventy-seven of their aircraft, 1,074 men, and one 12,000-ton carrier were no more, but they had shot down 66 aircraft, killed 543 men, and sunk a tanker, a destroyer, and a 42,000-ton fleet carrier.

Strategically, however, the victory was to the United States. The Battle of the Coral Sea was the first real check given to Japan's lightning conquests. The Japanese invasion of Port Moresby was canceled. No less important, the enemy's carrier strength was reduced at a crucial time. It was very difficult for them to replace any carrier, even the light *Shoho*. It was even more difficult to replace the dozens of trained and experienced pilots who had been killed. The majority of those came from *Zuikaku*, and until they were replaced she was effectively noncombatant. Similarly,

Shokaku needed a month's repairs; so for several weeks, the Imperial Navy was reduced by not one carrier, but three.

Those lost weeks were critical, because it was then that Admiral Yamamoto was refining the plan which he was convinced would make or break Japan and its war effort. This plan contained two cardinal objectives: control of the whole Central Pacific region and decisive battle with the U.S. fleet. Naturally the place and the time, chosen by him, should be the most favorable for Japan. The place was the tiny atoll of Midway, close to the International Date Line, halfway across the Pacific. The time was the first week of June 1942, when exactly six months would have elapsed since the attack on Pearl Harbor. "I shall run wild considerably for the first six months or a year," the admiral had said earlier; and no one could deny he had been true to his word. "But," he had added, "I have utterly no confidence in the second and third years."

His masters would have done well to heed his warning. But despite the manifold cultural differences between Japan and the West, some aspects of human nature are pretty universal, and one of those is what the ancient Greeks used to call hubris, overweening pride born of spectacular success. Even with the setback of the Coral Sea, the overall Japanese success had been so much easier and so much greater than even they had imagined, that now the idea of defeat seemed impossible. Yamamoto knew it was not: The limits of national resources were self-evident. But he did believe that if his ships could pull it off this time, they could bring the end of the war—and a Japanese victory—very close indeed.

His plan was complex, involving five distantly separated, closely coordinated fleets—an advance submarine force; a diversionary force aimed at the Aleutian Islands in the north Pacific; a Midway Attack force tasked with reducing the atoll's defenses; an invading transport force; and, bringing up the rear, the main body. From the 72,000-ton superbattleship *Yamato* with her unsurpassed armament, the main body was under Yamamoto's personal command; and altogether, the fleets he was mobilizing constituted the largest armada Japan had ever sent forth—162 major warships, against which Admiral Nimitz could muster no more than 76.

For the monstrous Japanese strength, Midway was, in itself, a ridiculous little target: 39 feet above sea level at its highest point, with only two square miles of dry land in its six-mile diameter. But in 1942, 1,100 miles from Pearl Harbor, it was the most westerly possession of the United States still in American hands; and that gave its two component islands a strategic importance out of any proportion to their actual size.

To its possessor, the atoll offered the possibility of midocean refueling and repairs for any ship or aircraft. If it belonged to Japan, the Imperial Navy could attack Hawaii easily; could threaten the U.S. West Coast;

could dominate the central as well as the west Pacific; and could crack American communication lines to the southwest Pacific. Those consequences were sure to be as clear in Pearl Harbor as in Tokyo, so Yamamoto was confident that if the U.S. fleet did not sortie to counter the Aleutian invasion, it would be absolutely certain to come out against a Japanese-held Midway. On the other hand, if it did try to prevent the Aleutian invasion, it would be swiftly cut off from any return to Oahu. One way or another, therefore, a major battle—probably a decisive one— was bound to occur.

The sixteen advance submarines would form a picket line between Oahu and Midway, ready to signal the U.S. fleet's sortie. While the Aleutians were attacked, the Imperial Navy's four remaining fleet carriers (*Kaga, Okagi, Hiryu,* and *Soryu*) under Vice Adm. Chuichi Nagumo would approach Midway from the northwest, launch an aerial strike against the atoll, and pulverize its defenses in preparation for the landing of an invasion force of 5,000 troops approaching simultaneously from the southwest. Coming in from the west, the main body would then be fresh and ready to trap and annihilate any counterattacking fleet. As Admiral Nimitz remarked later, "There was nothing petty about Japanese planning."[4]

But grand as it was, the strategy contained one demand over which Yamamoto could exercise no final control, and one assumption which was never seriously questioned. The demand was for clockwork punctuality from all the constituent fleets—including the U.S. fleet; the assumption was that no one outside the naval command, and especially no American, knew anything about the operation. In neither area was the military planner's eternal question posed: "What if it goes wrong?" Yet in any naval operation, even more than in a land operation, punctuality is impossible to guarantee. To base a plan on interweaving punctuality is to invite tragedy in through the front door; and a delay occurred at the very beginning of the operation. The picketing submarines were two days late leaving Japan. They reached their stations safely and took up watch; but there was nothing for them to see, for they were gazing in the wrong direction—the U.S. ships had already passed them by. As for the assumption of U.S. ignorance, it could not have been more wrong; for in Oahu, Nimitz knew very nearly as much about the operation as Yamamoto did himself.

In the middle weeks of May 1942, Comdr. Joe Rochefort and his codebreaking colleagues excelled themselves. Today, the clearest possible demonstration of their labors is contained in the National Archives in Washington, where, in row upon row of cardboard boxes, uncountable thousands of decoded messages are stored—a historian's Klondike. Some have become very famous; at intervals still others emerge, discovered and often put into context for the first time.

One of the very famous messages is the "fresh water" broadcast that gave the first certain indication an attack would be launched on Midway. Early in March 1942, Rochefort's team had guessed that a target designated "AF" in Japanese naval messages might be Midway. As the designator appeared more and more frequently over the following weeks, positive identification became essential. Rochefort laid an elementary snare. From Midway itself, an emergency radio signal was broadcast in plain English, saying that the garrison's supply of fresh water was running dangerously low. To make it more convincing, an immediate reply said that supplies were on their way; and within two days Rochefort picked up the Japanese response, broadcast from Wake—AF was running short of water, and the invasion force should take its own. Simple and brilliant: AF was definitely Midway. Almost two weeks before Admiral Nagumo's carriers sailed, Nimitz was able to prepare the atoll's defense.

But the trick was more than just a lucky guess, as is shown by one of the archives' documents, released in the early 1980s and referring to events of November 1941. In the middle of that month, members of the Japanese embassy in Washington had flown to Guam, Hawaii, Midway, and Wake to assess U.S. defenses. On the eighteenth, their report, entitled "The State of American Alert," was intercepted on its way to Tokyo.

"In Guam and Hawaii," the report said, "no special precautions were taken in regard to passengers. At Midway and Wake curtains were drawn over the windows of the plane before landing on the water, and over the windows of the boat in which we went ashore."

On both islands their movements were very restricted; and when they were allowed out of their hotel, "since it was night, and raining, we could not see anything along the way." All in all, they could report only one definite piece of information—"the lack of pure water on Wake and Midway."[5] So the identification of AF was not merely luck on Rochefort's part or gullibility on the Japanese side. He knew how limited their knowledge of Midway was; and they responded to the one message about it which they knew might easily be true.

The code breakers' guiding principle was that any code devised by one human brain could be broken by another; but although the broad outline of the Midway plan was clear, its exact dates and times were secured in an intractable new code. The forces available to Nimitz were too few to allow error. After seventy-two hours of unremitting effort from Rochefort and all his experts, the new code remained silent as a tomb. Rochefort himself was to see Nimitz the next morning, May 24, with his results. That final night he grappled again with the jumble of figures—a weird, almost uncanny, private, silent battle in the hours of darkness, as one man focused every ounce of his mental powers against the encrypt.

It is not surprising that cryptology both fascinates and repels; to those outside that esoteric world, it can seem close to witchcraft. And in some way Rochefort's unusual and powerful brain conquered, and forced its opponent to speak. He was late for his appointment with Nimitz; but when he got there, he was able to say that on June 3—ten days' time—the Aleutians would be attacked, with Midway assaulted by aircraft carriers on June 4.

The differing jobs of code breakers and intelligence personnel are sometimes confused. The job of intelligence staff is to collate, assess, and interpret information supplied from many sources, of which broken codes are one, and from that information to offer predictions to the command. Predictions do not form the primary part of a code breaker's job; instead, they deal in matters of fact. Rochefort's superlative mind had supplied the matters of fact, and now Comdr. Edwin T. Layton (leader of Nimitz's intelligence staff) made a prediction: "They'll come in from the northwest on a bearing 325 degrees and they will be sighted at about 175 miles from Midway, and the time will be about 0600 Midway time."[6]

As events proved, the accuracy was astounding. He was only 5 degrees out on bearing and 5 miles out on distance, and he was precisely right on the time. The carriers of the Nagumo Force (which, in six months of unbroken conquest, had traveled 50,000 miles) were sighted just before 6 A.M. Midway time, bearing 320 degrees, 180 miles away from their target.

Less than two hours previously, Admiral Nagumo had had his staff's own intelligence assessment promulgated throughout his fleet: "It is assumed there are no enemy carriers in the waters adjacent to Midway." The contrast with the U.S. intelligence effort could scarcely have been greater—for by then the three U.S. carriers of Task Forces 16 and 17 were a mere 300 miles from the atoll. An almost unbelievably high degree of skill had led them there; to return victorious, they would need luck as well. And luck came to them throughout that day.

The first fragment of fortune had already occurred: Through small technical problems, three of seven enemy scout planes failed to take off on time. Two never did get off, and the last, delayed for half an hour, was slated to search the very sector in which the U.S. carriers lay.

Nevertheless, for four hours (from shortly after 6 A.M. until a few minutes after 10) there seemed to be no question of luck for the Americans; it was merely endurance and retaliation, often suicidal. Every plane on Midway began taking off the moment Nagumo's aircraft were detected on radar. In the twenty-five minutes they were above the atoll, the attackers dropped upon it nearly 30 tons of bombs. The destruction, though correspondingly massive, was still far less than the total obliteration Yamamoto's plan demanded, and a second strike was called for. But by then the U.S. counterattack was under way, shore-based torpedo bombers showing all too clearly that the island had not been subdued.

While gunfire and fighter aircraft kept the torpedo bombers at bay, Nagumo made a crucial decision. He had not anticipated any need for a second strike; rather, he had expected the U.S. ships to rally to Midway's aid. Accordingly, the ninety-three aircraft he had kept in reserve on board were already armed with torpedoes; but since he had received no report of any U.S. warships in the vicinity, it seemed safe to allow a second strike. This meant the reserve airplanes' weaponry needed to be changed. To prepare for a land attack, they had to be taken down from the flight deck to the hangar deck, their torpedoes removed and replaced with bombs, and the planes themselves returned to the flight deck. At 0715 he gave the order. It would take about an hour to carry out.

Minutes later came the United States' second fragment of luck. Nagumo's delayed scout plane had at last sighted the U.S. task forces; but it reported them to be cruisers and destroyers. In the Nagumo Force, the rearming proceeded, while outside, the waves of torpedo bombers kept up their vain assault. By 0820 the rearming of Nagumo's reserve planes was nearly complete. In three separate waves, a total of fifty-two U.S. aircraft had attacked the Japanese carrier force. But these were old, slow planes; they had no fighter cover; and very few survived. On board one of the carriers, a Japanese officer observed how "their distant wings flashed in the sun. . . . Occasionally one of the specks burst into a spark of flame and trailed black smoke into the water."[7]

The fourth wave came droning in to its doom, and as it did, two other things happened at once. To the astonishment of everyone (including its captain) a U.S. submarine surfaced right in the middle of the Japanese fleet. Simultaneously, that fatefully delayed scout plane radioed a shocking new message: "Enemy accompanied by what appears to be a carrier." The scout was uncertain, but further messages in swift succession indicated a size of force which was bound to contain a carrier—and it was only 200 miles away. For the first time, Nagumo knew that a truly capable enemy was close at hand.

Meanwhile the submarine U.S.S. *Nautilus,* after a quick glance around, fired one torpedo and dived, pursued by a torrent of depth charges. A destroyer was detailed to hunt and kill—and in the carriers, the rearming of the aircraft, which was barely finished, was flung into reverse: They were going to have to attack ships, not the island, after all. But this meant another hour of toil, during which it became starkly clear that every second counted. In the haste, torpedoes and bombs were not stowed, but literally scattered around; and suddenly the sky was filled with fighters. Gunfire burst out until the aircraft were recognized as the returning first attackers of Midway, some damaged, all virtually unarmed, and all low on fuel. Recovery began at once, but by 0905 it was still incomplete. It was then that Nagumo decided he must attack the enemy's carrier. The decision deviated from Yamamoto's grand plan; but there was nothing else he could do. With recovery complete at 0917, the Nagumo Force changed course by 90 degrees and started toward its enemy.

That enemy included not one carrier, as he supposed, but three: *Enterprise* and *Hornet,* which had launched Doolittle on his raid over Tokyo, and *Yorktown,* still considerably battered from the Coral Sea encounter. She had been assessed then as needing ninety days' repairs, but in just three days in Pearl Harbor, dockyard workers laboring around the clock had patched her up sufficiently for battle again. Her damaged compartments were braced with timber, very few of her watertight doors worked, and three of her boilers could not be repaired. Yet in such desperate need, the jury-rigging had to be enough.

In addition to those from Midway, unprotected torpedo bombers from *Yorktown* and *Hornet* were shot down without harming the Japanese. The total confusion in the air—with many U.S. fighters losing track of the bombers they were meant to guard—kept the outcome of the battle still in the balance. With Nagumo's change of course, one group of protected bombers missed his fleet entirely and, as its fuel ran out, was forced to land as best it could on or around Midway. Elsewhere, led by Lieutenant Comdr. Clarence McClusky, another double group of thirty-seven planes from *Enterprise* was quartering the ocean in vain, way over their safe fuel limits. But at five minutes to ten, there fell to that group the last fragment of luck the U.S. would need: At that moment, 19,000 feet below them, they saw one solitary Japanese destroyer heading north. This was the one which had been hunting for *Nautilus.* The submarine had escaped; now the frustrated destroyer was returning to its fleet.

McClusky had no idea what it had been doing or why it was all alone, but he had a very good idea of where it might be going. His aircraft gave chase, and suddenly the target was there—the entire Nagumo Force, vulnerable in a way it never should have been. Constant maneuvering to avoid the torpedo bombers had thrown the fleet into disarray: Now it was a loose collection of ships scattered over the ocean, their mutual gun protection reduced. Most of its aircraft were on board. The few that were in the air had been held low by all the previous abortive bombing attacks; the flight decks were cluttered with aircraft and fuel hoses; on the invisible hangar decks, unstowed bombs and torpedoes lay scattered around. McClusky and his followers did not hesitate. Five or ten minutes more, and the first freshly fueled Zeros would have taken off. Their engines were warming up, the carriers were turning into the wind, and on board the flagship *Akagi* the air officer had just given the order to commence launch. For many Japanese sailors and airmen, the last sounds they heard on earth were the klaxons' warning shrieks, followed almost instantly by the high scream of bombs hurtling down. Under the impact of two and four direct hits, respectively, *Kaga* and *Akagi* shook with crashing explosions. McClusky's men slammed their aircraft out of their near-vertical 70-degree dive, and even as they flashed over and past the ships, another squadron from *Yorktown,* led by Lt. Comdr. Maxwell Leslie, hurtled in toward *Soryu* and hit her three times.

The combined attacks took a total of just six minutes. In those six minutes the battle became as decisive as any in Japanese naval theory. Three of Nagumo's four carriers (*Akagi, Kaga,* and *Soryu*) were destroyed. The fourth, *Hiryu* ("Flying Dragon") survived a few hours more, and, roaring and twisting and spitting fire like the dragon for which she was named, she sent out the one really successful Japanese air strike, which found and fatally hit *Yorktown.* The U.S. Navy also lost a destroyer (*Hammann*), approximately 150 aircraft, and 300 officers and men. But in addition to its four carriers, the Imperial Navy had lost a heavy cruiser (*Mikuma*), 322 aircraft, and about 5,000 officers and men, as well as suffering severe damage to other ships.

For the Imperial Navy it was a defeat without precedent in the Pacific War; for the U.S. Navy, an equally unprecedented victory. At its focus it was a battle of the utmost brevity; a staggering amount of destruction was packed into those central six minutes. "Something must be left to chance," said Nelson before Trafalgar—a view Nimitz shared entirely. "You will be governed," he told his tactical commanders before Midway, "by the principle of calculated risk." Nevertheless, the six minutes were the result of weeks of planning and brilliant insight; and without that and infinite daring, the lucky chances would have counted for little.

Japan had snatched the initiative at Pearl Harbor; and though Midway, June 4–6, 1942, was not in itself a war-winning battle, it was there that the U.S. snatched the initiative back, moving from the defensive to the offensive phase of the war, and fully into the age of naval air power. "You who have participated in the Battle of Midway today," said Nimitz to all the U.S. survivors, "have written a glorious page in our history. I am proud to be associated with you."

When Yamamoto made his formal apology to the emperor, perhaps both those men experienced a chill of foreknowledge; for both had tried to prevent Japan's entry into the war, and no doubt both saw in Midway the realization of Yamamoto's prophecy. There had been exactly six months of running wild; now, for Japan, there could be no confidence in the future.

13

★

CONFUSION AND FURY

*I*n the Atlantic, however, the initiative remained with the Axis. On June 11, five days after Midway, Admiral Dönitz's U-boats augmented Operation Paukenschlag by mining parts of the U.S. East Coast. On June 20 Germany announced that the submarine war off the U.S. would now be completely unrestricted; and on July 5 the tragedy of PQ17 took place. En route from Iceland to the USSR, the convoy of twenty-two American and eleven British merchantmen was ordered to scatter; and in that unprotected position, twenty-three of its ships were sunk. But while Dönitz rejoiced, an exchange of telegrams between Berlin and Tokyo, intercepted and decrypted by U.S. intelligence, emphasizes how crucial the first eighteen months after Pearl Harbor were for both the Axis and the Allies.

The first telegram, dated July 9, 1942, came from Berlin. It told Paul Wenneker (Germany's naval attaché in Tokyo) that the Middle East and Indian Ocean "should take precedence over Pacific as points of concentration for Axis sea warfare."[1] On May 4, British troops had landed on Madagascar, capturing the large harbor at Diégo Suarez. Now Wenneker was to do his best to persuade the Imperial Navy westward, to link with Rommel in North Africa and cut Allied supply lines from India to the Middle East and from Australia to the USSR. Wenneker sent his reply to Berlin on August 1:

> If the enemy's goal is "Hitler first," then "England first" must be the goal of the Axis, after Russia has collapsed. The Japanese Navy

would be able to carry on submarine and carrier warfare with all means available in the west Indian Ocean and South Africa after the middle of August. . . . Germany and Italy are to understand clearly that the possible acquisition of the Red Sea or the Persian Gulf is a question which could never concern the Japanese.[2]

The second half of the reply was cryptic. It was almost certainly meant to indicate that, after a final Axis victory, Japan would not claim territories outside the agreed spheres of influence even if it had helped to conquer them; but it could also have indicated a Japanese unwillingness to project naval power as far as the Red Sea. Even the first half was ambiguous: Couched in the conditional tense, it was not framed as a definite promise to action; but it certainly implied that, only two or three weeks later, Japan expected to be both able and willing to return to the Indian Ocean and complement the German-Italian campaigns in the Mediterranean and North Africa.

Both Germany and Japan had conducted their parts of the world war on the basis of opportunistic lightning strikes, without any great consideration of overall patterns or priorities, and (especially in the case of Japan) without any preexisting grand strategy for a long war. The Germans had realized belatedly that to win a global war, they would have to fight it globally, not as separated regional conflicts. The Japanese came to the same realization even later and optimistically hoped it was not too late. Yet while Germany was attempting to unite the conflict in Europe and the Middle East with that in the Far East and the Pacific, Japan had been completely carried away by its own success. The junction of the Axis could have happened already—when Japan attacked British naval forces in the Indian Ocean, Madagascar was entirely controlled by Vichy France and could have been a ready base. However, the early, easy Japanese conquests had encouraged its navy to take its rampage further into the Pacific than originally intended: Its defensive ring had expanded eastward like a steel balloon, remaining hollow and unsupported within. Midway had pierced the balloon. If Allied pressure continued, it would collapse; and though it was not spelled out, an absence of Allied pressure was the condition implicit in Wenneker's telegram.

In contrast to the overdue Axis effort to join its two wars together, the Allies had fought with the rough concept of a global war from the moment Hitler declared war against the U.S., if not from the moment when Pearl Harbor was attacked. That such a thing was possible was due in large part to the U.S. Navy's broad prewar planning, and particularly to the thinking behind Rainbow 5. After Pearl Harbor the framework for Anglo-American policy coordination was established swiftly, with the creation in January 1942 of the Combined Chiefs of Staff (CCS) in Washington. Since there were no British ships left in the Pacific at all, the CCS gave direction of the Pacific War to the U.S. Joint Chiefs of Staff (JCS). Command in the north, south, and central Pacific Ocean went to Adm. Chester Nimitz, Kimmel's replacement at Pearl Harbor, with the southwest Pacific allocated to MacArthur. On March 14, the JCS decided to maintain a policy of active defense in the Pacific, while building up U.S. strength in Britain for Allied offensive operations against Germany.

The hurt and shame of Pearl Harbor was so great that U.S. naval leaders had to think in very rational and large terms if they were to resist the instinctive desire to ignore Europe and throw everything at Japan immediately. That was certainly their first desire, and it might have prevailed if Hitler had not gratuitously declared war against the United States. Thereafter, painful as the decision was for U.S. Navy leaders, it (and all transatlantic cooperation) would have been much more difficult had they not already come to the point, pre–Pearl Harbor, of accepting Germany as the first priority.

But the magnificent June victory at Midway changed the emphasis. Nimitz and King considered it vital to capitalize on the success, in order to prevent Japan digging in to its conquests and becoming ever harder to remove. Against that, King also recognized that defeating Dönitz's U-boats in the Atlantic was an essential step toward victory over Germany. He also had to remember constantly that not only Churchill but (with the main exception of General MacArthur) the U.S. Army too was more interested in the prospect of land operations on the other side of the Atlantic than it was in the watery Pacific.

The Army's proposal (made by General Marshall in April 1942) was for a preliminary Anglo-American invasion of northern France, code-named "Sledgehammer," to take place by September and to be followed in spring 1943 by a second, larger invasion, code-named "Roundup." Churchill reluctantly accepted this, feeling he could not refuse the first major offer of direct aggressive aid from "our cherished Ally, without whose aid nothing but ruin faced the world."[3] But his memory of the slow, dismal trench warfare of World War I spoke stubbornly against gaining a mere toehold on the Continent. So in the summer of 1942, he counseled that more haste into Europe would bring less speed, and proposed an indirect approach via either Norway or North Africa.

The U.S. Navy's attention was thus demanded by three theaters at once—the Pacific, the Atlantic, and either Europe or North Africa. While General Marshall assumed that the Midway victory would need no immediate follow-up and could release troops for Europe, Churchill tried to withdraw from an autumn cross-Channel commitment, and Admiral King simultaneously put forward a plan (code-named "Watchtower") to attack the Pacific island of Rabaul. Located in the Solomons, a thousand miles northeast of Australia, it was one of the forward sections of Japan's defense perimeter and perilously close to the U.S.-Australian supply lines.

With all the conflicting views of grand strategy, Roosevelt had a further domestic consideration to bear in mind: the presidential election, due in November. In both Britain and the U.S., wide sections of the public were losing confidence in the political leadership of the war—many times British people had heard Prime Minister Churchill say that a given stronghold was secure, only to see it fall shortly thereafter, while Americans longed either to fight Japan all out or to open a second front against Germany as soon as possible. In mid-July 1942, therefore, when the president sent Marshall and King to confer with Churchill in London, it was with stern warnings and reminders:

"The defeat of Japan does not defeat Germany. . . . American concentration against Japan this year or in 1943 increases the chance of complete German domination of Europe and Africa." Loss of the Middle East would invite "joining hands between Germany and Japan and the probable loss of the Indian Ocean." Holding the Middle East meant operations "definitely" either in the eastern Mediterranean and Persian Gulf, or in Morocco and Algeria. And, demanding speed of decision, unity of plans, and attack combined with defense, the president concluded with a hope for "total agreement within one week of your arrival."[4]

He got it—indeed, after his strong words and clear preference, anything else would have been astonishing. King and Marshall accepted the principle of a North African invasion, and on July 24 Operation Torch was born.

Other principles of the U.S. Navy were changing too: Facing a severe shortage of manpower, further reserves in the population had to be tapped, not always to general naval contentment. On July 30, Congress authorized the establishment of the WAVES (Women Accepted for Volunteer Emergency Service), and only six weeks earlier, a young man named Bernard Robinson had been commissioned as an ensign in the U.S. Naval Reserve. He was the first black man ever to become an officer in the U.S. Navy.

Women had served as naval nurses from time to time since the War of 1812, but it was not until 1908 that the Navy Nurse Corps was officially established.[5] Following the creation of the Naval Reserve on August 29, 1916, World War I brought the "Yeomanettes"—officially, "Yeomen (F)"—to work alongside men in shore jobs. Many people, morally troubled that women should seem to be directly involved in warfare, questioned the legality of enrolling women, and the Navy Department had to scrutinize the act of August 29 thoroughly to make sure. Nothing was found against it ("On the contrary," said a departmental letter to all naval district commandants, "it is believed that their enrollment was contemplated"), and by the end of the war over 11,000 women had been enlisted.[6] But there was no opportunity for them to make a career of naval life; by the summer of 1919, all had been released from active duty, and a generation passed before women served in the Navy again.

When the chance returned, women did not let it go. The 1942 act envisaged a goal of 10,000 enlisted women with 1,000 officers. Recruiting lists were so oversubscribed, and the service given was so valuable, that by the end of the war there were 8,000 officers and 70,000 enlisted women on active shore duty, with a further 8,000 under training. "The WAVES," said Secretary of the Navy James V. Forrestal, "have released enough men for duty afloat to man completely a major task force," and he was not exaggerating. The enlisted men and male officers made available were estimated as sufficient to crew ten battleships, ten aircraft carriers, twenty-eight cruisers, and fifty destroyers—figures which express simply and clearly the women's contribution. Without them, the Navy's fighting sea service would have been that much smaller, that much weaker.

The contribution which blacks could make was obviously no less than that of anyone else, but it was much more contentious. A year before the attack on Pearl Harbor, the influential black newspaper *Pittsburgh Courier* was convinced not only that war would come, but that blacks would not be allowed to fight. "The War Department and the Navy Department plans for the coming war DEGRADE you," it said. "They would make war without you if they could."[7] But they could not. During World War I, the Navy had employed blacks, but only as stewards or mess attendants or in supply vessels; no other role was permitted. Certainly this reflected the prevailing shore conditions of social segregation and second-class citizenship; yet it was odd all the same, for blacks had served actively, often in fighting roles, ever since the time of John Paul Jones. During the War of 1812, one sixth of the fleet's manpower was black; during the Civil War, a quarter of the Union Navy's sailors were black; at the beginning of the war with Spain, nearly 10 percent of *Maine*'s dead were blacks. Yet less than twenty years later, blacks were not allowed to fight for the Navy; and to *The Pittsburgh Courier* at least, this meant that the Army and Navy "challenge your right to citizenship."[8]

Though it took another world war to adjust the balance, 1942 brought the previously unheard-of opportunity for blacks to become naval officers as well as seamen. One of the first was Samuel L. Graveley from Richmond, Virginia—the segregated South—who joined in September 1942. "My eyes were open," he remembered later. "I knew the conditions."[9]

The conditions were usually (though not always) continued segregation and discrimination, intentional or unintentional, open or disguised. Boot camp was all black, with all white officers; after training, blacks' shore

accommodation was separate from whites', and sea opportunities were
sharply limited. The destroyer escort U.S.S. *Mason* and the submarine
chaser PC 1264, in which Graveley served, were manned almost entirely
by blacks—a cautious official approach which was excused (not unreason-
ably) by the view that the Navy was not a social laboratory, especially
when it was actually fighting a war.

Of those early, confused days, when blacks were barely half tolerated,
Graveley later said wryly, "I knew how to act"—though not always well
enough. Shortly after gaining his commission, he was arrested by naval
police for impersonating an officer. Nevertheless, it was a white who told
him he ought to go for a commission and whom Graveley came to regard
as the founder of his career. For the young Graveley, who joined expecting a short war and hoping only to survive and learn a useful trade, stayed
to become the U.S. Navy's first black vice admiral.

His first flag rank came in June 1971; one year later, women started
to become flag officers as well, when Alene B. Duerk was made rear
admiral in charge of the Nurse Corps. Though the advance of women had
been a little slower, it had been comparatively painless; but by 1971 racial
discrimination within the fleet had scarcely diminished since World War
II, and racial tensions in the 1970s were far worse. Even so, during that
decade the U.S. Navy could truthfully claim that it included more active
members of more minorities than ever before—not only black, but Americans of every other nonwhite descent as well: Filipino, Puerto Rican,
Guamanian, Indian, Mexican, Chinese; and in 1986 there was at least one
name on the list of inactive naval reserve flag officers which few in World
War II would have dreamed could ever figure. At the time of the attack
on Pearl Harbor, many Hawaiian-born Japanese lived in Oahu, and as
objects of scapegoat suspicion (along with thousands of first- and second-
generation Japanese immigrants on the West Coast), most were arrested.
One of those was a dentist, arrested when he was partway through giving
Mrs. Thomas Moorer a course of treatment; yet forty years after the war,
by pure but pleasant coincidence—for he was no relation to the arrested
dentist—the commander of the Naval Dental Clinic at San Diego was
Rear Adm. Haruto W. Yamanouchi, U.S.N.

By the summer of 1942, Admiral King itched to hit the Japanese again.
In spite of the "Germany first" doctrine, and before Operation Torch (the
invasion of North Africa) had been agreed on, he used Byzantine machi-
nation to win JCS approval for Operation Watchtower, the attack on the
Solomon Islands group. The assault would initially focus on the island
of Guadalcanal, where the Japanese were known to be building an airfield. On August 7, 1942, King received a message from Nimitz: "At last
we have started."[10]

Several times in the final weeks before launching the attack, King had had doubts—preparations for Torch were severely limiting his Pacific resources, yet he knew that Japanese forces in the Solomons were being strengthened. The dilemma was that, though waiting could increase his own power, Japanese power could be increased still more. He decided, therefore, to accept the existing odds; but he could never have foretold how long and perilous the battle would become, nor how "Guadalcanal" would eat into the souls of those who fought there. Shortly after Pearl Harbor, Roosevelt selected Samuel Eliot Morison as official historian of the United States' naval war. Throughout the course of the war, Morison visited and served in all the combat areas, and of Guadalcanal he wrote, with vivid simplicity:

> For us who were there, Guadalcanal is not a name but an emotion, recalling desperate fights in the air, furious night naval battles, frantic work at supply or construction, savage fighting in the sodden jungle, nights broken by screaming bombs and deafening explosions of naval shells.[11]

From Tokyo on August 28, the German naval attaché, Paul Wenneker, signaled to Berlin: "The enemy is in possession of the airfield [on Guadalcanal] which was under construction by the Japanese."[12] In fact, the airfield had been seized on the very day of the first assault, three weeks earlier. The Japanese had only just finished building it and had planned to celebrate its completion the following day. In memory of Maj. Lofton Henderson, a Marine torpedo plane leader killed at Midway, its new owners promptly named the place Henderson Field. The name would become famous.

"In this way," Wenneker continued, "the enemy has an advantage." This was a considerable understatement. In peacetime, Henderson Field had been a worthless stretch of muddy jungle. In war, cleared and squashed flat by bulldozers, then floored with steel mats, its geographical location made it invaluable, an almost priceless asset for whoever held it.

"Fighting," said Wenneker tersely, "is being continued." Again, this was a considerable understatement. For six months the airfield became the focus of battering assaults and counterassaults. Bombed and bombarded almost without interruption from air, land, and sea, uncountable tons of high explosive fell on and around it—in one night alone, a pair of Japanese cruisers fired fifteen hundred shells at it. Rain, disease, and fatigue all took the death toll higher still for Japanese and Americans alike; but, once they had gotten it, the U.S. kept the precious, dreadful place—and kept it operational.

In that hellish half year, there were six major and many lesser naval battles around Guadalcanal: Savo Island, the Eastern Solomons, Cape

Esperance, Santa Cruz, Guadalcanal itself, and Tassafaronga. Near-legendary names were created—Ironbottom Sound, the macabre nickname for the gulf where five Allied heavy cruisers, three Japanese destroyers, and a Japanese heavy cruiser were sunk; the Slot (New Georgia Sound, in the middle of the Solomons); and the Tokyo Express, Japanese destroyers running men and supplies in almost every night. Altogether, the Imperial Japanese Navy lost eighteen warships in those battles: a carrier, two battleships, four heavy cruisers, and eleven destroyers. The U.S. Pacific Fleet lost twenty-three ships (two carriers, seven heavy cruisers, and fourteen destroyers), and an Australian cruiser was sunk as well. Sixteen hundred Americans were killed and 4,200 wounded; but some 15,000 Japanese were killed in action, while a further 9,000 died of disease.

It was not long before the Americans understood that they could have lost the entire underprepared campaign at the very beginning. Only a day after their first landings, the Battle of Savo Island took place—the worst defeat the U.S. Navy had suffered in its whole history. The circumstances were these.

The initial landings on August 7, 1942, had been a great success; surprise enabled some 10,000 marines and many tons of supplies to be landed by a combined American-Australian naval force against comparatively light local opposition. Moreover, Japanese naval surface forces based 700 miles away at Rabaul were scattered that day, supporting other convoys, while their naval aircraft were preparing for a bombing raid on Papua. The latter rapidly reorganized themselves and, during the afternoon of August 7 and morning of August 8, subjected the landed Americans and their defending forces to a series of heavy air attacks. By the time these ended in the late afternoon of August 8, 20 percent losses of his aircraft made Vice Adm. Frank J. Fletcher, the American officer in tactical command, decide to withdraw his carriers to a safer distance, out of range of the island. Without waiting for confirmation from his distant superiors, Fletcher simply told them he was going, and went. This left his subordinates close at hand in a tricky position: The landing was not yet complete, and they had no air cover for the following day. So, on the evening of August 8 (much to the disgust of Marine Maj. Gen. Alexander Vandegrift), Rear Adm. Richmond Kelly Turner felt obliged to say that in the morning he too would have to withdraw his transports and cruisers.

At midnight, when the tense meeting between Turner and Vandegrift ended, there was at any rate no sign of any Japanese surface force in the area. Nevertheless, crews on the Allied ships were kept on watch, nominally in an alert state. The problem was that they had been kept in that state for several consecutive days. Those who were off watch were sound asleep, and those who were on watch, equally dog-tired, were almost asleep. This was not their fault, but the fault of a system in which no better method had yet been devised.

The combined result of all these factors was shattering. Unknown to anyone there, a force of Japanese cruisers was approaching; and at 1:42 in the morning it attacked.

"At the time the battle began, I was not on watch," one young ensign, Elmo Zumwalt, Jr., recalled later. "I was asleep, but a class-mate came down and woke me to see the battle. We saw four huge fires. All of us on the ship cheered diligently, absolutely convinced that these were Japanese ships going down."[13]

They were not. Only a few hours later, in the morning, young Zumwalt and his colleagues learned the appalling truth: What they had seen, and cheered so heartily, were the death throes of the Australian heavy cruiser H.M.A.S. *Canberra* and the three U.S. heavy cruisers U.S.S. *Vincennes, Quincy,* and *Astoria.* Over a thousand sailors lay dead on the seabed among the wrecks, and the place became known as Ironbottom Sound. Only a single U.S. cruiser (U.S.S. *Chicago*) survived, albeit with her bows almost blown off, and only one (*Quincy*) had been able to react fast enough to offer any significant resistance. But by great good fortune her resistance proved crucial, for one of her pitifully few shots hit the Japanese flagship, the heavy cruiser *Chokai,* in the charthouse. This lucky shot, apparently uncannily accurate, persuaded Japanese Vice Adm. Gunichi Mikawa that the opposition would be stronger than he had hoped, and so he turned away. He knew that he had already secured a remarkable victory; that was something no one could ever deny. What he did not realize was that, if he had continued to press his attack, he could have sunk all the U.S. transport vessels and no doubt most of the remaining warships; and if that had happened, Operation Watchtower would have collapsed forthwith.

That was something Mikawa could not have been expected to guess. As he returned northward with his force to Rabaul, well satisfied, he encountered a U.S. destroyer—one of a patrol which had missed him before—and had a go at that for good measure. He was probably not much concerned when it escaped into the cover of a heavy rainstorm; one destroyer more or less made little difference overall. But then he met another member of the patrol: a submarine (*S-44*). It had not seen him before; he did not see it now, and it made up to some extent for its earlier omission by carrying out a neat, efficient attack. "One torpedo, one ship" was a German submariner's maxim, and with one torpedo, *S-44* sank the heavy cruiser *Kako.*

The next stage in the region's naval contest was not long delayed: the Battle of the Eastern Solomons on August 24, 1942. The opposing fleets were large. In spite of his questionable actions off Guadalcanal, Frank

Fletcher still led the U.S. forces, now with a much enhanced force under his command: three carriers, a battleship, five heavy and two light cruisers, 254 aircraft, and eighteen destroyers. Against him, with the intention of reinforcing the Japanese troops on Guadalcanal, were another three carriers (including *Zuikaku* and *Shokaku,* two veterans of Pearl Harbor, and the lighter *Ryujo*), three battleships, no less than thirteen heavy and three light cruisers, thirty-one destroyers, a dozen submarines, a seaplane transporter, and four troop transporters. But despite this enormous surface and subsurface superiority, the Japanese carriers had only 168 aircraft among them.

If it had been possible to maintain the U.S. air superiority, it could have been (and perhaps would have been) a decisive factor; but when the time came, Fletcher had only two thirds of his aircraft at hand, because one of his carriers had had to be detached for refueling and was 240 miles away. Tactically inconclusive, that day's battle produced no immediately clear-cut victory for anyone. Fletcher's flagship, the carrier *Enterprise,* was subjected to a serious assault and extensively damaged by three bomb hits, but not sunk; the same happened to the battleship *North Carolina.* Likewise, the Japanese seaplane carrier *Chitose* was badly damaged but remained afloat. However, the Japanese losses included 90 of their 168 aircraft and the light carrier *Ryujo.*

At the beginning of the year, the Imperial Navy had had ten carriers totaling just over 238,800 tons' displacement; *Ryujo* was the sixth to go down. On the other hand, six more were commissioned into service during the year as a whole, and it was not difficult to suppose that Japan's shipyards would keep pace with demand: Once, in 1918, they had even established a world record by building a 5,800-ton merchant ship in only twenty-nine days. However, on hearing his admirals' reports of the action, the Japanese naval commander in chief Isoroku Yamamoto was well aware of their deeper statistical significance. Nearly 150,000 tons of carrier shipping had been lost; only a little over 123,000 tons had been built in replacement. That gave a net loss of nearly 26,400 tons—nearly 9 percent in four months—and, far worse, the replacement ships were all conversion jobs made from submarine support vessels and passenger liners. With the Pacific war only nine months old, the Imperial Navy was already having to scratch around and take what it could get for carriers. As the war developed, its net losses of purpose-built carriers, aircraft, and trained pilots became a continuing hemmorhage.

Another action soon followed, of equal tension but lesser ultimate consequence. With the nighttime Battle of Cape Esperance (October 11–12, 1942), the U.S. Navy's gradual increase in skill and technology seemed to be confirmed; an efficient surface warning radar gave them earlier notice of the Japanese approach than the Japanese had of them, and afterwards the Americans thought for a while that they had managed to sink four heavy cruisers and four destroyers. In fact, they had sunk one of three enemy heavy cruisers and one of two enemy destroyers, and by misdirected fire had managed to cripple one of their own destroyers and sink another; the battle was later described rather accurately as "a moderate material success."

The struggle for Guadalcanal was still unfinished. Throughout this time, on the jungled, humid island, savage fighting had continued between the U.S. Marine Corps and the Japanese—the one side resolutely maintaining Henderson Field as an American-owned operational concern, the other doing its utmost to dislodge the invaders. At sea, the next encounter took place just a fortnight after Cape Esperance—the Battle of the Santa Cruz Islands, October 26, 1942. (Its somewhat cumbersome title, incidentally, distinguishes it from the much earlier Battle of Santa Cruz, fought in 1657 off the island of Tenerife by British and Spanish ships.) The 1942 battle involved the bulk of Japan's Combined Fleet—four battleships, eight heavy and two light cruisers, four aircraft carriers, and twenty-nine destroyers—against two U.S. carrier groups centered on U.S.S. *Enterprise* and U.S.S. *Hornet.*

For each side the strategic targets remained unchanged. The Japanese intended, first, to continue the support and reinforcement of their army on Guadalcanal as it strained to evict the Americans from Henderson Field and, second, to fly in naval aircraft as soon as that was accomplished. The Americans intended to stop them doing either. Tactically, of course, both sides intended to sink as many enemy ships and down as many enemy planes as possible; and overall the tactical victory went to the Japanese. Their light carrier *Zuiho* was driven out of the action, crippled by dive-bombing scout planes from *Enterprise;* the big fleet carrier *Shokaku* was severely damaged by dive-bombers from *Hornet* and required nine months of repairs. But *Enterprise* was badly damaged too, and *Hornet* was sunk.

She took an extraordinary amount of punishment before finally going under. Two Japanese torpedoes, three 500-pound bombs, and two kamikaze hits turned her into a blazing wreck; but they did not sink her. Eight U.S. torpedoes did not sink her either. She had to be abandoned and was found by Japanese destroyers more than ten hours later, still on the surface and still ablaze. They managed to sink her—at last; but her endurance was a great tribute to her builders.

Her loss was a serious blow: The battleship *South Dakota* and one damaged carrier were the only U.S. capital ships left to keep the supply lines to Guadalcanal open. Against that, the more positive assessment was that at least the supply lines *were* still open; the Japanese strategic objective had failed, and Henderson Field was still in American hands.

Moreover, the Combined Fleet had lost so many carrier planes that now it had fewer than a hundred remaining—and the critical phase of the fight for Guadalcanal was about to begin.

It was called, simply and appropriately, the Battle of Guadalcanal, but it was not one battle alone; rather, it was an intermittent series of actions fought from shortly after midnight on the night of November 12–13 until the morning of the fifteenth. In the two weeks following the Battle of the Santa Cruz Islands, both sides rushed in as many supplies and reinforcements as they possibly could. On the other side of the world, Operation Torch was likewise getting into top gear as Eisenhower's soldiers waded through the surf onto African shores. At the same time, code breakers in Pearl Harbor discovered that Japan's next great assault on Guadalcanal was set for November 13. During the four days needed to establish the United States' first transatlantic beachhead, thousands more troops were convoyed into Guadalcanal; and in the early hours of November 13, just as predicted, the Imperial Navy's Eleventh Battleship Division, accompanied by a light cruiser and fourteen destroyers, came thundering down the Slot, heading for Henderson and a new bombardment. And the only opposition, under Rear Adm. Daniel J. Callaghan, was five cruisers and eight destroyers.

One of the Imperial Navy's key weaknesses was an addiction to tightly timetabled plans, in which everything had to dovetail for the whole to succeed. On this occasion, without radar and covered by a heavy rainstorm, the Battleship Division temporarily lost its way. When the mistake was corrected, the commanding officer (Vice Adm. Hiroaki Abe) realized they would be several hours late in making the bombardment. But if it did not take place, the entire offensive plan would be ruined. So they pressed on, loaded their guns with 14-inch bombardment shells—and then, on the brink of letting rip, found Callaghan's line of ships placed straight across their bows.

"There followed," said Admiral Nimitz after the war, "a half-hour melee which for confusion and fury is scarcely paralleled in naval history."

"The ships fought at close quarters, almost falling aboard each other," recalls Comdr. Masataka Chihaya, staff officer in the flagship *Hiei*—adding that he and his colleagues desperately wished for old-fashioned rams on their battleships' bows.

It was a real helter-skelter match. Four U.S. destroyers were sunk, two severely damaged; all the U.S. cruisers were similarly damaged, one so much she had to be scuttled; two Japanese destroyers were sunk, three were damaged; and the battleship *Hiei* suffered so badly that soon after dawn on November 13, she too had to be torpedoed by her own consorts, as Chihaya witnessed. And her bombardment had not taken place.

The following night (November 13–14), a squadron of cruisers and destroyers did manage to bombard and damage the field but were unable to wreck it as they had hoped to. During the day of the fourteenth, eleven Japanese troop transports were sighted heading for the island. Under repeated attacks, seven were sunk; the other four carried grimly on. Night came—November 14–15—and with it yet another bombardment force, including *Hiei*'s sister ship *Kirishima.*

It would be their last attempt. The U.S. squadron awaiting them included two battleships, *South Dakota* and *Washington.* In the opening clash, a Japanese destroyer was badly damaged and later scuttled; two U.S. destroyers were swiftly sunk and another two crippled. Soon afterward, the battleships saw each other—and at that moment something went wrong with *South Dakota*'s electrical systems. As she sheered blindly out of line, unable to train or fire her guns, she came under withering fire from the heavy enemy ships, and a total of thirty-four torpedoes were fired at her. None of them hit, but many of the shells did. However, in concentrating on her, the Japanese fatally ignored *Washington,* whose radar-controlled 16-inch guns suddenly blanketed *Kirishima,* reducing her to a nearly unmanageable wreck.

The Japanese withdrew. Sea and air belonged to the Americans. When daylight came, *Kirishima*—like her sister *Hiei*—was torpedoed by her own consorts; and as the morning of the fifteenth wore on, the nearly 4,000 soldiers from the four transports that had gotten through to the island were shuttle-bombed by aircraft from the very field they had been meant to capture. None survived, nor did any of the supplies they brought.

The island was almost priceless, but not completely so. With the end of this battle the Japanese felt they had paid enough. They sent no more heavy ships to Guadalcanal and made only one more major attempt to supply it. Rather than risk losing more transports, eight destroyers approached on the night of November 30 with towed drums of ammunition, food, and medicines. Shortly before midnight, they ran into a far more powerful U.S. force—six destroyers, one light cruiser, and four heavy cruisers. Hastily cutting their tows adrift, the Japanese engaged and fought brilliantly. In this—the Battle of Tassafaronga, the last major naval action around Guadalcanal—one of the Japanese destroyers was sunk; but in return they severely damaged three of the U.S. heavy cruisers and sank a fourth. The Japanese might have lost the naval battles for Guadalcanal; they had certainly not yet lost the war.

Nor, indeed, had they completely lost the island of Guadalcanal. It was not until February 9, 1943, six full months after the first U.S. landings, that Admiral Halsey (by then supreme commander of all forces involved in Watchtower) was able to report the island's final conquest; for no one had imagined how fiercely the Japanese would cling to their positions. That harshest of lessons was well learned, and often repeated, until the black sands of Iwo Jima turned red.

Nevertheless (though it seems something of a paradox) the tenacity of the Japanese, matched ounce for ounce by the determination of the Americans, was one of the factors which gave Guadalcanal its great value. The Americans learned a great deal about their enemy, and, while neither side would willingly relinquish the fight, the United States was steadily gearing up to full wartime production of material and trained personnel and was already strong enough to fight simultaneously on another continent. The Japanese could not; and dissipating their strength in Guadalcanal virtually ensured that they would never be able to join hands with Germany. A Japan victorious on that little far-off scrap of land might well have found itself substantially unopposed until after Germany's defeat; but Japan defeated at Guadalcanal instead found itself alone and subject to unremitting, increasing pressure on all sides.

14

*

BRAVO!
KEEP AT IT!

*O*n August 21, 1942—two weeks after the American landings at Guadalcanal and a week before Wenneker reported their capture of its airstrip—the war diary of U-boat High Command gave an unhappy sketch of the Battle of the Atlantic:

> The numerical strengthening of enemy flights [and] the appearance of a wide variety of aircraft types located with an excellent location device against U-boats have made U-boat operations in the eastern Atlantic more difficult. . . . Besides daily reconnaissance it is now known that there are some especially long-range aircraft types which are used for convoy escort. . . . This has made the operation of boats very much more difficult, in some cases no longer worthwhile. This worsening of the operational situation must, if continued, lead to unsupportable losses, to a decline in successes and so to a decline in the prospects of success of the U-boat war as a whole.[1]

The long-range aircraft mentioned in the diary were Liberators; the "location device" was radar. The principles of radar were as well known in Germany as in Britain—indeed, the first experiments with radio detection were made in Düsseldorf in 1903, and it seems likely that the first use of gunnery radar in action was in May 1941, by the battleship *Bismarck*. Furthermore, from the French Admiral Darlan, Admiral Dönitz had received a radar detector (Metox) which gave his submariners warning of impending aircraft attack. But Metox operated only on 1.5 meter wavelengths, and in 1940, the British invention of the magnetron made possible the use of much shorter wavelengths. These not only produced greater range, definition, and accuracy, but also were undetectable by Metox. In addition, Allied warships were being provided with high-frequency direction finders (an invention unknown in Germany), enabling them to home in on U-boat broadcasts. The oceanic battle was becoming an electronic war.

A further Allied policy refinement was introduced as well: Following statistical demonstration, it was decided to reduce the numbers of convoys but increase their size, thus giving the wolf packs fewer targets. Yet against that, despite their own losses, the number of operational U-boats in the Atlantic was still increasing steadily, and with it the number of Allied ships sunk. Until Allied air and surface cover could be increased to cover completely the "black pit," or "black gap" (the mid-Atlantic area which convoys were still obliged to face almost entirely alone), there could be no final respite from the U-boat.

But there *could* be a second front against Germany. Since July 24, 1942, Allied commanders had argued over the form of Operation Torch. Finally, agreement was reached on September 5. "Hurrah!" said Roosevelt; to which Churchill gruffly replied, "O.K., full blast."[2]

In most of its fighting aspects, Torch was, of course, a land operation, and as such is properly the province of a military narrative, not a naval one. But the Allied soldiers did not spring from the soil like dragon's teeth, nor did they swim to North Africa—though some, struggling ashore through the coastal surf, might well have felt they had swum all the way. From west to east, the agreed sites for invasion were Casablanca (on French Morocco's Atlantic coast) and the ports of Oran, Algiers, and Bône (on the Algerian coast). It was vital for the Allies to capture the ports relatively intact: Every division of men required 600–700 tons of supplies a day, quantities which could not possibly be brought in across beaches. From the outset both Churchill and Roosevelt hoped to make the invasion an "all-American show," since it was judged that the substantial Vichy French forces in North Africa would oppose a British landing, but might possibly welcome the United States. However, while the U.S. Army was able to contribute 113,000 troops, the U.S. Navy's growing commitment in the Pacific limited the direct naval escort and support the U.S. could provide. The Americans at that time referred to an operation between different forces of one nation as "joint," and to one between forces of more than one nation as "combined"; the British called both "combined." And in the end, Torch grew into something wholly new—a true joint and combined operation. The majority of the troops were American; the majority of the ships were British; and each nation put in about the same quantity of air power.

Three other developments—the escorts, the command, and the sheer size of it—made this an operation of a different order than anything earlier. It was the biggest single convoy operation ever mounted: Altogether about 650 warships and transports were used. To help protect them, light escort carriers were available for the first time, and were put to effective use in antisubmarine patrols. It was also the first operation in which command was unified at all times. Traditionally, an amphibious operation maintained the division of services: The admiral commanding afloat and the general commanding ashore remained equal and independent throughout; neither could actually order the other to do anything. But in Torch that was changed.

To people outside the services, chains of command can be difficult to grasp, and even for people inside they can be difficult to explain in a simple fashion. But with Torch it is worth making the effort, for a system was devised which meant that, at any given stage in the operation, there was only one chain of command, combining sea and land; and the system proved so effective, it became the model for later Anglo-American operations in Europe.

For the purpose, the Atlantic Ocean was divided down the meridian of 40 degrees west. On the western side of that line (the U.S. half of the ocean) the CNO (Admiral King) had authority over all shipping. Responsible to him was Adm. Royal E. Ingersoll, the commander in chief of the U.S. Atlantic Fleet; and responsible to Ingersoll was Rear Adm. Kent Hewitt, commander of the Western Naval Task Force. In these vessels (102 warships and transports) the main section of U.S. troops (86,000 men) were brought directly from the United States. Thus, until 40 degrees west, King was in ultimate control; then the second chain of command took over.

After 40 degrees west, Hewitt's responsibility through Ingersoll to King ended. Instead, Hewitt and his men (whether soldiers or sailors) became responsible to British admiral Andrew Cunningham, and through him to Gen. Dwight D. Eisenhower, commander in chief of all Allied forces, sea and land. This chain lasted until the soldiers were landed; then the third chain took effect, which was perhaps the most remarkable. For, once the soldiers were on shore, Hewitt's responsibility changed again. Eisenhower remained supreme commander, but Admiral Cunningham was no longer the middleman; instead, not only the soldiers, but *also* Hewitt and his sailors, came under Gen. George S. Patton.

It may sound a little confusing at first. But it was a great deal less confusing than anything else would have been, cutting through traditional interservice parishes in a most unorthodox way; and (at least to those who took part and understood what rivalries had been dropped or overcome to achieve it) it was vastly encouraging—because armed forces which could stop defending their own privileges and cooperate in such a way must surely be irresistible.

And they were. In the clearest possible advertisement of conquest, Roosevelt and Churchill met in conference at Casablanca on January 14, 1943. From the initial landings on November 8, victory in Morocco and Algeria had come in days; Tunisia, separated from Europe only by the 90-mile Sicilian Channel and rapidly reinforced by Germany, had to wait until the spring.

One reason for the swift success of Torch was the extraordinary luck its massive convoys had in crossing the seas. Effective Allied secrecy and faulty German intelligence resulted in scarcely a ship being sunk, for the main U-boat packs which normally lay across the Bay of Biscay had been diverted to ambush a trade convoy south of the Azores. Nevertheless, November 1942 brought the heaviest Allied losses at sea for the entire war (700,000 tons sunk by U-boats alone, with a further 100,000 tons by other causes) while in January 1943, the U-boats reached their greatest operational strength. Two hundred and twelve of them were at sea: three in the Black Sea, twenty-one in the Arctic, twenty-four in the Mediterranean, and 164 scattered through the Atlantic.

While Stalin's armies continued to fend off German assaults on Stalingrad, his Allied colleagues had to decide their own next steps. Once again the U.S. Army urged a cross-Channel invasion of Europe; once again Churchill and his staff refused, adamantly favoring peripheral attacks; and Admiral King, openly doubting the British commitment to Japan's defeat, put in strong words for the Pacific. With that came agreement—eventually. Any cross-Channel operation in 1943 was excluded. "Adequate forces" (whatever that meant, and no one was sure) would be allocated to the Pacific and Far East. The route to Italy would be opened by Operation Husky—an invasion of Sicily, in preference to Sardinia, and a precursor of the island-hopping strategy which would develop in the Pacific.

At the same time, it was agreed that the best available men should confer as soon as possible on antisubmarine measures. For these decisions alone, Casablanca would have been an important encounter; but two further elements made it one of the most momentous meetings of the age. Since the summer of 1942, the Allies had pooled their extensive researches on atomic fission, and at Casablanca Roosevelt was able to confirm to Churchill in person that the first successful nuclear chain reaction (a fission of uranium isotope U-235) had taken place six weeks before, on December 2, 1942. It was also at Casablanca that, at the president's urging, the two men agreed to announce a new joint policy on January 24, 1943, the day after their conference ended. They would fight only for the unconditional surrender of the Axis powers—no terms, no negotiation; only absolute victory and absolute defeat. In later years, Fleet Admiral Nimitz spoke for many British and American people when he showed the shock he had felt then:

> Not even Napoleon at the height of his conquests ever so completely closed the door to negotiation. To adopt such an inflexible policy was bad enough; to announce it publicly was worse. The policy of Unconditional Surrender ran counter to the earlier insistence of British and American leaders that they were fighting not the people but the leaders who misled them. . . . Today's enemy might be needed as tomorrow's ally. And a war pushed to the point of complete victory might ruin victor as well as vanquished.[3]

On March 1, 1943, about a hundred people met secretly in Washington at the invitation of Admiral King. One in five was an admiral or a general, all came from the armed forces of Canada, Britain, and the United States, and among them they knew all there was to know about antisubmarine warfare. And more than ever, Karl Dönitz represented their joint enemy, for on January 31 he had become Grand Admiral, commander in chief of the German navy.

In King's opening address to the Washington Convoy Conference, he stressed the importance of keeping supplies going both to Britain, "as the citadel of the war effort against Germany," and to the USSR: "Russian convoys must be provided for in any plan that the United States may be expected to accept."[4] On March 13 the conference ended with agreement that all Allied resources in the Atlantic would be pooled and the ocean divided into areas of responsibility. But only three days later, off the east coast of Newfoundland, the U-boats scored a record kill: twenty-two Allied merchantmen totaling over 146,000 tons for the loss of a single submarine. A gleeful message came from U-boat High Command: "Bravo! Keep at it! Carry on like that!"[5]

Worldwide sinkings of Allied ships that month approached 630,000 tons—not far short of the previous November's peak of 700,000 tons and far more than the half-million tons a month deemed necessary in Dönitz's estimate of May 1942. However, in September 1942 that estimate had been drastically revised upwards to 1.3 million tons; and U-boat losses were beginning to rise—nineteen in February 1943, fifteen in March, a half dozen in the first ten days of April. On April 11 the Grand Admiral reported to Hitler: "My great anxiety . . . is that the U-boat war will fail if we do not sink more ships than the enemy builds," and then made the extraordinary assertion that between 100,000 and 200,000 tons sunk a month would achieve his goal.[6] Such a figure would have had a cumulative effect on Britain alone, but it could not seriously touch joint Allied production; for whatever reason, Dönitz's view of the war was becoming unrealistic.

On the other side of the world, the other naval half of the splintered Axis was also losing touch with reality. On Guadalcanal, the U.S. Marines emerged battered and malaria-ridden but victorious on February 9. Churchill then called them "the glorious Marines"—they had indeed come a long way since 1776, when Benedict Arnold called them "the refuse of every regiment."

Within two weeks, with the Army's Forty-third Division, they moved on to occupy the Russell Islands (60 miles northwest of Guadalcanal), which had another precious fighter airstrip. Early in March, as the Convoy Conference sat in Washington, U.S. and Australian aircraft intercepted a sixteen-ship Japanese convoy taking supplies and reinforcements to its beleaguered comrades in Lae, on the northern coast of New Guinea. In the Battle of the Bismarck Sea, as it became known, five U.S. planes were lost; but twenty Japanese planes were shot down, eight transports and four destroyers were sunk, and 3,600 Japanese soldiers died. It was the last time the Imperial Navy tried to reinforce that section of New Guinea.

Three weeks later, however, Admiral Yamamoto authorized a huge air counteroffensive in the southwest Pacific. With over three hundred aircraft, it was the largest air armada created by the Imperial Navy, and, beginning on April 7, it harried American forces for a week. As reported to Yamamoto, the results were impressive: 134 U.S. planes shot down and twenty-five transports, two destroyers, and a cruiser sunk. The true U.S. loss was much less: only twenty-five aircraft, a destroyer, a corvette, a tanker, and two transports. But the admiral (who was nicknamed "the Peacock" in the U.S.) accepted the reported figures with satisfaction, called the operation off, and prepared to embark on a morale-raising tour of the troops. It was his last journey.

U.S. naval intelligence was often superbly efficient, and one of its most spectacular coups was to arrange the killing of Yamamoto. Yet it was not very difficult: The hard work—learning how to read Japanese codes—had been done long before, and Yamamoto's broadcast schedule was read almost as easily by the Americans as by the Japanese. Knowing the commander in chief's habit of strict punctuality, eighteen P-38 fighters from Guadalcanal had only to be in the right place at the right time: four hundred miles away in the skies over Bougainville at 9:34 A.M. on April 18, 1943. There, just as announced on the supposedly secret Japanese radio network, were six fighters escorting two Mitsubishi bombers. In one of those sat Admiral Yamamoto; in the other, his chief of staff, Adm. Matome Ugaki. In moments, nine planes were spiraling down in flames toward sea and land: one P-38 and all the eight Japanese.

Yamamoto's strenuous attempts to prevent war had by then been universally ignored or forgotten, and both at home and abroad he was viewed purely as the man who had launched the attack on Pearl Harbor and who had directed the Imperial Navy's subsequent six fantastic months. His body was recovered from the wreck and his ashes taken reverently home to Japan; but his death was a blow from which the Imperial Navy never properly recovered, and a magnificent stroke for the Allies. "Congratulations Major Mitchell and his hunters," Vice Adm. William Halsey signaled when he heard the result. "Sounds as though one of the ducks in their bag was a peacock."

Back in the Atlantic, in spite of the severe losses to Atlantic U-boats in March, the work of the Convoy Conference was not in vain—indeed, those very losses concentrated Allied attention on the problem wonderfully. Very-long-range Liberator aircraft were taken from the glamorous but ineffective strategic bombing of Germany and moved to Newfoundland and Iceland to augment existing Catalinas. From those bases they soon achieved full daylight coverage of the "black pit" southeast of Greenland—the most vulnerable section of the North Atlantic, the British-Canadian area of responsibility.

U-boats were forced to operate only underwater, but they still covered the area thickly. On April 28 the westward-bound convoy ONS-5 (forty-two ships) encountered a picket line which summoned a pack of fifty-one submarines. In typical U-boat fashion, the ensuing battle ran over several days. One merchantman was lost at once. By the evening of May 5, eleven more merchantmen and two U-boats had been sunk; but then fog came on, and the advantage of invisibility was turned. Radar and high-frequency direction-finding revealed the submarines when they could see nothing; and by dawn the following day, four more were sunk.

In the next three weeks another dozen convoys crossed the "black pit" with a total loss of only five ships. In the same period the wolf packs lost a further thirteen of their number to air and surface escort attacks, and over May as a whole Dönitz's submarine fleet was reduced by forty-one. U-boat command had never experienced so great a loss. The offensive was withdrawn from the North Atlantic, and except for sporadic, isolated attacks, it did not return.

Instead it moved to the central Atlantic (the area of American responsibility) and the adjacent Bay of Biscay. But Biscay was covered by British air patrols with the advanced 10-centimeter wavelength radar, proof against Metox; and the central Atlantic was covered by the American Tenth Fleet.

The Tenth Fleet had no ships of its own at all. It was one of Admiral King's creations, an administrative unit supervised by himself and run by Rear Adm. Francis ("Frog") Low. Theoretically responsible to Admiral

Ingersoll, in practice Frog Low became the U.S. Navy's main authority controlling the direction and monitoring the movement of ships in the central Atlantic; the administration of antisubmarine warfare training programs; the research and development of antisubmarine warfare techniques and technology; and the accompanying intelligence effort. Between him and Grand Admiral Dönitz, the central Atlantic lay like a poker table. In that game of nerves and deadly skill, as the convoys steamed to and from the Mediterranean and North Africa, Low used all the Allies' high-scoring cards: escort carriers, destroyers, and aircraft, with radar, bombs, guns, and new weapons. Prime among these were the forward-throwing "hedgehog" and "squid" contact explosives (which, unlike the astern-thrown depth charge, enabled a ship to keep sonar contact with its target during attack) and "Fido," the new antisubmarine homing torpedo.

Without examples to follow, these "hunter-killer groups" devised their tactics almost as they went along; and they developed into a winning hand. On May 14, 1943, Dönitz acknowledged to his submarine commanders that the Allies had contrived to "rob U-boats of their most valuable characteristic, invisibility."[7] Five days later the Grand Admiral's submariner son Peter was killed when his U-boat, *U-954,* was bombed. "If there is anyone who thinks that fighting convoys is no longer possible," said Dönitz, "he is a weakling and no real U-boat commander. The Battle of the Atlantic gets harder, but it is the decisive campaign of the war."[8] At the end of May, without difficulty and without discussing where the resources would come from or what alternatives there might be, he persuaded Hitler to authorize a program of increased submarine construction; and early in July plans for a new type of prefabricated boat were shown to him. He was overjoyed: "With this," he cried, "we begin a new life!"[9]

His faith in the U-boat remained infinite; he knew well how close to starvation and defeat it had brought Britain in the First World War. He hoped to introduce sonar torpedoes which would home on a ship's propellers. He hoped to enable U-boats to recharge their batteries underwater by giving them a snorkel to breathe through. But Dönitz was deluding himself. In practical terms the Battle of the Atlantic was already over; Germany's tonnage war had been lost to greater material production and superior electronics. Yet with those factors left out, his theory was sound: The submarine, "by continuously sinking ships with war materials and supplies . . . must subdue the enemy by a continual blood-letting."[10] And in the Pacific, the U.S. Navy was beginning to put Dönitz's theory into effective practice against Japan.

15

★

ACTION AGAINST A RETREATING ENEMY

*I*t is well known that, by good fortune, the United States' aircraft carriers were absent from Pearl Harbor when the Japanese attack took place, and it has become a truism to add that after the attack, for want of other ships, the U.S. Navy was obliged to devise a carrier-based strategy. The graceful shapes of the ships themselves; the superficially glamorous nature of carrier warfare; the spectacular, highly visible successes achieved by the Navy when it had not intended to center its war on carrier vessels at all—these are all factors which make it easy to forget that that was not the only radical change forced on U.S. naval doctrine. Throughout the Pacific and its war, U.S. submarines were used in a way never planned for before Pearl Harbor and, for their numbers, made a disproportionately great contribution to final victory.

Unrestricted submarine warfare by Germany had been one cause of the United States' entry into the First World War, and until Pearl Harbor, U.S. submariners still thought in terms of civilized international conventions limiting their own use. But only a few hours after the attack, orders came from Washington lifting all restrictions on undersea war against Japan: Warships and merchant ships alike could be attacked without warning. It was not just an instinct for revenge, but a realistic review of resources; apart from carriers, submarines were the major type of warship immediately available. For the same reason, when Chester Nimitz (himself a submariner) took command of the Pacific Fleet on the last day of

1941, he did so in Pearl Harbor on board the submarine *Grayling,* surrounded by the wreckage of surface ships.

On December 7, 1941, the U.S. Navy had 111 submarines operational, of which fifty-one were in the Pacific: seven actually in Pearl Harbor, another operating locally, a further fourteen either in transit between Pearl Harbor and the West Coast or on the West Coast for training or overhaul; and twenty-nine more in the Philippines. U.S.S. *Gato* typified those built in or after 1941: 1,500 tons' surface displacement, 312 feet long, a cruising radius of 12,000 miles, a crew of about eight officers and eighty men, twenty-four torpedoes, ten tubes—six for'ard and four aft—with a 3-inch gun on deck and up to four light automatic weapons. "This," Nimitz wrote later, "was the type of boat that carried the war to Japan."[1]

But though the first Japanese victim was found quickly (a freighter, sunk off the coast of Indochina on December 16, 1941), the boats were plagued by defective equipment. An extreme episode took place in July 1943, when Lt. Comdr. (later Vice Admiral) L. R. Daspit, commanding *Tinosa,* found and fired at a 19,000-ton tanker—one of the largest Japanese merchant targets of the war. From the first spread of four torpedoes, only two exploded. Eleven of *Tinosa*'s twelve remaining torpedoes were launched, but as the enraged Daspit reported, "They were all good, solid hits, and all duds!"[2]

More than eighteen months after Pearl Harbor, it was a dismal level of technical achievement; fortunately, though, Daspit had the sense to hold back his last torpedo and return it to Pearl Harbor for inspection. By then, Charles Lockwood (who, as naval attaché in London, had written so scathingly about Kimmel) was an admiral and in charge of the Southwest Pacific Submarine Force. Only the month before *Tinosa*'s frustrating experience, Lockwood had banned the use of magnetic exploders; they had been so unreliable, they verged on being absolutely reliable failures. Now, the examination he ordered revealed that the alternative contact exploder was as defective—its firing pin broke if it hit straight on. No one could tell how many good hits had been wasted through these faults; but very few were wasted thereafter.

Turning their torpedoes into effective weapons was (not surprisingly) the most important single development for U.S. submarines, but the vessels also underwent several other improvements, and the doctrine of their use changed as well. At first it was cautious: Commanding officers were allowed to make only submerged daylight attacks, without using the audibly pinging, echo-ranging sonar. However, the boats themselves were gradually equipped with night periscopes, periscope range finders, enhanced radar, reliable torpedo data computers, and improved camouflage—though they had begun the war painted all black, it was discovered that light gray made a disguise good enough to allow nighttime surface attacks. Little by little, submarines were made more efficient and effective than ever before; and by the autumn of 1943 they had five distinct functions.

The foremost of these was cutting enemy supply lines. The next three (not directly combatant) were photo reconnaissance, lifeguarding during air strikes, and scouting to report enemy movements. Linked to the latter, they were ready to intercept and attack emerging enemy forces; and their last function was to pursue, intercept, and attack fugitive enemy shipping fleeing a target area.

They were always called boats then; but today's submarines have grown so large that the term can only be used affectionately, and they are called ships, which is really more appropriate. Among the comparatively small "boats" of the Pacific war, however, some established impressive individual records. In two separate four-day periods, *Batfish* sank three Japanese submarines and *Harder* three destroyers. *Archerfish* sank the 68,000-ton aircraft carrier *Shinano* (the biggest in the world) when the carrier was on her maiden voyage; and in the month of May 1944, *England* sank no less than six submarines—a feat which prompted the notoriously anti-British Admiral King to signal: "There'll always be an *England* in the United States Navy."[3] (There has been, too, at least as far as the end of the 1980s; *England,* CG-22, was then a guided missile cruiser.) And U.S. submariners rescued a total of 504 downed airmen, including one who was then the Navy's youngest commissioned pilot— Ensign George Bush, later president of the United States.

Such men—Bush was one of them—found they had to remain on board their rescuing submarine for days or weeks before their eventual return to port. Under the sea they found a way of life and death completely unlike their previous experience. With the exception of periods on the surface, usually at night, their view of the outside world (previously as wide as eyes would allow) was suddenly limited to a privileged peep through a periscope, a look at a radar screen, a listen on earphones. Added to the claustrophobic constriction was the frustration of having no definite job, no direct part in the team—a feeling definitely at its worst if the submarine came under attack.

"We got depth-charged; we got bombed," Bush said later. "That depth-charging got to me. It just shook the boat. . . . Those guys would say, 'Oh, that wasn't close.' It didn't bother them, but it bothered me."[4]

Yet if the submariners were not going to reveal any nervousness to someone from another branch of the Navy, privately they would write of it freely. One noted in his diary:

Any other person who says he is not afraid under similar circumstances is a damn liar. Each time [a depth charge] went off it resembled a low rumble of thunder, a jar, and then it seemed as if someone were throwing tons of gravel against the outside of the boat, or rattling chains against the hull. Then afterwards a quiet that seemed to shout at you. . . . I haven't any idea how many were in this barrage because I was too busy and scared to keep count. They were all close and must have been six hundred pounders, as the boat would bob like a cork after each one. . . . They were doing a very thorough job of stirring up every foot of the area in which we might be. I don't have the least idea how many came at us, but there was no let up all day.[5]

After an especially vicious attack, the same submariner wrote: "We were taught a lesson yesterday—there's two parties to this war." Fifty-two U.S. submarines were lost in the course of the war, thirty-six known to Japanese action; and at the end of the war 260 remained in commission. But compared to the figures for U-boats, the numbers were small, and favorable to the United States: Germany built 1,175, of which 781 were sunk. That is, while the United States lost a sixth of its submarines, Germany lost more than two thirds. As for Japan, through the course of the war its navy had 197 operational submarines, excluding midgets; and of those 197, only forty-nine survived to be surrendered at the end of the war—a loss of three quarters of the operational force.

Three final statistics testify to the disproportionate value of U.S. submarines in the Pacific war. They sank 55 percent of the total merchant tonnage and 29 percent of the total warship tonnage lost by Japan; but the crews of the submarines amounted to only 1.6 percent of the U.S. Navy's entire manpower.

This was Dönitz's dream of the tonnage war, at work and working. Woven through the figures of profit and loss, victory and defeat, is the curious way in which the Pacific submarine war mirrored the Battle of the Atlantic. As island nations, both Britain and Japan could be starved into submission by the destruction of their overseas supply lines, and by using unrestricted undersea combat from the outset, the U.S. Navy effectively adopted Dönitz's central strategy of tonnage warfare. Warships and merchant ships alike were fair game, for each contributed to the enemy's war effort: As the Grand Admiral had said the other way around, "the enemy powers' shipping is one large whole. It is therefore immaterial where a ship is sunk—in the end it must be replaced by a new ship."

Yet if Dönitz came close to starving Britain, the U.S. Navy actually did starve Japan; for while the U.S. Navy adopted a German-style strategy, the Japanese navy held fast to an outdated British-style view. This was not entirely surprising: Britain's Royal Navy had been tutor to the Japanese Navy's first generation of leaders, from the 1890s to the 1920s, and many of the Western navy's ideals and attitudes had transplanted readily to the East. One British admiral expressed his country's opinion of early submarines in a famous phrase—furtive and invisible, they were "underhand, unfair, and damned un-English." But they worked far too well to be ignored; like them or not, one had to condescend to fight them. Hence came convoys, depth charges, centimetric radar, escort carriers, and all the rest. Unfortunately for the Japanese navy, however, it never entirely rid itself (until it was far too late) of the double-sided attitude that merchant shipping was not a legitimate target.

On one side, this meant that the Japanese began to use convoy only in April 1942. That time lapse was comparable to the belated adoption of the system by the United States, but there was a difference—within the Sea of Japan, merchant ships sailed in peacetime habits (unescorted, lit, and alone) as late as June 1945, when a wolf pack of nine U.S. submarines penetrated the Strait of Tsushima. The other side of the same attitude meant that the Japanese navy used its submarines almost exclusively as adjuncts to fleet operations, as scouts, and even (in the later stages of the war) in the inappropriate role of supply boats to garrisons otherwise cut off. U.S. merchant shipping was rarely attacked; it was regarded as worth neither the risk nor the effort. But as Admiral King remarked after the war, "If the Japanese had done what they could have done, they might have raised hell with the West Coast–Hawaii convoys. Thank the Lord they did not understand or learn much about managing U-boats from the Nazis."[6]

"The danger inherent in any report confined to one aspect of the war," said Vice Adm. Forrest Sherman subsequently, "is that it may mislead the reader into forgetting that the conflict was won by a combination of ground, naval, and air forces, each of which carried its share of the common burden."[7]

The truth of the remark belies its generosity, for Sherman was a member of that most public and memorable group, the carrier commanders. As further conferences of the Allied leaders made and confirmed decisions on the continued prosecution of the global war, its conclusion became more and more clearly inevitable; and certain milestones marked its approach. The Battle of Midway had been one of the first, when the United States moved from the defensive to the defensive-offensive in the Pacific. Operation Torch was another, the turning of the tide of the European land war against the Axis.

Trident, the second Washington conference (May 12–25 1943), coincided with the effective end of the Battle of the Atlantic. At this conference, Churchill's repeated wish for more peripheral attacks on Germany through the Balkans was finally defeated; but at last there was an agreed provisional date for the cross-Channel invasion of France, set for May 1,

1944. It was further agreed that following the capture of Sicily, Italy would be defeated, and that military aid to China would be increased. (In the same way as the convoys to Russia were maintained in order to keep German armies weaker in the west, so Japan's still undeclared war against China tied down a vast number of Japanese land forces.) The conference's most urgent decision was put into effect almost at once: Operation Husky, the Allied invasion of Sicily (July 9–August 17, 1943) led directly to the invasion and simultaneous secret surrender of Italy on September 3. As the battle for Sicily was ending, Churchill and Roosevelt met again in Quebec (August 14–24) for their Quadrant conference. The date of the following year's cross-Channel invasion was confirmed, and at the same time (after much argument from General MacArthur earlier on) a dual offensive for the Pacific was agreed.

The background to this was basically that MacArthur had wished to lead the U.S. advance on Japan up through New Guinea toward the Philippines, in what would be mainly an Army operation; the Navy would be merely auxiliary, transporting troops, bombarding shores, and guarding communications. The U.S. Navy naturally envisaged a more active role for itself. Years before, pondering the possibility that one day the Philippines might be lost, naval officers had decided the central Pacific would offer the best route for the islands' reconquest: It was direct, it contained no large land masses, and even if enemy forces defended it island by island, they would necessarily be small, scattered, and fragmented.

The Quadrant conference adopted a compromise which took rather more of the Navy's plan than MacArthur's. To maintain the present offensive and to protect Australia, the general's forces would continue up through New Guinea, as he wanted; but it would no longer be the main offensive. Instead, it would support and gradually converge with a naval push through the central Pacific. MacArthur was disgusted, accepted the decision with bad grace, and turned his attention once more to current affairs—the existing dual advance (begun in June) against Rabaul, Japan's great stronghold at the north of New Britain.

Unification of command, which had worked so well in Operation Torch, played no part in this advance, except on the adjoining edges of two separate command areas—Admiral Halsey's South Pacific and MacArthur's Southwest Pacific. Running through the Solomon Sea and Coral Sea, the dividing line between the two command areas was also the center line of the whole operation. The layout was like an open book: New Britain and Papua–New Guinea lay on the left-hand page, the Solomon Islands on the right-hand. Rabaul was perched like some poisonous insect at the top of the spine. Between them, Halsey and MacArthur aimed to snap the pages shut and crush Rabaul.

They began on June 30 with simultaneous invasions: MacArthur's men into Milne Bay, at Papua's southeastern end, and the islands of Kiriwina and Woodlark in the Solomon Sea; Halsey's men into the New Georgia group of islands in the central Solomons. From those points, the general's objective was to advance some 450 miles northwest up the north coast of Papua to the Huon Peninsula, then, from the port of Fischhafen, to move across northeastward to New Britain. At the far end of the 300-mile-long island lay Rabaul. The admiral's objective was to control all islands up to and including Bougainville, the most northerly large island of the Solomons group, thus bringing bombers within range of Rabaul. His route (northwestward from the central Solomons) was shorter, more direct, and, in the Japanese estimation, more immediately threatening.

Almost at once the reinforcing Tokyo Express—defunct since Japan's loss of Guadalcanal—was revived, and on July 5–6, 1943, the first of a rapid-fire series of summer and autumn naval battles took place. This, the Battle of Kula Gulf, was a distinct Japanese victory. The Battle of Kolombangara followed exactly a week later, fought in almost exactly the same place and with similar results: An American cruiser, *Helena,* was sunk at Kula Gulf, and a New Zealand cruiser, *Leander,* disabled at Kolombangara. And between the two battles, the Japanese successfully landed 2,000 soldiers on Kolombangara island. Both these were night battles—a long-standing specialty of the Japanese navy, for which it was probably better trained than any other navy in the world. In the days (or rather, in the nights) before radar, such training had given it a real advantage; but the very quality of the training and its past successes were partly why the possibilities of radar were ignored in Japan. Now those nights of dark ascendancy were passing: On August 6–7, on the waters separating the islands of Kolombangara and Vella Lavella, six U.S. destroyers met four Japanese destroyers, sank three of them, and put the fourth to flight.

The Battle of Vella Gulf (which Nimitz called "a little classic of naval warfare") was won not merely by superior numbers, but by superior equipment—the radar the Japanese denied themselves—and an imaginative adaptation of very old tactics. Carried out by Comdr. Frederick Moosbrugger, the attack was planned by Arleigh Burke, then a captain. Warned by a search plane of the enemy approach and soon locating them on radar, Moosbrugger followed Burke's arrangement and divided his destroyers into two teams. The first, running on a course parallel and opposite to the Japanese, passed them, launched torpedoes, turned away, and reversed course to match the enemy. The second turned across the enemy bows, and just as the torpedoes reached their calculated targets, both teams of destroyers opened fire. Under the simultaneous attack of torpedoes beneath, guns ahead, and guns abeam, three of the Japanese destroyers (and some 1,800 soldiers and sailors) blew up instantly. Later on, Burke described his tactical design simply as "hitting the enemy with one surprise after another" and explained he had gotten the idea after reading the tactics of Scipio Africanus in the Punic Wars.[8] The description was characteristically modest; but few naval commanders would even think of adapting tactics from a land campaign that had taken place more than two thousand years earlier.

It is worth taking time out from the war's chronological sequence to ponder Comdr. (later Admiral) Arleigh Burke, because his name and exploits have become so firmly lodged in the anecdotal lore of the Pacific. Born in 1901, he became a hero in 1943; he proved to be very long-lived; and, as almost anyone who has met him would testify, throughout that long life he remained a charming, genial, immensely courteous man— always very approachable, willing to give of his time to young officers and others who wished to meet him, even forty years and more after the war was over. There is probably no one else in the U.S. Navy's history who is accorded not only the respect, but also the affection which Burke has inspired. In that characteristic, he may be likened (without much exaggeration) to Nelson, whose personal memory in Britain and the Royal Navy is held even today in unequaled regard.

Burke was a brilliant commander of destroyers; he sank a lot of enemy ships in a dashing manner; he had a pleasing personality. Those are the things for which he is most widely remembered today, yet they are far from being the sum total of his naval career. In his own lifetime, the U.S. Navy created a class of vessel named after him—a most unusual honor for a living person—and the U.S. Naval Institute's annual essay competition, which any naval author is proud to win, was renamed the "Arleigh Burke Award." But when assessing Burke's achievements, it is important to remember that these distinctions were bestowed not only for his remarkable contributions in the Pacific war, but also because of his naval career thereafter, especially in Korea and (for a unique six-year term) as Chief of Naval Operations. This does not demean the real boldness and value of his Pacific war role. It does keep that role in perspective, in relation both to the Pacific war overall and to his subsequent career.

The Pacific war was certainly his proving ground. After it began, the expertise he had already gathered kept him—much against his will, but apparently immovably—far from the scenes of action, organizing the production of naval guns back in the continental United States. It was not until December 1942, after repeated requests for sea duty, that he convinced his superiors that someone else was available to do his shore work. In January 1943 they let him go, to take charge of Destroyer Division 43. He was then a commander and well aware that he had missed out on a lot of practical experience—for more than a year, while he had been chasing up guns on shore, his classmates had been fighting the Japanese at sea. He boarded his divisional flagship, the destroyer U.S.S. *Walker,* on February 14—St. Valentine's Day—which could prompt observations (not completely unjustified) about the beginning of a long love affair with destroyers. More to the point, it was only three weeks later that he encountered his first Japanese destroyer—and promptly sank it.

Burke spent the summer of 1943 as commander of all destroyers in the Slot, escorting troop transports. Coming under shore fire from Kolombangara, he was wounded in the back by a piece of shrapnel (and, less conventionally, had two ribs dislocated when a signalman fell off the mast and landed on him). Promotion to captain came in September, followed in October by assignment to command Destroyer Squadron 23; and it was with this squadron that Burke's name became justly famous. The previous squadron commander had been insufficiently aggressive (hence his removal), but the individual ships and commanding officers were well trained and eager. Burke did not disappoint them: The schedule he set them was so full that within weeks they had nicknamed themselves "the Little Beavers." The name stuck—not surprisingly, because, after supplying gunfire support for the initial landings on Bougainville in November 1943, Burke and his five-ship squadron fought in twenty-two separate actions over the following four months. The squadron's credited tally of enemy craft sunk during that period was one cruiser, nine destroyers, one submarine, several smaller vessels, and some thirty airplanes.

In a single action, the Battle of Cape St. George (which took place on November 25, 1943—Thanksgiving Day), Burke's five destroyers sank three of five enemy destroyers which were evacuating troops from Bougainville, without loss to themselves. From an earlier report that he was proceeding to a scene of action at 31 knots, he, like his squadron, already had a nickname within the Navy; and after the victory, Thirty-One Knot Burke and the Little Beavers became known throughout the United States.

His personal performance as captain of the Little Beavers was so outstanding that in March 1944 he was made commodore—a rank which was phased out after the war—and appointed chief of staff to Vice Adm. Marc Mitscher (of whom more later) in the celebrated Fast Carrier Task Force 58. For many people, four months of exceptional activity would be enough to give distinction to a whole forty-year career, and certainly Burke's most famous deeds were done in that brief but hectic time with Destroyer Squadron 23. But they should not overshadow all the rest of his naval life: He still had a lot to give.

We left the story with Moosbrugger's victory, using Burke's plan, at the Battle of Vella Gulf (August 6–7, 1943). Two months later and only a few miles away, the Battle of Vella Lavella (October 6–7, 1943) appeared to turn the tables neatly. In this, a night action of six Tokyo Express destroyers against three U.S. destroyers, two of the U.S. destroyers had their bows blown off, one of those two was rammed by the third, and the Japanese capped their success by evacuating the island of Vella Lavella without molestation. No doubt they were exhilarated; it showed that some 2,800 miles from Tokyo, they were continuing to defend the homeland. But the success was temporary, and in later years that small engagement in a remote and obscure tropical sound attained a significance out of all proportion to its size—for it was the last time the United States lost a battle in the Pacific, and the last time Japan won.

Taken together, that fact, its place, and its date are a simple and vivid indication of the unceasing ferocity of Japanese defense. Between the invasion of New Georgia and the Battle of Vella Lavella, ninety-nine days had elapsed. In that time Halsey's advance had covered only about 120 miles, and very nearly two full years more would pass before peace returned to the Pacific.

On the other hand, if the Allied speed of advance through the remaining 2,800 miles or so to Tokyo had gone at the same speed as the advance through the Solomons, the war would have gone on at least another six years. In 1943 that seemed all too possible: When enlisted men looked forward to a victorious return home, they spoke of seeing the "Golden Gate in '48." But of course no war works like that, with a steady rate of progress in one direction or the other. The Battle of Vella Lavella shows how hard Halsey's advance had been to that point—and how rapid the overall advance against Japan became thereafter. And in large part, that was made possible by the success of an earlier experiment nearly 4,000 miles from the Solomons.

The experiment was the method by which Kiska was recaptured. Up in the farthest north Pacific, its occupation and the occupation of neighboring Attu were the sole benefits derived by Japan from the operation against Midway. Undertaken as a diversionary tactic to split the U.S. fleet in its defense of Midway, the islands' actual acquisition was entirely useless to Japan. The unfortunate soldiers ordered to occupy those frigid, desolate, fog-bound islands could be forgiven for viewing their task as a particularly twisted form of punishment—their sole consolation being the thought that, as representatives of Japan, they were in control of the U.S. territory nearest to the continental United States. That in turn was the sole reason why they had to be ejected; and in the middle of May 1943 the process began.

Supplies to the islands had already been cut off by the Battle of the Komandorskiyes (the last naval battle in history fought by surface ships and guns alone) and when the ships of Rear Adm. (later Admiral) Thomas C. Kinkaid approached the islands on May 11, 1943, he decided to ignore the more heavily defended Kiska for the time being and go first for Attu, even though it was almost 200 miles further from the United States. The campaign took eighteen days. At sea there were sporadic counterattacks by submarines and by aircraft flying 650 miles from Paramushir Island, south of Kamchatka; these were frightening but ineffective. One participant, Ens. Elmo R. Zumwalt, Jr. (who would become Admiral Zumwalt, Chief of Naval Operations) recalled in later years that he happened to be officer of the deck at the time:

> The look-out reported: "Aircraft coming in over the islands—they're Billy Mitchells." Just about this time was when we got our glasses on them. We could see things dropping. The look-out said: "They're dropping their spare tanks"—and then suddenly, almost with one voice, the shout was: "Jesus Christ!—The gas tanks are under way!—Torpedoes!—General Stations! Battle Stations!" The Japanese reported the next day that they had sunk a battleship and a light cruiser. They actually hit none of us.[9]

Onshore, though, the Japanese resistance became brutal in the extreme, as the defenders realized they had neither support nor hope. Holed up in the island's mountainous interior, their last thousand men came down unobserved in the predawn darkness of May 29 and launched a ghastly, vengeful suicide attack. Breaking through the U.S. lines and overrunning two command posts, they found a medical station, killed all the patients, and (when the last five hundred of their number were finally cornered) committed mass suicide by clutching grenades to their stomachs.

Gradually U.S. soldiers, sailors, and marines were learning the nature of the enemy. Appalled at the carnage, angered at their own unexpectedly high losses (600 dead, 1,200 wounded) and at the lack of preparation which put 1,500 more out of action (inadequate training, inappropriate equipment), they made ready to the last degree before approaching Kiska. Over 34,000 U.S. and Canadian soldiers (more than three times the force at Attu) were trained rigorously in arctic conditions. Twelve hundred tons of bombs were dropped on Kiska to soften it up, and battle ships bombarded its main camp and harbor in preparation for the assault on August 15; and all for naught. The assault was completely unopposed, for the island turned out to be absolutely empty. Every single enemy soldier had been spirited away, under cover of fog, by cruisers and destroyers.

It was with some embarrassment that Admiral King reported the bloodless recapture to the Combined Chiefs of Staff, the president, and the prime minister, meeting at the Quadrant conference in Quebec. Apart from the exposed deficiency of the United States' normally reliable intelligence service, the assault had been intended as a rehearsal for the Pacific war's expected amphibious tactics. But, knowing well that anyone can make mistakes, the British Chiefs offered no criticism; and in any case the campaign as a whole had demonstrated an intriguing strategy which offered the possibility of real acceleration across the Pacific. If a weakly defended island lay beyond a strongly defended one; if it were possible to bypass the strong one and take the weak; and if, most important, it were then possible to cut off completely the strong island's communications—then a direct attack on the strong island could be avoided altogether. Literally isolated, its defenders could be starved into submission.

Thus was born one of the most famous aspects of the Pacific war, the leapfrogging strategy. It is often confused now with the island-hopping strategy. That, however, was an earlier approach, used (for example) by Halsey in the first part of his Solomons campaign; it meant the capture of islands in order, hopping from one to the next. Leapfrogging was a radical change, but no single person was responsible for its invention. With intelligent people analyzing the same problem, the same solution will often appear to several minds at once, and to name only two, General MacArthur and Rear Adm. Theodore S. Wilkinson thought of the same thing independently and simultaneously. Halsey took it on quickly: After New Georgia, Wilkinson (under Halsey's command) bypassed Kolombangara for Vella Lavella. Both islands were swiftly evacuated by the Japanese, many moving to the defense of the southern end of Bougainville, the last large island in the chain. "Going into swampy jungles to fight the Japanese," Churchill once said to his own Chiefs of Staff, "is like going into the water to fight a shark."[10] Halsey's men did not have the option; but in Bougainville, at least the admiral was able to choose which swamp they would fight in.

The one he selected (again leapfrogging over the enemy defenses) was a bog called Torokina, halfway up the island's west coast and inland from Empress Augusta Bay. Drained, leveled, and transformed into an airfield by the noncombatant naval Construction Battalions (nicknamed Seabees, from their initials), it prompted the last major naval surface clash in the south/southwest Pacific, the Battle of Empress Augusta Bay during the night of November 1–2, when the initial landing was barely complete. Four Japanese cruisers and six destroyers came out from Rabaul; only three cruisers and five destroyers returned; and out of the force they met (four cruisers and eight destroyers under Rear Adm. Aaron S. Merrill), not one ship was sunk. The U.S. Navy really was coming to grips with the tactics of night action; and now, less than 300 miles northwest, the Japanese navy's great base was within range of fighter planes from Bougainville.

Three weeks later and 1,000 miles northeast, Rear Adm. Keiji Shibasaki faced the test of his favorite claim. Commanding 3,000 naval infantry (Japan's equivalent of Marines), he was ordered to defend Tarawa, a triangular atoll in the Gilbert Islands. To fortify Betio, a tiny island two miles long by three quarters of a mile wide at its broadest point, which is at the apex of Tarawa, he had constructed steel-reinforced concrete blockhouses with walls and roofs six feet thick; bombproof shelters, half underground and covered with interwoven levels of green coconut logs; pillboxes with field guns; emplacements with antiaircraft and coastal defense guns; trenches surrounded by steel, concrete, logs, and sandbags; a log seawall four feet high; and, meshed with the coral growing in the bright, clear, shallow water, a maze of concrete, metal, and barbed wire. Central to the little island and occupying half its length was the airfield which, as it gave the island value, also demanded defense. And when he surveyed it all, satisfied that he had done a thorough job, Shibasaki declared that a million men in a hundred years could never conquer Betio.[11] But in the space of four days (November 20–23, 1943) 18,300 U.S. marines and sailors proved him wrong.

More than a thousand of them died in the process, and only seventeen of the defenders survived. The death toll in the amphibious assault on Tarawa shocked Americans at home: So many men were killed, and so fast. Yet it was only the first of many such battles across the central Pacific. Each one was concentrated, brief, and vicious, and each offered the prize of an enormously extended area of permanent authority. The atolls provided staging posts, anchorages, and airstrips: Like medieval castles, they became bases for the projection of physical power across the surrounding region, threatening, dominating, and controlling. The carriers were their floating, mobile equivalent, and now a new one entered the U.S. fleet every week. When the battle for Guadalcanal was at its height late in 1942, the U.S. Navy had had only three carriers. One year later, as the central Pacific drive began, it had fifty. By the end of the war there were over a hundred carriers in the fleet, and as the momentum of production kept up, the fleet's momentum toward Japan increased.

From Tarawa and neighboring Makin in the Gilberts, the next targeted island chain was the Marshalls—600 miles closer to Japan and in a direct line for Tokyo. Its central atoll, Kwajalein, was also the main Japanese base in the archipelago, with two airfields and a seaplane base. But defending Kwajalein were four other bases, and after the savage experience of Tarawa, admirals Richmond Turner and Raymond Spruance agreed with Gen. Holland M. Smith of the Marines that time was needed to gather more strength and to assess the mistakes and lessons of Betio, their first big amphibious operation in the Pacific. All three men felt that two of the outlying Marshalls bases should be attacked first as a preliminary step toward Kwajalein. Nimitz thought otherwise. Willing to try the still unconventional leapfrog, he thoroughly alarmed his three commanders—in his opinion, Kwajalein should be assaulted directly.

At the same time as Tarawa fell, so did Bougainville, and on the other side of the Solomon Sea, MacArthur's advance paralleled Halsey's neatly. By October he had captured Finschhafen; on December 26 he assaulted Cape Gloucester, the westernmost point of New Britain. Rabaul had come under air attack already: On November 5 Halsey launched ninety-seven planes from *Saratoga* and the new light carrier *Princeton* against the island fortress, damaging eight ships in its harbor. Six days later the planes returned, accompanied by another 185 from the new carriers *Essex, Bunker Hill,* and *Independence.* By December the air attacks were constant, both from Bougainville and from New Guinea. Rabaul Island still held some hundreds of Japanese aircraft, as well as scores of thousands of troops still to be conquered or neutralized; but no shipping, either navy or merchant, remained in its harbor.

It was at the end of January 1944 that a most formidable new U.S. fleet arrived in the Marshalls—an expanded Fast Carrier Task Force, designated TF 58, commanded by Rear Adm. Marc A. Mitscher and composed of thirty-six destroyers, six cruisers, eight fast battleships, and twelve carriers with 750 aircraft. Joining land-based aircraft from the new fields in the Gilberts, they took wing against every base in the Marshalls and also against Eniwetok, another 300 miles nearer Japan. Simultaneously, the Fifth Amphibious Force was approaching with 53,000 soldiers and Marines, while at Funafuti in the Ellice Islands, 700 miles southeast of Tarawa, the Service Force Pacific Fleet turned the lagoon into a floating naval base, able to look after the fleets with everything from light repairs to steak-and-egg supplies and high explosives.

"Maybe we had too many men and too many ships for the job," Admiral Turner said later, "but I prefer to do things that way. It saved us a lot of lives."[12] He was right; the U.S. casualties were far fewer than at Tarawa. Against the scrupulous planning and enormous force deployed, the Japanese occupation of the atolls could not hope to survive. The invasion of Kwajalein Island itself was, in Nimitz's words, "as near perfection as any such operation was likely to attain," proceeding exactly on schedule. In only four days the conquest was complete, and Kwajalein, said General Smith, "looked as if it had been picked up to 20,000 feet and then dropped."[13]

The speedy success, and the large numbers of men uncommitted and still fresh for action, prompted Nimitz to order a further immediate stab forward—not to Eniwetok, whose aircraft had been utterly destroyed, but far beyond, to those bases which could threaten Eniwetok if it were taken alone. They lay in a crescent shape, from Ponape (600 miles southwest of Eniwetok) through Truk (700 miles distant) to Saipan in the Marianas, a thousand miles northwest.

Truk, a sunken volcano, contained one of the world's best natural anchorages in its circular crater. Chosen by Yamamoto as the operational base of the Imperial Navy's Combined Fleet, it had a reputation for impregnability and was likened in value and importance to Pearl Harbor and Gibraltar; but on February 10, 1944, hearing of the disaster in the Marshalls and the approach of TF 58, Adm. Mineichi Koga (Yamamoto's successor) withdrew the fleet from Truk and retreated 900 miles westward to the comparative safety of the Palau Islands. He left only two light cruisers and eight destroyers behind him, but with the small naval force, hundreds of aircraft and dozens of merchant vessels remained in Truk as well; and they are still there. One week after Koga's hasty departure, Mitscher's aircraft and Spruance's battleships *Iowa* and *New Jersey* blasted the planes and merchantmen to shreds. Seventy-five percent of the shore installations were destroyed, and 200,000 tons of naval and merchant shipping were sunk. The huge destruction brought those ships far greater fame than they could ever have gained otherwise. Today, collectively, they are not only an official war grave, but also—with the sweet, slow erosion of instruments of death—they have become celebrated as the breeding ground for innumerable forms of marine life where little existed before.

Throughout the previous autumn, while Halsey had fought in the Solomons and MacArthur in New Guinea, Russian armies had pressed further and further westward into Europe as British and American troops slowly advanced up Italy. The time came for the leaders to confer again. After a preliminary meeting in Cairo, Roosevelt and Churchill planned to go on to Teheran, there to meet Stalin for the first time together. The president traveled in the battleship *Iowa,* accompanied by the Joint Chiefs of Staff. On their second day out from Hampton Roads, 350 miles east of Bermuda, they were almost torpedoed. The culprit was not a U-boat but one of their escorting destroyers, U.S.S. *William D. Porter,* carrying out torpedo drill, and aiming (for greater realism) at *Iowa*'s No. 2 magazine. A live, fully armed torpedo was fired accidentally. *Iowa* evaded it, leaving it to explode astern, and General Arnold (one of Admiral King's JCS colleagues) deliberately made King even more infuriated than he already was by asking him facetiously: "Tell me, Ernest, does this kind of thing often happen in your Navy?"

But all understood what the consequences could have been. As the president himself noted: "Had that torpedo hit the *Iowa* in the right spot with her passenger list of distinguished statesmen, military, naval, and aerial strategists and planners, it could have had untold effect on the outcome of the war and the destiny of the country."[14]

Out of those conferences came the firm decision to invade France in 1944, not only from across the Channel but also (simultaneously, if possible) from the south, squeezing the German armies against the blade of the Russians' bulldozer. During Europe's winter months, Anglo-American preparations forged onward for the invasion of Normandy, Operation Overlord; and Nimitz and MacArthur continued their steady progress through the Pacific.

With Rabaul surrounded and neutralized, MacArthur jumped forward to the Admiralty Islands, conquered them, jumped back to New Guinea again (400 miles ahead of his previous position, so bypassing a further 20,000 Japanese troops), and prepared to advance up the rest of the northern New Guinea coast, toward the Moluccas and his longed-for return to the Philippines. As he did so, TF 58 came to the Palaus in pursuit of the Combined Fleet, and, without any damage to itself, destroyed all land-based aircraft and any ships it could find. Ponape was shelled; carriers from the Fifth Fleet supported "MacArthur's Navy," the Seventh Fleet, in the return to New Guinea; and Gen. Holland Smith, Admiral Spruance, and Admiral Turner planned their attack on Saipan—Operation Forager. It would lead to the largest fleet operation in the Pacific war.

It is still startling to consider that such plans as Overlord and Forager could be made at the same time, on opposite sides of the world, for operations to be carried out almost simultaneously by the same allies. Overlord demanded 284 major combatant vessels, more than 4,000 landing craft and ships, more than 3,500 special types of amphibious craft, and 9,500 aircraft; and within twenty-four hours of its beginning at dawn on June 6, 1944, 176,000 troops were onshore. Forager took TF 58 (112 vessels covering 800 square miles of sea) followed by its amphibious force: 535 ships carrying over 80,000 Marines and nearly 50,000 soldiers. And on the same day as Overlord began, crowded into the narrow seas between England and France, the forces of Forager left the Marshalls en route for the Marianas, 1,500 miles northwest.

On June 11, 1944, TF 58 was 200 miles east of Guam in the southern Marianas. Mitscher began the air attack. Two days later his battleships began to bombard Saipan and neighboring Tinian; the day after that, air attacks began on the landing fields of Iwo Jima and Chichi Jima, as the bombardment of Saipan continued; and early on June 15 the invasion of Saipan commenced. At the same time, flying out of China, B-29 bombers dropped 221 tons of bombs on Kyushu, the southernmost island of Japan proper—the first direct attack on the homeland since the one-off Doolittle raid in April 1942. Intelligence reports from submarines stationed ahead indicated that a fleet battle was imminent: Fifty-five Japanese warships were leaving the Philippines in the direction of the Marianas.

On June 17 the commanders of the opposing fleets gave their battle orders. Their keynotes were very different. From the Japanese commander in chief came the old, stirring admonition used by their revered

Admiral Togo thirty-nine years earlier, before the decisive victory at Tsushima over the Russian fleet—"The fate of the Empire depends on this battle. Let every man do his utmost." Admiral Spruance, passing tactical command to Admiral Mitscher, used a far less romantic phrase: "Action against a retreating enemy must be pushed vigorously by all hands to complete destruction of his fleet."[15]

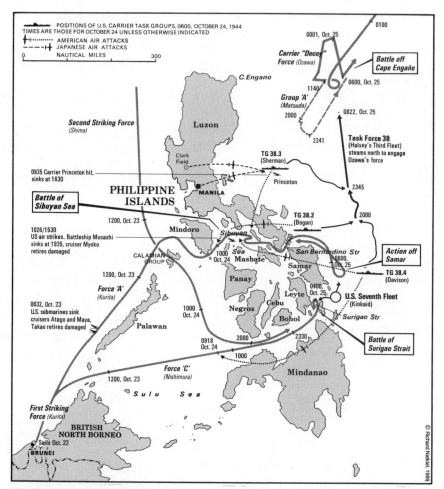

The Battle for Leyte Gulf (October 25–26, 1944) was composed of four separate battles—the Sibuyan Sea, Surigao Strait, Samar Island, and Cape Engaño. Together they covered an area larger than France, the battle involving more ships and men than had ever been deployed at one time anywhere.

16

★

A SEA FIGHT
BEYOND ALL OTHERS

*I*n private, Winston Churchill had rejoiced at the attack on Pearl Harbor: With the U.S. in the war, he had absolute confidence that eventually the Allies would win. "Hitler's fate was sealed. Mussolini's fate was sealed. As for the Japanese, they would be ground to powder. All the rest was merely the proper application of overwhelming force." And he remembered how an earlier British statesman, Lord Grey of Falloden, had likened the United States to a gigantic boiler—"Once the fire is lighted under it there is no limit to the power it can generate."[1]

The Battle of the Philippine Sea (June 19–20, 1944) showed vividly the truth of both Churchill's prophecy and Grey's proposition. Eighteen months previously there had been only three aircraft carriers in the whole U.S. Navy; now Task Force 58 alone contained fifteen, with 891 planes, all under Vice Adm. Marc Mitscher's command. And even this mighty force was not the total of the U.S. fleet which fought in the Philippine Sea that day. In addition to the carriers, the entire fleet (commanded by Vice Adm. Raymond Spruance) included seven battleships, twenty-one cruisers, and sixty-nine destroyers.

Approaching to do battle with them, Vice Adm. Jisaburo Ozawa's First Mobile Fleet contained nine carriers with 430 aircraft; but though he correctly estimated TF 58's strength as about twice his own, Ozawa did not regard it as an overwhelming force, for he expected that before he arrived, a third of it would have been destroyed by some five hundred land-based aircraft from the Marianas. He did not know that those five hundred had already been reduced to a mere thirty by unreported U.S. attacks; and he would never have imagined that before nightfall on the battle's first day, he would have lost two of his carriers and all but a hundred of his planes. Unknown to him, the force he faced on the morning of June 19 was already overwhelming; and the power of the "irresistible 58th," as another Japanese naval officer called it, was never more properly applied.[2]

At this point it is once again worthwhile stepping aside from the chronological flow to take a closer look at one man—this time, Marc Mitscher.

By mid-June 1944, as the Battle of the Philippine Sea approached, Commodore Arleigh Burke—fresh from the spectacular exploits of the Little Beavers—had been Mitscher's chief of staff for about ten weeks. The relationship between the two officers had not at first been easy. Mitscher resented Burke's appointment, seeing it as an imposition from on high, an unnecessary interference in an established team; Burke missed his Little Beavers, disliked staff work, and yearned to be back in operational command. But both men were too professional to bear grudges and build barriers, and in their separate ways they set about learning to work together. By May this process had advanced very markedly: "The boss," wrote Burke in a letter home, "is a good hard fighting little shriveled-up pleasant man . . ."[3]

It was an apt description, both of character and appearance— Mitscher's slight frame was topped by a deeply lined face with a rare smile, the gentleness of which belied his combative spirit. Burke could have added with perfect truth that his boss was taciturn often to the point of complete silence. But by then he had learned that behind the quiet front was something quite different—"he's full of fun . . . I admire him very much."

Mitscher was a supreme naval aviator and commander of naval aviators. He was then fifty-seven years old and had been a pilot most of his life—after graduation from the Naval Academy in 1910, he had become one of the first officers in the U.S. Navy to receive a pilot's certificate. As early as 1920 he had been in command of the Pacific Fleet's air detachment at San Diego; he had served on U.S.S. *Langley*—the first U.S. aircraft carrier—and was air officer of the third, U.S.S. *Saratoga*. After that he had progressed steadily through a variety of postings, all air-related, and just before the attack on Pearl Harbor had brought U.S.S. *Hornet* into commissioned service.

His Pacific war command experience already included *Hornet* in the Doolittle raid and at Midway; Noumea and the Solomons, with planes from the U.S. Navy, Army, and Marine Corps under him, along with others from the Royal New Zealand Air Force; naval air units on the U.S. West Coast; and most recently, Carrier Division 3.

In the six months since he had taken charge of the fast carriers, he had led them against the Marshalls, Truk, and New Guinea. His staff, whether they were career aviators or not, were all closely bonded to him; he did not care for yes-men, and one of his great gifts was the ability to form his subordinates, whoever they were, into a fully functioning team, encouraging them to challenge each other and himself if they felt a decision or line of argument was flawed. His pilots likewise trusted him implicitly, knowing that, as a former pilot himself, he would always do his utmost, within the limits imposed by battle, to make sure they got back safely. Not only had he repeatedly told them so himself, ever since the preparations for Midway; better than that, they had seen him do it, and as they approached the Philippine Sea, many pilots present already owed him their lives from past occasions. He was not always right and could not always rescue ditched airmen; but the important thing was that they knew he would always try his hardest for them. They, in return, always tried their hardest for him; and way beyond its imposing size and massive strength, it was these simple but crucial factors—experience, with mutual trust and confidence—which made Mitscher's carriers into the "irresistible 58th." And now once more he was leading them out to fight.

The action in this, the last and largest carrier conflict, came in two distinct phases: Ozawa's attack on June 19, followed by Mitscher's counterstroke on the twentieth. American radar contact was established at 10 A.M. on the nineteenth, with 150 miles separating the fleets. Twenty minutes later, Mitscher started to launch his entire complement of over 450 fighters, and "the Great Marianas Turkey Shoot" commenced. The U.S. airmen typically had two years' experience; their Japanese counterparts, after the deaths of veterans in Midway, Rabaul, and the Solomons, between two and six months. It was almost too easy: In eight hours of aerial combat, well over three hundred Japanese aircraft attacked, and well over two hundred were shot down or otherwise wrecked. During the same period, submarines attacked Ozawa's carriers, sinking two, including *Shokaku* from the Pearl Harbor assault force. Only thirty U.S. Navy planes were lost, and only slight damage was done to one or two of TF 58's vessels.

As night came on, Ozawa—accepting his surviving pilots' reports of great destruction in the enemy task force—withdrew to refuel; Mitscher recovered his aircraft; and during the night the fleets lost contact with one another. It was not until late next afternoon that a search plane finally located Ozawa's ships, 220 miles from TF 58—a distance well over the optimum attack range and certain to force returning pilots to land in the dark, which they were not trained to do. Nevertheless, Mitscher launched promptly: Within ten minutes, 216 aircraft were up and on their way. But no sooner was that done than the admiral received a further signal, correcting the previous one: The enemy was 300 miles away. For some minutes he pondered whether or not to recall the planes. He decided not to; and from that decision, the Battle of the Philippine Sea itself became both decisive and spectacular.

Mitscher had launched eighty-five fighters, seventy-seven dive-bombers, and fifty-four torpedo bombers. They sighted Ozawa's fleet at 6:20 P.M., a little before sunset. Seventy-five Japanese fighters flew defiantly up, and with the help of the fleet's antiaircraft guns, they succeeded in shooting down twenty U.S. planes. But two of the fleet's accompanying oil tankers were sunk; a third carrier was torpedoed, exploded, and sank; and when the struggle ended after dark, the surviving units of Ozawa's Mobile Fleet had a total of only thirty-five aircraft remaining.

By itself, the previous day's "Turkey Shoot" had been a severe blow to Japan. Added to the losses of land-based aircraft in the preceding few days, it gave the U.S. Navy complete air control in the Marianas; and when the lost carriers were added in as well, the full, decisive damage to Japan's navy became clear. Because of the Pearl Harbor attack and the subsequent wide-ranging victories of the same task force, it is easy to think of the Imperial Navy as a carrier-based fleet, as the U.S. Navy in the Pacific had become. But it was not, though Admiral Yamamoto would dearly have loved to have made it so. In 1941 the Imperial Japanese Navy included only twelve fleet carriers and a single escort carrier. In the course of the war, four new fleet carriers were built in Japan; four were converted from other vessels; and four escort carriers were converted from other hulls. Together, those twenty-five vessels were the total of Japan's important carriers in the entire war. But though three of the four escort carrier conversions existed in June 1944, only one of the new fleet carriers was complete then; and since the beginning of the war, an escort carrier and six fleet carriers had been sunk. In short, when Ozawa steamed toward TF 58, the Imperial Navy's whole stock of aircraft carriers was ten fleet vessels and four escorts. To lose three fleet carriers was, for Japan, catastrophic.

The damage figures were spectacular, and Mitscher's recovery of his returning aviators was equally so—an audacious act and a visual spectacle seen very rarely indeed, even in peace. While the aircraft had fought, his ships had raced toward them, to reduce the length of their return journey. Now, to help the pilots find the Task Force in the darkness, Mitscher ignored the risk of submarines and had every single carrier light switched on, including the searchlights, pointing vertically upward; and through the dark Pacific night, Task Force 58 shone out like a beacon proclaiming rescue and liberty.

. . .

In the few weeks before and after the Turkey Shoot, Saipan, Tinian, and Guam (the key islands of the southern Marianas) fell to the combined assaults of the U.S. Navy, Army, and Marines. Each capture entailed an appalling death toll, usually with ten or fifteen Japanese deaths for every American, as the emperor's troops (and his civilian subjects) attacked against impossible odds, or killed themselves rather than surrender. Saipan was the most terrible: 3,400 Americans dead and over 13,000 wounded; 24,000 Japanese dead from combat, estimated by the burials; and a number which could only be guessed at of suicides, as men and women threw themselves and their children over cliffs and into the sea. Some said hundreds, others thousands. For days afterward, U.S. Navy warships steamed through a sea of corpses.

The loss of Saipan on July 18 brought, in Japan, the resignation of General Tojo as prime minister and minister of war; and in Pearl Harbor, during the last week of the month, President Roosevelt met with General MacArthur and Admiral Nimitz to determine the rest of the U.S. route to Japan. The naval view held that MacArthur should take Mindanao, the southernmost of the Philippine Islands, with naval assistance. From there, air strikes could reduce Luzon, the northernmost of the Philippines, after which the forces of both Nimitz's Central Pacific and MacArthur's Southwestern Pacific commands would unite to invade Formosa and the Chinese coast. This would simultaneously cut Japan off from its East Indies supply zone by blockade and provide a suitable base for an invasion of its home islands, without the need for slogging up through the Philippines island by island. MacArthur disagreed, passionately and loudly insisting that the route must be through the Philippines. On military grounds, he pointed out that Formosa could be easily reinforced by the enemy, but that the Philippines could not, and the Filipino people were ready to revolt against the occupying Japanese. On political grounds, he maintained that his promised return had become a national commitment (at least in Filipino eyes) and that if it were deferred until after the fall of Japan, the United States would lose Filipino trust for ever.

The president was convinced by this, but Nimitz was not. Nevertheless, in the interests of harmonious cooperation, he gave way. While he still believed the Philippines would be a slow route, he accepted that Formosa could bring greater losses, realized that the general could make its conquest very disagreeable, and was certain that slowly or quickly, Japan would fall. Admiral Halsey was directed to take over the Central Pacific Fifth Fleet from Vice Admiral Spruance. When he did so, the Fifth was renamed the Third, and Vice Admiral Mitscher's TF 58 became TF 38—an administrative measure which confused the Japanese intelligence service mightily, causing them to believe there were two massive fleets taking turns at attacking them. Halsey's instructions were to capture

Ulithi Atoll, Peleliu, and Yap (halfway between Guam and the Philippines), and then to support MacArthur's forces in the capture of Morotai and the Talaud Islands, between New Guinea and the Philippines. Thus the central Pacific and southwest Pacific drives would converge. November 15, 1944, should see MacArthur in Mindanao; December 20 would bring the beginning of an invasion of Leyte, the Philippines' central island. By then, a final decision would have been made on whether to island-hop to Luzon or leapfrog to Formosa. One or the other would be attacked as soon as possible, probably early in 1945.

That, at any rate, was the schedule agreed by the Combined Chiefs of Staff, the president, and the prime minister when they met again in Quebec for the Octagon conference (September 12–16, 1944). But while they sat and conferred, Admiral Halsey was busy preparing for the invasions of Peleliu and Morotai. His method was to knock out airfields and shipping in the central Philippines which could threaten the invasions. He was highly successful: Two hundred Japanese aircraft, a dozen freighters, and a tanker were destroyed for the loss of eight U.S. Navy aircraft and ten airmen. And he discovered sensational news—there appeared to be hardly any other ships or aircraft in the Philippines at all. On hearing this, Nimitz, MacArthur, the Combined Chiefs of Staff, and the two Allied leaders agreed without hesitation to Halsey's suggestion: Leyte should be invaded as soon as possible. The plan was brought forward by two months and a new date set—October 20, 1944.

When that morning came, it began as a pleasant one. The sky at Leyte was clear, the sea calm, the surf light, and the naval bombardment (beginning on the dot of seven) very heavy. Three hours later the first troops landed, followed by their commanding officer, wading ashore through knee-deep water. Anyone who expressed surprise that Douglas MacArthur did not actually walk on the water kept their voices down as his voice was broadcast round the island: "People of the Philippines! I have returned."

The role of conquering hero must be an enjoyable one, and for a man of his theatrical temperament, it was impossible to resist. It was always easy (in his absence) to make fun of MacArthur and his taste for melodrama; but fortunately he was a good general. Otherwise he would have been merely a pretentious clown. It was equally easy to caricature the Japanese—buck-toothed, yellow-skinned, slant-eyed, stunted fanatics— and certainly their army, originally trained by the Prussians, was in general a vicious and brutal force. In contrast, their navy had been, at least until Yamamoto's death, an honorable force, and by Western standards a fair opponent; and its existence ended with sad, heroic grandeur. For the invasion of Leyte, the U.S. Navy used the largest fleet the world had ever known to that date: 842 vessels, of which 261 were combat ships from destroyers to aircraft carriers. To counter them, the Imperial Japanese Navy was able to muster sixty-four warships all told. "You must all remember," said their commanding officer as they prepared to head out to battle, "that there are such things as miracles."

There was nothing else to hope for. Since Admiral Halsey's air strikes a month earlier, Peleliu had been assaulted, and (on October 18) declared secure, although fighting continued there. Ulithi and Morotai had been taken unopposed; and between October 13 and 16, at a cost of seventy-nine U.S. Navy planes and sixty-four airmen, Halsey and Mitscher's carriers had destroyed over five hundred Japanese aircraft. That encounter (the Battle off Formosa) was the war's largest single air battle. The Battle for Leyte Gulf became the largest naval battle ever fought anywhere in history.

When the Japanese fleet received its orders, the inhabitants of Tokyo were celebrating the first public victory holiday in over two years. The "victory" touted to the population by government propaganda was the Battle off Formosa, in which, it was claimed, all of Halsey and Mitscher's carriers had been sunk. The Imperial Navy knew better; its officers and men were aware that they would probably not win against the U.S. Navy at Leyte. Nevertheless, they would try; and in one part of their complex three-part plan, they succeeded. In a second part they came close to success and should have been victorious. It was only in the third part that they were defeated absolutely; yet overall, the great battle was a defeat of such proportions that their fleet never again posed an active threat, and the U.S. Navy became supreme throughout the Pacific.

The plan was characteristically Japanese, similar to the Midway plan. But it was not uniquely a Japanese style; the U.S. fleet commanded by Spruance at Saipan had used a similar arrangement. In each case a diversion was created to distract the defenders from the main assault, and attacking forces were divided to surprise and entrap. The difference—the final outcome of victory or defeat—lay in the availability and use of intelligence. At Midway, that entire advantage lay with the Americans and was used to devastating effect. At Saipan the Japanese had no such benefit, and after the Turkey Shoot, Spruance was much criticized for refusing to chase and annihilate Ozawa's fleet. But his decision then was wise, first, because his primary orders were to cover the Saipan landings, not to chase ships and, second, because he did not know if there were other Japanese ships around to interfere with the landings. And his wisdom was underlined by the events at Leyte.

SHO-1 (as the Imperial Navy's plan was named) called for the simultaneous approach of three separate fleets from north, south, and west toward Leyte Gulf. One fleet would enter the gulf from the south through the Surigao Strait. Another would approach from the north, attract American warships away, and remove the invading force's sea cover from the gulf. From the west, meanwhile, the main fleet or Center Force would penetrate the San Bernadino Strait, descend on the gulf, join with the Southern Force, defeat any remaining U.S. ships, and surround the invaders onshore.

The Americans, despite their enormous numerical advantage, had one disadvantage which came at least halfway to being crucial. The wrangle between Admiral King and General MacArthur over a unified Pacific command had never been resolved. While the central Pacific and southwestern Pacific drives were geographically separated, King's refusal to let MacArthur command Nimitz, and MacArthur's refusal to be commanded by Nimitz, had not been matters of final urgency. Now, however, the two drives had successfully converged, and command was still divided. The Seventh Fleet ("MacArthur's Navy," under Adm. Thomas Kinkaid) was still responsible to MacArthur. The Third Fleet, under Halsey, was still responsible to Nimitz. And with the divided command, Nimitz issued ambiguous orders to Halsey. The Third Fleet was to "cover and support forces of the Southwest Pacific"; but "in case opportunity for destruction of major portion of the enemy fleet offers or can be created, such destruction becomes the primary task."[4]

Kinkaid, for the Seventh Fleet, took the "cover and support" of the Third Fleet to mean that he need not prepare for a naval action. Halsey read it differently; and as his then chief of staff, Rear Adm. (later Admiral and CNO) Robert B. Carney acknowledged later: "We didn't know Kinkaid's situation as well as we should have."[5]

All day long on October 20, soldiers, Marines, and equipment surged onto Leyte Island against light shore opposition. There was no opposition at sea, and MacArthur's headquarters predicted there would probably be none later; the two unlit straits leading into the gulf, Surigao and San Bernadino, were reckoned to be too narrow and hazardous for the passage of warships without radar. By midnight on October 21, 132,000 men and 200,000 tons of equipment had been landed on Leyte, and by midnight on October 22, the amphibious stage of the operation was over. Gen. Walter Krueger and the Sixth Army were engaging the 60,000 Japanese scattered over the island, but in the gulf, where there had been hundreds of vessels, only twenty-eight Liberty ships and twenty-five landing ships were left. It seemed the Army's prediction that there would be no naval conflict was going to come true—something Halsey, for one, did not want. However, at 1:16 A.M. on October 23, the submarines *Darter* and *Dace,* patrolling 500 miles west of Leyte Gulf, made radar contact with the enemy Center Force under Adm. Takeo Kurita. At 1:28 *Darter* torpedoed and sank the heavy cruiser *Atago,* Kurita's flagship. Minutes later the heavy cruiser *Takao* was hit and put out of action; and as *Atago* went down, *Dace* sank a third heavy cruiser, *Maya.* Five hours after the first sighting, Halsey received the news with delight. The Battle for Leyte Gulf was on, and first blood had gone, with a vengeance, to the U.S. Navy.

Many years later Admiral Carney remarked: "That Bay of Leyte thing has been written and rewritten till hell won't have it." He was right—indeed, the same could be said of almost any battle in the Pacific war, starting with Pearl Harbor. But Leyte was different, and only a man who actually took part in it, and who has seen all the wild descriptions by people who were not there, is entitled to speak so casually. The overall conflict was composed of four widely separated engagements: the Sibuyan Sea, the Surigao Strait, Cape Engaño, and Samar Island. By normal standards of wartime, each was a full-fledged battle in its own right; each had its own character; and in each there was an aspect of distinct and outstanding importance.

The first (the Battle of the Sibuyan Sea) began at 0810 on October 24 with the sighting of Admiral Kurita's Center Force (minus the victims of *Darter* and *Dace*) as it approached the central, almost inland waters of the Philippines. Kurita had five battleships (including the 72,000-ton superbattleships *Yamato* and *Musashi*), seven heavy cruisers, two light cruisers, and thirteen destroyers. For air cover he was relying on land-based planes; but the officer commanding those (Vice Adm. Shigeru Fukudome) considered their best use was directly against some of Halsey's carriers. From Luzon he launched three waves of fifty to sixty planes each, most of which were shot down. One of them, evading everything, did sink the light carrier *Princeton,* but Fukudome had misjudged the situation badly: He had nothing to spare for Kurita's protection, while Halsey had more than enough to fend Fukudome off and attack Kurita at the same time. Five separate strikes (259 sorties) were flown against the Center Force with a success that would have warmed Billy Mitchell's heart—four of the five battleships were hit and damaged, one heavy cruiser was put out of action, and (at 1935) the supposedly unsinkable *Musashi* was destroyed. Plowing determinedly ahead even when her foredeck was under water, she seemed to be executing an almost perfect submarine-type dive. It took nineteen torpedoes and seventeen bombs to sink her; but impressive and durable as she was, in the end she showed only—like the *Prince of Wales* and *Repulse*—that even the largest ships would be defeated if they had no air cover.

No U.S. plane was present to see *Musashi*'s final roll to port, but shortly afterward a lone scout flying overhead reported that the Center Force had turned westward again and was retreating. Admiral Halsey was overjoyed, for late in the afternoon, other scouts had discovered

Ozawa's Northern Force. Composed of four carriers (survivors of the Philippine Sea), two battleships, three cruisers, and nine destroyers, it was the last of the Japanese fleets to be sighted—ironically, because Vice Adm. Ozawa had made every effort to be detected. Despite its impressive size and apparent threat, as a carrier force it was a sham: After the attrition of past weeks and months, there were only 116 aircraft in the force, and most were piloted by men so inexperienced they could take off from a carrier but not land back on board again. Unaware of the force's real weakness, Halsey quite reasonably saw only the threat, and in his name, Carney sent a message to Kinkaid and the Seventh Fleet: "Am going north with three groups to attack enemy carrier force at dawn."[6] With that, the most controversial section of the Battle for Leyte Gulf commenced.

Seven hours after the sinking of *Musashi* and over 200 miles away from the Sibuyan Sea, as Halsey's TF 38 was racing northward, the all-night Battle of Surigao Strait began. By dawn the following day (October 25) Rear Adm. Jesse B. Oldendorf and the Seventh Fleet Bombardment and Fire Support Group had concluded a stunning, classic, and (if such a word can be used for war) elegant victory. This is how it happened.

Moving up the strait in accordance with the official schedule, the Japanese Southern Force was divided into two. This division was not at all according to plan. One part of the force (composed of two battleships, a cruiser, and four destroyers) was commanded by Vice Adm. Shoji Nishimura; the other (composed of two heavy cruisers, one light cruiser, and four destroyers) was commanded by Vice Adm. Kiyohide Shima. The two men were meant to work together at Surigao but had been rivals ever since academy days, and as they proceeded up the strait they did not even communicate. According to Shima, who survived, maintaining radio silence seemed more important, especially since—although he knew the battle plan better than Nishimura did—Nishimura was senior to him and would therefore have had to take overall command if they had made contact with each other. It was convoluted reasoning, to say the least; and Nishimura could not reply to it later, for he did not survive the battle. Leading his ships in line ahead 40 miles in front of Shima, he steamed directly into Oldendorf's well-laid snare. First came picket lines of torpedo boats, a gauntlet along both edges of the strait; then, at its northern end, came two tranverse flanking lines of cruisers; and finally, bridging the cruiser lines and completely blocking the entrance to the gulf were six battleships—most of them victims of Pearl Harbor, refloated, repaired, and revengeful.

Thus, Oldendorf's horizontal line barred Nishimura's vertical in a perfect crossing of the T, enabling all the U.S. battleship guns to bear simultaneously on the leading Japanese vessel: Nishimura's own flagship, the battleship *Yamashiro*. Given the faultless disposition of Oldendorf's vessels, the issue was never in doubt, even before his battleships opened fire at 0352. One U.S. destroyer was put out of action after nineteen hits, including accidental ones from friendly ships; but that was the only damage to any U.S. vessel. However, of Nishimura's force, only a single destroyer survived.

Shima's introduction to the battle some hours later was a torpedo hit to his light cruiser, followed by a sight of the burning wrecks of his old rival's ships, one of which he rammed. He also attempted to torpedo an island, thinking it was an enemy vessel, and at last, choosing discretion over valor, beat what one can only call a somewhat ignoble retreat.

Meanwhile, Kurita's Center Force had reversed its own seeming retreat, and at the same time as Shima turned tail from Surigao, the Center Force emerged cautiously from the tortuous San Bernadino Strait into the Pacific. Surprised to find no ambush awaiting him, Kurita turned down the eastern side of Samar Island and headed for Leyte Gulf itself. Despite the loss of *Musashi,* he still had eleven destroyers, two light cruisers, six heavy cruisers, and four battleships, including the stupendous *Yamato.* Simultaneously, Halsey's fleet carriers were still speeding north; so all that lay between Kurita, the gulf, and the invaders' beachhead was Rear Adm. Thomas Sprague's Task Group 77.4, one of the Seventh Fleet's subgroups. TG 77.4 was made up of three task units, nicknamed Taffy 1, 2, and 3, each consisting of four to six CVEs (carrier vessels, escort), three or four destroyers, and four destroyer escorts. It was commonly said that CVE stood for Combustible, Vulnerable, Expendable; and even together, the three Taffys were a weak, exposed little force which was never intended to go quite so directly in harm's way. But at 0645 on October 25, Rear Adm. Clifton Sprague, commanding Taffy 3 (the most northerly of the three units and over a hundred miles from any possible help) saw the shocking, unexpected sight of the masts of the Imperial Japanese Navy's Center Force approaching over the horizon. At 0658 the fleets were less than 20 miles apart; Kurita's battleships opened fire; and moments later the first gigantic splashes exploded astern of Taffy 3 as 14-inch, 16-inch, and *Yamato*'s mammoth 18.1-inch shells sought their diminutive targets.

This encounter, the Battle off Samar, lasted two hours and thirteen minutes and was one of the most remarkable displays of sheer bravery in the U.S. Navy's history. *Yamato* could make over 27 knots, 10 knots better than the escort carriers' top speed. After the war it was discovered that by Japanese estimates the U.S. "baby flattops" were running at an impossible 30 knots. "I knew you were scared," said one of Clifton Sprague's colleagues then, "but I didn't know you were that scared!"[7]

Japanese confusion of that sort was an important factor in the battle:

Kurita and his officers fully expected to see Halsey's TF 38 with its fast fleet carriers, cruisers, and destroyers. From the beginning, they made the easy blunder of identifying what they actually saw with what they thought should be there; this meant their perspective of the battle was wrong from the start. The weather was a second important factor: For a time, an east wind enabled Sprague to launch aircraft while fleeing from the huge enemy, and occasional rain squalls added to the smokescreens his ships made, giving the vessels some brief minutes of cover. Yet the most important factor, without which the others would have counted for nothing, was the extraordinary courage and gallantry of the U.S. aircrews and ships' crews.

At 0706, said Sprague, "it did not appear that any of our ships could survive another five minutes"; but at that moment they were able to take cover under a squall, and from 0716 the unit's three destroyers, its aircraft, and (from 0742) even its destroyer escorts fought a brilliant rearguard action. Orders from two of the commanding officers caught the battle's essence. In the destroyer *Johnston*—a small vessel—Comdr. Ernest E. Evans told his men: "Prepare to attack major portion of Japanese fleet"; and in the destroyer escort *Samuel B. Roberts*—an even smaller vessel—Lt. Comdr. R. W. Copeland warned his own crew it would be "a fight against overwhelming odds from which survival could not be expected, during which time we would do what damage we could."[8]

At the same time, all available aircraft were attacking (individually, since there was no time to coordinate them) with torpedoes; with bombs as small as 100 pounds, when the torpedoes ran out; and, when even the bombs ran out, with dry runs to distract the Japanese gunners from the escort carriers.

One of the little carriers, *Gambier Bay,* was shelled beyond recovery and sank; *Johnston* was lost after three 14-inch, three 6-inch, and numerous other hits; *Hoel,* one of the other two destroyers, sustained over forty hits, including some from 16-inch shells, before she too sank; and the destroyer escort *Samuel B. Roberts* was lost as well. But together with the unit's own aircraft and others flying in from Taffy 1 and Taffy 2, the damage they inflicted was far out of proportion to their size and theoretical threat: *Three* of Kurita's heavy cruisers were sunk, a fourth heavily damaged.

A final crucial factor was a spread of six torpedoes fired by the destroyer *Heermann* at *Yamato* in the first attack. The superbattleship reversed course to avoid them, and then for ten minutes found them running parallel to her on either side. From that time on, Kurita lost any tactical control of the battle—because of those maddening torpedoes, running alongside like tracker dogs, he could not turn back to the battle. At 0911, out of touch with most of his own force and with the U.S. "fleet carriers," he concluded that the enemy had escaped and called off the action. His last two heavy cruisers were closing to point-blank range when they received the order. Suddenly, to their utter bewilderment, the men of Taffy 3 saw the great ships turn from the chase; and on the bridge of Sprague's flagship *Fanshaw Bay* a signalman shouted, "Goddammit, boys, they're getting away!"

Of course, it was an absurd thing to say, but its very absurdity captured the vigorous spirit behind that remarkable engagement. The phrase quickly became as telling a part of American naval history as any since the days of John Paul Jones.

However, Taffy 3 had been lucky as well as brave. Everyone knew it and resented it: They should not have had to depend so much on fortune. With Oldendorf hard at work replenishing his ships with fuel and ammunition, Halsey and TF 38 should have been there to protect them. Another phrase became famous (or notorious) that day—a signal from Nimitz which reached Halsey at 1000: WHERE IS, REPEAT WHERE IS TF 38? THE WORLD WONDERS. The answer was, over 300 miles north, busy fighting the fourth battle that made up Leyte Gulf—the Battle off Cape Engaño.

Admiral Ozawa's Northern Force was composed of seventeen ships: four carriers, two hybrid carriers (battleships partially converted to carriers), three light cruisers, and nine destroyers. Of the 116 planes originally in them, less than thirty now remained; the others had all gone in vain attacks or in attempts to reveal the decoy fleet's position, and had landed ashore or ditched. Opposing this force, TF 38 included 64 ships and 787 planes. At about 0800 on October 25 (just after Sprague, far in the south, had had to commit his destroyer escorts to the attack against Kurita) the first of six air strikes from TF 38 reached Ozawa's near-empty carriers. The U.S. planes encountered an unexpectedly furious and accurate antiaircraft barrage. Nevertheless, a destroyer and a carrier were sunk in short order, and Ozawa's flagship *Zuikaku* (the sole surviving veteran of Pearl Harbor) was so damaged that to retain effective command, the admiral had to shift his flag to a light cruiser. The second U.S. wave disabled another carrier, which later sank; the third finally disposed of *Zuikaku;* and the fourth sent the fourth carrier down. Neither the fifth nor the sixth waves accomplished further sinkings: The two hybrid carriers survived and, with the remaining cruisers and destroyers, scurried away northward. But their bitter task as sacrificial decoy had been successfully completed; the fast U.S. carriers had been diverted from the defense of Leyte Gulf.

If Admiral Kurita had meanwhile pressed the assault on Taffy 3, he could have broken through to the gulf, fulfilling his part of the plan just as Ozawa had fulfilled his own. Kurita could not have linked with the

Southern Force—it had gone—but he could have wrought infinite damage against the half-ready U.S. Third Fleet and the undefended shore. Had he done so, Japan's eventual national defeat would still only have been delayed, not averted; but its naval losses in the Battle for Leyte Gulf could have been much less and those of the U.S. Navy much more. In total, the U.S. Navy lost one light carrier, two escort carriers, two destroyers, and one destroyer escort. Japan lost two battleships, one super-battleship, four aircraft carriers, six heavy cruisers, four light cruisers, and nine destroyers. Because of this battle, its tactics for the rest of the war were the tactics of despair, and its navy's role was that of a mere auxiliary.

William Halsey inspired enormous loyalty among his officers and men. His press nickname, Bull Halsey (linked to his name, his pugnacious appearance, and his character) was never used in the fleet; General MacArthur, who got on very well with him, was the only person who ever called him "Bull" to his face. Carney recalls that he and his colleagues called Halsey " 'Admiral Bill,' sometimes; 'Sir,' mostly. If we were skylarking ashore, we'd call him 'Sir Butch.' " But, adds Carney, "about Admiral Bill himself—he had one quality which to my mind stood out above everything else. If things went well, he couldn't wait to give credit to all his subordinates. If things went badly (and after all you can't fight for 2½ years as we did, all the time, without something going wrong), he took the responsibility immediately, himself. This had a great deal to do with the blind following that he had."

The wording of Nimitz's signal (WHERE IS TF 38? THE WORLD WONDERS) infuriated Admiral Halsey, especially since it had been sent for information to other admirals too. Nimitz had not meant it to be insulting; the final words, "the world wonders," were inserted by the enlisted communicator as padding to lessen the chance of decryption by the enemy. Such padding was mandatory, but the actual words used to pad any signal were up to the individual radio operator. The one who had sent the offending signal always claimed he thought of the words without considering their meaning; the one who received it explained he was unsure whether they formed part of the message or not. The explanations were accepted, but for years afterwards, the episode expressed the reaction of many people outside TF 38: that Halsey had been duped into neglecting his protective duty and had risked much of the operation to satisfy his own well-known detestation of the ships which had attacked Pearl Harbor. Within TF 38, the view was markedly different:

"We were all convinced that without naval air, the Japanese Navy was out of the picture, from here on, no matter what happened," Admiral Carney remarked subsequently. "And that was the decision, to go after the carriers. We didn't know how thin they were at that particular point."

Of course, in hindsight the assumption was wrong, but it was legitimate. On the other hand, Halsey made an equally wrong assumption about the defense strength left in Leyte Gulf; and since he had not corrected an earlier signal sent to Kinkaid and Nimitz, they both thought one group from TF 38 had been left to guard the gulf. In addition, his unwilling and belated dispatch of fast battleships back to the south meant, first, that they could give no practical protection in the south and, second, that part of the Northern Force and part of the Center Force (for what their remnants were worth) survived, when one or the other could have been destroyed completely. Such were the faults on one side; on the other was the ambiguous nature of Nimitz's orders.

Questioned informally on the subject almost four decades later, Admiral Carney observed simply: "You can argue both ways. But if you're sitting there with all the [vast amount of] information being given to you . . ."

Carney's justification of his former admiral ended with a short, expressive silence; and once again, he was right. The challenge to any critic is whether, under the same circumstances, he could have done any better.

Contemplating the history of other navies, a British naval person naturally tends to recall and apply the touchstone phrases of the Royal Navy; and as the Second World War drew to its end, some of those touchstones gained a particular aptness for the U.S. Navy. General MacArthur once said that Halsey could become "a greater man than Nelson ever dreamed of being."[9] Halsey admitted he was flattered and left it modestly at that, not seeing himself as part of the heroic world of MacArthurian legend.

But Nelson would probably have been glad to acknowledge the spiritual kinship. "In case Signals can neither be seen nor perfectly understood," he said before the Battle of Trafalgar on October 21, 1805, "no Captain can do very wrong if he places his ship alongside that of an Enemy." The British admiral's words then were an appropriate pre-echo to the Battle off Cape Engaño on October 25, 1944; and there, U.S. Admiral Halsey followed Nelson's spirit closely.

Indeed, the entire Battle for Leyte Gulf would have fascinated Nelson; he would have found much in common with his own thinking. In 1805, he decided that "no day can be long enough to arrange a couple of fleets, and fight a decisive battle, according to the old system"—that is, the system of maneuvering large numbers of slow ships into line ahead while the enemy did the same, and then sailing past each other to exchange broadsides. At Trafalgar, therefore, he had deliberately divided his fleet into three separate lines. The principle behind this entirely novel arrangement, which, though extremely risky, worked perfectly, was that two British lines would cut off the middle and rear thirds of the French line;

the remaining British line would fight where it could be most useful; and the forward third of the French line would be unable to turn and re-form before it was too late. "I look with confidence," he said, "to a Victory, before the Van of the Enemy could succour their Rear."

Thus he improved the numerical odds of ship-to-ship combat. But more important, he effectively turned one battle into two, fought and won simultaneously and separately, before the third began. Conceiving such a strategy, to be carried out in a few square miles, he would have recognized and responded instantly to the strategy at Leyte, where four constituent battles were fought in an area larger than France. He would have praised Oldendorf's neatly professional crossing of the T in the Surigao Strait—the last time that tactic was used. He would have admired the bravery of Clifton Sprague and Taffy 3 in the Battle off Samar. One might guess that in the Battle of the Sibuyan Sea, he would have agreed at once with the exponents of naval air power (Halsey, Mitscher, and Yamamoto as well) that in this new age, a battleship without air cover was powerless. And he would not have pretended that luck was unnecessary: "Something must be left to chance," he said before Trafalgar. "Nothing is sure in a Sea Fight beyond all others."[10]

With just a slight change in emphasis, those last words could not be more apt. At Trafalgar and at Leyte, empires were made and broken; but the Battle for Leyte Gulf became incomparable. In every way it was—and will probably remain forever—"a sea fight beyond all others."

17

★

LORDS OF THE OCEAN, LORDS OF THE AIR

*I*n 1780—a full generation before Trafalgar and the beginning of British maritime world dominance—John Paul Jones wrote: "The English Nation may hate me, but *I will force them to esteem me too.*"[1] On October 27, 1944, one day after the Battle for Leyte Gulf, Winston Churchill wrote to President Roosevelt: "Pray accept my most sincere congratulations, which I tender on behalf of His Majesty's Government, on the brilliant and massive victory gained by the sea and air forces of the United States over the Japanese in the recent heavy battles."[2]

The graceful compliment was more than just a felicitation of victory from one friend and ally to another; it marks the date (so far as one can be given) when Britain acknowledged that the Royal Navy had lost its ancient primacy and that the mantle of global supremacy at sea was passing to the U.S. Navy.

After Pearl Harbor, Churchill had found comfort in Lord Grey's simile likening the United States to a boiler capable of producing unlimited power. The same Lord Grey wrote elsewhere that "the British Army should be a projectile to be fired by the British Navy."[3] Leyte broke Japan's Imperial Navy almost entirely, and with virtually no ships left to fight, the U.S. Navy was able to concentrate the greater part of its colossal strength in projecting the U.S. Army and Marines ever closer to Japan's home islands.

As 1945 opened, U.S. invasion forces approaching Lingayen Gulf on the northern Philippine island of Luzon came under proud, despairing, dreadful attack from kamikaze pilots, one of whom sank the escort carrier *Ommaney Bay*. These self-sacrificing men (they never considered themselves as anything so dishonorable as mere suicide pilots) had found their first victim at Leyte Gulf, when one of their number sank the escort carrier *St. Lô*. Determined not to surrender and unconcerned about individual survival, they saw their fatal attacks as an inevitable and logical final phase, which they believed might yet bring victory. Through the final twelve months of the war, kamikaze attacks inflicted damage on at least 300 Allied ships, of which about forty were sunk. In achieving that, however, some 2,000 Japanese pilots and planes were destroyed. To U.S. sailors it was a peculiarly horrible form of attack, wasteful, futile, and signifying nothing inevitable except the approaching defeat of a fanatic enemy.

As land fighting continued in the Philippines and beyond, the U.S. Marine Corps came truly into its own. The warships surged northward, bombarding, protecting, assaulting, supplying, transporting; but the prolonged and bloody battles for Iwo Jima (the volcanic island fortress-airstrip dominated by Mount Suribachi) and for Okinawa (the last hurdle, only 360 miles short of Japan)—those battles belonged to the Army and the Marines, but most of all to the Marines. The Navy lost nearly 900 men at Iwo; the Corps almost 6,000. "A yard by yard advance against a tough, resourceful enemy who allowed no let-up, and who used his terrain to extract the maximum price in blood"—such was Iwo Jima, attacked on February 19, 1945, and secured on March 16.[4] The Okinawa landings (April 1, Easter Sunday, 1945) involved the largest armada in history, surpassing even that of Leyte Gulf: 1,450 Allied ships of all types. Among them was a new Task Force, TF 57. Composed of two battleships, four carriers with almost 250 aircraft, five cruisers, and eleven destroyers, this—the "forgotten fleet"—was a clear sign of the Allies' rolling successes in the Atlantic and Europe; for these were Royal Navy ships, at last able to participate (albeit in a limited way) with their friends in the Pacific.

For the 100,000 Imperial soldiers dug deeply into caves and tunnels throughout the island of Okinawa, the only available tactic was to defend their stronghold in the fiercest possible manner, to the death. The unmatched savagery of the fighting onshore in the eighty-two-day campaign for the island was reflected by the final official casualty list: 7,374 Americans dead, 31,807 wounded, 230 missing; 107,539 Japanese counted dead (including an estimated 42,000 civilians killed by both sides), a further 23,764 Japanese assumed dead in caves, and 10,755 who surrendered.

For the Imperial Navy and its air force, no other tactic remained but self-destruction. Winston Churchill learned later from Admiral King that about 1,900 kamikaze air attacks (the great majority of all such attacks) were made in the Okinawa campaign, sinking thirty-four destroyers and small craft and damaging about two hundred other ships; and six days after the Okinawa landings came the symbolic death of the Imperial Japanese Navy.

Yamato, its greatest and most graceful ship, left the Inland Sea in company with a light cruiser and eight destroyers on the evening of April 6, 1945. Their destination was Okinawa; their purpose was to sink whatever ships they could en route, and on arrival to beach themselves, if necessary, as instant fortresses. Since that voyage, the legend has taken root that *Yamato* had only enough fuel for a one-way voyage, a kamikaze mission to assured destruction. Comdr. Masataka Chihaya, ex–Imperial Navy, was present at the meeting to decide the superbattleship's fate, and denies the legend; yet whatever the truth, *Yamato*'s destruction was assured in any case, for she had no air cover.[5] If air power had never been discovered and exploited, *Yamato* would have inaugurated a new age of battleship building, as *Dreadnought* had done in 1906. But before Japan chose war, Admiral Yamamoto had used a Japanese proverb as a warning to his countrymen: "The fiercest serpent may be overcome by a swarm of ants." And at twenty-three minutes past two o'clock on the afternoon of April 7, 1945, swarms of U.S. Navy aircraft (900 planes in all) overcame the biggest battleship in history, the ship whose name was the ancient name for Japan.

So the Imperial Navy of Japan died. Five days later, on April 12, 1945, the Allies suffered one of their saddest losses, when Franklin Delano Roosevelt, the longest-serving president of the United States, died suddenly of a severe cerebral hemmorhage. Churchill was grief-stricken: "I feel a very painful personal loss," he wrote, "quite apart from the ties of public action which bound us so closely together. I had a true affection for Franklin."[6]

From Stalin too came a message of condolence: The late president's "friendly attitude . . . to the USSR will always be most highly valued and remembered by the Soviet people."[7]

The British prime minister was disconcerted, however, to discover that Roosevelt had not kept Harry Truman (his vice president and successor) fully informed on inter-Allied diplomacy; for as Churchill later observed, "This proved of grave disadvantage to our affairs."[8]

At that moment, though, nothing could impede the sweep to victory. On May 1 Grand Adm. Dönitz issued a historic Order of the Day: "German armed forces! My comrades! The Führer has fallen." No mention was made of Hitler's squalid suicide; the implication was that he had died in battle.

"The Führer has appointed me," Dönitz continued, "as his successor as Head of State and as Commander in Chief of the armed forces. I take over command of all arms of the services with the intention of continuing the battle against the Bolshevists [and] against the English and Americans . . ."[9] Six days later, the German High Command surrendered unconditionally.

It had been predicted that defeating Japan would take a further eighteen months. Among the Joint Chiefs of Staff there had been much debate over the surest and quickest way to do so. The three broad alternatives (in general supported by the U.S. Navy, Army, and Air Force, respectively) were to blockade, to invade, or to bomb strategically. Blockade and strategic bombing were already under way, as crucial waterways were mined and cities razed by fire; and on May 25, 1945, seeing no method more certain, the JCS set November 1 as a date for invasion.

The timetable was set for the Plain of Tokyo to be in Allied hands by March 1946. The Allied forces available were far larger than the total of armies, navies, and air forces which had been ranged against Nazi Germany. Off the coasts of Japan, from July 10, Halsey's TF 38 roamed almost completely freely, bombarding and bombing at will. Added to its 105 ships on July 17 were twenty-eight British warships, designated TF 37. Together, TF's 37 and 38 formed the strongest naval strike force in the history of the world.

The last major warship sunk on either side during the Second World War went down in the early hours of July 30, 1945, taking with her nearly nine hundred men. While Halsey's task forces enthusiastically shelled and bombed whatever units remained of the Imperial Navy, there was a double irony in this final sinking: first, because the victim, *Indianapolis* (onetime flagship of the Fifth Fleet), was a U.S. heavy cruiser, torpedoed by the Japanese submarine *I-58* en route from Tinian to the Philippines; and second, because *Indianapolis* had just delivered to Tinian the component parts of "Little Boy," the Hiroshima bomb.

Dropped on Hiroshima on August 6, 1945, and on Nagasaki three days later, the world's first (and, one may devoutly hope, last) atomic bombs to be used in warfare did not in themselves defeat Japan. Beyond any shade of doubt, that defeat would have occurred without them, but at a cost which no one could or can definitely calculate. In making the decision to invade Japan, the Joint Chiefs of Staff warned their political masters to be ready to accept the loss of perhaps 1.5 million Allied lives. No one could say how many Japanese would be killed or would kill themselves; possibly ten times as many, possibly more. Certainly the nation would have continued to resist as long as the emperor willed it. Plans and preparations for invasion were made because until July 16, 1945, when the first test atomic bomb was exploded at Alamogordo, New Mexico, President Truman could not be sure the new, millennial weapon would actually work. On that day, at the beginning of the Terminal conference with Churchill and Stalin at Potsdam in Germany, Truman received the macabre message indicating test success: "Babies satisfactorily born." Knowing now that it would work, still "no one could yet measure the immediate military consequences of the discovery, and," as Churchill wrote eight years later, "no one has yet measured anything else about it."[10] But there could be no question about using it, and the Potsdam Declaration was uncompromising—without immediate and unconditional surrender, "the alternative for Japan is complete and utter destruction."[11]

Surrender might have come earlier, and the explosions might have been avoided, if the Potsdam Declaration had included a clear, continuing role in postwar Japan for Emperor Hirohito. The bombs might also have been unnecessary if the USSR (still neutral toward Japan, and already approached by the Japanese to act as a peace mediator) had accepted that role. But with at least 78,000 people instantaneously obliterated at Hiroshima on August 6, 1945, with a further minimum figure of 35,000 people wiped out in a single flash at Nagasaki on August 9, and with a Russian declaration of war and invasion of Manchuria on the same day, only the proudest and most prejudiced of Japanese could deny the reality of defeat and the awful truth of the Allied ultimatum.

There were those who would have denied it; an army coup designed to kidnap the emperor and refuse surrender was only narrowly averted. However, after the assurance that the emperor would remain on the throne (subject to Allied authority), capitulation came at last. Shortly after 6 A.M. on August 15, 100 miles from Tokyo, Admiral Halsey received the signal "Suspend air attack operations" and bellowed with joy. After infinite cost on many fronts, the most terrible war in history was ending.

On September 2, 1945, twenty-three aircraft carriers, a dozen battleships, twenty-six cruisers, 116 destroyers and escorts, a dozen submarines, and 185 smaller vessels—a total of 374 warships, the great majority of them units of the U.S. Navy—lay at anchor over the greater part of a hundred miles from the top of Tokyo Bay down into Sugami Bay.

No one present could see more than a section of the whole Allied fleet, but for those people, the knowledge that it continued far beyond the range of sight made the gathering of warships all the more impressive. It was a demonstration of more naval power than anyone could have imagined four years before. In his message of congratulation to all the men under his command, Nimitz added a cautionary note. With victory achieved, he wisely said: "The use of insulting epithets in connection with the Japanese as a race or individuals does not now become the officers of the United States Navy."[12]

As the representatives of Japan waited on the decks of the battleship

Missouri, the atmosphere was punctiliously correct but icy cold. For all present, it was impossible to forget in a moment the years of real hate; but MacArthur used his gift for rhetoric to echo and amplify Nimitz's message, and looked forward from that day to a time of eventual reconciliation. "It is my earnest hope," he declared, "indeed, the hope of all mankind, that from this solemn occasion a better world shall emerge out of the blood and carnage of the past—a world founded upon faith and understanding, a world dedicated to the dignity of man and the fulfillment of his most cherished wish for freedom, tolerance and justice."[13]

All the delegates signed their names, in order: the Japanese delegation first, followed by MacArthur, Nimitz, and (for Britain) Adm. Sir Bruce Fraser. Signatures were appended for China, Russia, Australia, Canada, France, the Netherlands, and New Zealand. "Let us pray that peace be now restored to the world and that God will preserve it always," said MacArthur. "These proceedings are now closed."[14] And with those uncharacteristically simple words, he marked the end of World War II.

Almost exactly 169 years earlier, on September 6, 1776, at the height of the War of Independence, the British admiral Sir George Collier had been waiting to set sail from Long Island for Halifax. Everything was ready, but the wind refused to blow and his ships could not move. Referring to Boreas, the ancient god of the north wind, Sir George penned a good-humored, philosophical letter to a friend: "Though we are Lords of the Ocean, we are not so of the Air," he said, "and we must patiently wait till Mr Boreas gives us a Passport to Proceed."[15]

Late in 1945, Fleet Adm. Ernest J. King was presented with an illuminated leather-bound text. It read, in part:

> As your friends and colleagues in the great struggle which has just ended, we, the British Chiefs of Staff, send you our sincere good wishes on the occasion of your retirement from your post as Chief of Naval Operations of the United States Navy. Under your leadership as Commander-in-Chief, the United States Navy has grown, with unprecedented speed, into the most powerful in all the world. . .[16]

They signed themselves friends and colleagues, and were proud and happy to do so; yet in a century and a half, what a distance the U.S. Navy had traveled. Born in an era when none would dare challenge the might of Britain's Royal Navy and hope to survive, by the end of 1945 the U.S. Navy had become a fleet incomparable in history, second to none at last—Lords of the Ocean, and Lords of the Air as well.

PART SIX

RESHAPING

1 9 4 5 – 1 9 6 3

★

The first twenty postwar years contain
a most perplexing form of peace;
and in these decades of Cold War,
limited war, and global reorganization,
the U.S. Navy enters its third age.

18

★

THE ELIMINATION OF
WAR ITSELF

"Surely for the coming generation, and probably for generations to come, use and control of the seas in war will be decisive." On March 12, 1947, Rear Adm. William S. Parsons was writing to a woman at a college in Virginia, a lady much concerned about the possibility of yet another war. She felt that the huge size of the U.S. Navy might of itself be a provocation; but "at this portentous time," Parsons explained, "our Navy has the great responsibility of leadership in sea power which for generations was carried by England. Its size is dictated more by the vastness of the oceans over which control would be exercised than the strength of possible animate adversaries."[1]

Parsons was right to call the time "portentous." The Second World War turned the world not upside down, but on its side. For navigators, the prime meridian still ran through the London suburb of Greenwich, north and south; for every other person and purpose, it seemed to run east and west. The age of the Great Powers was over; the age of the Superpowers was beginning, and the most important line in the world ran between Washington and Moscow.

On the day Parsons wrote his letter to Virginia, President Truman sent a message to Congress asking for aid for Greece and Turkey, countries which Britain could no longer protect from Communist-inspired civil war and Soviet hopes of land. The message also outlined Truman's view of the United States' postwar foreign policy: He intended "to support freed peoples who are resisting attempted subjugation by armed minorities or by outside pressures." This (the "Truman doctrine") was the nearest thing to a declaration that the Cold War ever had. And for any American naval officer, there was much more to make the time portentous. Despite Parsons's words to his correspondent, the U.S. Navy—having secured its greatest victory—was actually coming closer to extinction than at any time since 1865.

Just two weeks earlier, Secretary of the Navy James V. Forrestal had remarked in public that the U.S. Navy had "more or less inherited from Britain the job of keeping the sea lanes open and stabilising areas from which exports come."[2] Parsons's letter echoed the official naval line—a line which most people within the service understood and agreed with. After the Second World War, as Forrestal indicated, the U.S. Navy was able and willing to take over from the debilitated Royal Navy, perhaps to inaugurate a new century of worldwide stability at sea—a Pax Americana, descendant of the Pax Britannica of 1815 to 1914.

But the United States' own view of its navy was drastically different. Led emotionally by the return of peace and intellectually by the arguments of soldiers and aviators, the nation was passing through one of the strongest of its recurring bouts of antinavalism. At the end of the war, the U.S. Navy included 1,194 major combatant vessels, 1,256 amphibious transports, over 41,000 aircraft, and almost 3.4 million active personnel. In total, these made it nearly double the size of the Royal Navy and all the navies of the British Empire put together. But beginning at once, the process of demobilization (though it seemed lengthy to those involved) was conducted so swiftly, efficiently, and thoroughly that within three years only 267 major combatant vessels remained active.[3]

The U.S. Navy's very successes in the war now counted against it. The fleets of Germany, Italy, and Japan were destroyed; there was no other likely enemy afloat; and with no one left for it to fight, many people saw no obvious reason for its continued existence. Other factors followed the same plausible direction. The League of Nations died quietly on April 19, 1946, superseded by the United Nations, the world's new great hope for international cooperation and the avoidance of conflict; and over all lay the deadly promise of the Bomb.

In the rosy dawn of the atomic age, nuclear superweapons appeared to many to have completely removed the need for anything as antiquated and vulnerable as battleships or even aircraft carriers: Their day of dominance now seemed to have been brief indeed. A single atom bomb, exploded underwater at the Pacific atoll of Bikini in 1946, produced a column of water half a mile across with a mushroom top two miles in diameter, and sank or very severely damaged seventy-three surplus warships (ex-German, ex-Japanese, and U.S.) anchored there. Such bombs could be delivered by very-long-range aircraft or possibly even by rockets—Hitler's V-2 rocket attacks on London had shown the way with conventional high explosive. People vaguely understood that the attendant risks of atomic war were greater than those of conventional war, and it was easy to see that international Communism, pushed by Soviet Russia, was moving to fill the power vacuum left by Germany and Japan. But there was little prospect of the USSR having its own nuclear weapon before 1955. The United States had peace, prosperity, and apparently complete security, and it was hoped that by 1955 the new Atomic Energy Commission would have reached an agreement banning the use of nuclear power except for peaceful purposes. This was a heady mix. It seemed to revive (with a far greater chance of success) President Wilson's dream of a world where all nations could live at peace—for as Bernard Baruch (U.S. representative to the Atomic Energy Commission) said:

> Who can doubt, if we succeed in controlling the atomic weapon, that we can go on to the control of other instruments of mass destruction? The elimination of war itself is within the range of possibility.[4]

This hope was somewhat dented when the Soviet Union's foreign minister, Andrei Gromyko, refused the proposed nuclear control, stating that the necessary verification process would be an unacceptable intrusion into the USSR's private affairs. But ordinary Americans were not very much dismayed.[5] The reply merely deepened their wariness and suspicion of the onetime ally of convenience without denting their huge confidence in themselves, their superweapon, and their ability and willingness to use it if necessary.

Simultaneously, members of the U.S. Army Air Force found arguments supporting their own favorite dream: that all military and naval aviation should be joined into one force, distinct from Army or Navy. Army, Navy, and Air Force would then be unified into a single department of government with a single chief of staff and a single secretary to administer them all. Since the USSR had no oceangoing navy to speak of but relied for military power on its armies, the proposal for unification was broadly supported by the U.S. Army. The Navy would be given a new role, appropriate to the age of strategic bombing, as a useful ferry service. Brig. Gen. Frank Armstrong, an aviator, put it very bluntly at an Armed Forces Staff College dinner early in 1947:

"You gentlemen," he declared to assembled Army and Navy officers, "had better understand that the Army Air Force is tired of being a subordinate outfit, and is no longer going to be a subordinate outfit. It was a predominant force during the war. It is going to be a predominant force during the peace, and you may as well make up your minds, whether you like it or not, that we do not care whether you like it or not: The Army Air Force is going to run the show."

The Marines ("a small, fouled-up army talking navy lingo") would go into the Army, where they belonged. Armstrong reckoned the fleet would have "nothing but a couple of carriers which are ineffective anyway, and . . . will probably be sunk in the first battle." It followed, therefore, that "the Navy is going to end up by only supplying the requirements of the Army, Air, and Ground Forces too."[6]

Such remarks were hardly calculated to make friends, though they might influence people, and an official disclaimer from the Pentagon did not mollify hurt naval feelings: To be told that Armstrong's comments "were intended to be entirely humorous" simply implied that the Navy was stuffy, pompous, and could not take a joke. But Armstrong's tactless words did summarize Army Air Force lobbying which had been going on since 1943; and it was no laughing matter on either side.

During the war, the AAF had established itself as virtually a separate service, with its commanding general an equal member of the Joint Chiefs of Staff alongside the Army's chief of staff and the CNO. Moves to unify the forces began in 1942 and found wide popular support—it sounded like a commonsense solution to interservice rivalry and duplicated effort. At first influential naval men favored unification as well, for they understood that the fleet would retain its own air force and Marine Corps, and the benefits of unified command in wartime were apparent. Gradually, though, the Army's and AAF's very different ideas became clear; and when he was vice president, Truman left no doubt of his view. In an article entitled "Our Armed Forces *Must* Be United," he wrote:

> Our scrambled military setup has been an open invitation to catastrophe. . . . The nation's safety must have a more solid foundation. An obvious first step is a consolidation of the Army and Navy that will put all of our defensive and offensive strength under one tent and one authoritative, responsible command.[7]

If that were to be the future of the U.S. armed forces, then Artemus L. Gates (assistant secretary of the Navy for air) had a bright idea—the Navy itself could provide the matrix of a merger: "It can operate on sea, under the sea, in the air, in amphibious operations, land," he explained. "This force by itself can police the world. It is the nucleus around which can be built one force."[8]

It was a simple and effective concept which deserved more attention than it got. Unfortunately for Gates (who otherwise would have come out of obscurity as a reforming genius), Vice Adm. John S. McCain's reaction to merging, though cynical, was more accurate: "No matter how fair the words, or beguiling the phraseology, and regardless of intent . . . the Army banks on controlling the individual who will head this single unit; and historically, they will be correct in that assumption." And in a perceptive aside, the admiral added: "This will appeal to the grand American illusion that wars can be fought cheaply."[9]

But as debates developed and quarrels flared between these different groups of strong-willed men, the Army Air Force wrong-footed the Navy from the start. By taking the initiative, the Army Air Force at once placed the Navy on the defensive. Because of its superficial logic and broad public appeal, the proposed unification plan could not be rejected out of hand and certainly could not be ignored; either course would suggest that the fleet was led by cranky reactionaries thinking only of their own careers and not of the good of the nation. Counterproposals had to be made to limit the possible damage; yet again, the United States' real and continuing need for a navy had to be explained. And the counterproposals had to be crystal clear; if they were not, they too would suggest selfishness and a deliberate attempt to confuse.

Of course, there *were* elements of individual self-interest underlying the Navy's general sense of alarm, but there were at least as many in the Army and AAF attack. That was neither the problem nor the point. What really worried naval men was that their colleagues in the other forces, professionals like themselves, must have failed (apparently thoroughly) to understand the lessons of the recent war. The first among those lessons was that none of the services could have won the war alone. The postwar Navy accepted this as fundamental, but the AAF believed that with atomic weapons, it could win any war single-handed. If not, the Army reckoned itself to be fully capable of completing the task.

There was no naval opposition to unified command in the battlefield. Instead, opposition focused on the principle of unified policy; on the fear of unsympathetic, uncomprehending Army control by which one man could be given near-dictatorial powers; and in the plain disgust that a fleet which had become the most powerful in history could seriously be considered for demotion to a glorified ferry service and nothing else.

Unfortunately, to rather a large extent, the Navy had only itself to blame for the awkward situation. The shame of Pearl Harbor, lingeringly analyzed by hearings and inquiries, argued against its ability to be ready for war at sea. Its subsequent wartime growth and conquest argued against the very need to be ready. The postwar absence of an immediate enemy and the possession of a nuclear monopoly argued against any continuing need for a fleet at all. And the existence of all those apparently decisive antinaval arguments emphasized the uncomfortable fact that ever since the States had become a politically united, continental nation, the Navy had never been very good at educating public opinion to an understanding of the continent's need for sea power. Its thinkers had influenced naval people around the world far more than citizens at home. Henry L. Stimson (Franklin Roosevelt's secretary of war) expressed this neatly when he wrote of "the peculiar psychology of the Navy Department, which frequently seemed to retire from the realm of logic into a dim religious world in which Neptune was God, Mahan his prophet, and the United States Navy the only true Church."[10]

Truman's vice-presidential conviction did not alter when he became president; on December 19, 1945, he recommended that Congress should "adopt legislation combining the War and Navy Departments into one single Department of National Defense." A little later, he added (despite his known views, and his rank as commander in chief) that naval men were entirely free to express their opinions on the subject.

Taking him at his word, one rear admiral promptly observed that "when the next war comes, we will need the finest army and air force in the world, because with a greatly weakened navy, submerged under army control, the fighting will be on our own shores."[11]

On hearing this remark so contrary to his beliefs, the president immediately ordered the Navy to confine its views to factual testimony, without emotive assertions.

His order was useful as far as it went, for emotion tends to color any discussion even remotely connected with ships. But the order did not go far enough: With the Navy partly muzzled, Truman left the Army and AAF free to say whatever they pleased, emotive or not. When a further presidential order in May 1946 told the War and Navy departments to get on with it and come to an agreement, it was plain what kind of an agreement the president hoped to see. And by the middle of the summer of 1947, after a history of 149 years, the Department of the Navy ceased to exist in its own right.

The National Security Act of 1947, signed by President Truman on July 26, centralized the nation's armed forces into the National Military Establishment; but it did not actually merge them. Under the circumstances, the Navy did a great deal better (or a great deal less badly) than anyone would have anticipated a year or two earlier. The act created a separate Air Force, but specifically retained naval aviation as a fleet function, as well as keeping the Marine Corps under the naval umbrella. All three forces now came under a single civilian secretary of defense, one of whose tasks was to "eliminate unnecessary duplication or overlapping in the fields of procurement, supply, transportation, storage, health, and research." Below him, each department had its own secretary with executive powers within that department, and with the right (after informing the defense secretary) to report directly to the president.

This was very much less than the Army and AAF had wanted, very much less than the Navy had feared; and most of the credit (or responsibility) for that lay with five men: Robert P. Patterson, ex–secretary of war; James V. Forrestal, ex–secretary of the Navy and now the first secretary of defense; Maj. Gen. Lauris Norstad and Vice Adm. Forrest P. Sherman, both aviators; and Ferdinand Eberstadt, a lawyer and, at different times in the Second World War, chairman of the Army and Navy Munitions Board and vice chairman of the War Production Board.

Patterson and Forrestal knew, liked, and respected each other from their common war experience as cooperating undersecretaries. Close to their respective services but, as civilians, not part of them, they were able to approach the problem without partisan attitudes. After they had arrived at a tolerable degree of compromise, Sherman and Norstad tackled the details; but it was Eberstadt who, at Forrestal's request, provided the workable blueprint.

In a 250-page report, he supported coordination in preference to full unification, and proposed "a complete realignment of our governmental organizations to serve our national security in the light of our new world power and position, our new international commitments and risks, and the epochal new scientific discoveries."[12] Rather than a single, potentially dictatorial chief of staff reporting to one overall secretary, the Joint Chiefs of Staff should be given statutory recognition and should report to individual service secretaries, each with cabinet status. A Military Education and Training Board should be established, along with a Central Research and Development Agency; the Army and Navy Munitions Board should be expanded; a Central Intelligence Agency should be created; a National Security Resources Board was recommended; and, following the British model of the Committee for Imperial Defence, war strategy and peace aims should be blended in a National Security Council.

Every one of the proposals became part of the 1947 act, without major changes. The only additions were the creation of the single secretary above the three departmental secretaries and the formal establishment of a War Council, informally developed during the world war and consisting of the JCS and the various secretaries. The act as a whole was the most comprehensive document ever produced on U.S. defense policy—and most of it, fundamentally, was by Eberstadt.

For those with long memories, the event resonated with echoes from nearly a century and a half before. In 1801, at the end of the Quasi-War with France, the U.S. Navy's Peace Establishment Act had been passed. Just as in World War II, the United States' victory then had created lasting reputations for individual men and ships; with peace, the Navy came close to dissolution when there seemed no further need for it; and one man (Benjamin Stoddert, the Navy's first secretary) had been mainly responsible for its preservation, drafting the bill which passed almost unchanged into the act of 1801. It was apt, then, that under Forrestal (the last secretary of the Navy and first secretary of defense) one man should also have been mainly responsible for drafting the act which, once again, ensured the victorious fleet's survival in peace.

Yet the absurdity was that Eberstadt's report was finished and pub-

lished in the autumn of 1945. If the Army and AAF had been prepared
to view it not as a supplement to their plans but as the real alternative
which it was, two years' wrangling between the services might have been
avoided.

Those first two postwar years were a busy period for the Navy, quite apart
from the unification row. Despite the fleet's rapidly dwindling size, the
range of its peacetime responsibility and activity became very wide. During the winter of 1946–47, Operation Highjump took place—America's
first major Antarctic expedition since the war, under the technical direc-
torship of the nation's foremost expert on the region, Adm. Richard E.
Byrd. Arctic exploration and exercises with surface, air, and submarine
forces also took place throughout the decade and into the 1950s. In Japan,
Naval Forces Far East formed part of General MacArthur's unified
command in occupation; and in the Mediterranean, the force which
would become the Sixth Fleet began to take shape, effectively reestablishing the old Mediterranean Station as Britain's naval presence in that sea
diminished.

But the immediate postwar first essentials were mineclearing in European and Pacific waters; transporting 2 million U.S. troops back home;
and transporting a further 400,000 Chinese, Japanese, and Korean troops
from places where the war had stranded them to their respective home-
lands. David F. Emerson (then a young officer and now a retired vice
admiral) recalls how he and his men "started carrying Chinese Nationalists north from Hong Kong to Chinwangtao to fight the Communists.
Those first Chinese were nowhere near as disciplined as the defeated
Japanese; and the quality of the Chinese got lower and lower. My last run
was made with what could only be called a rabble. . . . The Japanese were
under the control of their officers—it was impressive. With the Chinese,
it was sheep-herding. That's the difference in discipline. We'd take them
up to Chinwangtao, and the Chinese Communists were very close, and
they [the transported Nationalists] would go over and surrender. . . . It
was discouraging."[13]

Where China was concerned, the U.S. had indeed become discouraged,
and with reason. Throughout the war, the self-styled generalissimo of
China (Chiang Kai-shek) and his Nationalists had been treated as full
allies by the Western powers. Apart from its long-standing commercial
relations with the West, China had been the first victim of Japanese
aggression, commencing in 1937, and subject to intermittent Communist
uprisings since the 1920s. During the war Chiang's armies could not have
kept going without almost constant aid from the West, deemed worthwhile if only as a means of keeping Japanese troops away from the Pacific
and southern theaters. But, defeated again and again by the Japanese,
Chiang and his armies became increasingly unreliable and ineffective.

When the war against Japan ended, full-blown civil war broke out in China between Nationalists and Communists; Britain could no longer afford to assist Chiang; and Truman (sensing that the generalissimo was less and less trustworthy) was equally unwilling to carry on throwing good money after bad. By 1948 the United States had given Chiang's government $4.5 trillion in money and equipment to support its fight; but much of the money was purloined by corrupt Nationalists, and much of the equipment was abandoned by them, only to be captured and used by the Communists.

By the end of 1948, Truman had had enough. In February 1949 all the remaining U.S. soldiers and sailors were withdrawn from China. Two months later Nanking fell to Mao Tse-tung; in May Shanghai was taken; and by October, the whole of mainland China—the world's most populous country—was under Communist control. And that only capped other events which made 1949 one of the most formative years of the Cold War period.

Though it had spread rapidly to other parts of the world, the geographical heart of political conflict still remained in Europe, which had been uncertainly divided by the Yalta and Potsdam conferences. With Germany split in two, Berlin (the nominal capital of a nominally single country) lay deep inside the Soviet Zone. Since April 1948 the Russian blockade of Berlin had been in force—all land routes to the city from the West had been closed as Stalin attempted to squeeze the Western Allies out of eastern Germany altogether.

To counter this, some of Truman's military leaders advocated an armed drive on Berlin; others even proposed a nuclear attack on the USSR. Instead, with his French and British allies, the president instituted the famous airlift of supplies to the beleaguered city. It continued throughout the winter of 1948–49, with up to nine hundred flights a day bringing in hundreds of thousands of tons of cargo. Simultaneously, an Anglo-French postwar alliance (under the Dunkirk Treaty) was extended to include Belgium, the Netherlands, and Luxembourg and renamed the Western Union. Early in April 1949, France, Britain, and the United States agreed to merge their German zones of occupation, and (as a temporary measure, pending the reunification of the whole country) the Federal Republic of Germany came into being, with Bonn as its capital. At the same time, members of the Western Union met in Washington with representatives of Iceland, Portugal, Norway, Italy, Denmark, Canada, and the United States, and on April 2, 1949 the North Atlantic Treaty Organization was created. Contrary as ever, the French called it OTAN, but the title was less important than the fact that for the first time in its history, the United States had committed itself in peacetime to a full military alliance with other nations.

Within a month Moscow called off the Berlin blockade. Now augmented by road and rail transport, the airlift of supplies to the still-nominal capital of all Germany continued throughout the summer, in order to build up stores for the following winter. On September 30 it came to an end—exactly one week after a frightening announcement from President Truman. On September 23 he revealed that the United States' nuclear monopoly had come to an end as well: Russian scientists had succeeded in exploding their country's first atomic bomb.

Thus, in the space of a year, the fundamental reshaping of the postwar world was completed. The globe was broadly divided between a Communist East and a democratic West; the dreadful possibility of nuclear destruction was extended to every nation in the Northern Hemisphere; the countries of western Europe were joined in a transatlantic commitment with Canada and the United States. In an alliance whose major halves were separated by 3,000 miles of ocean, it would appear self-evident that naval power must form a part of the joint defense at least equal to that of the other two services; but in the United States, throughout those tense and memorable months, the Navy was being hammered once again—far harder than before—by the Army, the Air Force, and the new secretary of defense.

In those recurring periods when neither president nor people especially favored the Navy, it always required a strong, articulate supporter to provide a balance. James Forrestal (the first secretary of defense) had been one such; his successor, Louis A. Johnson, was distinctly not. Like Ferdinand Eberstadt, Johnson echoed a key character from the U.S. Navy's early days—Albert Gallatin, President Jefferson's secretary of the treasury, notorious in naval circles as the man who (in 1802) cut the defense budget by 40 percent and the naval budget by more than 50 percent. Gallatin had allocated a defense ceiling of under $3 million; Johnson set a limit of under $15 billion. The number of zeros after the dollar sign had changed, but the principle was similar and the equation was simple: A desire to save money, plus a disbelief in the need for naval defense, equaled naval cuts.

Everything had changed in a century and a half, yet the result was the same. In 1802 Gallatin's argument against the Navy had been based on geography, neutrality, and the abolition of the national debt. His assertions had been that if the United States owed no money, then others would have no motive to attack it; that in any case, it was too far away to be attacked directly by anyone; and that no one would be so dastardly as to attack the merchant ships of a neutral nation. In 1949 Louis Johnson's view was pure Army and nuclear Air Force. The Marines should become part of the Army; naval aviation should merge with the Air Force. He acknowledged that much had been achieved by the Navy but maintained that its fighting life was now over; the time had come for it to change into a seaborne auxiliary support force.

The new secretary of defense took office on March 28. On April 14 he issued his Consolidation Directive No. 1, subjecting active and retired military personnel and civilian employees to censorship. On April 18 the keel was laid of a 65,000-ton aircraft carrier, *United States,* a prototype designed to enable the development of high-performance, nuclear-capable naval attack aircraft over the following twenty years. But on April 23, without consulting the secretary of the navy or the CNO, Louis Johnson canceled *United States.*

The battle over the roles of the services—which most people thought had been settled by their merger in 1947—broke out again with renewed venom and greater bitterness than before. The naval secretary (John L. Sullivan) resigned in protest at Johnson's high-handed action, only to be replaced by a puppet of Johnson's choosing. Gen. Omar Bradley (chairman of the JCS) gave the Army's scathing attitude: Naval leaders, including the victors of the Pacific war, were " 'Fancy Dans' who won't hit the line with all they have on every play unless they can call the signals."[14] The Air Force championed its large and very costly B-36 intercontinental bomber; and, in what newspapers called the "Revolt of the Admirals," the Navy fought back, repeating the need for a balanced force, pointing out that the propeller-driven aircraft was incapable of self-defense against jet fighters, and alleging dozens of improprieties by both Johnson and the secretary of the Air Force in its procurement.

For the umpteenth time, professionals—experts—were at one another's throats again. In the public view, as one admiral remarked, "The Supreme Court deliberates, the Congress legislates, the Joint Chiefs of Staff just bicker."[15]

But the issues at stake were of potentially vital national importance: The everlasting twin questions of internal and external naval policy— what the Navy should be and what it should do—now extended to include the concept of total national defense, and were complicated rather than simplified by the new sciences of warfare.

Allowing no doubt of his answer to those questions, Secretary Johnson continued to exert his authority. In August he ordered the Navy's force of large carriers to be cut from eight to four, with similar reductions in carrier aviation groups, escort carriers, antisubmarine air squadrons, patrol squadrons, Marine Corps air squadrons, cruisers, destroyers, and submarines.

If the cuts were carried out, one might reasonably wonder what would be left of the U.S. Navy. Defying the censorship imposed by Consolidation Directive No. 1, Capt. John Crommelin, U.S.N., announced in public that, surely and not very slowly, the Navy was being dismantled behind the nation's back. Under Johnson's regime, going public like that was not a good career move. It might not be a matter for the Supreme Court, but it became a matter for two sets of congressional hearings, held under the chairmanship of Carl Vinson in August and October 1949; and by the end of the hearings, it certainly looked as if the Navy had lost the so-called "Battle of the Potomac." Crommelin was sent into retirement along with two vice admirals (William Blandy, commander in chief of the Atlantic Fleet, and Gerald Bogan, commander of the First Task Fleet, Pacific Fleet) who had supported him.

Adm. Arleigh Burke was then a captain. Later, thinking back to those days, he observed with wry accuracy: "We Americans . . . we want a complete solution to every problem."[16]

For his own part in putting the Navy's case, Burke would have been barred from flag rank had it not been for President Truman's personal intervention. Adm. Louis E. Denfeld, Chief of Naval Operations, was sacked ("Number 1 victim," said the Navy League, "to the new thought control in the United States") and the cancellation and cuts remained in force.[17] But it was only weeks after the August hearings (and five years earlier than originally thought possible) that the Russians exploded their bomb. The October hearings opened with that terrible shadow in the background; and simultaneously, Mao Tse-tung's victory in China darkened the shadow further. Directed to provide a comprehensive report on national strategy, the National Security Council did so.

Its reply (NSC-68) stated that, in the light of the USSR's new nuclear capability and its existing superiority in conventional forces, the United States must have "rearmament and rehabilitation of forces" in a "rapid and sustained build-up" of conventional strength "in order that it may not have to be used." Estimating that its program would cost $50 billion (more than three times the sum allocated by Johnson for all the forces together in 1949), the council issued a warning: "The United States and the other free countries do not now have the forces in being and readily available to defeat local Soviet moves with local action, but must accept these reverses or make these local moves the occasion for war—for which we are not prepared."[18]

On April 12, 1950, Truman ordered the council to work out the practical details of the program. Little more than ten weeks later, at 4 A.M. on June 25, Communist troops marched unopposed from north to south across the Thirty-Eighth Parallel, and the Korean War began.

What on earth now? "We hope and strive for a system which will prevent the use of atomic weapons," Captain Parsons had written in his letter to Virginia in 1947. "But we must assume that with or without international control, a major war will end with one or both sides using them."[19] Suddenly and horribly, it looked as though the time had come.

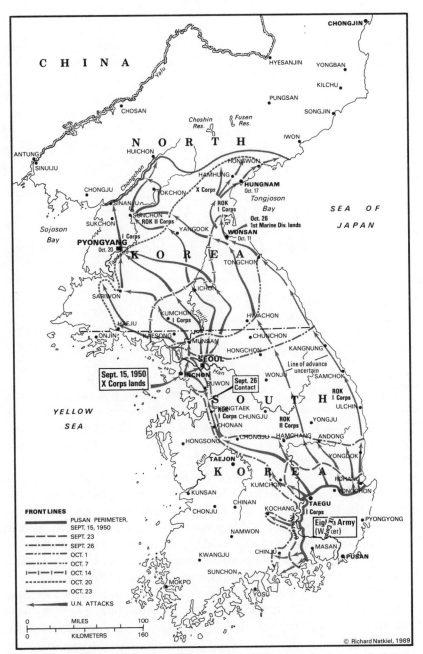

The Korean War ended in stalemate. Without complete Allied control of the sea, however, United Nations and Communist officials alike realized that a swift Allied defeat would have been inevitable.

19

★

UNDER WAY
ON NUCLEAR POWER

"What people can't understand is the weather in Korea. You can't believe, even the people who have been up in Canada can't believe, how cold it is in Korea. It was 25 below zero, and a very high wind. Winds come sweeping down there. . . . The winds are terrific, they come down from Siberia, the snow comes down horizontally and it's frozen, it's not like snowflakes, it's ice."[1]

Still bruised from the "Battle of the Potomac," Arleigh Burke was appointed deputy chief of staff to Vice Adm. Charles Turner Joy, commander of the U.S. Naval Forces Far East. In Korea he found his constant belief confirmed—that "things never go right in any kind of war operation."[2] Korea demonstrated vividly how distant a sophisticated theory of warfare could be from actual combat. Even in the 1980s, guarding northeast Greenland's uninhabited wastes, the Sirius sledge patrol used Enfield rifles made in the United States in 1917 for the simple reason that they worked in the cold. If they froze, the breech could be kicked open. When the modern automatics taken to Korea froze, they were of no more use than a club.[3]

Bernard Baruch had spoken of the possibility of eliminating war—a happy optimism which showed exactly the mental trap into which the United States had fallen. It was in sole possession of the "ultimate" weapon, and it seemed impossible that anyone else, armed only with conventional weapons, would dare fight at all. When the atomic monopoly was broken, the idea of a nuclear exchange was so ghastly that it seemed impossible that either side would wish to fight with anything *except* conventional weapons. Against that, no commander was going to refuse using nuclear weaponry if it looked as if his side could thereby win a war.

But what if it simply brought escalation? Today, knowing full well that nuclear war was not the outcome, we have to remember that in 1950 there was no such promise. The novel, unwelcome questions facing war planners were whether victory through conventional means was possible, and whether victory though the alternative means—unlimited nuclear war—would be worthwhile.

When the Korean War commenced, those questions had not been answered, and all that could be said for sure was that the United States was not ready for a limited conventional war, especially in Asia. The idea, said Gen. Matthew Ridgway, "never entered our councils."[4]

Separating the Yellow Sea and the Sea of Japan, the two Koreas hang suspended from the northeast mainland of China. Neither is a large country; each is about 180 miles wide and 240 miles long at its greatest. Their artificial and unintentional division along the Thirty-eighth Parallel had been established toward the end of the Second World War as a military administrative convenience, to simplify the surrender of Japanese troops: Those in the mountainous, industrial north would give up to the Russians, those in the agricultural south to the Americans. Unlike in Germany, however, there was no wartime intention on the part of the Allies to create two zones of occupation. Yet though both Russian and American troops had withdrawn from North and South by the end of 1948, Korea's permanent division had already come about: The ex-Allies' political differences, surfacing even before the war had ended, precluded free elections in the North, while in the South, the Republic of Korea was established under an elected president.

Had the war been fought only by North and South, Korea would have been reunited; but it would have been under Communist rule, for the North would certainly have won. After their withdrawal in 1948, the Russians had left an organized and well-armed North Korean army of 135,000, including 25,000 men trained by Russians and experienced from fighting Chiang's Nationalists in China. At the same time South Korea's army included 100,000 largely untrained, lightly armed, and inexperienced men. But among the many oddities of the Korean War are the facts that neither side ever surrendered and neither side won. After more than three years of fighting, an armistice was agreed on on July 25, 1953. Signed eight days later, it established a demilitarized zone along the existing battle lines—very close, as it happened, to the original division along the Thirty-eighth Parallel. And South Korea's unexpected ability to withstand the North was solely due to the other odd (indeed, unique) factor of that war: Namely, that on June 27, 1950 (two days after the invasion) the United Nations adopted President Truman's resolution that member nations should help South Korea to "repel the armed attack." At least until 1990, when the possibility emerged of a U.N.-sanctioned war against Iraq, the Korean War remained the only war ever sanctioned by an international organization other than a military alliance.

To a greater extent than usually remembered, it was an international effort to push back Communism physically: British and U.S. carriers (U.S.S. *Valley Forge* and H.M.S. *Triumph*) were the first to launch air strikes against the invaders, and during the war 5,017 Britons were killed, wounded, or listed missing, along with 12,000 men from fifteen other nations. But it is scarcely unjust if people recall Korea as being mainly another U.S. war. For one thing, the first-ever commander in chief of U.N. forces was Douglas MacArthur, created General of the Army and recalled to active service in Korea from working on his life's greatest achievement, the democratization of defeated Japan. For another thing, South Korea and the United States provided 90 percent of the frontline soldiers and endured correspondingly high losses—over 54,000 Americans were killed and over 100,000 wounded. Yet even those figures pale compared to the South Korean military and civilian casualties: 415,000 dead, 429,000 wounded, 460,000 missing. With all those dead, lost, or injured, the constant official U.S. references to this conflict as a "police action" seem demeaning. In addition, a further 900,000 Chinese and 520,000 North Korean troops were killed or wounded. When such figures could come out of a local, limited, conventional war, it became possible to start imagining the hideous worldwide death toll escalation could bring.

For the United Nations, the dread of shared atomic destruction, and wholesale poisoning of the globe were the main factors inhibiting escalation. Using the West's still limited stocks of nuclear weapons could invite a Soviet attack elsewhere, possibly in Europe. Presumably the same dread was felt by Soviet Russia, which allowed its client states to do the actual fighting. But just after the war, Arleigh Burke produced his own analysis of it, and one of his beliefs was that "this could have been an experimental war." Today, the suggestion evokes the fear felt by many Americans in the 1950s—the fear of callous, sinister, and subtle manipulation by Moscow.

"The enemy had a very small Navy and Air Force," Burke pointed out then. "Many variables of warfare were not present. This may have been done purposely by the enemy to permit a careful testing of their theories of one variable, i.e., the Army, under controlled conditions. . . . If so, Russia was conducting the experiment, while we, as laboratory assistants, contributed; and, if we are wise, will learn just as much."[5]

It was not so much a question of learning as of relearning, and the Navy amply justified its continued life as a fighting force with its own air and amphibious capability. The first North Korean drive south was speedy: By August 5, 1950, less than six weeks after their invasion, the People's Army had overrun more than three quarters of South Korea. In another month the area of resistance had shrunk still further, until it came down to the "Pusan perimeter," a rough quarter-circle arc radiating 50 miles from the port of Pusan in the country's southeast corner. By then, the U.S. Seventh Fleet (commanded by Vice Adm. Arthur D. Struble) had evacuated all U.S. civilians to safety. More important for the prosecution of the war, a U.N. naval blockade, under the command of Admiral Joy, was established around the whole of South Korea. Later, Burke underlined "another simple point, that is so obvious that people have forgotten it. We had absolute control of the sea around there. It was never contested in Korea. If our control of the sea had been contested just a little bit . . . Korea would have been lost very fast."[6]

Russia's Admiral of the Fleet, Sergei Gorshkov, agreed: "Without the extensive active employment of the Navy," he wrote, "the interventionists [the U.N. forces] would hardly have been able to avoid a military defeat in Korea. The Navy . . . considerably influenced the course of the war as a whole."[7]

On the very night of the invasion by the North, the South Koreans themselves had shown the reality of a northern seaborne threat. During the night of June 25–26, the South Korean navy's one and only patrol craft, delivered from America just a few weeks previously, intercepted and challenged a large freighter approaching Pusan from the northeast. As the merchant ship fled, fire was exchanged—the freighter was armed with concealed guns. Eventually it was sunk, and then its purpose was discovered: It was carrying 600 North Korean soldiers for an intended attack on Pusan.

U.S. aircraft carriers brought effective air power to Korea more rapidly than the Air Force could. Shore bombardment by cruisers, destroyers, and battleships (of which *Missouri* was the sole example in commission at the start of the war) proved cheaper and more accurate than aerial bombing. The Marines were credited with inventing the use of helicopters for rescue missions. Beyond the fundamental requirement of sea control, the Navy also took the war to the enemy, swiftly and directly, in the celebrated amphibious landing at Inchon—"a hell of a place to have a landing," Admiral Burke recalls. "Extremely high tides, shallow water, just one narrow channel, high cliffs to scale . . . [but] that was the only area that was geographically suitable, to get far enough behind the enemy lines."[8] Located on South Korea's west coast, only 35 miles south of the Thirty-eighth Parallel, the success of the Inchon landing on September 15 was such that the tide of war swung heavily in favor of South Korea:

By the third week of October, the Communist forces had retreated, and U.N. forces had advanced, to 120 miles north of the Thirty-eighth Parallel.

The leapfrog landing (approved by the JCS only on the third time of asking) was General MacArthur's idea, taken from the Pacific war experience. To him was due much of the credit for its success. But, working on the unreliable principle that a success may be repeated, he insisted that another landing should be made at the east coast port of Wonsan. Only 120 miles away by land, Wonsan is 850 miles by sea from Inchon. Soldiers had to be transported by sea, and before they could be landed, Wonsan's shallow, 400-square-mile harbor had to be swept clear of mines. Inchon had been mined as well (as all other South Korean ports would have been without the blockade), but Inchon's high tides, which forced a very narrow "window" of dates for the landings there, had one benefit: As the tide went down, mines came to the surface. At Wonsan they did not.

In the Second World War, over three hundred minesweepers had been used for the Normandy landings. In the battle for Okinawa, the area of sea to be swept was comparable to that of Wonsan, and over a hundred sweepers had been used. At Wonsan itself, a total of about thirty sweepers was available—a dozen U.S. vessels and twenty, with their crews, from the defunct Imperial Japanese Navy.

Since the world war, the latter had been employed in sweeping the Inland Sea and were vastly experienced; but they brought several drawbacks with them. The first was the enormous difficulty of communication: Only one of their number spoke English, and none of the Americans spoke Japanese. Next, the Japanese techniques were somewhat different—the Japanese sweepers had no mother ship carrying spares and so on, and the Americans did not have suitable parts for them. Another problem was that the Japanese were there entirely voluntarily—when one of their ships was lost, three more decided to leave, and did so, without anyone being able to stop them. And underlying it all was an inevitable lack of trust, which forced the American sweepers to check-sweep any channel the Japanese claimed to be clear. Burke, who had to organize the arduous and diplomatically ticklish Wonsan operation, described it later as "just God-awful."[9]

The port was secured by the Marines on October 26, but the operation's very success showed its doubtful military value. It meant that U.N. and South Korean troops were divided across the country, and their penetration beyond the Thirty-eighth Parallel prompted the introduction of Chinese Communist soldiers into the war. China, understandably, could no more tolerate an alien force near the Yalu River (its border with North Korea) than the U.S. would along the Rio Grande, its border with Mexico.

So on December 10, 1950, just fifty days after the Marines had taken it, Wonsan was evacuated. Two weeks later, the port of Hungnam (50 miles further north) was also evacuated. Protected by *Missouri*'s bombardment, a fleet of over a hundred vessels removed 91,000 Korean civilians and 105,000 U.N. troops. Seventeen thousand vehicles and over a third of a million tons of supplies were also embarked; then, in a series of massive explosions, the dock installations were deliberately blown up.

It was clear to everyone that without sea control, this echo of Dunkirk would not have been possible; nearly 200,000 people would have been in the gravest peril. And gradually it also became clear to everyone that this was a war no one could win. Had the Koreas been an island, there would have been no problem—the United Nations would have won through its dominant sea power. As it was, the U.N. force could be supplied indefinitely by sea, and the North Korean and Chinese force likewise by land. Slowly the swings of fighting and fortune settled to an inert stalemate in the center; and although there were repeated flare-ups of conflict, from the first time peace was proposed to the final armistice, the Korean War began to fizzle out. It lasted just over three years (June 25, 1950 to August 2, 1953) and was an unusual war for at least three reasons—it was the first and only one so far to have been sanctioned by the United Nations; and the first war of the nuclear age. It must also be one of the few wars in history which ended mainly because both sides decided there was nothing to be gained from carrying on.

As far as the U.S. Navy was concerned, however, much was gained from the conflict in Korea. The Navy's credibility and its physical size were substantially restored by the unexpected need for flexible, conventional warfare. Five days after the first invasion, it had little more than 380,000 active personnel—one eighth of its World War II peak. The first year of Korea brought it up again to over 730,000, with a similar increase in active ships; more than three hundred were recommissioned from Second World War mothballed stock, bringing the fleet to some eleven hundred active vessels. And after Korea, neither men nor ships were flung back into reserve with the cheerful abandon of 1945; throughout the 1960s and into the 1970s, the United States was always served by at least 600,000 active naval personnel.

At the same time, the U.S. Army, Air Force, and Marine Corps grew in proportion. This rearming of the United States was, in Winston Churchill's opinion, the most important outcome of the Korean War. In a way, it had been a rather old-fashioned war. More often than not, the tactics, the weapons, and the ships had been created and used in the Second World War—and many of the men, too, were veterans of the Pacific, Atlantic, or European theaters. But while the war in Korea was being fought, the U.S. Navy's most important single technological development ever was approaching, a development thoroughly in keeping with the new presidential doctrine for the 1950s.

Stalin died on March 5, 1953. The day before, supported by the largest popular vote to that date, General Eisenhower became the thirty-fourth president of the United States. Truman had taken the Monroe Doctrine and turned it inside out; Eisenhower took the Truman Doctrine and extended it enormously, promising economic and military assistance to any nation threatened by Communist subversion and (in place of the lost nuclear monopoly) promising "massive retaliation" in the event of a Soviet nuclear attack. And the U.S. Navy would become the main channel of retaliation—for the fleet was going nuclear.

"The cleverest, the most cunning and the rudest man in the whole United States Navy"—in a fleet with over 700,000 personnel at the time, the description was sharply barbed. But it was not difficult to live with a reputation for extreme irascibility and unnecessary discourtesy when, as with Adm. Hyman G. Rickover, it was balanced by a free acknowledgement of brilliance, even from those whom he had most antagonized.[10]

As liaison officer between Vice Adm. Earle Mills (postwar chief of the Bureau of Ships) and the Atomic Energy Commission (on which the U.S. Navy depended for the development of a nuclear reactor plant), the then–Captain Rickover began the work which would absorb him, passionately, for the rest of his long life: transforming the steam-powered U.S. Navy into a nuclear-powered fleet. When the secretary of the Navy announced that 1955 was the "birthdate of a new United States Navy," he was not overstating the matter; and though no one person can be credited with that rebirth, the one who could take much of the credit was Rickover. As his friends in the Navy and Congress acknowledged, he was abusive, manipulative, impatient, ill-tempered, stubborn, arrogant, and capable of enraging more people in a shorter time than anyone who never met him would believe possible. As his enemies in the Navy and Congress acknowledged, he was close to being a genius. And they all acknowledged him as the "father" of America's nuclear navy.

The shift from steam to nuclear power was as radical as the shift from sail to steam had been, and came much faster. The U.S. Navy began its third age just after 11 A.M. on January 17, 1955, when the 3,530-ton submarine U.S.S. *Nautilus* made a signal no other vessel had ever made: UNDER WAY ON NUCLEAR POWER.[11]

The last of the world's major navies to enter the steam age, the U.S. fleet was the first to use nuclear propulsion. By then it was also able to deliver nuclear weapons: In February 1951, the Mediterranean (Sixth) Fleet was provided with its first nuclear-capable AJ-1 Savage heavy attack aircraft. Because of their large size, they were based on land at Port Lyautey, Morocco; but as nuclear warheads were made smaller and lighter, it became possible to fit them to missiles, and in May 1954 the first nuclear-tipped Regulus missile was declared operational.

The subsonic, turbojet-powered Regulus I was only part of the Navy's post–Second World War technological growth. Missile experiments began immediately after the war with the Loon (its design borrowed from the German V-1), the Regulus I, and the supersonic, ramjet-powered Rigel. Although some submarines, cruisers, and small carriers were adapted to launch them, the large, awkward missiles were all comparatively short-lived. In 1955, when Adm. Arleigh Burke became Chief of Naval Operations, he appointed Rear Adm. William F. Raborn, Jr., to begin developing Polaris ballistic missiles—submarine-launched, guided by a very accurate inertial navigating system, and first deployed in 1960. As the development of Polaris began, 60,000-ton supercarriers of the *Forrestal* class were added to the fleet at the rate of one a year, incorporating three new British inventions—the mirror landing system, the angled flight deck, and the steam catapult. Displacing 78,000 tons when fully loaded, each ship could carry about eighty-five aircraft, including the A4D Skyhawk with its atomic weapons and the heavy A3D Skywarrior, bearing hydrogen bombs.

The latest addition to the world's grotesquely swelling arsenals, the first H-bomb was tested in 1952 on the innocent Pacific atoll of Eniwetok—already the joint grave of many Japanese and American soldiers, sailors, airmen, and Marines. Truman announced the bomb's existence in his final State of the Union address in January 1953. Eight months later Stalin's successor, Georgi Malenkov, observed with satisfaction that the U.S. had not regained a nuclear monopoly; a Russian hydrogen bomb had been developed as well, and was in production.

It seemed the motto of the U.S. Navy's new age was "nukes with everything." Development of the nuclear-warhead antisubmarine torpedo was commenced, along with the atomic depth charge, the atomic antisubmarine rocket, the BT-3A(N) Terrier shipborne nuclear-warhead antiaircraft missile (among others), and of course the ships themselves. In 1958 Admiral Burke predicted a 1970s nuclear fleet that would include thirty cruisers and frigates, six aircraft carriers, seventy-five attack submarines, and fifty Polaris submarines. By the beginning of the 1960s, taking only the key vessels and their completion dates, the fleet included U.S.S. *George Washington* (1960), the first nuclear-powered submarine to test Polaris and the first too to carry it operationally; U.S.S. *Long Beach* (1961), the first nuclear-powered cruiser, armed with guided missiles; U.S.S. *Bainbridge* (1962), the first frigate with nuclear propulsion; and U.S.S. *Enterprise* (1961), the first nuclear-propelled carrier, displacing

76,000 tons and powered by eight reactors. A second *George Washington*–class submarine and eleven more attack submarines had been commissioned; seven further ballistic-missile submarines and another eighteen attack submarines had been authorized and were being built. Burke's prediction appeared to be on course to fulfillment.

In the quest to find the limits (if any) of the new and seemingly inexhaustible source of energy, trials, tests, and demonstrations continued to reshape every traditional view of the world and war. Two outstanding achievements and two oft-repeated exercises encapsulate all the experiments.

The first came at 11:15 P.M., Washington time, on August 3, 1958, when, after an eleven-day voyage from Pearl Harbor, *Nautilus* reached the North Pole and continued—submerged—to complete an astonishing pioneer voyage from Pacific to Atlantic across the top of the world.

The second came in the spring months of 1960: Under the command of Capt. Edward L. Beach (later as distinguished a writer as he was a sailor), U.S.S. *Triton* accomplished history's first underwater voyage around the world. Nigh on 6,000 tons' standard displacement, 447½ feet long, *Triton* was then the world's largest existing submarine. In twelve weeks (February 16 to May 10, 1960) she voyaged 36,000 miles—from the Atlantic around the Horn to the Pacific, across to the Philippines, onward to the Cape of Good Hope, and north to Europe before her final return home—at an average speed of 18 knots throughout; and except for two brief interruptions, she was submerged the entire time.

Remembering the voyages of men like Magellan and Sir John Franklin, these frontier-breaking voyages by the first nuclear submarines have almost an air of fantasy about them, a sense of infinite ability—the dreams of Jules Verne come to life. If nothing else, the new power source transformed submarines from submersible craft into true underwater vessels; now only human endurance limited the time they could spend below the waves. But as Adm. Stansfield Turner recalls, other exercises showed vividly how the same infinite ability could create a nightmare. In May 1962, as captain of the destroyer U.S.S. *Rowan,* he was 200 miles west of Christmas Island, in the central Pacific:

> I knew that at five o'clock in the morning there was going to be another nuclear explosion. I will never forget that experience, because when the explosion went off, I didn't see a loom of light bright in the east, the direction of the explosion; I found the entire sky from zenith to horizon was illuminated. One nuclear explosion—but it was enough for a prolonged daylight, not just a flash. . . . We weren't close enough to hear, but all of a sudden, it went from total dark to total light.[12]

Turner witnessed several nuclear-test air explosions, at distances varying from 20 to 800 miles. The most distant, only a few weeks after the Christmas Island test, was also the most sinister. Traveling from Christmas Island to Hawaii, Turner was informed that a high-altitude air test was going to take place over Johnston Island.

It was a little after sunset. It wasn't fully dark, but it was night-time. This bomb went off at high altitude and as far as I could see, the entire sky turned red. I could see white stars through the redness— it was the most eerie scene I believe I'll ever see. The magnitude of it—not just a red streak in the sky, but the whole sky was red. . . . Instead of the blue night sky with white stars in it, you have a red sky with white stars.

It used to be said that a red sky at night was a shepherd's delight; but no more. Shaking his head in amazement at the memory of that bizarre and sinister vision, Admiral Turner added simply: "It really tells you what mankind has created, in terms of enormity of power."

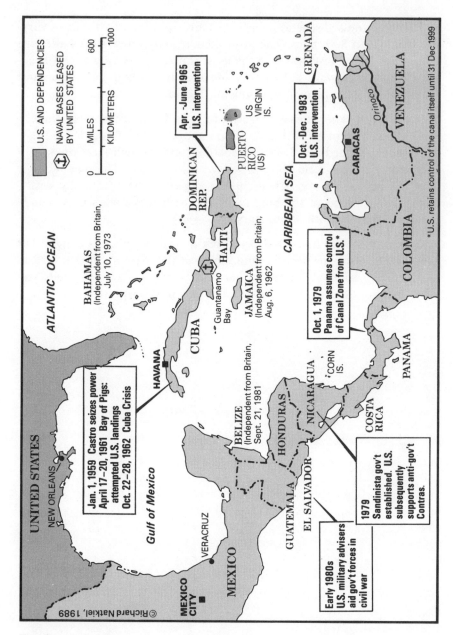

Despite every effort to impose the Monroe Doctrine, in the second half of the twentieth century the Caribbean remained as volatile—and, to the United States, as potentially threatening—as ever.

20

★

EYEBALL TO EYEBALL

*T*he swift development of a nuclear-propelled, nuclear-armed fleet sucked away funds from conventional building. Fortunately—or so it seemed—the large existing reservoir of World War II stock covered conventional naval needs. As the worldwide Cold War contest of ideology continued after Korea, there were many such needs; and the first turned out to be only a curtain raiser for the United States' longest hot war.

By 1954, an eight-year-old insurrection in French Indochina had matured into unrelenting guerrilla war. To begin with, it had seemed merely a part of the crumbling colonialism, or evolving independence, which was affecting nations throughout the Third World. Had it been so, perhaps the United States might never have become involved in Vietnam; but given that the insurgents, led by Ho Chi Minh, were Communists, a direct confrontation with the United States was almost inevitable sooner or later. In fact, the United States had already financed 80 percent of the French counterinsurgency effort, to the tune of $400 million in 1953 alone; and when ten battalions of French troops were besieged at Dien Bien Phu in the early months of 1954, President Eisenhower and his secretary of state, John Foster Dulles, made ready to assist. The U.S. Air Force could not do it—their B-29 bombers could not guarantee to miss the beleaguered French—so three attack carriers, *Essex, Wasp,* and *Boxer,* moved to the South China Sea, offering nearly a hundred instantly available aircraft each. Their accuracy was not in question, but Eisenhower did not want the United States to go it alone. He asked the British to join in. They refused; so the aircraft stayed on the carriers, and after fifty-five days of constant Communist artillery bombardment, the French garrison was overwhelmed.

Soon afterwards France admitted defeat and Vietnam, like Korea, was divided into a Communist North and democratic South. The division prompted huge shifts of population. Now in the role of servant as well as defender of those opposed to Communism, U.S. warships began a four-month operation called "Passage to Freedom," evacuating thousands of vehicles, scores of thousands of tons of goods, and over 300,000 people from north to south.

In the same year, Marines stood by to render direct assistance in an American-backed invasion of Guatemala from Honduras, overthrowing an infant Communist government. In the Far East, after a British airliner was shot down by Communist Chinese fighter aircraft, two carriers of the U.S. Seventh Fleet moved in, were challenged by fighters, and shot down a pair of them in turn. Soon there were further Far Eastern tussles involving the two republics of China: the mainland People's Republic, all 3.7 million square miles of it, and Chiang Kai-shek's Taiwan, the 23,000-square-mile island known improbably but officially as the Republic of China. The two are separated by the 100-mile-wide Strait of Formosa. On the mainland side of the strait, virtually within a stone's throw of the People's Republic, were the two small islands of Quemoy and Matsu—claimed and occupied, despite their geographical position, as part of Chiang's republic in Taiwan.

It was highly unlikely that Chiang's troops would be able to enjoy uninterrupted possession of the islands for very long—especially since, with Soviet help, the Red Chinese navy was becoming a respectable fleet. Although still limited to a coastal defense capability, it contained destroyers, minesweepers, submarine chasers, torpedo boats, and some twenty medium-sized attack submarines. Backed by a substantial army and mainland shore defenses, the time came, late in August 1958, for a Communist attack on Quemoy, occasioned by a visit there of the Nationalist defense minister.

The Communists made their disapproval of this visit clear by bombarding the island with 40,000 high-explosive shells in two hours. Equally clear, from reconnaissance by U.S. naval aircraft, were the abnormally large numbers of Communist warships in nearby mainland ports. What followed was effectively a maritime version of the Berlin Airlift: Not wishing to commit the nation to direct military action but determined not to let Red China expand, even to so small and close an island, Eisenhower instituted a policy of passive assistance—supplying Quemoy, under fire when necessary, by sea.

The sealift, like the airlift, became a test of nerve, with the advantage very much on the U.S. side—submarine pickets were established, and to the one carrier group already in the vicinity a further six carriers were soon added, including one hunter-killer antisubmarine group. Among this large force were nuclear-capable aircraft, which, when connected with an earlier and much-publicized remark of Eisenhower's, gave everyone pause for thought.

As commander of NATO in 1951, two years before he came to the presidency, he had stated unequivocally that if the "net advantage of their use was on my side" in war, he would use nuclear weapons "instantly."[1] Of course, the United States and China were not at war: For both sides, this face-off in the Strait of Formosa was a gamble. But on one occasion, mainland Chinese artillery bombardment came so close to U.S. warships that the vessels felt obliged to withdraw—they were there to manage a crisis, not to precipitate a war by allowing themselves to be hit—and the very closeness of their own shooting unsettled the authorities in mainland China. If they did hit a U.S. ship, there might be war, and they could not be sure that Eisenhower, as president, had changed the priorities he had held as NATO commander. So their direct assault on Quemoy was abandoned, and in its place the Communists adopted a new, odd, and almost gentlemanly way of making their point—the island would be bombarded every other day. This lasted several years, and looking back, seems like rather a good arrangement; it meant that no one forgot the differences between the island and the mainland, but supplies could easily be brought in, and no one had to get hurt at all.

These distant crises were important, but existed mostly on the fringes of U.S. spheres of interest. The Guatemalan affair, which had provoked a quick and heavy U.S. response, was something of an exception; the Caribbean region still figured as highly in U.S. defensive thinking as at any time since the Navy had begun to clear it of pirates in 1823. And after Turkey and Greece joined NATO in 1952, the Mediterranean effectively became a part of the United States' East Coast waters, with the Sixth Fleet as the front line against Communist intrusion. The importance of the fleet was shown by the Defense Department's growing habit of giving it the newest and best ships and aircraft; and on July 15, 1958 (less than six weeks before the Quemoy bombardment) it was put to dramatic and effective use, when U.S. Marines first entered Lebanon.

In a pattern still depressingly familiar well over thirty years later, Beirut and Tripoli were subject to daily and nightly riot and civil violence. The area's legacy of hate, created when Israel was carved out of the existing Arab nations, was complicated by the permutations of three militant religions (Judaism, Islam, and Christianity) and at least three broad political views (pro-Soviet, pro-Britain and United States, and independent, which could mean pro-nobody or anti-everybody). It was, as it remains, in an almost permanent state of crisis.

But even where instability has become a way of life, some events are more visibly critical than others; and one such was the assassination, on the morning of July 14, 1958, of King Faisal and Crown Prince Abdul Illah of Iraq. The assassins were officers from their own military, supporters of the recently formed pro-Soviet United Arab Republic, which was composed of Egypt, Yemen, and Syria. President Chamoun of Lebanon looked like a good candidate for murder as well, and not only in his own eyes. Eisenhower responded quickly to Chamoun's cry for help—at 6 P.M. Washington time, the American president telephoned Admiral Burke, his Chief of Naval Operations, and ordered him to land Marines at Beirut thirteen hours later.

The first contingent was there at 7:04 A.M. Washington time on July 15—just four minutes overdue—as Eisenhower went on national television to announce the event. Aircraft from the attack carrier *Essex* (soon to be ordered out to Quemoy) covered the unopposed landings. By midday on July 16 there were 5,000 Marines ashore; four days later, as Army and Air Force personnel arrived, the number of U.S. military men in Beirut rose to nearly 14,000, with 10,000 of them in a four-square-mile area in and around the airport. Operation Bluebat, as it was called, was the largest single deployment of U.S. servicemen since the Korean War.

It could have gone badly wrong. Despite the soldiers' high level of training and practice, it took several days longer than expected to airlift them in. In their three months in Lebanon, only one American was killed by hostile fire; but had there been any opposition on the beaches, from any source, Marine deaths would have been many and immediate. Nevertheless, the deployment was successful as an exercise in injecting localized force to aid foreign policy and protect national interests. In Eisenhower's view, it showed "in a truly practical way that the United States was capable of supporting its friends" and simultaneously could avoid involving itself in other countries' domestic politics. Lebanon did not become a neocolonial base for the restoration of the Iraqi monarchy, as some had predicted; and in October, when the Lebanese government decided it could handle matters and asked the U.S. forces to leave, they did so, as had been promised from the beginning.

Overall, the demonstration of ability to fulfill intent—the proof that the United States could do what it said it would do—was timely. Bluebat at least partly erased a large question mark which had been placed over the anti-Communist rhetoric of U.S. foreign policy by three recent events: the Suez crisis, the Hungarian uprising, and the launch of Sputnik. It is worth taking a glance at all three.

First, the seizure of the neutral Suez Canal by Egypt's pro-Soviet

President Nasser (July 26, 1956) resulted directly from the removal, one week earlier, of an offered U.S. loan of $56 million to start construction of the Aswan dam. The offer was canceled by Secretary of State Dulles, angered because Nasser had not only asked for a cheaper offer from Moscow, but also had mortgaged the country's cotton crop to spend $200 million on arms from Soviet-bloc nations.

Obviously this was disagreeable to Dulles; but to cancel the offered loan without warning, as he did, was ham-fisted too. The error was compounded by the British Prime Minister Sir Anthony Eden and the French Foreign Minister Christian Pineau; at the beginning of September, they informed Dulles and Eisenhower that they planned a military invasion of the canal zone, but omitted to say when. At the end of October, Israeli forces launched a successful attack on Egypt. Ships of the U.S. Navy Sixth Fleet were able to evacuate 1,500 U.S. citizens from Egypt; and at that point the U.S. leaders were told that a thousand British and French paratroops were about to be dropped into Egypt.

Neither Dulles nor Eisenhower cared to have been kept (apparently deliberately) in the dark; and when threatening noises issued from the Soviet Union, they started diplomatic moves to stop the whole business. In that, at least, they succeeded; but Nasser held on to the canal.

At the same time (October 1956), the people of Hungary rebelled against Soviet control of their country. Harshly suppressed, the short-lived rebellion seemed to many in the United States and Europe to be an ideal opportunity to redraw the boundaries of the Communist world. So it was, superficially; and when Eisenhower reacted with only sympathetic platitudes, there was widespread disappointment.

As for Sputnik, it was little more than a metal football which bleeped; but orbiting the globe and bleeping from space, it shocked the Western world rigid, for despite their nuclear bombs, the Russians were not supposed to be a people of such technological sophistication.

With unpleasant clarity, it followed that if they could make a rocket powerful enough to escape gravity, they could also make one powerful enough to take an H-bomb across the ocean. In the West, questions tumbled over each other in their haste to be asked: How much warning would be given? Could a rocket be shot down? Where might it fall? Was there any protection? How many bombs did they have, anyway? What about Europe? Massachusetts? California? Texas? And so on. It was a formative moment for the democracies, as all understood together that though "massive retaliation" might destroy an enemy, there might also be a rather limited number of friends left afterwards.

And then came Khrushchev, Castro, Cuba—and the Bay of Pigs. Most people probably have moments when, prompted by some unexpected trigger of memory, they involuntarily relive an acutely embarrassing experience and groan inwardly or aloud with the thought of it. Today the Bay of Pigs is still such a thing for Americans old enough to remember; for this—the last foreign policy initiative of the aging Eisenhower and the first inheritance of his glamorous young successor, John F. Kennedy— was deeply embarrassing to the American nation.

The ship's name *Essex* is an ancient, honorable, and adventurous one in the U.S. Navy. Under Edward Preble, in 1799, U.S.S. *Essex* was the first American warship to penetrate the Indian Ocean. In 1812 she was the first ever to capture a British warship; in 1813, the first to round the Horn and achieve the Pacific. A century and a half later, U.S.S. *Essex* was still busy and venturesome: launching aircraft to guard the Lebanon landings, steaming down to Quemoy to overawe the Chinese, and now (in April 1961) providing escort to and aerial reconnaissance over the United States' newly Communist neighbor, Cuba.

This is how the situation had developed. In the sixty-three years since *Maine* had blown up in Havana harbor, Cuba had been chronically unstable, but also (until 1959) unthreatening. In 1902, three years of U.S. military government of the island ended with the creation of the Republic of Cuba, which was nominally independent but agreed (under the "Platt Amendment") to accept U.S. intervention in case of domestic upheaval. This agreement was invoked twice in periods of political unrest (1906–9 and 1917–23) and fitted well with Theodore Roosevelt's corollary to the Monroe Doctrine: "If we intend to say 'Hands off [the Caribbean]' to the powers of Europe," he had observed in 1904, "then sooner or later we must keep order ourselves."[2]

Thirty years after that, his namesake and relative Franklin Roosevelt had a very different view: the so-called "Good Neighbor" policy, given idealized form in the declaration of the Montevideo Conference of December 1933. In that same year, a young sergeant named Fulgencio Batista y Zaldicar led a successful coup in Cuba. In 1934 the Montevideo Declaration was unanimously endorsed by the U.S. Senate. Among other things, it said explicitly that "no state has the right to intervene in the internal or external affairs of another."[3] The Platt Amendment was therefore withdrawn. For a further six years, Batista ruled Cuba through a series of figurehead presidents, until in 1940 he became president himself. He retired in 1944; went to live in Florida; returned to power through another military coup in 1952; and thereafter Cuba degenerated swiftly into a brutal, corrupt dictatorship.

Over the decades, U.S. investment in Cuba had grown to near-colonial proportions. During Batista's regime, 40 percent of its sugar production, 80 percent of its utilities, and 90 percent of its mining were owned by Americans, while at Guantanamo in the southeast (only 50 miles from the site of their victory over Admiral Cervera in 1898) the U.S. Navy had a leasehold base. All this was very useful and profitable to Americans, but Batista's rule disgusted them. Americans wanted the island to have a more liberal, democratic ruler; but the existing political arrangements meant that any change would have to be a Cuban initiative. So it was that when Fidel Castro began his (second) period of guerrilla warfare against Batista in 1956, then ousted the dictator on New Year's Day, 1959, and made himself president, he was hailed in the United States as a true liberator.

This made the jolt to the United States all the more severe when the liberator collectivized agriculture, expropriated the banks, the sugar estates, and other major industries; closed churches, imprisoned opponents, sent a quarter of a million Cubans into voluntary or involuntary exile abroad; and, in 1961, declared himself a Marxist-Leninist, with Cuba a Communist state.

Cuba and the continental United States are separated by only 150 miles of sea. The distance from Havana to the nearest U.S. island, Key West, is even less—a trifling 90 miles or so. Suddenly and disconcertingly, foreign policy ceased to be a concept remote from the lives of ordinary Americans. For the inhabitants of Florida in particular, to awaken and find Communists sitting virtually on one's doorstep was a very disagreeable experience.

In its whole history, Cuba had never had a democratic choice of any sort, nor any chance to learn how to govern itself freely—the only alternatives it had ever known were anarchy or tyranny. But now, with at least a quarter million exiles ready to stand up and confirm that they had had no democratic choice in the matter, no one outside the island could imagine that for the majority of Cubans, Communism might seem to offer a better way of life than any they had known hitherto.

Given the island's history, there was of course the chance that if, in time, enough people came to dislike Castro's methods, he would be overthrown too. Indeed, by the end of President Reagan's second term in office in 1989, there actually were more Cubans living in Miami than in Havana—but Castro, still firmly in power, had become Latin America's most durable dictator. And back in 1961, the chance that he might be ousted was not one which President Kennedy was prepared to take. Instead, Kennedy chose to carry out Eisenhower's bequest.

Thus, on the morning of April 17, 1961, U.S.S. *Essex* and five U.S. destroyers positioned themselves off the Bay of Pigs on Cuba's south coast, ready to cover an invasion of returning exiles. The exiles had been trained and armed in the United States; the six freighters transporting their ground troops were leased by the CIA and escorted by U.S. warships; the B-26 bombers of their air troops were built in and flying from the United States. Altogether it looked as though the Montevideo Declaration that "no state has the right to intervene in the internal or external affairs of another" was being interpreted very loosely indeed. But it was not thrown out of the window completely: Officially, there was no U.S. involvement. Just five days earlier, Kennedy had stated that he would not try to get rid of Castro by force, and to support the story, *Essex* and her companions were forbidden to join any fighting. If the exiles were victorious, the question of how they would avoid imposing their own tyranny was not an issue: They would welcome open U.S. protection and did not doubt that their countrymen still living in Cuba would rise up in immediate support of their landing.

It did not quite work out that way. Say "Bay of Pigs" in a word-association game today, and most Americans will reply "Fiasco." The phrase has become automatic, but is nonetheless true. "Probably the most mismanaged military operation in U.S. history" was a courteous description, but "the most screwed-up operation" (as a White House adviser called it) was closer to the national view.[4]

Just about everything that could go wrong did go wrong, starting with the CIA's misinterpretation of aerial photographs of the landing site. Cuban exiles said firmly that blurry shapes offshore were coral reefs, but to the CIA, seaweed or cloud shadows seemed more likely. Of course they were coral, and they impeded the landing badly. Other problems included motorboats whose engines did not work, lack of maps, and old, slow aircraft; but worst was the resident islanders' unexpected reluctance to be freed from Communism. That, together with Castro's personal detailed knowledge of the area and control of communications, made the invasion's humiliating defeat inevitable.

On April 24, President Kennedy admitted that the United States had been deeply involved. At home, the shameful confirmation that he had been lying outright was partly mitigated by the fact that he had at least "come clean." Abroad, friends were disappointed and enemies delighted; Castro was sufficiently ruffled to ask for increased Soviet protection; and Khrushchev was so emboldened that (remarking "The Monroe Doctrine has outlived its time and has died a natural death") he offered Castro the very best local weapons he had.[5]

These soon formed a daunting arsenal, including at least twenty-five Ilyushin-28 nuclear-capable bombers; an indeterminate number of medium-range nuclear missiles, each 52 feet long, able to fly 1,200 miles, and visibly pointing toward the United States; and half a dozen bases in preparation for long-range missiles with a 2,500-mile functional radius. Scattered around Cuba, the missile and bomber sites threatened every state, and virtually every city, in the United States. Of course, in the USSR there already were intercontinental missiles quite capable of hitting the United States; but they were not within imaginable distance and you did not see spy-plane photographs of them on television and in the news-papers. For post–World War II babies, now teenagers, the Cuban Missile Crisis was their first experience of real fear.

The first photographs were taken on October 14, 1962, by a high-flying U-2 surveillance plane. To understand them, one had to know what one was looking for and at; an untrained person might have thought they showed nothing more than fields and roads. But to trained eyes the shapes were immediately recognizable: security fences, vehicle revetments, bunk-ers, launch pads, stacks of construction materials. Low-level photographs were still more vivid—as clearly as the surrounding trees and tracks, the machinery could be seen: fuel trailers, missile transporters, firing tables.

It was a far more serious threat than the mere communization of Cuba. The danger lay not so much in the missiles themselves, though they were more than sufficiently perilous. The danger was one of precedent: Allow this, and anything could follow. West Berlin, immured since the previous year, would become not just a tempting, but a practical, target for Soviet expansion. Western Europe would seem open to attack from the Soviet Union's superior conventional forces. Any state or island in the Americas or any part of the Western Hemisphere would be vulnerable. But in marked contrast to the Bay of Pigs, Kennedy, having taken professional advice from the Joint Chiefs of Staff, this time made a masterly response.

Under his administration, the principle of flexible response had already begun to be developed—a move away from the "massive retaliation" of Eisenhower's time, in which nuclear weapons would be used "instantly," to the concept of their use as a last resort. And as first resort in the Cuban Missile Crisis, President Kennedy called upon the Navy.

One hundred and eighty-three U.S. Navy ships (including eight aircraft carriers and carrying over 30,000 Marines) were ordered from the rein-forced Atlantic Fleet into the Caribbean, with the support of the NATO allies and the Organization of American States. Units from Argentina, Venezuela, and the Dominican Republic joined them, emphasizing the unanimity of the Western Hemisphere. The vessels' objective could have been neither simpler nor more nerve-wracking: They were ordered to prevent the importation into Cuba of any further Soviet military supplies. All suspect ships would be stopped and their cargoes inspected. In every way except in name, a blockade was to be instituted. Since, under interna-tional law, a blockade could be used only in wartime, this was instead called a quarantine—and what echoes of naval history it evoked. Stop and search: the issue which had brought Britain and the U.S. to war in 1812. Quarantine: Franklin Roosevelt and his call for a quarantine of the fascist nations before World War II became a fully global war.

About thirty-six hours' warning was given before the quarantine came into effect at 9 A.M., Washington time, on Wednesday, October 24, 1962.

With twenty-five ships bearing Soviet military supplies known to be en route for Cuba, there was time (but not a lot) for the USSR to decide how to react. Six Soviet submarines were already in the vicinity, but this was the sum total of Soviet naval units present. The United States possessed absolute command of the sea around Cuba. In addition, Kennedy let it be known that B-52 bombers armed with nuclear bombs were on standby; 156 intercontinental ballistic missiles were ready to be launched against the Soviet Union; and Polaris-armed submarines were in position. The quarantine itself was, he pointed out, a peaceful act: Any aggressive initiative would have to come from Moscow, and U.S. forces were prepared for anything—anything from a full invasion of the island to an all-out nuclear assault on the USSR.

He also explained that an aggressive initiative did not have to be as crude as an attack. An aggressive initiative would be anything which did not demonstrate absolutely peaceful cooperation. If Soviet surface ships refused to submit to stop-and-search procedures, or if submarines refused to respond to the international code signal IDKCA ("Surface or be destroyed"), it would be considered an aggressive initiative.

Early on Wednesday morning, October 24, eight Soviet freighters were approaching the quarantine line, a submarine stationed underwater between two of them. Accompanied by her hunter-killer, U.S.S. *Essex* issued the challenge.

The freighters stopped. The submarine surfaced. One by one, all six of the other submarines already in the area were challenged, and all came up. One by one, the other freighters stopped; some turned away of their own accord. Gradually it became evident that the Russians had lost their nerve—that the quarantine's authority was being accepted and respected. And as the news filtered into the United States, Secretary of State Dean Rusk voiced the relief of millions in a famous phrase: "We're eyeball to eyeball, and I think the other fellow just blinked."[6] Ships which penetrated the screening line did so because they were confident of the innocence of their cargoes. After searches confirmed it, they were allowed to proceed. The crisis was not over yet; on Cuba itself, building of the missile sites continued. But on Sunday, October 28, Khrushchev gave his public admission of defeat and informed Kennedy that "the arms which you describe as offensive" would be dismantled, crated, and returned to the Soviet Union.

Moscow's experiment had failed; yet trying it out had been a reasonable thing to do. The United States had backed off in a huff at Suez; had declined to support the Hungarian rebellion; was lagging in the newborn space race. Thus there was little evidence that it would stand any more firmly anywhere else. Now, though, the USSR and the rest of the world learned that there actually was substance and resolve behind U.S. rhetoric.

There was something else to learn as well. In Quemoy, the Communist Chinese navy had been as unable to compete as the Soviets had been off Lebanon or Cuba. In comparison to Cuba, U.S. actions in Quemoy and Lebanon were small; but all had succeeded, and the basic reason for their success—the common factor allowing the United States to respond swiftly, efficiently, and appropriately—was dominant sea power. In the USSR this lesson was clearly understood, and quickly absorbed.

PART SEVEN

RECKONING

1964 – 1991

★

*The United States' longest war becomes
the nation's first military defeat.
Subterfuge and deceit rule
in the White House.
The fleet declines alongside the morale of
the people; but the Soviet navy develops,
posing a new seaborne challenge
to the Western world.
Once again, the United States accepts the challenge.
Abruptly and unexpectedly, the
Cold War appears to be won.*

21

★

THAT BITCH OF
A WAR

*T*he year was 1964. In one single day, Khrushchev was toppled from power; Britain, bored with "thirteen years of Tory misrule," voted in a Labour Government; and China exploded its first atomic bomb to become (after the United States, Russia, Britain, and France) the world's fifth nuclear nation. Shortly afterward, Lyndon Johnson was elected president of the United States by the largest majority to date; the bombing of Vietnam intensified; and in the spring of 1965, as folk singers emphasized that the times they were a-changing, the international protest movement began to gain weight and strength. To some, the old order did seem to be rapidly fading; but as one veteran, Bob Muller, observes, "everybody remembers the tail end of the war. They don't remember that in 1964, '65, '66, '67, there was a lot of support in America for the Vietnam war."[1]

Born in 1945, Bob Muller was a twenty-four-year-old lieutenant in the Marine Corps when a North Vietnamese bullet passed through his chest and left him paralyzed from the waist down. In 1985, as president of the Vietnam Veterans of America association, he represented many middle-aged men who went as youths to fight in the nation's longest war.

By the time Kennedy was murdered in 1963, Vietnam was already an old war. During World War II, Ho Chi Minh had been the acknowledged leader of the Viet Minh, the main Indochinese resistance to Japanese occupation. But the goal was not mere ejection of the Japanese in order to live under French rule again; the goal was independence, as it had been when Filipinos had cooperated with the United States in the war against Spain in 1898. And, as had happened in the four-year Philippine insurrection against U.S. rule, when the anticipated independence of Indochina did not materialize, nothing changed for the Viet Minh except the face of the enemy. Fighting against French troops continued until the final massacre at Dien Bien Phu in May 1954. A peace conference at Geneva two months later produced the Geneva Accords, dividing Vietnam into North and South along the Seventeenth Parallel—a choice forced by the United States on the French, who would have preferred the Eighteenth Parallel, which ran along a naturally defensive line of hills. But even after the accords, the war did not cease; it merely went underground. While many northern refugees went South and many southerners went North, some groups of Viet Minh remained in the South to continue political and guerrilla resistance, while others operated from over the borders of neighboring Cambodia and Laos.

From the Asian pronunciation of the word "communist," the Viet Minh subversives became known as the Viet Cong. For them, the face of the enemy had changed once more, this time specifically into the form of Ngo Dinh Diem, appointed under the accords as president of South Vietnam. Slowly, but almost inevitably, the United States was drawn in. After the fortunes expended in useless support of the French, U.S. military advisers followed; after the advisers, Kennedy, in the autumn of 1961, began to ponder the use of U.S. troops. By mid-December of that year, in Operation Farm Gate, he authorized U.S. bombers (B-26's and SC-47's) and T-28 fighter-bomber trainers to fly combat missions against the Viet Cong. The first flew on January 13, 1962. By the end of the month, after more than two hundred sorties, they were approaching the Seventeenth Parallel.

The Geneva Accords had forbidden the introduction of bombers into Indochina; but the veto was only a minor problem. The Cuban Missile Crisis had shown that it was possible to institute an effective naval blockade outside of war, merely by calling it a quarantine. In the same way, it was a simple matter to call the bombers over Vietnam "reconnaissance bombers." Nor was it difficult to have them flown by Americans, because all that was required to make the flights legal was to have one South Vietnamese in each plane—even if the man was untrained and incapable through constant airsickness.

In 1960 there were 685 U.S. military advisers in Vietnam; by November 22, 1963, as a shocked world mourned the death of President Kennedy, the number had risen to 16,000. Vietnam, it seemed, demanded an ever-growing involvement from the United States—an involvement President Johnson had no intention of reducing. For as he said to his ambassador to South Vietnam, he was "not going to be the President who saw Vietnam go the way China did."[2]

"War," according to the 1978 edition of the *Shorter Oxford English Dictionary,* is "hostile contention by means of armed forces, carried on between nations, states, or rulers, or between parties in the same nation or state." This quite plainly happened in Vietnam. The dictionary's definition continues with many historical examples of the use of the word "war," either by itself or in conjunction with others; but the phrase "declaration of war" is not listed.

Another powerful document, the eighth section of the First Article of the U.S. Constitution—one of its original parts—explicitly gives to Congress the authority to declare war; the president may not take the nation to war without its consent. Unfortunately but effectively, President Johnson did precisely that, for the United States never made a declaration of war against Vietnam. Instead, there was the "Gulf of Tonkin Resolution."

Lying between North Vietnam and China, the Gulf of Tonkin was the scene in 1964 of repeated coastal raids by Southern Vietnamese torpedo boats against the North, and of skirmishes between the small vessels of both sides. In February of that year (against the advice of the Joint Chiefs of Staff), Secretary of Defense Robert S. McNamara ordered U.S. Navy destroyer patrols into the gulf. Six months later, on August 2, after one of the southern raids northwards, retaliating North Vietnamese boats attacked the U.S. destroyer *Maddox*—possibly by mistake. Two days later, in similar circumstances, U.S.S. *Turner Joy* was also fired on. Three days after that, with unanimous support in the House of Representatives and a vote of 88 to 2 in the Senate, Congress empowered Johnson to "take all necessary measures to repel any armed attack against the forces of the United States and to prevent further aggression."[3]

It was one of the least auspicious resolutions Congress ever passed. Although supporters of the developing war subsequently argued that the resolution was the "functional equivalent" of a declaration of war, it was also the functional equivalent of giving the president unlimited power, without regard to the requirements of the Constitution. Perhaps an overt declaration of war (for which Congress would have had to take responsibility in the proper way) would not have been passed; but the hawks would have saved themselves and their country much tribulation in the long run if they had argued the case in the short run. For one way or the other, the decision would have been reached in a manner visibly correct and constitutional, and indisputably legal.

Had Congress accepted its legitimate responsibility, instead of effectively passing the buck to the president, debate could have clarified the war's aims and purposes as well. But as Arleigh Burke recalls:

The unreal thing is that we were going to war and nobody realized when we went to war; we never called it a war. It just grew . . . so then maybe because we didn't know we were in a war, we didn't conduct a war. We ran things from back here—not altogether from the White House, but . . . there was no local responsibility, everything was ordered from here, and permission was asked to do things; you can't run a military operation that way.[4]

The admiral's words bring out a striking parallel between the conduct of the U.S. war in Vietnam and Britain's war against its rebellious American colonies. After the severe British defeat at Saratoga in 1777, Sir Guy Carleton, governor of Canada, wrote bitterly to London, saying:

This unfortunate event, it is to be hoped, will in future prevent Ministers from pretending to direct operations of war in a country at three thousand miles distance, of which they have so little knowledge as not to be able to distinguish between good, bad, or interested advices, or to give positive orders upon matters which, from their very nature, are ever on the change.[5]

Reminded of that observation—as much the key to Britain's defeat in the eighteenth century as to the United States' defeat in the twentieth— Burke commented ruefully: "I believe nobody has paid any attention to that."

"From my perspective in the Vietnam War, there could have been no war."[6] Capt. Joseph Kiel was a lieutenant commander at the time, working in U.S.S. *Hancock,* then the second-oldest carrier in the U.S. Navy. "Except for the amount of time we worked and the time that we were at sea, I did not experience any of the elements of war." Operating in the Gulf of Tonkin with a twelve-hour flying cycle every twenty-four hours was, for him, like an extended exercise. Nevertheless, "there was a lot of tension on board. When the pilots took off . . . one of the biggest complaints was that they would take off in bad weather, a life-risking situation even without the war; then once they got into North Vietnam, the restrictions were such that you had to look back and say, 'Why did I risk my life taking off in this 1,500-foot ceiling, go there, and worry about getting back, when I'm just going out here to do what I consider to be very little anyhow?' A prevailing perception on the ship was that it was a waste of time, a risk for no return."

Even if it did not really seem like war for Lt. Commander Kiel, for his pilots the risks were real enough. *Hancock* carried A-4's and F-8's. Both were older types of aircraft, with the F-8 Crusader particularly known for its difficult flying characteristics. In two cruises totaling seventeen months, the carrier lost some twenty planes and half a dozen pilots through deck crashes—many more than she lost from the war itself.

Some of the risks had a touch of black comedy, such as the occasion when the ship heeled as an F-8 was preparing to take off. The plane slid across the wet deck and came to rest with the cockpit and pilot sticking out over the sea. Thinking he had been going to plummet into the sea, the pilot had activated his ejector seat—but it had not worked, "so he was now sitting hanging out over the side of the ship in an ejection seat that hadn't gone, trying to decide whether or not he should unstrap. If it goes then, he's got problems." Gingerly, the man did unstrap, climbed out, and "slid his way back across the top of the aircraft" to safety.

Other risks, however, demanded difficult, immediate decisions—such as when the launch of an A-4 went wrong, and instead of flying away, the aircraft and its pilot fell "directly off the bow of the ship. The officer of the deck called out, 'Left full rudder!' trying to miss him. The commanding officer knew that there was no way we could do anything except mess up everybody else on deck, and he hollered out right away, 'Belay that order!' And with the decision, instantaneously, that man was dead. At the time it happened, I thought, *Jesus*—but that was the proper decision: Trying to swerve away from him would have done no good whatsoever, and every other aircraft on that deck would have been jeopardized."

Landing F-8's brought the greatest hazards: "They react very slowly to power changes, and by the time you realize, for instance, that you're low on glide slope and try to add power, sometimes it's too late . . . then the aircraft just slides off the runway in a ball of flame. The first thing that happens is that the aviation fuel spreads over the deck and catches fire; I have had the conn when the entire flight deck was on fire."

Kiel is the first to admit that, in spite of such episodes, on the whole his was a pleasant way to spend a war: "I never felt any uneasiness at all in the ship." Many thousands of other U.S. servicemen then and now would envy that—might, indeed, feel it suggests the U.S. Navy had no real war to fight in Vietnam. But the reason for Kiel's equanimity lay precisely in the Navy's sea control.

This was not the same as Mahan's concept of control of the sea. "To Mahan," Stansfield Turner explained, "control of the seas meant Nelson blockading the French in their ports, or if they dared to come out, destroying their fleet. That's no longer possible." During the Vietnam War, when he was a captain, Turner redefined Mahan's concept:

> With submarines and airplanes, I don't believe you can hope to do what Nelson did, to remove the enemy's presence from the seas. I could not get people to understand that control of the seas had

changed in that way, so I changed the name. "Sea control" is a more localized concept, controlling those parts of the seas you need to control.[7]

Gen. William Westmoreland (commander of U.S. forces in South Vietnam from 1964 to mid-1968) remembers that the country "had a coastline we estimate to be at least 1,200 miles long. . . . I can't say we sealed off the coast completely, but my guess is that we did it on the order of 80 to 90% of what would otherwise have occurred."[8]

In this and its other functions, Westmoreland ascribes to the Navy "a very significant role" in Vietnam, a judgment which (for good or ill) is no more than fair. The widespread impression of Vietnam as an exclusively land and jungle war derives directly from the Navy's sea control; and the fleet was not merely a passive presence. President Johnson's first attacks on North Vietnam, delivered during his announcement of the Gulf of Tonkin incident and two days before the resolution's dubious endorsement of such attacks, were air strikes from the carriers *Ticonderoga* and *Constellation,* with more than sixty planes bombing the port and oil installations at Vinh, just north of the Seventeenth Parallel.

As the struggle grew, U.S. warships were involved at every stage in their customary roles—amphibious mobility; coastal bombardment both north and south of the Seventeenth Parallel; logistic sealift (very little in the way of arms, armor, ammunition, food, and troops used in Vietnam arrived other than by sea); and "coastal interdiction," which was another way of describing a blockade.

Established in 1965 under the name Operation Market Time, the U.S. Navy's blockade of Vietnam was a three-fence arrangement. Long-range naval patrol planes, belonging to the Seventh Fleet and operating out of the Philippines and Vietnam itself, formed the first fence, 100–150 miles offshore. Closer in was a surface blockade of medium-sized vessels (Coast Guard cutters, minesweepers, and destroyer escorts) while a hundred or so PCFs (Patrol Craft, Fast—otherwise known as "swift boats") made up the innermost line. And from an idea by David F. Welch, one of Westmoreland's naval staff captains, a branch of naval operations was revived after lying untouched for a full century: riverine forces.

Lincoln's tribute to the Union Navy after the Civil War was just as apt for the united country's ships in Vietnam: "At all the watery margins they have been present. Not only on the deep sea, the broad bay, the rapid river, but also up the narrow muddy bayou, and wherever the ground was a little damp, they have made their tracks."[9]

In the deep south of South Vietnam lies the Mekong Delta, straddling the Tenth Parallel—420 miles below the "demilitarized" zone, the theoretical separation of North and South. With virtually all southern sea approaches denied to the Viet Cong, the Ho Chi Minh Trail through nominally neutral Laos and Cambodia became their main supply route: a slow and difficult overland trek leading to the natural communication line of the Mekong and its many tributaries and outlets. To counter this, Operation Game Warden was created on December 18, 1965. Its force was a large fleet of small fiberglass boats, only 28 feet long but heavily armed. Joining the staff of Commander Naval Forces Vietnam (ComNavForV) as assistant chief of staff, Operations, David Emerson remembers that "any boat the Navy had in Vietnam was a very powerful machine gun nest. Not only machine guns—some of them had mortars, and they could just overwhelm the enemy."[10]

Emerson's boss (newly appointed in 1968 to the rank of vice admiral and to the job of ComNavForV) was Elmo R. Zumwalt, Jr. Even further south than the Mekong, "on the Kwalun River, which cuts across the very bottom tip of South Vietnam," he set up a new kind of naval base to work against the Viet Cong, who had made the area their own. In Emerson's words: "He put an immense raft of thirteen barges together, out in the middle of the river. . . . The eventual idea was to build a base ashore; but in those days, when it first started, the jungle came right down to the bank. Scary as hell at night."

"From Sea Float, as we called it," Zumwalt wrote later, "swift boats and PBRs (Patrol Boats, River) could range up and down the river and it had a pad for helos as well. We supported it with three-inch gunboats. . . . It was protected from mines floated downstream or swimmers carrying demolition charges." Zumwalt was particularly proud of this unusual creation: "Under Sea Float's protection, [South Vietnamese] resettlement did begin," and farming and fishing returned to what had been a ruined area.[11]

After Sea Float came Sea Lords. This, Emerson recalls, was "interdiction as close to the borders of Cambodia as the Navy could get. The enemy, North Vietnamese army and Viet Cong, had immense base areas up in Cambodia. It was a very successful interdiction campaign." Central to this operation's second phase (code-named Giant Slingshot) were "little bases, called ATSB—Advanced Tactical Support Base. All they were were a bunch of sandbags, a place to fuel the boats, a place for the crews to sleep; water, food, that kind of thing. They generally came about every 20 kilometers along the riverbank." Each base would be home for perhaps ten PBRs, "and they'd go out every night and lie in the ambush position before dark, or right after dark, and sit there all night, quiet, and ambush. They were very, very successful. . . . You'd slide in, snuggle up to the bank, clear field of fire, and then you'd just stand watch. No smoking, try to be quiet and all the rest—the worst thing being the mosquitoes, my God!" In arcs around the ambush area, magnetic, acoustic, and seismic interference detectors were placed at ground level or in trees. "They were very handy. . . . If you got an indication, you knew there was something— you didn't know it was a man necessarily, but at least you were alerted." In Emerson's view, the Viet Cong could be "pretty goddamn dumb, too: They'd always cross at the same places. . . . You'd start shooting as soon as you had a good target."[12]

But Giant Slingshot, and every riverine operation, was still fraught with risk. As Zumwalt observed subsequently: "There is no body of accepted doctrine on the subject; the Naval Academy does not offer courses in it; indeed there is little empirical evidence from previous wars to draw upon. You have to make up riverine warfare as you go along."[13]

Alongside the reinvented warfare of the rivers, the Navy fought "on the deep sea, the broad bay," and (in ways Abraham Lincoln could never have conceived) in the air. From 1966 to 1968, it conducted Operation Sea Dragon, extending antishipping patrols north of the demilitarized zone to the Twentieth Parallel; in the same years, in Operation Rolling Thunder, it sent air strikes from carriers of Task Force 77 against selected North Vietnamese targets. In May 1972, restrictions were lifted on attacking Haiphong—the main harbor in North Vietnam and a prime entry for Russian and Chinese arms-bearing ships, not subject to the blockade. The excessively belated decision enabled Navy jets to mine, and effectively seal, the harbor entrance; and though it seemed an inverted achievement, the Navy participated as fully in the ending of the Vietnam War as it had in the creation and prosecution of America's involvement.

When, under Richard Nixon's presidency, moves began to try to return responsibility to the South Vietnamese for their own future, it was Admiral Zumwalt who initiated the program called ACTOV (Accelerated Turnover to Vietnam). This was designed "to turn the in-country U.S. naval operation over to the Vietnamese."[14] And at the very end, with ACTOV as complete as it could be, the nuclear carrier U.S.S. *Enterprise* and her consorts provided cover throughout the month of April 1975 for Operation Frequent Wind: the largest airborne withdrawal in history, as the U.S. acknowledged its defeat in Vietnam.

The last U.S. troops left Vietnam on March 29, 1975. Over the next five weeks, along with chartered civilian planes, Air Force and Navy aircraft airlifted 130,000 South Vietnamese troops and civilians out of the shell-shocked wreck of their wretched country. For those who remained when the United States had gone, there was only one choice left: Within hours of the airlift's completion, South Vietnam formally surrendered to the North and the Viet Cong.

Thinking back to Korea, Arleigh Burke said with regret and emphasis: "We did not learn, because we did the same damn thing in Vietnam. We had control of the sea and we had control of the air, but we didn't use them and we lost the war in Vietnam. Not primarily because of that. Primarily because we didn't want to fight a war. We fought a holding action, and you can never win with a holding action . . . because you aren't trying to win."[15]

The common Southeast Asian theater caused many people to assume the wars in Korea and Vietnam were similar; but their differences far outweighed any similarities. Instead of massed forces outfacing each other along a hundred-mile front, as in Korea, the land and river war in Vietnam became a lunatic nightmare hunt of hide-and-seek against a guerrilla enemy who could merge invisibly with the indigenous population. Instead of a peninsula which could be blockaded on three of its four sides, Vietnam presented an immense coastline, a narrow battlefield, and three bordering nations (Laos, Cambodia, and China) which, while forbidden to U.S. forces, were used for supply and sanctuary by the North Vietnamese and Viet Cong. And instead of a war sanctioned by international agreement, Vietnam was not even sanctioned by national agreement.

"I knew from the start that I was bound to be crucified either way I moved," President Johnson admitted.[16] Unlike Kennedy, identified with the cosmopolitan, urban, industrial northeast of the United States, Johnson's interest lay more with the rural, agricultural southwest. On election to the presidency in his own right, his main political desire was to create a "Great Society" in the United States—to introduce Medicare for old people; widespread federal assistance for schools for young people; full voting power for black people; and a policy of nondiscrimination toward immigrants. He also believed that international Communism had to be contained to prevent it spreading worldwide, a belief widely shared by other political leaders, military leaders, and citizens. But there was a body of opinion strong enough to delay or derail even the most liberal reforms, if those reforms went hand in hand with a commitment to an escalating involvement in a small and distant war of little apparent importance to America. Later, Johnson reflected on the dilemma he had faced:

> If I left the woman I really loved—the Great Society—in order to get involved in that bitch of a war on the other side of the world, then I would lose everything at home. But if I left that war and let the Communists take over South Vietnam, then I would be seen as a coward and my nation would be seen as an appeaser, and we would both find it impossible to accomplish anything for anybody anywhere on the entire globe.

After he had tried to achieve both, by welcoming the Great Society at the front door while ushering in war at the back, it was easier to see the losses than the gains. The billions of dollars expended counted for far less than the U.S. lives lost (nearly 60,000) and the fearful, wary view of the United States engendered among the rising generation in allied nations. At home, the same generation was split against itself and its elders. American soldiers, sailors, marines, and airmen returning home found themselves treated not as heroes but as custodians of a national shame, while those who had not fought, through luck or evasion, learned a deep distrust of the established order and rejoiced in savage satire of their country's competitive materialism.

Among martial leaders, there was a shared view of the reasons for failure. Burke: "We did not fight that war in the enemy's territory. Most all of the rules of war we violated in Vietnam."[17]

Westmoreland: "It would have been better if there had been a single operational commander for Southeast Asia. But that was not compatible with the doctrine and the views of the Joint Chiefs of Staff at the time."[18]

Zumwalt: "The rules of engagement . . . almost certainly would preclude major ground action north of the Demilitarized Zone, and thus would make a decisive victory over the North Vietnamese unlikely."[19]

Adm. Thomas R. Wechsler, commander, Naval Support Activity, Danang: "The commanders recognized the kind of war we were in and thought that [President Johnson's] message was completely out of tune. They knew we weren't going after North Vietnam, and that we were just going after the Vietcong or the North Vietnamese Army in the South, and how difficult that was, and how partial the victory was likely to be. The President's talk . . . just was not the sort of talk that represented a real understanding of what was going on."[20]

Lt. Gen. Victor H. Krulak, USMC, Commander of the Fleet Marine Force Pacific: "Our national policy assumed that all-out American air and sea operations against the North Vietnamese ports, airfields, and transportation systems would risk galvanizing the Soviets—and perhaps the Chinese, too—into participation in the conflict. . . . The strategy was futile—analogous to pushing a wet noodle. . . . The costly, blood-sapping, grinding battles were blows in the air."[21]

For most of the enlisted men and junior officers, however, questions of high policy did not occur: "Never once, all the time I was in Vietnam, did I have a political discussion as to why we were there. It was irrelevant. You don't fight a war on the basis of politics, you fight it on the basis of survival."[22] From his wheelchair, Bob Muller speaks forcefully. "The villages that we operated around were not sympathetic to us; they were hostile to us. Every time we passed, we'd get sniper fire; they would obviously know where the booby traps were, and the mines; and the people simply looked at us with a look that was not one of welcoming a liberator, but rather was fear or hatred. I was injured, and so it's harder for me to speak out against the war—because," he concludes with bitter energy, "I'm saying that what happened to me was for *nothing.*"

22

★

WE MUST HAVE
NATIONAL GOALS

*A*fter any war, it was more or less expected that the Navy would decline in numbers of ships and personnel. For it to decline while a war was in progress was unheard of; but that was another of the unfortunate distinctions of the war in Vietnam. Five and ten years earlier, funds had been directed toward the building of nuclear-powered vessels at the expense of conventional ones; World War II stock was still in good order then and perfectly able to make up the difference. In 1968, at the height of the Vietnam War, the fleet included 428 surface ships and 146 submarines. But, attempting to disguise the true financial cost of the conflict, both the Johnson and Nixon administrations had reduced new naval building severely and had channeled the money saved into other parts of the war effort. During the second half of the 1970s, both birds came home to roost—old World War II ships were reaching the end of their useful lives, and because of the Johnson-Nixon curtailments, there were no new ships to replace them. By 1978 the fleet's stock of active surface ships and submarines had fallen to 217 and 119, respectively.

From his "brown water" post as Commander Naval Forces, Vietnam, Admiral Zumwalt had been elevated (on July 1, 1970) to the Navy's top job as Chief of Naval Operations—a somewhat unexpected appointment since he was still only forty-nine years old, and since the Vietnam command was not seen as the kind of major post which usually preceded the CNO's four-year term. But his abilities had made him a rear admiral two years before he was technically old enough to be one; and his running of the ACTOV program was so closely in line with Congress's wish to "Vietnamize" the war that his appointment, though controversial, was readily passed.

He took charge of a navy already depleted in hardware and low in morale. Few sailors ever think their fleet has enough ships or that those they have are good enough; the grumble is so commonplace that it does not usually become serious. Even if it is serious, it need not affect morale adversely if the work at hand is seen to be worthy; inadequate ships then become part of the challenge—problems (as Admiral King wrote back in March 1941) that should be "dealt with as 'enemies' to be overcome. . . . We must do all we can with what we have."[1] But the depressing combination of deteriorating ships and an unpopular war wears down even the most self-confident.

Naturally, a navy reflects to a large extent the standards and attitudes of the society which it serves and defends. U.S. attitudes in the early 1970s could hardly have provided less psychological support to naval personnel. Gung-ho sailors could deride the peace-loving hippie culture and the militantly antimilitarist yippies, but, as opposition to uniformed authority became a middle-class adult preoccupation as well, it was impossible for the fleet not to be affected. Capt. Joseph Kiel (then a lieutenant commander) remembers that "a lot of the junior officers during the Vietnam war were in just to get their service out of the way"—scarcely the best attitude with which to fight a war.[2] Young men, joining for the shortest possible time, brought in civilian habits. "For example," Capt. Roger Barnett recollects, "in California there was a marijuana law passed. . . . If you were caught with marijuana in your possession of less than one ounce, it was considered to be for personal use, and the fine was in the order of a parking ticket. That was the way the sailors were being treated out in the community." In the Navy, however, the same offense carried "a very severe penalty—you were liable to be kept on board for two months and fined a half a month's pay for two months. Sailors had great difficulty understanding the difference and why it existed."[3]

Other social changes brought more tension, and even conflict, in the fleet. For one thing, greater material affluence enabled a growing percentage of enlisted men to own their own cars and houses. "I certainly didn't welcome that," Barnett observes, "from a very narrow point of view of shipboard good order and discipline, of the loyalty of the crew to the ship. When I joined the Navy, all the enlisted men lived on board; the ship was home. This was a very severe cultural change—when the ship was no longer a home, but a place to go and work. This caused great stresses that didn't exist before." However, such problems were strictly the Navy's own business, private matters for shipboard management. Others were glaringly public. "The first and worst explosion," wrote the new CNO, "occurred aboard CVA 63, U.S.S. *Kitty Hawk.* "⁴ By mid-October 1972, the carrier had been on station in the Pacific for eight months, setting a new record for aircraft sorties for one deployment, while support at home for the Vietnam War was at its lowest ebb. Suddenly the combined strains came to a flashpoint: For nine hours during the night of October 12–13, some 200 of the 5,000-strong crew rampaged and rioted through the ship. Sixty men ended up needing medical treatment; three were so badly injured they were flown to shore hospitals.

Four days later, in Subic Bay, Manila, another riot broke out in the oiler *Hassayampa.* Mercifully, it was shorter and less violent; but the clashes were not over. On November 3, the eve of the presidential election, a confrontation began on the carrier U.S.S. *Constellation.* This one entirely lacked physical violence; yet that made it all the more difficult to cope with. It lasted six days, overlapping the election in which Richard Nixon was returned for a second term as president, and it was the clearest possible protest against the Navy's institutional racism. "You can be black *and* Navy too," said a recruiting slogan. But, as Zumwalt was told by a group of junior officers whose task was to study reenlistment rates among minorities, " 'You can be black *or* Navy too' more truly represents the situation in our Navy today."⁵

Racism was the only link among the three separate episodes. In comparison with the third, those in *Kitty Hawk* and *Hassayampa* were straightforward affairs—physical outbursts bred from exhaustion, resentment, and frustration and brought under control in accordance with naval discipline. Six men from the oiler and twenty-six from the carrier were charged—all, as it happened, were black. The incidents attracted passing press interest, but the one in *Constellation* attracted full attention from the media, and fury from the president. It was a much more politically conscious event than the others: The 144 protesters included both blacks and whites. Nixon saw them on television giving clenched-fist salutes and was so enraged that through Kissinger (who "all but shrieked at me," wrote Zumwalt), he ordered the CNO to discharge them all dishonorably at once. The order was illegal, first, because such discharge could come only after a lengthy court-martial and, second, because (in a complicated series of actions and reactions) the protesters' only technical breach of naval regulations was to be a few hours' absent over leave, which could not possibly result in dishonorable discharge.

For the fleet, for his own job, and for the protesters, it was lucky that the CNO was a highly political admiral. The illegality of Nixon's order enabled Zumwalt to follow the prompting of his own conscience and ignore the commander in chief. The announcement that a special congressional subcommittee would be formed to investigate "alleged racial and disciplinary problems" in the fleet gave him the chance to air his own views on the Navy's program of racial integration publicly. He knew full well that doing so might cost him his job—"Armed with the ammunition provided by the race riots and sabotage," *Time* reported on November 27, 1972, "many admirals have shown their own lack of discipline by campaigning for Zumwalt's ouster." Nevertheless, he was determined to go ahead: "I considered the tumult not as a warning to take a defensive posture," he wrote, "but as an opportunity to nail equal treatment for minorities and women so firmly into the Navy that anyone would have trouble removing it."[6]

Indeed, the "tumult" was to a large degree directed against him personally. Zumwalt, apart from being political, was that thing most navies find highly suspicious: a forward-looking admiral. From the time of his inauguration as CNO he had issued scores of orders (nicknamed "Z-grams") in which he tried to bring the Navy up to date in its human attitudes. Since the loss of World War II's urgency, it had become riddled with "Mickey Mouse" regulations—"things that were put in under the guise of good order and discipline that were really just . . . to piss people off," in Captain Kiel's words. "He got rid of a lot of those."[7]

The effect of some of the Z-grams was so contentious and considerable that they became the main feature for which Zumwalt's period as CNO is remembered. Z-57 and Z-66 gained particular fame, or notoriety, among a wide public—the former ("Demeaning and Abrasive Regulations, Elimination of") because in its critics' view, it brought "permissiveness" into the fleet; and the latter ("Equal Opportunity in the Navy") because it stated specifically: "Ours must be a Navy family that recognizes no artificial barriers of race, color or religion. There is no black Navy, no white Navy—just one Navy—the United States Navy."[8]

Z-57 dealt with small, unnecessary problems surrounding the lives of naval personnel; for example, every naval base now had to be able to cash a check—even that simple facility had not been universally available before. It also allowed men to wear work clothes in base canteens and established many other little bits of common sense in place of trivial, unhelpful restrictions. However, the item which became most famous was its permission for sailors to grow their hair "long" (that is, all the way to the top of the collar) and to grow beards, mustaches, or sideburns. It was odd this should have attracted so much praise and opprobrium, because regulations already stated that beards and mustaches were permissible; the only innovation was sideburns. But, true to form and contrary to the advice of his regional commanders in chief, the CNO gave the news a fanfare of publicity. To help recruiting and reenlistment, the fleet needed a new image. It got one: Newspapers latched onto the story, and suddenly the United States had a "mod Navy."

"A very challenging and stimulating time of sociocultural changes," is how Roger Barnett remembers it—perhaps a charitable description from one of the middle-ranking officers (he was then a lieutenant commander) who had to administer the new look. He acknowledges that "it was very painful. . . . There was a lot of resentment; people in the chain of command were confused." Joseph Kiel agrees: "It probably went a little bit too far, because it did take away some of the discipline. . . . A lot of the older officers and the older enlisted men, the chief petty officers, did feel threatened by this new laxity."

Necessary but too much, too quickly—some still adamantly disagree, but that has become a typical assessment of Z-57. Z-66 picked up another area where the Navy sadly distinguished itself: the neglect of particular needs of minority groups, especially blacks. Commanding officers and squadron commanders were now obliged to appoint either an officer or a senior petty officer as special assistant for minority affairs, and to grant him direct access to their offices. In addition, this Z-gram ordered the provision of ethnic foods, appropriate grooming aids, barbers and beauticians appropriately trained, and books, magazines, and records by and about black Americans—changes which, in their spectacular simplicity, emphasized how little thought had previously been given to such needs.

Z-66 was issued on December 17, 1970. Close to two years later, the riots and confrontations in *Kitty Hawk, Hassayampa,* and *Constellation* emphasized how little attitudes had altered in the meantime. Publicly and angrily, Zumwalt reminded his admirals that real changes took more than a legislative program: "It is self-deception to think that . . . Navy personnel come to us fresh from some other place than our world—that they come untainted by prejudices."[9]

Both inside and outside the service, America's attitudes damaged it; and so did the new low of national standards. Within weeks of the outbreaks, in January 1973, the Watergate trials began. Stoutly declaring "I am not a crook," Richard Nixon hung on to office until August 8, 1974. Then, rather than face impeachment, he went into history as the first American president to resign his post.

Public distrust of and disenchantment with the uniformed services extended now to government. Gerald Ford, Nixon's vice president and successor, suffered not only by association with the disgraced ex-president but also because, within a month of coming to office, he granted Nixon, who had been facing criminal prosecution, a full pardon. Ford's approval rating fell overnight from 71 percent to 50 percent. Soon, whatever his other qualities, he began to be seen as little more than a bumbling caretaker. In 1976 Georgia Democrat Jimmy Carter became the thirty-ninth President of the despondent United States, and in the Navy or outside it, a hope for the future seemed to arise. It was clear to all that he was a deeply moral man, and honest morality was craved; it was remembered that he had been a naval officer, and though he had not made it a career, there seemed a plausible chance he might favor the fleet for old times' sake at least.

By 1978 Carter was halfway through his first term in office—a suitable time for us to pause and make a brief review of the contemporary state of the U.S. Navy in relation to its major competitor. And whether (as his friends asserted) Carter was turning out to be too good a man for the Oval Office or whether (as his least harsh critics said) he was merely a naive and sentimental president, it was not an encouraging picture.

The century-long Pax Britannica had been possible because from 1815 to 1914 the Royal Navy had no practical challengers. The twentieth-century Pax Americana faced a potential challenger almost as soon as it began: the growing, well-guided navy of Soviet Russia. During the Second World War (the "Great Patriotic War," as the Russians called it), the Soviet navy played a comparatively small part, being only a modest fleet of coastal ability. In the immediate postwar years (as in the United States and Britain) the Soviet military establishment found the recently created and apparently potent force of strategic bombing a very attractive proposition for their future defense. All three countries experienced the same pressure from their respective air forces to enhance national air power at the expense of sea power—an argument which, in view of its location, was particularly persuasive in the Soviet Union. Yet by coincidence, in all three countries and at almost the same time, naval leaders of unusual caliber were appointed and were able to prevent their service from becoming stepsister to the air force. In the United States, it was the new Chief of Naval Operations, Adm. Arleigh Burke; in Britain, it was the new First Sea Lord, Adm. Lord Louis Mountbatten; and in Russia, it was the new commander in chief of the Soviet Navy, Adm. Sergei Gorschkov.

Burke and Mountbatten were both appointed in 1955, Gorschkov in 1956. Lord Louis served as First Sea Lord for four years and as Chief of the Defense Staff for a further five. Burke (uniquely among CNOs) served not for the usual four years but for six. Gorschkov served as commander in chief of the Soviet Navy for no less than twenty-nine years; as Albert Gallatin had once observed, "time was necessary to build ships of war."

Seven years was not enough; in 1962, at the time of the Cuban Missile Crisis, Gorschkov's fleet was not significantly larger than the U.S. Navy in numerical terms. But the United States had twenty-eight aircraft carriers and the Soviet Navy had none, and its distribution of units in other categories still meant it was not a serious rival. However, from Gorshkov's viewpoint, the overt lesson taught in Cuba—that sea power could determine the outcome of a contest between world powers—was timely. It was a lesson he knew by heart already; he had observed the U.N. use of sea power in Korea and remarked how, without it, it "would hardly have been able to avoid a military defeat." Perhaps it could be seen as an instance (though rather odd in an atheistic society) of loving one's enemy—his perceived enemy not only threatened, but also defined and justified, his own existence. Cuba gave Gorshkov the opportunity to convert those of his masters who remained unconverted; and by 1978, as the U.S. fleet went ship by ship to the breaker's yard, twenty-three years of continuous development and production had given Sergei Gorshkov a magnificent navy.

By then the Soviet fleet had twice (in 1970 and again in 1975) demonstrated its enormous latent power to the world. While the United States frittered its strength away in Vietnam, Admiral Gorshkov directed "Okean" and "Okean II"—the largest global exercises ever undertaken by any navy. Two hundred ships took part in the 1970 Okean deployment, 220 in Okean II, on each occasion operating in coordination in the Black Sea, the Mediterranean, the Baltic, and (more ominously and impressively) in the Pacific, the Atlantic, the Indian Ocean, and the Arctic Ocean. In numbers of units, moreover, the participating vessels represented only about one quarter to one third of the total Soviet fleet. Some of the navy's traditional defensive characteristics still remained: Very strong on conventional submarines, it also contained a high percentage of missile-armed patrol boats and was only just beginning to introduce aircraft carriers. But the Okean deployments proved that it could operate successfully in all parts of the world at once—and therefore, if so directed, aggressively.

Already it had expanded its areas of regular deployment, most noticeably within the Mediterranean. There, in 1967, 1970, and 1973, the presence of Soviet warships had had a marked effect on Middle Eastern politics. During the Arab-Israeli war of 1967 and the Jordanian crisis of 1970, Russia's Fifth Eskadra was strong enough to prevent intervention by the U.S. Sixth Fleet—which, had the conditions of the 1950s still obtained, would certainly have taken place.

A still more dramatic change in the local naval balance was introduced by the Yom Kippur war of October 1973. The initial heavy attack (200 aircraft, 600 tanks, and 70,000 troops) was launched by Egypt against Israel on the Jewish people's annual Day of Atonement. However, within two weeks, as Israeli forces fought back, 20,000 soldiers of the Third Egyptian Army were trapped on the West Bank of the Suez Canal. At that point, having effectively fought a proxy war by supplying their respective allies with arms and ammunition, both superpowers called for a cease-fire. The trapped Egyptians would not surrender; the surrounding Israelis would not allow a "mercy mission" of food, water, and medicine to be delivered; and so the Russians proposed sending in a joint Soviet-

U.S. force, reserving the option of unilateral action if the United States declined. The proposal *was* turned down, whereupon the size of the Fifth Eskadra was rapidly increased from its usual level of about fifty-five vessels. The Sixth Fleet was also strengthened, to sixty-five vessels; but opposing it now were ninety-eight Soviet ships.

This triggered a worldwide U.S. troop alert—the first since Kennedy's assassination. This, of course, was in the midst of the Watergate crisis, and (marking how low President Nixon's stock had sunk at home) doubts about the alert's validity were widely and publicly expressed in the United States. In the Navy, though, there was not the slightest doubt—as Vice Adm. Daniel Murphy (commanding officer, Sixth Fleet) put it, his ships and the Russians' "were, in effect, sitting in a pond in close proximity, and the stage for the hitherto unlikely 'war at sea' scenario was set. . . . Both fleets were obviously in a high readiness posture for whatever might come next, although it appeared that neither fleet knew exactly what to expect."[10]

It was the most tense situation U.S. warships had been in since the end of World War II. Eventually, though—in what appeared to be something of an anticlimax—the matter was resolved when the combatants agreed to a cease-fire and withdrawal supervised by the United Nations. But this happened only because the United States forced it on Israel; and that happened only because (again in Admiral Zumwalt's words) "we lacked either the military strength or the stable domestic leadership—one or the other might have been enough—to have supported the Israelis."[11] With foreboding, U.S. naval officers realized that for the first time, their own power in the Mediterranean had been outnumbered by the Soviet Union.

The U.S. Navy's material change was visible in almost every category. In 1968 there had been 31 carriers; in 1978 there were 21. Cruisers had diminished from 34 to 26; amphibious vessels from 77 to 36; conventional submarines, staggeringly, from 72 to 10; and destroyers (the major class of overage World War Two ships) from 227 to 64.

These recent memories (Vietnam, the Okeans, Yom Kippur) form a background to the midterm review of President Carter and his policies; and underlining them was the plain fact that, by shrinking as its competitor had grown, the U.S. Navy included a total of 436 major warships (those over 250 feet in length), while the Soviet Navy included 740.

To some extent the disparity was deliberate—that is, a consciously accepted risk had been taken in the early 1970s, when the cost of maintaining the U.S. stock of World War II warships became prohibitive. As the elderly destroyers and others were scrapped, further categories in the U.S. fleet had remained steady or had even grown: In the ten years since 1968, the quantities of frigates and missile-armed patrol boats had increased marginally, from 50 and 130 to 64 and 135 respectively; there were a constant 41 nuclear ballistic submarines; and the number of nuclear nonballistic submarines had more than doubled, from 33 to 68. In the summer of 1978, the outgoing CNO, Adm. James Holloway, stated his belief that the U.S. Navy was still stronger than the Soviet fleet. The United States' considerable advantage in aircraft carriers (21 versus three) gave it a greatly superior ability to project sea-based air power, and though the Soviet Union possessed 294 submarines to the United States' 119, the Soviet figure included 172 conventional boats, while only 30 American boats were nonnuclear.

The redoubtable Admiral Rickover was not impressed, and he informed Congress that given the choice, he would rather command the Soviet submarine fleet—if it came to a war, he would want to win, and was sure he would have a better chance on the other side. He and Zumwalt (Holloway's predecessor) had had many disagreements, centering on Zumwalt's preference for conventional ships, which were very expensive, against Rickover's predilection for nuclear ships, which were extremely expensive. But on the question of the United States' chances in a sea war against the USSR, they agreed that the United States would probably lose. "The odds are," said Zumwalt later, "that we would have lost a war with the Soviet Union if we had had to fight it any year since 1970; the navy dropped to about a 35% probability of victory."[12]

Two of the U.S. Navy's twenty-one carriers were of the new, giant *Nimitz* class—1,090 feet long overall, with a full load displacement of 91,400 tons. Capable of carrying over ninety aircraft and helicopters, and (with the power of two A4W nuclear reactors) of steaming at 33 knots, *Nimitz* (CVN-68) and her sister *Dwight D. Eisenhower* (CVN-69) could do almost anything—project air power deep into enemy territory; control the sea; hunt submarines. But they and the third of the class, *Carl Vinson* (CVN-70), had suffered from the Vietnam involvement. Funds for *Nimitz* had first been set aside in 1966, with her commissioning due in 1971, to be followed at two-year intervals by her sisters. Yet she was not commissioned until 1975; *Dwight D. Eisenhower* was likewise four years overdue; in 1978 *Carl Vinson* was barely half built; and their price was escalating. *Nimitz* cost $1.881 billion; in 1978 it was predicted that the others would easily cost more than $2 billion each.[13]

Despite the cost, a fourth vessel of the class was planned. As Stansfield Turner observed: "Economy is not an overriding concern in military matters. . . . Economy is only one factor and often a subsidiary factor. If you can survive you don't need to be economical."[14] Congress did not agree. In March 1977 it decided not to underwrite the initial costs of a fourth *Nimitz*-class carrier; and to the Navy's dismay, President Carter accepted the decision without question.

One year later—our final note in this midterm review—Carter revealed his alterations to the Ford administration's last five-year naval building plan, covering 1979–84. Instead of the intended 156 ships, only 70 would be built. To Congress, the cuts seemed so shockingly large that, changing its collective mind, a fourth *Nimitz*-class carrier was speedily voted in as an addition for 1979. Equally speedily, the president vetoed this.

He was fully entitled to do so, of course. But even a simple comparison of the Soviet and U.S. navies showed how huge the gap had become. In 1978 the U.S. Navy still had twenty-one carriers; the Russians by then had three. That looked pretty comfortable. But in every other category of major surface warship the Soviet fleet outnumbered that of the United States, with a total of 446 units against the United States' 217. Further, the Soviet submarine fleet included 84 nuclear ships against the United States' 68, and 58 ballistic nuclear ships against the United States' 41, with the overall totals being 294 Soviet submarines to 119 U.S. ones. Thus, when 1978 ended, U.S. naval men could view 1979 only with worry, disappointment, and confusion, their sole certainty being that— after years of progressive depletion of the service—Carter was not the longed-for messiah. The problem was that while everyone could see the gap, not everyone could agree on how best to fill it. "You cannot run a military campaign by changing your mind every morning," said Arleigh Burke. "We must have national goals."[15]

Building priorities had to be determined by interpreting the statistics; but anyone could (and many people did) spend days, months, even years arguing over comparative tables of U.S. and Soviet naval power. The reckoning of the fleets could be attempted in a wide variety of ways, starting with the total number of units above a given length—usually 250 feet—to count as a "major warship." A slight refinement might compare the numbers of surface and subsurface units in each navy. Matching the number in a given class with its nearest equivalent type brought the process a little further. But relative displacements could also be compared and could make a substantial difference; and the same was true with comparisons of weaponry and endurance.

In varying combinations, the figures could be shunted around to a remarkable degree, producing very different results; and these were only the statistical facts. Other far less easily determinable factors needed to be put into the equation as well, each altering it yet again—comparisons of purpose, known or assumed; of geography; and most difficult of all, of the character, training, and motivation of the sailors involved. Given the possible permutations of even these most basic elements in the naval equation, it is scarcely surprising how much bitter disagreement and utter perplexity surrounded their interpretation; but until they were interpreted to a majority agreement, effective legislation on building priorities could not be passed.

The nation and its leaders were, in brief, once again facing the unchanging questions of any naval nation, the questions of external and internal naval policy—what a navy is for and how, therefore, it should be composed. These are decisions which cannot be taken lightly, for whatever answers are reached, their effects last for decades. President Carter's defense secretary, Harold Brown, had stated the administration's assessment of the Navy's prime war purpose: to protect the sea lanes of communication between the United States and Europe. At first sight (especially from a European point of view) there was much to commend the assessment—in both world wars, the survival of Europe had hinged on long-drawn-out naval battles in the Atlantic.

From this assessment it followed that sea control, rather than the projection of seaborne air power, was a priority. As it happens, sea control does not require such large carriers as the projection of air power does; therefore, the extremely expensive fourth member of the *Nimitz* class could safely be abandoned. In its place and confirming his secretary's words, the president proposed a series of medium-sized conventional carriers. Both men asserted that these would be suitable for the rest of the century. If they were built, they would *have* to be suitable, for in spite of their smaller size and cheaper propulsion, they would still not be bargain-basement ships. The money and effort of design and construction would have been spent, and the ships would probably last anything up to forty years.

Nevertheless, the president's neatly interlocking proposals for a smaller fleet centered on smaller carriers were logically faultless—*if* wartime protection of the Atlantic sea lanes were all the Navy would have to do. But turning the thesis around revealed a glaring fault: A smaller fleet centered on smaller carriers could *only* protect the sea lanes.

The implied policy changes were radical. Optimistic as he was about the Navy's existing attack capability, Admiral Holloway, Carter's CNO, was already less certain about its ability to control the sea, and on hearing Carter's plan, he made its implications plain. If the plan were adopted, by the end of the century the U.S. Navy would contain no more than 420 ships. It could have no other important wartime task beyond sea lane protection; and it would not even be able to fulfill its established peacetime tasks.

With opposing sides marshaled for the remaining two years of Carter's presidency, decisions concerning the Navy's future were set to have an important part in the next election. But as Iran ran riot, as the USSR invaded Afghanistan, and as U.S. citizens were taken hostage, the president's vacillating, ineffective use of sea power seemed to characterize all that had gone wrong with U.S. foreign policy in the preceding fifteen years.

The Iranian revolution provided 1979 with a particularly inauspicious start, for the revolutionaries were given their chance by one of Carter's best-intentioned policies. The repressive habits of the last ruling shah (habits he had been able to maintain only with U.S. military aid) offended the president's deeply held belief in human rights. By demanding and getting some liberalization of the regime before allowing further arms sales, Carter unwittingly took the lid off many years of Iranian resentment. By dispatching a carrier battle group to the Arabian Sea in March, he hoped to reduce the revengeful harassing of U.S. residents in Iran; but by refusing to state the battle group's purpose in public, he did not get the message through to Teheran. A regime more sophisticated than that of revolutionary Iran, a regime wiser in the ways of worldly politics, would have seen the possibility of a threat and might have altered its actions; but the Iranians either needed the threat spelled out before they could understand it, or else did not believe anything would come of it, or else simply did not care.

Badly as the year had begun, it ended far worse. In August the president was informed that Soviet forces might invade Afghanistan. Preoccupied elsewhere, he did not act on the information. On November 4, the showdown the Iranians appeared to be seeking came when the U.S. embassy in Teheran was stormed by militant students and sixty-six American personnel were taken captive. Four days later, Congress resuscitated the canceled *Nimitz*-class carrier; this time the president agreed to it. Six days after that (November 14, 1979), he ordered another carrier group to the Arabian Sea; on November 17 thirteen of the hostages in Teheran were released. It began to look as though, panicked and disorderly as it was, the presidential policy might be working, and on November 21 a further carrier group was sent to the Arabian Sea. But by December 8 the remaining fifty-three hostages had been imprisoned almost five weeks and were no closer to freedom.

It was then—three months after he had first received information of a possible Soviet invasion of Afghanistan—that Carter took up the subject and issued a warning to the Soviet Union. Over the following nineteen days the warning was repeated four times; but on December 27 the invasion took place.

"The Americans cannot protect themselves. . . . They cannot pretend to a navy."[16]

"I had hoped to get on board a ship of war which might at least not be sneered at."[17]

The former comment was written by Lord Sheffield in 1783; the latter came from a disappointed American ensign in 1881. One had to go back a long way to find when last the United States, its foreign policies, and its warships had been held in such contempt as in 1979.

"The present navy of the United States . . . has raised us in our esteem."[18]
That observation was made by John Adams in 1800.

With his descendants, he would have wept in humiliation if he had seen the events of April 1980. By then, though there were twenty-seven U.S. Navy ships positioned in the Arabian Sea, the hostages still remained captive. On April 27 U.S.S. *Nimitz* launched eight RH-53D helicopters as part of a rescue raid coordinated with U.S. Air Force transports flying out of Egypt. Ending with the breakdown of three helicopters, the collision of a fourth with one of the transports, and the death of eight rescuers, the abortive, farcical attempt did less than nothing to raise the United States in its own, or the world's, esteem.

Another president might possibly have weathered the setbacks; at another time, Carter himself might have done so. If the raid had worked, he would probably have coasted home in the November elections that year. But coming after fifteen years of confusion, defeat, and demoralization, and with the hostages now scattered in various locations beyond military rescue, the failure did more than any other single factor to confirm Jimmy Carter's presidential demise.

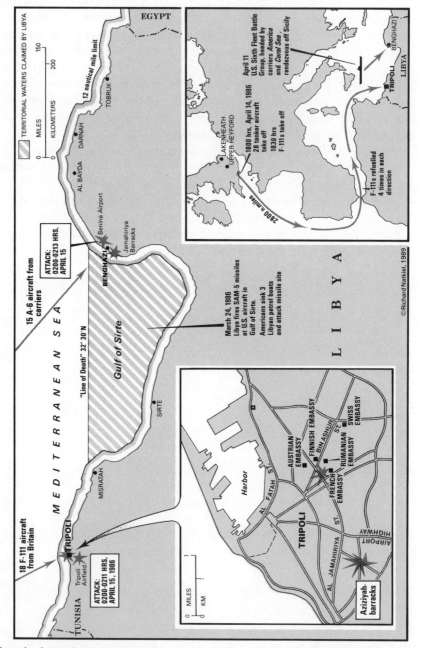

Seemingly anxious to settle ancient scores, Tripoli in the 1980s showed itself as truculent as it had been nearly two hundred years before, and provoked a similar response.

23

★

WE MUST . . . NOT
APPEAR AS TERRORISTS

*A*nd so, not for the first time in his life, Ronald Reagan took center
stage. There was a refreshing clarity, certainty, and directness in the
United States' new naval catechism: Neither the newly elected but elderly
president nor his young and energetic secretary of the Navy, John F.
Lehman, Jr., displayed a single public doubt about the direction in which
they would take the country and its fleet.

During the summer of 1981, Lehman stated that by the 1990s, the
United States should have "outright maritime superiority over any power
or powers which might attempt to prevent our free use of the seas and
the maintenance of our vital interests worldwide."[1] Outright maritime
superiority! That was really telling them. And the thirty-eight-year-old
secretary had already publicly defined the size of the fleet he believed
necessary. On the day of his swearing-in (February 5, 1981) he had
specified the target: 600 ships, to include fifteen carrier battle groups, 100
nuclear attack submarines, and (most surprisingly and controversially)
four surface battle groups focused on renovated World War II battleships.

Furthermore, in the spring of 1981, the use of U.S. warships had
already changed from that of the Carter years. As Syria and Israel struck
at each other in the air, the carrier U.S.S. *America* was held in the eastern
Mediterranean after her scheduled departure date, with the openly declared purpose of showing U.S. strength. And just a few months later, in

the high summer, the U.S. Navy provided a most vivid example of its new guiding policies, shooting down two Libyan jets over the Gulf of Sidra.

For those with long memories, the Libyan episode of August 1981 brought clear echoes of the U.S. Navy's earliest years and its wars (at the turn of the nineteenth century) against the pirates of Barbary. It was also an exact reversal of President Carter's policy in the region. Since 1973, Colonel Gadhaffi—the modern-day bashaw of Tripoli—had claimed the entire Gulf of Sidra as a Libyan territorial possession, far beyond the internationally accepted limit of 12 nautical miles. To make it quite clear that the United States, at least, did not accept the colonel's claim, the Sixth Fleet had continued to exercise annually in the gulf—until 1980, when Carter stopped it, perhaps fearing to cause an international incident in an election year, or perhaps because the hostages were still being held in Iran. Under Reagan and Lehman, the exercises took place again; and when World War III did not break out, even critics admitted that international law had been upheld.

The new-look Navy was not going to be cheap, and there was much lost time to be made up. For the second half of fiscal year 1981, a supplement of $2.9 billion was added to Carter's sums; and for fiscal year 1982, where Jimmy Carter had provided $6.6 billion, the Reagan-Lehman navy received a cool $11.6 billion. It was entertaining to speculate on what one might do privately with a salary increase of $5 billion; but the jokes that suddenly arose had a sharp cutting edge when journalists discovered that the U.S. Navy was paying exorbitant prices for the most commonplace articles. In the *Milwaukee Journal*'s cartoon entitled "Defense Department Hall of Fame," four pedestals displayed the $659 ashtray, the $404 socket, the $436 hammer, and the "multimillion-dollar nut"—a goofy-looking purchaser from the military procurement offices. The sardonic jokes came thick and fast; not since the days of Josephus Daniels had the Navy been the butt of so many lampoons. But the politician who cannot turn a problem into a challenge, and overcome it, does not last long. Lehman did just that. Far from trying to deny the undeniable, he acknowledged the revelations, appeared glad they had been made, supplied explanations, and (most important) set in motion a public program to improve the situation. American taxpayers might have an expensive navy, but they were going to be convinced it was good value as well.

To earn its keep and enhance its image, it worked harder and more dramatically each year. Lehman was secretary of the Marine Corps as well, and between August 24 and September 20, 1982, 800 U.S. Marines evacuated 12,000 members of the Palestine Liberation Organization (PLO) from Beirut as invading Israeli forces approached the city. Nine years earlier, during the Yom Kippur war of 1973, the tension generated between Soviet and U.S. naval forces in the Mediterranean had triggered a worldwide nuclear alert. With comparable Mediterranean conditions in 1982, one of the most intriguing aspects to outside observers of the operation was the muted reaction from Moscow. On the opposite side of the world, during September and October, the new, tough U.S. approach was underscored by the exercises of two carrier battle groups in the north Pacific and near the Aleutians; and as far as the other superpower's reaction was concerned, it began to look—just a little—as though this was an approach which worked.

At the same time, something stirred much closer to the United States than either Lebanon or the Aleutians. In the little Central American country of El Salvador (barely 250 miles long by 100 miles across), the hum of Marxist revolution resonated from across the border with Nicaragua. Salvadorean revolutionaries were being supplied with arms from Cuba and Nicaragua, both of which were being supplied in turn by Russia.

Ever since President Monroe's first enunciation of his doctrine (in 1823), the United States had had a formally declared interest in the region, emphasized by Theodore Roosevelt's "corollary" of 1904—"If we intend to say 'Hands off' . . . then sooner or later we must keep order ourselves." From shortly after Reagan's inauguration, small groups of U.S. military advisers had been present in El Salvador; in early February 1983, 1,600 American troops joined Honduran troops in exercises; on May 27 of that year, the first American death in El Salvador took place, with the assassination of a lieutenant commander from the U.S. Navy's SEAL (sea, air, and land) covert operations group; and from summer 1983 to spring 1984, U.S. carrier groups exercised off both coasts of Nicaragua, while the recently recommissioned battleship *New Jersey* took station off the coast of El Salvador.

The interception of a Soviet arms-supply ship to Nicaragua showed that blockade or "quarantine" could be instituted, if necessary; but in the minds of some Congressmen and many citizens, memories of failure in Vietnam overshadowed those of success in Cuba. The natures of the terrain, of the prospective enemy, and of the United States' apparently escalating involvement were altogether too similar to those in Southeast Asia for popular confidence, and throughout Reagan's first administration, Central American instability remained a chronic and obvious problem.

But as that turbulence continued, the year 1983 became brutally and theatrically memorable for two short, sharp episodes: the slaughter of Marines in Beirut and the invasion of the Caribbean island of Grenada.

Following the PLO evacuation of 1982, the Marine detachment had left Beirut as promised. After only nine days, however, they were obliged to return as part of an international peace-keeping force; and on October 23, 1983, they themselves became the target of a suicide bomber, driving a truck laden with thousands of pounds of explosive. Two hundred and forty-one marines and sailors died and 71 were injured—a casualty list close to that of the war-provoking explosion on U.S.S. *Maine* in 1898, and exceeded in recent years only on January 31, 1968, when 246 American servicemen had died on the first day of the North Vietnamese Tet Offensive.

Grenada came a mere two days later, on October 25, and from a British point of view was a highly offensive operation. As Admiral Zumwalt described it shortly afterwards: "Grenada was on the way to becoming a very sturdy Gibraltar for the Soviet Union, and it was one where the President could, with very low casualties, reverse the picture quickly—unlike Nicaragua, which would cost him many casualties."[2]

This was all true, as a quick glance at Grenadan history shows; but it left out one rather important factor. After a couple of centuries as a British colony, the 133-square-mile island had become independent in 1974. Since then, it had been tormented by vicious political rivalries which culminated on October 19, 1983, in the murder of the left-wing president by a Communist general. Soviet aid had already provided a naval base, a barracks, storage facilities, and military training areas; and though the island is a full 1,600 miles from Florida, it covers the southern entrance to the Caribbean from the Atlantic. To let it become a "Russian Gibraltar" was obviously intolerable to Reagan, so with eleven other U.S. warships, the aptly named carrier *Independence* took 1,900 marines and army rangers to Operation Urgent Fury—"a very superior action," Zumwalt remarked, expressing Americans' general opinion as (with only eighteen U.S. fatalities) the island was swiftly brought out of Communist rule.

One of the important effects of the operation was to disprove the theory that Marxist revolution was irreversible, and senior U.S. diplomats and military men were surprised, baffled, and disappointed when their major ally, Britain, expressed deep disapproval of the whole business. The reason for this was simple, but unfortunately very few Americans (even those who should have known better) had grasped it beforehand. Grenada, though no longer a British colony, was still a member of the Commonwealth; Queen Elizabeth remained its head of state. Naturally—whatever the motives or consequences—for the United States to invade a part of the Commonwealth without so much as a by-your-leave was bound to be received with considerable displeasure in Britain.

Worse still, as far as British politicians were concerned, was the fuel it gave to the otherwise quiescent feeling in Britain that Reagan's United States was unpalatably bossy, unreliable, and trigger-happy. But perhaps worst of all for a country which (as the Falklands/Malvinas conflict of

1982 had shown) still felt possessive and protective about the last scattered remnants of its empire, the British eventually realized that unlike the Falkland islanders, the Grenadans did not mind the invasion—indeed, rather the contrary. Two years after it, the Queen and Prince Philip visited the island, and *The Times* of London acknowledged with some dismay that "Ronald Reagan would have pulled bigger crowds. He is revered, and so is his money. . . . Loyalties are now to Washington, not London."[3]

But, diplomatic mishaps and bruised feelings notwithstanding, by the spring of 1984 (with the next presidential election in sight) John Lehman's ebullient confidence had not diminished one bit: "We have," he said, "by virtually every measure, *tremendously* increased readiness. . . . By every single measure, statistic, and common sense we're a tremendously improved force."[4]

The word "we" in the last sentence indicates one reason for the respect he enjoyed in the fleet: Not only did he support it vigorously and coherently, he also identified with it passionately, to the extent of undertaking an annual tour of active duty with both the Marines and the Navy in his capacity as a reserve officer.

His assessment could not be denied—from the 470 ships of 1980, the Navy had already expanded to 516, with 115 more under contract to be built. Yet of course he could be, and frequently was, criticized:

"The program he's so successfully promoting," asserted Robert Komer (an assistant secretary of defense under Carter), "would lead to a strategic disaster in the event of a major conflict with the Soviet Union."[5]

Coming from a political opponent, such remarks were to be expected. Less expected, however, was criticism from within Lehman's own party and the Navy itself. A bitter argument took place between Lehman and Paul Thayer (deputy secretary of defense and chairman of the Pentagon's Defense Resources Board), with Thayer demanding an $18 billion cut on proposed naval expenditure over the next five years. Eventually a $700 million saving was agreed on; but the shipbuilding program remained intact. Simultaneously, criticism of Lehman's own strategic beliefs came from within the Navy. Prime among these beliefs was the "forward strategy," which would take a sea war with the Soviet Union the traditional defensive line of the G-I-UK gap (the seas between Greenland, Iceland, and the United Kingdom) and on into the Norwegian Sea:

"I take an oath," he said solemnly, "to defend Norway as if it was . . . Long Island. It makes no sense to turn the Norwegian Sea and the Baltic over to the Soviets in time of conflict if we can win in the northern flank with aggressive policies and aggressive defiance."[6]

"I have yet to find an admiral who would even attempt it," Stansfield Turner remarked dismissively. "Our carrier forces would clearly not survive a thrust against Murmansk," Zumwalt added. "I'm in strong opposition to the strategy of planning to charge them in. . . . The Soviet Union in that kind of war would use tactical nuclear weapons against them."[7]

United in their criticism of the forward strategy, the same two admirals disagreed over Lehman's recommissioning of the battleships. The first of the four vessels, *New Jersey,* was ready for use early in 1983; the second, *Iowa,* followed in April 1984. After her work off El Salvador, *New Jersey* (the world's largest single source of naval firepower) steamed to Lebanon, and, in order to deter further attacks on Marine positions by the Druze militia, proceeded to bombard the shore with 16-inch shells. In Admiral Turner's opinion, Reagan's tough talking was not only cheaper, but at least as effective: "The big battleships are not an entire mistake, but they're an extremely expensive way to get what was wanted; and in Lebanon . . . they were totally useless."

Naval gunfire is not designed to hit a target the first time, but through lack of spotters, the 16-inch salvoes achieved no hits on any targets. However, Admiral Zumwalt still assessed the Lebanese deployment as "very useful" and offered another view of the ships themselves: "Recommissioning the battleships is the kind of nonoptimal thing one has to do when you would lose a war if you had to fight it, and you therefore have to move quickly, and can't have the luxury of starting from the keel and building the optimal thing."

Denying the charge that they were expensive toys for outdated admirals, he saw them as "the most survivable ship afloat today, because of the immense armor protection; and though any ship could be destroyed by a nuclear weapon, the battleships can survive more conventional hits than even the aircraft carriers." The giant vessels were not merely taken out of reserve and put back on the line; a thoroughgoing renovation included the addition of launchers for thirty-six Tomahawk cruise missiles, each either nuclear-tipped with a range of 1,500 nautical miles, "or lesser but very-long-range capability with conventional warheads." Altogether, as Zumwalt pointed out, "that is a very potent capability to bring power to bear."[8]

Overall, he believed the recommissionings improved Western chances in a war with the Soviet Union by about 5 percent; and whether or not the analysis is accepted, the ships do have an enormous psychological value at least. Somehow, even if one knows the latent power of an aircraft carrier, extremely large guns remain even more impressive—as the British saw for themselves in 1985. In the major transatlantic exercise Ocean Safari, traditional convoy escort activities were combined with advances by carrier battle groups from NATO's Striking Fleet Atlantic into the very fjords bordering the Norwegian Sea, both testing and demonstrating the forward strategy. As the exercise drew to its close, the battleship U.S.S. *Iowa* provided a spectacular display of firepower in the western approaches to the English Channel. A broadside of nine 16-inch shells may be a rarity, but when it occurs, it is very daunting indeed.

Ocean Safari was only one of more than a hundred major U.S. naval exercises in the course of 1985. Early in the year, Admiral James D. Watkins, Chief of Naval Operations, observed that "America is at peace, but it is a violent peace."[9] By then, forty years had passed since the end of World War II—nineteen years more than had elapsed between the two world wars. Whether the continuing avoidance of global conflict was due to the combined deterrent capability of nuclear power and very large conventional sea, air, and land forces, or whether the savagery of World War II was in itself the effective deterrent, Watkins's observation was all too accurate. Violence was still thriving, but under other names—low-intensity conflict, undeclared war, unconventional warfare, war without fronts—and in the course of 1985, on land and sea and in the air, the U.S. State Department logged almost seven hundred international terrorist incidents. As was said at a conference of ships' Marine detachments in Norfolk, Virginia: "If you don't think it can happen to *you,* on *your* watch, you better get out of the Corps."[10]

In bomb or gun attacks as far apart as Greece, Spain, and San Salvador, U.S. servicemen were killed or injured. More often than not, there was no possibility of direct, active retaliation nor any apparent solution beyond continually increased vigilance. In their own war of independence, the early Americans had used guerrilla warfare and terrorist tactics against the superpower of the day; but even to the more reflective of their descendants, the thought was no consolation, and for most it was irrelevant. In the age of violent peace, all that was relevant was anger, fear, and frustration—not even a private citizen could travel or live abroad in safety. Hence came the jubilation after the capture of the *Achille Lauro* seajackers—WE BAG THE BUMS! yelled the New York *Daily News* in headlines, accurately reflecting the national feeling that the United States, so long apparently impotent despite its monstrous power, had given a comeuppance to terrorism at last.

As usual, there was criticism too; but if the critics of this operation had been able to give it a detached, professional assessment, even they would have agreed that it was very smoothly done. The background was that on October 7, 1985, four young Palestinian passengers had taken over the *Achille Lauro* cruise liner at gunpoint, demanding the release of fifty Palestinians held in Israel. As the air wing of U.S.S. *Saratoga* went on alert, U.S.S. *Scott* (a guided missile destroyer) shadowed the captured vessel. On October 8 the terrorists sought sanctuary in the Syrian port of Tartus. This was refused, and one elderly, crippled passenger was murdered—a representative (as both a Jew and an American) of the Palestinians' greatest loathing. Off Port Said on the afternoon of October 9, the terrorists accepted a deal (strongly opposed by U.S. diplomats in Cairo) whereby they would go free if the ship and its remaining passengers were safely returned. In the morning of October 10, President Hosni Mubarak of Egypt asserted that they had already left his country for an unknown destination. However, American intelligence soon confirmed that they were still in Egypt and preparing to fly to Tunis; and President Reagan agreed that, as long as no innocent lives were threatened, *Saratoga*'s aircraft should make ready to capture the escaping terrorists in midair.

At 8:15 P.M. the carrier launched an E-2C Hawkeye (airborne early warning) aircraft. Two hours later, the Egyptian airliner bearing the terrorists took off. Steaming in company with *Saratoga* was the cruiser *Yorktown,* whose sophisticated Aegis combat system and SPY-1A radar showed everything in the air from the central Ionian Sea to beyond the North African coastline. Another Hawkeye, seven F-14 Tomcat fighters, and an EA-6B Prowler (electronic warfare) aircraft were launched from *Saratoga;* and eighty miles south of Crete, four of the Tomcats surrounded the airliner above, below, and behind it, forcing it to change course and land at Rome airport.

Under international law, the capture of *Achille Lauro* was not an act of piracy, although most people around the world would have said it was. The distinction was that the act was committed not by one ship against another for private gain, but by a political organization for political ends. Nor was the midair snatch of the terrorists piratical, though even some of the United States' allies questioned its legality. Nevertheless, for once (with the exceptions of President Mubarak, who was deeply embarrassed, and the Italian government, which was faced with the problem of sorting out the legal and diplomatic niceties), most U.S. allies praised the act for the same reason as Americans themselves did—at last someone was doing something about terrorists, who had had their own way for far too long.

If one took a very long historical perspective, however, it was also fair to say that after almost two centuries, relations between the United States and Tripoli were back to where they had started. Apart from its archaic vocabulary, a letter written at the beginning of the nineteenth century by Benjamin Stoddert (the first secretary of the U.S. Navy) to Thomas Truxtun (one of his foremost captains) could have been a message from President Reagan to the Sixth Fleet. *"It is conceived,"* Stoddert had written, *". . . that such a squadron cruising in view of the Barbary Powers will have a tendency to prevent them from seizing on our commerce, whenever passion or a desire for plunder might incite them thereto."*

Since May 15, 1801, when Tripoli ludicrously declared war on the far-distant United States, there had been almost a tradition of terror between the two countries. Officially, the Tripolitan War ended in 1805 and the Barbary Wars as a whole in 1815. But thirty years earlier (in February 1785) *The Times* of London referred to the United States' original flag as "the Thirteen Stripes, against which the Barbarians have sworn eternal enmity." Despite the midair snatch, which showed that the United States could be pushed too far, Gadhaffi's Libya kept that tradition alive in 1985 by bombing the airports of Rome and Vienna.

"The Moors," said Edward Preble in 1804, *"are a deep designing artful treacherous set of villains, and nothing will keep them so quiet as a respectable naval force near them."*[11]

In January 1986, two carrier battle groups (centered on U.S.S. *Coral Sea* [CV-43] and U.S.S. *Saratoga* [CV-60] and commanded by Vice Adm. Frank B. Kelso II) began OVL-I: Operations in the Vicinity of Libya. Their area of activity was limited to north of latitude 32 degrees 30 minutes north. Stretching roughly from Misurata (south of Tripoli) to Benghazi, the line—pretentiously named the "Line of Death" by Gadhaffi—enclosed the Gulf of Sidra (also known as the Gulf of Sirte); and, said the colonel, any U.S. ship or aircraft crossing the line would be attacked and destroyed.

OVL-I lasted from January 26 to 30, with Combat Air Patrols (CAPs) on constant watch. On the first morning a group of Libyan MiG-25 Foxbats approached one of the CAP stations, were intercepted, and moved away. Other intercepts took place thereafter, but without direct confrontation. In the four days of OVL-II (February 12–15) about 160 such encounters took place, with several Foxbats (escorted by U.S. Navy Hornets) flying over *Coral Sea.* OVL-III lasted a week (March 23–29) and deliberately pushed further south. The two carrier battle groups were joined by a third, centered on U.S.S. *America* (CV-66). Materially, her arrival made the Sixth Fleet the strongest it had been for years; and her name gave equally important symbolism to the Freedom of Navigation Operations about to take place.

On March 24, as part of a surface action group, the guided missile cruiser U.S.S. *Ticonderoga* (CG-47) crossed the "Line of Death" into waters recognized by almost everyone except the Libyans as free and international. In the early afternoon, as CAP aircraft approached the extreme range of a surface-to-air missile (SAM) site on the Libyan coast, two SAMs were shot at them. They missed; but now that the fleet had been shot at, its Rules of Engagement permitted retaliation.

That evening, an approaching missile patrol boat was sunk by one of *America*'s A-6 aircraft. During the night, the land-based SAM site was attacked and struck twice by HARMs (High-speed Anti-Radiation Missiles) from *Saratoga*'s A-7's. By the morning, one missile corvette had been sunk and another severely damaged by Rockeye and Harpoon missiles from A-6's launched by *Saratoga* and *Coral Sea.*

Throughout the following day (as *The Times* of London reported): "Libyan state radio broadcast the sound of street demonstrations, in Tripoli and Benghazi, and government-sponsored parades in which shrieking young men promised to stage suicide attacks against the Americans."[12]

"Europe fearful as Arabs back Gadhaffi—Kremlin sees world security threatened by conflict," said other headlines. Libya's proxy attacks did not cease. A Berlin discotheque crowded with off-duty U.S. servicemen was bombed; a TWA airliner was blown up. In 1801, after humiliation in the Mediterranean, the U.S. naval captain William Bainbridge declared he would never return to Barbary "with *tribute* except it be from the *mouth of a cannon;*" and on April 10, 1986, OVL-IV began—Operation El Dorado Canyon, the instantly famous and notorious U.S. air raid on Libya.[13]

Its designated targets were Benina air base near Benghazi; military barracks in Benghazi itself; the Sidi Bilal training area and Al Azziziyah barracks at Tripoli; and Tripoli's military airport. The night attack was a complete surprise—both Tripoli and Benghazi had street lights on as normal. It was a surprise to the rest of the world as well, and in that lay the apparent incompleteness of its success, at least in the short term.

Among the few world leaders who knew beforehand of the raid were British Prime Minister Margaret Thatcher and French President François Mitterand. Thatcher, in one of the operation's most controversial aspects, had permitted the use of Royal Air Force bases in Britain for USAF aircraft augmenting the carriers' strength; Mitterand had forbidden them to overfly French airspace. Only one of the dozens of aircraft used was lost—shot down, according to the Libyans; lost through technical failure, according to the Americans. All the designated targets were hit, but in spite of the much-vaunted pinpoint accuracy of the aircraft and their missiles, so were the Tripoli embassies of France, Finland, Austria, Switzerland, and Iran, as well as civilian areas of the city. Among the civilian dead (perhaps as many as a hundred Libyans plus many foreign nationals) was one of Gadhaffi's adopted children—a sad little victim whose death Gadhaffi promptly exploited for propaganda.

But over the previous few years, the U.S. position had repeatedly been made clear. "State-sponsored terrorism," said a Department of Defense Commission after the Beirut bombing of 1983, "is an important part of the spectrum of warfare."[14]

"We must reach a consensus in this country," said Secretary of State George P. Shultz in October 1984, "that our responses should go beyond passive defense."[15]

"We cannot and will not abstain from forcible action," said Reagan's national security adviser, Robert C. McFarlane, in March 1985, "to prevent, preempt, and respond to terrorist acts when conditions merit the use of force."[16]

By April 1986, the United States had reached the consensus Shultz desired, and had no intention of backtracking. And that national determination posed, in turn, a new, double diplomatic and military problem for the country and the rest of the world; for beyond national consensus, international consensus was needed. One side of the problem was expressed by the deputy director of the State Department Office of Counter-Terrorism: "Until now, some of the allies have been conspicuous in their reluctance to form a multi-lateral agreement to fight terrorism. In future we would prefer to consult an existing anti-terrorist structure before considering U.S. action. . . . Without such an organization, we would have little choice but to proceed with our own crisis plans."[17]

The United States would go it alone, if necessary. But the other side of the same problem was expressed by the president himself: "We must be careful that we do not appear as terrorists ourselves."[18]

During the remainder of President Reagan's second term in office, it often seemed that the U.S. Navy was on an irresistible up-and-up—and up, as exemplified on May 6, 1986. On that date, three U.S. Navy nuclear submarines (*Ray* [SSN-653], *Hawkbill* [SSN-666], and *Archerfish* [SSN-678]) surfaced at the North Pole—the first time vessels of any navy had done such a thing. On October 25 the same year, the fleet's latest nuclear carrier (*Theodore Roosevelt* [CVN-71]) was commissioned, bringing U.S. carrier strength to fifteen active ships; and between November 5 and 11 the biggest news of U.S. Navy port visits for the year was when the cruiser *Reeves* (CG-24), the destroyer *Oldendorf* (DD-972), and the frigate *Rentz* (FFG-46) went to Qingdao—formerly Tsingtao—in the People's Republic of China.

By the end of 1987, the entire U.S. Navy contained 509 ships. A year later, that total had risen to approximately 588—figures which would suggest that the Reagan-Lehman 600-ship Navy was on target for completion. But naturally it was a very expensive target. The statistics of funding, the billions upon billions of dollars, were so huge as to be almost meaningless on any normal scale, but a couple of smaller figures help make the larger ones understandable. The new carrier *Theodore Roosevelt* was due for shock damage tests in November 1987. The sum set aside for preparations was $26.7 million, while damage repair afterwards was budgeted at $18 million. Big money indeed; and that was only for one set of tests and repairs on one ship. As the U.S. budget deficit continued to spiral to incomprehensible levels—fueled in large part by defense spending—not only the domestic economy but the global economy felt the effects. Cost-cutting exercises became ever more vigorously debated, with the forces, particularly the Navy, seen as prime targets for economy.

Only a few months after President Reagan had left office (to be succeeded by his vice president, George Bush, once the youngest commissioned pilot in the U.S. Navy) Adm. Carlisle Trost, the Chief of Naval Operations, felt bound to emphasize (in May 1989) that: "We cannot maintain our commitments in other areas of the world with fewer than 15 deployable carriers. Fiscal austerity must not be allowed to weaken the force structure that supports our national strategy of forward-based coalition defense."[19]

Put more simply, the admiral was saying: Our job is necessary, and we know how to do it; but we must have the money to do it with. Phrased in the style of the late 1980s, this was only the latest version of one of the U.S. Navy's—or any navy's—most ancient combat. Britons might remember how in 1966, Christopher Mayhew (later Lord Mayhew) had resigned from the post of navy minister (equivalent to secretary of the Navy) over the "East of Suez" row. The question then was whether or not the Royal Navy's existing role should be maintained. "The Navy," said the Labour Party's 1964 manifesto, "has been run down to a dangerously low level, and is now pathetically inadequate in number of ships in commission, in manning, and in the most modern types such as nuclear-powered tracker submarines."[20]

Having won the election under Harold Wilson (later Lord Rievaulx), the Labour Government's duty was, in Mayhew's view, plain: "We must increase the Navy's resources or reduce its commitments." But neither happened; the commitments were maintained and defense expenditure was reduced by one sixth. Early in 1966, unable to change his colleagues' minds, Mayhew resigned, as did Adm. Sir David Luce, the First Sea Lord—the equivalent of CNO.

"The basic mistake of the defence review has been the classic crime of peace-time British governments, of giving the armed forces too large tasks and too few resources," said Mayhew in his resignation speech. "The overseas departments have laid down a proud defence role for Britain, the Treasury had laid down a humble defence budget for Britain and the servicemen 'carry the can.' This has all happened before . . ."[21]

And would again, as Admiral Trost could testify. In the second half of the 1980s, what one might call the villain of the peace (at least from the Navy's point of view) was Gramm-Rudman. To give it its full title, this was the Gramm-Rudman-Hollings Balanced Budget and Emergency Deficit Control Act of 1985 (Public Law 99-177), designed to run for five years. In February 1985 Lehman gave a confident review of his first four years as secretary of the Navy:

The course to re-establish maritime superiority set [in 1981] has not wavered. . . . We have achieved an effective balance between building for the future and making the fleet we have today a maximum-ready fighting force. These results have already added enormously to our ability to deter Soviet adventurism and to stabilize the peace. The Fleet and the Fleet Marine Force are more ready to go in harm's way than at any time in postwar history. Our friends and adversaries alike know this.[22]

But by 1986, another expert analyst put the secretary's dilemma bluntly: "If Gramm-Rudman stays in force for the full five years, the U.S. Navy will suffer its greatest defeat since Pearl Harbor."[23] On April 11, 1987, Lehman too resigned, and his successor (James H. Webb, an ex-Marine) lasted less than a year, resigning on February 22, 1988. "He stayed as long as he could," said one analyst, "watching budget cutters set adrift the administration's 600-ship goal."[24]

And while fighting for funds at home, the U.S. Navy was having to fight for peace abroad. If 1986 was the year of Libya, 1987 was certainly the year of the Gulf. The war between Iran and Iraq, as bloody and prolonged as the First World War, forced the navies of many nations to escort and protect their merchant ships in the area—especially oil tankers, regarded as fair game by both belligerents. British, French, Russian, Italian, Dutch, and even Belgian warships were engaged in this; for the Belgians, it was the first time they had operated out of their home area. U.S. warships were also on patrol, but not as actively, until March 7, 1987. On that date, President Reagan allowed eleven Kuwaiti tankers to reflag as U.S. vessels. Taking on the Stars and Stripes, they were able to expect active U.S. Navy protection; and since Kuwait was supporting Iraq's war effort (and working out of Kuwait, the tankers were contributing to that), it meant that U.S. warships were suddenly far more closely involved than before.

The first Gulf attack against the U.S. Navy came on May 17, 1987, 80 miles northeast of Bahrain. The victim was the frigate *Stark;* the attacker was, unexpectedly, an Iraqi F-1 mirage jet armed with two Exocet missiles. It appeared later that the Iraqi, able only to see *Stark*'s blip on his radar, assumed she was a tanker: The attack was an "unfortunate mistake." It certainly was for the thirty-seven American crew members who were killed.

Just over two months later came the second attack. The victim this time was the supertanker *Bridgeton,* one of the reflagged Kuwaiti vessels, in the first Gulf convoy to be escorted by the U.S. Navy. The weapon was a simple 250-pound floating mine, but it blew a hole ten meters by five through the ship's 27-millimeter steel plating and sent shrapnel right through the main deck, 90 feet away and also 27 millimeters thick. The plating on the escorting frigate, *Crommelin,* was less than half as thick; had she been hit, she would almost certainly have sunk. *Bridgeton,* however, was able to complete her voyage; and though no one knew for sure who the attacker was, it was the Iranians who broadcast cheerfully that "the hand of God" had been at work.

If so, it was working in a mysterious way, for on September 21, 1987, a helicopter from the frigate U.S.S. *Jarrett* caught an Iranian boat, *Iran Ajr,* in the act of laying a field of horned contact mines identical to the one which had damaged *Bridgeton.* Still familiar from movies of World War II, these old-fashioned weapons (which followed a Russian design of 1908) were not the only echo of earlier conflicts: The U.S. Navy's role in the Gulf, often compared to that of the Marines in Lebanon, was also very like the Neutrality Patrol in the western Atlantic of 1940–41. It had all the stresses, strains, and risks of war, without the relief of being able to initiate action; so when *Jarrett*'s helicopter caught the minelayers red-handed, they legitimately attacked at once and with gusto, rapidly sinking the craft.

Less than a month went by before there came another opportunity for legitimate retaliation. The Iranians were discovered to be using old oil platforms, close to or straddling international shipping lanes, as coordination centers for their attacks on neutral merchantmen. On October 19, 1987, four U.S. destroyers approached the most active of these old platforms, gave its occupants sufficient warning to evacuate, and then poured over a thousand armor-piercing and high explosive shells into it. It was target practice rather than warfare, and, to the crews of U.S.S. *Kidd, Leftwich, John Young,* and *Hoel,* highly satisfactory; they left the platform a blazing, crumpled wreck, completely useless for any purpose whatsoever. No more speedboat attacks, minelaying, or communications from that one, at any rate; but the mine danger continued. Not for nothing have they been called "weapons that wait." Once laid, mines can last for decades, until they are either swept or break free and float away (whereupon simple ones like those laid by Iran become a completely undiscriminating hazard). There is, of course, a third possibility: Still moored in position, the mine can fulfill its function and blow up a ship, which is what happened to the frigate *Samuel B. Roberts* on April 14, 1988.

This was the first of three major events affecting the U.S. Navy in the Gulf that year, and one in which some people may have seen the hand of God at work again; for although the ship was blown almost in half— with 15 feet of her keel destroyed and a hole 30 by 23 feet punched in her side—and although there were some serious injuries, not one person was killed, and the frigate herself was saved.

The mining led, four days later, to Operation Praying Mantis, an attack on two more old oil platforms being used as military bases. Led by the nuclear carrier U.S.S. *Enterprise,* this in turn developed into the largest naval battle conducted by U.S. ships since World War II, in which several Iranian warships—some gunboats and one cruiser—were sunk. Afterward, two of the U.S. aviators involved pointed out that it was "not a demonstration of sophisticated tactics against a formidable threat,"[25] which was true. What it did demonstrate, however, was that Iran's behavior was becoming an increasing gamble. Admiral Trost drew a further moral: "We spent a lot of effort and taxpayers' dollars the last seven years to achieve the level of readiness that we enjoy today," he said after the battle. "What our people saw was an opportunity for the first time under hostile conditions to use both their sensors and their weapons, and they worked as advertised."[26]

But however advanced the sensors and weapons, they were used and directed by humans, who could still be all too fallible. The U.S. Navy's third and final major Gulf episode of 1988 came on July 3—the *Vincennes* incident. The date was important: Being the day before the United States' Independence Day, it was widely expected that Iran would launch an attack against some U.S. representative, "the Great Satan." The vessel (a guided missile frigate) was comparatively new to the area—she had arrived on May 16—but was manned by a very highly trained crew, aided by the Aegis weapon system. Focused on SPY-1A radar, which has four large-screen displays, and Standard missiles, the system is designed for fast, accurate differentiation between hostile and friendly aircraft. On the morning of July 3, 1988, U.S.S. *Vincennes,* with only two guns capable of engaging surface targets, began to be harassed by a number of small, fast Iranian gunboats. Shots were exchanged, and one of *Vincennes*'s two guns jammed. To keep the remaining one bearing on the speedy gunboats, she had to carry out a series of violent course changes. In this confusion, an aircraft was detected flying from Iran on a course directly toward *Vincennes* and apparently losing altitude—a classic approach for an attack, possibly a suicidal one. Deciding the aircraft was indeed aggressive, *Vincennes* shot it down; whereupon it was discovered to be Iran Air's Flight 655, with 290 civilian passengers and crew on board, all of whom were killed.

By coincidence, three separate high-ranking study groups were attempting even then to work out the shape of the future U.S. Navy and the consequences of what had been called a "revolution at sea." The term, coined by Vice Adm. Joseph Metcalf III, was shorthand for the U.S. Navy's technological developments over the foregoing decade, and in particular the Reagan years. These developments meant that already, the total volume of space in which a warship could fight had been vastly extended:

"...*up,*" said Metcalf, "to 100,000 feet, to the limits of today's surface-to-air missiles . . . *out* on the wings of a cruise missile to 1,200 miles, and *down* thousands of feet to the limits of the deepest diving submarine."[27]

The investigation following the *Vincennes* incident was detailed, long, and public, and was able to conclude only that it was the kind of tragic accident inevitable in the stress of combat. This was certainly a correct conclusion, yet there was a sad irony attached. A warship could fight in a far greater space than ever before, but the technological advances which made that possible had one insurmountable drawback—in the end, the mass of information coming in from that space had to be analyzed, interpreted, and acted upon by people. And the incident demonstrated that however brilliant their machines, however well trained the crew, people were still as frail as always.

During the Reagan years, human frailty of another sort came much to the fore in the unsavory shape of the spy. Not a diplomat or journalist carrying out work "incompatible with his status"—that was par for the course—but a traitor willing to sell his country's secrets for money, for revenge, or even simply for thrills. By their end, the 1980s were known as "the decade of the spy." The U.S. Navy did not have a monopoly on these weak individuals—others were discovered working for both the Army and the Air Force—but there were more naval spies than any others.

Perhaps the most pathetic of them was Samuel L. Morison, grandson of Rear Adm. Samuel E. Morison, the man personally chosen by President Roosevelt as the official historian of the U.S. Navy's role in World War II. The young Morison, an analyst at the Naval Intelligence Support Center in Maryland, sold satellite pictures of the half-built Soviet aircraft carrier *Tbilisi* to the British magazine *Jane's Defence Weekly.* The pictures did not tell the Soviets anything they did not know (apart perhaps from the striking clarity of U.S. satellite photography), but they were highly classified, and it seemed that Morison's motive was an attempt to gain an editorship on the magazine. If so, it was a sad way to try to emulate his distinguished grandfather; all he got was two years' incarceration and a ruined reputation.

Certainly the most cynical of all the decade's spies was John A. Walker, Jr. "If I had access," he said after he had been caught, "color it gone."[28] For seventeen years he led a ring, subsequently very widely publicized, which included his brother Arthur, son Michael and best friend Jerry Whitworth. The three older men received life sentences; Michael Walker received the lesser penalty of twenty-five years, because in a plea bargain his father acted as the main witness against Whitworth. It was not much use for Whitworth to hope for loyalty from a friend whose main pleasure was systematic betrayal.

From the naval and national point of view, the worst aspect of this case in particular was not the simple sense and fact of betrayal, but the impossibility of accurately assessing the damage. During the period 1985–88, according to Dr. Robert M. Gates (ex–deputy director of Central Intelligence, later President Bush's deputy national security adviser), "we . . . discovered more penetration of the U.S. defense and intelligence than at any time in our history."[29] This was not a result of mere paranoia, finding invented or imagined spies, and though Gates could be confident only that the last had not been found, his words could be construed in a more positive way as well. Spies will continue as long as there are different political systems; but perhaps, in the late 1980s, the U.S. forces had simply become better at finding them out. And perhaps that was why there appeared to be more spies in the Navy than either of the other forces: It may be that when it came to finding spies out, the Navy was better than the others.

Thus, when the U.S. Navy entered its third hundred years, it looked rather like business as usual—still learning new methods of combat, still fighting for funds, still defending the national interests abroad, still trying to keep its secrets secret. The principles remained the same, unaltered since 1775; only the scale had grown.

But how astonishing that growth had been! From the chunky little "gondola" *Philadelphia* sunk by the British in Lake Champlain in 1776 to the 95,000-ton nuclear-powered carriers of the *Nimitz* class of 1975; from 1783, when Lord Sheffield wrote that "the Americans . . . cannot pretend to a navy," to 1940, when in London it was "impossible to overstate the jubilation in official and unofficial circles" caused by the news that Roosevelt was sending fifty overage destroyers "to help Great Britain in her hour of peril." By 1989, a little way into its third century (and well into its third age, from sail, to steam, to nuclear power) the U.S. Navy was one of the world's most potent forces for war or for peace.

24

★

BEYOND THE
PILLARS OF HERCULES

*T*he Mediterranean gained its name in the days of ancient Rome, when that sea was regarded as literally the middle of the known world. In the same era the Strait of Gibraltar, the western Mediterranean's narrow outlet to the open Atlantic ocean, was known as the Pillars of Hercules—the northern pillar being the Rock of Gibraltar itself and the southern, the Moroccan headland on which modern-day Ceuta stands. The distance between the two is a mere 11 miles or so; thereafter, the Strait comes down to only 6 miles in width. Marking the end of the enclosed, almost tideless Mediterranean, the Pillars of Hercules were at that time the limit of safely navigable seas, and "to go beyond the Pillars of Hercules" meant to voyage into strange waters and possible danger, knowing only that the unknown lay ahead. In the summer of 1989, swept by an unforeseen and increasingly powerful current from the east, the U.S. Navy approached its own Pillars of Hercules and found itself propelled willy-nilly on a voyage toward the unknown.

During his unparalleled twenty-eight years as foreign minister of the USSR, Andrei Gromyko had become known in the West as "Mr. *Nyet.*" In 1985 he had become head of state, with Mikhail Gorbachev as General Secretary. In 1986 the U.S. Navy published its new "Maritime Strategy"—a bold outline which dictated, in the event of war with the Soviet Union, fast, aggressive moves against the potential enemy's coasts and fleets, designed to keep conflict as far from the U.S. coasts as possible. Some hailed it as a strong, daring doctrine; others castigated it as crazily irresponsible. Then in 1987 came the first sign of movement toward the unfamiliar; suddenly everyone in Europe and America knew at least two more words of Russian—*glasnost* and *perestroika,* political openness and economic restructuring. Secretary Gorbachev admitted that the Soviet Union was in profound economic difficulty, partly caused by the cost of naval and military competition with the United States. At the end of 1987, he and President Reagan signed a treaty reducing (by a very small percentage) their nations' nuclear stockpiles; almost exactly one year later, only a month after President Bush's election, Gorbachev—having become head of state in place of Gromyko—announced that the Red Army would be cut by 10 percent. With the current running hard, the Pillars of Hercules, boundary markers of the familiar world, were fast approaching; and in 1989 they hurtled by.

It was a year of wonder and astonishment. In almost every communist country around the world, the ruling system came under powerful challenge from the people it ruled. In China there was savage repression; elsewhere, communism seemed to crumble in the face of concerted popular demands for democracy. The extraordinary became the norm: In July, Soviet warships docked as honored guests at the U.S. naval base of Norfolk, Virginia—the first time such a visit had ever taken place. Later in the year the compliment was returned, with U.S. warships accepting an invitation to visit Vladivostok; yet the culmination of the year came in November with an event which by then was inevitable, but which was still almost unbelievable: the political opening and beginning of the physical destruction of the Berlin Wall. With this, the single most significant event in world history for a generation, two more new words were on all English-speaking lips—"peace dividend."

From the U.S. Navy's point of view, this was the peril beyond the Pillars. Splendid as it sounded, the peace dividend was only a fancy term for defense cuts, and everything in the Maritime Strategy had been based on the indefinite continuation of the forty-year-old Cold War between East and West. The year had also brought (on April 19) a considerable and mysterious tragedy—an explosion in the No. 2 turret of the battleship U.S.S. *Iowa,* in which forty-seven American sailors were killed. A naval investigation, which placed the blame on the actions of a suicidal individual sailor, was itself called swiftly into question; criticism came from many groups, including the House Armed Services Committee. Able to challenge the Navy's credibility in this specific tragic incident, its more general critics found themselves doubly armed. The Cold War had become the Cold Thaw. No more enemy, so no more need of expensive armed forces. Mentally spending in advance the money that would be saved, politicians and pundits outside the forces began debating what should go first.

But this had happened before, back in the time of President Jefferson, when Albert Gallatin was secretary of the Navy and, seeing no use for a navy in peacetime, cut its budget in half. To conclude the Herculean metaphor, the U.S. Navy in 1990 rapidly recognized that although a strange new ocean stretched ahead, its dangers were not completely unfamiliar. The rocks and reefs of naval cuts had frequently threatened before. There was obviously no going back, and certainly there would be cuts, perhaps deep ones, in all the services; certainly there would be wrecks and casualties. Yet with seamanlike precaution, the worst of the hazards might be avoided.

So it was back to the old, old naval question, first posed in American history by John Adams in 1775: "What think you of an American Fleet?" In other words, is the Navy necessary? Is it affordable? How should it be composed? For every naval nation, these are the unchanging questions of external and internal naval policy, the questions of need, function, and structure. The arguments have always been long; the answers have never been simple. In 1986 the U.S. Navy had defined the purpose of its existence in terms which, by 1990, appeared to be out of date. Knowing full well it was not going to be disestablished overnight, it understood just as well that its role for the 1990s and beyond must be redefined. If not, then undoubtedly it would suffer greater proportional cuts than its sister—and rival—services.

Proposals were correspondingly robust, including the suggestion that perhaps the U.S. Army was no longer necessary. With only a tiny likelihood of a massive conventional armored assault being necessary in any part of the world, the Army and the Marines were in competition for one limited mission; so why have both? If the suggestion was not entirely serious, it was not entirely frivolous either; because not only U.S. naval policy, but every part of national defense policy (and, by extension, NATO's policies) required rethinking.

For the U.S. Navy this meant a return to first principles. The Chief of Naval Operations, Adm. Carlisle Trost, defied critics of the Maritime Strategy by stating clearly that it was "a concept of operations rather than a war plan . . . based on three broad principles governing the global employment of naval forces." He listed these three principles as *deterrence*—convincing any potential enemy that an attack against the United States would not be worthwhile; *forward defense*—the ability, if deterrence failed, to deploy forces very rapidly to a crisis area, thereby giving the United States the widest number of policy options; and *alliances*. So far from being the foreign entanglements that early Americans had sought to avoid like the plague, Trost pointed out that since World War II, the United States had built agreements of mutual security with over forty nations worldwide, and said simply: "By defending our allies we defend ourselves."[1]

The admiral's full statement—long, detailed, thoughtful, and thought-provoking—was published in the May 1990 issue of the *United States Naval Institute Proceedings*. That issue may well be seen by future historians of the U.S. Navy as the real marker for the commencement of the fleet's third century. Excelling even the Institute's own customary standards, it brought together exceptionally high-caliber professional and specialist reviews and forecasts of events, covering every major aspect of U.S. maritime thought at the time—arms control (military and naval), the continuing question of the battleships, naval strategy, the drug war, the Marine Corps, the Coast Guard, law enforcement, the U.S. merchant fleet, U.S. naval aircraft, the Soviet Navy, world naval developments, and the planned additions to the U.S. Navy.

A few extracts provide the flavor, and a fair summary, of the key naval thoughts. Colin Gray, chairman of the National Institute for Public Policy, opened with a sensible disclaimer—"No one can, or should attempt to, predict the future in detail." But it was part of his job and those of all the other experts to have a go at predicting, at least in general terms. One of Gray's most important observations was that amid all the uncertainties which beset American policymakers and defense planners, there was one thing of which they could be sure:

> For virtually all military purposes between the (airborne) dispatch of perhaps a battalion of elite troops and the launching of some modest fraction of central nuclear firepower, U.S. maritime power is the critical "enabler," not just facilitator, of effective U.S. participation in conflict.[2]

In other words, without its Navy, the United States could exert little influence beyond its own coastline. George Washington had said practically the same thing in 1781: "It follows then, as certain as that night succeeds the day, that without a decisive naval force we can do nothing definitive—and with it, everything honorable and glorious."

Ambassador Edward L. Rowny, special adviser to the President and secretary of state for arms control matters, continued the 1990 discussion:

> In terms of geography alone, the United States as a maritime nation must maintain its ability to operate freely in critical ocean areas in

order to reinforce and sustain U.S. and allied forces around the world and to ensure our economic survival. In contrast, the Soviet Union is a dominant land power. . . .

As the world becomes increasingly polycentric, the traditional naval missions of peacetime presence and crisis response will not change. Regional conflicts, as well as nonstate actions, such as international terrorism and drug trafficking, will require employment of U.S. naval forces unrelated to the U.S.-Soviet balance. In addition, the proliferation of increasingly sophisticated high technology weapons throughout the Third World (such as ballistic missiles and chemical weapons) will require a modern navy capable of defending against threats to the United States and our Allies . . . the fact that the Soviet Union may appear less threatening does not lessen the need for a strong U.S. Navy. Neither does it reduce U.S. global commitments.[3]

John Paul Jones would have agreed: "In time of Peace," he wrote in 1779, "it is necessary to prepare, and be *always prepared,* for War by Sea." In 1990 Admiral Trost stressed in addition that if the apparent Soviet threat had diminished, it had not gone away:

Despite Soviet pronouncements of naval force cutbacks, Soviet naval *capabilities* are improving. Under the guise of arms reductions, they are scrapping old units that have limited military utility. Having addressed the problem of block obsolescence, the Soviet Navy will emerge as a smaller, but thoroughly updated and modern force, more sustainable and extremely difficult to defeat. . . . We must remember, as we have learned so many times in the past, that political intentions can change overnight, while naval force structure, once relinquished, takes much longer to rebuild.[4]

Gallatin had been one of the reluctant first to learn that lesson: "It would be a very economical measure," he had written glumly, "for every naval nation to burn their navy at the end of a war, and to build a new one when again at war, if it were not that time was necessary to build ships of war."

Trost's remark about Soviet naval reductions referred to another aspect of Gorbachev's policy. Having decided unilaterally to get rid of a noticeable number of its naval units, the Soviet Union (as Ambassador Rowny noted) "continues to push naval arms control at every opportunity." Whereas U.S. arms control criteria ("enhancing national security, reducing the risk of war, and strengthening global stability") were met by agreements on reducing conventional forces in Europe (CFE), defense and space talks (DST), and strategic arms reduction talks (START), the ambassador observed that in contrast "recent Soviet arms control proposals for limiting general-purpose naval forces and operations simply do not meet these standards." His reaction was straightforward: "The best answer to any call for formal talks specifically designed to develop arms control agreements involving naval forces is just to say 'No.' "[5]

Lest it be thought that these extracts reflect only naval professionals repeating naval dogma, at least one other should be noted as well. In January 1990, in Vienna, Gen. Mikhail Moiseyev (chief of the Soviet General Staff) confirmed to his U.S. counterpart that Soviet military forces were being restructured and modernized with the intent of making them "smaller, better and more efficient." Reflecting that "we have worldwide commercial and security interests that require a strong, capable navy that can serve those interests," the U.S. officer said to Moiseyev: "I am willing at any time to discuss our Navy, but I am not prepared to negotiate restraints, controls, or reductions in our Navy." And the U.S. officer—chairman of the Joint Chiefs of Staff—was not a naval man at all, but Gen. Colin Powell of the U.S. Army.[6]

With cross-service support like that, the U.S. Navy could know it was not in terminal danger. No one doubted that cuts would come, but "that," said General Powell, "is something that we and our allies must discuss"— it was not Soviet business and would certainly not be formally linked with, or even necessarily reflect, unilateral Soviet cuts. Apart from anything else, certain large U.S. Navy cuts were already in effect; its budget for 1988 was $100.3 billion, a sum which by 1989 dropped to $97.7 billion—a steep reduction of $2.6 billion in plain figures. Fiscal year (FY) 1990 saw that partly restored, to $99.6 billion, and on January 29, 1990, Secretary of Defense Richard Cheney requested Congress to provide $99.5 billion for FY 1991. He also announced the deactivation, in addition to already planned ones, of two nuclear cruisers and five nuclear attack submarines over the following four years, as well as the retirement of the battleships *Iowa* and *New Jersey.* Against that, no fewer than 168 vessels ranging from mine hunters to ballistic submarines and aircraft carriers—in themselves a substantial and balanced fleet that most other naval nations would envy—were in various stages of construction, and there were no plans to abandon any. By the end of FY 1991, the secretary declared, the U.S. Navy would have 546 battle force ships, including fourteen deployable carriers and thirteen active and two reserve carrier air wings.[7]

Summarizing the revised uses to which this still enormous fleet would be put, an official naval statement said: "Our primary defense concerns will increasingly be associated with our interests in the Pacific, the Middle East, the Caribbean Basin, and Southwest Asia; in other words, during the 1990s, no front will be "central.' "[8]

After forty years of knowing exactly who the most likely enemy was, having to be so imprecise was a strange sensation; and yet that very imprecision indicated a more hopeful future than had been possible at any time in the previous forty years. Overall, therefore, it seemed that although the fleet had been forced beyond the Pillars of Hercules and out of its familiar surroundings, nevertheless it was navigating its new waters pretty safely. It had plenty of experience to call on, and though its old certainties had gone, it had adjusted its task accordingly to continue giving a service appropriate to national and Allied needs.

Thus the professional forecasters came to their conclusions. Writers of history are not meant to make forecasts, but, coming toward the conclusion of this book, perhaps one single forecast may be drawn from history: namely, that the U.S. Navy is likely to last a great deal longer than the Soviet Navy.

There are no laws in history, merely patterns; yet in the course of history those patterns can have the strength of laws. About 3,600 years ago, Minoan Crete established what was effectively the world's first navy with an offensive capability. Ever since then, one very simple pattern that has been observable worldwide is this: Because the sea is their lifeline, maritime nations with coastlines or seaboards longer than their land frontiers have generally developed and organized their ships, sooner or later, into fleets with an offensive capability. In contrast, seafaring nations with land frontiers longer than their coastlines have scarcely ever developed their fleets beyond a defensive capability; they have not had the need to.

Throughout World War II and the succeeding decade, the Soviet Navy was essentially a coastal defense force; and that, it may reasonably be said, was and is its natural form, for it conformed to the 3,600-year-old pattern. But in 1956 Sergei Gorshkov was given control of the Soviet fleet. He retained control for twenty-nine years, until his retirement (in December 1985) in the rank of Admiral of the Fleet. He was then seventy-five years old and was replaced by Admiral of the Fleet Vladimir Chernavin, eighteen years his junior. Gorschkov died shortly afterwards. Under his leadership—and with the political will which enabled it—the Soviet Navy had been transformed, with a rate of growth and progress even more impressive than that of the U.S. Navy. In less than thirty years it had changed from the Soviet Union's traditional coastal defense force into a force of seriously offensive potential. As such, it bucked the pattern of the past, having developed beyond the Soviet Union's natural geographical constraints. And it is notable that in this century only one other naval nation of major significance has done that: namely, Germany, under both the kaiser and Hitler. Young and ambitious (Germany was united into one nation only in 1871), it twice deliberately created a war-capable fleet; yet with a coastline far shorter than its land frontiers, this was in defiance of its own geography. The Soviet Union, united only in 1922, is still a young country; it certainly has been ambitious; and navally speaking, its geographical constraints are similar to those of Germany.

When one considers those constraints and the Soviet Union's many deep internal divisions of language and culture, it is clear that the Soviet Union's existing navy is not a "natural" creation, developed in line with a recognizable pattern of human response to the physical world, a pattern as old as civilization. Rather, it is an artificial construct built in defiance of that pattern, with its origin and continued existence made possible only by the exertion of a most powerful political will and an enforced unity.

On the other hand, with the end of the Mexican War of 1846–48, the United States collectively became a continental island; and since the end of the Civil War, its political unity has never been in serious doubt. These factors alone meant that from then on, there was a strong likelihood that sooner or later the United States would develop a nationally organized fleet with offensive capability. The essential difference between the U.S. Navy and the Soviet Navy was that the U.S. Navy's development to that stage conformed to the historic pattern. As such, it can properly be seen as a natural growth rather than an artificial construct, with a corresponding likelihood of a longer life. Since 1956, forces other than military have made the Soviet Navy what it is; forces other than military work constantly toward its demise; and similar forces work just as constantly to the sustenance of the United States' armed fleet.

Back in 1914, the Navy League of the United States wrote a famous prescription. If "Kings, Oligarchs, Race Antipathies, Unfair Competition, Land Grabbing, Injustice and Sin" were abolished, and if "The Rule of the People, A Satisfactory World Tribunal, Justice, Charity, and A Changed Human Nature" were established, then there would be peace on Earth. If not, then "Ad interim: MAINTAIN A STRONG NAVY."

It remains sound advice. Indeed, the first part of the prescription— "Oligarchs, Race Antipathies, Unfair Competition, Land Grabbing, Injustice and Sin"—summarizes well the mood and actions of Iraq's President Saddam Hussein when, in the summer of 1990, his forces invaded Kuwait. It scarcely needs to be added that, apart from economic sanctions, the world's only means of rapid retaliation was naval power; and in the large multinational fleet that soon assembled in the Gulf, with warships from France, Britain, Australia, Canada, the Soviet Union, and others, the U.S. Navy was predominant.

For only the second time in its existence, the United Nations Organization was in complete agreement: Iraqi troops must completely evacuate Kuwait by midnight, New York time, on January 15, 1991. If they did not do so voluntarily, the twenty-eight-nation coalition massed against them was authorized to use every means, including force, to remove them. By January 16, every nonmilitary option had been exhausted. Diplomacy was at an end; even a personal appeal from Javier Pérez de Cuéllar, secretary general of the U.N., to Saddam Hussein, had been ignored. The deadline had passed; the Gulf trembled on the edge of a war whose like no one could imagine; and Commodore Christopher Craig, commander of British naval forces in the region, spoke to his sailors. He and they, he said, were about to face the most testing period of their lives; and he added: "May God go with you, as you go in harm's way."

Simple enough words; but to anyone who heard and recognized them, they gave a surging echo of John Paul Jones and all the naval events of two hundred years and more—two centuries of rivalry and alliance at sea. *"I intend to go in harm's way. . . . The English nation may hate me, but I will force them to esteem me too."* By 1991 the esteem Jones had dreamed of had been real, and mutual, for fifty years. Now, in those tense and melancholy hours, supported by their allies in the coalition, the two great navies stood once again side by side, ready to defeat a dictator. But no one could know what would happen next.

If humankind is not designed for Utopia, it is not designed for standing still either, and for a writer of history, it is a tricky thing to finish the story of a great institution which is still very much alive; the story itself is unfinished. But newspapers and journals are the proper place for recording the U.S. Navy's most recent changes and for predicting its future form and functions; and out of all the possible endings for this book, one—as good as any, and better than most—was reached 3,000 miles away from Washington and Annapolis, in the pretty little English county town of Lewes, in East Sussex.

The date was July 4, 1990—the 214th birthday of the United States of America, and an important (though much younger) anniversary in the present writer's life; the place was the Bull House, now a charming restaurant and once (for a period of seven years) the home of Thomas Paine. His name, though widely remembered in America, is generally forgotten in Britain—perhaps because, like John Paul Jones, he was British-born, yet vigorously took up the cause of American independence. Tom Paine chose the pen, rather than ships or guns, as his weapon; yet in the support of individual liberty, he was willing to take up arms if need be, and the words he wrote in 1791 remain apt for the U.S. Navy two hundred years later:

> I am thus far a Quaker, that I would gladly agree with all the world to lay aside the use of arms, and settle matters by negotiation; but unless the whole world will, the matter ends, and I take up my musket and thank heaven He has put it on my power.[9]

The U.S. Navy continues. But here, for the time being, the matter ends.

SOURCE NOTES

★

Publication details can be found in the bibliography.

ABBREVIATIONS:

AHC	*American History Told by Contemporaries* (A. B. Hart, ed.)
LoC	Library of Congress, Washington, D.C.
LMCC	*Letters of Members of the Continental Congress* (E. C. Burnett, ed.)
NA	National Archives, Washington, D.C.
NDAR	*Naval Documents of the American Revolution* (W. B. Clark, ed.)
NDBW	*Naval Documents Related to the United States Wars with the Barbary Powers, 1797–1804* (D. Knox, ed.)
NDQW	*Naval Documents Related to the Quasi-War Between the United States and France* (D. Knox, ed.)
NHFMC	Naval Historical Foundation Manuscript Collection in the Library of Congress
PJA	*Papers of John Adams* (R. J. Taylor, ed.)
PRO	Public Records Office, Kew, London
SNA	Secret Naval Attaché Documents on the Probability of the Outbreak of War (National Archives microfilms, Washington, D.C.)
SND	*Select Naval Documents* (H. W. Hodges and E. A. Hughes, eds.)
USNIP	*United States Naval Institute Proceedings*

BOOK ONE: WOOD AND CANVAS 1775–1881

CHAPTER 1: WHAT THINK YOU OF AN AMERICAN FLEET?

1. Washington to Lafayette, late 1781: *NDAR*, v. 1, p. xvii.
2. *NDAR*, v. 1, p. 1236.

3. Morison, S. E., *Oxford History of the American People,* p. 234.
4. *NDAR,* v. 1, p. 1289n; Clark, W. B., *George Washington's Navy,* p 3.
5. *PJA,* v. 3, p. 214.
6. *Ibid.,* v. 3, p. 400.
7. Brewington, "American Naval Guns 1775–1785," no. 1, p. 12.
8. William Whipple to John Langdon, July 8, 1776: *LMCC,* p. 5.
9. Samuel Cooper to Benjamin Franklin, Sept. 17, 1776: *NDAR,* v. 6, p. 36.
10. James Warren to John Adams, Aug. 11, 1776: *PJA,* v. 4, p. 445.
11. Richard Henry Lee to Samuel Purviance, Jr., Oct. 11, 1776: *LMCC,* p. 124.
12. Brewington, *op cit.,* p. 17.
13. *NDAR,* v. 1, p. 36. In *John Paul Jones: A Sailor's Biography,* Morison gives *Alfred's* tonnage as 350.
14. *NDAR,* v. 6, p. 149.
15. Chapelle, *The History of the American Sailing Navy,* pp. 72, 542.
16. *PJA,* v. 3, p. 235.
17. J.A. to William Cooper, Jan. 4, 1776: *ibid.,* v. 3, p. 394.
18. J.A. to David Sewall, June 12, 1776: *ibid.,* v. 4, p. 251.
19. James Warren to J.A., Aug. 11, 1776: *ibid.,* v. 4, p. 445.
20. John Landon to Josiah Bartlett, Aug. 19, 1776: *NDAR,* v. 6, p. 229.
21. Samuel Cooper to Benjamin Franklin, Sept. 17, 1776: *ibid.,* v. 6, p. 871.
22. J.A. to James Warren, Aug. 21, 1776: *ibid.,* v. 6, p. 256.
23. William Hooper to Josiah Hewes, Jan. 1, 1777: *LMCC,* p. 200.
24. *AHC,* pp. 497–9.

CHAPTER 2: THE REBEL FLEET WAS ATTACKED AND DESTROYED

1. Westcott, *American Sea Power since 1775,* p. 7.
2. Instruction promulgated in Maryland, undated: *NDAR,* v. 6, p. 1485.
3. Beck, *The Correspondence of Esek Hopkins,* p. 45.
4. *Ibid.*
5. *Ibid.,* p. 22.
6. J.A. to Samuel Adams, Aug. 16, 1776: *LMCC,* p. 53.
7. John Paul Jones to Robert Morris, Sept. 4, 1776: *NDAR,* v. 6, p. 686.
8. Morison, S. E., *John Paul Jones,* p. 169.
9. J.P.J. to Robert Morris, Sept. 4, 1776: *NDAR,* v. 6, p. 686.
10. J.A. to Elbridge Gerry, ca. June 7, 1775: *PJA,* v. 3, p. 23.
11. Syrett, *Shipping and the American War, 1775–83.* p. 7.
12. Keppel to Admiralty, May 3, 1778: James, *The British Navy in Adversity,* p. 122; Maj. L. Floyd to Lord Herbert re Admiral Barrington, Sept. 30, 1779: *SND,* p. 148.
13. Edward Dilly to J.A., May 3, 1775: *PJA,* v. 3, p. 2.
14. William Eden (Lord Auckland) to Lord George Germain re Shuldham, Sept. 27, 1775: James, *op cit.,* p. 32.
15. Carleton to General Burgoyne, Oct. 12, 1776, re Battle of Lake Champlain: *NDAR,* v. 6, p. 1274.
16. Kempenfelt to Middleton, Jan. 18, 1770: *SND,* p. 173.
17. Governor Tryon to Shuldham, Nov. 16, 1775; PRO, Adm. 1, p. 350.
18. Gale to Deane, Nov. 9, 1775: *NDAR,* v. 2, pp. 953–6.
19. Cited in Kemp, *The History of Ships,* p. 192.
20. Hopkinson, F., "Battle of the Kegs": *AHC,* pp. 562–5.

21. Garnier to Vergennes, July 5, 1776: *NDAR,* v. 6, p. 467.
22. Starke: *ibid.,* v. 6, p. 63.
23. Brewington, "American Naval Guns 1775–1785," no. 1, p. 12.
24. Benedict Arnold, Oct. 1, 1776: *NDAR,* v. 6 pp. 1082–3.
25. Cited in Heinl, *Soldiers of the Sea,* p. 5.
26. Mahan, *Major Operations of the Navies,* p. 18.
27. Arnold to Gates, Oct. 10, 1776: *NDAR,* v. 6, p. 1197.
28. Joshua Pell, Jr., diary, Oct. 10, 1776: *ibid.,* v. 6, p. 1198.
29. George Pausch, journal, Oct. 10, 1776: *ibid.,* v. 6, p. 1254.
30. Gates to Schuyler, Oct. 15, 1776: *ibid.,* v. 6, p. 1277.
31. James, *op cit.,* p. 51.
32. Carleton to Howe, Oct. 20, 1776: *NDAR,* v. 6, p. 1336.
33. Starke: *ibid.,* v. 6, p. 1244.
34. Carleton to Burgoyne, Nov. 17, 1777: James, *op cit.,* p. 61.

CHAPTER 3: WITHOUT A RESPECTABLE NAVY

1. Committee of Secret Correspondence to Wickes, Oct. 29, 1776: *NDAR,* v. 6, pp. 1400–1.
2. Committee of Secret Correspondence to Franklin: *LMCC,* p. 182.
3. Wickes to Commissioners in Paris: Knox, *A History of the United States Navy,* p. 19.
4. Heinl, *Soldiers of the Sea,* p. 7.
5. Morris to William Whipple, Sept. 4, 1777: *LMCC,* p. 475.
6. Hotham to Howe, Oct. 9, 1777: PRO, Adm. 1, p. 488.
7. Nicola to Penna. Committee, July 6, 1775: *NDAR,* v. 1, p. 831.
8. J.A. to David Sewall, June 12, 1776: *PJA,* v. 4, p. 251.
9. Hotham to Howe, Oct. 9, 1777: PRO, Adm. 1, p. 488.
10. Wallace to Hotham, Oct. 17, 1777: *ibid.*
11. J.P.J. to U.S. government: *SND,* p. 179.
12. J.A., diary, May 13, 1779: Morison, *John Paul Jones,* p. 201.
13. J.P.J. to Marine Committee, Jan. 21, 1777: *ibid.,* p. 87.
14. Caroline Edes: *ibid.,* p. 281.
15. Franklin to J.P.J.: *ibid.,* p. 91.
16. J.P.J. to John Wendell, Dec. 11, 1777: *ibid.,* p. 115.
17. Commissioners to J.P.J., Jan. 16, 1778: *ibid.,* p. 125.
18. J.P.J. to Marine Committee: *ibid.,* p. 125.
19. *Ibid.,* p. 139.
20. Selkirk to J.P.J., June 9, 1778: *ibid.,* p. 152.
21. J.P.J. to Le Roy de Chaumont: *ibid.,* p. 182.
22. Landais to J.P.J., Aug. 24, 1779: *ibid.,* p. 210.
23. For the timing of this exchange, see *ibid.,* p. 231.
24. *AHC,* p. 590.
25. J.P.J. to Vice Adm. Vicomte de Kersaint, 1791: *SND,* p. 182.
26. Reaction dated Oct. 12, 1779: Morison, *op cit.,* p. 258.
27. *Ibid.,* p. 258.
28. *Ibid.,* p. 323.
29. *Ibid.,* p. 336.

CHAPTER 4: I HAVE BEEN FORCED . . . TO SURRENDER

1. *AHC*, p. 514.
2. James Madison, July 7, 1781: *AHC*, p. 608.
3. George Washington to John Laurens, Jan. 15, 1781: *AHC*, p. 596.
4. Hood to Sir George Jackson, Sept. 6, 1781: *SND*, p. 175.
5. Graves memorandum: James, *The British Navy in Adversity*, p. 293.
6. *AHC*, p. 615.
7. J.P.J. to Kersaint, 1791: *SND*, p. 182.
8. Sheffield, "Observations on the Commerce of the American State," 1783: Field, *America and the Mediterranean World*, p. 32.
9. Humphreys, D., "Poem on the Future Glory of America": *ibid.*, p. 33.
10. J.P.J. to John Jay: Morison, *John Paul Jones*, p. 402.
11. Adams and Jefferson: Field, *op cit.*, p. 34.
12. For the full text of the Constitution, see (for example) the *Oxford Companion to American History*, pp. 889–906.
13. Field, *op cit.*, p. 36.
14. J.P.J., 1780: Morison, *op cit.*, pp. 415–16.
15. Robertson, *The Spanish Town Papers*, p. 105.

CHAPTER 5: OPEN HOSTILITIES

1. Minister to Secretary of State Pickering, Dec. 1793: Westcott, *American Sea Power Since 1775*, p. 28.
2. Humphreys to Knox, 1793: Westcott, *ibid.*, p. 24.
3. Order-in-Council, Nov. 6, 1793: *The Times* (London), Jan. 2, 1794.
4. Morison gives an excellent brief account of the difficulties of handling a square-rigger in Chapter 4 of *John Paul Jones.*
5. A wooden corvette bearing the name *Constellation* and advertised as both a "frigate" and the "oldest ship of the U.S. Navy" is preserved in Baltimore. She is well worth visiting, but, with all due respect to the people of Baltimore, she is by no means one of the "six original frigates." Her main authentic distinction is that she was "the last sailing man-of-war designed and built for the United States Navy," to quote Chapelle, *The History of the American Sailing Navy*, p. 466. The argument of *Constitution* versus *Constellation* should have been long put to rest by pp. 466–9 of his analysis.
6. *The Times* (London), Oct. 14, 1795.
7. *Ibid.*, Mar. 24, 1795.
8. American State Papers, Naval Affairs, v. 1, pp. 25–8.
9. Adams to Congress: *The Times* (London), June 26, 1797.
10. *Ibid.*, June 24, 1797.
11. *Ibid.*, June 5, 1798.
12. *Ibid.*, Aug. 21, 1798.
13. *Ibid.*, Aug. 11, 1798.
14. *Ibid.*
15. *Ibid.*, Mar. 28, 1799.
16. Truxtun to Stoddert, May 19, 1799: *NDQW*, v. 3, pp. 212–13.
17. Dillon, *A Narrative of My Personal Adventures, 1790–1839*, v. 1, p. 377.
18. Stoddert to Spotswood, Mar. 20, 1801: *NDQW*, v. 7, p. 149.
19. Truxtun to Stoddert, Apr. 6, 1799: *ibid.*, v. 3, p. 24.

20. Albion, R. G., *Makers of Naval Policy, 1798–1947,* p. 46.
21. *Ibid.*
22. *Ibid.,* p. 40.
23. *NDBW,* v. 1, p. 12.
24. Knox, *A History of the United States Navy,* p. 55; and others.
25. *Annals of the 5th Congress,* pp. 2823–32, 2859–71.

CHAPTER 6: A SQUADRON OF OBSERVATION

1. Sharrer, G. T., "The Search for a Naval Policy, 1783–1812," in Hagan, *In Peace and War,* pp. 38–9.
2. Albion, *Makers of Naval Policy, 1798–1947,* p. 183.
3. *Ibid.,* pp. 184–5.
4. *Ibid.,* p. 297.
5. Albion and Pope, *Sea Lanes in Wartime,* p. 135.
6. Field, *America and the Mediterranean World, 1776–1882,* p. 47.
7. *NDBW,* v. 1, p. 432; Fowler, *Rebels Under Sail,* p. 66.
8. *NDBW,* v. 1, p. 470; Albion, *op cit.,* p. 298.
9. *NDBW,* v. 1, pp. 465–9; Albion, *ibid.*
10. *NDBW,* v. 1, pp. 428–9.
11. *Ibid.,* pp. 460–1.
12. *Ibid.,* p. 480.
13. *Ibid.,* p. 470.
14. Cited, Fowler, *Jack Tars and Commodores,* p. 76.
15. Albion, *op cit.,* p. 184.
16. This account is based on McKee, *Edward Preble,* and Fowler, *op cit.,* pp. 88–9.
17. *NDBW,* v. 3, p. 70.
18. *The Times* (London), Sept. 26, 1785.
19. *Ibid.,* Feb. 18, 1785.
20. *NDBW,* v. 3, p. 172.
21. *Ibid.,* p. 174.

CHAPTER 7: SOMETHING DRASTIC

1. Maclay, *A History of the United States Navy,* v. 1, p. 258.
2. Midshipman Charles Morris, Jr., log: NA, RG45, App. D, No. 22.
3. *NDBW,* v. 4, p. 153.
4. Adams, *History of the United States,* v. 2, p. 431; Albion, *Makers of Naval Policy, 1797–1947,* p. 285.
5. *NDBW,* v. 4, p. 153.
6. *Ibid.,* v. 6, pp. 214, 297.
7. *Ibid.,* v. 6, p. 392.
8. Adams: Albion, *op cit.,* pp. 184–5.

CHAPTER 8: MUCH SENSATION IN AMERICA

1. "A Freeholder," "A Short Essay upon the Present Mode of Impressing Men into the Sea-Service," p. 6. Subsequent quotes on impressment are from the same source unless otherwise stated.
2. *The Times* (London), Jan. 7, 1794.
3. Hansard, Feb. 18, 1811.
4. *The Times* (London), Feb. 28, 1799.

5. *NDAR*, v. 1, p. 1041.
6. Morison, S. E., *Oxford History of the American People*, p. 378.
7. *NDBW*, v. 6, pp. 114–5.
8. McKee, *Edward Preble*, pp. 309–10.
9. Sprout, H. and M., *The Rise of American Naval Power, 1776–1918*, p. 67.
10. Maloney, L., "The War of 1812," in Hagan, *In Peace and War*, p. 54.
11. *Ibid.*, p. 49; NA, RG45, letters to Naval Secretary from Captains, Rodgers to Hamilton, Sept. 1, 1812.
12. Log of U.S.S. *Constitution*, Aug. 20–21, 1812: NA, RG45, E.392, D-27.
13. Dacres's comments are from his letter to Vice Adm. H. Sawyer, Sept. 7, 1812: PRO, Adm. 1, pp. 502, 541 (also in Fowler, *Jack Tars and Commodores*, pp. 173–4). The times given in *Constitution*'s log occasionally differ by one hour from those in Dacres's account. I have therefore excluded them to avoid confusion.
14. *The Times* (London), Mar. 20, 1813.
15. Morris, C., *Autobiography:* Knox, *A History of the United States Navy*, p. 85.

CHAPTER 9: THE LAKE AND THE SEA SERVICE

1. Madison to General Dearborn, Oct. 7, 1812: Knox, *A History of the United States Navy*, p. 86.
2. Brock to Prevost: *ibid.*, p. 111.
3. Morison, S. E., *Oxford History of the American People*, p. 386.
4. Maclay, *History of the United States Navy, 1775–1893*, v. 1, p. 423.
5. Fowler, *Jack Tars and Commodores*, p. 189.
6. Jones to Chauncey, Jan. 26, 1813: NA microfilm M149.
7. Howarth, *Sovereign of the Seas*, p. 121.
8. Longfellow, "My Lost Youth," stanzas 3 and 5.
9. *The Times* (London), Oct. 22, 1813.
10. Perry to Jones, Aug. 4, 1813: NA microfilm M147.
11. Jones to Madison, Oct. 26, 1814: LoC, J.M. papers, series 1; also Maloney, M., "The War of 1812," in Hagan, *In Peace and War*, p. 60.
12. Dillon, *A Narrative of My Personal Adventures, 1790–1839*, v. 2, pp. 277–8.
13. Fowler, *op cit.*, pp. 196–7.

CHAPTER 10: THE AMERICANS TAUGHT US A LESSON

1. Jones to Lowndes, Chairman of the House Naval Committee, Feb. 2, 1814: Albion, *Makers of Naval Policy, 1798–1947*, p. 186.
2. *Naval Chronicle*, v. 32, pp. 243–5; also Fowler, *Jack Tars and Commodores*, pp. 250–1.
3. Cochrane to Gloucester, Sept. 3, 1814: NHFMC.
4. Macdonough to Jones, Sept. 11, 1814: Fowler, *op cit.*, p. 240.
5. Wellington, Nov. 4, 1814: Morison, *Oxford History of the American People*, p. 398.
6. Dillon, *A Narrative of My Personal Adventures, 1790–1839*, v. 2, p. 325.
7. Rodgers, W. T., personal journal, 1813–15: entries for June 25, 1814, June 28, 1814, July 1, 1815, Oct. 30, 1815, NHFMC.

CHAPTER 11: OUR PEACEFUL CONFEDERACY

1. Chase, P., journal 1818–19: NHFMC.
2. Extracts from Monroe's 1824 report: Sprout, H. and M., *The Rise of American Naval Power, 1776–1918*, p. 99.

3. Wilkes, C., Jr., journal on Ship *O'Cain,* 1823: NA, RG45, E.392, D-39.
4. Adams to Congress, Dec. 5, 1826: *Messages and Papers of the Presidents,* v. 2, pp. 361–2; Sprout, *op cit.,* p. 102.
5. Macon: *Register of Debates,* 19th Congress, 2nd session, p. 521; Sprout, *ibid.,* p. 103.
6. Hayne: *Register of Debates, ibid.,* pp. 351, 353; Sprout, *ibid.,* p. 103.
7. Jackson to Congress, Dec. 8, 1829: *Messages and Papers of the Presidents, op cit.,* v. 2, pp. 437–8; Sprout, *ibid.,* p. 105.
8. Morison, S. E., *Oxford History of the American People,* p. 444.
9. Woodbury to Congress, *Annual Report, 1832: American State Papers,* Class VI (Naval Affairs), v. 4, p. 160; Long, D. F., "The Board of Navy Commissioners," in Hagan, *In Peace and War,* p. 67.
10. Browning, R. L., journal 1835–38 on U.S.S. *Vincennes:* NHFMC.
11. *American State Papers* (Military Affairs), v. 6, p. 400; Sprout, *op cit.,* p. 108.
12. *Messages and Papers of the Presidents,* v. 3, pp. 306–7; *ibid.,* p. 107.

CHAPTER 12: DISPUTES AND COLLISIONS

1. Paulding, *Literary Life of James Kirk Paulding,* p. 278; cited, Albion, *Makers of Naval Policy, 1797–1948,* p. 190; Hagan, *In Peace and War,* p. 65; Sprout, *The Rise of American Naval Power, 1776–1918,* p. 114.
2. *New York Herald,* Jan. 23, 1878; Albion, *ibid.,* p. 190.
3. Paulding, *op cit.,* p. 69; cited, *ibid.,* p. 58.
4. Wilkes Exploring Expedition: NA, RG45, E.25, A4, para. 11, v. 1.
5. Wilkes to Southard, Aug. 22, 1838: NA, RG45, E.25, A4.
6. *Ibid.*
7. Clough, A. H., "Where Lies the Land."
8. Wilkes to Southard: NA, RG45, E.25, A4.
9. Wood: *Hansard,* ser. 3, XLV, col. 1221; Brodie, *Sea Power in the Machine Age,* p. 22.
10. *Congressional Globe,* 27th Congress, 2nd session, 1841–2, p. 859; Smith, G. S., "An Uncertain Passage" in Hagan, *op cit.,* p. 86.
11. Upshur to Tyler, Report for 1841: Knox, *A History of the United States Navy,* p. 159.
12. Clough, A. H., "Say Not the Struggle Naught Availeth."

CHAPTER 13: WE WILL GREET YOU WITH BLOODY HANDS

1. Price, *Origins of the War with Mexico,* p. 69.
2. *Ibid.*
3. Bayard, *A Sketch of the Life of Commodore R. F. Stockton,* App. E, pp. 94–8; cited, *ibid.,* p. 13.
4. Stockton to Henshaw, Feb. 5, 1844: *ibid.,* pp. 81–3, 73.
5. McMaster, *A History of the People of the United States,* v. VII, p. 323: *ibid.,* pp. 28–9.
6. Schouler, *History of the United States,* v. IV, p. 498: *ibid.,* p. 36.
7. Jones, *Memoranda and Official Correspondence Relating to the Republic of Texas, Its History and Annexation,* p. 48: *ibid.,* pp. 111, 113.
8. Morison, S. E., *Oxford History of the American People,* p. 561.
9. Conner to his wife, May 29, 1846: David Conner papers, Franklin D. Roosevelt Library; Bauer, *The Mexican War, 1846–48.* p. 109.
10. Bancroft to Conner, May 13, 1846: cited, *ibid.,* p. 108.

11. Morris to Conner, Sept. 21, 1846: *ibid.,* p. 116.
12. Morison, S. E., *"Old Bruin,"* p. 211.
13. *Ibid.,* p. 216.
14. *Ibid.,* p. 220.
15. *Ibid.,* p. 221.
16. Bauer, *op cit.,* p. 363.
17. Lincoln to the House of Representatives, Jan. 12, 1848: Price, *op cit.,* p. 92.
18. Grant, *Personal Memoirs,* v. 1, pp. 53–5; cited, *ibid.,* p. 95.
19. Bauer, *op cit.,* p. 369.
20. Dana, *Two Years Before the Mast,* p. 48.
21. Melville, *Moby Dick,* pp. 9–10.

CHAPTER 14: SHOCKS, AND THROES, AND CONVULSIONS

1. Johnson, D. N., journal, Dec. 19, 1841: Peterson, *Smithsonian Miscellaneous Collections,* v. 136, no. 2, pp. 29–30.
2. *Ibid.,* p. 19.
3. Rowan, S. C., journal, Aug. 10, 1843: NA, RG45, E.392, D-67.
4. Johnson, D. N., *op cit.,* pp. 14–23, 53–4, 72, 80–1, 90.
5. Morison, S. E., *"Old Bruin,"* p. 155.
6. *Ibid.,* p. 156.
7. Buchanan, F., July 22, 1847: *ibid.,* p. 237.
8. Coppée, H.: *ibid.,* p. 251.
9. Perry to Secretary Kennedy, Dec. 14, 1852: *ibid.,* p. 261.
10. *Ibid.*
11. Orders to Perry, Nov. 5, 1852: *ibid.,* p. 284.
12. Perry to J. C. Delano, Dec. 18, 1851: *ibid.,* p. 273.
13. Perry to Navy Department, Mar. 20, 1854: *ibid.,* p. 361.
14. Perry, "Narrative": *ibid.,* p. 324.
15. Secretary Dobbin to Perry, Sept. 19, 1854: *ibid.,* p. 411.
16. Lincoln, Peoria speech, Oct. 16, 1854: Morison, S. E., *Oxford History of the American People,* p. 595.
17. Lincoln, opening speech of senatorial campaign, June 16, 1858: *ibid.,* p. 595.
18. South Carolina State Legislature declaration, Dec. 20, 1860: *ibid.,* p. 607.

CHAPTER 15: MANY EXCITING SUNDAYS

1. Lincoln's inaugural address, Mar. 4, 1861: Morison, S. E., *Oxford History of the American People,* p. 610.
2. Scharf, *History of the Confederate States Navy,* p. 20.
3. *Ibid.,* p. 17.
4. *Ibid.,* p. 137.
5. *Ibid.,* p. 43.
6. *Ibid.*
7. *Ibid.,* p. 150.
8. Davis, C., to C. S. Bushnell: Niven, *Gideon Welles,* p. 368.
9. Morison, S. E., *"Old Bruin,"* p. 258.
10. Mahan to Newcome, Oct. 10, 1861: Mahan papers, 1861–1913, NHFMC.
11. Scharf, *op cit.,* p. 44.
12. Mallory to Buchanan, Feb. 24, 1862: *ibid.,* p. 155.
13. Dahlgren, *Memoir of John A. Dahlgren,* pp. 358–9; Niven, *op cit.,* p. 405.
14. Porter, J. L., Apr. 8, 1862: Scharf, *op cit.,* p. 151.

15. Welles, *Diary,* v. 1, pp. 62–4.
16. Log of U.S.S. *Monitor,* Feb. 25–Sept. 10, 1862: NA, RG45, E.392, App. D, No. 110.
17. Welles, *op cit.,* v. 1, p. 65.
18. Scharf, *op cit.,* p. 169.
19. Welles, *op cit.,* v. 1, pp. 65–6.

CHAPTER 16: VICKSBURG MUST OF NECESSITY FALL

1. Train, S. F. (Acting Assistant Paymaster, U.S.S. *Ino,* Feb. 5–June 3, 1862), journal: NA, RG45, E.392, D-108. All of Train's comments are from this.
2. Mahan, *Admiral Farragut,* p. 125.
3. *Ibid.*
4. *Ibid.,* p. 147.
5. Smith, M. L.: *ibid.,* p. 145.
6. Perkins, G. H.: *ibid.,* pp. 151, 159.
7. Farragut: *ibid.,* p. 96.
8. Pinckney, N., to his wife, Mar. 29, 1863: Pinckney papers, 1830–78, NHFMC.
9. Farragut: Mahan, *op cit.,* p. 208.
10. *Ibid.,* p. 211.
11. *Ibid.,* p. 217.
12. *Ibid.,* pp. 223–4.
13. *Ibid.,* p. 224.
14. *Ibid.*
15. *Ibid.,* p. 232.
16. Pinckney to his wife, Apr. 6, 1863: *op cit.*
17. Grant to Farragut: Mahan, *op cit.,* p. 227.
18. Pinckney to his wife, May 30, 1863: *op cit.*
19. Welles, *Diary,* v. 1, p. 364.

CHAPTER 17: THE REBS . . . HAVE GOT GOOD COURAGE

1. Smith, D. A.: Smith papers, 1863–1905, NHFMC. All of Smith's subsequent comments come from this source.
2. Welles, *Diary,* v. 1, p. 497.
3. Scharf, J. T., *History of the Confederate States Navy,* p. 799.
4. *Ibid.,* p. 570.
5. Davis's intransigence: Morison, S. E., *Oxford History of the American People,* pp. 693–4.
6. Farragut: Scharf, *op cit.,* p. 765.
7. Welles, *op cit.,* v. 2, p. 231.
8. *Ibid.,* p. 273.
9. Grant at Appomattox: Morison, S. E., *Oxford History of the American People, op cit.,* p. 700.
10. Welles, *op cit.,* v. 2, p. 278.
11. Lincoln to J. C. Conkling, Aug. 26, 1863: Basler, *The Collected Works of Abraham Lincoln,* v. 6, pp. 409–10; cited Wegner, D. M., "The Union Navy," in Hagan, *In Peace and War,* p. 124.
12. Bulloch, *The Secret Service of the Confederate States in Europe,* v. 1, p. 22; cited Merli, F. J., "The Confederate Navy," *ibid.,* p. 136.
13. Scharf, *op cit.,* pp. 51–2.

CHAPTER 18: SO NEGLECTED OF LATE YEARS

1. Paget, *Naval Powers and Their Policy,* pp. 173–5.
2. King, *Warships and Navies of the World.*
3. Mahan to C. H. Fitzhugh, June 7, 1911: Mahan papers, 1861–1913, NHFMC.
4. *Ibid.,* Oct. 24, 1912.
5. *Ibid.,* postscript.
6. Schuster, "Voyage of U.S.S. *Hartford* to the Far East, 1865": Personal diary, Aug.–Dec., NHFMC.
7. Welles, G., *Annual Report, 1865,* pp. xiv–xv.
8. Bell to Welles, Feb. 7, 1866, squadron letters, NA, RG45; Johnson, R. E., *Far China Station,* p. 126.
9. Porter: General Orders Nos. 93 (Mar. 11, 1869), 128 (June 11, 1869), 131 (June 18, 1869); Albion, *Makers of Naval Policy, 1798–1947,* pp. 201–2.
10. This and the quotations in the following two paragraphs are from Still, *American Sea Power in the Old World,* pp. 56–7.
11. Clift, C. W., journal, log No. 426, May 29, 1869, Mystic Seaport: Johnson, *op cit.,* p. 146.
12. The Nice and Villefranche quotations are from Still, *op cit.,* various pages.
13. Ammen, "Purposes of a Navy," in *The United Service,* v. 1, pp. 245, 253.
14. This and the quotations in the following two paragraphs are from Still, *op cit.,* pp. 34, 56, 31.
15. Schufeldt to Bell, Nov. 22, 1866: Johnson, *op cit.,* p. 130.
16. Sperry to father, Mar. 3, 1885: Sperry papers, 1885–99, NHFMC.
17. Rowan to Robeson, Jan. 4, 1870: Johnson, *op cit.,* p. 149.
18. *Nation,* Nov. 20, 1875: Still, *op cit.,* p. 69.
19. This and the quotations in the following three paragraphs are from Albion, *op cit.,* pp. 74–6, 317.
20. Mahan, *The Influence of Sea Power upon History.*
21. Welles, G., July 24, 1865: *Diary,* 186–69, v. 2, p. 340.
22. Stevens, A. F., *Congressional Globe* 41–2, 3539; cited Buhl, L. C., "Maintaining an American Navy," in Hagan, *In Peace and War,* p. 152.
23. Welles, G., July 24, 1865: *Diary, op cit.,* v. 2, p. 341.
24. Mahan, *op cit.,*

BOOK TWO: STEAM AND STEEL 1881–1991

CHAPTER 1: APPROACHING UNDER STEAM

1. George: Spector, *Professors of War,* p. 7.
2. T.R.: Sprout, *The Rise of American Naval Power, 1776–1918,* pp. 227–8.
3. Long: *ibid.,* p. 229.
4. Isherwood: *ibid.,* p. 199.
5. Rowan, S. C.: Rowan papers, NA, RG45, E.392, 67.
6. Porter: Sprout, *op cit.,* p. 196.
7. Fiske: *ibid.,* p. 198.
8. Porter: *ibid.,* p. 195.
9. Mahan: Spector, *op cit.,* p. 8.
10. Chandler on Naval War College, Oct. 6, 1984: *ibid.,* p. 25; Luce, *Writings,* p. 49.
11. Rhode Island General Assembly, Aug. 26, 1775: *NDAR,* v. 1, p. 1236.

12. Luce and Whitney: Spector, *op cit.*, pp. 39, 18, 55.
13. Luce on science of naval warfare: *ibid.*, p. 55.
14. Luce and Sherman: *ibid.*, p. 17.
15. Mahan: *ibid.*, p. 38.
16. Mahan: *ibid.*
17. Mahan: *ibid.*, p. 44.
18. Ramsay: *ibid.*, p. 61.
19. De Long references are all from "The Ice Journals," NA, RG45, E.392, 148.
20. Peary to his mother: Weems, *Peary*, p. 84.
21. Whitney and Peary: *ibid.*, p. 75.
22. Sampson: Spector, *op cit.*, pp. 84–5.
23. Mahan: *ibid.*, p. 84.
24. Luce: *ibid.*, pp. 47–8.
25. Porter: Buhl, L. C., "Maintaining an American Navy," in Hagan, *In Peace and War*, p. 166.
26. Herbert, *Annual Report 1893:* Sprout, *op cit.*, p. 219.
27. Albion, *Makers of Naval Policy, 1798–1947*, p. 321.

CHAPTER 2: A FEELING OF UNEASY EXCITEMENT

1. Wainwright: Spector, *Professors of War*, p. 83.
2. T.R. on Dewey: O'Toole, *The Spanish War*, p. 102.
3. Watson, E. H.: NA, RG45, E.392, D-149.
4. New York *World:* O'Toole, *op cit.*, pp. 124–5.
5. Rickover: *ibid.*, p. 400.
6. *Evening Journal:* *ibid.*, p. 126.
7. T.R. to Dewey, Feb. 25, 1898: Sargent, *Admiral Dewey and the Manila Campaign*, p. 10.
8. Dewey notebook, Navy Yard Museum display, Washington, D.C.; NA, RG45, E.992, D-151.
9. Sen. Redfield Proctor: O'Toole, *op cit.*, pp. 146–7.
10. Queen María Cristina: *ibid.*, p. 147.
11. Dewey: Sargent, *op cit.*, p. 16.
12. Gomez Nuñez, S., June 2, 1899: Gomez Nuñez, *The Spanish-American War*, p. 9.
13. Dewey's departure from Hong Kong: Sargent, *op cit.*, p. 19.
14. Montojo: O'Toole, *op cit.*, p. 179.
15. Joint resolution: *ibid.*, pp. 171–2.
16. Cervera: Cervera y Topete, *The Spanish-American War*, p. 123.
17. Bermejo: *ibid.*, p. 24.
18. T.R. on Kettle Hill: O'Toole, *op cit.*, p. 317; "parlor jingo," p. 162.
19. Carpenter to his mother, May 3, 1898: Carpenter papers, NHFMC. Later Carpenter quotes from same source.
20. Julian, diary, 1897–99: Julian papers, NHFMC. Later Julian quotes from same source.
21. T.R.: O'Toole, *op cit.*, p. 297.
22. *Castilla:* Sargent, *op cit.*, p. 106.
23. *Ibid.*, p. 35.
24. *Diario de Manila*, May 4, 1898: *ibid.*, p. 115.
25. Montojo: *ibid.*, pp. 107–8.

26. Gridley: *ibid.,* p. 36.
27. Fullam, cable to *The Herald,* Paris: Correspondence 1863–1905, Fullam papers, Box 8, NHFMC.

CHAPTER 3: TO CHEER THE SPANISH

1. *New York Herald:* Gomez Nuñez, *The Spanish-American War,* p. 14.
2. Blanco: O'Toole, *The Spanish War,* p. 173.
3. Cervera: *ibid.*
4. Long: *ibid.,* p. 220.
5. Very to SecNav, quoting Benet: NA, RG45, M.167, M.1114.
6. Long: O'Toole, *op cit.,* pp. 228–9.
7. Sims to Bureau of Navigation, June 15, 1898: NA, RG45, M.167, M.1114.
8. Graham, G. E.: O'Toole, *op cit.,* p. 329.
9. Evans, Capt. R. D.: "The Sea Fight at Santiago, as seen from the *Iowa*" (original draft): Evans papers, NHFMC; and slightly different version in O'Toole, *ibid.,* pp. 329–30.
10. Cervera: Cervera y Topete, *The Spanish-American War.*
11. Concas: O'Toole, *op cit.,* p. 329.
12. Cervera: Laffin, *Americans in Battle,* p. 82.
13. Evans: "Sea Fight," *op cit.*
14. *Ibid.*

CHAPTER 4: SUCH A FLEET . . . SUCH A DAY

1. *Edinburgh Magazine:* Still, *American Sea Power in the Old World 1865–1917,* p. 135.
2. Picot, G., Institut de France: *ibid.*
3. O'Toole, *The Spanish War,* p. 339.
4. McKinley: Costello, *The Pacific War,* p. 21.
5. T.R.: O'Toole, *op cit.,* p. 377.
6. T.R.: *ibid.,* p. 392.
7. T.R.: Still, *op cit.,* pp. 157, 137.
8. Gray: O'Toole, *op cit.,* p. 385.
9. McKinley: *ibid.,* p. 386.
10. T.R.: Turk, R. W., "Defending the New Empire," in Hagan, *In Peace and War,* p. 189.
11. Sargent: *ibid.,* p. 190.
12. T.R.: *ibid.,* p. 192.
13. *Neueste Nachrichten:* Still, *op cit.,* p. 146.
14. *Pester Lloyd:* ibid., p. 145.
15. Seward to Welles, Dec. 3, 1864: Welles, *Diary, 1861–69,* v. 2, p. 191.
16. T.R.: Okamoto, S., *The Japanese Oligarchy and the Russo-Japanese War,* p. 119.
17. T.R.: White, *The Diplomacy of the Russo-Japanese War,* p. 162.
18. T.R.: *ibid.*
19. Kennan to T.R.: Esthus, *Theodore Roosevelt and Japan,* p. 130.
20. *Mainichi Shimbun:* ibid., p. 134.
21. Togo: Howarth, S., *Morning Glory: A History of the Imperial Japanese Navy,* pp. 104–5.
22. T.R. on California: Esthus, *op cit.,* p. 130.
23. Fisher: Howarth, D., *The Dreadnoughts,* p. 44.
24. T.R.: Albion, *Makers of Naval Policy, 1798–1947,* p. 216.

25. T.R.: Costello, *op cit.*, p. 5.
26. d'Anethan, Baron, *The d'Anethan Despatches,* pp. 389–93; Howarth, *op cit.*, p. 111.
27. *Ibid.*
28. Halsey: Halsey, *Admiral Halsey's Story,* p. 13.
29. *The Times* (London): Howarth, S., *op cit.*, pp. 109–10.
30. Lansdowne: Still, *op cit.*, p. 137.

CHAPTER 5: HOW TO TELL SHIPS FROM AUTOMOBILES

1. Duvall: Braisted, *The United States Navy in the Pacific,* p. 61.
2. T.R. to Taft: *ibid.*, p. 3; Sprout, *The Rise of American Naval Power, 1776–1918,* p. 279; Albion, *Makers of Naval Policy, 1798–1947,* p. 328.
3. Taft's inaugural address: Braisted, *op cit.*, p. 10.
4. T.R. to Taft: *ibid.*, p. 12.
5. Calhoun: *ibid.*, pp. 81–2.
6. Reuterdahl: Albion, *op cit.*, pp. 218, 337.
7. House Naval Committee Minority Report: Sprout, *op cit.*, p. 291.
8. Bernhardi, General F. von, *Germany and the Next War,* p. 24.
9. Mahan to FitzHugh, Jan. 18, 1913: Mahan papers, 1861–1913, NHFMC.
10. Daniels: Sprout, *op cit.*, pp. 303–4.
11. Mahan to FitzHugh, Mar. 9, 1912: Mahan papers, NHFMC.
12. "Ad Interim": Rappaport, *The Navy League of the United States,* p. 13.
13. Navy League: *ibid.*, pp. 44–45.
14. Wilson on Jefferson: *ibid.*, p. 32.
15. Wilson to Congress: *ibid.*, p. 46.
16. Daniels: Sprout, *op cit.*, p. 313.
17. Benson to Sims: Morison, S. E., *Oxford History of the American People,* p. 862.

CHAPTER 6: WOW! BUT IT WAS GREAT WORK

1. Kerrick, *Military and Naval America,* pp. 221–2; Mitchell, *History of the Modern American Navy,* p. 137.
2. Wilson to Daniels, May 21, 1915: Albion, *Makers of Naval Policy 1798–1947,* p. 68.
3. Wilson to Manhattan Club, Nov. 4, 1915, printed as Navy League pamphlet No. 39: Rappaport, *The Navy League of the United States,* p. 51.
4. Kaplan, *The Conduct of Inquiry: Methodology for Behavioural Science,* p. 28; Booth, *Navies and Foreign Policy,* p. 100.
5. *Naval Investigation, 1920* (Report of testimonies before subcommittee of Senate Naval Affairs Committee, 66th Congress, 2nd Session), p. 3213; Sprout, *The Rise of American Naval Power, 1776–1918,* p. 353, n. 27.
6. *Life,* May 20, 1915.
7. Sprout, *op cit.*, p. 331.
8. Kaiser to Admiral von Müller, Mar. 10, 1916: Herwig, *"Luxury" Fleet: The Imperial German Navy, 1888–1918,* p. 165.
9. Kitchin, C. (Dem., N.C.), Aug. 15, 1916: Sprout, *op cit.*, p. 339.
10. Beech to Lt. Leigh Noyes, U.S.N., Mar. 14, 1917: NA, RG38, II A2, E.45, p. 23.
11. Wilson to Congress, Apr. 2, 1917: Morison, S. E., *Oxford History of the American People,* pp. 859–60.
12. Jellicoe and Sims: Sims, *The Victory at Sea,* p. 9.

13. Holtzendorff's prophecy: Newbolt, H., *Naval Operations,* p. 346.
14. Pratt to Sims, May 6, 1917: Braisted, *The United States Navy in the Pacific, 1897–1941,* v. 1, p. 296.
15. Pratt to CNO, June 7, 1917: *ibid.,* p. 296.
16. Duff to Jellicoe, Apr. 26, 1917: Gretton, *op cit.,* p. 133.
17. Miller, C. R., diary, Apr. 27–28, 1917: Miller papers, NHFMC.
18. All Grider references are from his diary: Springs, *War Birds.*
19. Brodie, *Sea Power in the Machine Age,* p. 317, n. 48.
20. Breckinridge, H. L., *New York Times,* June 11, 1919; Rappaport, *op cit.,* p. 77.
21. Sims: *Naval Investigation, 1920,* p. 3297; Sprout, *op cit.,* p. 352, n. 25.
22. Badger, Adm. C. J., U.S.N., to SecNav, July 13, 1917: Braisted, *op cit.,* p. 300.
23. Munro to Cooke, Mar. 18, 1918: Papers of Rear Adm. H. D. Cooke, U.S.N., NHFMC.
24. Jones on Fanning: Office of the CNO, *Dictionary of American Naval Fighting Ships,* v. 2, p. 388.
25. Carney, R. B., Lt. Comdr. (later Admiral and CNO): All Carney references on this episode from Carney, "The Capture of the U-58," in *USNIP,* Oct. 1934, pp. 1401–1404.
26. T.R. to SecNav, Mar. 28, 1895: Albion, *op cit.,* p. 359.
27. Army-Navy Board on aircraft, Apr. 1898: *ibid.,* p. 360.
28. Wainwright to Fiske: Fiske, *Midshipman to Rear Admiral;* cited *ibid.,* p. 362.
29. Callan, J. L., journal, Jan. 1916: Callan papers, Box 1, NHFMC.
30. *Ibid.*
31. Bernhardi, Gen. F. von, *Germany and the Next War,* pp. 234–5.
32. Grider: Springs, *op cit.,* p. 155.
33. Callan, journal, *op cit.*
34. *Ibid.*
35. Grider: Springs, *op cit.,* pp. 150, viii, 31, 11, 43.
36. *Ibid.,* pp. 150–1.
37. *Ibid.,* pp. 160–1.
38. *Ibid.,* p. 163.
39. Smith, S. F., notebook, Nov. 11, 1918: Smith papers, NHFMC.
40. Callan, journal, *op cit.*

CHAPTER 7: THE BATTLES OF THE FUTURE

1. Herwig, *"Luxury" Fleet: The Imperial German Navy, 1888–1918,* p. 250.
2. Freedom of the seas: Roskill, *Naval Policy Between the Wars,* v. 1, p. 80.
3. Statistics of U.S. capital ships: Sprout, *Towards a New Order of Sea Power,* pp. 51–3. See also Roskill, *ibid.,* pp. 71–2.
4. Lloyd George to House: Sprout, *ibid.,* p. 62.
5. House to Lloyd George: *ibid.,* p. 60.
6. Royal Navy shipping statistics: Mitchell, *History of the Modern American Navy,* p. 261.
7. Churchill's warning: Rappaport, *The Navy League of the United States,* p. 94.
8. House, July 1919: Sprout, *op cit.,* p. 86.
9. Benson to Daniels, Nov. 20, 1918: Roskill, *op cit.,* p. 99, n. 4.
10. Benson's staff, Apr. 9, 1919: Albion, *Makers of Naval Policy, 1798–1947,* p. 225.
11. Wilson's prediction: Morison, S. E., *Oxford History of the American People,* p. 882.

12. Wilson on the press: Braisted, *The United States Navy in the Pacific,* v. 1, p. 165.
13. *Ibid.,* p. 337.
14. Payne to London: Roskill, *op cit.,* p. 169; Daniels to commander in chief, Asiatic Fleet, Mar. 28, 1918: Braisted, *op cit.,* p. 360.
15. Wilson to Geddes, Oct. 16, 1918: Roskill, *op cit.,* p. 133.
16. Curtiss: Albion, *op cit.,* p. 361.
17. Steele to Mayo, Mar. 28, 1919: Roskill, *op cit.,* p. 244, n. 4; the figures are from *ibid.,* pp. 234, 244.
18. General Board, June 23, 1919: *ibid.,* p. 116.
19. Final Report of Admiralty Post-War Questions Committee, Mar. 27, 1920: *ibid.,* p. 115.
20. Braisted, *op cit.,* p. 512.
21. Fullam, W. F., *New York Herald,* Sept. 29, 1919, p. 274: Fullam papers, NHFMC.
22. Sims-Lodge-Sims letters, Feb. 10–14, 1921: Roskill, *op cit.,* p. 248.

CHAPTER 8: SEEDS OF MISUNDERSTANDING AND GRAVE TROUBLE

1. Planning Section memo 21: Trask, D. F., "In a World at War," in Hagan, *In Peace and War,* p. 213.
2. Borah, W. E.: Sprout, *Towards a New Order of Sea Power,* p. 117.
3. Harding, Mar. 4, 1921: *ibid.,* p. 129, n. 30.
4. Lee to INA, Mar. 16, 1921: *The Times* (London) Mar. 17, 1921; *ibid.,* p. 129; Roskill, *Naval Policy Between the Wars,* v. 1, p. 229, n. 1.
5. Yardley, *The American Black Chamber,* p. 187.
6. *Ibid.,* p. 164.
7. *Fortnightly,* CXIII (June 1920), p. 849: Rappaport, *The Navy League of the United States,* p. 86.
8. Kelley, P. H.: Braisted, *The United States Navy in the Pacific,* v. 1, pp. 300–1.
9. Lee, May 19, 1921: *ibid.,* p. 554.
10. Hughes, Nov. 12, 1921: Sprout, *op cit.,* pp. 156–7.
11. Yardley, *op cit.,* p. 208.
12. *Ibid.,* p. 209.
13. *Ibid.,* p. 211.
14. Delegation to the president, Feb. 9, 1922: Engely, *The Politics of Naval Disarmament,* p. 2.
15. Fullam, W. F., "The Passing of Sea Power and the Dawn of a New Naval Era in Which Battleships Are Obsolete," in *McClure's Magazine,* June 1923.
16. Menoher, Apr. 14, 1921: Braisted, *op cit.,* p. 514.
17. Knox, D. W.: Rosen, P. T., "The Treaty Navy," in Hagan, *In Peace and War,* p. 223.
18. Data on carrier conversions: Roskill, *op cit.,* p. 335, n. 1.
19. Eberle Board of Inquiry, report, Jan. 17, 1925: *ibid.,* p. 399.
20. Peary, diary, Apr. 6, 1909: Weems, *Peary,* p. 270.
21. Wilbur, annual report: Roskill, *op cit.,* p. 458.
22. *Ibid.,* pp. 58–9 and footnotes.
23. General Board report to ONI, Apr. 21, 1927: *ibid.,* p. 502.
24. Jellicoe: *ibid.,* p. 516.
25. Sebald, *With MacArthur in Japan,* p. 29.
26. MacDonald to King George V, Apr. 12, 1930: Roskill, *op cit.,* v. 2, p. 65.

27. *ONI Monthly Bulletin,* v. XII, no. 6: *ibid.,* p. 149.
28. Navy League on Hoover: Rosen, "The Treaty Navy," in Hagan, *In Peace and War,* p. 232.
29. League of Nations: Scott, *The Rise and Fall of the League of Nations,* p. 228.
30. Grey, Mar. 7, 1932: Bassett, *Democracy and Foreign Policy,* pp. 192–3.
31. Taylor to Pratt, Mar. 6, 1932: Taylor papers, NHFMC.
32. May 15 incident: Pelz, *Race to Pearl Harbor,* p. 10.
33. Enabling Act: "Questions on German History" (Catalogue of Historical Exhibition in the Reichstag), pp. 312–15, Bundestag, Bonn, 1984.
34. Taylor, Apr. 18, 1933: Taylor papers, NHFMC.
35. Pratt to F.D.R., June 9, 1933: Roskill, *op cit.,* v. 2, p. 163.
36. F.D.R. to Swanson: Pelz, *op cit.,* p. 79.

CHAPTER 9: OUR CITIZENS DO NOT WANT WAR

1. Araki to Japanese Foreign Office, Nov. 1933: Pelz, *Race to Pearl Harbor,* pp. 34–5.
2. Fushimi, Prince H.: *ibid.,* p. 18.
3. Letters protesting U.S. Navy Pacific Maneuvers, Feb.–May 1935: NA, RG38, III, Alg. No. 159.
4. Nye report, June 24, 1935: Dull, P. S., *A Battle History of the Imperial Japanese Navy, 1941–45,* p. 365.
5. Naval Attaché Tokyo, Mar. 1, 1937: SNA microfilm 975, location N-1-5.
6. Naval Attaché Tokyo, May 22, 1937: SNA microfilm 975, (2) 10-40-3.
7. Naval Attaché Paris, Sept. 20, 1937: *ibid.,* location I-1-7.
8. F.D.R.: Albion, *Makers of Naval Policy, 1798–1947,* p. 344.
9. Yarnell, Sept. 27, 1937: *ibid.,* p. 345.
10. Grew, *Ten Years in Japan,* p. 211.
11. Yarnell, diary, Feb. 9, 1938: Yarnell papers, Box 3, NHFMC.
12. Nazi plebiscite: "Questions on German History" (Catalogue of Historical Exhibition in the Reichstag), pp. 336–7, Bundestag, Bonn, 1984.
13. Naval Attaché Tokyo, Apr. 13, 1938: SNA microfilm 975, (2) 10-40-3.
14. Naval Attaché Berlin, June 22, 1938: *ibid.*
15. Naval Attaché Tokyo, June 1938: *ibid.,* location N-1-21.
16. Munro to Cooke, Aug. 10, 1938: Cooke papers, NHFMC.
17. Naval Attaché Tokyo, Nov. 28, 1938: SNA microfilm 975, report No. 26.
18. Naval Attaché Tokyo, Jan. 25, 1939: *ibid.,* location N-1-30.
19. *Ibid.*
20. F.D.R.: Goralski, *World War Two Almanac, 1931–45,* p. 78.
21. Naval Attaché Tokyo, Apr. 10, 1939: SNA microfilm 975, location N-1-38.
22. Stimson to Hull, Apr. 5, 1939: Lash, *Roosevelt and Churchill, 1939–41,* p. 32.
23. Naval Attaché Tokyo, Apr. 25, 1939: SNA microfilm 975, location N-1-42.
24. Report of Joint Planning Committee, Apr. 21, 1939: Major, J., "The Navy Plans for War," in Hagan, *In Peace and War,* pp. 245–7.
25. Yarnell, diary, Sept. 3, 1939: Yarnell papers, NHFMC.
26. Smith, diary, Sept. 3–4, 1939: Smith papers, NHFMC.
27. Naval Attaché Rome, Sept. 4, 1939: SNA microfilm 975, location K-1-40.
28. Chamberlain to F.D.R., Oct. 4, 1939: Lash, *op cit.,* p. 70.
29. Hitler, speech, Nov. 23, 1929: *ibid.,* p. 80.
30. Naval Attaché Berlin, Nov. 27, 1939: SNA microfilm 975, location L-1-25.
31. F.D.R. to W. A. White, Dec. 14, 1939: Lash, *op cit.,* p. 85.

CHAPTER 10: IF YOU ATTACK US . . . WE SHALL CRUSH YOU

1. Munro to Cooke, Jan. 27, 1940: Cooke papers, NHFMC.
2. *Ibid.*
3. Estimated statistics of I.J.N., Nov. 15, 1939: Mitchell, *History of the Modern American Navy,* pp. 354–5.
4. *Osaka Mainichi,* Jan. 11, 1940: Naval Attaché Tokyo, Feb. 15, 1940, SNA, microfilm 975, location N-2-59.
5. *Ibid.*
6. Mussolini to U.S. Ambassador: Goralski, *World War Two Almanac, 1931–45,* p. 111.
7. Stark to C.O. Pacific Fleet: Major, J., "The Navy Plans for War," in Hagan, *In Peace and War,* p. 250.
8. Naval Attaché Rome, May 10, 1940: SNA, *op cit.,* location K-2-53.
9. Lord Lothian to Lady Astor, May 20, 1940: Lash, *Roosevelt and Churchill, 1939–1941,* p. 132.
10. Ito in *Contemporary Japan:* Naval Attaché Tokyo, May 14, 1940, SNA, *op cit.,* location N-2-64.
11. Munro to Cooke, Jan. 4, 1940: Cooke papers, *op cit.*
12. F.D.R. to University of Virginia, June 10, 1940: Morison, S. E., *Oxford History of the American People,* p. 995; Goralski, *op cit.,* p. 119.
13. Munro to Cooke, June 30, 1940, July 27, 1940: Cooke papers, *op cit.*
14. *New York Times,* Sept. 5, 1940.
15. Lloyd George to Maisky: Lash, *op cit.,* p. 217.
16. Lewin, *The American Magic,* p. 44.
17. Naval Attaché Rome, Oct. 14, 1940: SNA, *op cit.,* location K-2-69.
18. Kimmel to Coburn and to Leahy, Jan. 29, 1941; to Herron, Jan. 31, 1941; to Stark, n.d.; Kimmel papers (Corr. 1.29.41–3.23.44), U.S. Naval Academy Library.
19. Naval Attaché Berlin, SNA, *op cit.,* location L-1-25.
20. Grew, diary, Jan. 27, 1941: Grew, *Ten Years in Japan,* p. 318.
21. Grew on Nomura: *ibid.,* p. 303.
22. Naval Attaché Rome, Mar. 24, 1941: SNA, *op cit.,* location K-2-82.
23. Stark to Kimmel, Apr. 3, 1941: Major, *op cit.,* p. 258.
24. King, fleet order, Mar. 24, 1941: Buell, T. B., *Master of Sea Power,* p. 136.
25. Stark to King, Apr. 4, 1941: *ibid.,* p. 137.
26. Naval Attaché Tokyo, Apr. 25, 1941: SNA, *op cit.,* location N-2-89.
27. Naval Attaché Tokyo, June 29, 1941: *ibid.*
28. Naval Attaché Tokyo, Aug. 21, 1941: *ibid.,* location G-397.
29. Naval Attaché Tokyo, Aug. 23, 1941: *ibid.,* location N-2-96.
30. F.D.R., Sept. 11, 1941: Abbazia, *Mr. Roosevelt's Navy,* p. 229.
31. U.S.S. *Belknap* war diary, Sept. 14, 1941: *ibid.,* p. 231.
32. Stark to Hart, Sept. 22, 1941: *ibid.,* p. 250.
33. Coffin to Cooke, Sept. 23, 1941: Cooke papers, *op cit.*
34. Report on *Reuben James:* Abbazia, *op cit.*
35. Stark to Hart, Nov. 7, 1941; Ickes, diary; Thomsen, Oct. 17, 1941: *ibid.,* pp. 306, 277.
36. Stark to Kimmel, Nov. 14, 1941 (received Nov. 20, 1941): Kimmel papers, *op cit.*
37. Stark to Nomura: Major, *op cit.,* p. 261.

38. Kimmel to Stark, Dec. 2, 1941; Stark to Kimmel, Nov. 25, 1941: Kimmel papers, *op cit.*
39. Knox, SecNav *Annual Report* 1941: Mitchell, *op cit.,* p. 389.

CHAPTER 11: THOSE SPLENDID SHIPS—LOST

1. Moorer: conversation with the author, Aug. 9, 1984.
2. Benbrookes: conversation with the author, Feb. 6, 1982.
3. Peterson: information courtesy of his nephew, Capt. G. I. Peterson, U.S.N., transcript of Mutual Network/KGMB broadcast (Apr. 3, 1942) and conversation with and letter to the author, Mar. 25, 1985.
4. Kimmel to Stark, Dec. 12, 1941: Kimmel papers (Corr. 1.29.41–3.23.44), U.S. Naval Academy Library.
5. Hate letters to Kimmel: *ibid.*
6. Lockwood on Kimmel, Dec. 8, 1941: Lockwood papers, NHFMC.
7. Masefield, "Ships," lines 77–80.
8. Pearl Harbor intelligence: Casey, *The Secret War Against Hitler,* pp. 7–9.
9. Lockwood, Dec. 12, 1941: Lockwood papers, *op cit.*
10. Dönitz, Dec. 9, 1941: Padfield, *Dönitz: The Last Führer,* p. 266.
11. Dönitz, Feb. 7, 1942: *ibid.,* p. 268.
12. Stark and Marshall: Albion, *Makers of Naval Policy 1798–1947,* p. 572.
13. Dönitz, war diary, Apr. 19, 1942: Padfield, *op cit.,* p. 269.
14. Dönitz to Hitler, May 14, 1942: *ibid.,* p. 272.
15. Pound to King, May 18, 1942: Buell, T. B., *Master of Sea Power,* p. 290.
16. Wynn, ASW report, Apr. 1942: Padfield, *op cit.,* p. 273.
17. King, press release: Buell, *op cit.,* p. 290.

CHAPTER 12: DISTANT WINGS

1. I.J.N. on Moresby intercepted, Mar. 28, 1942: Costello, *The Pacific War,* p. 247.
2. Inouye: *ibid.,* p. 252.
3. Crace: *ibid.,* p. 256.
4. Nimitz: Nimitz and Potter, *The Great Sea War.*
5. Message on fresh water: NA, RG45, SRNA, 000175.
6. Layton: Costello, *op cit.,* p. 278.
7. Fuchida: *ibid.,* p. 294.

CHAPTER 13: CONFUSION AND FURY

1. Kriegsmarine (Km) Berlin to Wenneker, July 9, 1942: NA, RG45, 7, SRGL, 0164.
2. Wenneker to Km Berlin, Aug. 1, 1942: NA, RG45, 7, SRGL, 0368.
3. Churchill, *The Second World War,* v. 4, pp. 289–90.
4. F.D.R. to Hopkins, Marshall, and King, July 16, 1942: *ibid.,* pp. 398–400.
5. Langley, H. D., "Women in a Warship, 1813," *USNIP,* Jan. 1984, pp. 124–5.
6. *All Hands* magazine, Aug. 1975 (Navy Bicentennial Issue), p. 70.
7. *Pittsburgh Courier:* Wynn, *The Afro-American and the Second World War,* p. 22.
8. *Ibid.*
9. Graveley: conversation with the author, Aug. 21, 1984.
10. Nimitz to King, Aug. 7, 1942: Buell, T. B., *Master of Sea Power,* p. 221.
11. Morison, S. E., *The Struggle for Guadalcanal;* Churchill, *op cit.,* v. 5, pp. 20–1.
12. Wenneker to Km Berlin, Aug. 28, 1942: NA, RG45, 7, SRGL, 0429.
13. Zumwalt: conversation with the author, July 5, 1984.

CHAPTER 14: BRAVO! KEEP AT IT!

1. War diary, U-boat High Command, Aug. 21, 1942: Padfield, *Dönitz: The Last Führer,* pp. 279–80.
2. F.D.R. to W.S.C., Sept. 5, 1942; W.S.C. to F.D.R., Sept. 6, 1942: Churchill, *Second World War,* v. 4, p. 487.
3. Nimitz and Potter, *The Great Sea War,* p. 129.
4. King, Mar. 1, 1943: Buell, T. B., *Master of Sea Power,* p. 292.
5. U-boat High Command, Mar. 16, 1943: Padfield, *op cit.,* p. 309.
6. Dönitz to Hitler, Apr. 11, 1943: *ibid.,* p. 312.
7. Dönitz to U-boat commanders, May 14, 1943: *ibid.,* p. 331.
8. Dönitz to U-boat commanders, May 20, 1943: *ibid.,* p. 333.
9. Dönitz on sectional U-boats: *ibid.,* p. 345.
10. Dönitz to all U-boat officers, May 23, 1943: *ibid.,* p. 335.

CHAPTER 15: ACTION AGAINST A RETREATING ENEMY

1. Nimitz and Potter, *The Great Sea War,* p. 402.
2. Daspit on duds: Polmar, *The American Submarine,* p. 59.
3. King on *England:* Nimitz and Potter, *op cit.,* p. 414.
4. Bush on submarines: interview with E. B. Furgurson, *The Washingtonian,* Aug. 1985.
5. Diary from U.S.S. *Snook,* June 22–July 7, 1943: Lockwood papers, NHFMC.
6. King on I.J.N. subs: Buell, T. B., *Master of Sea Power,* p. 299.
7. Sherman: Polmar, *op cit.,* pp. 68–71.
8. Burke: Nimitz and Potter, *op cit.,* p. 292.
9. Zumwalt: conversation with the author, July 5, 1984.
10. Churchill, *The Second World War,* v. 4, p. 702.
11. Shibasaki on Betio: Nimitz and Potter, *op cit.,* p. 325.
12. Turner on Marshalls: Costello, *The Pacific War,* p. 451.
13. Smith on Kwajalein: *ibid.,* p. 450.
14. King et al. in *Iowa:* Goralski, *World War Two Almanac, 1931–45,* p. 289.
15. Spruance: Costello, *op cit.,* p. 478.

CHAPTER 16: A SEA FIGHT BEYOND ALL OTHERS

1. Churchill, *The Second World War,* v. 5, pp. 539–40.
2. Chihaya, M.: Untitled, unpublished MS of his part in the Pacific war; Chihaya private possession.
3. Burke on Mitscher: cited in Howarth, S., *Men of War.*
4. Nimitz orders: Nimitz and Potter, *The Great Sea War,* p. 379.
5. Carney: conversation with the author, Feb. 9, 1982.
6. Carney to Kinkaid for Halsey: Nimitz and Potter, *op cit.,* p. 382.
7. Sprague's colleague: Morison, S. E., *The Two-Ocean War,* p. 461.
8. Copeland: *ibid.,* pp. 456–9.
9. MacArthur on Halsey: Halsey, *Admiral Halsey's Story,* p. 186.
10. Nelson: Howarth, D., *Trafalgar: The Nelson Touch,* p. 73.

CHAPTER 17: LORDS OF THE OCEAN, LORDS OF THE AIR

1. Jones: Morison, S. E., *John Paul Jones,* pp. 415–6.
2. W.S.C. to F.D.R., Oct. 27, 1944: Churchill, *The Second World War,* v. 6, p. 162.
3. Grey: *Lord Fisher: Memories,* ch. 1.
4. Iwo Jima: Morison, S. E., *The Two-Ocean War,* p. 521.

5. Chihaya on *Yamato:* conversations with the author, Dec. 81.
6. W.S.C. to Hopkins on F.D.R.: Churchill, *op cit.,* v. 6, p. 413.
7. Stalin to W.S.C. on F.D.R.: *ibid.,* p. 421.
8. W.S.C. on Truman: *ibid.,* p. 418.
9. Dönitz, order of the day, May 1, 1945: Padfield, *Dönitz: The Last Führer,* p. 455.
10. W.S.C. on A-bomb: Churchill, *op cit.,* v. 6, p. 553.
11. Potsdam Declaration: *ibid.,* p. 557.
12. Nimitz: Costello, *The Pacific War,* p. 597.
13. MacArthur: Morison, S. E., *op cit.,* p. 575.
14. MacArthur: Costello, *op cit.,* p. 601.
15. NDAR, v. 6, p. 1520.
16. British chief of staff: Buell, T. B., *Master of Sea Power,* pp. 505–6.

CHAPTER 18: THE ELIMINATION OF WAR ITSELF

1. Parsons to Miss Lysbeth W. Muncy, Sweet Briar College, Va., Mar. 11, 1947: Parsons papers, Box 3, NHFMC.
2. Forrestal, Feb. 20, 1947: *The Times* (London), Mar. 1, 1947.
3. Statistics on U.S.N. demobilization: Breemer, *U.S. Naval Developments,* p. 17.
4. Baruch: address to AEC at Lake Success, Dec. 5, 1946: Albion, *Makers of Naval Policy, 1798–1947,* pp. 612–13.
5. Gromyko at Lake Success, Mar. 5, 1947: *ibid.*
6. Armstrong: *ibid.*
7. Truman: *ibid.,* p. 603.
8. Gates: *ibid.,* p. 600.
9. McCain: *ibid.,* p. 601.
10. Stimson: *ibid.,* p. 597.
11. Truman: *ibid.,* p. 609.
12. Eberstadt: *ibid.,* p. 606.
13. Emerson: conversation with the author, July 13, 1984.
14. Bradley: Schratz, P. R., "The Admirals' Revolt," *USNIP,* Feb. 1986, pp. 64–71.
15. Orem, Vice Adm. H.: *ibid.*
16. Burke: conversation with the author, Aug. 7, 1984.
17. Navy League on Denfeld: Rappaport, *The Navy League of the United States,* p. 197.
18. NSC-68: Allard, D., "An Era of Transition," in Hagan, *In Peace and War,* p. 304.
19. Parsons to Muncy: Parsons papers, Box 3, NHFMC.

CHAPTER 19: UNDER WAY ON NUCLEAR POWER

1. Burke: *Oral History,* v. 1, Special Series Interview 3, pp. 217–8, U.S. Naval Historical Center, U.S. Navy Yard, Washington, D.C.
2. Burke: *ibid.,* Interview 1, pp. 22–3.
3. Sirius patrol: Boesgaard, N. E., "Patrolling the Icy North," *Jane's Defence Weekly,* v. 5, no. 22, June 7, 1986, pp. 1055–7.
4. Ridgway: Anderson, *U.S. Military Operations, 1945–1984,* p. 35.
5. Burke to McDill, 1953: *Oral History,* Interview 1, p. 10.
6. Burke: *ibid.,* Interview 3, p. 185.
7. Gorschkov: Kennedy, F. D., "The Creation of the Cold War Navy," in Hagan, *In Peace and War,* p. 305.

8. Burke: *Oral History, op cit.,* Interview 3, p. 15.
9. Burke: *ibid.,* p. 44.
10. Rickover: My specific source does not wish to be named, but from the admiral's history, very senior sources, and brief personal contact, the description seems accurate.
11. *Nautilus:* Polmar, *The American Submarine,* p. 111.
12. Turner: conversation with the author, Aug. 6, 1984.

CHAPTER 20: EYEBALL TO EYEBALL

1. Eisenhower: Anderson, *U.S. Military Operations, 1945–1984,* p. 68.
2. T.R.: Turk, R. W., "Defending the New Empire," in Hagan, *In Peace and War,* p. 192.
3. Montevideo Declaration: Morison, S. E., *Oxford History of the American People,* p. 967.
4. Bay of Pigs: Anderson, *op cit.,* p. 96.
5. Khrushchev: *ibid.,* p. 102.
6. Rusk: Kennedy, F. D., Jr., "The Cold War Navy," in Hagan, *op cit.,* p. 324.

CHAPTER 21: THAT BITCH OF A WAR

1. Muller: conversation with the author, Aug. 29, 1984.
2. L.B.J.: Siegel, *Troubled Journey,* p. 172.
3. Congress: *ibid.*
4. Burke: conversation with the author, Aug. 7, 1984.
5. Carleton to Burgoyne, Nov. 17, 1777: James, *The British Navy in Adversity,* p. 61.
6. Kiel: conversation with the author, July 9, 1984.
7. Turner: conversation with the author, Aug. 6, 1984.
8. Westmoreland: interview with D. Chamberland, *USNIP,* July 1986, pp. 45–8.
9. Lincoln to Conkling, Aug. 26, 1863: Morison, S. E., *"Old Bruin,"* p. 211.
10. Emerson: conversation with the author, July 13, 1984.
11. Zumwalt: Zumwalt, *On Watch,* p. 39.
12. Emerson: conversation, *op cit.*
13. Zumwalt: *op cit.,* p. 38.
14. Zumwalt: *ibid.,* p. 36.
15. Burke: *Oral History,* v. 1, Special Series Interview 3, p. 186, U.S. Naval Historical Center, U.S. Navy Yard, Washington, D.C.
16. L.B.J.: Siegel, *op cit.,* p. 171.
17. Burke: *Oral History, op cit.*
18. Westmoreland: interview with Chamberland, *op cit.*
19. Zumwalt: *op cit.,* p. 35.
20. Wechsler: *Oral History,* Interview with P. Stillwell, Sept. 20, 1984, May 20, 1985, USNI; "As I Recall . . . Vietnam," *USNIP,* Nov. 1985, p. 86.
21. Krulak: "A Conflict of Strategies," *USNIP,* Nov. 1984, pp. 84–90.
22. Muller: conversation with the author, Aug. 29, 1984.

CHAPTER 22: WE MUST HAVE NATIONAL GOALS

1. King: Buell, T. B., *Master of Sea Power,* p. 136.
2. Kiel: conversation with the author, July 9, 1984.
3. Barnett: conversation with the author, Aug. 24, 1984.

4. Zumwalt: Zumwalt, *On Watch,* p. 217.
5. Zumwalt: *ibid.,* p. 220.
6. Zumwalt: *ibid.,* p. 256.
7. Kiel: conversation with the author, *op cit.*
8. Zumwalt: *op cit.,* p. 204.
9. Zumwalt: *ibid.,* p. 236.
10. Zumwalt: *ibid.,* p. 447.
11. Zumwalt: *ibid.,* p. 448.
12. Zumwalt: conversation with the author, July 5, 1984.
13. Statistics on *Nimitz,* etc: Lyon, H., "U.S. Warships," in Bonds, *American War Power,* pp. 135–6.
14. Turner: conversation with the author, Aug. 6, 1984.
15. Burke: conversation with the author, Aug. 7, 1984.
16. Sheffield: Field, *America and the Mediterranean World,* p. 32.
17. U.S.N. ensign, 1881: Still, *American Sea Power in the Old World,* pp. 56–7.
18. Adams, 1800: Knox, *A History of the United States Navy,* p. 55.

CHAPTER 23: WE MUST . . . NOT APPEAR AS TERRORISTS

1. Lehman: Breemer, *U.S. Naval Developments,* p. 30.
2. Zumwalt: conversation with the author, July 5, 1984.
3. Grenada: Thomas, C., *The Times* (London), 1985.
4. Lehman: Interview with J. D. Hessman and V. C. Thomas, Jr., *Sea Power,* Apr. 1984, pp. 15–34.
5. Komer: Connell, J., *Sunday Times* (London), Nov. 11, 1983.
6. Lehman: *ibid.*
7. Turner: *ibid.;* Zumwalt: conversation with the author, *op cit.*
8. Turner: conversation with the author, Aug. 6, 1984; Zumwalt: conversation, *op cit.*
9. Watkins: Report to the House Armed Services Committee, Feb. 7, 1985.
10. Marines: Helle, R. B., "Defeating Terrorism," *USNIP,* July 1986, p. 50.
11. Preble: *NDBW,* v. 3, p. 70.
12. Libya: Fisk, R., *The Times* (London), Mar. 26, 1986.
13. Operation El Dorado Canyon: *USNIP.*
14. Department of Defense Commission: Sloane, S., "TWA Flight 847: Learning Hard Lessons," *USNIP,* Feb. 1986, pp. 78–9.
15. Shultz, address in Park Avenue Synagogue, New York City, Oct. 25, 1984: *ibid.*
16. McFarlane, "Terrorism and the Future of Free Society": *ibid.*
17. Borg, P., *Jane's Defence Weekly,* Apr. 26, 1986, p. 739.
18. Reagan: *USNIP,* Nov. 1985, pp. 10–12.
19. Trost: *USNIP,* May 1989, p. 34.
20. Labour manifesto: Mayhew, *Time to Explain,* p. 169.
21. Mayhew resignation: *ibid.,* p. 173.
22. Lehman: *Report . . . on the Fiscal Year 1986 Military Posture of United States Navy and Marine Corps,* Feb. 1985, p. 16.
23. Gramm-Rudman: Truver, S. C., "Gramm-Rudman and the Future of the 600-Ship Fleet," *USNIP,* May 1987, pp. 110–123.
24. Webb: Kennedy, F. D., Jr., "U.S. Naval Aircraft and Weapon Developments in 1987," *USNIP,* May 1988, p. 195.
25. Operation Praying Mantis: Langston, Capt. B., and Bringle, Lt. Comdr. D.,

"Operation Praying Mantis—The Air View," and Perkins, Capt. J. B., III, "The Surface View," *USNIP,* May 1989, pp. 54–65, 66–70.

26. Trost: *ibid.,* p. 65.
27. Metcalf: Metcalf, Vice Adm. J., III, "Revolution at Sea," *USNIP,* Jan. 1988, pp. 34–9.
28. Walker: Polmar, N., and Allen, T. B., "The Decade of the Spy," *USNIP,* May 1989, pp. 107–9.
29. Gates: *ibid.,* p. 109.

CHAPTER 24: BEYOND THE PILLARS OF HERCULES

1. Trost, C.A.H., "Maritime Strategy for the 1990s," *USNIP,* May 1990, p. 93.
2. Gray, C., "Tomorrow's Forecast: Warmer/Still Cloudy," *USNIP,* May 1990, pp. 40–43.
3. Rowny, E. L.: "Arms Control at Arm's Length," *USNIP,* May 1990, p. 58.
4. Trost: *op cit.,* p. 95.
5. Rowny: *op cit.,* pp. 57–8.
6. Powell, C., "Crystal Balls Don't Always Help," *USNIP,* May 1990, p. 64.
7. Morton, J. F., "The U.S. Navy in 1989," *USNIP,* May 1990, p. 166.
8. *Ibid.*
9. Paine, T., "The Rights of Man," 1791; cited on the menu of the Bull House, Lewes, East Sussex, England.

BIBLIOGRAPHY

★

Location details of materials cited in this book—manuscripts, interviews, periodicals, official histories, and secondary published works—are given in the notes. This list of published works does not include every work consulted (and certainly does not include everything written on the U.S. Navy), but it may be helpful for further reference. Experts may be surprised at some of the entries; although none is frivolous, some are lightweight. However, even the lightweight ones are useful and generally accurate; and the list is meant not only for experts, but also for people who simply enjoy reading about the U.S. Navy, and who might wish to read a little more.

Abbazia, P.: *Mr. Roosevelt's Navy: The Private War of the U.S. Atlantic Fleet, 1939–1942* (Naval Institute Press, 1975).

Adams, J.: *Papers of John Adams,* (4 v.) (R. J. Taylor, ed.) (Harvard University Press, 1979).

Adamson, H. C.: *Halsey's Typhoons* (Crown Publishers, New York, 1967).

Albion, R. G.: *Makers of Naval Policy, 1798–1947* (R. Reed, ed.), (Naval Institute Press, 1980).

———, and J. B. Pope: *Sea Lanes in Wartime: The American Experience, 1775–1942* (George Allen and Unwin, 1943).

Alford, J. (ed.): *Sea Power and Influence: Old Issues and New Challenges* (Gower and Allanhead, 1980).

Ammen, D.: *The Navy in the Civil War: The Atlantic Coast* (Charles Scribner's Sons, 1883).

———: *The Old Navy and the New* (J. B. Lippincott, 1891).

Anderson, K.: *U.S. Military Operations, 1945–1984* (Hamlyn, 1984).

Anethan, Baron d': *The d'Anethan Despatches from Japan, 1894–1910* (G. A. Lensen, ed.) (Sophia University and Diplomatic Press, 1967).

Baldwin, H. W.: *The American Navy* (George Allen and Unwin, 1941).

Basler, R. P. (ed.): *The Collected Works of Abraham Lincoln* (10 v.) (Rutgers University Press, 1953–55).

Bassett, R.: *Democracy and Foreign Policy: A Case History—The Sino-Japanese Dispute, 1931–33* (Frank Cass and Co., 1968).

Bates, W. W.: *American Marine: The Shipping Question in History and Politics* (Houghton, Mifflin, 1893).

Bauer, K. J.: *Surfboats and Horse Marines: U.S. Naval Operations in the Mexican War, 1846–48* (U.S. Naval Institute, 1969).

———: *The Mexican War 1846–48* (Macmillan, 1974).

Beach, E. L.: *The United States Navy: 200 Years* (Henry Holt & Co., 1986).

Beck, A. S.: *The Correspondence of Esek Hopkins* (Rhode Island Historical Society, 1933).

Beers, H. P.: *The U.S. Naval Detachment in Turkish Waters, 1919–24* (Office of Records Administration, U.S. Navy Department, 1943).

———: *The American Naval Occupation and Government of Guam, 1898–1902* (Office of Records Administration, U.S. Navy Department, 1944).

Bernhardi, Gen. F. von: *Germany and the Next War* (tr. Powles, A. H.) (Edward Arnold, 1914).

Bird, H.: *Navies in the Mountains: The Battles on the Waters of Lake Champlain and Lake George, 1609–1814* (Oxford University Press, 1962).

Blair, C.: *Silent Victory: The U.S. Submarine War Against Japan* (Lippincott, 1975).

Bonds, R. (ed.): *American War Power* (Corgi, 1981).

Booth, K.: *Navies and Foreign Policy* (Croom Helm, 1977).

Borklund, C. W.: *Men of the Pentagon: From Forrestal to McNamara* (Praeger, 1966).

Boynton, C. B.: *The History of the Navy During the Rebellion* (Appleton and Co., 1867).

Braisted, W. R.: *The United States Navy in the Pacific, 1897–1941* (2 v.) (University of California Press, 1958).

Breemer, J. S.: *U.S. Naval Developments* (Nautical & Aviation Publishing Co. of America, 1983).

Brewington, M. V.: "American Naval Guns, 1775–1785," in *The American Neptune,* v. 3, nos. 1 and 2, Jan. and Apr. 1943.

Brodie, B.: *Sea Power in the Machine Age* (Princeton and Oxford University Press, 1941).

Brogan, H.: *Longman History of the United States of America* (Longman Group Ltd., 1985).

Brown, A. C. (ed.): *Operation: World War III* (Arms and Armour Press, 1979).

Buell, A. C. (ed.): *Narrative of John Kilby, Quartergunner of the U.S.S.* Bonhomme Richard (n.p., n.d.; 1904?).

Buell, T. B.: *Master of Sea Power: A Biography of Fleet Admiral E. J. King* (Little, Brown, 1980).

Burnett, E. C. (ed.): *Letters of Members of the Continental Congress,* v. 2: *July 5, 1776–Dec. 31, 1777* (Carnegie Institute, 1923).

Cagle, M. W., and F. A. Manson: *The Sea War in Korea* (U.S. Naval Institute, 1957).

Carse, R.: *Blockade: The Civil War at Sea* (Rinehart, 1958).

Casey, W.: *The Secret War Against Hitler* (Simon and Schuster, 1989).

Cervera y Topete, P.: *The Spanish-American War: A Collection of Documents Relative* to the Squadron Operations in the West Indies (anon tr. from Spanish) (Office of Naval Intelligence, U.S. Government Printing Office, 1899).

Chapelle, H. I.: *The History of the American Sailing Navy: The Ships and their Development* (W. W. Norton & Co., 1949).

Churchill, W. S.: *The Second World War* (6 v.) (Cassell, 1948–54).

Clark, J. J., and D. H. Barnes: *Sea Power and Its Meaning* (F. Watts, 1968).

Clark, W. B.: *George Washington's Navy* (Louisiana State University Press, 1960).

—— (ed.): *Naval Documents of the American Revolution,* (6 v.) (U.S. Navy Department, 1964 on).

Clephane, L. P.: *History of the Naval Overseas Transportation Service in World War One* (Naval History Division, Washington, D.C., 1969).

Coker, C.: *United States Military Power in the 1980s* (Macmillan, 1984).

Cooper, J. F.: *History of the Navy of the United States of America* (2 v.) (Richard Bentley, 1839).

Corbett, J.: *History of the Great War: Naval Operations* (rev. ed.) (Longmans, 1940).

Costello, J.: *The Pacific War* (Rawson Wade, 1981).

Dana, R. H., Jr.: *Two Years Before the Mast* (Harper & Row edition, 1958).

Davidonis, A. C.: *The American Naval Mission in the Adriatic, 1918–1921* (Office of Records Administration, U.S. Navy Department, 1943).

Davis, V.: *Postwar Defense Policy and the U.S. Navy, 1943–46* (2 v.) (University of North Carolina Press, 1962, 1966).

Dictionary of American Naval Fighting Ships (Naval History Division, Washington, D.C., 1963).

Dillon, W. H.: *A Narrative of My Personal Adventures, 1790–1839* (M. A. Lewis, ed.) (Navy Records Society, 1953, 1956).

Dixon, N. F.: *On the Psychology of Military Incompetence* (Cape, 1976).

Dull, P. S.: *A Battle History of the Imperial Japanese Navy, 1941–45* (Stephens, 1978).

Dupuy, T. N.: *Numbers, Predictions and War: Using History to Evaluate Combat Factors and Predict the Outcome of Battles* (MacDonald and Jane's, 1979).

Elliott, P.: *Allied Minesweeping in World War Two* (Stephens, 1979).

Engely, G.: *The Politics of Naval Disarmament* (tr. Rhodes, H. V.) (Williams and Norgate, 1932).

Esthus, R. A.: *Theodore Roosevelt and Japan* (University of Washington Press, 1967).

Fane, F. D., and D. Moore: *The Naked Warriors* (Appleton-Century-Crofts, 1956).

Field, J. A., Jr.: *America and the Mediterranean World, 1776–1882* (Princeton University Press, 1969).

Forester, C. S.: *The Naval War of 1812* (Michael Joseph, 1957).

Fowler, W. M., Jr.: *Rebels Under Sail: The American Navy During the Revolution* (Charles Scribner's Sons, 1976).

——: *Jack Tars and Commodores: The American Navy 1783–1815* (Houghton Mifflin, 1984).

Friedman, N.: "US Naval Radars: A Look Ahead," in *Defence,* v. 12, no. 6, June 1981.

Gomez Nuñez, S.: *The Spanish-American War: Blockades and Coast Defense* (anon. tr. from Spanish) (Office of Naval Intelligence, U.S. Government Printing Office, 1899).

Goralski, R.: *World War Two Almanac, 1931–45* (Hamish Hamilton, 1981).

Gorshkov, S. G.: *The Sea Power of the State* (Pergamon Press, 1979).

Greger, R.: *The Russian Fleet, 1914–17* (tr. Gearing, J.) (Ian Allen, 1972).

Grew, J. C.: *Ten Years in Japan* (Hammond, Hammond & Co, 1944).

Grider, J. G.: *War Birds* (ed. E. W. Springs) (n.p.; Fort Mill, S.C., 1951).

Hagan, K. J. (ed.): *In Peace and War: Interpretations of American Naval History, 1775–1984* (Greenwood Press, 1984).

Hailey, F., and M. Lancelot: *Clear for Action: The Photographic Story of Modern Naval Combat 1898–1964* (Duell, Sloane & Pearce, 1964).

Halsey, W. F., and J. B., III: *Admiral Halsey's Story* (McGraw-Hill, 1947).

Harmann, G. K.: *Weapons That Wait: Mine Warfare in the U.S. Navy* (U.S. Naval Institute Press, 1979).

Hart, A. B. (ed.): *American History Told by Contemporaries,* v. 2: *The Building of the Republic, 1689–1783* (MacMillan, 1898).

Hart, R. A.: *The Great White Fleet* (Little, Brown, 1965).

Heinl, R. D.: *Soldiers of the Sea: The U.S. Marine Corps, 1775–1962* (U.S. Naval Institute Press, 1962).

Herwig, H. H.: *"Luxury" Fleet: The Imperial German Navy, 1888–1918* (Allen and Unwin, 1983).

Hessen, R.: "The Admiralty's American Ally, 1914–18," in *History Today,* Dec. 1971.

Hodges, H. W., and E. A. Hughes: *Select Naval Documents* (Cambridge University Press, 1922).

Holmes, W. J.: *Double-Edged Secrets: U.S. Navy Intelligence in the Pacific During World War Two* (U.S. Naval Institute Press, 1979).

Hood, M.: *Gunboat Diplomacy 1895–1905: Great Power Pressure in Venezuela* (Allen & Unwin, 1975).

Hooper, E. B.: *Mobility, Support, Endurance: A Story of Naval Operational Logistics in the Vietnam War, 1965–1968* (Naval History Division, Washington, D.C., 1972).

———, D. C. Allard, and O. P. Fitzgerald: *The U.S. Navy and the Vietnam Conflict,* v. 1: *The Setting of the Stage to 1959* (Naval History Division, Washington, D.C., 1976).

Howarth, D.: *Trafalgar: The Nelson Touch* (Collins, 1969).

———: *Sovereign of the Seas: The Story of Britain and the Sea* (Atheneum, 1974).

———: *The Dreadnoughts* (Time-Life Books, 1979).

Howarth, S.: *Morning Glory: A History of the Imperial Japanese Navy* (Hamish Hamilton, 1983).

———, ed.: *Men of War: Great Naval Leaders of World War Two* (Weidenfeld & Nicolson, 1991).

James, W. M.: *The British Navy in Adversity: A Study of the War of American Independence* (Longmans, Green & Co, 1926).

Johnson, D. N.: *The Journals of Daniel Noble Johnson (1822–1863), U.S. Navy* (M. L. Peterson, ed.) (Smithsonian Miscellaneous Collections, v. 136, no. 2, Smithsonian Institution, 1959).

Johnson, R. E.: *Far China Station: The U.S. Navy in Asian Waters, 1800–1898* (U.S. Naval Institute Press, 1979).

Kaplan, A.: *The Conduct of Inquiry: Methodology for Behavioural Science* (Chandler, 1964).

Kemp, P. (ed.): *Oxford Companion to Ships and the Sea* (Oxford University Press, 1976).

———: *The History of Ships* (Orbis, 1978).

Kerrick, H. S.: *Military and Naval America* (Doubleday, 1916).

King, J. W.: *Warships and Navies of the World* (A. Williams & Co., 1881).

Knox, D. W.: *A History of the United States Navy* (G. P. Putnam's Sons, 1936).

——— (ed.): *Naval Documents Related to the Quasi-War Between the United States and France,* (7 v.) (U.S. Government Printing Office, Washington, D.C., 1935–1938).

——— (ed.): *Naval Documents Related to the United States Wars with the Barbary Powers, 1797–1804,* (6 v.) (U.S. Government Printing Office, Washington, D.C., 1939–1944).

Koenig, W. J.: *Americans at War: From the Colonial Wars to Vietnam* (Bison Books, 1980).

Laffin, J.: *Americans in Battle* (J. M. Dent & Sons, 1973).

Lash, J. P.: *Roosevelt and Churchill, 1939–1941* (André Deutsch, 1976).

Lehman, J. F., Jr.: *A Report by Honorable John F. Lehman, Jr., Secretary of the Navy, on the Fiscal Year 1986 Military Posture of the United States Navy and Marine Corps* (U.S. Government Printing Office, 1985).

Lenton, H. T.: *American Gunboats and Minesweepers* (MacDonald and Jane's, 1974).

Lewin, R.: *The American Magic* (Hutchinson, 1982).

Livezey, W. E.: *Mahan on Seapower* (University of Oklahoma Press, 1947).

Lopez, L.: "The United States Marine Corps in the 1980s," in *International Defence Review,* v. 14, no. 4, 1981.

Luce, S. B.: *Writings* (J. D. Hayes and J. B. Hattendorf, eds.) (U.S. Naval War College, Rhode Island, 1975).

Lundeberg, P. K.: *The Continental Gunboat* Philadelphia *and the Northern Campaign of 1776* (Smithsonian Institution, 1966).

Macartney, C. E.: *Mr. Lincoln's Admirals* (Funk & Wagnalls, 1956).

Maclay, E. S.: *A History of the United States Navy, 1775–1893* (2 v.) (D. Appleton and Co., 1894).

Mahan, A. T.: *The Influence of Sea Power upon History, 1600–1783,* (Sampson, Low, 1890).

———: *Sea Power in Relation to the War of 1812* (Little, Brown and Co., 1897).

———: *The Major Operations of the Navies in the War of American Independence* (Sampson, Low, Marston & Co, 1913).

———: *Admiral Farragut* (Appleton, 1892).

———: *From Sail to Steam: Recollections of Naval Life* (Da Capo Press, 1968).

Martinez, O.: *The Great Landgrab: The Mexican-American War, 1846–48* (Quartet, 1975).

Mayhew, C.: *Time to Explain* (Hutchinson, 1987).

McKee, C.: *Edward Preble* (U.S. Naval Institute Press, 1972).

Melville, H.: *Moby Dick* (Harper, 1857).

Mitchell, D. W.: *History of the Modern American Navy from 1883 to Pearl Harbor* (Knopf, 1946).

Moore, J.: *Seapower and Politics* (Weidenfeld and Nicolson, 1979).

Morison, E. E.: *Admiral Sims and the Modern American Navy* (Russell & Russell, 1968).

Morison, S. E.: *The Maritime History of Massachusetts, 1783–1860* (Houghton Mifflin, 1921).

———: *The Struggle for Guadalcanal* (v. 5 of *History of U.S. Naval Operations in World War II*) (Little, Brown, 1949).

———: *The Two-Ocean War* (Little, Brown, 1963).

———: *John Paul Jones: A Sailor's Biography* (Time-Life Books, 1964).

———: *Oxford History of the American People* (Oxford University Press, 1965).

———: *"Old Bruin": Commodore Matthew C. Perry, 1794–1858* (Oxford University Press, 1968).

Morris, C.: *The American Navy: Its Ships and Their Achievements* (Hutchinson, 1898).

Morris, E.: *Corregidor: Nightmare in the Philippines* (Hutchinson, 1982).

Nash, H. P., Jr.: *The Forgotten Wars: The Role of the U.S. Navy in the Quasi-War with France and the Barbary Wars, 1794–1805* (A. S. Barnes, 1968).

Nelson, D. D.: *The Integration of the Negro into the United States Navy* (Farrar, Straus and Young, 1951).

Newbolt, H.: *Naval Operations,* v. 4 (Longmans, Green, 1928).

Nimitz, C., and E. B. Potter: *The Great Sea War* (Harrap, 1962).

Niven, J.: *Gideon Welles: Lincoln's Secretary of the Navy* (Oxford University Press, 1973).

Okamoto, S.: *The Japanese Oligarchy and the Russo-Japanese War* (Columbia University Press, 1970).

O'Toole, G.J.A.: *The Spanish War: An American Epic, 1898* (W. W. Norton & Co., 1984).

Owsley, F. L., Jr.: *The C.S.S. Florida: Her Building and Operations* (University of Pennsylvania Press, 1965).

Padfield, P.: *Dönitz: The Last Führer* (Panther Books, 1985).

Paget, J. C.: *Naval Powers and Their Policy,* (Longmans, 1876).

Patterson, A. J.: *The Other Armada* (Manchester University Press, 1960).

Paulding, W. I.: *Literary Life of James Kirk Paulding,* (Charles Scribner, 1867).

Pelz, S. E.: *Race to Pearl Harbor* (Harvard University Press, 1974).

Polmar, N.: "Building the United States Fleet, 1947–67," in *Brassey's Annual,* 1966.

———: *The American Submarine* (Nautical & Aviation Publishing Co. of America, 1981).

Potter, E. B.: *The United States and World Sea Power* (Prentice-Hall, 1955).

———: *Nimitz* (U.S. Naval Institute Press, 1976).

Prange, G. W.: *At Dawn We Slept* (McGraw-Hill, 1983).

Preston, A., D. Lyon, and J. H. Batchelor: *Navies of the American Revolution* (Leo Cooper/Bison Books, 1975).

Price, G. W.: *Origins of the War with Mexico: The Polk-Stockton Intrigue* (University of Texas Press, 1967).

Quarles, B.: *The Negro in the American Revolution* (University of North Carolina Press, 1961).

Rappaport, A.: *The Navy League of the United States* (Wayne State University Press, 1962).

Reynolds, C. G.: *Famous American Admirals* (Van Nostrand Reinhold, 1976).

Richmond, H. W.: *The Navy in India* (Benn, 1931).

Robertson, E. A.: *The Spanish Town Papers: Some Sidelights on the American War of Independence* (Cresset Press, 1959).

Roosevelt, T.: *The Naval War of 1812* (Putnam's, 1901).

Roskill, S. W.: *The Strategy of Sea Power: Its Development and Application* (Collins, 1962).

———: *Naval Policy Between the Wars,* v. 1: *1919–1929,* (Collins, 1968).

Ryan, P. B.: *First Line of Defense: The U.S. Navy Since 1945* (Hoover Institution Press, 1981).

Sargent, N.: *Admiral Dewey and the Manila Campaign* (Naval Historical Foundation, 1947).

Scharf, J. T.: *History of the Confederate States Navy* (Joseph McDonough, 1894).

Scott, G.: *The Rise and Fall of the League of Nations* (Hutchinson, 1973).

Sebald, W. J., with E. Brines: *With MacArthur in Japan* (Cresset Press, 1965).

Serig, H. W.: "The *Iowa* Class Needed Once Again" (in *U.S. Naval Institute Proceedings,* May 1982).

Siegel, F. F.: *Troubled Journey* (Hill and Wang, 1984).

Sims, W. S.: *The Victory at Sea* (U.S. Naval Institute Press, 1984).

Spector, R. H.: *Professors of War: The Naval War College and the Development of the Naval Profession* (Naval War College Press, 1977).

Sprout, H. and M.: *The Rise of American Naval Power, 1776–1918* (Princeton University Press, 1939).

———: *Towards a New Order of Sea Power* (Princeton University Press, 1940).

Still, W. N., Jr.: *American Sea Power in the Old World, 1865–1917* (Greenwood Press, 1980).

Syrett, D.: *Shipping and the American War, 1775–83* (University of London, 1970).

Taylor, A.J.P.: *The Course of German History* (Methuen, 1976).

Tily, J. C.: *The Uniforms of the United States Navy* (Thomas Yoseloff, 1964).

Tsipis, K., A. H. Cahn, and B. T. Feld (eds.): *The Future of the Sea-Based Deterrent* (Massachusetts Institute of Technology, 1973).

Weems, J. E.: *Peary* (Houghton Mifflin, 1967).

Welles, G.: *Diary, 1861–69* (H. K. Beale and A. W. Brownsford, eds.) (3 v.) (W. W. Norton & Co, 1960).

Westcott, A. F. (ed.): *American Sea Power Since 1775* (Lippincott, 1952).

Wheeler, G. E.: *Prelude to Pearl Harbor* (University of Missouri Press, 1968).

White, J. A.: *The Diplomacy of the Russo-Japanese War* (Princeton University Press, 1964).

Wintringham, T.: *Weapons and Tactics* (Penguin, 1973).

Wynn, N. A.: *The Afro-American and the Second World War* (Elek Books, 1976).

Yardley, H. O.: *The American Black Chamber* (Ballantine Books, 1981).

Zumwalt, E., Jr.: *On Watch* (Quadrangle, 1976).

PERIODICALS

American Neptune
Armed Forces Journal International
Brassey's Annual Defence
Hansard
History Today
International Defence Review
Jane's Defence Weekly

Royal United Services Institute Journal
Sea Power
The Independent (London)
The Sunday Times (London)
The Times (London)
The Washingtonian
United States Naval Institute Proceedings

INDEX

★